Counseling Children and Adolescents

Counseling Children and Adolescents gives students the information they need to prepare for work in both school and clinical mental health settings (two CACREP—Council for Accreditation of Counseling and Related Educational Programs—specialty areas). This text includes not only content related to developmental and counseling theories but also information on evidence-based practices across the continuum of care, diagnosis and treatment of youth, and current trends such as integrated care, mindfulness, and neuroscience. Unique to this book are sections on both the instructional and behavioral Response to Intervention (RtI) model and PBIS, examples of evidence-based practices used across settings such as Student Success Skills, Check & Connect, and trauma-focused CBT, and a review of common mental health-related disorders most often seen in youth and treatment recommendations. Ethical and legal implications are infused throughout the book, as are CACREP learning outcomes. Instructors using this textbook can also turn to its companion website to access test questions for each chapter. Expansive and practical, *Counseling Children and Adolescents* fills a gap in counselor preparation programs and provides an important resource that can be used across specialty areas and coursework.

Jolie Ziomek-Daigle, PhD, is an associate professor in the school counseling program at the University of Georgia. She is a licensed professional counselor (LPC) and has published extensively in the areas of child and adolescent mental health and the use of evidence-based practices in school settings.

Counseling Children and Adolescents

Working in School and Clinical Mental Health Settings

Edited by Jolie Ziomek-Daigle

Routledge
Taylor & Francis Group

NEW YORK AND LONDON

First edition published 2017
by Routledge
711 Third Avenue, New York, NY 10017

and by Routledge
2 Park Square, Milton Park, Abingdon, Oxon, OX14 4RN

Routledge is an imprint of the Taylor & Francis Group, an informa business

© 2017 Jolie Ziomek-Daigle

The right of the editor to be identified as the author of the editorial material, and of the authors for their individual chapters, has been asserted in accordance with sections 77 and 78 of the Copyright, Designs and Patents Act 1988.

Library of Congress Cataloging-in-Publication Data
Names: Ziomek-Daigle, Jolie, editor.
Title: Counseling children and adolescents : working in school and clinical mental health settings / edited by Jolie Ziomek-Daigle.
Description: First Edition. | New York : Routledge, 2017. | Includes bibliographical references and index.
Identifiers: LCCN 2016059880| ISBN 9781138200579 (hardcover : alk. paper) | ISBN 9781138200586 (pbk. : alk. paper) | ISBN 9781315466736 (e-book)
Subjects: LCSH: Children--Counseling of. | Teenagers--Counseling of.
Classification: LCC BF637.C6 C637198 2017 | DDC 158.3083--dc23
LC record available at https://lccn.loc.gov/2016059880

ISBN: 978-1-138-20057-9 (hbk)
ISBN: 978-1-138-20058-6 (pbk)
ISBN: 978-1-315-46673-6 (ebk)

Typeset in Akzidenz Grotesk
by Saxon Graphics Ltd, Derby

Visit the companion website: www.routledge.com/cw/ziomek-daigle

This book is dedicated to my husband, Chris, my children, Brennan, Chance, and Vivienne, and my parents. You make my life and work more meaningful and provide inspiration every day.

Contents

List of Figures

List of Tables

Acknowledgments

First, I would like to recognize the authors of this textbook and thank them for their unique insight, expertise, and contributions to each chapter. These authors are a group of talented researchers and scholars and I appreciated getting to know each one better. I thank Anna Moore for her openness and willingness to explore a new text in the area of counseling children and adolescents and for seeing this one as unique. Working with Nina Guttapalle during the copy editing and production stages of the book has been an absolute pleasure. Thank you, Nina, for your patience and flexibility as I made final decisions. I would also like to acknowledge Tameka Oliphant for helping me organize the text and the reviewers who provided excellent suggestions and generated new ideas for me to consider.

I would also like to acknowledge my colleagues and students at the University of Georgia. Many of these individuals understand my passion for counseling children and adolescents and inspire me with new ideas and avenues for research. Finally, I would be remiss if I did not acknowledge my family for giving me opportunities to do the work I love and for providing the very best of "real world" examples.

PART I

Introduction and Developmental Considerations Pertaining to Counseling Children and Adolescents in School and Clinical Mental Health Settings

CHAPTER 1

Introduction to *Counseling Children and Adolescents*

Christopher T. Belser

We worry about what a child will become tomorrow, yet we forget that he is someone today.

Stacia Tauscher

CHAPTER OBJECTIVES

After reading this chapter, you will be able to:

■ define childhood and adolescence
■ recognize how counseling children and adolescents differs from counseling adults
■ understand various models of child and adolescent development
■ apply developmental models to counseling scenarios

INTRODUCTION

Welcome to the exciting world of child and adolescent counseling. Whether you are reading this textbook for a graduate class or for your practice as a counselor, you yourself were once a child and then an adolescent, and, as you will discover throughout this chapter and throughout the book, there are distinct developmental reasons why you are reading this text at *this* stage of your life and not when you *were* a child or adolescent.

WHO ARE CHILDREN AND ADOLESCENTS?

Childhood and adolescence are distinct periods within the lifespan, although exact age ranges can vary slightly based on the source. Childhood is often divided into at least three sub-stages. The infant/toddler years (ages 0–3) are marked by significant physical and cognitive development as well as dependence on caregivers (American Academy of Pediatrics [AAP], 2016). These trends continue during the preschool years (ages 3–5) as children develop more independence and start preschool. The school-age years (ages 6–12), also called middle childhood, are signified by increases in independence, cognitive development, physical growth, social engagement, and maturation. Sometimes, the school-age years are broken into two smaller stages known as middle childhood (ages 6–8) and late childhood (ages 9–11) to help clarify developmental tasks (Centers for Disease Control and Prevention [CDCP], 2016).

Adolescence, also known as the teenage years, is a time of raging hormones, increased social and romantic interests, marked desire for independence and autonomy, and preparation to leave the family of origin (AAP, 2016). The age range for adolescence also varies based on the source of information. The World Health Organization (WHO, 2016) generally considers adolescence to include ages 10–19, but has also noted that age may be more related to the biological changes occurring during adolescence than the social and emotional changes. The CDCP defines adolescence as the time between ages 12 and 17 and divides the period into two groups: Young teens (ages 12–14) and teens (ages 15–17). Siegel (2013) noted that the brain development processes occurring during this timeframe continue until around age 24, which makes a case for adolescence encompassing more than just the teenage years. The developmental models described later in this chapter will help provide context for other processes that are happening within childhood and adolescence.

HOW DOES COUNSELING A CHILD DIFFER FROM COUNSELING AN ADULT?

Johnson, Rasbury, and Siegel (1997) posited that levels of development account for the differences between children and adults. These developmental differences will influence the content and focus of counseling sessions as well as the modality of counseling delivery. Unlike adults, who can actively comprehend and verbally engage with a counselor, children are often limited in their ability to adequately communicate, comprehend, and make meaning of their experiences (Landreth, 2012; Piaget, 1962). As you will see in the case study below, a child will likely make sense of an experience, such as a traumatic event, in a quite different way from an adolescent or an adult. For example, a child may not fully understand the death of a loved one as a permanent event, and, instead, may not be able to differentiate it from that person leaving for work or for a long trip.

Similarly, children may not emotionally know how to respond to a situation and may not have the emotional vocabulary with which to process their experiences (Landreth, 2002). As such, counselors will need to tailor their counseling approach to the developmental needs of the child. Landreth (2012) described play as children's natural means of communicating with other children and adults. Because play provides an avenue for children to express themselves, it is commonly used as a therapeutic method with children (Bratton, Ray, Edwards, and Landreth, 2009; Kottman, 2011; Landreth, 2012; Taylor and Bratton, 2014). Incorporating play into counseling or engaging in formal play therapy allows the counselor to meet the child's needs while being sensitive to developmental abilities.

Although there are multiple perspectives on the age ranges, childhood usually refers to the period from birth to approximately age 12 and adolescence usually refers to the teenage years. Both periods are marked with physical, cognitive, and social growth, typically increasing in complexity with age. These differences set children and adolescents apart from adults. Counselors must keep these developmental considerations in mind when working with children and adolescents to ensure that interventions are tailored to the client. One such example of this is play therapy, which is often used with children, due to their limited verbal and cognitive abilities. The following case example illustrates some of these differences within the context of family grief.

Case Study: The Knight Family

The Knight family is comprised of James (41-year-old father), Sheri (39-year-old mother), Sam (15-year-old son), and Shay (5-year-old daughter). They are a hardworking, middle-class American family, but their world is turned upside down after the tragic loss of one of the family members. While he was driving home from work one day, James was hit by a driver who ran a red light, and died as a result of the injuries he sustained. All of the other members of the family, devastated by the loss, are left to pick up the pieces and move on.

Sheri is now a widow. At first she is shocked at the sudden loss of her partner and angry at the other driver, but she knows that she has to hold her family together and be there for her children at this time. At night, she cries herself to sleep, and feels empty without James. She is afraid of how her children will handle his death, concerned about whether she will be able to continue to raise them by herself, and worried about taking on the responsibilities of both parents. As time moves on, she must cope with the changes to her social life, as she is no longer a member of a couple.

After hearing the news about his father, Sam does not cry. Instead, he withdraws and becomes very angry. He misses his dad, but does not want to admit it. At the same time, he feels very guilty that the last conversation he had with his dad that morning on the way to school was an argument—James had told Sam he was not ready to get his driver's permit. Instead of saying goodbye that morning after getting out of the car, Sam had just slammed the door and walked away. Sam knows he is the "man of the house" now but cannot get past the anger. He wants to be helpful, but snaps at his mom and sister every time they try to talk with him.

Shay does not really understand what is going on, but knows that everyone is sad. She tells Sheri that she wants her daddy to tuck her in, like he always does. When Sheri says that he will not be able to, Shay asks if it is because she did not pick up her toys, and whether he will come back if she is "good enough." Over the next few days and nights, she does not want anyone to leave the house for fear that he or she will not come back, and she has nightmares about her mommy leaving too.

Each member of the family has lost the same person, yet each of them is experiencing loss differently. Sheri's grieving process is influenced by her roles as wife and mother; additionally, she is deeply concerned about what will happen long term. Sam and Shay are both concerned about their mother; however, their grief process is more egocentric. For Sam, he feels guilt about the argument he had with his father; Shay believes that if her behavior is good enough her father will come back and be able to tuck her in. Sam knows what happened to his father, but Shay is unable fully to comprehend the concept of death. These differences in the family members' grieving process are the result of their development.

Whereas a family intervention may be warranted for the Knights, we will examine each as an individual client in order to highlight the differences in how a counselor would approach working with each member. Sheri will be able to verbally talk about her feelings, and a counselor would likely work with her on how to cope with her husband's death (i.e. a trauma-focused therapy), how to support her family, and how to move forward with the changes that will be occurring. Sam will likely be resistant to counseling and will need a counselor who is patient and focused on building a rapport before helping him work through his guilt and grief. It will be important for his counselor to recognize the surface-level grief responses (e.g., withdrawal, acting out, vacillating between being irritable and wanting to be helpful) and also explore the underlying feelings. For Shay, a play-based approach to counseling, such as sand tray, puppets, or drawing, may help her process thoughts and feelings she may not even know she has. A counselor working with her would need to have specialized training in utilizing these counseling media with children.

The developmental nuances of each family member shapes his or her grief responses and ultimately how counselors would work with each. But what impacts human development? Are these differences solely explained by stage models related to various aspects of development, or does environment play a factor? The following sections will explore different models related to child and adolescent development. We begin with Bronfenbrenner's Ecological Theory.

BRONFENBRENNER'S ECOLOGICAL THEORY

Bronfenbrenner (1977) posited that individual biological factors strongly influence a child's development. He also noted that development is shaped by the interactions between these environmental factors and between environmental and biological factors. Bronfenbrenner's Ecological Theory describes the multiple environmental levels that impact human development. These environmental levels are often depicted as a set of concentric circles with the individual in the middle; circles that are smaller and closer to the center are meant to represent the environments that more closely interact with a person on an individual level (Bronfenbrenner, 1977). Table 1.1 provides a description and examples of each level in order of smallest to largest.

More recently, Bronfenbrenner and Evans (2000) discussed societal changes that have resulted in children's varied developmental experiences. These societal factors, such as increases in single-parent households, the prevalence of school violence, and the educational achievement gap, impact children's development at various levels within the bioecological model. Moreover, examining these changes within the context of the various bioecological systems provides another element within more traditional stage models of development (e.g., Piaget, Erikson, Kohlberg). Writing about school counseling, Galassi and Akos (2007) described this as contextual development and

Table 1.1 Levels of Bronfenbrenner's Bioecological Theory

Level	Description	Examples
Individual	Representative of each person separately; factors include gender, race, sexual orientation, age, health, etc.; interacts reciprocally with microspheres	■ an able-bodied 14-year-old transgendered African American female ■ a 5-year-old cisgender White male with a learning disability
Microsystem	The smallest systems that interact with individuals, typically within their immediate surroundings; interacts reciprocally with individuals; the most influential systems on child development	■ family of origin ■ school ■ neighborhoods/communities
Mesosystem	Refers to the interactions between microsystems; these have indirect influences on children	■ communication between a child's teacher and parents ■ interaction between households of parents with joint custody
Exosystem	Refers to interactions between a person's immediate context (i.e. individual or microsystem level) and environments in which the individual is not a member; these have indirect influences on children	■ a parent receiving a shift change at work ■ school board enacting a new discipline policy
Macrosystem	Refers to the beliefs and values of the individual's society or culture that can change over time; these have a trickle-down effect that can ultimately impact the child	■ Baby Boomer generation vs. Millennials generation ■ rural conservative environment vs. urban liberal environment
Chronosystem	Refers to life transitions, life events, and socio-historical changes that can shape or alter a person's experience	■ starting preschool ■ September 11

noted that viewing a child's environment from this perspective can shed light on the more individualized experience of that child and how it impacts his or her development.

Case Study: Jamie

Jamie is a 9-year-old female in the second grade. She lives with her mothers, Dana and Grace, who recently got married after being together for more than 15 years. Jamie also has a 12-year-old brother, Joseph. Several of Jamie's classmates have been teasing her after they learned of her parents' recent wedding; one female classmate said Jamie was weird because of this, and another male classmate told Jamie that his dad had said that Jamie's parents were gross. The bullying that Jamie is receiving escalated when her parents formally changed her last name to reflect both parents. At first, Jamie did not want to tell her parents about what was happening at school because she was afraid they would decide to homeschool her, like they did with Joseph when he was in elementary school. After several weeks, Grace noticed that Jamie seemed sad and asked her if anything was going on. Jamie reported what her classmates had been doing, which prompted her parents to set up a meeting with Jamie's teacher, Ms. Light. The teacher indicated that she had not witnessed anything, assured that she would keep watch for any acts of bullying, and encouraged Jamie to report these incidents to her or another teacher. Ms. Light referred Jamie and her parents to the school counselor, Mr. Walters, who asked if Jamie would like to be a part of a small group for students who have had similar experiences with their peers.

Within the above example, Jamie represents the individual. She is a part of several microsystems, including her family, her school, her peer groups, and the counseling small group. Mesosystems within this example include the inter-action between Jamie's parents and her teacher and the interaction between Jamie's parents and the school counselor. The interaction between Jamie's classmate and his father and the interaction between Jamie's teacher and the school counselor would be examples of exosystems in action. Jamie was raised in a macrosystem that welcomed same-sex parented families, whereas her peers seem to have been raised in an environment that does not; similarly, although the example only includes two faculty perspectives, the school environment does appear to be welcoming and inclusive. One event represent-ing changes in the chronosystem would be the national legalization of same-sex marriage, which likely impacted Jamie's parents' decision to marry; conflicts occurred after this event due to varying macrosystemic views, which trickled down into the microsystems of which Jamie is a member.

We will revisit this example later in the sections related to other developmental theories.

DEVELOPMENTAL CONSIDERATIONS

Before discussing the more traditional developmental theories, it is important to note that development does not progress at the same rate for everyone. These differences can be connected to biological, genetic, environmental, and social factors (Silk, Redcay, and Fox, 2014; Smith, Chein, and Steinberg, 2013; Steinberg, 2004). Common developmental categories include cognition, language, motor co-ordination, social interaction, and adaptive skills (National Center for Learning Disabilities [NCLD], 2015). In cases of *typical* develop-ment, children's accomplishment of developmental milestones occurs within a predictable course, meaning that development is occurring as expected. Conversely, *atypical development* refers to cases in which accomplishment of these milestones occurs outside of predictable patterns (NCLD, 2015). Parents and educators of a child who displays evidence of atypical develop-ment should take note of what is occurring with the child in order to help professionals determine if the situation is related to a developmental delay or a disorder (e.g., ADHD, Autism Spectrum Disorder). A third concept, *asynchro-nous development,* refers to cases in which one area of development (e.g., cognition) is highly advanced in comparison to other areas of development;

this concept is often used within the context of gifted students (Alsop, 2003; Bailey, 2011; Silverman, 1994). Each of these situations presents a different developmental context for children, and these considerations help shape the discussion of developmental theories.

Cognitive Development

Piaget (1977) proposed a developmental stage theory that explains individuals' ability to acquire, make sense of, and use knowledge. Within his theory, he noted that learning can occur through *assimilation*, in which an individual integrates new knowledge into existing thought structures, and *accommodation*, in which an individual takes in new knowledge and alters these existing thought structures (Berger, 2008). For example, if a child who believes that all animals lay eggs learns that the ducks she sees in the pond also lay eggs, she will assimilate this information into her existing cognitive schema related to animals. However, when the same child learns that her pet dog does *not* lay eggs, her existing cognitive schema related to animals will have to adjust to accommodate for this new knowledge. According to Piaget (1977), cognitive ability becomes more advanced over time in cases of typical development. He classified this development into the following four distinct stages:

- sensorimotor stage (birth–2 years)
- preoperational stage (2–7 years)
- concrete operational stage (7–12 years)
- formal operational stage (12 years–adulthood)

The age ranges associated with each stage are somewhat flexible, even in accounting for typical development. In the *sensorimotor stage*, children learn by their physical interactions with the world (e.g., touching, sucking) and by developing habits (e.g., smiling in the presence of a parent). During this stage, children also begin to understand object permanence, meaning that they can understand that an object still exists even though the object is out of sight (Piaget, 1977). The *preoperational stage* is known for the emergence of symbolic thought, which is crucial to play; with symbolic thought, one object can stand for another object (e.g., a broom can represent a horse). During this stage, children can primarily see only from their perspective and cannot reason through steps or processes forward and in reverse. During the *concrete operational stage*, children develop the ability to think logically, process through steps forward and in reverse, develop systems of classification, and consider the perspectives of others. Finally, the *formal operational stage* is marked by the development of hypothetical and deductive reasoning and the ability to consider long-term effects of actions. It is important to note that this abstract thinking continues to develop into adulthood and that not all adults fully develop this ability.

Counselors must account for differences in cognitive development when working with children and adolescents. Taking into account one's cognitive abilities will help counselors tailor interventions appropriately. This is especially important when discussing consequences of certain behaviors; younger children may only be able to consider immediate consequences of a certain behavior (e.g., getting a time out, receiving a treat), whereas older children and adolescents may be able to think more abstractly about future consequences of the same behavior. In cases of atypical or asynchronous development, the counselor will need to determine what the child's cognitive abilities are and how to adjust interventions accordingly.

Psychosocial Development

Erikson's (1963) theory of psychosocial development highlights crises, or developmental tasks, that an individual must accomplish over the course of his or her lifespan. In each stage, an individual must successfully complete the associated crisis. The individual may advance to a later stage without mastering an earlier stage; however, the earlier crisis will more than likely reappear until the individual masters it. The table below defines each of Erikson's eight stages. Although all eight stages do not relate to childhood and adolescence, it is important for counselors to be aware of crises that a child or adolescent will face later; moreover, this may help the counselor be able to better work with parents and caregivers.

As you can see, psychosocial development begins very individually focused and gradually shifts to include other individuals. The first two stages are

Table 1.2 Erikson's stages of psychosocial development

Age	Psychosocial Crisis	Key Task
Birth–2 years	trust vs. mistrust	Developing comfort with the surrounding environment (e.g., building relationships with primary caretakers)
2–3 years	autonomy vs. shame	Mastering the surrounding physical environment (e.g., toilet training)
3–5 years	initiative vs. guilt	Initiating actions rather than imitating actions (e.g., initiating play by oneself)
6–12 years	industry vs. inferiority	Developing one's sense of self-worth by refining skills (e.g., developing an athletic or artistic ability)
12–18 years	identity vs. role confusion	Integrating many life roles into one's self-image (e.g., using values and interests to determine future goals)
19–35 years	intimacy vs. isolation	Learning to make long-term commitment to another person (e.g., developing a long-term romantic relationship)
35–65 years	generativity vs. stagnation	Seeking satisfaction from self and others through productivity (e.g., having a stable and successful career)
65 years +	integrity vs. despair	Reviewing life accomplishments, dealing with loss, and preparing for death (e.g., examining influence on one's family, developing a "bucket list")

centered on acclimating oneself to the surrounding environment, with particular focus on establishing safety and independence. Once that independence is established, children are able to take initiative, try new experiences, and determine what they are good at; inability to master these tasks will likely lead to struggles during the adolescent years when individuals are trying to make sense of who they are in relation to others. Within this fifth stage, adolescents must come to terms with various aspects of themselves and integrate them into an identity with which they are secure. Having a strong sense of identity will assist an individual with later stages in which romantic relationships, careers, and families are important.

As with cognitive development, it is imperative for counselors to assess the psychosocial development of clients and students. These developmental crises, if not resolved, can lead to distress and ultimately shape a presenting issue for counseling. Although there are age ranges associated with each task, keep in mind that a child or adolescent may not have fully mastered an earlier task, which is now causing them concern in a later stage.

MORAL DEVELOPMENT

Kohlberg (1981) proposed a theory of moral development based on his findings after posing hypothetical moral dilemmas to individuals and examining the reasoning behind their responses. As a result, he organized his theory into six stages across three levels, with higher levels demonstrating more advanced and individualized moral reasoning. Table 1.3 provides more information about the levels, motivations, and stages.

Understanding children's level of moral development will give insight on the motivation for their behavior. Particularly related to counseling, this may also help the counselor gauge the extent to which the child sees the world from an egocentric perspective; moreover, the level of moral development may impact the child's ability to show empathy. As moral development is linked

Table 1.3 Kohlberg's theory of moral development

Level	Motivation	Stages
Level 3: Postconventional (teenage years to adulthood)	Individuals are motivated by internalized standards and duties	Stage 6: What action is consistent with my values while respecting others at the same time? Stage 5: Are there exceptions to some rules in certain situations?
Level 2: Conventional (school-age years)	Individuals are motivated by performing "right" roles and duties within society	Stage 4: What should I do to follow the rules? Stage 3: What should I do to gain approval from others around me?
Level 1: Preconventional (infancy and preschool)	Individuals are motivated by external rewards and events	Stage 2: What should I do to get a reward I want? Stage 1: What should I do to avoid being punished?

to the child's ability to cognitively think through a scenario, children and adolescents identified as gifted often display a heightened moral sensitivity to larger issues that affect society (e.g., nuclear war, environmental issues, poverty [Silverman, 1994]). Just like psychosocial development, children's moral reasoning can become a presenting problem for counseling if the individual's expected outcome does not match with the actual outcome (e.g., expecting approval from a parent after good behavior and not getting it); moreover, the counselor should be mindful that a child who engages in particular behaviors in order to please adults may attempt the same pattern with the counselor. As such, conversations pertaining to moral development are essential to counseling children and adolescents.

Attachment Theory

Bowlby (1973, 1980) posited that during infancy children form bonds with their caretakers to attain a sense of comfort and security. For most children, who successfully form secure attachments, the desire for proximity wanes over time as the child develops a sense of independence; however, the child may return to the caretaker in times of distress or crisis (Zilberstein, 2014). Children do not always develop a secure attachment with their caretakers; in fact, researchers have identified three additional maladaptive attachment styles that can shape the individual's future relationships and interactions with others (Ainsworth, Blehar, Waters, and Wall, 1978; Main and Solomon, 1990). In all, the four identified attachment styles are:

■   secure
■   anxious–avoidant
■   anxious–ambivalent
■   disorganized

The attachment style can evolve over time, and individuals can display different attachment styles toward different people, although most people have one dominant attachment style (Zilberstein, 2014).

Whereas those with secure attachment styles tend to develop typically, those with insecure attachment styles are at risk of interpersonal and intrapersonal conflicts. Those with an anxious–avoidant attachment style tend to ignore caregivers and loved ones and often show little emotion; as individuals with this attachment style mature, they may rely on self-soothing, refrain from showing emotion, and avoid help-seeking behaviors (Zilberstein, 2014). Anxious–ambivalent attachment stems from the child internalizing mixed messages from the caretaker—an unpredictable wavering between being nurturing and being unavailable; as a result, the child may become equally unpredictable, wavering between being distrustful and being clingy (Zilberstein, 2014). Finally, the disorganized attachment style is marked by a child's fear of the caretaker's unpredictable nature; these interactions, common in situations of abuse or neglect, can leave the child dependent upon the caretaker, but simultaneously fearful of him or her (Zilberstein, 2014).

Because attachment styles extend beyond infancy, the counselor should attempt to determine the child's primary attachment style, as this will shed light on how the child interacts with others, including the counselor. The attachment style may be contributing to the child's presenting concern or may cause the child difficulty in getting help for the presenting concern. Once again, involving the caregivers in treatment may provide more information about the reason for the child's insecure attachment, or may help correct the insecure attachment.

Object Relations Theory

Based in Freudian theory, Object Relations Theory theorizes that, beginning in infancy, children direct instinctual needs (e.g., food, comfort) at "objects" (Wagner, 2008). These objects can be external (e.g., the child's mother) or internal (e.g., the child's mental representation of his or her mother). Object Relations theorists are more concerned with the internal objects that children create, as these tend to provide more context of how children perceive the world around them (Wagner, 2008). For example, from the perspective of Object Relations Theory, if a child grows up with parents who are controlling and verbally abusive, this will be reflected in the way the child conceptualizes caregivers; in turn, as the child grows and has more experiences out in the world, he or she may expect the other people in the world to be cold and possibly abusive. Winnicott (1965) held that a secure mother–infant relationship is pivotal to the child's ability to shift from dependence on caretakers to independence in adulthood. Winnicott also promoted the use of transitional objects (e.g., the security blanket, the favorite toy) as a means of easing the transition from dependence on the primary caregiver as a source of security; he believed that these objects help the child individuate from the mother.

Because internal objects are based on the child's subjective interpretation of his or her environment, they can also be inaccurate. For example, a child might only remember negative qualities (e.g., discipline and limit setting) of a parent and overlook the positive qualities. These errors may impact the child's relationship with his or her caregivers later in life and may impact the child's relationships with others later in life. These relational problems may factor into presenting issues for counseling and/or may impact how the individual copes with other problems. Depending on the counselor's theoretical orientation, assessing childhood relationships may be warranted to help understand current relational functioning.

The last several sections have provided an overview of a variety of developmental models. Bronfenbrenner's Ecological Model relates development to the biological and environmental contexts in which one exists. Stage models of cognitive, psychosocial, and moral development provide a framework for evaluating an individual's development against what is considered *typical*. Other models, including Attachment Theory and Object Relations Theory, consider how experiences beginning in infancy and early childhood impact an individual's connections with other individuals and perspectives on the world around them. Individually, these models explain different aspects of development; however, they can be examined together to help gather a more comprehensive perspective of a person. The following section revisits the case of Jamie, which was previously discussed only within the context of Bronfenbrenner's Model.

Case Study: Jamie Revisited

If we revisit the case of Jamie, we can begin to examine her situation through a developmental lens. Regarding cognitive development, she would fall within Piaget's Concrete Operations Stage. One example of evidence is that she is able to think about what logical consequences may occur if she reports the bullying to her parents. Based on what she knows about her brother's experience in school, she has deduced that homeschooling may be a possible consequence of reporting the behavior. She may not yet fully understand the magnitude of her parents' marriage within the context of society.

From a psychosocial perspective, Jamie is in the industry vs. inferiority stage. Another hesitation with her sharing the information is possibly that she wanted to solve the problem on her own; because she was unable to do so, she may feel less efficacious, which makes the counseling small group an important environment for her. At the same time, she may have felt a moral obligation to follow the rules (e.g., reporting instances of bullying to an adult), while at the same time wanting to protect her parents from the mean comments made by peers.

Based on the example, Jamie more than likely has a secure attachment to her parents. She attempted to deal with her problem on her own but went back to her mother when her efforts did not work. Regarding Object Relations, there is not a lot of evidence to provide context of Jamie's conceptualization of her parents. She does know, however, that they are helpful and nurturing in times of trouble and also that they have the authority to change her school situation; this may provide context of a secure and balanced view of them.

These developmental models provide additional context to Jamie's situation and allow the reader to understand various processes that are at work. It is imperative to remember the environmental contexts in which Jamie resides. Focusing only on the stage models discussed later in this chapter may shed light on Jamie's internal process with the presenting issue; however, her situation does also occur in an environment where macrosystemic views seem to be at odds. The school counselor who will be working with Jamie in the small group setting must keep both perspectives in mind. Doing so will allow him to ensure that the counseling interventions account for what is developmentally appropriate and possible for Jamie, while also considering how the world around her impacts the situation.

Case Study: Toby

Toby is a 13-year-old African American male, currently in the sixth grade. He is an only child who lives with his single father, Darrell. After receiving a recommendation from Toby's school, Darrell decides to bring Toby to counseling with Shayna, a 36-year-old White female mental health counselor in community agency. During the initial meeting with Shayna, Darrell provides background on their family. When Toby was 3, his mother left, and Toby has only had contact with her once, on his 8th birthday. Darrell and Toby previously lived in a large city, where Toby attended a school comprised mostly of students of color. Darrell's recent job change required them to move to a suburb with a largely different demographic. Toby's new school is predominantly White, including the faculty. Darrell informs Shayna that Toby was recently in a fight, which is one of the few times in his educational history that he has been "in trouble" at school; Toby's principal recommended counseling because of this incident and because Toby has had trouble "fitting in."

Over the course of Toby's meetings with Shayna, he becomes more comfortable talking with her about the differences between his old school and his new school. He talks of being called names, being asked questions about his race, and generally feeling out of place. The fight he had with a classmate started because one of his classmates made a joke about his hair being different. Toby said that he reported it to his teacher, but "she didn't do anything," so he defended himself. He has reported finding friends, including both Black and White students, and noted that some of his teachers have been very supportive. However, he does feel singled out by some of the school's faculty because of his race. Their goals for counseling include processing Toby's identity development, learning self-advocacy skills, and identifying pro-social strategies for handling bullies.

Toby's microsystems include his relationships with his father, with his friends at school, with his teachers, with Shayna, and with the student he fought; most of these are positive relationships, but the negative ones are causing him numerous issues. It also must be noted that these lower levels are where issues related to race have more immediately affected Toby. At the mesosystemic level, we can see the interactions between Toby's family and his school and between Toby's family and Shayna, among others. At the exosystemic level, Toby has been impacted by the change in his father's job, and possibly by his new school's disciplinary policies. One example of a macrosystemic concern is the potential for differences in the city in which Toby previously lived and the suburb in which he currently lives; due to the demographic differences, there are possibly political and ideological differences that trickle down to lower levels. The chronosystem in which Toby exists includes several key incidents, such as his mother leaving, his family's move, and his fight with the classmate.

Developmentally, Toby is an adolescent likely transitioning between concrete operations and formal operations. From a psychosocial perspective, other adolescents at his age are in the stage of identity vs. role confusion; this developmental stage has been made especially important because he is now having a harder time fitting in due to his move and the resulting change in his peers. Regarding moral development, Toby appears to be in Stage 5 of the postconventional level (Level 3)—he is developing his own moral code and is testing moments in which there may be exceptions to the rules (e.g., first reporting his peer to the teacher, then fighting). Toby seems to have a secure attachment style, but it is not known how his mother leaving early in life has affected him. This same relationship with his mother may also be a factor from an Object Relations perspective, in that Toby may have a preconception of how to relate to adult females. At the same time, his relationship with his father *appears to be very secure and supportive, as evidenced by his father willingly responding to a recommendation by the school to seek counseling.*

As with the case of Jamie, these models help provide a better understanding of Toby. Viewing him from the various stage models allows for comparisons to typical development based on his age and his peers. However, the contextual development revealed through Bronfenbrenner's model may provide more insight into Toby's situation. As his counselor, Shayna cannot ignore the demographic and geographic changes in his immediate systems, as these are salient to his presenting issue. Similarly, she cannot ignore the larger macrosystemic changes and how these have impacted him and will continue to impact him. Another important consideration is the system in which the counseling relationship resides. Unlike Jamie working with her school counselor, Toby is working with a mental health counselor in an agency outside of the school setting; this has direct implications for the structure of the counseling relationship and what can be worked on in counseling.

SUMMARY

Children and adolescents are distinctly different from each other and from adults. These differences are vitally important considerations for counselors, as counselors should be tailoring interventions to the unique situations of clients based on what is developmentally and environmentally appropriate. This chapter introduced bioecological systems as a framework for surveying the environmental context within which clients live. Additionally, this chapter examined several models of human development and explored the varying rates at which individuals can pass through these stage models. Counselors, both in school settings and mental health settings, who work with children and adolescents must be knowledgeable of how environmental and developmental factors impact their clients so that they can provide the best care possible.

The key points that have arisen in this chapter are as follows.

- Childhood is often divided into three stages: (a) infant/toddler years, (b) preschool years, and (c) school-age years.
- The school-age years are sometimes divided into middle and late childhood.
- Play provides a developmentally appropriate medium for children to express themselves.
- Child development is impacted by a variety of factors, including biology and the environment.
- Bronfenbrenner's Bioecological Theory identifies six environmental levels: (a) individual, (b) microsystem, (c) mesosystem, (d) exosystem, (e) macrosystem, and (f) chronosystem. The closer the system is to the individual, the more directly the system impacts the individual.
- Development can occur according to predictable patterns (i.e. typical) or outside of predictable patterns (i.e. atypical); additionally, development can occur asynchronously when one area is developing at a much faster rate than others.

- Cognitive development refers to the changes in how an individual processes information; this occurs within four stages: (a) sensorimotor, (b) preoperational, (c) concrete operations, and (d) formal operations.
- The eight stages of psychosocial development are associated with developmental tasks, or crises, that must be mastered by the individual.
- The levels and stages of moral development provide context for the changes the process by which individuals make decisions about moral issues; moral reasoning typically becomes more complex with age and development.
- Attachment Theory helps explain how secure and insecure bonds with caregivers in childhood impact interpersonal relationships later in life.
- Object Relations Theory is concerned with how children construct subjective objects representing people and things in their lives, such as caregivers; these objects can also impact expectations for future interpersonal relationships.
- Child and adolescent counselors must consider the developmental and environmental context of clients in order to provide appropriate services.

Additional Resources

ASCA Why Elementary School Counselors: https://www.schoolcounselor.org/school-counselors-members/careers-roles/why-elementary-school-counselors
ASCA Why Secondary School Counselors: https://www.schoolcounselor.org/school-counselors-members/careers-roles/why-secondary-school-counselors
ASCA Why Middle School Counselors: https://www.schoolcounselor.org/school-counselors-members/careers-roles/why-middle-school-counselors
Association for Play Therapy: http://www.a4pt.org/
Play Therapy Outcome Research Database: http://evidencebasedchildtherapy.com/research/

Suggested Readings

Bronfenbrenner, U. (1981) *The ecology of human development: Experiments by nature and design.* Cambridge, MA: Harvard University Press.
Capuzzi, D. and Gross, D. R. (2014). *Youth at risk: A prevention resource for counselors, teachers, and parents,* 5th ed. Alexandria, VA: American Counseling Association.
Cook-Cottone, C., Kane, L. S., and Anderson, L. M. (2015). *The elements of counseling children and adolescents.* New York: Springer.
DeKruyf, L., Auger, R., and Trice-Black, S. (2013). The role of school counselors in meeting students' mental health needs: Examining issues of professional identity. *Professional School Counseling* 16 (5), 271–282. http://dx.doi.org/10.5330/PSC.n.2013-16.271
Juntunen, C. L. and Schwartz, J. P. (2016). *Counseling across the lifespan: Prevention and treatment,* 2nd ed. Thousand Oaks, CA: Sage.
Kaffenberger, C. and O'Rorke-Trigiani, J. (2013). Addressing student mental health needs by providing direct and indirect services and building alliances in the community. *Professional School Counseling* 16 (5), 323–332. http://dx.doi.org/10.5330/PSC.n.2013-16.323
Levy, T. M. and Orlans, M. (2014). *Attachment, trauma, and healing: Understanding and treating attachment disorder in children, families, and adults,* 2nd ed. Philadelphia, PA: Jessica Kingsley.

Mendaglio, S. and Peterson, J. S. (2007). *Models of counseling gifted children, adolescents, and young adults.* Waco, TX: Prufrock Press.

Roaten, G. K. and Roaten, D. J. (2012). Adolescent brain development: Current research and the impact on secondary school counseling programs. *Journal of School Counseling* 10 (18), 1–27. Retrieved from: http://jsc.montana.edu/articles/v10n18.pdf

Shoukouhi, A. M., Limberg, D. and Armstrong, S. A. (2014). Counseling preadolescents: Using developmental cues to guide therapeutic approach. *International Journal of Play Therapy* 23 (4), 217–230. http://dx.doi.org/10.1037/a0038146

Sink, Christopher. (2011). *Mental health interventions for school counselors.* Belmont, CA: Brooks/Cole.

Sommers-Flanagan, J. and Sommers-Flanagan, R. (2007). *Tough kids, cool counseling: User-friendly approaches with challenging youth.* Alexandria, VA: American Counseling Association.

Trice-Black, S., Bailey, C. L., and Riechel, M. K. (2013). Play therapy in school counseling. *Professional School Counseling* 16 (5), 303–312. http://dx.doi.org/10.5330/PSC.n.2013-16.303

Glossary

Accommodation: Refers to a process in cognitive development in which newly acquired knowledge does not fit within existing cognitive schema, resulting in changes in the cognitive schema

Adolescence: A period roughly between the ages of 12 and 18; known for puberty, hormonal changes, and a desire for independence

Assimilation: Refers to a process in cognitive development in which newly acquired knowledge is incorporated into an existing cognitive schema

Asynchronous development: A process in which one area of human development is much more advanced than other areas; often discussed within the context of gifted students

Atypical development: A process in which one or more areas of human development are advancing outside of predictable patterns

Childhood: A period roughly between birth and age 12; known for significant development and shifts from dependence on the primary caregiver to more independent functioning

Chronosystem: In Bioecological Theory, the system which accounts for temporal changes and significant events

Crises: In psychosocial development, the tasks that must be accomplished at each level

Exosystem: In Bioecological Theory, the system in which the individual's microsystems interact with environments of which the individual is not a member

Macrosystem: In Bioecological Theory, the system in which societal norms, beliefs, and values shape the environment and trickle down to more proximal systems

Mesosystem: In Bioecological Theory, the system in which an individual's microsystems interact with each other

Microsystem: In Bioecological Theory, the most proximal system to the individual; represents the various systems of which the individual is a member

Objects: Refers to real or imagined people, things, or concepts around which children shape their concept of reality; during infancy, instinctual needs are often directed at them

Play: Refers to the developmental language of children

Typical development: A process in which areas of human development are advancing according to predictable patterns

References

Ainsworth, M. D. S., Blehar, M. C., Waters, E., and Wall, S. (1978). *Patterns of attachment: A psychological study of the strange situation*. Hillsdale, NJ: Erlbaum.

Alsop, G. (2003). Asynchrony: Intuitively valid and theoretically reliable. *Roeper Review: A Journal on Gifted Education* 25 (3), 118–126.

American Academy of Pediatrics (2016). Ages and stages. Retrieved from https://www.healthychildren.org/English/ages-stages/Pages/default.aspx

Bailey, C. L. (2011). An examination of the relationships between ego development, Dabrowski's theory of positive disintegration, and the behavioral characteristics of gifted adolescents. *Gifted Child Quarterly* 55 (3), 208–222. doi:10.1177/0016986211412180

Berger, K. S. (2008). *The developing person through the lifespan*, 7th ed. New York: Worth Publishers.

Bowlby, J. (1973). *Attachment and loss: Separation*, vol. 2. New York: Basic Books.

Bowlby, J. (1980). *Attachment and loss: Loss, sadness, and depression*, vol. 3. New York: Basic Books.

Bratton, S. C., Ray, D. C., Edwards, N. A., and Landreth, G. L. (2009). Child-centered play therapy (CCPT): Theory, research, and practice. *Person-Centered and Experiential Psychotherapies* 8 (4), 266–281. doi:10.1080/14779757.2009.9688493

Bronfenbrenner, U. (1977). Toward an experimental ecology of human development. *American Psychologist* 32 (7), 513–531.

Bronfenbrenner, U. and Evans, G. W. (2000). Developmental science in the 21st century: Emerging questions, theoretical models, research designs, and empirical findings. *Social Development* 9 (1), 115–125.

Centers for Disease Control and Prevention (2016). Middle childhood (6–8 years of age). Retrieved from http://www.cdc.gov/ncbddd/childdevelopment/positiveparenting/middle.html

Erikson, E. (1963). *Childhood and society*. New York: Norton.

Galassi, J. P. and Akos, P. (2007). *Strengths-based school counseling: Promoting student development and achievement*. New York: Routledge.

Johnson, J. H., Rasbury, W. C. and Siegel, L. J. (1997). *Approaches to child treatment: Introduction to theory, research, and practice*, 2nd ed. Boston: Allyn & Bacon.

Kohlberg, L. (1981). *The philosophy of moral development*. San Francisco, CA: Harper & Row.

Kottman, T. (2011). *Play therapy: Basics and beyond*, 2nd ed. Alexandria, VA: American Counseling Association.

Landreth, G. L. (2012). *Play therapy: The art of the relationship*, 3rd ed. New York: Brunner Routledge.

Main, M. and Solomon, J. (1990). Procedures for identifying infants as disorganized/disoriented during the strange situation. In M. T. Greenberg, D. Cicchetti, and E. M. Cummings (eds.), *Attachment in the preschool years: Theory, research, and intervention* (pp. 121–160). Chicago, IL: University of Chicago Press.

National Center for Learning Disabilities (2015). Early identification: Normal and atypical development. Retrieved from http://www.ldonline.org/article/6047/

Piaget, J. (1962). *Play, dreams, and imitation in childhood*. New York: Routledge.

Piaget, J. (1977). *The development of thought: Equilibration of cognitive structure*. New York: Viking Press.

Siegel, D. J. (2013). *Brainstorm: the power and purpose of the teenage brain*. New York: Penguin Putnam.

Silk, J. S., Redcay, E., and Fox, N. A. (2014). Contributions of social and affective neuroscience to our understanding of typical and atypical development. *Developmental Cognitive Neuroscience* 1–6. doi:10.1016/j.dcn.2014.02.002

Silverman, L. K. (1994). The moral sensitivity of gifted children and the evolution of society. *Roeper Review: A Journal on Gifted Education* 17 (2), 110–116.

Smith, A. R., Chein, J., and Steinberg, L. (2013). Impact of socio-emotional context, brain development, and pubertal maturation on adolescent risk-taking. *Hormones and Behavior* 64, 323–332. doi:10.1016/j.yhbeh.2013.03.006

Steinberg, L. (2004). Cognitive and affective development in adolescence. *Trends in Cognitive Science* 9 (2), 69–74. doi:10.1016/j.tics.2004.12.005

Taylor, D. D. and Bratton, S. C. (2014). Developmentally appropriate practice: Adlerian play therapy with preschool children. *The Journal of Individual Psychology* 70 (3), 205–219.

Wagner, W. G. (2008). *Counseling, psychology, and children*, 2nd ed. Upper Saddle River, NJ: Pearson Education.

Winnicott, D. W. (1965). *The maturational process and the facilitating environment: Studies in the theory of emotional development.* New York: International Universities Press

World Health Organization (2016). Adolescent development. Retrieved from http://www.who.int/maternal_child_adolescent/topics/adolescence/development/en/

Zilberstein, K. (2014). The use and limitations of attachment theory in child psychotherapy. *Psychotherapy* 51 (1), 93–103. doi:10.1037/a0030930

CHAPTER 2

Counseling Children in School and Clinical Mental Health Settings

Malti Tuttle, Christy Land, and Lauren Moss

There is in every child at every stage a new miracle of vigorous unfolding, which constitutes a new hope and a new responsibility for all.

Erik Erikson (1950)

CHAPTER OBJECTIVES

After reading this chapter, you will be able to:

- better understand the different developmental domains of children between 4–8 years old
- explain the stage-specific developments of 4–8-year-old children
- more clearly understand children within this age range's counseling needs
- apply your knowledge to the provision of age-appropriate counseling services

---

INTRODUCTION

Childhood is a time of new experiences, wonder, and inquisitiveness. During this stage of life, children are continuously gaining new skills, knowledge, and abilities (Wood, 2007). As children navigate through this stage, there may be a time where they face challenges requiring support through counseling services. Therefore, this chapter contains different developmental domains pertaining to children between the ages of 4–8 years and explains the developmental stages specific to this age group. The purpose of the chapter is to highlight these significant developmental domains and stages while guiding counselors' understanding of children within this age group in order to provide appropriate counseling services. Additionally, case studies are provided focusing on young children receiving counseling services in clinical mental health and school settings, especially since counseling services between both agencies differ from one another. Clinical mental health and school counselors often work collaboratively to support children; however, limited knowledge is known to each counseling professional in regards to how the other operates in their setting, since clinical mental health and school counselors operate within different parameters. Therefore it is imperative as well as beneficial for both to

Table 2.1 Role of clinical mental health and school counselors

Clinical Mental Health Counselors	School Counselors
■ advocate for children ■ work in offices, hospitals, mental health facilities ■ are credentialed and/or licensed ■ counsel children and adults ■ provide in-depth therapeutic counseling services ■ charge for counseling services ■ may accept insurance/Medicaid ■ adhere to ethics ■ receive court orders referring children for counseling	■ advocate for children ■ work in K–12 schools ■ are certified or licensed by state Departments of Education as school counselors ■ counsel children in grades K–12 ■ provide services under academic, social/emotional, and career domains ■ refer children to clinical mental health counselors for in-depth therapeutic counseling services ■ receive a salary from the school district and do not charge for counseling services provided to children ■ adhere to ethics as well as school district policies

Sources: ASCA, 2012; Gladding, 2013.

understand each other's roles, strengths, and limits as practitioners. Clinical mental health counselors are practitioners who are credentialed and/or licensed, charge clients, Medicaid, or insurance companies for counseling sessions, and provide therapy, whereas school counselors are certified, do not charge for counseling services, refer students to clinical mental health counselors for in-depth counseling services, and carry additional roles in the school setting other than counseling (ASCA, 2012; Gladding, 2013). This chapter will further provide information to identify developmental domains and stages pertaining to children between the ages of four to eight years old, understand clinical mental health counselor and school counselor services based on the parameters of the profession, and conceptualize internal and external factors that contribute to childhood behaviors and manifestations. Table 2.1 has been provided to lay out the roles of clinical mental health and school counselors.

DEVELOPMENTAL THEORIES

Developmental theories provide insight and a foundation for the purposes of understanding childhood growth and gauging milestone attainment. Two theorists who have significantly contributed to the childhood development field are Erik Erikson and Jean Piaget. Erik Erikson is known for his Personality Theory and Jean Piaget for his Cognitive Developmental Theory. Erickson's Personality Theory highlighted "the psychosocial aspects of behavior: attitudes and feelings toward the self and toward others," as well as identifying eight psychosocial stages (Broderick and Blewitt, 2015, p. 11). Children in this age group, 4–8 years old, fall under the psychosocial stages of initiative vs. guilt and industry vs. inferiority. The initiative vs. guilt psychosocial stage includes children between the ages of 3–6 years old and specifies children at this time focus on mirroring adult roles; the industry vs. inferiority psychosocial stage encompasses children between the ages of 6–12 years old, who desire to grasp academic material and perform on the same level as other children (Broderick and Blewitt, 2015).

Jean Piaget's Cognitive Developmental Theory stated children learn and develop at their own pace and adults should foster this process. Additionally, Piaget recognized four stages of development instead of eight, in comparison to Erikson. The preoperational stage included children between the ages of 2–7 years old and stated the thought process generally is centered around a specific aspect instead of several ideas (Broderick and Blewitt, 2015). The concrete operational stage included children between the ages of 7–12 years old and during this stage children's logical thinking skills are increasing at a quicker rate than the previous stage (Broderick and Blewitt, 2015).

Reflection Activity

Before reading further about the childhood developmental stage, reflect on what you currently know and understand about children between the ages of 4–8 years old. Recall what you previously learned about children in this age group and your experiences from when you were a child. Reflecting, unpacking individual experiences and prior knowledge, and recognizing assumptions assist individuals to visualize and conceptualize childhood development. A chart has been provided to write down thoughts to assist for this reflection activity.

Me as a child	What I know about childhood developmental stages

1. What memories of childhood between the ages of 4–8 stand out for you?
2. What are children capable of doing during this stage of their lives?
3. What activities did you enjoy participating in during the ages of 4–6 and 6–8? What similarities and differences do you notice?
4. Describe your school experience.

Exercise 2.1

Childhood (Ages 4–8)

Early childhood is the developmental stage where children grow and meet specific milestones indicating whether appropriate developmental domains have or have not been achieved. The Centers for Disease Control and Prevention (CDC) defined milestones as "things most children can do by a certain age", such as playing, speaking, and jumping. Gross and fine motor movement is often included in milestones. However, children may develop at different stages compared to their peers, therefore counselors should be mindful of this when working with children between the ages of 4–8. Specifically, school counselors who work with children in a school setting would be an asset in the role of an advocate to students by reflecting and utilizing their knowledge of developmental stages while consulting with school personnel, parents, and in their own practice. Additional factors such as family, language, culture, ability, socio-economics, education of parents, exposure to cultural experiences, and trauma impact child development. Therefore, clinical mental health and school counselors should be able to demonstrate best practices by providing counseling services through a social justice lens when considering all developmental areas of each child they counsel. Counselors who have received their education from a Council of Accreditation of Counseling and Related Educational Programs (CACREP) institution are equipped with the skills, techniques, and knowledge base to work in the best interest of children.

Childhood is filled with new experiences where children play individually and/or with others, fantasize, begin to gain motor skill control and usage, and recognize letters, numbers, and sounds. Children between the ages of 4 to 8 years old generally are socialized by attending school such as pre-school, pre-kindergarten, and elementary school or activities where they interact and engage with other children and adults. These opportunities allow children to adapt to different surroundings, personalities, activities, and routines. During these years, the main concepts children gain involve learning to interact with adults and peers, follow directions and rules, and learning academic subjects. Younger children first learn basic skills such as holding a pencil or crayon, recalling the alphabet and shapes, and gaining balance. Older children have more developed language and math skills, demonstrate increased vocabulary, and engage in more friendship-building activities than their younger peers.

Younger children are navigating various transitions such as attending school, playing at friends' homes, and participating in extracurricular activities. These transitional events allow children to socialize, gain independence from their parents, build connections with other people outside of the family, and engage in recreation. Children between the ages of 4 and 6 years old may attend pre-kindergarten prior to enrolling in public school. Some states do not require students to enroll in kindergarten until they are 6 years old, so the age range of formal education enrollment can vary (National Center for Educational Statistics, 2015). Children between the ages of 5 and 8 years old attend formal education such as early childhood education centers or elementary school. Younger children who never attended school prior to the elementary setting may face an increased sense of separation anxiety and difficulty comprehending school rules, culture, and expectations.

Parents during this time decide whether to enroll their child in home school or a regular school setting such as public, private, or Montessori. Some parents select home schooling for their children instead of the regular school setting since there is more flexibility in the day. Home schooling is structured differently since the parent is able to decide on the curriculum, daily schedule, method of delivery of instruction, as well as instructing their own children or joining other home school groups. Regular schools differ than home schooling based on various factors. These factors include student enrollment size, mandated curriculum, and specific schedule implemented to follow during the day. Therefore, children who have been home schooled may at first face challenges transitioning to the regular school setting due to the vast differences. The larger class size, less flexibility, new structure of the educational setting, and separation from the parent may cause frustration and anxiety. School counselors who understand the difference between home school and the regular school settings are pivotal in supporting children in coping and managing during this transition.

Generally older children who have previously attended school or participated in extracurricular activities transition more smoothly in comparison to their younger counterparts. Children between the ages of 6 and 8 years old are accustomed to attending school for longer hours, engaging in tasks, following rules, and interacting more independently. Clinical mental health and school counselors working with children would benefit during the intake stage by soliciting information of when the child first started interacting with peers and formal schooling. This glimpse of insight may also provide vital information in conceptualizing the child as well as contributing to interventions for a treatment plan.

Case Study: Jose

Below is a case illustration about a 5-year-old named Jose. While reading, reflect on poignant factors such as age, culture, family, education, student advocacy, and social justice considerations the school counselor may utilize when addressing the concerns referred by the teacher. Additionally, focus on the role of advocacy in the realm of supporting the student based on developmental and culturally appropriate counseling interventions.

Jose, a 5-year-old Latino male, was referred to the school counselor by his kindergarten teacher. The teacher expressed concern by stating Jose does not interact with other students, does not respond to her when she asks him questions, cries each day, cannot hold a pencil to write, hides under his desk, and walks around the classroom to get supplies without raising his hand to ask for permission. The students in the class prefer to stay away from Jose because they feel he is not following the rules and does not complete his work. They do not want to associate with someone who is considered to be a troublemaker. The teacher expresses she is concerned about Jose's developmental functioning, academic success, and social/emotional wellbeing. The school counselor follows up on the teacher's referral and finds out Jose's family moved to the United States in July prior to the start of school and do not speak English. Furthermore, Jose never attended any type of formal education prior to enrolling in Kindergarten. It is evident Jose's lack of schooling, English acquisition, and knowledge of school culture has created a barrier to being successful in the classroom.

Process Questions

1. How can the school counselor utilize the background information provided to support Jose? (CACREP G.3.h.)
2. What factors are available to determine the types of support Jose will need to be socially, emotionally, and academically successful? (CACREP G.2.b.; CACREP G.3.f)
3. What are some social justice considerations to be mindful of prior to providing counseling interventions? (CACREP G.3.f; CACREP G.3.h)
4. What primary intervention(s) should the school counselor consider implementing when creating a treatment plan? (CACREP G.2.a; CACREP G.2.g)

Children between the ages of 4–8 years old experience various developmental changes during this stage of their lives. Each child develops differently; however, specific developmental stages are recognized for the purpose of identifying milestone attainment. Therefore clinical mental health and school counselors should remain mindful and abreast of current research focusing on childhood developmental stages. The following section further expounds on developmental stages by addressing physical development in childhood. Additionally, abilities, tasks, physical growth, and medical considerations for the age group will be discussed.

PHYSICAL DEVELOPMENT IN CHILDHOOD

Children between the ages of 4–8 are continuously growing taller and gaining weight, but at a slower pace compared to infants and toddlers (Ziomek-Daigle and Land, 2016). They are able to gain balance and navigate moving around on their own while able to perceive spatial boundaries in order to avoid colliding with others. During these years, children are able to independently or with the assistance of an adult grasp gross motor skills such as locomotor skills, manipulative skills, and nonlocomotor skills (Kostelnik, Soderman, and Whiren, 2011). Examples of these skills include beginning to throw and catch balls, draw shapes, kick, stretch, and sway (Breslin, Morton, and Rudisill, 2008). Ease and fluency of mastering these skills are based on the age of the child. Older children generally are able to master maneuvering these skills compared to their younger peers.

Additionally, Breslin, Morton, and Rudisill (2008) discuss that children at this age engage in basic grooming skills, which include bathing, dental hygiene, brushing hair, getting dressed, and undressed, and hand washing. Older children maintain a longer attention span and are more independent than their younger peers. Children between the ages of 6 to 8 years old are able to move around on their own, write their names and sentences, spell words, follow directions involving a few steps, and retain larger chunks of information. However, parents may receive a recommendation for their child to be examined by a physician if there is distinct difficulty with gross motor skills mastery.

This time of life involves several doctor appointments and visits since children grow quickly, biological ailments emerge, and children become sick more often due to germ exposure while being around other children. Medical evaluations involve physicians conducting and monitoring child development for the purpose of verifying and identifying possible biological factors inhibiting milestone achievement. Further, checkups by the pediatrician may detect onset of childhood diseases and disorders such as juvenile diabetes, obesity, food allergies, asthma, and autism that often are detected at this age. Children during this developmental stage may be identified with speech and language impairments, vision problems, and/or Attention Deficit Hyperactivity Disorder (ADHD), which may lead to special education services or 504 accommodations in the school setting.

Additionally, schools expect children to be immunized when enrolling in school; however, vaccinations have been a controversial debate. The Centers for Disease Control and Prevention (CDC, 2016) issued a 2016 recommended immunization schedule stating between the ages of 4 to 6 years old, children should have their fifth dose of diphtheria, tetanus, and acellular pertussis; fourth dose of inactivated poliovirus; second dose of measles, mumps, rubella (MMR); and second dose of varicella. However, parents' opinions vary between children receiving an exorbitant amount of vaccines, unnecessary vaccines, mandatory vaccinations for all children, and no vaccinations for children (Campbell, 2015). This debate was sparked due to speculation and research that vaccines lead to autism in children, and even though schools desire all children to be immunized, parents have the flexibility and freedom to submit immunization waivers to the schools.

Brainstorming Activity

Clinical mental health and school counselors receive majority of the same training during graduate school in terms of counseling courses. However, each counseling professional is able to practice in the realm of their work setting and parameters of their job. School counselors do not provide long-term therapeutic services in the school setting whereas clinical mental health counselors are able to see clients on a regular basis in their work setting. Additionally, school counselors are unable to diagnose in the school setting and treat the child, but clinical mental health counselors do so in their practice. Based on this information, a scenario of a child who is 8 years old is provided. Brainstorm how a school counselor and a clinical mental health counselor would approach this case given their respective work sites.

Case Study: Thomas

Thomas is an 8-year-old male in the third grade. He has difficulty staying focused, engaging with peers, and maintaining eye contact. His classroom teacher mentioned he also has not been able to engage with the other students and is worried he is not able to make friends. The example she

Exercise 2.2

provided is that Thomas does not initiate engagement with his peers during recess and does not accept invitations to play. His parents have stated he has a hard time when his routine is changed without prior notice. Thomas's parents and teacher have pondered if there are any underlying issues that may be contributing to his challenges. The mother has been reading about autism, but has some questions she would like to ask in order to gain further information and guidance. As a result, the parents have requested a meeting with the school counselor to discuss their concerns.

1. How would a school counselor approach working with Thomas?
2. What limitations does the school counselor have in this scenario?
3. How would a clinical mental health counselor approach working with Thomas, in comparison to a school counselor?
4. Discuss how the school counselor and clinical mental health counselor are able to work in tandem with the same student.

Children during this stage gain independence while achieving balance and moving around by themselves. Gross motor skills development provides children with the abilities such as throwing and catching, drawing shapes, and kicking (Breslin, Morton, and Rudisill, 2008). Additionally, children may be referred to a physician if certain skills and abilities are not achieved or mastered by a particular age. Several contributing factors for a referral to a physician may be related to childhood diseases, disorders, or impairments. The next section on cognitive development addresses concepts such as childhood imagination, abstract and tangible thinking, and problem solving.

COGNITIVE DEVELOPMENT IN CHILDHOOD

The cognitive development for children in this age group varies significantly. Children between the ages of 4–6 generally function differently from their 6–8-year-old peers. This is due to several factors such as age and milestones achieved during child growth. Additionally, as a reminder, children may develop rapidly, delayed, or at the same rate as their peers, which must not necessitate immediate alarm (Wood, 2007). However, parents should schedule regular appointments and checkups with their child's pediatrician to remain aware of their child's development.

Children between the ages of 4–6 years old are energetic, with a zest for life. They have a great sense of imagination and often embellish stories. However, abstract concepts are too vague to comprehend at this age level. Their desire to play and affinity for music intersect for learning opportunities through combining instruction on routines, letters, and numbers (Wood, 2007). Children also need positive affirmation from adults while they are learning new tasks and trying new experiences. Adults can support children during this stage by modeling appropriate behaviors, reading stories while pointing out pictures, and providing opportunities to interact with other children.

Children between the ages of 6–8 years are inquisitive, ask questions, and participate in new activities. Their inquisitive minds lead them to explore how objects are made and work. These children have a greater attention span than their younger peers. However, these children still have short attention spans compared to children older than them. They are able to interact and engage with other children while working on tasks. Additionally, they are able to discuss their thoughts while problem solving and identify challenges. Computers and technology are of special interest, since games, videos, and programs are opportunities for hands-on learning (Wood, 2007). It is imperative counselors working with children between the ages of 4 to 8 years old be mindful in recognizing children in the same age group have significantly differing abilities based on their being either younger or older members of this group.

Reflection Activity

1. Recall when you were between the ages of 4–8. What types of songs and activities did you sing and perform when learning new concepts and materials?
2. How did this differ from when you were 4–6 years old to when you were 6–8 years old?

Exercise 2.3

Brainstorm Activity

Now that you have reflected on your own experiences, brainstorm how a clinical mental health counselor and a school counselor can build rapport with children in this age group. Keep in mind young children are not able to sit down for a long time, based on their cognitive development.

1. What types of strategies can clinical mental health and school counselors utilize during rapport building?
2. What tools, objects, and/or activities would be ideal to have in a counseling office for rapport building?
3. How could a balance between sitting and movement be achieved during the rapport-building process?

Exercise 2.4

Social/Emotional Development in Childhood

Children between the ages of 4–5 years old begin to establish friendship groups, name call and brag, and use their imagination while transitioning into more detailed play (Poppe, Werth, Guzman, Brand, Fox, Crandall, Durden, and Pitt, 2011). Children who demonstrate prosocial behaviors such as "helping, cooperating, sharing, and showing concern" generally develop positive relationships with others throughout their lives (Eisenberg, Fabes, and Spinrad, 2006; Scrimgeour, Davis, and Buss, 2016, p. 102). Often times, the sharing of friends result in turmoil amongst children at this age, causing social/emotional angst. Therefore, school counselors and clinical mental health counselors can support childhood social/emotional development by providing counseling services that foster skills that build friendship, empathy, and social development. Small-group counseling may be beneficial to this age group to best address social skills, bonding, and communication.

Children at this age generally express feelings through play in lieu of talk since identifying feelings may be too abstract of a concept to verbalize (Gladding, 2011). Therefore, capitalizing on the integration of expressive arts and/or play therapy in the counseling practice would be beneficial for clinical mental health and school counselors in their work with children in this age group. Examples of expressive arts include but are not limited to role play, singing, drawing, puppets, drama, literature, and music (Gladding, 2011). Kottman (2011) further reiterated the importance of play therapy by stating children who face challenges such as "attachment disorder, attention-deficit/hyperactivity disorder (ADHD), autism spectrum disorders, mood disorders, learning disabilities, speech difficulties, and children in residential treatment centers may be appropriate candidates for play therapy if it is combined with other treatment strategies" (pp.17–21). Therefore, expressive arts and play therapy interventions provide clinical mental health and school counselors tools to work with children in avenues other than talk therapy to support children in each developmental stage.

Case Study: Natalia

The case study below is a school counseling case illustration for elementary school.

Natalia, a 6-year-old first grader, has been receiving school counseling services for demonstrating aggression towards peers. She has been pushing and kicking other students in class when wanting to be selected first, or if things do not go her way. The teacher and administration, after consulting with the parents, referred Natalia to the school counselor. The school counselor met with the teacher and spoke with the parents on the telephone. Additionally, the school counselor reviewed Natalia's cumulative file for additional details. During the first counseling session, Natalia and the school counselor focused primarily on the intake and rapport-building process. Once rapport had been built, the focus of the sessions revolved around positive self-esteem and appropriate peer interactions such as demonstrating respect to other students, anger management, self-affirmation, and self-regulation.

The school counselor consistently followed up with the parents, teacher, and Natalia to gain perspective from all parties. Based on the information collected, the school counselor utilized her theoretical orientation to facilitate her counseling interventions in order to guide her approach. The use of theory is pivotal in all types of counseling settings; therefore the school counselor strategically selected the interventions based on a theoretical framework.

Additionally, the school counselor and Natalia's teacher collaborated to work as a team to best serve Natalia. The plan was for the school counselor and Natalia to meet once a week for 7 sessions for duration of 30 minutes. The format for the counseling sessions varied based on Natalia's needs. Furthermore, based on Natalia's age, the school counselor utilized expressive arts, play, music, books, games, talk, and role play. Throughout the sessions, skills such as managing emotions, building self-esteem, making friends, and decision-making were addressed. After the seven counseling sessions, the school counselor would evaluate whether Natalia had met her goals, or would need to be referred for clinical mental health counseling.

Process Questions

1. Discuss the importance of school counselor, parent, and teacher collaboration during the counseling process. (CACREP G.2.b; CACREP G.3.1)
2. How can the school counselor further provide counseling services considering Natalia's age and developmental stages? (CACREP G.3.f; CACREP G.3.h)
3. How can the clinical mental health counselor further provide counseling services considering Natalia's age and developmental stages? (CACREP C.2.j.)
4. How would you identify goals for Natalia's treatment plan if she were your client? (CACREP C.2.d.; CACREP C.2.j; CACREP G.2.g.; CACREP G.3.f.; CACREP G.3.h)

Case Study: Sanjeev

This case study is a clinical mental health case illustration for a mental health setting.

Sanjeev, an 8-year-old boy, has recently started receiving clinical mental health counseling. His parents sought counseling due to remarks he consistently made at home and school. Sanjeev would talk about not having friends, feeling lonely and unimportant, and not liked by anyone. His parents became increasingly concerned since he appeared to be depressed and did not want to engage in activities with peers or family members.

Prior to meeting, the clinical mental health counselor discussed with the parents the billing process, which included a flat fee of $100 per hour. Insurance was not accepted and the family's gross income was too high, therefore they did not qualify for a sliding-scale fee. Additionally, the clinical mental *health counselor informed the parents of the cancellation policy, which states clients who need to cancel a session must notify the counselor 24 hours prior to the session, otherwise they will be charged the full fee of a session.*

Once Sanjeev's parents agreed to the terms, an appointment was made to meet with the clinical mental health counselor. The first counseling session consisted of the clinical mental health counselor conducting an intake session. The counselor asked the parents about their family history, background, Sanjeev's developmental milestones, and school performance. Currently, Sanjeev meets with his clinical mental health counselor once a week for a one-hour session. During the first few sessions, the clinical mental health counselor and Sanjeev identified specific goals to be addressed during the therapeutic process. Sanjeev stated he would like to feel liked by his peers and gain more friends. These goals were tracked by Sanjeev using a rating scale of 1 to 10 to gauge his perceptions as well as through anecdotal insight provided by him and his parents. He will also join a group during the summer to work with other children who have similar needs. The group will meet for eight weeks and the topics addressed will include friendship skills, social skills, self-esteem, and emotional regulation.

Process Questions

1. What factors are necessary for the counselor to consider when developing a treatment plan? (CACREP C. 3. a; CACREP C. 3. b)
2. What needs should the counselor focus on when determining goals for treatment? (CACREP C.2.c.; CACREP C.2.d.; CACREP C.2.j.)
3. During the intake process, what poignant questions would you ask the parents and Sanjeev while collecting information to develop a treatment plan and goals? (CACREP C.1.c.; CACREP C.2.j)

Reflection Activity

Exercise 2.5

Reflect back to when you were between the ages of 4–8 years old. Think about your relationships with peers from when you were 4–6 years old and 6–8 years old. Where your relationships the same or different? How did you manage making new friends and sharing friends?

Application

As a final exercise, an application activity has been provided. Based on each developmental stage, complete the chart indicating what factors clinical mental health and school counselors should be cognizant of at this time and what types of counseling interventions and supports would be appropriate.

Developmental Stage	1. counseling considerations 2. clinical mental health counseling interventions and supports 3. school counseling interventions and supports
Physical	1. counseling considerations 2. clinical mental health counseling interventions and supports 3. school counseling interventions and supports
Cognitive	1. counseling considerations 2. clinical mental health counseling interventions and supports 3. school counseling interventions and supports
Social/Emotional	1. counseling considerations 2. clinical mental health counseling interventions and supports 3. school counseling interventions and supports

Exercise 2.6

SUMMARY

Milestones are set to determine the development of children; however, milestones can be achieved at different times during childhood based on various factors. These factors include family, language, culture, ability, socio-economics, education of parents, exposure, and trauma. Therefore it is imperative clinical mental health counselors and school counselors remain cognizant of cognitive, social/emotional, and physical development when conducting an intake process and providing counseling services. Further, counselors should be mindful to view each child through a social justice lens in order to demonstrate ethical practice.

Table 2.2 Childhood developmental milestones

Physical Development	Cognitive Development	Social/Emotional Development
■ grows taller ■ gains weight ■ gains navigation and balance ■ basic grooming skills ■ catches and throws balls ■ draws shapes	■ short attention span ■ learns through movement ■ inquisitive ■ asks questions ■ problem solving ■ identifies challenges	■ builds friendships ■ name calls and brags ■ behaviors may be predictors of future patterns ■ play and expression

Additional Resources

American Diabetes Association: http://www.diabetes.org/diabetes-basics/type-1/
American School Counselor Association: www.schoolcounselor.org
Association for Play Therapy: http://www.a4pt.org/
Centers for Disease Control and Prevention: www.cdc.gov
Kids Health: http://kidshealth.org/en/parents/medical/
Migration Policy Institute: http://www.migrationpolicy.org
PBS Parents: www.pbs.org/parents
The National Coalition of Creative Arts Therapies Associations: www.nccata.org

Suggested Readings

American School Counselor Association (2016). The school counselor and students with disabilities [position statement]. Retrieved from: https://www.schoolcounselor.org/asca/media/asca/PositionStatements/PS_Disabilities.pdf

Hall, J. G. (2015). The school counselor and special education: Aligning training with practice. *Professional Counselor: Research and Practice* 5(2), 217–224. Retrieved from: http://tpcjournal.nbcc.org/the-school-counselor-and-special-education-aligning-training-with-practice/

Martinez, A. and Lasser, J. (2013). Thinking outside the box while playing the game: A creative school-based approach to working with children and adolescents. *Journal of Creativity in Mental Health* 8(1), 81–91. DOI: 10.1080/15401383.2013.763688

Owens, D., Thomas, D., and Strong, L. A. (2011). School counselors assisting students with disabilities. *Education* 132, 235–240.

Peterson, J. S. (2015). School counselors and gifted kids: Respecting cognitive and affective. *Journal of Counseling and Development* 93 (2), 153–162. DOI: 10.1002/j.1556-6676.2015.00191.x.

Glossary

504 accommodations: Section 504 of the U.S. Rehabilitation Act 1973 helps parents of physically or mentally disabled children in public schools to ensure that a child has customized educational plans and will be treated fairly at school, for example by having suitable seating, more time in exams etc.

Childhood: The ages of 4–8 years old

Cognitive development: The process of the brain learning, thinking, and growing during childhood

Expressive arts: Creative medium utilized in counseling to convey feelings, thoughts, experiences, and change

Milestone: A significant achievement in gaining a new skill or ability during childhood

Physical development: The process of the body's organs, bones, and motor skills developing during childhood

Play: Physical activity representing outward expression of feelings and fantasy

Prosocial behaviors: Behaviors demonstrating kindness and good citizenship towards others

Rapport building: The process of starting the counseling relationship between a counselor and client based on trust and positive connections

Social/emotional development: The process of building connections, relationships, and identifying emotions during early childhood

References

American School Counselor Association (2012). *The ASCA National Model: A Framework for School Counseling Programs*, 3rd ed. Alexandria, VA: Author.

Broderick, P. C. and Blewitt, P. (2015). *The life span: Human development for helping professionals*, 4th ed. Upper Saddle River, NJ: Pearson Education.

Campbell, A. W. (2015). Vaccines: Both sides of the same coin. *Alternative Therapies in Health and Medicine* 21 (4), 8–10.

Centers for Disease Control and Prevention. Child development. Retrieved from: http://www.cdc.gov/ncbddd/childdevelopment/positiveparenting/preschoolers.html

Centers for Disease Control and Prevention (2016). Recommended immunization schedules for persons aged 0 through 18 years: UNITED STATES, 2016. Retrieved from: http://www.cdc.gov/vaccines/schedules/downloads/child/0-18yrs-child-combined-schedule.pdf

Gladding, S. T. (2011). *The creative arts in counseling*, 4th ed. Alexandria, VA: American Counseling Association.

Gladding, S. T. (2013). *Counseling: A comprehensive profession*, 7th ed. Upper Saddle River, NJ: Pearson Education.

Kostelnik, M. J., Soderman, A. K., and Whiren, A. P. (2011). *Developmentally appropriate curriculum: Best practices in early childhood education*, 5th ed. New York, NY: Pearson.

Kottman, T. (2011). *Play therapy: Basics and beyond*, 2nd ed. Alexandria, VA: American Counseling Association.

National Center for Education Statistics. State education reforms. Retrieved from: https://nces.ed.gov/programs/statereform/tab5_1.asp

Poppe, L, M., Werth, L. A., Guzman, J. M., Brand, G. L., Fox, M. S., Crandall, L., Durden, T.R., and Pitt, R. (2011). Ages and stages: 3-, 4- and 5-year-olds .G2106. Faculty Publications from CYFS. Paper 76. http://digitalcommons.unl.edu/cyfsfacpub/76

Wood, C. (2007). *Yardsticks: Children in the classroom—ages 4–14*, 3rd ed. Turners Falls, MA: Northeast Foundation for Children, Inc.

Ziomek-Daigle, J. and Land, C. W. (2016). The elementary school. In J. Ziomek-Daigle (ed.), *School counseling classroom guidance: Prevention, accountability, and outcomes* (pp. 38–52). Thousand Oaks, CA: Sage Publications.

CHAPTER 3

Counseling Older Children and Young Adolescents in School and Clinical Mental Health Settings

Christy Land, Malti Tuttle, and Lauren Moss

As middle school educators, we have students for the shortest amount of time, and they change the most in those three short years. They come to us as young children from elementary school and leave us as young adults ready to take on the world.

Hilda Wilkins, former middle school principal

CHAPTER OBJECTIVES

After reading this chapter, you will be able to:

- describe and identify attributes of normal and abnormal cognitive, physical, and social/emotional development of older children and young adolescents (aged 11–14)
- integrate theoretical knowledge to practical application through the examination of the unique roles that school counselors and clinical mental health counselors play in supporting young people during this developmental timeframe
- construct suggestions regarding case management for adolescent clients (based on case studies provided in the chapter)

INTRODUCTION

For older children and young adolescents, at the start of the middle school years (approximately ages 11–14), this fast and furious developmental period represents a brand new frontier during this developmental timeframe. Highly differentiated changes occur in physical, cognitive, and social/emotional development. These developmental advancements, coupled with demanding schedules, rigorous academic environments, and the aspiration to find a social niche, may create the "storm" of mental and emotional turmoil for many young people during this developmental span. In fact, DeKruyf, Auger, and Trice-Black (2013) found an "emergence of data regarding the high prevalence of mental health needs among K–12 students and the dismally low proportion of students who receive proper mental health services for those needs" (p. 271). Therefore, it is critically important for both clinical mental health and school counselors to understand the developmental challenges that older children and younger adolescents may face. Helping professionals must be prepared to collaboratively support young people to overcome various barriers to success during the middle school years and the approximate ages of 11 to 14.

The following chapter will discuss typical and atypical physical, cognitive, and social/emotional development of older children and young adolescents. Two case studies are discussed and process questions are provided to the reader. Chapter questions, chapter activities, a glossary of terms, chapter references, and suggested readings are also included. After reading this chapter, students will be able to describe and identify attributes of normal and abnormal cognitive, physical, and social/emotional development of older children and young adolescents. Further, students will be able to integrate theoretical knowledge to practical application through the examination of the unique roles that school counselors and clinical mental health counselors play in supporting young people during this developmental timeframe.

OLDER CHILDHOOD (AGES 9–11)

Older children, aged 9–11, exert a growing independence as they navigate the many physical, emotional, and cognitive changes that rapidly occur during this time span. There are typical milestones of development associated with every age group. Awareness and understanding of these milestones is important when working with children in a variety of settings. Similarly, it is important that both school counselors and clinical mental health counselors have a comprehensive understanding of the vast array of developmental challenges that may arise during this time period.

Physical Development in Older Children

The process of adolescent physical development and sexual maturation is a process that takes several years to complete and is fueled by changes in one's glandular and hormonal systems (APA, 2002; Broderick and Blewitt, 2015). The pituitary and endocrine glands stimulate hormone production, estrogen in females and testosterone in males, triggering the start of many physical changes in older children. The beginning of puberty corresponds with the adolescent growth spurt, which according to Broderick and Blewitt (2015) is "a rapid increase in size accompanied by changes in the shape and proportions of the body" (p. 328). Pubertal onset in older childhood is marked by the development of breasts in young females, typically around the age of 10, and by the testicular enlargement for young males around the age of 11 (Bright Futures, 2016). Initial outward signs of puberty in older children also include the appearance of pubic hair in both males and females (Broderick and Blewitt, 2015). Hair may also begin to grow under the arms and on the chest and face of young males (Advocates for Youth, 2016).

As hormone production increases, older children may also experience other physical changes during this developmental time period, such as an increase in sweating and body odor and changes in the skin, resulting in an oily appearance or the development of acne (Advocates for Youth, 2016). Older children may complain of "growing pains" as their joints ache due to their widening hips in females and broadening shoulders in males (Advocates for Youth, 2016). Their young bodies are preparing for years of continuous physical growth.

Obesity, caused by an imbalance of calorie intake versus calorie output, is on the rise and is a public health crisis both nationally and internationally (Karnik and Kanekar, 2012). Specifically, childhood obesity is defined as having a Body Mass Index above 95 per cent in comparison to children of the same age and same sex, and results in a magnitude of physical, behavioral, and social/emotional problems for obese children (Karnik and Kanekar, 2012). Obese children may experience a host of physical problems to include: a) cardiovascular problems, b) high blood pressure, c) asthma and/or sleep apnea, and d) are at risk of developing diabetes (Karnik and Kanekar, 2012).

School, community, and home-based interventions are critical to addressing this health crisis and protecting young people from a lifetime of physical and emotional challenges related to obesity (Karnik and Kanekar, 2012). For example, schools can offer and encourage young people to choose healthy food items and build in multiple opportunities for physical activity. Some comprehensive school counseling programs incorporate programs that address health and wellness into their work with students. As another example, a school counselor may facilitate a small group that focuses on making healthy choices and building self-esteem, or partner with the Parent Teacher Organization (PTO) to bring a trademarked program such as Girls on the Run (Girls on the Run, 2016) to the school. Community agencies may sponsor health and wellness fairs or "walk to school days." Such activities encourage family bonding and a family approach to making healthy choices—it is important that parents and guardians model healthy balanced eating and an active physical lifestyle.

Exercise 3.1

Brainstorming Activity

You are working with a student/client and you have concerns about her physical health. Specifically, you are concerned that the child may be classified as obese. The child appears to be significantly overweight and breathes heavily when walking in and out of your office. The child shares with you that she is not physically active and often complains of not feeling well.

1. Considering your future work setting, how would you approach the parent or guardian to discuss your concerns? (CACREP C.1.c; CACREP G.2.b)
2. Considering your future work setting, what more systemic interventions may you consider? (CACREP C.3.b; CACREP G.2.g)
3. In your future professional role, what type of partnerships or collaborative relationships would you want intentionally to develop to address an issue such as childhood obesity proactively? (CACREP C.3.d; CACREP G.2.b)

Development in older children (aged 9–11) encompasses significant changes physically, cognitively, and socially/emotionally. Physical growth during this developmental time period marks the beginning of older children's sexual maturation as their bodies begin to show outward and inward indicators of this advanced physical development. Older children may experience hormonal changes triggering advancement of this physical bloom. The following section discusses cognitive development, with special attention to cognitive deficits in older children and the role technology may play during this time span.

COGNITIVE DEVELOPMENT IN OLDER CHILDREN

Although the brain has reached approximately 95 per cent of its peak size by the age of 6, this "muscle of thinking" continues to develop significantly during older childhood (Broderick and Blewitt, 2015). Older children begin to make great strides in terms of gross and fine motor skills and present more like young adults able to handle responsibilities and manage multiple, fairly complex tasks. Cognitively, older children are able to apply logic and reasoning to concrete events—a stage termed by Piaget and widely known as the 'concrete operational stage' (Broderick and Blewitt, 2015).

Over the course of this concrete operational period older children can think about a situation from multiple perspectives, allowing them to identify reversible relationships and draw logical conclusions, which are hallmarks of this developmental stage. However, the advancement of an older child's logical thinking is contingent upon numerous factors, including cultural considerations, prior experiences, formal education, and general areas of interest (Broderick and Blewitt, 2015: Pressley and Hilden, 2006).

A child's intellectual abilities, deficits, and/or potential learning problems may become increasingly evident with the rise in academic demands and responsibilities (Bright Futures, 2016). To take a case in point, between 5 and 10 per cent of school-aged children are diagnosed with attention deficit disorder (ADD) and show atypical variation in cognitive development (Broderick and Blewitt, 2015; Brown, 2015). ADD is a developmental impairment, impacting the brain's self-regulation system, posing a variety of challenges for children. Individuals impacted by ADD may exhibit deficits in cognitive function in the following areas:

- activations (organizing tasks/materials)
- focus
- effort
- managing emotion and frustration
- working memory and recall, and
- monitoring self-action (Brown, 2009)

Professionals working with children and adolescents must remain aware of the presenting problems and challenges associated with attentional difficulties as intervention and support both academically and socially can help children with ADD reach their full potential.

Given the technological advances in today's society we must also consider the impact of exposure to electronic media on perceptual and cognitive development of young people. Therefore, the question remains, "How does exposure to technology impact cognitive development in children?" (Bavalier, Green, and Dye, 2012; Hsin, Li, and Tsai, 2014). While some technology is designed to enhance learning and other technology platforms are created for entertainment reasons, the outcomes are unpredictable and often not aligned with the intended purpose (Bavalier, Green, and Dye, 2012). For example, playing video games may, in fact enhance memory, attention, motor control, visual processing, and overall cognition (Bavalier, Green, and Dye, 2012; Subrahmanyam, Kraut, Greenfield, and Gross, 2000). Therefore, young people's use of technology must be closely monitored, and not only the amount of time and the technology platform they are using, but the impact of engagement with various forms of media.

The Center for Disease Control (2016) recommends that parents talk to their children about their specific uses of technology and with whom they are interacting on the internet. Parents should also develop rules *with* their children for the use of technology and regularly monitor their child's technology use by checking his or her devices and search history (CDC, 2016). Further, parents should talk to others and strive to educate themselves on new websites, social media platforms, and online interaction (CDC, 2016). School counselors and clinical mental health counselors can play an important role in educating parents, students, and the community on the dangers of technology, including cyberbullying and online predators. Through education, parents will have the information to inform their decision making and help their child learn to use technology appropriately and in positive ways.

Exercise 3.2

Reflection Activity

Given the clear positive and negative impacts that technology use can have on older children, consider and discuss the following:

1. What are your personal experiences with technology? Discuss both your positive and negative experiences. (CACREP C.2.j; CACREP G.3.f)
2. What are your personal beliefs about older children's (aged 9–11) use of technology? (CACREP C.2.j; CACREP G.3.f)
3. If you were going to develop guidelines for the use of technology for this age group, what would they include? (CACREP C.3.b; CACREP G.3.h)
4. In what ways can school counselors and clinical mental health counselors work to educate parents and young people about technology? (CACREP C.2.a; CACREP C.3.b; CACREP G.1.d; CACREP G.2.b)
5. How could school counselors and clinical mental health counselors collaborate on this important issue? (CACREP C.2.a; CACREP G.1.d)

Many factors—socio-cultural, formal education, parenting styles—play a role in the cognitive advancement of older children. During this time period an older child's abilities and deficits may become clearer, as his or her responsibilities and academic demands increase. Technology can be a resource for young people and aid in their cognitive development; however, parents, educators, school counselors, and clinical mental health counselors must remain cognizant of the dangers and potential negative impacts of technology. The next section will discuss the social/emotional development of older children and expand upon the role that physical and cognitive development plays in a young person's social and emotional development.

SOCIAL/EMOTIONAL DEVELOPMENT IN OLDER CHILDREN

Social and emotional development in older children consists of two components: Self-esteem and self-concept. Self-esteem involves the belief that one holds of oneself and attributes (i.e., appearance, intelligence) and self-concept is the evaluation of one's self-esteem (APA, 2002). Self-esteem develops uniquely for each individual and may remain stable in older childhood through young adolescence or increase or decrease, depending on numerous factors (APA, 2002). Young people may experience a decrease in self-esteem if there is a discrepancy in in what they believe they should be like and how they are evaluating themselves at the time.

Changes in one's physical and cognitive development as well as peer and family relationships all play an integral part in young people's self-esteem. The older children become, the more value they place on how their peers view them, impacting both their self-concept and self-esteem (Broderick and Blewitt, 2002). Older children may begin to evaluate themselves internally in comparison to their peers (Broderick and Blewitt, 2002). For example, "How does my math performance compare to that of my peers?" or "Am I as good at soccer as my sister?" Strategies, such as positive reinforcement and high levels of encouragement, should be used to protect and enhance children's self-esteem (Broderick and Blewitt, 2002). A school may incorporate programs to recognize students' gains and not just focus on programs that recognize students who receive all As or who have a perfect attendance record. Schools may also incorporate programs that recognize students' acts of kindness and service and provide opportunities for students of all ability levels to be successful. Clinical mental health counselors may find a strengths-based approach to be an effective strategy in counseling older children. Using a strengths-based approach, mental health counselors are able to conceptualize client issues based on strengths and virtues of the client as opposed to the "problem" and what is not working (Smith, 2005).

Case Study: Allen

The following is a school counseling case illustration.

Allen is an 11-year-old African American sixth-grade male. His academic record indicates average cognitive functioning in all areas. Anecdotal feedback on his report cards (K–5) indicates that Allen has historically struggled with staying on task and maintaining focus and attention, especially in the areas of reading and English Language Arts (ELA). Allen's sixth-grade teachers have noticed an increased level of frustration in the classroom, especially in these two areas. His teacher's observations are consistent with previous feedback in that Allen appears to be unfocused, unengaged, and Allen is not able to meet expectations in Reading and ELA at this time. When his teachers redirect Allen or try to work with him one-on-one, Allen is exhibiting signs of increased frustration and anger. Most recently, in class, Allen threw his pencil, ripped up his paper, and screamed at his ELA teacher, refusing to do any work. His teachers requested a meeting with Allen's parents and the school counselor to discuss their concerns as they are worried about Allen's overall functioning, especially with the increase in demands and rigor in middle school.

Allen lives at home with mom, dad, and an older brother, who is a sophomore in high school. Allen's parents are happy to meet with the teachers and the school counselor as they share similar concerns. Allen's parents state they have noticed an increased level of frustration when Allen is asked to do homework—especially work that requires reading and writing—since he started middle school. In fact, Allen's parents told the school counselor that he became so distraught last week during homework time that he threw his glass of milk across the room and broke the glass. Allen's parents shared that Allen plays soccer and he has historically gotten along well with his peers. However, they have noticed over the last several of weeks that Allen has not wanted to play outside as much and prefers to stay in his room, which is unlike him. It is decided that the school counselor will observe Allen in the classroom and speak to him individually. Allen's parents, teachers, and the school counselor will meet again in the next couple of weeks to reassess and devise a plan of action to support Allen.

Process Questions

1. Based on Allen's needs and current cognitive, physical, and social/emotional development, what key areas should the school counselor consider during the classroom observation? (CACREP G.2.d; CACREP G.2.g)
2. Given's Allen's cognitive developmental stage, academic history, and presenting problems, what potential learning issues may need to be considered? (CACREP G.2.g)
3. During the follow-up meeting, what type of referrals may the school counselor need to provide to the parents to meet Allen's learning and social/emotional needs comprehensively? (CACREP G.2.b)

Exercise 3.3

Reflection Activity

Reflect on your own physical, cognitive, and social/emotional development during older childhood (ages 9–11).

1. Does anything stand out to you about your physical development? (CACREP C.2.j; CACREP G.3.f)
2. Did you experience any developmental delays or atypical development in your cognitive development? If so, what? (CACREP C.2.j ;CACREP G.3.f)
3. What do you remember about your peer group during this time period in your life? (CACREP C.2.j; CACREP G.3.f)
4. How do you think your own development as an older child will inform your work as a future professional school counselor or clinical mental health counselor? (CACREP C.2.j; CACREP G.3.f)

Older children experience an array of physical, cognitive, and social/emotional developmental changes from the ages of 9–11. Even typical development may cause varying forms of distress for young people. It is critical, then, that school counselors and clinical mental health counselors understand the various challenges that older children may encounter during this time and use their knowledge and skills to support and intervene as appropriate.

YOUNG ADOLESCENCE (AGES 12–13)

Young adolescence is a significant time period where older children start to shift from the immaturity of childhood into the realm of mature adulthood (Hashmi, 2013). This time period is sometimes viewed as a transitional stage encompassing physical, cognitive, and social/emotional transitions, and serves as a springboard to independence. As young adolescents begin to exert a more mature physical appearance and growing independence, they still need support, guidance, and nurturing from their parents and adults in their lives.

Physical Development in Young Adolescence

Most often, physical development during the adolescent years is associated with the onset of puberty, "raging" hormones, and a rapid growth spurt. This biological transformation is the most observable sign that adolescence has begun (Hashmi, 2013). There are changes in the height and weight of males and females during young adolescence. Over a four-year span during adolescence, physical development is rapid. Both males and females grow approximately 10 inches; males gain approximately 42 pounds and females about 38 pounds (Broderick and Blewitt, 2015, p. 328).

This developmental period is marked by the onset of menstruation (menarche) for females at the age of 12 or 13 and for males by the punctuated enlargement of the testes at age 11 or 12. Males experience their first ejaculation (spermarche) at around the age of 13 as well as eventual changes in the voice. Physical changes in both males and females are fueled by hormones, genetics, and environmental factors (Broderick and Blewitt, 2015; Hashmi, 2013).

This time period is significant, as research indicates that young girls who are not prepared for the changes their body will undergo during puberty may face difficulties with menstruation (APA, 2002). Koff and Rierdan (1995) interviewed 157 ninth-grade females and found that the young ladies wanted assurance and support from their mothers and to hear the personal experiences of their own mothers, framed positively. Additionally, the young girls expressed a desire to be informed about the logistics of hygiene during menstruation and preferred that their fathers not comment on their physical changes. Instead, the girls preferred that their mothers speak privately with their fathers about the physical changes associated with puberty that the girls were experiencing (Koff and Rierdan). Similarly, young males reported feeling confused when they were not prepared for the experience of their first ejaculation (Stein and Reisser, 1994). Older children and adolescents will be more prepared and more likely to experience physical changes in a positive manner when they are educated about such developmental milestones early on.

Further, during this time period, physical appearance becomes increasingly important to young people, and both males and females may spend a significant amount of time focused on their physical appearance (APA, 2002). When young adolescents express concern about their physical appearance, adults should take the time to listen and try to understand the concern in context. This will help this adolescent to feel comfortable in sharing concerns in the future (APA, 2002). Adults should be especially aware of females that physically mature early and males that physically mature later than their peers (APA, 2002). When adolescents experience premature or delayed pubertal development, research indicates that these young people are more likely to become depressed and experiment with risky behaviors such as substance abuse, sexual activity, and eating disorders (APA, 2002; Mendle, Turkheimer, and Emory, 2007; Stice, Presnell, and Bearman, 2001).

Sexuality and Sexual Preference in Young Adolescence

During puberty, adolescents experience for the first time a strong and urgent sexual desire, similar to that of an adult (Broderick and Blewitt, 2015). Therefore, during this time period, a young person's sexual interest naturally peaks, and they may begin to explore with sexual fantasizing, masturbation, and—for some adolescents—sexual experiences (Broderick and Blewitt, 2015). Sexual orientation, or the preference for sexual partners, also emerges during young adolescence. Young people may develop a conscious awareness for their sexuality and how they want to express their individual sexual orientation (Advocates for Youth, 2016).

Table 3.1 identifies common sexually related behaviors for children and adolescents (Kellogg, 2010). This table may serve as a useful tool for help to determine if a child or adolescent's sexually charged behavior is problematic or a typical part of development. However, consideration should be given to more common behaviors that are done in excess and may be interfering with daily activities of children and adolescents. For example, it is noted as common for males aged 10–12 to touch their genitals at home in private. However, if an 11-year-old male is spending a substantial amount of time in his room masturbating and missing sports practice and social activities, this would be cause for concern. It is important for mental health professionals, parents, educators, and other adults to convey the message that healthy sexual development is a part of normal, natural human development.

Table 3.1 Age-appropriate behaviors in children and adolescents

Age	2–5	6–9	10–12
Behaviors	More common ■ explores private parts at home and in public ■ stands too close to other persons ■ tries to look at persons when they are nude ■ discusses bodily functions	More common ■ touches genitals at home ■ tries to look at persons when they are nude ■ may try to mimic dating behavior (e.g. kissing, touching, holding hands) ■ explores private parts with peers (e.g. playing doctor) ■ uses sexually explicit language without understanding the meaning	More common ■ very interested in opposite sex ■ wants to view nudity on television or social media ■ knows more about sex ■ tries to look at pictures of nude persons ■ touches anogenital area at home ■ seeks more personal privacy ■ may begin to shows signs of sexual attraction to peers and interest in romantic-type relationships
Behaviors	Less common (15–20%) ■ very interested in opposite sex ■ masturbates with hand ■ hugs adults that are not known well ■ shows anogenital area to adults ■ masturbates with hand and shoes ■ interest in the opposite sex	Less common (8.5–13%) ■ very interested in opposite sex ■ knows more about sex ■ masturbates with hand ■ tries to look at pictures of nude persons ■ talks about sexual acts and watches sexual acts on television	Less common (6–8%) ■ stands too close to other persons ■ tries to look at persons when they are nude ■ talks flirtatiously

Sources: Kellogg, 2010, p. 1235; The National Child Traumatic Stress Network (2009). Sexual development and behavior in children: Information for caregivers. Retrieved from: http://nctsn.org/nctsn_assets/pdfs/caring/sexualdevelopmentandbehavior.pdf

Reflection Activity

Reflect on your physical development as a young adolescent, giving special consideration to pubertal milestones, and consider the following.

1. Do you remember a parent or other trusted adult speaking with you about puberty and the changes that your body would undergo? (CACREP C.2.j; CACREP G.3.f)
2. Can you remember the feelings that you experienced with your changing physical appearance? (CACREP C.2.j; CACREP G.3.f)
3. Was going through puberty a positive or negative experience for you? Why? (CACREP C.2.j; CACREP G.3.f)
4. Did you talk to your friends, peers, or siblings about the changes that you experienced in your physical development? (CACREP C.2.j; CACREP G.3.f)
5. What do you remember about your own sexual identity development? (CACREP C.2.j; CACREP G.3.f)
6. How will your experiences as an adolescent impact your practice as a professional school counselor or clinical mental health counselor? (CACREP C.2.j; CACREP G.3.f)

The physical development of young adolescents highlights their shift from children to young adults as their sexual maturation advances in parallel with their bodies. Young adolescents may experience sexual urges and engage in typical and atypical sexual behavior throughout this period in their life. School counselor and clinical mental health counselors play a significant role in supporting and promoting healthy physical and sexual development during this time. The next session will delve into the cognitive and social/emotional transitions that young adolescents experience from the ages of 12–13.

COGNITIVE DEVELOPMENT IN YOUNG ADOLESCENCE

Cognitive efficiency, memory, and processing speed continually improves until young adulthood. Young people begin to think about endless possibilities instead of what is real and concrete (Hashmi, 2013). This is largely in part due to their advancement in logical and higher-order thinking skills and more in-depth understanding of their own internal experiences. This is known as metacognition—thinking about one's own thinking or the process of thinking, resulting in an increased introspection (Hasmi, 2013).

According to Piaget, this cognitive developmental time period beginning at about 11–12 years old marks the beginning of the formal operational thought stage (Piaget, 1954). This more elaborate formal thought process enables young adolescents to think more abstractly, use reasoning, and identify relationships on a higher level. This ability to think more abstractly and think critically will positively impact young people in their capacity to manage their academic tasks (Broderick and Blewitt, 2015).

With the advancement in cognition and rapid neurobiological adaptations, adolescence is a sensitive period for processing emotional information (Broderick and Blewitt, 2015). The adolescent brain is still developing and may not be equipped to handle the challenge of integrating and processing both cognitive and emotional information. Therefore, adolescents may find themselves in situations where they are "literally" ahead of their time, in that their cognition is not in alignment with their physical and pubertal development (Silk et al., 2009). Adolescents may have an especially difficult time managing stress during this developmental period.

Despite their vastly increasing cognition, most adolescents still need direction from adults in their life (APA, 2002). Trusted adults should use this developmental time period as an opportunity to model positive decision making and effective problem solving (APA, 2002). However, even with proper guidance, adolescents may demonstrate faulty decision making, resulting in engaging in risky behaviors such as experimentation with drugs and/or alcohol (APA, 2002).

Social/Emotional Development in Young Adolescence

Middle school students are changing biologically, cognitively, and in the development of their self-concept (Harris and Petrie, 2002; Wigfiled, Lutz, and Wagner, 2005). During middle adolescence, as young people are beginning puberty, increasingly engaging in abstract thinking and higher-order thinking processes, the development of self-concept takes center stage (Wigfield, Lutz, and Wagner, 2005). Young adolescents may develop a positive social/emotional identity through experimentation with different types of behavior, dress, and social outlets (APA, 2002). Through this complex exploration, young adolescents may begin to develop their moral self as a means to enhance their self-concept through acting in responsible ways consistent with their individual belief system (Broderick and Blewitt, 2015). Young people should be encouraged to explore, in their own unique way, as they continue to develop their self-esteem and moral belief system.

However, the middle school years are a time of great risk socially, when students often need help identifying and managing their emotions (Harris and Petrie, 2002). Green (2007) argued that incidents of bullying are quite common in middle school students, as many of these young people are rapidly changing before transitioning into high school. This transformative developmental period when coupled with hormonal changes may result in undesirable negative behaviors. Such negative behaviors are often observed in the school setting in the form of insults, put downs, exclusion, and threats—bullying behaviors (Olweus, 2007). The effects of bullying range may from loss of opportunity to loss of life. Depression, suicidal ideation, isolation, low self-esteem, and lack of hope are just a few of the characteristics evident in young people victimized as a result of bullying (Klomek et al., 2008; Lieberman and Cowan, 2011; Pranjic and Bajraktarevic, 2010). Klomek et al. (2008) and Dracic (2009) found that frequent exposure to bullying was directly related to high risk of depression, suicidal ideation, and suicide attempts compared to students not victimized. Scholars assert that anxieties, feelings of being unsafe, loss of concentration, migraine headaches, being unable to start/finish a task, and fear of going to school are consequences of being repeatedly bullied (Dracic, 2009; Klomek et al., 2008).

Mental health counselors should be cognizant of signs and symptoms associated with bullying and encourage their clients to share about their peer relationships and/or experiences with bullying. School counselors, as advocates, may act as part of the solution to combat bullying and spearhead bullying prevention efforts. School counselors must be proactive and implement school-wide programs to meet the needs of all students that are preventive in nature and comprehensively send the message that bullying is not acceptable (ASCA, 2012; Griffin, 2012). Moreover, all students and clients must know that they can reach out to a trusted adult if bullying occurs so that they can receive support, guidance, and encouragement and feel a sense of wellness and belonging in schools, which is critical to developing self-confidence and a sense of wellbeing (Griffin, 2012).

School–family–community collaboration is defined as

> collaborative relationships in which school counselors, school personnel, students, families, community members and other stakeholders work jointly to implement school and community based programs and activities that improve student academic achievement directly within schools, and indirectly by attending to the needs that may be hindering students and families from these accomplishments.
>
> (Griffin and Steen, 2010, p. 77)

Furthermore, the focus on serving students and families must move beyond individual challenges to external factors that are barriers to success (ASCA, 2012; Griffin and Steen, 2010; Lieberman and Cowan, 2011; Young et al., 2009). School and mental health counselors may partner to offer a parent education workshop on bullying or to develop a mentoring program between individuals in the community and schools.

Austin, Reynolds, and Barnes (2012) recommend that an agency have an identified role in crime prevention and intervention and be a part of a local school's bullying prevention efforts. Specifically, it is recommended that secondary school resources, such as coaches and other enrichment teachers, be an integral component of school-wide bullying prevention efforts (Austin, Reynolds, and Barnes, 2012; Lieberman and Cowan, 2011). Such components promote school and community involvement and encourage students to develop a sense of community and connectedness. Furthermore, when young people have strong connections with adults, they tend to be more resilient and are less likely to be emotionally wounded if bullied (Davis and Nixon, 2011).

Case Study: Amy

The case study below is a clinical mental health case illustration.

Amy is a 13-year-old White female eighth-grade student. Amy attends an academically rigorous middle school and performs above average academically in the classroom and on standardized tests. Amy is a competitive gymnast, which often requires weekend travel to competitions. Amy is also heavily involved with her church and has a strong peer group that she has associated with since early elementary school. Amy has experienced physical and emotional symptoms associated with anxiety off and on since the beginning of sixth grade; however, she has received no formal counseling or medical intervention for anxiety. Amy's level of anxiety has become problematic recently and she has started to miss school and gymnastics practice, resulting in her falling behind in all areas and causing her anxiety to spiral more out of control.

Amy is close to her mother and describes her anxiety as feeling "out of control." Amy further describes her anxiety as feeling sick, like she is going crazy, and not wanting to leave the house. Amy's mother has tried a number of approaches to help Amy feel better and "coax" her into going to school and practice, with little to no success. Amy's mother has decided that Amy is in crisis and makes her an appointment with a licensed professional counselor, as she is concerned for her immediate wellbeing.

Process Questions

1. Considering Amy's presenting problem and developmental considerations, discuss primary considerations of the intake process. (CACREP C.3.a; CACREP C.2.a)
2. Discuss the importance of Amy's developmental history as relevant to her presenting problem. (CACREP C.2.g)
3. In developing a treatment plan for Amy, what would be the primary and secondary goals, based on Amy's presenting problem? (CACREP C.2.b)

While young people may appear physically advanced during the adolescent time period, their cognitive and social/emotional intelligence is not that of a young adult. Therefore, young adolescents will continue to need guidance and support from their parental figures, and will benefit from clear expectations and boundaries. School counselors and clinical mental health counselors, in collaboration, can work to educate parents on challenges and important topics.

SUMMARY

Older children and young adolescents experience a myriad of changes related to their physical, cognitive, and social/emotional development. Professional school counselors and clinical mental health counselors must be familiar with typical and atypical developmental patterns and deficits. Access to counseling services both at school and in the community are necessary to ensure a young person's academic success and social/emotional wellbeing.

Additional Resources

Association for Play Therapy: http://www.a4pt.org/
Girls on the Run: https://www.girlsontherun.org/
The National Resource Center on ADHD: www.help4adhd.org
The National Resource on ADHD: http://www.chadd.org/
Understood: https://Understood.org

Suggested Readings

Burnham, J. J. (2009). Contemporary fear of children and adolescents: Coping and resiliency in the 21st century [Special Issue]. *Journal of Counseling and Development* 87, 28–35.

Burnham, J. J. and Lomax, R. G. (2009). Examining ethnicity and fears of children and adolescents in the United States: Differences between Caucasian, African American, and Hispanic populations. *Journal of Counseling and Development* 87, 387–393.

Conger, R. D. and Chao, W. (1996). Adolescent depressed mood. In R. L. Simons (ed.), *Understanding differences between divorced and intact families: Stress, interaction, and child outcome*. Thousand Oaks, CA: Sage.

DeKruyf, L., Auger, R. W. and Trice-Black, S. (2013). The role of school counselors in meeting students' mental health needs: Examining issues of professional identity. *Professional School Counseling* 16 (5), 271–282.

Gruman, D. H., Marston, T., and Koon, H. (2013). Bringing mental health needs into focus through school counseling program transformation. *Professional School Counseling* 16(5), 333–341.

Liu, W. M. and Clay, D. (2002). Multicultural counseling competencies: Guidelines in working with children and adolescents. *Journal of Mental Health Counseling* 24 (2), 177–187.

Glossary

Adolescent growth spurt: A rapid increase in size accompanied by changes in the shape and proportions of the body

Attention deficit disorder: A developmental impairment, impacting the brain's self-regulation system, posing a variety of challenges for children

Bisexual: Preference for sexual partners of the same and of the opposite sex

Estrogen: Feminizing hormone

Heterosexuality: Preference for sexual partners of the opposite sex

Homosexuality: Preference for sexual partners of one's own sex

Menarche: Term used to describe the onset of menstruation in young females

Piaget's Concrete Operational Stage: The ability to apply logic and reasoning to concrete events

Sexual orientation: The preference for sexual partners

Spermarche: Term used to describe the first ejaculation in young males

Testosterone: Male hormone

References

Advocates for Youth (2016). Growth and development: Ages 9–12. Retrieved from: http://www.advocatesforyouth.org/parents/155?task=view

American Psychological Association (2002). *A reference for professionals: Developing adolescents.* Washington, DC: American Psychological Association.

American School Counselor Association (2012). *The ASCA National Model: A Framework for School Counseling Programs,* 3rd ed. Alexandria, VA: Author.

Austin, S. M., Reynolds, G. P., and Barnes, S. L. (2012). School leadership and counselors working together address bullying. *Education School Leadership* 1·33 (2), 283–291.

Bavalier, D., Green, C. S., and Dye, M. W. (2012). Children, wired for better or worse. *Neuron* 67 (5), 692–701. doi:10.1016/j.neuron.2010.08.035.

Bright Futures, 2016. Guidelines for health, supervision of infants, children, and adolescents. Retrieved from: https://brightfutures.aap.org/Bright%20Futures%20Documents/17-Middle_Childhood.pdf.

Broderick, P. and Blewitt, P. (2015). *The life span: Human development for helping professionals.* Upper Saddle River, NJ: Pearson.

Brown, T. (2009). ADD/ADHD and impaired executive functioning in clinical practice. *Neuroscience and Neuropsychology of ADHD* 1, 37–41.

Brown, T. (2015). ADHD: From stereotype to science. *Educational Leadership* 10, 52–56.

Center for Disease Control (2016). Kids and technology: Tips for parents in a high-tech world. Retrieved from: http://www.cdc.gov/media/subtopic/matte/pdf/cdcelectronicregression.pdf.

Davis, S. and Nixon, C. (2011). What students say about bullying. *Education Leadership* 9, 18–23.

DeKruyf, L., Auger, R., and Trice-Black, L. (2013). The role of school counselors in meeting students' mental health needs: Examining issues of professional identity. *Journal of Professional School Counseling* 16 (5), 271–282.

Dracic, S. (2009). Bullying and peer victimization. *Materia Socio Medica* 21 (4), 216–221.

Freedman, D. S., Khan, L. K., Dietz, W. H., Srinivasan, S. R., and Berenson, G. S. (2001). Relationship of childhood obesity to coronary heart disease risk factors in adulthood: The Bogalusa Heart Study. *Pediatrics* 108 (3), 712–718.

Girls on the Run (2016). Girls on the Run. Retrieved from: https://www.girlsontherun.org/.

Green, G. (2007). Bullying: A concern for survival. *Education* 128 (2), 333–338.

Griffin, C. (2012). Bullying: It's a very big deal. *District Administration* 48 (4), 64.

Griffin, D. and Steen, S. (2010). A social justice approach to school counseling. *Journal for Social Action in Counseling and Psychology* 3 (1), 74–87.

Hashmi, S. (2013). An age of storm and stress. *Review of Arts and Humanities* 1(2), 19–33.

Hsin, C.-T., Li, M.-C., Tsai, C.-C. (2014). The influence of young children's use of technology on their learning: A review. *Educational Technology and Society* 17 (4), 85–89.

Karnik, S. and Kanekar, A. (2012). Childhood obesity: A global public health crisis. *International Journal of Preventative Medicine* 3 (1), 1–7.

Kellogg, N.D. (2010). Sexual behaviors in children: Evaluation and management. *American Family Physician* 10 (82), 1233–1238.

Klomek, A. B., Sourander, A., Niemela, S., Kumpulainen, K., Piha, J. Tamminen, T., Almqviest, F., and Gould M. S. (2008). Childhood bullying behaviors as a risk for suicide attempts and completed suicides: A population-based birth cohort study. *Journal of the American Academy of Child Adolescent Psychiatry* 48, 254–261.

Koff, E. and Rierdan, J. (1995). Preparing girls for menstruation: Recommendations from adolescent girls. *Adolescence* 30, 795–781.

Lieberman, R. and Cowan, K. (2011). Bullying and youth suicide: Breaking the connection. *Principle Leadership* 10, 12–17.

Mendle, J., Turkheimer, E. and Emery, R. (2007). Detrimental psychological outcomes associated with early pubertal timing in adolescents girls. *Developmental Review* 2 (27), 151–171. doi:10.1016/j.dr.2006.11.001.

Olweus, D. (2007). *Bullying prevention program teacher guide*. Center City, MN: Hazelden.

Piaget, J. (1954). *The construction of reality in the child*. New York: Basic Books.

Pranjic, N. and Bajraktarevic, A. (2010). Depression and suicide ideation among secondary school adolescents involved in school bullying. *Primary Health Care Research and Development* 11, 349–362.

Pressley, M. and Hilden, K. (2006). Cognitive strategies. In W. Damon and R. M. Lerner (series eds.), *Handbook of child psychology: Vol 2. Cognition, perception and language*, 6th ed. (pp. 511–556). Hoboken, NJ: Wiley.

Silk, J. S., Siegle, G. J., Whalen, D. J., Ostapenko, L. J., Ladouceur, C. D., and Dahl, R. E. (2009). Pubertal changes in emotional information processing: Pupillary, behavioral, and subjective evidence during emotional word identification. *Developmental Psychology* 21 (1), 7–26. doi:10.1017/S0954579409000029.

Smith, E. J. (2005). The strengths based counseling model. *The Counseling Psychologist* 34 (13), 13–76. doi: 10.1177/0011000005277018.

Stein, J. H. and Reiser, L. W. (1994). A study of White middle-class adolescent boys' responses to "semenarche" (the first ejaculation). *Journal of Youth and Adolescence* 23, 373–384.

Striegel-Moore, R. H. and Cachelin, F. M. (1999). Body image concerns and disordered eating in adolescent girls: Risk and protective factors. In N. G. Johnson, M. C. Roberts, and J. Worell (eds.), *Beyond appearance: A new look at adolescent girls*. Washington, DC: American Psychological Association.

Subrahmanyam, K. Kraut, R. E. Greenfield, P. M., and Gross, E. F. (2000). The impact of home computer use on children's activities and development. *Children and Computer Technology* 2 (10), 123–144.

Wigfield, A., Lutz, S., and Wagner, A. L. (2005). Early adolescent development across the middle school years: Implications for school counselors. *Professional School Counseling* 9 (2), 112–119.

Young, A., Hardy, V., Hamilton, C., Biernesser, K., Sun, L., and Niebergall, S. (2009). Empowering students: Using data to transform a bullying prevention and intervention program. *Professional School Counseling* 12 (6), 413–420.

CHAPTER 4

Counseling Adolescents in School and Clinical Mental Health Settings

Lauren Moss, Christy Land, and Malti Tuttle

Don't laugh at a youth for his affectations; he is only trying on one face after another to find a face of his own.

Logan Pearsall Smith

CHAPTER OBJECTIVES

After reading this chapter, students will be able to:

- discriminate between normal and abnormal developmental milestones and behaviors for adolescents age 14–18;
- construct suggestions regarding case management for adolescent clients (based on case studies provided in the chapter);
- maintain fundamental understanding of the mid to late adolescent developmental stage.

INTRODUCTION

Anna opens her closet. "I hate everything in this stupid closet!" she screams as she storms out of her room. Upon her mother asking what's upsetting her, Anna mumbles, "You pick the most immature clothing for me. Everything about this family is stupid. I wish I lived with Ashley and her parents. They are so cool; they let her do whatever she wants! I'm so tired of looking and feeling like a baby. I just want to grow up, already."

While this scenario may sound stressful or concerning, situations like this are often part of typical adolescent development. This chapter discusses various developmental domains most pertinent to adolescents aged 14–18, most notably physical, cognitive, and social/emotional development. With respect to adolescent physical development, sexual maturation and puberty for both males and females are discussed. Regarding cognitive development, the chapter presents core concepts of abstract thinking, personal values development, and identity development. Cognitive challenges and limitations are also presented with an emphasis on how learning or cognitive disabilities may impact adolescence and, subsequently, the work of counselors in school and

clinical mental health settings. Within the domain of social/emotional development, this chapter highlights the importance of self-concept and self-esteem
in the social/emotional development of adolescence and furthermore explains
adolescent norms with respect to peer and parent/caregiver relationships.
Accordingly, it offers case studies focused on adolescents receiving counseling
services in school and clinical mental health settings.

ADOLESCENCE (AGES 14–18)

Due to the uniqueness of each individual's condition and process, scholars
and practitioners vary regarding how they conceptualize adolescence.
Generally speaking, helping professionals consider the age span of 14–18
years as the *mid- to late adolescence* developmental period (Coleman and
Hendry, 2011). As the final phase before one becomes a legal adult, this
stage in life can be qualified by a number of physical, cognitive, and social/
emotional benchmarks. Overall, this developmental stage consists of
milestones such as the maturation of the physical body, cognitive refinement
in areas of intellectual and interpersonal interest, and movement toward
social and emotional independence. While this stage is typically comprised of
many exciting life choices and developments, it can also create a significant
amount of angst and dissonance for young people as they wrestle with
determining personal priorities and making life-changing decisions regarding
important topics such as education, peer groups, and family relationships
(Coleman and Hendry, 2011).

Physical Development

Physical growth and development is a significant indicator of mid- to late
adolescence. Adolescents in this stage typically experience *puberty* in the
form of sexual maturation and growth to their adult height. Despite many
schools' efforts to address human growth and development in the academic
curriculum, many adolescents remain unsettled and unprepared for the
changes that come with puberty (Coleman and Hendry, 2011). Therefore, in
order to best support adolescents through this developmental time, counselors must be informed about what is typical development during this stage
versus markers that may indicate premature, delayed, or abnormal physical
development.

   The process of *sexual maturation* takes several years to occur, yet it is
difficult to name precisely when childhood ends and adolescence begins. A
relatively predictable series of physical changes articulate the pubescent
process, which include a number of genetic and environmental factors that
influence the onset and progression of adolescents' physical development.
Overall, during mid-adolescence, most youth are in the midst of a growth spurt,
which involves accelerated changes in the physical body. By late adolescence
(around the age of 17 or 19 in girls and 20 for boys) most individuals have
reached their full adult height (Coleman and Hendry, 2011). In adolescents
developing typically, sexual development involves maturing to the point of

reproductive ability (Gilmore and Meersand, 2014). For both male and female adolescents, this stage also involves the development of secondary sexual characteristics such as body hair. These drastic, and sometimes rapid, changes often precipitate overwhelming feelings for adolescents.

Some adolescents become frustrated that they are not physically maturing at the same rate as their peers, while others will feel embarrassed by early maturation. Many adolescents find physical growth and development embarrassing to discuss with adults, yet they often desire answers to questions they have about the unfamiliar changes they experience. Therefore, counselors in the school and clinical mental health settings must maintain therapeutic factors (e.g. unconditional positive regard, genuineness, and empathy) to ensure adolescent clients feel comfortable and supported as they navigate their unique growth and maturation processes.

Sexual Maturation and Puberty

Spanning all adolescent stages, puberty comprehensively affects bodily systems, including male and female reproductive systems. While different for each individual, the physical changes associated with sexual maturation and puberty typically progress gradually and culminate in mid- to late adolescence. Several critical maturation and pubescent processes for adolescent girls include breast development, secondary body hair growth (e.g. pubic and underarm hair), changing body shape, and becoming fertile. Similarly, adolescent boys also grow and develop to sexual maturation through puberty, punctuated by the enlargement of testicles and scrotum, development of secondary body hair (e.g. underarm, pubic, and facial hair), changing body shape including penis growth, and becoming fertile.

Females

According to the American Association of Pediatrics, girls typically note the first signs of puberty when small lumps (called breast buds) develop under each nipple (Bashe and Greydanus, 2003). While this development is typically noted at the age 9 or 10, they may appear earlier or later. For most girls, the second sign of puberty comes in the form of hair in the pubic area. When pubic hair first begins to appear it is scant, straight and fine, but becomes thicker, curlier, and coarser as maturation continues. By late adolescence, pubic hair covers the pubic area and inner thighs. Typically about two years after pubic hair emerges, adolescent girls also begin to grow underarm hair (Bashe and Greydanus, 2003). Throughout adolescence, as these bodily changes occur, girls' overall body shape changes. In early adolescence, many girls note a generally 'softer' body, especially in the midsection, as part of normal development. By mid- to late adolescence, the body creates a more mature figure by redistributing fat from the waist to the breasts and the hips. Regardless of the rate or progression of physical changes, girls become fertile when they experience their first menstruation (which usually occurs about one and a half or three years after the onset of puberty).

Males

For boys, the start of puberty is noted by testicle and scrotum growth. As the testicles continue to grow through late adolescence, the skin of the scrotum changes by enlarging to accommodate the growing testicles, while the skin becomes darker, thinner and hangs from the body (Bashe and Greydanus, 2003). Boys' genitals grow to adult size by late adolescence. Boys are considered capable of procreation upon their first ejaculation, approximately a year after the testicles begin to enlarge.

The scrotum is normally the first location to sprout secondary body hair, but soon after it can also typically be spotted at the base of the penis, followed by the whole pubic region, and, finally, by mid- to late adolescence, around the thighs, with a line of hair growing up to the navel. About two years after pubic hair growth begins, facial hair begins to grow, and leg, arm, and underarm hair thickens. By late adolescence, chest hair is often present (Bashe and Greydanus, 2003).

As *secondary body hair* continues to emerge, boys usually also begin a growth spurt in stature and height, the peak of which tends to occur during late adolescence. At this time, boys' larynx and vocal cords also enlarge, ultimately deepening the voice. During this growth spurt, boys' body proportions change from gangly to mature, as their trunk and legs expand. Boys' growth spurt is musculoskeletal in nature and they continue to develop muscle mass long after girls do. By late adolescence, a boy's body composition is normalized at around 12 per cent fat, which is less than half that of the average girl's (Bashe and Greydanus, 2003).

Table 4.1 Physical indicators of puberty and sexual maturation

	Onset of Puberty	*General Changes in Body*	*Secondary Body Hair*	*Reproductive Maturity*
Females	Noted by development of breast buds	Begins with a "softer" body and ends with mature figure noted by fat redistribution to breasts and the hips	Begins with pubic hair, which expands to inner thighs and under arms	Noted by first menses
Males	Noted by testicle and scrotum growth	Body proportions change from gangly to mature as the trunk and legs expand musculoskeletally; voice deepens	Begins with hair on the scrotum, followed by the base of the penis and whole pubic region and inner thighs, with a line of hair growing up to the navel; chest and facial hair present by late adolescence	Considered capable of procreation upon their first ejaculation

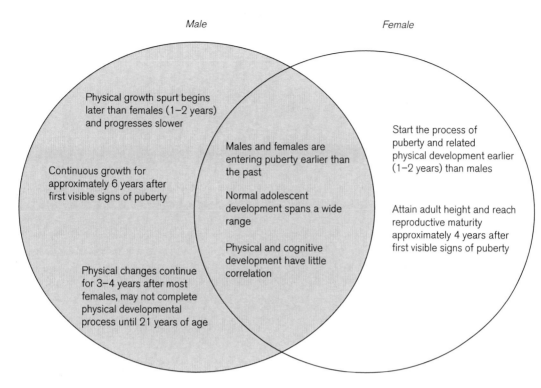

Male   *Female*

Physical growth spurt begins later than females (1–2 years) and progresses slower

Continuous growth for approximately 6 years after first visible signs of puberty

Physical changes continue for 3–4 years after most females, may not complete physical developmental process until 21 years of age

Males and females are entering puberty earlier than the past

Normal adolescent development spans a wide range

Physical and cognitive development have little correlation

Start the process of puberty and related physical development earlier (1–2 years) than males

Attain adult height and reach reproductive maturity approximately 4 years after first visible signs of puberty

Figure 4.1 Adolescent similarities and differences by gender

Physical Development Summary

There are many physical changes occurring for adolescence during the window of 14–18 years of age. Counselors in the school and clinical settings must remain mindful of typical as opposed to atypical adolescent development in order to appropriately support and intervene, if necessary. For example, understanding the general differences in scope and sequence for male and female development is important, yet counselors must consider that each individual is unique and different. Therefore, a holistic approach to conceptualizing the physical maturation of adolescents offers the best approach. Knowing when to consult doctors, pediatricians, and other mental health colleagues will help the counselor know when and how to take appropriate action when working with youth in the mid- to late adolescent stage. To gauge your understanding of this process, consider the following.

- As a school counselor you are working with a 15-year-old female student. She has disclosed concerns to you because all of her friends have started their periods, but she has not yet experienced her first menses. She is concerned something is wrong with her body. How would you respond to her? With whom would you discuss the issue further, if anyone?
- As a clinical mental health counselor, you have been seeing a 17-year-old male client, David. David talks often and at length about how excited he is

for college next year so that he can be on a college campus and "have a lot of sex." How might you approach working with David to discuss and process the urges he feels?

COGNITIVE DEVELOPMENT

Equally as profound as adolescents' physical changes during this stage of development are the shifts in the ways they are able to process information cognitively and make sense of the stimuli around them. Developmentally, typical adolescents move from concrete thinking patterns to having the ability to abstractly deconstruct and analyze concepts. Accordingly, during mid- to late adolescence, intellectual interests gain importance, particularly in the areas of abstract thinking, development of personal values, and the increased emergence of individual identity. Some cognitive concerns such as learning or developmental disabilities might also present unique challenges for adolescents aged 14–18. Counselors can help adolescents find their way through the cognitive developmental process during this exciting, and sometimes overwhelming, time of life.

Abstract Thinking

As the adolescent brain grows and develops, adolescents experience drastic changes in their cognitive thought processes and patterns (Teipel, n.d.). By mid- to late adolescence, youths have experienced the transition from concrete to *abstract thinking* and are increasingly able to conceptualize and process complex ideas, consider future possibilities, experience metacognitions, and empathize with others. Generally, the cognitive shifts adolescents experience by late adolescence completely alters their ability to think about themselves and how they are situated in, and interact with, the world around them. However, adolescents in the mid-to late stage may revert to concrete cognitions when experiencing trauma or stress. Overall, counselors working with youth in mid- to late adolescence should remain mindful of significant developments adolescents experience in abstract thinking, which can be summed up as the following:

- increased ability in sophisticated thought patterns and skills, e.g.:
  - considering possibilities
  - thinking more about the process of thinking
  - contemplating concepts and situations in relative terms rather than absolutes
  - thinking in multiple dimensions
- clearer understanding of cause–effect relationships
- ability to apply/practice new thinking skills through humor and debate

Personal Values

As adolescents develop the ability to think abstractly, they concurrently shape their *personal value system*. While most adolescents in the mid- to late stage still benefit from positive adult guidance to support their decision making, adolescents naturally wish to assert the thoughts and ideas they generate as their unique model for personal values. For example, adolescents often require care-giver boundaries and emotional support while also yearning for space and autonomy to make decisions about topics such as social choices and routines, the selection of recreational and leisure activities, and how much time they allot to academic, social, familial, and recreational pursuits.

By late adolescence, individuals become adept at understanding abstract concepts such as personal dignity, self-esteem, goal-setting and acquisition, and cultural traditions. Adolescents also develop a sense of values and behaviors that best reflect how they conceptualize abstract concepts such as values, religion, and moral decision making. For example, by late adolescence, individuals maintain an understanding of the principles of justice that underpin moral behavior. Accordingly, adolescents question and assess beliefs from their childhood and family in addition to those of the peers and adults around them in order to craft a personal ideology that resonates best with them as individuals. The identification of personal values and behaviors helps to inform social/emotional decisions and development in adolescence.

Counselors working with youth in mid- to late adolescence should keep in mind that the shift in cognitive ability can create intense cognitive dissonance for youth. For example, adolescents in this stage critically and carefully consider the behaviors, decisions, and social patterns of others (peers and adults) around them and consider how those behaviors could possibly fit into their own value system. As this process of dissonance, curiosity, and self-discovery unfolds, adolescents determine what best fits into their personal value structure. This may challenge norms from the family of origin. It will be important for counselors to support this process in a way that helps youth safely to develop their unique sense of self. Counselors should remain aware of important developmental themes often evident during this developmental period, such as:

- development of personal ideals
- selection of role models
- interest in moral reasoning
- increased ability to understand and rationalize various perspectives
- personal morals taking shape based on social order and agreements
- questioning social conventions
- reconsidering traditions from family of origin
- contemplation of the social behaviors of peers and adults outside of the family of origin and consider integrating into personal value system

A Personal Sense of Identity

By mid- to late adolescence, youth have moved from considering themselves as an extension of their parents to exploring and understanding their own unique qualities, abilities, and perspectives. This allows them to develop a clearer sense of self as an individual who can connect and become valued by other people and groups. Specifically, by this stage, adolescents have whittled their sense of self around abstract social/emotional questions such as:

- Who am I?
- Where do I fit in to the world around me?
- Am I able to give and receive love? If so, to/from whom, and how?
- What are my skills, abilities, and talents?

Based on the answers to these questions, adolescents refine their sense of identity around topics such as gender, physical attributes, sexuality, race, ethnicity, heritage, etc. Accordingly, individuals in the advance stages of adolescence typically enjoy expressing their various identities and trying on alternative identities through temporary means such as style of dress, accessories, music selection, hair style, mannerisms, and lifestyle choices.

As adolescents explore various identities and ways in which to understand and express them, there is the possibility of internal and external conflict around how they go about "trying on" and integrating various identities. Even by late adolescence, youth may struggle to identify an authentic sense of self amid the vast sea of possibilities. Subsequently, it is natural for the way they feel and behave in various situations to be self-involved, dramatic, unrealistic, introspective, or even egocentric (Arnett, 2004).

Challenges and Limitations to Cognitive Development

Sometimes youth experience various challenges to cognitive development. Threats to learning that are severe enough to meet diagnosable criteria typically fall into one of two broad categories: Developmental disability or learning disability (Backenson et al., 2015). Counselors working with youth should remain aware of the possibility of a developmental disability or learning disability for adolescent clients who present unusual or significant challenges regarding their cognitive development. The following sections point to criteria counselors may find helpful when considering if they should provide a screening to assess for a developmental or learning disability. Counselors in both the school and clinical mental health settings might also find it appropriate to refer adolescents to an alternative mental health specialist (e.g. psychologist) if they recognize assessment is needed for a particular adolescent and that assessment is out of the scope of the counselor's training.

Developmental Disabilities

A *developmental disability* is a severe, chronic disability attributable to mental (or a combination of mental and physical) impairments that are likely to present indefinitely and result in substantial functional limitations in three or more areas of life activity (e.g. self-care, receptive/expressive language, learning, self-direction, capacity for independent living, and economic self-sufficiency) (Backenson et al., 2015). Due to the manner in which developmental disabilities mitigate life functions, they are typically recognized and diagnosed prior to mid-/late adolescence. Youth with developmental disabilities tend to require a plethora of supports, therapies, and accommodations in the community, home, and school settings.

Learning Disabilities

Quite different from developmental disabilities, learning disabilities do not impact intellectual functioning, and therefore are not always addressed prior to mid-/late adolescence. The term *learning disabilities* is used to describe disorders that impact one's ability to interpret what he or she sees and hears or link information from different parts of the brain (Backenson et al., 2015; Siegel, 1989). A learning disability may only impact one part of an individual's cognitive functioning and, therefore, it is often tedious to discriminate between an adolescent with a learning disability and one with typical cognitive functioning. For example, an adolescent with a disability such as dyslexia (a specific learning disability that effects one's ability to read efficiently) might mask or compensate for the disability by spending an exorbitant amount of time on assignments involving reading.

If a school or clinical mental health counselor suspects an undiagnosed developmental or learning disability in an adolescent, it is important to explore the topic with parents and, ultimately, the client to co-construct the best course of subsequent action. The following table is provided to help counselors discriminate between developmental and learning disabilities. It also provides language for counselors to use when processing and discussing cognitive challenges and limitations with clients.

Table 4.2 Indicators of developmental and learning disabilities

Developmental Disabilities	Learning Disabilities
Limited intellectual potential	Atypical acquisition, retention, processing, understanding and/or expression of information
Reduced ability to transfer information	Maintains intellectual ability to learn and process information
Reduced ability to think critically/solve problems	Disability may have an ongoing (but manageable) impact on work, school, social relationships, self-esteem, and daily life
Typically receive education (and ultimately live) in a protected/supported environment	Typically maintains a "normal" academic and career placement but likely has difficulty in particular academic area(s) (e.g. literacy)
May work in supported employment or lack employment	Maintains age-appropriate peer–peer friendships
Often remain in K–12 educational settings until the age of 21	Leaves K–12 education at typical time
Difficulty articulating goals	May struggle emotionally with goal-setting due to current challenges or past failures
Therapeutic, personal, and academic goals typically center around increased life skills/independence	Goal setting typically centers around appropriate academic and post-secondary placement

Table 4.2 continued

Developmental Disabilities	Learning Disabilities
Low level of ability in all/most areas	Abilities may seem to be inconsistent (e.g. very strong in math skills but significant struggles with literacy or vice versa)
May have language/literacy and behavioral challenges	May display behavioral challenges due to academic frustration

Cognitive Development Summary

Counselors in school and clinical mental health settings provide a unique type of support for youth in mid- to late adolescence, particularly with respect to the cognitive developments experienced during this time. It can be challenging for young people in this stage to comprehend fully how they are changing and growing in their mind. Indeed, the ability to think about this topic is in and of itself evidence that one has matured cognitively! Therefore, support in processing the changes in abstract thinking, personal values, individual identity development, and cognitive developmental challenges may prove extremely helpful for both adolescents and their families. However, counselors certainly may face challenges when helping adolescents around this developmental theme. Therefore, you may want to process your understanding of this theme by considering how you might handle the following situation(s).

- You are a high school counselor eating lunch with two teachers (one math teacher and one language arts teacher) when the math teacher suddenly asks "Do you know why Maggie Jones might be struggling so much in my class?" Before you have a chance to respond, the English teacher chimes in "Maggie? Well, she's my top student!" Later, you look at Maggie's cumulative record and notice that she has historically performed well academically in her humanities classes, but profoundly struggled in math and science. How might you interpret this information? Might there be any follow-up needed? If so, with whom?
- In a session with Brandon, a 16-year-old client you see for clinical mental health counseling, he becomes very agitated, expressing that he "Doesn't even know who he is anymore" because the things he used to be good at, like "basketball and school," he now "sucks" at. He says he is now too short for basketball and that academic work has become too challenging since starting high school. How might you continue your work with Brandon? What follow-up questions might you have for him? What type of informational or directed responses may be appropriate?

SOCIAL/EMOTIONAL DEVELOPMENT

As adolescents mature physically and cognitively their social/emotional development also takes shape. By mid- to late adolescence, youth are honing their ability to cope with stress and manage emotions with others, and reflect on life experiences. Mid- to late adolescence is the first time youth possess the cognitive capacity to sort consciously through who they are and what makes them uniquely different from others.

Self-Concept and Self-Esteem

As they process how to conceptualize their unique identity, adolescents consider their *self-concept* (i.e. the beliefs they hold about themselves). Included in adolescents' self-concepts are: Beliefs about their attributes; their roles and goals; and their interests, values, and beliefs (Smetana, 2011). Furthermore, adolescents in this stage consider their *self-esteem* (evaluating how they feel about their self-concept). Figure 4.2 offers a visual containing various examples of low, mid-, and high self-concept and self-esteem to normalize expected themes and related concepts as they work with clients in mid-/late adolescence.

Self-Esteem (feelings about own self-concept)	**High Self-Concept** e.g. "I am really smart. Probably the smartest in the school!"	**High Self-Concept** e.g. "I am extremely athletic. I play sports every season because I dominate in every sport I try."	**High Self-Concept** e.g. "I am a very devout Christian. I have explored various faiths and churches, but mine is the best by *far*."
	Low Self-Esteem e.g. "I hate being so smart. It makes it too hard to relate to my peers. I'd much rather be of average intelligence."	**Mid-Self-Esteem** e.g. "It's fine being so talented at sports. Sometimes I wish I had more free time, but overall I'm pretty thankful for my athletic skills."	**High Self-Esteem** e.g. "I love that I am such a devout Christian. Becoming Christian was the best thing that ever happened to me!"
	Mid-Self-Concept e.g.: "I am an average basketball player."	**Mid-Self-Concept** e.g. "I will probably make an average plumber when I grow up and get a job."	**Mid-Self-Concept** e.g. "I recently became part of the Democratic party."
	Low Self-Esteem e.g.: "It is devastating to me that I am an average basketball player."	**Mid-Self-Esteem** e.g. "I feel like becoming a plumber is an OK job. Maybe not the best, but it will pay the bills, and I'll enjoy the work for the most part."	**High Self-Esteem** e.g. "I love the Democratic party. Democrats are the *best*!"
	Low Self-Concept e.g. "I am horrible at spelling."	**Low Self-Concept** e.g. "I am really—and I mean *really*—bad at math!"	**High Self-Concept** e.g. "I really think I can become an amazing information technologist. I am a whiz with computers!"
	Low Self-Esteem e.g. "I hate that I am horrible at spelling."	**Mid-Self-Esteem** e.g. "Being bad at math isn't that big of a deal. I go in for tutoring enough that I should pass, which is good enough for me."	**Low Self-Esteem** e.g. "I hate that I could be an amazing information technologist. It seems like such a dorky job and I don't think I would be paid well at all."

Self-concept (belief held about self)
- attributes (e.g. athletic/ smart)
- roles and goals (e.g. future occupation)
- interests, values, and beliefs (e.g. political and religious beliefs)

Figure 4.2 Self-concept and self-esteem

When thinking about self-esteem, it is important for counselors in the school and mental health settings to consider that an evaluation of self-esteem includes *global* self-esteem, referring to how much adolescents approve of themselves overall. In the case of global self-esteem, imagine averaging the total sum of all areas of self-esteem (attributes, roles and goals, and interests values and beliefs). While an individual may be low or high in one or more areas, the concern of global self-esteem is the general state of self-esteem. *Specific* self-esteem refers to how they feel about specific parts of themselves (Smetana, 2011), for example, how good they feel about their ability to play basketball, memorize times tables, or socialize with peers.

Self-esteem is very dynamic, particularly for mid- to late adolescents. For example, when considering Figure 4.2, it is easy to imagine how the client with low self-esteem quoted in the upper left-hand corner ("I hate being so smart. It makes it too hard to relate to my peers. I'd much rather be of average intelligence") might experience a shift in self-esteem after attending a summer camp with other adolescents who are similarly gifted and talented. Likewise, the client with mid-level self-esteem in the bottom center of the figure ("Being bad at math isn't that big of a deal. I go in for tutoring enough that I should pass, which is good enough for me") might find a change in his or her self-esteem if he or she was suddenly faced with a challenging concept and then, rather than making Cs in math, was failing. In this instance, it would not be unlikely for the individual's self-esteem to drop.

Low self-esteem develops when a gap exists between an adolescent's self-concept and what he or she believes he or she ought to be (Coleman and Hendry, 2011; Smetana, 2011). Researchers have linked a number of characteristics to low self-esteem in adolescence, including:

- depression
- low energy
- rejecting one's appearance
- resistance to compliments
- regular feelings of insecurity or inadequacy
- maintaining unrealistic expectations of achievement/success
- maintaining doubts about the future
- extreme shyness
- avoidance of situations where expressing individuality or points of view are anticipated
- consistently conforming to what others expect or desire
- submissive behaviors

Since low self-esteem is also associated with negative outcomes such as mental health disorders (e.g. depression, eating disorders, delinquency, and adjustment problems) it is important for counselors and caregivers to help adolescents acquire a realistic sense of identity by providing appropriate levels of challenge and support as the adolescent approaches different ways of interacting, appearing, and expressing one's self. While increasing global self-esteem can prove challenging, there are several ways in which counselors can operationalize this goal. A few suggested action items include:

- identify targeted areas of importance to the adolescent (e.g. learning to ride a bike, learn a language, or ask a peer on a date);
- encourage adolescents to face problems to build self-efficacy (e.g. try different interpersonal skills or problem solving skills).

Relationships with Peers

One of the most notable shifts in adolescence is the social migration from the family to peer group. As a means of increasing independence, adolescents are attracted away from their families of origin toward peer groups consisting of other adolescents. Peer groups provide several functions to adolescence, from normalizing the growth and development processes to offering a point of reference for adolescents' sense of identity. In this way, adolescents are able to hone their personal moral valuing system and more clearly determine how they are different from their adult care-givers.

By mid- to late adolescence, peer groups are often comprised of mixed gender, and there is often more acceptance of individual differences (i.e. appearance, activities of interest, beliefs, etc.). As adolescents move into the final years of the adolescent developmental process, intimate dyadic relationships (e.g. one–one friendships and romantic relationships) are typically noted. Depending on an individual adolescent's identities, importance may also be placed on peer groups with other adolescence with the same identity (e.g. race, community, etc.).

Overall, peer groups also provide influential stimuli to adolescents in the areas of social status, popularity, prestige, etc. Therefore, counselors working with adolescents in the school and mental health settings can provide great support for clients by serving as a non-parental adult support person by which adolescents may seek and acquire guidance to support their peer and social decision making. Given the profound impact peers can have on social developmental processes, counselors serving youth in this way have a huge privilege and responsibility to ensure that adolescents develop healthy social decision-making and relationship-building skills.

Relationships with Parents/Caregivers

It is natural for youth to establish independence from their families of origin during adolescent development, particularly by mid- to late adolescence. Contrary to what parents may perceive, this natural progression does not indicate a degeneration of the parent–child relationship, or that caregivers have become less important to the adolescent. In fact, it simply indicates that a healthy new stage of development has begun.

When consulting with parents, counselors who work with adolescents should reassure parents and youth around this natural process. It is helpful to reassure parents that it is developmentally appropriate for adolescents to forge new, more mature relationships with peers, but also that the intensified focus on peers does not mean that parents are less significant to adolescents. In fact, adolescents often still aim to identify with parents closely (albeit covertly), while concurrently differentiating how they are unique and different. A few tips counselors can use when consulting with the parents and caregivers of adolescents include:

- talking to parents about the importance of positive peer relationships during adolescence and encourage parents to do the same with their children;
- reassuring parents that their child's increased preoccupation with peers is healthy and natural;
- discussing with parents how adolescents' peer groups help them explore the world—and who they are in the world—outside of the family system;
- if needed, support children in developing social skills appropriate for adolescence (e.g. beginning conversations, offering compliments, being a good listener, confidentiality, etc.).

Social/Emotional Development Summary

Helping adolescent youth make meaning of their social/emotional development is complex. Emotional development is extremely abstract and an adolescent's feelings can change day to day, or even more often. Additionally, the social landscape(s) of adolescents' worlds are equally volatile. Continued support, empathy, and understanding from the adults around them—counselors and parents in particular—can help adolescents emerge from the later adolescent developmental stages with healthy peer and family relationships and their self-concept and self-esteem in tact. However, achieving this end goal requires grace and skill from counselors working with adolescents in the school and mental health settings. Take a moment to reflect on your reading and consider how you might best support clients in the following situations.

- Working at your desk one afternoon you receive a phone call from the mother of your 14-year-old client Chloe. Chloe's mom sounds as if she has been crying and shares that she is feeling helpless. Chloe just screamed at her and said, "I hate you and this entire family! I don't like anything about the way I grew up. I'm going to be the exact opposite of *you* when I'm an adult!" Keeping the best interest of your client, Chloe, in mind, what can you do for or say to her mother on the other end of the line?
- As a school counselor, you've known Sam his whole freshman year. He's always been a stand-out student, great athlete, and kind person. The first week of Sam's sophomore year, you pass him in the hall. You almost don't recognize him. Sam has grown out his hair, dyed it blue, and added several facial piercings over the summer. How should you react/respond? What type of follow-up do you feel is most appropriate?

A CLOSE LOOK AT CASES

The following cases provide you with a deeper look at some of the issues 14–18-year-old adolescents might face during their developmental processes.

Subsequently, it is likely for counselors in school and mental health settings to process similar situations with adolescents and their parents. Consider each of the following cases and the accompanying process questions to consider how you might respond to/manage each case.

Case Study: Jenna

This case study reflects a clinical mental health counseling case in which Jenna, in her early adolescence, faces a dilemma.

Jenna is a 15-year-old Chinese American female ninth-grade student. As second-generation immigrants, her father is a high-profile business executive and her mother is self-employed and operates a small high-end interior design company. Her family identifies as upper class and resides in New York City. Jenna is an only child and attends an exclusive private high school designed to prepare students for top colleges and universities. Academically, Jenna is high achieving, and takes honors classes in all core content areas. She also plays the cello and actively performs in the school orchestra. Jenna is classically trained in ballet and takes classes privately at the New York City Ballet's youth program—an opportunity her mother takes great pride in.

Historically, the circumstances surrounding Jenna's upbringing have appeared "picture perfect." During a recent pediatrician appointment, Jenna was diagnosed with scoliosis, a condition which affects the curve of the spine. Jenna's doctor believes they caught her scoliosis early enough to take measures that will limit the impact the condition will have on her physical growth and development. The doctor referred Jenna to a specialist to fit her for a back brace, which she will need to wear 23 hours per day to be sure to stop the incorrect growth of her spine. Concerned about the impact this intervention will have on Jenna's ballet training and social/emotional development including self-esteem, Jenna's parents arranged for private counseling.

Process Questions, Section 1

1. Considering Jenna's presenting problem and current developmental stage, what considerations would be important to consider during the intake process? (CACREP C.3.a; C.2.a)
2. Discuss the importance of Jenna's developmental history as relevant to her presenting problem. (CACREP C.2.g)
3. In developing a treatment plan for Jenna, what would be the primary and secondary goals based on Jenna's presenting problem? (CACREP C.2.b)

Ultimately, at her doctor's recommendation, Jenna takes several months' break from ballet and continues seeing you for clinical mental health counseling. During one session, Jenna reveals that she does not want to continue with ballet, even if she gets her doctor's permission to return to this activity. When you respond with the statement "Explain more about your decision," Jenna shares that she now has time for her other hobbies, like cello, and even has time to "hang out" with new friends she met in an after-school group created for students with medical challenges. Finally, she shares that she has gained 10 pounds since she stopped dancing. She says that at first it felt "weird," but that now she's excited because she can wear a "real" bra and got her first period a few weeks ago. She admits that ballet was likely hard on her body and she's enjoying life without the activity, but that she is fearful to share her feelings with her mother, who is so proud of her accomplishments and potential as a ballerina.

Process Questions, Section 2

1. Based on how treatment is progressing, do you see a need to shift the treatment goals you originally created with Jenna? (CACREP C.2.g; C.3.b)
2. Whom, if anyone, might you want to consult with further regarding Jenna's case? (CACREP C.2.a; C.3.d; C.3.e)
3. What physical, cognitive, and/or social/emotional themes might you note at this juncture, given Jenna's case? (CACREP C.1.c)

As you continue counseling Jenna, she shares with her mother that she does not wish to continue with ballet. Her mother is disappointed, and their relationship is strained, but they continue to work through their differences, sometimes more gracefully than others. Additionally, Jenna enjoys participating so much in the group for students with medical challenges that she and a friend she met in the group have asked the facilitating teacher if she could help start a similar support group at the elementary school that feeds into her high school. She is very energized by the idea of helping younger students and tells you, her counselor, that "in some ways, scoliosis is the best thing that ever happened" to her.

Process Questions, Section 3

1. Given Jenna's case to date, what physical, cognitive, and social/emotional changes have you noted? (CACREP C.1.c)
2. At this time of adolescent development, what themes appear most prevalent for Jenna?
3. What would be your recommendations regarding how to proceed with Jenna at this point? (CACREP C.1.c; C.2.c)

Case study: Miguel

This second case study is a school counseling illustration concerning 17-year-old Miguel.

Miguel is a late-teens Mexican–American male student in eleventh grade at a suburban high school in Pennsylvania. Due to a plethora of mushroom farms in the region, many under-documented migrant workers settle in the area due to their ability to work year-round in the indoor mushroom houses, which was the case for Miguel's parents. Miguel is an English Language Learner (ELL). His native language is Spanish. He is currently fluent in spoken English, but he struggles with his written expression in both Spanish and English. Miguel has no notable physical developmental abnormalities.

Miguel's cumulative academic record indicates above-average cognitive ability in math and average cognitive ability in all other academic areas. Historically, he has earned all As in math and science classes, and Bs and Cs in the humanities. The school counselor became familiar with Miguel during annual advisement. Otherwise, Miguel presents as a reserved student who is not widely involved in school extracurricular groups, but who appears to have a small group of close friends.

During his junior advisement session, the school counselor asks Miguel about his postsecondary aspirations. Miguel shares with the school counselor that he really doesn't know what he wants to do with his "life" after high school, but that most of the friends in his peer group plan to get jobs at the mushroom farm where his parents work, so he imagines that's what he will end up doing. When the counselor probes Miguel further to discuss what he would do if he could do "anything he wanted" after high school, he describes a career in information technology or computer programming.

Process Questions, Section 1

1. Based on Miguel's needs and current development, what critical elements should the school counselor consider as she continues to support Miguel's post-secondary success? (CACREP G.1.c; G.2.b; G.2.c)
2. Given Miguel's cognitive developmental stage, academic history, and presenting problems, what additional information might be helpful for the school counselor to acquire? (CACREP G.2.g)
3. When planning how to proceed with Miguel, what type of referrals may the school counselor need to provide to appropriately meet Miguel's developmental needs? (CACREP G.2.b)

Upon seeing Miguel in the hallway a few weeks after the junior advisement session, you say "Hey Miguel, how's it going?" simply to build rapport as you would with all students. However, Miguel replies, "Not so good. I just found out last night that my Dad lost his job at the mushroom farm. I don't know what we're going to do. He lost his salary and our health insurance." Shocked, you aren't sure how to respond, but know that this could have an impact on Miguel's immediate situation as well as his wellbeing.

Process Questions, Section 2

1. Given your latest interaction with Miguel, what developmental concerns (physical, cognitive, social/emotional) do you have for Miguel? (CACREP G.2.g)
2. What would be your next course of action, if any, for supporting Miguel's developmental needs? (CACREP G.2.k; G.3.d; G.3.j)
3. With whom, if anyone, would you want to collaborate regarding Miguel's current status given his current developmental state? (CACREP G.2.k; G.3.d; G.3.j)

As the school year progresses, you are intentional about maintaining communication with Miguel. Miguel's father ultimately landed a new, better paying, job at another local mushroom farm. However, the job loss from earlier in the year stuck with Miguel. Additionally, Miguel recently started dating a girl, Regina, with whom he really connects. In some of your most recent interactions with him, Miguel has made statements like "I don't know if I'm like my friends and family as much as I used to be. I think I might want to go to Tech (the local technical college) next year, like Regina. She is studying medical billing and said there is a 95-per cent job placement rate for people who complete their medical billing program. And the jobs pay well, too." He also shared, "Tech has a computer programming course of study there and Regina thinks I could finish it in two years if I stay focused. I'm not sure if I can afford it, but it sounds interesting."

Process Questions, Section 3

1. How has Miguel's social/emotional development shifted throughout his case? (CACREP G.2.g)
2. What is typical and/or atypical about Miguel's adolescent social/emotional development? (CACREP G.2.g)
3. As Miguel's school counselor, what might you do to support his cognitive development as he enters late adolescence? (CACREP G.2.k; G.3.d; G.3.j)

SUMMARY

Mid- to late adolescence, occupied by individuals in the 14–18 age range, is a complex time of growth and development. It is a stage wherein young people set long-term goals (often for the first time), become interested in the purpose of their life, increase their moral reasoning, and experience many social/ emotional changes, including increased preoccupation with self and desire for independence (State Adolescent Health Resource Center, 2013). Counselors in schools and clinical mental health settings are uniquely positioned to support young people as they navigate the nuanced landscape of mid- to late adolescence. With this privilege comes the responsibility for counselors to become familiar with adolescent developmental functioning.

Most notably, as this chapter indicates, counselors must remain aware of adolescents' physical development, including sexual maturation and puberty, for male and female clients, including how male and female physical development are parallel in many ways and altogether unique in others. Additionally, counselors are charged with mastering understanding of the basic cognitive developmental markers of adolescent development, including abstract thinking, personal values development, individual identity development, and possible cognitive challenges and limitations for some adolescent clients. Finally, counselors must also understand the complexities of adolescent social/emotions development such as the concepts of self-esteem and self-concept in addition to the nature of relationships with peers and parents during the unique stage of mid- to late adolescence. Therefore, counselors in school and clinical mental health settings should keep the following key points in mind when working with clients in the 14–18-year-old range.

- Adolescence is an exciting and sometimes trying time for everyone involved, but arguably most jarring for the individual experiencing it.
- When working with adolescent clients in the 14–18-year-old range, remember that there is no "one-size-fits-all" developmental process or procedure to approach adolescence.
- While setting goals and interventions to support adolescent client success, remain aware of typical developmental markers in the themes of physical, cognitive, and social/emotional development.
- Be sure to function proactively with adolescent clients in the 14–18-year-old age range without falling victim to the sometimes volatile nature of the adolescent developmental process.
- Always consult with other mental health experts, medical doctors, and parents when their insight is in the best interest of the adolescent client.

Additional Resources

HealthyChildren.org: https://www.healthychildren.org/English/ages-stages/teen/Pages/Stages-of-Adolescence.aspx

Johns Hopkins Bloomberg School of Public Health Center for Adolescent Health: http://www.jhsph.edu/research/centers-and-institutes/center-for-adolescent-health/

National Institute of Health, MEdLine Plus Website on Adolescents: https://www.nlm.nih.gov/medlineplus/ency/article/002003.htmJohns

World Health Organization Adolescent Development: http://www.who.int/maternal_child_adolescent/topics/adolescence/dev/en/

Suggested Readings

Arnett, J. J. (2004). *Emerging adulthood.* New York: Oxford.

Backenson, E. M., Holland, S. C., Kubas, H. A., Fitzer, K. R., Wilcox, G., Carmichael, J. A., and Hale, J. B. (2015). Psychosocial and adaptive deficits associated with learning disability subtypes. *Journal of Learning Disabilities* 48 (5), 511–522.

Bashe, P. and Greydanus, D. E. (2003). *The complete and authoritative guide for caring for your teenager.* American Academy of Pediatrics.

Coleman, J. C. and Hendry, L.B. (2011). *The Nature of Adolescence*, 4th ed. New York: Routledge.

Gilmore, K. J. and Meersand, P. (2014). *The Little Book of Child and Adolescent Development.* Oxford: Oxford University Press.

Smetana, J. G. (2011). *Adolescents, Families, and Social Development: How Teens Construct Their Worlds.* Chichester: Wiley-Blackwell.

Glossary

Abstract thinking: Complex cognitions beyond the concrete (e.g.: complex ideas and future possibilities)

Developmental disability: Severe, chronic disability that is likely to persist indefinitely and substantially impacts functional limitations in three or more areas of life activity (e.g.: self-care, receptive/expressive language, learning, self-direction, capacity for independent living, and economic self-sufficiency)

Global self-esteem: Level to which someone approves of themselves

Learning disability: Disorder that impacts one's ability to interpret what he or she and hears or links information from different parts of the brain in a way that may only impact one part of an individual's cognitive functioning

Mid to late adolescence: Developmental period between the ages of 14 to 18 years old

Personal value system: Unique model for living generated by one's own experiences, feelings, and worldview

Puberty: Developmental period evidenced by sexual maturation and growth to adult height

Secondary body hair: Body hair that appears during puberty (e.g. underarm, facial, and pubic hair)

Self-concept: Beliefs individuals hold about themselves

Self-esteem: The evaluation of how one feels about their self-concept

Sexual maturation: Series of physical changes that articulate the pubescent process, including the onset and progression of adolescents' physical development

Specific self-esteem: How someone feels about specific parts of him or herself

References

Arnett, J. J. (2004). *Emerging Adulthood.* New York: Oxford.

Backenson, E. M., Holland, S. C., Kubas, H. A., Fitzer, K. R., Wilcox, G., Carmichael, J. A., and Hale, J. B. (2015). Psychosocial and adaptive deficits associated with learning disability subtypes. *Journal of Learning Disabilities* 48 (5), 511–522.

Bashe, P. and Greydanus, D. E. (2003). *The complete and authoritative guide for caring for your teenager.* American Academy of Pediatrics. New York: Bantam.

Coleman, J. C. and Hendry, L. B. (2011). *The Nature of Adolescence*, 4th ed. New York: Routledge.

Gilmore, K. J. and Meersand, P. (2014). *The Little Book of Child and Adolescent Development.* Oxford: Oxford University Press.

Siegel, L. S. (1989). IQ is irrelevant to the definition of learning disabilities. *Journal of Learning Disabilities* 22 (8), 469–478.

Smetana, J. G. (2011). *Adolescents, families, and social development: How teens construct their worlds*. Chichester: Wiley-Blackwell.

State Adolescent Health Resource Center (2013). Understanding adolescence: late adolescence. Downloaded from: http://www.amchp.org/programsandtopics/ AdolescentHealth/projects/Pages/AdolescentDevelopment.aspx

Teipel, K. (n.d.). *Understanding adolescence: Seeing through a developmental lens*. State Adolescent Health Resource Center, Konopka Institute, University of Minnesota.

PART II

Theoretical Orientations and
Ethical and Legal Issues Pertaining
to Counseling Children and
Adolescents in School and
Clinical Mental Health Settings

CHAPTER 5

Counseling Theories Specific to Children and Adolescents

Natoya Haskins and Taryne Mingo

It is estimated that 13–20 percent of children living in the United States experience a mental health issue in any given year and that $247 billion is spent by the government to meet these needs. Because of the impact on children, families, and communities, counseling approaches with specific applications to children become imperative.

CDC, 2013

CHAPTER OBJECTIVES

After reading this chapter about counseling theories, processes, and techniques, students will be able to:

- identify various psychoanalytic, humanistic, behavioral, and postmodern counseling approaches that address the mental health of children and adolescents
- recognize the role of the family systems and its application when working with children and adolescents
- understand the differences and similarities across theories and their applications
- apply the counseling process and techniques of specific theories while counseling children and adolescents in school and mental health settings

INTRODUCTION

More children and adolescents are receiving counseling than any other time in history. Researchers indicate that more than 400 approaches exist to address the clinical needs of this population. All approaches appear to have some level of therapeutic effectiveness when compared to no treatment.

PSYCHOANALYTIC THERAPY

Psychoanalytic theory, first developed by Sigmund Freud, is a deterministic model of personality development. Behavior is determined by internal forces and instinctual drives that are experienced throughout the first years of life (Freud, 1955). The personality involves three aspects—id (the pleasure principle), superego (the ideal principle), and ego (the reality principle) (Elliot, 1994; Freud, 1955). The priority of the ego is self-perseveration by managing the needs and demands of the id and the superego (Thompson, Rudolph, and Henderson, 2004). Because children are typically reliant on their parental figures to guide their decisions, a child's ego creates a superego that is based on parental influence and guides the child for the remainder of his or her life (Thompson et al., 2004). Neurotic anxiety is often caused when the id takes over and potentially creates a negative consequence. For example, when a child skips school to be with friends, the pleasure (the id) of skipping school overrules the reality (the ego) of what will happen—that the school will contact his or her parents, and they will be disappointed. To deal with neurotic anxiety and protect the ego, individuals use defense mechanisms. Defense mechanisms, through unconscious thought, distort the reality to decrease undesirable feelings and/or challenging interactions.

Freud developed his theory of personality based on a set of sequential stages grounded on the individual's desire to achieve pleasure and by unique developmental skills (Freud, 1949). The developmental stages encompass

Table 5.1 Defense mechanisms

Defense Mechanism	Description	Example
Denial	Barring an anxiety provoking external stimulus from awareness	Amy is suspended for bullying, but doesn't believe she is a bully
Repression	Barring an anxiety provoking internal stimulus from awareness	Randy can't remember when his brother died
Projection	Placing unacceptable thoughts or impulses in yourself on to someone else	Seth gets mad at his teacher when he is really mad at the other students in his class
Displacement	Taking out impulses on a safer substitute	When Sally gets mad at her mother, she breaks a glass by throwing it
Sublimation	Channeling unacceptable impulses in a socially acceptable way	John seems to always be engaged in a physical altercation, he decides to join a boxing gym and the wresting team
Reaction formation	Converting the unacceptable impulse into its opposite	Billy says that he is fine when he doesn't make the basketball team but really he is angry
Regression	Returning to a previous more childish stage of development	Charlie started sucking her thumb again after her parents' divorce
Rationalization	Supplying a logical or rational excuse for a shortcoming	Christy states "I always study for my test, but everyone usually cheats, so it's not a big deal that I cheated on this one"
Identification	Imitating traits of another person	Whitney starts to dress and act like a local celebrity, but fails to realize the changes

oral, anal, phallic, latency, and genital. The *oral stage*, birth to 18 months, is characterized by the sucking reflex and the focus is on weaning and the child becoming less dependent. If the process does not begin to help the child develop his or her own identity, due to his or her lack of trust of the caregiver, he or she will experience mistrust, rejection, unhealthy dependency, and/or fixation with oral activities (Henderson and Thompson, 2015). The *anal stage*, 18 months to 3 years, focuses on the search for control and power through the toilet training process. If the child has challenges during this stage he or she may be characterized as stubborn or organized (anal retentive) or giving or messy (anal expulsive). During the *phallic stage*, 3 to 6 years, the focus is on the genital area and differences between males and females. The Electra complex (a child desires his or her mother sexually), Oedipus complex (a child desires his or her father sexually), penis envy (a girl desires to have the genitals of her father), and castration anxiety (boys are afraid their fathers will castrate them for loving their mothers) are phenomenon that are often witnessed during this stage. In the latency stage, 6 years to puberty, the child's focus is primarily on developing skills and garnering information. Children typically engage in same-sex friendships and sexual interest is repressed. The genital stage, puberty and beyond, is characterized as the sexual awakening, and adolescents begin to feel attraction. A critical aspect of this stage is the development of romantic relationships and the rejection or acceptance that adolescents may experience as they try to navigate this phase.

The Counseling Process

The overarching goals of the counseling process are twofold—to make the unconscious conscious and to strengthen the ego. According to Arlow (1995), the psychoanalytic counseling process includes four phases—*opening phase, development of transference, working through transference*, and *resolution of transference*. The *opening phase* involves two stages. In the initial stage, the counselor interviews the child to determine what the presenting problem entails. The counselor then decides if the issue is appropriate for analysis. The counselor then explains the therapeutic process to the child. The counselor begins to record the sessions, ensures that conscious and unconscious material is captured, and comprehensive case notes are kept. During this process, the child may share dreams, thoughts, free associations, fantasies, projections, and early recollections.

The next phase, the *development of transference*, the counselor uses the client's feelings for him or her to show how the child's responses and interpretations in the present represents the same ways he or she has responded to a significant person in his or her life in the past. This will allow the child to develop more self-awareness and learn how to respond differently. During this phase, counselors should also consider any countertransference that they may be experiencing in relation to unresolved feelings related to significant others in their own lives. If this is an issue, counselors should work through the unresolved feelings immediately so that they will not influence the interpretation of the child's transference (Arlow, 1995).

The *working through transference* phase typically corresponds with the preceding phase. This phase often starts with remembering a critical incident in life, which then allows the counselor and child to gain deeper insight. Overtime, the process evolves and allows for further understanding, clarity, and awareness (Arlow, 1995). At this point in the process, the counselor may encounter resistance from the child. Exploring and working through this resistance is critical to this process.

The *resolutions of transference* is the last phase of the counseling process. After the child works through transference and develops more insight, the counselor identifies a date to terminate the counseling. This phase is designed to help children work through any anxiety they may experience in detaching from the counselor. It is not uncommon that additional recollections or fantasies are revealed during this process. It is imperative that the counselor explores these and helps children understand that there will always be deeper insights and awareness that they can glean throughout their lives.

Psychoanalytic Techniques

Maintain the Analytic Framework

Maintain neutrality and objectivity, consistency of sessions, and the amount of time dedicated for each session, clearly presenting fees, and procedures and processes related to ethics codes. This is considered a critical technique in psychoanalytic work.

Free Association

Counselors encourage children to say whatever comes to mind, regardless of how difficult or painful, irrational, or unrelated it appears. This technique is used to open the door to the unconscious, which may include fantasies, motivations, and desires. The counselor would then help the child to identify and understand these free associations as they relate to various aspects of his or her life.

Interpretation

The purpose of interpretation is to facilitate the discovery of unconscious information. The counselor focuses on identifying, exploring, and educating the child about the meaning of free associations, dreams, and fantasies.

Dream Analysis

This technique is designed to uncover unconscious thoughts and feelings that may cause unresolved problems. During sleep, individuals' defenses are lowered, and repressed feelings and experiences come to the surface. During a session, the counselor will help the child transform manifest content (i.e.

COUNSELING THEORIES   81

more acceptable meaning of the dream) to latent content (i.e. unconscious or hidden meaning of the dream).

Working through Resistance

Resistance is anything that gets in the way of change or prevents insight. The counselor should create a safe space wherein he or she points out and interprets resistance/resistant behaviors to help the child begin to examine the role of his or her resistance. Resistance should not be looked at as a roadblock to counseling, but as a means to help the child develop insight.

Analyzing Transference

Transference allows children to re-experience feelings and thoughts that may be hidden related to significant relationships in their lives. The counselor encourages the child to express thoughts, feelings, behaviors, beliefs, and wants that have been buried in his or her unconscious.

Psychoanalytic theory encompasses the exploration of unconscious and its role on behavior, interpretation of countertransference and transference within the counseling experience, and the influence of the anxiety on a child's personality. Techniques, primarily used to uncover the unconscious, include free association, analytic framework, dream analysis, interpretation, and analysis of transference and resistance. While psychoanalytic theory is often criticized for its lack of empirical support and deterministic perspective, many theorists (e.g., neo-Freudians) have used Freud's concepts and basic assumptions to develop additional psychoanalytic theories, such as Adlerian therapy.

ADLERIAN THERAPY

Adlerian therapy, developed by Alfred Adler, is built on the premise that within a social setting individuals' decisions and thoughts serve as a function to move them toward a goal. Adlerian therapy is based on six assumptions (Adler, 1978; Dreikurs, 1953):

1. Behavior is based on the social context and meaning is derived based on this context;
2. Personality is based on the notion of holism and not segmented parts;
3. Individuals are unified moving toward a goal;
4. Every behavior serves a purpose;
5. Each person has the innate drive for self-improvement; and
6. Behavior is based on how we learn to view life.

In addition, Adlerian counselors view personality as encompassing heredity and social interactions as well as how the individual makes meaning of his or her heredity (e.g. heritage, culture background, historical experiences) and social interactions (e.g. interactions within their community and with family and friends).

Consequently, birth order and sibling relationships are critical in understanding behavior (e.g. purpose and goal) and can influence behavior (Adler, 1978; Corey, 2013). The oldest child becomes a model child, bosses younger siblings, and exhibits high achievement. The second child is typically the opposite of the oldest child and often seeks to excel in the areas in which the first-born fails. The middle child is often in a challenging position, as the child often feels left out; however, sometimes he or she will take on the role of peacemaker. The youngest child is the baby and spoiled, which can contribute to helpless behavior, although in the end he or she may develop unique skills and outshine his or her siblings. The only child shares several characteristics with the oldest child—he or she may be a high achiever; however, he or she may have challenges related to sharing and may become overly dependent on parents and adults in general.

The Counseling Process

Adlerian counselors typically see children's behavior as an attempt to reach four goals:

To get attention, to get power, to get even, and because they feel inadequate. For teens, Dinkmeyer and McKay (1997) indicate that these goals of misbehavior may encompass excitement (e.g. alcohol, sex), peer acceptance and pressure, superiority, and machoism. The counselor focuses on teaching and encouraging clients to help them develop courage and self-confidence to address these goals of misbehavior. The counseling process involves four phases: *forming a relationship, conducting a lifestyle assessment, obtaining understanding and insight,* and *reeducation or reorientation* (Dreikurs, 1967). The forming a relationship phase focuses on the counselor working collaboratively with the client. The primary focus initially is on the person in the counseling session and not the issue or problem. In forming this relationship, the counselor listens with empathy, using nonverbal and verbal encouragers (e.g., leaning in posture, minimal encouragers). The counselor also displays respect, hope, and unconditional positive regard as he or she discusses the client's experiences, strengths, and triumphs. During this phase, the counselor will help the client develop counseling goals.

The second phase, conducting a lifestyle assessment, is the assessment stage. Subjective and objective interviews are used in this phase. A subjective interview allows the client to share his or her story. The counselor will listen with interest and curiosity and will then use the story to help the client to view him or herself as the expert, so that he or she can then deepen the story. This interview allows the counselor to begin to see themes in the life of the client and start to develop a hypothesis about what is helpful for the client and what contributes to the concerns in the client's life (Bitter, Christensen, Hawes, and Nicoll, 1998). The objective interview purpose is to determine when the issues started, what the precipitating events were, social and familial experiences, and why therapy at this point. This data also includes the child's family constellation, interactions with peers and adults, experiences at school, early recollections, and wishes (Corey, 2013).

At the next phase, obtaining understanding and insight, the counselor interprets the lifestyle assessment. The counselor presents these interpretations as tentative using open-ended questions (e.g. Is it possible that …? Might it be that …?). This helps the counselor and child to come to an understanding regarding the client's motivations. The counselor also assists the child in understanding the limitations of lifestyle and its impact on his or her current behaviors. The last phase is reorientation and reeducation, which focuses on helping the child make a different decision and move toward new life goals. The counselor will help the child look for new possibilities and alternatives to his or her current lifestyle and uses encouragement to affirm and validate the child's new choices.

Adlerian Techniques

Basic Counseling Skills

Restatement is a technique that is used throughout the counseling process for clarity and understanding, for example, "So what I'm hearing is that your weekend wasn't as fun as you thought it would be because your father didn't have time to spend with you because he was working." Reflection is also used very often by counselors to help a child garner a deeper meaning related to the feeling he or she expresses. The counselor may say, "It seems like you were feeling confused and maybe a little frustrated and hurt when your father did spend more time with your brother and attended his soccer practices but missed yours."

Use of Natural and Logical Consequences

These can help children take responsibility for themselves. Natural consequences are results due to behavior. These results are not controlled or planned (Pryor and Tollerud, 1999)—for example, if a child does not play fairly with friends, the friends choose not to play with the child anymore. Logical consequences do not naturally occur but are intentionally planned and controlled by parents, teachers, or school personnel. For example, a child does not put his or her toys away, the parents put the child in timeout or the child receives three tardies at school, and then an after-school detention. Adlerian counselors use/apply (or encourage parents and teachers to use/apply) the following steps in counseling:

1. identify reasons for behaviors;
2. decide if this is the child's problem;
3. offer choices or alternatives;
4. follow through with the consequences; and
5. encourage the child regarding his or her positive choices.

Puppetry and Clowns

Puppetry allows children the chance to express themselves in ways that are consistent with their interests, values, beliefs, and developmental levels. Children can use puppets to explain what they feel is needed in their own lives and make their experiences individually rewarding (Egge, Marks, and McEvers, 1987). Counselors can use this technique at any point during the counseling process.

The "Could it be …?" Question

Adlerian scholars suggest the "Could it be …?" question can help a child to develop a deeper awareness regarding his or her behavior (Bitter et al., 1998; Dreikurs, 1967). For example, the counselor may ask, "Could it be that you want to express yourself in a way that does not create the negative consequences you are experiencing now?" Furthermore, the counselor may suggest the goal related to the child's behavior in a nonthreatening manner. This should be delivered in a caring way that conveys concern. This technique in turn could be used to help identify the goals of children's misbehavior.

Encouragement

Encouragement is the cornerstone of Adlerian counseling. It is imperative that counselors point out and validate the child's abilities and accomplishments (e.g., "Carlos, you worked hard at creating the artwork, I'm sure you will do well." Avoid using judgment or critique in your statements (e.g. "You did well—now, why can't you do that all of the time?").

Adlerian theory focuses on the role that social factors have on individuals' motivations and behaviors. The Adlerian counselor's goal is to assist a child in identifying mistaken beliefs and developing ways to address these beliefs regarding self, others, or life. The basic assumptions of Adlerian therapy include establishing a collaborative and respectful counseling relationship and cultivating the child's strengths and personal resources. Although Adlerian theory is lacking in terms of research and testability, its focus on social context makes it one of the first multicultural responsive approaches, paving the way for humanistic approaches.

EXISTENTIAL THERAPY

Existential counseling is viewed by most as more of a philosophy than a counseling approach; however, existential therapy can and is used singularly as an approach to counsel children using a relational framework (Henderson and Thompson, 2015; Yalom, 1980). It emphasizes choice, freedom, responsibility, and self-determination. Specifically, existential counselors focus on how children make meaning in their life and develop a purpose for their interactions

(May, 1958). Existentialism also allows children to begin to understand how they author their own lives by taking the perspective that a child can create his or her own path to follow. Existential counseling is based on six propositions of the human condition (Corey, 2013):

1. capacity for self-awareness, which denotes that all children have the ability to become more self-aware with the help of the counselor;
2. children should accept responsibility that accompanies their actions.;
3. children have the ability to preserve their uniqueness and can know themselves in relation to interacting with others.
4. children recreate and create themselves through their work in the classroom, interactions with friends and family, and extracurricular selections;
5. anxiety is a part of every child's experience; and
6. death gives every life significance and meaning.

The Counseling Process

The overall goal of existential counseling is to give children an opportunity to explore their own lives (e.g. purpose, anxiety, humanity, responsibility, and aloneness) and how they accept or ignore these aspects of their lives, which can lead to a deeper understanding of their own existence and behavior change (Corey, 2013). Other objectives the counselor may address in the counseling process include helping the child identify how he or she can live more fully and authentically. This can be accomplished when the counselor maintains a focus on the child's current experience and helps the child develop his or her purpose by recognizing factors that prevent him or her from feeling free or having freedom. In addition, the counselor helps the child to identify ways he or she is contributing to their current experience. These goals and objectives are addressed in a three-part process. In the initial phase, counselors help children recognize and discuss their assumptions and beliefs about the world (e.g. family, community, school). The children then specifically explore how they see themselves in the world. Children may do this through drawing, collages, poetry, or other forms of expressive arts. Next, the counselor instructs the child to reflect on his or her role in the problems he or she is currently experiencing. The counselor may use journaling, role playing, or Socratic dialogue to explore this content.

In the middle phase, children are urged to examine the significant influences on their life (e.g. peers, family, church, community, culture, society). This process potentially helps children to develop greater insight into what they want to change or how they might change their attitudes and, consequently, their behavior. Children are then better equipped to develop a more authentic existence.

The final phase in existential counseling encompasses assisting children in learning how to put what they have learned about themselves into action. The counselor will want to focus on helping children develop an action plan regarding ways they can interact with family, peers, teachers, and community that feels more authentic and provides more meaning for them. This phase will also aim to help the child take responsibility regarding these decisions. During this process, the counselor also helps children to discover their strengths and identify ways to put their strengths into practice as they live a more meaningful life.

Existential Techniques

While existentialism does not have specific techniques, selected interventions and techniques are guided by the understanding of humanity (Deurzen, 2002). Consequently, various techniques from other theories can be used to address the goals of the counseling process. Existential theorists indicate that the techniques or interventions used should be based on the counselor's personality and own counseling style as he or she attempts to explore and understand the experience of the child being counseled (Henderson and Thompson, 2015). The techniques that are used should be designed to expand on how children live their lives and develop awareness regarding their choices and actions.

The main goal of existentialism is self-awareness and examining concerns related to purpose and meaning. In addition, freedom and responsibility are available to all, and the counseling process can allow the child to experience his or her purpose freely. While techniques are not central to this approach, like other humanistic approaches (e.g. person-centered therapy, Gestalt therapy), the I–Thou relationship can significantly influence the outcome of the counseling process.

PERSON-CENTERED THERAPY

Person-centered therapy was pioneered by Carl Rogers and shares many concepts with existentialism. The basic assumptions of this approach include humanity being viewed as positive and people having the innate desire to become fully functioning, so the counselor can create an environment for growth while children can resolve their own problem as they are empowered. Children can actualize toward growth, wholeness, and independence—the child brings about change (Rogers, 1967). In person-centered therapy, children are viewed as having the resources to move toward change and the life or experience they desire. They can resolve their own issues without the counselor intervening with interpretation or guidance (Watson, Godman, and Greenberg, 2011). The person-centered counselor focuses on helping the child be fully present in the moment and completely experience that moment (Corey, 2013). In addition, the counselor facilitates a process where children can learn how to accept themselves fully and decide on what they want to change. The focus is on the child and not on the presenting problem.

The Counseling Process

The primary goal of person-centered therapy is for the child to develop greater independence and autonomy. Rogers (1961) hypothesized that necessary and sufficient conditions need to be in place for change to occur. This hypothesis included six components, three of which have been coined the core conditions (e.g., empathy, unconditional positive regard, congruence).

1. **Psychological contact.** This condition indicates that a relationship between the counselor and child is needed for the child to experience a positive change
2. **The child experiences incongruence.** Inconsistency exists regarding how clients see themselves and their experience. This creates vulnerability and anxiety.
3. **Counselor congruence.** Counselors are genuinely themselves in the relationship.
4. **Counselor unconditional positive regard.** Regardless of what the child does or has experienced, the counselor should be accepting and display no judgment regarding the child's decisions and actions.
5. **Counselor empathy.** The counselor shows understanding of the child's experiences and perspective and attempts to communicate this to the child.
6. **Child's response.** The child perceives through words and behaviors of the counselor that he or she has unconditional positive regard to some extent.

In the application of this process, the counselor uses the following methods to move the child toward growth:

- active and passive listening
- reflection feelings and meaning
- clarification
- summarization
- confrontation of contradictions
- open leads that allow the child to explore (Henderson and Thompson, 2015)

Person-Centered Techniques

Specific techniques beyond empathy, unconditional positive regard, and congruence are not used in person-centered therapy (Rogers, 1957). However, counselor A can use techniques if they help to enhance the "being together" of the counselor and the child. Active listening and reflection of feeling, presence, and immediacy are also valuable tools for counselors who practice person-centered therapy.

Empathy

The counselor displays accurate empathy, which implies that the counselor will feel the child's experiences as if they were his or her own. The counselor should use multiple perspectives of empathy to empathize accurately with the child—*subjective empathy* (i.e. what it feels like to be the client), *interpersonal empathy* (i.e. understanding the point of view and conveying this perspective to the child), and *objective empathy* (i.e. depend on outside sources) (Clark, 2010).

Unconditional Positive Regard

The counselor values and accepts the child without placing judgements or stipulations regarding this acceptance. This is conveyed by counselors indicating that it is normal for children to have their own views and that they value their perspectives. In this respect, children feel free to be themselves and move toward being their authentic selves.

Congruence

Counselors are real and authentic in their interactions with the child, but also in their daily lives. The authenticity indicates that their inner experience matches their external experience. Consequently, the counselor is able to discuss their feelings, thoughts, and reactions openly with the child. The counselor should reflect on the impact of sharing these thoughts and reactions prior to sharing in preparation for the child's response.

Reflection of Feeling

This technique allows the counselor to convey empathy. For example, Hallie shares that she has lived in four foster homes in the last year and that she is very sad. The counselor stating "Hallie, it sounds like you might be feeling alone and maybe even abandoned and angry" could help the child to see that the counselor understands her perspective and worldview.

Active Listening

The counselor should be attentive to the child during the session, specifically, engrossed in what the child is sharing, how he or she is behaving, and his or her overall presence (Cain, 2010). In being present, the counselor displays active listening, respect, and acceptance. These responses all should be genuine and not forced.

Immediacy

Immediacy can be used to display congruence by specifically discussing what is going on in the session between the child and counselor. The counselor might discuss how he or she is experiencing the child. For instance, Michael is uncharacteristically quiet. The counselor might say, "Michael, you seem really quiet today, and its making me feel like you may not want to share."

Person-centered therapy's central assumption is that all individuals have the ability to self-actualize and all have the ability to make decisions independently, based on their authentic selves. While person-centered counselors do not rely on specific techniques, they hold that three core conditions are necessary for change to occur: Empathy, unconditional positive regard, congruence. Other humanistic approaches such as gestalt therapy may rely on additional techniques to address the needs of the child.

GESTALT THERAPY

Gestalt therapy, a humanistic phenomenological approach, was designed on the supposition that children are best understood in the context of their environment and that children have the ability to self-monitor once they gain an awareness of their environment around them (Perls, Hefferline, and Goodman, 1951). The child should focus fully on being who he or she is right now rather than attempting to be who he or she *thinks* he or she should be. Consequently, counselors focus on awareness, choice, and responsibility.

Gestalt therapy is comprised of several principles: *Holism, field theory, figure-formation process*, and *organismic self-regulation* (Corey, 2013). Holism is defined as seeing nature as a complete, whole entity, that is the sum of its parts. For example, the counselor would want to find out about the child's experiences, physiology, thoughts, feelings, fantasies, and dreams. The counselor may then emphasize those aspects that fall within the figure (i.e. aspects that are most salient) or the ground (i.e. aspects that are outside of awareness). Field theory indicates that individuals must be seen in their environments or social contexts. The figure-formation process involves how individuals organize themselves from moment to moment and how the figure emerges from the ground and deal with unfinished business. Organismic self-regulation occurs when the figure or ground is disturbed by a need or emerging interests of the child. During the counseling process, the counselor may face several types of resistance in the form of boundary disturbances (see Table 5.2).

Table 5.2 Boundary disturbances

Types of Boundaries	Description	Examples of Behaviors
Introjection	To accept uncritically others' beliefs without making them congruent with one's own	Believe that those in authority know what is best for us
Projection	Disown aspects of self by assigning them external to self	See themselves as victims of circumstances
Retroflection	Turning back on to self what we would like to do to someone else	Individuals who self-mutilate or self-injure
Deflection	Distraction so it is difficult to maintain contact	Speak through or for others
Confluence	Blurring between the environment and self	High need to be accepted and liked

Counseling Process

The Gestalt counseling process is for many not a sequence of agreed-upon steps, but techniques and experiments that allow the child to gain an awareness in the here and now. However, Fiebert (2012) identified four stages that counselors can use to apply Gestalt in counseling sessions. Stage one, emergence of the problem, helps children to assume responsibility for their feelings, thoughts, sensations, and create a connection between their verbal and nonverbal behaviors. The counselor does not interpret or evaluate the child's behavior. At the end of this stage, the child should be able to express feelings and sensations in the here and now. Stage two, working with external polarities, the counselor begins the process when the child explores the tensions in his or her life. The counselor may ask the child to engage in a dialogue with a parent or sibling, where the child can bring hidden feelings into awareness. In addition, counselors may ask the following: What were the major issues with this person? What feelings or agendas are connected to this relationship? What solutions would they like to see?

Stage three, working with internal polarities, focuses on tensions that are maintained and reinforced by entrenched behaviors. The counselor's aim is to help the child give voice to each side of the polarity and discuss the thoughts, feelings, bodily responses and sensations that are connected to the polarities. The final stage, integration, allows the child to celebrate his or her ability to unify all aspects of him or herself. The final stage is evolving and typically happens throughout the lifespan.

Gestalt Techniques and Exercises

Empty Chair Technique

This technique assists children in externalizing the polarities that have caused them to cut off pieces of themselves in an attempt to try to pacify others or fit within societal norms. The counselor uses two chairs and has the child be the top dog (e.g. authoritarian, bossy, demanding), then switch seats to be the underdog (e.g., victim, defensive, helpless, weak). The counselor then helps the child to integrate both aspects.

Changing Questions into Statements

Children are able to be more authentic and real in this process when the counselor has them use this method in their counseling sessions. For example, instead of asking, "Do you think that I should try to be myself with my friend the counselor would encourage the child to say, "I should try to be myself with my friend."

"I" language

The counselor will urge the child to own his or her statements by using "I" language instead of using general words like "you." For instance, Randy may say, "It feels like you always have to fit in with everyone if you want to be accepted," the counselor will have Randy substitute "I" for "you" and state "It feels like I always have to fit in with everyone if I want to be accepted." The substitution allows Randy to own his actions and take responsibility.

Substituting "won't" for "can't" and "what" and "how" for "why"

This substitution allows clients to take responsibility and move toward changing how they see themselves. For example, the counselor might hear "I won't do my homework" from children, but will have them say "I can't do my homework," which then focuses the responsibility on them.

The Reversal Exercise

Behaviors and symptoms often manifest as reversals of their true impulses. The counselor may ask a child who is isolating him or herself to talk to at least three classmates this week. This technique allows the child to face the thing that causes the most anxiety.

The Rehearsal Exercise

Individuals tend to use internal rehearsal when they are faced with various challenges. A counselor can help children discuss times when they do internal rehearsal (e.g. when they walk into a room with people they don't know; before they take a test or do a presentation). This helps children to see how often they use this and the counselor can examine why they use these exercises. For example, the child at a new school may rehearse, saying to herself, "I will introduce myself—'I'm Sarah and I'm new here,'—and then I'll ask 'What's your name?' That should break the ice."

The Exaggeration Exercise

Non-verbal behaviors may have important meanings. Consequently, the counselor asks the child to exaggerate a movement or posture or repeat a gesture. This helps the child to see easily the emotion behind the behavior. For example, the counselor may ask Shane, who is slouching, to exaggerate and then name the slouching behavior or give it an emotion.

Staying with the Feeling

Individuals often want to move away from unpleasant feelings. The counselor encourages the child to stay with the feelings and help him or her go deeper. In addition, the session may also entail helping the child to go deeper and exploring resistance or boundaries to deepening the identified feeling. For example, the counselor may say, "Your tears start, and then you try to move on to a safer topic like your grades. I wonder what feelings and thoughts are coming?" and "What makes you want to move away from those feelings?"

Gestalt, a phenomenological experiential approach, aims to help children reintegrate all aspects of themselves by developing an enhanced awareness of every facet of themselves and their environment. The goal of the gestalt counselor is to devise experiments that allow the child to develop great awareness and determine which aspects of his or her life are most important in his or her current functioning. Like other humanistic approaches, Gestalt therapy is focused on deeper awareness of self and the relational aspects of the counselor–client dyad; however, the various exercises and experiments may be overwhelming for some humanistic counselors. As a result, counselors that are more comfortable with being active and directive during counseling experience may lean more toward the behaviorism paradigm.

BEHAVIORAL THERAPIES

Behavior therapy is in a singular approach but it is comprised of various theoretical perspectives with common basic assumptions. The common assumption encompasses the following (Anthony and Roemer, 2011):

- the theories rely on the scientific method and assessment processes
- behavior is viewed as overt actions and internal processes
- the focus is on behavior change in the here and now
- clients actively participate by doing
- insight is not necessary for behavior change
- behaviors are viewed as functional
- behavioral interventions are supported by empirical research, and
- behavior therapy is time limited

Traditional behavior therapy encompasses classical conditional, operant conditioning, and social learning theory (Corey, 2013). *Classical conditioning* focuses on behavioral responses that have been created by pairing a neutral stimulus with a respondent behavior (e.g. a dog salivates at the presentation of food; then a neutral stimulus, in the form of a ringing bell, is added with the presentation of food—eventually, the dog will salivate when the bell rings, even if food is not present). In *operant conditioning*, individuals behave in a particular way based on the consequences associated with that behavior. For example, if children are involved with an altercation at school, then they are suspended and/or grounded, and this punishment will lessen the chances that the behavior will reoccur. The *social learning approach* involves the interactions between the environment (e.g. social context), personal factors (e.g. beliefs, values, assumptions, expectations), and behavior. For instance, Leon can learn leadership skills by surrounding himself with other children who display effective leadership skills. A newer approach to behavioral therapy is *mindfulness and acceptance based cognitive behavior therapy*. This approach aims to consider mindfulness, acceptance, the counseling relationship, values, spirituality, and emotionality (Corey, 2013; Herbert and Forman, 2011). Mindfulness helps train the child to be present fully in their experience, even when presented with distractions. Acceptance involves embodying one's current experience without judgement. The goals of mindfulness and acceptance therapy are to cultivate acceptance and mindfulness as well as encourage values that create a consistent life. In addition, the counselor may help the child with understanding difficulties and strategies for change, increase awareness, and behavioral flexibility.

The Counseling Process

The behavioral therapy process is four-fold: Identify the problem through a behavioral assessment, employ behavioral techniques, implement a plan, and assess the progress. The identification process involves using interviews, reports and ratings, observations, and physiological method. Interviews focus on gaining information regarding what, when, where, how, and how often. Reports and ratings typically include self-report assessments and rating scales related to the child's behavior. Observations of the child's behavior are a critical aspect of the behavioral assessment. Observations can take place in either a natural or simulated setting. Physiological methods are used by a medical doctor to determine biological concerns that may be contributing to the identified problem (Anthony and Roemer, 2011).

Negotiating goals involves the counselor and the child in determining which goal(s) related to the problem they should work towards. All identified goals should be specific, achievable, and measurable. The aim of all goals should be to eliminate maladaptive behaviors and learn effective behavior patterns. Next, the counselor uses varied behavioral techniques to help the child achieve his or her goal. These techniques, which will be discussed in the next section, do not aim for the child to gain insight regarding his or her behavior—rather, the focus is solely on the behavior.

Behavioral Techniques

Reinforcement

Reinforcement can be positive or negative and aims to increase the targeted behavior. Positive reinforcement involves adding something of value to the child (e.g., toy, playtime, money) as a consequence of the behavior. Negative reinforcement focuses on the removal of something that created an unpleasant response (e.g. adverse stimuli) to produce a more beneficial result, for example, a child putting on sunscreen in the morning (behavior) to prevent being burned (removal of adverse stimuli).

Extinction

Extinction is withholding reinforcement to eliminate the connection between the problematic behavior and positive support. For example, every time a child cries, the parents give in; however, when they employ extinction, they do not give into the child's demands when he or she cries.

Punishment

Positive punishment and negative punishment can potentially help decrease a problematic behavior. With positive punishment, an unpleasant stimulus is added when the problematic behavior is presented, for example, Emily is given extra chores as a response to her misbehavior. Negative punishment focuses on removing the reinforcing stimulus to decrease the problematic or target behavior. For example, Hareem, who misbehaves, is not allowed to attend the school dance.

Relaxation Methods

Relaxation processes are often used with other behavioral techniques. Typically, children are given instructions on how to relax. The counselor may then provide guidance on how to breathe and think pleasant thoughts. They focus on experiencing the tension and holding it, then gradually letting it go. Relaxation procedures can be used with anxiety, panic disorders, stress, and other physiological ailments.

Systematic Desensitization

A classical conditioning technique, systematic desensitization allows the children to imagine on a gradient more anxiety-arousing stimuli or situations. As a result, children become less sensitive to anxiety-producing stimuli. For example, a counselor is working with Ron, a child who has a fear of dogs. The counselor may start with talking about dogs, then show a picture or have Ron draw a picture of a dog, then show a video, followed by presenting a stuffed dog, then bring in a dog on a leash, all the while exploring how Ron's anxiety is diminishing.

In vivo *Exposure*

Rather than imagining anxiety, through *in vivo* exposure, the child actually experiences the feared situation in real life, having gradually developed a hierarchy of situations with the counselor that allow this. The counselor talks about how the child can address difficulties that arise in each situation. The counselor may join the child in the situation, if necessary.

Flooding

Flooding includes both *in vivo* or imaginal exposure to anxiety-evoking stimuli for an extended amount of time. While the child experiences some anxiety during the process, his or her fears that something bad will happen are not realized.

Social Skills Training

Skills training in behavior therapy is used to enhance children's social interactions. Children that are involved in social skills training are working on developing communication strategies that are proper and useful. Counselors may use modeling, assertive training, behavior rehearsal, psychoeducation, and feedback.

Behavior therapy is designed to change a specific observed behavior and counselors use many techniques to address the behavior change. Behavior therapy has been empirically supported as an effective approach for many disorders (e.g. phobias, post-traumatic stress disorder, substance abuse, anxiety disorders) and child-based issues (e.g. academic, truancy, insubordination). While traditional behavior therapy has been critiqued as not addressing the emotionality and cognitive processes associated with behavior change, cognitive behavior therapy, a contemporary behavior therapy approach, integrates behavior with actions and emotions.

COGNITIVE BEHAVIORAL THERAPIES

Various cognitive behavioral therapies are included within this approach to counseling. Rational emotive behavior therapy (REBT) and cognitive therapy (CT) are the most researched and identifiable cognitive behavioral therapies; consequently, this section will focus primarily on REBT and CT. The shared characteristics include the following (Beck, 2011)—(a) they aim at changing cognitions to create new feelings and behaviors; (b) the counselor is directive; (c) a collaborative client–counselor relationship; d) psychological distress is due to cognitive distortions and dysfunction, e) they are time limited; and f) interventions target the noted problem. Interventions in both approaches are based on a psychoeducational model and the central assumption that helping a child to reorganize self-statements will manifest in a change in behavior (Corey, 2013). REBT and cognitive therapy will be described in more detail below.

REBT

REBT, developed by Albert Ellis in 1955, was the first CBT approach and continues to be viewed as a primary approach in this area. REBT counselors attribute a child's psychological problems to rigid beliefs (Ellis, 1996). However, children have the potential for rational thinking if they stop blaming self or others. Children's cognitions typically fall within three categories: "I must do to win the approval … or I'm no good", "Other people must treat me well … if they don't they are no good", and "I must get what I want … if I don't life is no good" (Ellis, 2001; Henderson and Thompson, 2015).

The Counseling Process

ABC theory is a cornerstone in REBT and helps counselors understand the thoughts, feelings, and behaviors of children. It also presents a counseling process that allows irrational thoughts to become rational. A is the activating event, B is the belief, C is the emotional or behavioral consequences, D focuses on implementing the disputing intervention, E is the effect of the intervention, and F is the new feeling that emerges (Corey, 2013). REBT counselors first identify a child's irrational beliefs. Then, the counselor implements an intervention to teach the child to dispute the beliefs and substitute logical and rational beliefs. Lastly, the counselor evaluates the effects of disputing the child's irrational beliefs.

For example, Sally fails an exam (A). Sally says "I'm stupid, I'll never be able to pass this course" (B). She feels depressed (C). The counselor uses cognitive methods to dispute this irrational belief (D). Sally begins to think differently about failing the exam (E) and begins to feel less depressed (F).

Cognitive Theory

Cognitive theory was developed by Aaron Beck. Beck believed that depressed people have a negative view of themselves, the world, or their future. Such negative schemas are what depressed individuals use to interpret all events and experiences. From a cognitive theory perspective, negative schemas are always present, unconscious, and typically become activated during stressful events. Emotional difficulties tend to cause children to distort reality (Beck, 2011). Cognitive distortions lead to faulty assumptions and misconceptions. Table 5.3 displays the types of cognitive distortions that children may experience.

Table 5.3 Cognitive distortions

Distortions	Descriptions	Examples
Arbitrary inferences	No support for conclusions	Joe starts at a new school and thinks that everyone will dislike him
Selective abstraction	Conclusion based on one experience	Kim gets one B this semester and then feels like she will never make the A honor roll again
Overgeneralization	Extreme beliefs based on one incident and then applying them to dissimilar situations	Erin doesn't make the basketball team, he then believes he will never make the team or any other team
Magnification and minimization	Perceiving a situation in a greater or lesser light than it should be	Angie accidentally bumps into someone in the school hall, she thinks that she will be expelled for "fighting"

Counseling Process

In cognitive therapy, the counseling process includes three phases (Beck, 2011; Corey, 2013). The first sessions focus on the counselor explaining cognitive theory and how negative cognitions contribute to distress. The middle sessions aim to teach the child to identify, evaluate, and replace negative automatic thoughts with more positive cognitions. Throughout this process, the counselor is a collaborator. In the final aspect of counseling, the counselor helps to solidify gains and focuses on preventing recurrence of the maladaptive thoughts. By solidifying the gains, the child can broaden the range of identified negative thoughts and strengthen more positive cognitions.

Cognitive Behavioral Techniques

Cognitive behavioral counselors often use the same techniques discussed in the behavioral therapy section. However, some additional techniques are used to address the unique cognitive and emotional aspects of CBT.

Disputing Irrational Beliefs

The counselor actively disputes the child's irrational beliefs and teaches the child how to do this outside of the counseling session. The child discusses a "must" or "should" or "ought" with the aim of minimizing or removing the irrational thought. To accomplish this, the counselor may help the child learn to tell him or herself the following: "If I don't get straight As, I am not less intelligent." "If everyone doesn't friend me on social media, I am still a good person." "If I am different, it may be difficult, but I can graduate."

Relational Emotive Imagery

The aim of this technique is to establish new emotional patterns (Ellis, 2001). The counselor asks the child to imagine the worst thing that could happen to him or her and then the emotions he or she would experience as a consequence of this image. The counselor then teaches the child how to experience new emotions in response to imagining the said situation. By changing their emotions, children's behaviors typically can change.

Shame-attacking Exercises

Irrational beliefs typically create feelings of shame, guilt, and anxiety (Ellis, 1996; Henderson and Thompson, 2013). Consequently, counselors can implement exercises that can help children decrease the shame associated with how they behave. For example, if Lee says "Everyone is looking at me," the counselor may assign homework that encourages Lee to sing loudly or dress in "attention getting" attire. This exercise can help children see that many people are not paying attention to them, which can potentially help to increase self-acceptance.

Changing One's Language

The counselor supports the child in changing "must" and "should" language to preferences. For example, instead of saying "I must be the captain of the cheer-leading squad" change to "I would like to be the captain ... but it wouldn't be terrible if I'm not." This change can help children to think and behave differently.

Alternative Interpretations

Applying processes that help the child to see alternative ways of viewing his or her experiences is critical to cognitive behavioral approaches. A counselor may ask "What are other ways of looking at this situation?" "What other emotions might someone experience in this experience?" Or "What evidence exists that counters your perspective?"

Cognitive behavior emphasizes dysfunctional thinking as a primary factor in cognitive dysfunction. In addition, cognitive behavior therapists emphasize clients' cognitions, observable behaviors, changing perceptions, and measurable outcomes of therapy. Cognitive therapists work at a deeper level of cognition to change a child's basic beliefs about him or herself, his or her world, and other people. Traditional CBT offers a wide range of intervention techniques and is empirically sound; however, the importance of relational factors are minimized. In this regard, reality therapy, another CBT approach, pointedly integrates the merits of relational factors within a CBT frame.

REALITY THERAPY

Reality therapy, based on choice theory, posits that all living things control how they see the environment and their behavior within this environment (Powers, 1973). In addition, counselors see all individuals as needing to connect with others, and behavior is designed to meet one or more of their five basic needs (Wubbolding, 2000). Reality therapists believe that human dysfunction exists due to children's inability to connect with at least one other individual in their quality world (i.e., it consists of images, activities, events, beliefs, etc.) (Glasser, 1998). Behavior is a child's ways of having his or her needs met. Consequently, counselors that use a reality therapy lens posit that children are responsible for how they behave.

Reality therapists do not focus on behaviors such as fault finding, complaining, blaming, or criticizing (Glasser, 2000). Rather, reality therapists use five characteristics to help children understand their own needs: Emphasizing choice and responsibility; rejection of transference; keeping therapy in the present; avoid focusing on symptoms; and challenging traditional views of mental illness (Glasser, 2000). Consequently, counselors assist children to accept responsibility and identify their role in the change process.

The Counseling Process

The goals of reality therapy include reconnecting with people in children's quality world and helping children meet their psychological needs for power, freedom, and fun (Corey, 2013). These goals are met in such a way that they do not infringe on the needs of others. The focus is on responsibility and choices; the obligation of choosing goals and following through with them are on the child. Reality therapists work to build a good relationship with clients and to ensure that children see them as a person to help them make changes. Reality counselors typically use the WDEP system to guide their counseling process. The WDEP system— the acronym stands for: W = wants and needs; D = direction and doing; E = self-evaluation; P = planning (Wubbolding, 2000)—describes the basic method of reality therapy and through implementation of skillful questioning by the counselor it assists children in understanding and accepting responsibility in how they meet their needs (Wubbolding, 2000). Table 5.4 displays specific ways counselors can utilize WDEP throughout the counseling process.

Table 5.4 WDEP

WDEP Components	Description	Questions During Counseling
Wants	Discover what the child wants and hopes related to the five basic needs	■ What do you want? ■ What do you want instead of the problem? ■ What is your picture of a quality life, relationship, etc.? ■ What do your family/friends want for you? ■ What do you want from counselling?
Doing	Explore what the child is currently doing or what his or her current behaviors are and what the child envisions as the overall direction for life	■ What are you doing? (acting, thinking, feeling, physiology) ■ When you act this way, what are you thinking? ■ When you think/act this way, how are you feeling? ■ How do your thoughts/actions affect your health?
Evaluation	Examine the behavior, wants, perceptions, directions, and plans to determine if what the child is doing is allowing him or her to get what he or she wants	■ Is what you are doing, helping you get what you want? ■ Is it taking you in the direction you want to go? ■ Is what you want achievable? ■ Does it help you to look at it in that way? ■ How hard are you prepared to work at this? ■ Is your current level of commitment working in your favor? ■ Is it a helpful plan?
Planning	Create plans that are simple, attainable, measurable, immediate, involved, controlled, committed, continuous; in a manner that allows the child to take responsibility for his or her behavior	■ What are you prepared to do/think differently that will take you in the direction you want to go? ■ Are you clear about what you are going to do? ■ Is it achievable? ■ How will you know you have done it? ■ Can you start doing it immediately? ■ Is it in your control? ■ Are you committed to doing it?

Reality Therapy Techniques

Reality therapists do not focus on explicit techniques. However, they may use some of the following.

Questioning

Questions can be used to help clients explore their wants, needs, and perceptions. They are also conducive in understanding how the client thinks, gathering information, giving information and making sure it's understood, and in helping clients to take more effective control. For example, the counselor may ask, "How does this current behavior get you what you want?" or "You say that you want to have more friends. What might you need to do differently to get this want and need met?"

Being Positive

Reality therapists take many opportunities to reinforce the constructive planning of their clients and their success in following through on their plans. Reality therapists may turn negative occurrences into positive ones by taking advantage of opportunities to communicate hope to clients.

Metaphors

When clients talk, they sometimes use metaphors such as "When I got caught, the whole world fell apart." Therapists listen to those metaphors and respond to the metaphor: "What happened when the world fell apart?"

Humor

Because humor is spontaneous and idiosyncratic, it can only occur at a particular moment in which it fits in naturally. Humor is part of friendly involvement—therapists can sometimes laugh at themselves, which encourages clients to do the same.

Confrontation

When clients don't follow through on plans, confrontation is unavoidable. Not accepting excuses, being positive, and using humor can be ways of confronting clients.

Paradoxical Techniques

When clients are reluctant to carry out plans or resist making plans, sometimes paradoxical techniques can be used. They are among the most difficult techniques for therapists to use because they are counter-intuitive. Reframing the way clients think about a topic can help them believe a previously undesirable behavior is desirable (like "spitting in the client's soup"—Corey, 2013). Another paradoxical technique is to prescribe a symptom such as telling an anxious person to schedule times when they are anxious.

A primary goal of reality therapy is to help clients connect or reconnect with people in their quality world. In this regard, the reality therapist functions as a teacher or mentor and challenges clients to examine their choices and current behaviors. Through questioning, reality therapists engage clients in a self-evaluation process so they can evaluate their behaviors, perceptions, wants, needs, and action plans. Although reality therapy considers the relational world of the child, many other cultural and systemic concerns may still be overlooked. Postmodern approaches attempt to address this limitation.

POSTMODERN THERAPIES

Counseling theories that fall within the postmodern or social constructionism paradigm share the premise that people make their own meaning through multiple realities. Six major assumptions undergird these theoretical applications (Gergen, 1985; Corey, 2013). First, counselors value the child's reality without disputing whether it is accurate or rational. Second, reality is largely a function of the situations in which people live. Next, knowledge is socially constructed. Fourth, stories and the use of language create meaning. Fifth, the range of truths is limited due to the effects of specific historical events. Last, the range of truths is limited by the dominant culture. The counselor is viewed as a collaborator and consultant and the child is viewed as the expert in his or her life. Two postmodern approaches that have received considerable attention in counseling children, solution-focused brief therapy and narrative therapy, are included here.

Solution-Focused Brief Therapy

The key concepts of solution-focused brief therapy include the following (De Shazer, 1988; Berg and Miller, 1992): Therapy is grounded in a positive orientation, the past is minimized, focus is on what is working, the counselor helps the child to find exceptions to the problem, and the emphasis is on finding the solution. The basic assumptions of solution-focused therapy encompass some of the same aspects as the overarching paradigm of social constructionism (De Shazer, 1985), for example, people can create their own solutions, the client is the expert, the counseling process is collaborative, and the counselor has a not knowing stance. Other assumptions unique to a solution-focused brief include: The problem itself may not be relevant to finding a solution, people can create their own solutions, and small changes lead to large changes (De Shazer, 1988).

The Counseling Process

Solution-focused therapy counseling goals are to change the frame of reference of the situation, to alter the behavior related to the problem, and uncover and apply the child's strengths and resources (De Shazer, 1988). The counselor uses five steps to meet these goals (De Shazer and Dolan, 2007). In the first step, the child is given a chance to describe his or her problem. Next, the counselor collaborates with the child to identify specific goals for the counseling process. The counselor then asks the child to talk about the times when the problems are not present or less severe. As the counselor and child end the solution-focused discussion, the counselor provides a summation of the session, offers encouragement, and recommends what the child might do before the next meeting. In the last step, the counselor and the child assess the progress toward the agreed-upon goals using a rating scale. The therapist and client evaluate the progress being made in reaching satisfactory solutions by a rating scale.

Solution-Focused Techniques

Pre-therapy Change

Individuals who decide to attend counseling typically begin making changes in their lives (Henderson and Thompson, 2015). Consequently, pre-therapy change questions are used during the first session to ascertain what a child may have done before the first session to address the problem. For example, a counselor may ask, "What have you done since you made the appointment that has made a difference in your problem?"

Exception Questions

Exception questions allow the child to begin to see times when the problem was not an issue or not as difficult. The exceptions can help the child see potential solutions. A counselor may ask, "When was a time when this was not happening?" or "Can you talk about when you did not respond in this manner?"

Miracle Question

The miracle question can help children identify the goals they would like to address. It can take many forms—for example, the counselor might say, "A miracle happens tonight while you are asleep, Reuben, and the problem that you discussed at the beginning of counseling has disappeared while sleeping, when you wake up tomorrow morning, what could be a change you notice?

This change might cause you to say, 'Wow, something must have happened—the problem is gone!'" (Berg and Dolan, 2001, p. 7.)

Scaling Questions

It is important for the child to evaluate his or her own progress, and the use of scaling questions by the counselor allows the child to do this. This technique is used in three ways throughout the therapeutic process. First, it is used as an assessment during each session. Scaling questions are also used to let the child know that his or her evaluation is more important than the counselor's. Additionally, it focuses on the discussions of solutions, exceptions, and new changes in their life. A counselor might ask, "On a scale of 0 to 10, with zero being the worst you have felt related to the problem and 10 indicating that the problem is solved, where would you say you are?" The counselor may follow up with, "What made it a 3 and not a 1?" or "What would help you go from a 5 to a 6?"

Solution-focused therapy is primarily a strengths-based approach with a future orientation. This approach allows counselors to support children in developing resilience and building on their own personal resources. While this approach has potential for marginalized populations and children, scholars have critiqued solution-focused therapy as being more of a technique and less of a counseling theory due to its vague counseling process and theoretical assumptions as well as limited empirical support. In contrast, other postmodern approaches, such as narrative therapy, have provided clear theoretical assumptions and detailed counseling processes.

Narrative Therapy

Narrative therapy, developed by White and Epston in the 1970s and 1980s, is based on the premise that meaning is derived from various stories that individuals view as truth. These stories are influenced by dominant cultural narratives, which are internalized by individuals and tend to work against the narrative that the individual wants to live. Uniquely, narrative therapy sheds light on how power, knowledge, and dominant narratives are negotiated in society and families (White, 1989). Narrative therapy allows the child to create an identity separate from oppressive dominant narratives. The concepts that undergird narrative therapy include the following: Listening to the child with an open mind, encouraging the child to share his or her story, not getting stuck in the problem-saturated story, maintaining a curious respectful stance, and helping the client to see that he or she is not the problem, but the *problem* is the problem (White, 1995).

The Counseling Process

Using a six-stage process, the counselor collaborates with the child to help him or her to describe his or her experience in new and fresh language and start the process of creating new meaning related to thoughts, behaviors, beliefs, and feelings (White and Epston, 1990). First, the counselor collaborates with the child to name the problem. Next, the counselor helps to separate the child from the client using alternative meanings. Third, the counselor investigates how the problem disrupts or dominates the child's life. Fourth, the counselor searches for exceptions to the problem. In the fifth stage, the counselor speculates about the type of future the child could have as a new competent person. The final aspect of the process would allow the child to create an audience to support the new story.

Narrative Therapy Techniques

While narrative therapy does not specify techniques as separate from the counseling process, below are listed three "techniques" or processes that are used (Corey, 2013; White and Epston, 1990).

Questions

Narrative therapists use questions to garner the experiences of the child rather than just information. The counselor asks questions using curiosity, openness, and a "not knowing stance." Incorporating questions helps the child explore various aspects of his or her life experiences and dismantle problem-saturated stories.

Externalization

Externalization is a process of separating the person from identifying with the problem. These conversations aim to free the client from identifying with the problem. Externalizing allows the child to recognize when he or she does deal successfully with the problem.

Deconstruction and Creating Alternative Stories

To create new stories, the current and previous ones have to be deconstructed. Consequently, the counselor uses possibility questions to help the child see a new future and explore what it might be like to live differently within a new narrative. To solidify the new story, the counselor helps the child find a new audience, for example, finding a school or community group that will validate the new story.

Narrative therapy has been used in the counseling profession to assist individuals in reauthoring their personal stories. A narrative counselor provides individuals with a safe place to separate themselves from the problem. In addition, it allows a child to see that he or she has the power to develop his or her own narrative and become the narrator of his or her life. Counselors can further address the systemic concerns by infusing family into the counseling process.

FAMILY SYSTEMS THEORY

Family systems theory began to develop in the 1960s and 1970s (Broderick, 1993) to address the rising counseling needs of families (Dore, 2008). Family systems theory is an approach to understanding family dynamics and roles, household and family structural configurations, communication relationships, and boundary lines in the family and between the family and others (Bowen, 1978).

While family systems therapy is comprised of many counseling approaches (see Table 5.5), the primary assumptions of family systems theory include nonsummativity (which reasons that the sum of the family's interactions is greater than the behaviors of individual family members), interrelational connections, circular causality (the notion that each action within the family causes a reaction within the family), communication, family rules and boundaries, and homeostasis (Corey, 2013). Every family uses boundaries and rules to organize themselves, which also helps to provide stability (Collins, 2012). Communication is critical to the interactions within family and typically helps convey information and dictate the type of relationship that exists between family members (Corey, 2013). In terms of family boundaries, most families present in an open manner, which allows individuals from outside of the family to join and communicate with the family or individual family members while still maintaining rules, stability, and healthy boundaries.

The Counseling Process

To begin the family counseling process, all family members must be in attendance. The counselor starts the counseling process by first focusing on the presenting problem or identified client (typically one of the children) (Anderson, 1988). As the family engages, the counselor listens for dysfunctions within the family system (e.g. boundary issues, structural disturbance, role confusion). The counselor's goal is to expose the family to a new way of making meaning of what is taking place as well as finding different ways to experience one another (Bowen, 1978). Consequently, this allows the family to determine the function of the problem within the family, neutralize the scapegoat or the individual(s) that is blamed for the problem, decrease the guilt, increase empathy regarding divergent perspectives, challenge and dismantle nonfunctional roles, and develop new agreement for living in a healthy and stable family. During this process, the counselor observes roadblocks to change in the family and helps the family experiment with new ways of

Table 5.5 Family therapy approaches

Theory	Key Concepts	Goals	Techniques
Multi-generational therapy	■ differentiation of self ■ triangulation	■ change individuals ■ end generational cycles ■ limit anxiety ■ increase differentiation	■ genograms
Human validation therapy	■ family rules ■ openness in communication ■ nurturing triads ■ family mapping	■ open communications ■ enhance self-esteem ■ encourage growth ■ transform extreme rules	■ empathy ■ touch communication ■ sculpting ■ role playing
Experiential therapy	■ intuitive approach ■ techniques secondary ■ pragmatic ■ interventions intensify the here and now	■ individual autonomy and belonging ■ achieve intimacy ■ express self freely ■ support creativity	■ co-therapy ■ self-disclosure ■ confrontation ■ use of self as change agent
Structural therapy	■ family structure ■ structural failings	■ change structure reduce symptoms ■ modify rules ■ create appropriate boundaries and subsystems	■ joining ■ unbalancing ■ tracking ■ boundary making ■ enactments
Strategic therapy	■ solve problems in the present ■ problems are "real" ■ process-focused	■ change behavioral sequences ■ shift family organization ■ move toward correct stage of development	■ reframing ■ directive and paradox ■ pretending ■ amplifying ■ enactments

engaging with one another (Anderson). The counselor then communicates concerns and identifies hidden information or secrets, which can help to ameliorate tension within various relationships in the family (Minuchin, 1974).

Family Systems Techniques

While various theories of family counseling are used (see Table 5.5), several techniques are implemented that are shared by most family counseling approaches. Anderson (1988, p. 4) identified 10 such techniques:

1. **Sequencing**. Ask questions like who does what, when? When kids are fighting, what is mother doing? Father?
2. **Hypothetical questions**. Who would be most likely to stay home if mother got sick? Which child can you visualize living at home as an adult?
3. **Scaling reports**. On a scale of most–least, compare one another in terms of anger, power, neediness, happiness.

4. ***Family map***. Organize information about the generational development of a family that reveals the powerful transmission of family rules, roles, and myths (Bowen, 1978).
5. ***Reframing***. Describe negative behavior in different ways. Acting out, for example, can be described as displaced anger from an unresolved family conflict.
6. ***Tracking***. How does a family deal with a problem: "What was it like for you when …?" rather than "How did you feel when …?" These kinds of questions help keep the focus on the family rather than on the individual.
7. ***Sculpting***. Create a still picture of the family that symbolizes relationships by having members position one another physically. This technique helps to cut through intellectualized defenses, and allows nonverbal members to express themselves.
8. ***Eco map***. Organize data about the family's total environment and their relationship to it.
9. ***Paradoxical intervention***. Instruct a family to do something they don't expect and observe how the family then changes by rebellion or noncompliance. This approach is not appropriate in crisis situations such as violence, grief, or suicide, or for families with minimal resistance. It is reserved for highly resistant and rigid families and is clearly an advanced therapeutic skill.
10. ***Unbalancing***. Support an individual or subsystem at the expense of others. This modifies family structure and introduces the possibility for alternative ways of living together.

Children are best understood within the scope of the family system. Family counseling can help children cultivate healthy relationships with family members and address family concerns that are influencing their behavior, feelings, and thoughts. Family counseling can help to reposition the child, moving him or her from the center to focus on the parental dynamics and family structures.

Table 5.6 Counseling theories chart

Theories	Techniques	Application with Children
Psychoanalytic therapy	■ interpretation ■ dream analysis ■ free association ■ analysis of resistance ■ analysis of transference	Use with: Psychological pain Settings: Mental health and intensive group counseling settings
Adlerian therapy	■ data gathering: family constellation, early recollections, personal priorities ■ encouragement	Use with: Preventive and many conditions Settings: Parent–child counseling, family counseling, individual counseling in school, substance abuse, and juvenile detention settings

Table 5.6 continued

Theories	Techniques	Application with Children
Existential therapy	■ no unique techniques, but counselors can borrow from other approaches	Use with: Developmental issues or transitions and those who need help with life meaning; crisis Settings: Individual, group, family, mental health settings
Person-centered therapy	■ active listening ■ reflection of feelings ■ use of the three core conditions: empathy, unconditional positive regard, congruence	Use with: Crisis, parent child relations, groups with diverse backgrounds Settings: Individual, group, family, community programs
Gestalt therapy	■ experiments ■ I/Thou dialogue	Use with: Crisis, psychosomatic disorders, behavior problems Settings: Individual, family, mental health
Behavior therapy	■ reinforcement ■ shaping ■ modeling ■ systematic desensitization ■ relaxation methods ■ flooding ■ social and assertion skills ■ mindfulness and acceptance methods	Use with: Phobias, depression, trauma, behavioral issues, stuttering Settings: Individual, group, family
Cognitive behavior therapy	■ Socratic dialogue ■ collaborative empiricism ■ debating irrational beliefs ■ homework ■ alternative interpretation ■ new coping skills ■ changing one's language ■ role playing ■ imagery ■ confronting faulty beliefs	Use with: Depression, anxiety, relational issues, stress, skill training, substance abuse, eating disorders, panic attacks, test anxiety Settings: Individual, groups, school, mental health settings
Reality therapy	■ WDEP ■ skillful questions	Use with: Relational issues, empowerment concerns, many issues Settings: Individual, group, family, school, mental health settings
Postmodern approaches	■ change talk ■ miracle question ■ scaling question ■ externalizing ■ letter writing	Use with: Adjustment issues, anxiety, depression, eating disorders, family distress, relational issues Settings: Individual, group, school, mental health settings

Although the theories discussed in this chapter have divergent assumptions and change process, all have been used effectively in addressing the needs of children and adolescents. Each has its own merit and individually or integratively may be used to address developmental, academic, social, and behavioral challenges with these age cohorts. The general counseling process discussed below can be used with every approach listed above.

OVERVIEW OF THE COUNSELING PROCESS

Initial Stage

The initial stage of the counseling process is to begin developing a safe and supportive environment, especially in terms of trusting the school or mental health counselor to help children and adolescents process through difficult issues or transitional times. It will also be pertinent for the school or mental health counselor to disclose his or her legal responsibility to break confidentiality should children disclose any information that would suggest a risk to their safety. This is considered an important first step in building the counseling relationship and remaining honest and genuine about the counseling process and the role of the counselor. In addition, recognizing the uncertainty of ongoing counseling sessions or potential changes in the counseling process is important in building a strong foundation. Addressing or at least acknowledging this possibility in the initial and forming stages of counseling is necessary in developing a safe and trusting relationship because it provides a net of security if the child moves or is introduced to a new counselor.

Working Stage

Once children develop a supportive foundation with the school or mental health counselor, they are usually more willing to talk about issues that are important to their perceived needs. From a developmental perspective, children are still learning basic skills related to peer conflict and problem solving, and any technique or intervention used by school or mental health counselors should be specifically tailored to their age or cognitive developmental level. By incorporating basic skills throughout the counseling process, children and adolescents are better prepared to express their concerns or frustrations in a safe environment. Some challenges specific to children who have experienced trauma may include resistance to opening up and talking about their experiences. Therefore, the goal of the school or mental health counselor, at the working stage of the counseling process, is to help children overcome these challenges through the processing of one's emotions across a variety of outlets, such as play therapy or expressive arts therapy.

Termination Stage

In an effort to prepare children and adolescents for the termination stage of the counseling process, the school or mental health counselor will inform their students or clients weeks before their last counseling session. Having covered a variety of topics over the course of their counseling sessions (i.e. relationship building, coping with anxieties, anger, and self-esteem, and preparing for future difficult situations), children and adolescents will have developed skills to assist them during the absence of counseling sessions. The goal of the school or mental health counselor during the termination stage of the counseling process is to assist children and adolescents in continuing to set goals that will benefit them socially, emotionally, and academically. Progress will be consistently recognized by the school and mental health counselor as children begin to accept the ending of the counseling process. The overall goal for children and adolescents through counseling sessions will be to help them heal from previous traumas or work through life challenges or transitions, recognize access to support during difficult times, and have the ability to be successful in future endeavors.

Case Study: Kendra

The following is a child-centered school-setting case study.

Kendra is an eight-year-old African American female student who has recently begun her third-grade year at Kingsbury Elementary School and who lives in one of the poorest neighborhoods in the rural south with her mother, father, and two siblings. Kendra is the middle child, yet oldest girl in her family, and, as a result of her parents' work schedules, is pressured by her parents to look after her older brother and younger sister. When her brother, a year older than Kendra, and her younger sister get into trouble at school or at home, Kendra is physically punished by her parents for failing to maintain a close watch on her two siblings. In addition, Kendra frequently witnesses her father's physical attacks on her mother when he becomes intoxicated after work, and consist-ently feels obligated to keep her siblings a safe distance away from their dad's rages and care for her mom once he calms down. Kendra has developed a positive relationship with her school counselor since kindergarten and meets with the school counselor frequently to talk about her concerns at home.

Kendra is brought to the school counselor by her third-grade teacher because she refused to follow directions in class, yelled at her teacher and classmates, and put her head down on her desk, unwilling to speak or look at anyone. Prior to walking out and leaving Kendra in the counselor's office her teacher added that Kendra never brings in her homework or has her agenda book signed and will be spending time in in-school suspension if this behavior continues. Dr. Austin, Kendra's school counselor, greets Kendra warmly and invites her to join her in a coloring activity at a nearby table. Kendra has talked with Dr. Austin since she was in kindergarten, and each time she visits her office she reaches for her favorite coloring book that Dr. Austin keeps for her on a nearby shelf.

Counseling Perspective

According to the National Coalition Against Domestic Violence (NCADV), 1 out of every 15 children is exposed to domestic violence each year. Children who are exposed to violence can be impacted physically, mentally, emotionally, and academically, and the effects can either be long-term or short-term. Emotionally, children often become fearful, depressed, anxious, and angry. They may develop Post-Traumatic Stress Disorder and/or participate in self-injurious behaviors. Some physical reactions children may experience are physical abuse, stomachaches, headaches, bedwetting, and sleep deprivation. Often, children lose the ability to concentrate, which can dramatically affect their performance in school. These emotional disturbances paired with a lack of concentration amount to many obstacles for success. It becomes very easy for students to fall through the cracks if underlying issues are not addressed. Many times these children develop behavior problems and emotional difficulties that follow them into adulthood. They will also most likely have an unhealthy view of relationships that has the potential to fall into the cycle of domestic violence (either as a victim or a perpetrator).

There are many societal issues that create problems among students in our schools, and witnessing violence at home is one that has the potential to effect children negatively in a variety of ways. As school counselors, there are several ways we can approach students who have been impacted, including individual and group counseling in the school setting. Since verbal and/or physical abuse is so common, there is likely to be several students in a school with similar experiences. This case study example is intended to assist future counselors interested in working with elementary-aged children who have been exposed to violence and traumatic situations across three theoretical approaches.

Person-Centered Theory

Operating from a person-centered theoretical (PCT) approach, Dr. Austin has already established a trusting relationship with Kendra since her first years of elementary school, and as a result has been identified by Kendra as an adult she can trust with her concerns. In addition, Dr. Austin has provided Kendra an opportunity to claim space in her office, and her coloring book, which she recognizes exists solely for her and no other student, and will be available to her when she needs it. Dr. Austin's ability to provide a supportive and trusting relationship for Kendra sets the stage for potential growth for Kendra. Upholding the principles of PCT, Dr. Austin does not talk to Kendra about the concerns expressed by the teacher who brought her to the counseling office, but, instead, waits for Kendra to begin their dialogue or asks Kendra what is on her mind.

These steps promote openness to discuss real issues with the student without their immediate need to become defensive or fear getting in trouble for telling the truth. Maintaining a trusting relationship is key, including not assigning blame or judgment once the child admits to wrongdoing. For example, if Kendra admits to yelling at her teacher and classmates, the school counselor's role is to acknowledge what was said and reflect the emotion and statement back to the student without criticizing. In addition, if Kendra is not forthcoming about the concerns that brought her to the counseling office, and, for example, begins talking with Dr. Austin about something other than what was stated by her teacher, the counselor's role is to remain present with the current topic mentioned by the student. According to the person-centered theory (PCT) approach, by providing the core conditions, which include maintaining that trusting relationship with the student, Kendra will eventually talk about the issues taking place in the classroom or any outside contributing factors that are creating the behaviors seen in the classroom.

Existential Theory

From a more directive approach, Dr. Austin can assist Kendra in helping her recognize how she can be responsible for her actions despite her struggles in school and at home, those "givens of life" (Corey, 2013) that continue to happen beyond her control. Similarly to person-centered theory, Dr. Austin will not focus her meetings with Kendra on various techniques, but help Kendra understand what she needs to be happy despite her environmental situations. In addition, she will help Kendra to find a balance between all that she feels makes her unhappy or feels unfair with all that does make her feel happy or can lead to future positive outcomes.

From an existential approach, Dr. Austin can help Kendra become more self-aware or attuned to how external factors (e.g. home environment) may be impacting her decisions and behaviors in the classroom. More importantly, Dr. Austin, through their meaningful relationship, can help Kendra realize that while she may have a good reason to misbehave in her classroom that does not mean she has to continue these behaviors. For example, Dr. Austin can encourage Kendra to point out all of people in her school building that she trusts to take care of her. Through this activity Dr. Austin demonstrates that while Kendra's obligation to care for her siblings at home is beyond her control, there are a number of individuals who are willing to take care of her and see her reach her full potential. Dr. Austin's role is to teach Kendra that all is not lost, that anxiety and difficulties are a part of life and short-lived, and can be life lessons that will teach her how to make choices that will benefit her future.

Narrative Therapy

Using empathy, unconditional positive regard, and congruence, Dr. Austin builds a rapport and creates an environment that allows Kendra to feel connected and understood in a way that she may not have experienced in the past (White, 1995). Furthermore, Dr. Austin embraces Kendra's language and meaning-making system and searches for opportunities to empower Kendra. Then, Dr. Austin focuses on helping Kendra see herself as separate from the problem. To begin this process, Dr. Austin uses questions that help Kendra articulate how the problem has impacted her life and relational experiences.

Separating the problem in such a way helps Kendra begin to externalize the problem. In addition, Kendra can start to create internal agency regarding her life and begin to understand what influences the problem and how her family maintain the problem.

Dr. Austin then asks Kendra to discuss significant life events, to examine the sequences of these events, and explicitly illuminating precursors and results of the events. Dr. Austin can then begin the process of linking oppressive narrative to the new narrative that Kendra would like to create as not someone who is hopeless and inferior but to someone who is strong and resilient. Finally, Dr. Austin develops opportunities for Kendra to have an audience to witness the changes and validate the new narrative (e.g., group counseling, mentoring, school group).

Process Questions

1. How should Dr. Austin respond to the teacher who brought Kendra to the counseling office in an effort to create a supportive environment and allow the teacher to feel her concerns were heard?
2. What cultural aspects in Kendra's presenting problem should be considered prior to implementing an existential therapeutic approach?
3. What social justice implications play a contributing role in Kendra's presenting problem, and how can school counselors advocate for Kendra?

Follow-up

Kendra visited Dr. Austin for six sessions. During this process, Dr. Austin also encouraged Kendra's family to seek counseling from outside sources. Kendra's family did begin family counseling, where Kendra also received individual counseling. In addition, Dr. Austin did contact child protective services due to the physical violence taking place in the home. As a result, the parents are also mandated to attend parenting classes and attend counseling. It has been two months since the first counseling session, and while Dr. Austin does not have scheduled counseling sessions with Kendra anymore, she does a check-in with her at least once a week. Over the last two months Kendra's grades have improved significantly. Her self-esteem and socialization skills have also increased.

Case Study: Benji

This second case study is a clinical mental health case study with an adolescent, Benji.

Benji is a 13-year old White male who was placed in foster care in the middle of his sixth-grade year after his grandmother passed away. His grandmother was given primary custody of Benji when his parents were incarcerated for a home burglary and drug charges related to the use of methamphetamine when he was in second grade. Benji currently has no living relatives who are able to care for him, and, as a result, had to be placed in a foster care home nearly 200 miles from where he grew up and attended school. Benji was known to be very close to his grandmother but displayed no emotions at her funeral and would withdraw from anyone who attempted to comfort him.

Presenting Problem

His foster parents describe Benji as quiet and non-social and say that he appears uninterested in making friends at his new school. He only engages in playing video games on the Xbox given to him by his foster parents when he comes home. Frustrated by his lack of attention and social behaviors, Benji's foster parents refer him to a mental health counselor, Dr. Jarrah, at a nearby counseling clinic. They expressed their desire to see Benji become more social and willing to engage with them at home. In addition, Benji's foster parents state that while they realize he is still grieving over the loss of his grandmother, they believe making friends at his new school may help him transition into his new environment, and hope Dr. Jarrah can assist him in making friends at school and transition to the new living situation.

Counseling Perspective

Fostering or adoption affects children across all ages, and there are some commonalities among students who have been fostered or adopted. Externally, these students are more likely to exhibit behaviors related to ADHD, Conduct Disorder, or Oppositional Defiant Disorder (Keyes et al., 2008). They are rated by teachers as being significantly more anxious (Keyes et al., 2008). They also have increased suicidal thoughts, and difficulty with attachment and relationships is highly likely (Keyes et al., 2008). Internally, many youth who are adopted face lifelong issues of abandonment and loss, rejection, trust, loyalty, shame, guilt, intimacy, identity, power, or mastery and control. To understand fully the needs of this group of children, it is critical to acknowledge adoption as "a long term life event process and psychosocial transition rather than a point-in-time occurrence" (Jordan and Dempsey, 2013, p. 44). Based on research that exists on the needs and struggles of students affected by fostering and adoption, an intervention is often necessary for these students to move toward healthy growth.

Gestalt Therapy

Through Gestalt therapy, Dr. Jarrah would help Benji achieve personal growth through an awareness task, which could potentially provide consensual validation and the instillation of hope. By helping Benji gain greater awareness and choice, his potential outcomes may include increased social skills, improved balance of individuality and connectedness, and an increased sense of self-responsibility. Helping Benji tap into any unfinished business, which means unacknowledged feelings that create emotional frustration and prevent positive emotional growth, will encourage Benji to talk about repressed feelings. This includes helping Benji acknowledge what Gestalt referred to as "blocked energy" (Corey, 2013). Once Benji can confront forms of defensive behavior he can then reshape these behaviors into more adaptable forms of behavior.

Mindfulness-Based Stress Reduction Therapy

By using Mindfulness-Based Stress Reduction therapy (MBSR), Dr. Jarrah can help Benji learn how to get in touch with his body and explore any feelings or emotions that he may be suppressing or intentionally avoiding. Helping Benji live in the present moment, relax, and de-stress his mind and body may encourage him to talk about his late grandmother, his parents, moving to a new home and school, and begin to develop coping strategies to adjust in his new environment. Dr. Jarrah is responsible for "establishing trust and creating a climate of safety" (Corey, 2013) as this will be key to encouraging Benji to open up and talk to him. MBSR is highly participatory on the part of the client, and therefore Dr. Jarrah will need to spend significant time building a positive relationship with Benji.

Adlerian Therapy

From an Adlerian approach, Dr. Jarrah must acknowledge the importance of a good client–therapist relationship, and provide Benji an equal opportunity to evaluate his needs and what is best for his future. Having Benji participate in the family constellation technique can provide Dr. Jarrah with a clear picture of how Benji sees himself in relation to his biological family and his current foster family. This technique can also help Benji open up about his emotions towards specific family members and how his perceptions of his family have hindered or strengthened him throughout his life. Once Benji is able to openly communicate with Dr. Jarrah and trust him with the areas of his life that he would like to change, Dr. Jarrah can assist Benji in striving towards a sense of balance or purpose in his new environment. Through increased awareness, Benji can effectively analyze his perception of reality and what meanings he has associated with specific people and events, and modify these perceptions so that he can strive for a lifestyle he finds more suitable to his future goals.

Process Questions

1. In Gestalt therapy there is very little focus on client's retelling of past events. How might Dr. Jarrah help Benji heal from his previous traumatic events from a Gestalt approach to counseling?
2. Considering how participatory Mindfulness-based Stress Reduction therapy can be, how long should Dr. Jarrah work towards building a supportive and trusting relationship with Benji from this approach?
3. Adlerian therapy posits that counselors should attempt to view the world from their client's frame of reference. In considering the case study example of Benji, should Dr. Jarrah attempt to counsel Benji from an Adlerian approach if he has never experienced foster care placement himself?

Follow-up

Benji has attended counseling with Dr. Jarrah for 12 sessions. Over the course of their time together Dr. Jarrah notes that Benji has become more comfortable with him. He hopes that the relationship that he has developed with Benji helps him to connect with other adults who show care and concern. Benji is still withdrawn in his interactions with his foster parents, but does seems to be showing some progress. He seems to be developing relationships with classmates and has joined a basketball team. In addition, his foster parents started attending some sessions with Benji and have discussed with Dr. Jarrah the possibility of adoption in the future. Benji continues to see Dr. Jarrah.

SUMMARY

This chapter has highlighted some of the most researched and applicable counseling theories, counseling processes, and techniques for school counselors and mental health counselors to use with children and adolescents. Applying these theories and techniques can enhance counselors' efficacy with children and adolescents as well as help counselors display more intentionality during their interactions with this population. The key points that arose are as follows.

■ Psychoanalytics focuses mainly on helping the counselor uncover the unconscious information that the child can work through.
■ The main focus in Adlerian therapy is to assist children in changing their mistaken beliefs about themselves, others, and life to engage more fully in society.
■ Humanistic therapies focus on personal development, growth, and taking responsibility regarding one's life. They assist children in identifying their strengths, using creativity, and making decisions in the "here and now."

- Behavioral and Cognitive Behavioral approaches are action-focused approaches that emphasize allowing children to turn understandings into new thoughts, behaviors, and feelings.
- Postmodern approaches challenge the traditional approaches to counselling and embrace the notion of multiple realities and that reality is socially constructed.
- Family counseling therapy should be considered for all children and adolescents as their behavior, thoughts, and feelings can only be clearly understood within the familial context. The family counseling process is where lasting change can take place for this population.

Additional Resources

American Academy of Child and Adolescent Psychiatry: www.aacap.org
American Academy of Pediatrics: Mental Health: Knowledge Exchange Network: www.aap.org
National Institute of Mental Health: https://www.nimh.nih.gov/index.shtml
Society for Adolescent Health and Medicine: http://www.adolescenthealth.org/Home.aspx
Society of Clinical Child and Adolescent Psychology: http://effectivechildtherapy.fiu.edu/professionals
The National Child Traumatic Stress Network: www.nctsn.org
WorryWiseKids.org: http://www.worrywisekids.org/

Suggested Readings

Blom, R. (2006). *The handbook of gestalt play therapy: practical guidelines for child therapists*. London: J. Kingsley.

Eyberg, S. M., Nelson, M. M., and Boggs, S. R. (2008). Evidence-based psychosocial treatments for children and adolescents with disruptive behavior. *Journal of Clinical Child and Adolescent Psychology* 37 (1), 215–237.

Fitzpatrick, M. R., and Irannejad, S. (2008). Adolescent readiness for change and the working alliance in counseling. *Journal of Counseling and Development* 86 (4), 438–445.

Flatt, N. and King, N. (2008). Building the case for brief psychointerventions in the treatment of specific phobias in children and adolescents. *Behaviour Change* 25 (4), 191–200.

Geller, J. and Dunn, E. C. (2011). Integrating motivational interviewing and cognitive behavioral therapy in the treatment of eating disorders: Tailoring interventions to patient readiness to change. *Cognitive and Behavioral Practice* 18 (1), 5–15.

Gil, E. and Rubin, L. (2005). Countertransference play: Informing and enhancing therapist self-awareness through play. *International Journal of Play Therapy* 14 (2), 87–102.

Jayne, K. M. and Ray, D. C. (2016). Child-centered play therapy as a comprehensive school counseling approach: Direction for research and practice. *Person-Centered and Experiential Psychotherapies* 15, 5–18.

Lincoln, A., Swift, E. and Shorteno-Fraser, M. (2008). Psychological adjustment and treatment of children and families with parents deployed in military combat. *Journal of Clinical Psychology* 64 (8), 984–992.

Lock, J. and Fitzpatrick, K. K. (2009). Advances in psychotherapy for children and adolescents with eating disorders. *American Journal of Psychotherapy* 63 (4), 287–303.

Meany-Walen, K., Kottman, T., Bullis, Q., and Dillman Taylor, D. (2015). Effects of Adlerian play therapy on children's externalizing behavior. *Journal of Counseling and Development* 93, 418–428.

Miller, L. D., Short, C., Garland, E. J., and Clark, S. (2010). The ABCs of CBT (cognitive behavior therapy): Evidence-based approaches to child anxiety in public school settings. *Journal of Counseling and Development* 88 (4), 432–439.

Milner, J. (2011). *Working with children and teenagers using solution focused approaches: Enabling children to overcome challenges and achieve their potential.* London: Jessica Kingsley Publishers.

Rotheram-Fuller, E. and Macmullen, L. (2011). Cognitive-behavioral therapy for children with autism spectrum disorders. *Psychology in the Schools* 48, 263–271.

Shillingford, M. A. and Edwards, O. W. (2008). Professional school counselors using choice theory to meet the needs of children of prisoners. *Professional School Counseling* 2, 62–65.

Talleyrand, R. M. (2010). Eating disorders in African American girls: Implications for counselors. *Journal of Counseling and Development* 88 (3), 319–324.

Thomas, D. A. and Gibbons, M. M. (2009). Narrative theory: A career counseling approach for adolescents of divorce. *Professional School Counseling* 12, 223–229.

Tsai, M.-H. and Ray, D. C. (2011). Children in therapy: Learning from evaluation of university-based community counseling clinical services. *Children and Youth Services Review* 33 (6), 901–909.

Glossary

Choice theory: All of our behavior is chosen as we continually attempt to meet one or more of the five basic needs (i.e., survival, love and belonging, power, freedom and fun) that are part of our genetic structure

Cognitive distortions: Ways that our mind convinces us of something that is not really true. These inaccurate thoughts are usually used to reinforce negative thinking or emotions—telling ourselves things that sound rational and accurate, but really only serve to keep us feeling bad about ourselves

Collaborative empiricism: Therapist and client become investigators by examining the evidence to support or reject the client's cognitions. Empirical evidence is used to determine whether particular cognitions serve any useful purpose

Defense mechanisms: Manners in which we behave or think in certain ways to better protect or "defend" ourselves from a full awareness of unpleasant thoughts, feelings and behaviors

Externalization: A process used in Narrative therapy by which the therapist helps a client to see that they are separate from their perceived character traits

I/Thou relationship: We move beyond personal issues, characters, social roles, etc., and see the uniqueness of each individual. This has the effect of moving people into a meaningful inter-personal encounter in which ideas and feelings can be expressed freely

Insight: The person in therapy is helped to develop new ways of thinking about his or her situation

Mindfulness: Maintaining a moment-by-moment awareness of our thoughts, feelings, bodily sensations, and surrounding environment without judging them as "right" or "wrong" in a given moment

Neurotic anxiety: The unconscious worry that we will lose control of the id's urges, resulting in punishment for inappropriate behavior

Paradoxical techniques: A therapeutic method wherein a patient is guided by the therapy professional to keep engaging in unfavored symptomatic behavior, and even escalate it, to express that the patient has voluntary control over them

Reinforcement: Stimuli that can strengthen or weaken specific behaviors. Rewards and punishment are used to change and reinforce people's behaviors

Social constructionism: A theory that examines the development of jointly constructed understandings of the world that form the basis for shared assumptions about reality

Socratic dialogue: The major therapeutic device is questioning through the Socratic method, which involves the creation of a series of questions to (a) clarify and define problems, (b) assist in the identification of thoughts, images and assumptions, (c) examine the meanings of events for the patient, and (d) assess the consequences of maintaining maladaptive thoughts and behaviors

Transference: The inappropriate repetition in the present of a relationship that was important in a person's childhood or the redirection of feelings and desires and especially of those unconsciously retained from childhood toward a new object

References

Adler, A. (1978). *The education of children*. Chicago: Regnery Publishing.

Arlow, J. A. (1995). Psychoanalysis. In R. J. Corsini and D. Wedding (eds.), *Current psychotherapies*, 5th ed. (pp. 15–50). Itasca, IL: F. E. Peacock.

Beck, J. S. (2011). *Cognitive therapy: Basics and beyond*, 2nd ed. New York, NY: Guilford

Berg, I. K. and Miller, S. D. (1992). *Working with the problem drinker: A solution-focused approach*. New York: Norton.

Bitter, J. R., Christensen, O. C., Hawes, C. and Nicoll, W. G. (1998). Adlerian brief therapy with individuals, couples, and families. *Directions in Clinical and Counseling Psychology* 8 (8), 95–111.

Bowen, M. (1978). *Family therapy in clinical practice*. New York: Jason Aronson.

Broderick, C. B. (1993). *Understanding family process*. Newbury Park, CA: Sage Publications.

Cain, D. J. (2010). *Person-centered psychotherapies*. Washington, DC: American Psychological Association.

Center for Mindfulness (Producer) (2014). The stress reduction program. Available from http://www.umassmed.edu/cfm/stress-reduction/

Clark, A. J. (2010). Empathy: An integral model in the counseling process. *Journal of Counseling and Development* 88 (3), 348–356.

Corey, G. (2013). *Theory and practice of counseling and psychotherapy*, 8th ed. Belmont CA: Brooks/Cole, Cengage Learning.

De Shazer, S. (1985). *Keys to solutions in brief therapy*. New York: Norton.

De Shazer, S. (1988). *Clues: Investigating solutions in brief therapy*. New York: Norton.

De Shazer, S. and Dolan, Y. M. (with Korman, H., Trepper, T., McCullom, E., and Berg, I. K.) (2007). *More than miracles: The state of the art of solution-focused brief therapy*. New York: Haworth Press.

Dinkmeyer, D. C. and McKay, G. D. (1997). *Systematic training for effective parenting [STEP]*. Circle Pines, MN: American Guidance Service.

Dore, M. M. (2008). Family systems theory. In B. A. Thyer, K. M. Sowers, and C. N. Dulmus (eds.), *Comprehensive handbook of social work and social welfare, volume*

2: *Human behavior in the social environment* (pp.431–462). Hoboken, NJ: John Wiley & Sons.

Dreikurs, R. (1953). *Fundamentals of Adlerian psychology.* Chicago: Alfred Adler Institute

Dreikurs, R. (1967). *Psychodynamics, psychotherapy, and counseling.* Collected papers. Chicago: Alfred Adler Institute.

Egge, D. L., Marks, L. J., and McEvers, D. M. (1987). Puppets and adolescents: A group guidance workshop approach. *Elementary School Guidance and Counseling* 21, 182–193.

Elliot, A. (1994). *Psychoanalytic theory: An introduction.* Oxford and Cambridge, MA: Blackwell.

Ellis, A. (1996). *Better, deeper, and more enduring brief therapy: The rational emotive behavior therapy approach.* New York: Brunner/Mazel.

Ellis, A. (2001). *Overcoming destructive beliefs, feelings, and behaviors.* Amherst, NY: Prometheus Books.

Fiebert, M. S. (2012). Stages in a gestalt therapy session and an examination of counselor interventions. *International Review of Social Sciences and Humanities* 2, 49–61.

Freud, S. (1949). *An outline of psychoanalysis.* New York: Norton.

Freud, S. (1955). *The interpretation of dreams.* London: Hogarth Press.

Gergen, K. (1985). The social constructionist movement in modern psychology. *American Psychologist* 40, 266–275.

Glasser, W. (1998). *Choice theory.* New York, NY: HarperCollins Publishers.

Glasser, W. (2000). *Reality therapy in action.* New York: HarperCollins Publishers.

Henderson, D. and Thompson, C. L. (2015). *Counseling children,* 6th ed. Belmont, CA: Thomson Brooks/Cole.

Herbert, J. D. and Forman, E. M. (2011). *Acceptance and mindfulness in cognitive behavior therapy: Understanding and applying the new therapies.* Hoboken, NJ: Wiley.

Jordan, C. and Dempsey, M. (2013). Exploring experiences of adoption: Emerging implications for therapeutic practice. *Counselling Psychology Review* 28 (1), 37–46.

Keyes, M., Sharma, A., Elkins, I., Iacono, W., and McGue, M. (2008). The mental health of US adolescents adopted in infancy. *Archives of Pediatrics and Adolescent Medicine* 162 (5), 419–425.

May, R. (1958). The origins and significance of the existential movement in psychology. In R. May, E. Angel, and H. R. Ellenberger (eds.), *Existence: A new dimension in psychiatry and psychology.* New York: Basic Books.

Perls, F., Hefferline, R., and Goodman, R. (1951). *Gestalt therapy: Excitement and growth in the human personality.* New York: Dell.

Powers, W. T. (1973). *Behavior: The control of perception,* 1st ed. Hawthorne, NY: Aldine de Gruyter Press.

Pryor, D. B. and Tollerud, T. R. (1999). Applications of Adlerian principles in school settings. *Professional School Counseling* 24, 299–304.

Rogers, C. (1961). *On becoming a person.* Boston: Houghton Mifflin.

Rogers, C. (1967). The conditions of change from a client-centered viewpoint. In B. Berenson and R. Carkhuff (eds.), *Sources of gain in counseling and psychotherapy* (pp. 71–85). New York: Holt, Rinehart & Winston.

Thompson, C. L., Rudolph, L. B., and Henderson, D. A. (2004). *Counseling children.* Pacific Grove, CA: Thomson/Brooks/Cole.

Watson, J. C., Goldman, R. N., and Greenberg, L. S. (2011). Humanistic and experiential theories in psychotherapy. In J. C. Norcross, G. R. Vandenbos, and D. K. Freedheim (eds.), *History of psychotherapy,* 2nd ed. (pp. 141–172). Washington, DC: American Psychological Association.

White, M. (1989). The externalizing of the problem in the reauthoring of lives and relationships. In Selected Papers, Dulwich Centre Newsletter. Adelaide, South Australia: Dulwich Centre.

White, M. (1995). *Reauthoring lives: Interviews and essays*. Adelaide, South Australia: Dulwich Centre.

White, M. and Epston, D. (1990). *Narrative means to therapeutic ends*. New York: Norton.

Wubbolding, R. E. (2000). *Reality Therapy for the 21st Century*. Philadelphia, PA: Brunner-Routledge.

Yalom, I. D. (1980). *Existential psychotherapy*. New York: Basic Books.

CHAPTER 6

Legal and Ethical Implications
Kimberly Hall and Lindon Ratliff

The disappearance of a sense of responsibility is the most far-reaching consequence of submission to authority.

Stanley Milgram

CHAPTER OBJECTIVES

This chapter will provide you with ethical and legal guidelines to help you
remain objective and guide these children and adolescents. Specifically,
you will be able to:

- understand and apply ethical standards of the counseling profession to counseling children and adolescents
- understand and apply previous legal proceedings to counseling
children and adolescents

INTRODUCTION

Stanley Milgram is perhaps best known for his obedience experiments
(Milgram, 1963). A participant walks into a laboratory believing that he or she
will be part of a study of memory and learning. After being assigned the role of
teacher, the participant is asked to teach word associations to another participant and to deliver electric shocks to the other participant. Despite cries of
pain, the participant in the teacher role continues to deliver these shocks
because the experimenter tells him or her that the shocks are not as unhealthy
or painful as they appear to be. Milgram found that 65 per cent of participants
continued to administer the shocks up to the highest levels.

How does this relate to counseling children? Counseling gives us great
power—our clients trust us deeply. We must be diligent to not abuse that power.

The idea that people would continue to deliver painful electric shocks to
another person simply because an experimenter told them to do so is quite
alarming and teaches us a valuable lesson. According to Milgram, when people
see themselves as being instruments of other people, then they no longer see
themselves as being responsible for their actions. They transfer that responsibility on to the person giving the orders.

How does this relate to counseling children? Counseling gives us great
power—our clients trust us deeply. We must be diligent to not abuse that power.

Children and adolescents, in particular, lean on us to guide them and direct them. We must be sure to guide them in the direction that is in their best interest.

Children and adolescents are vulnerable populations that require additional safeguards to ensure that they are being protected. Counseling these populations involves a great number of ethical and legal considerations that would not necessarily need to be considered for adult populations. Thankfully, counselors have ethical codes that provide guidelines and expected professional behaviors specifically when working with children and adolescents through national organizations such as the American Counseling Association (ACA), American Mental Health Counselors Association (AMHCA), and the American School Counselor Association (ASCA). All three of these professional associations provide excellent guidelines on how to address issues that may arise when counseling children and adolescents.

According to the American Counseling Association (2014), the core professional values of the counseling profession consist of the following:

- improving human development throughout life
- supporting diversity
- fostering social justice
- protecting the counselor–client relationship
- providing services in a competent and ethical manner

These core values provide the foundation for the ethical principles that guide our behaviors as counselors. These principles include the following:

- **autonomy**, or encouraging the right to control one's own direction in life
- **nonmaleficence**, or avoiding actions that could cause harm
- **beneficence**, or working for the good of a person as well as for society
- **justice**, or fostering fairness and equality
- **fidelity**, or honoring commitments
- **veracity**, or being truthful

These values and principles set the tone for the ethical guidelines developed by the ACA, AMHCA, and ASCA. The ACA Code of Ethics (2014) is a more general overview of ethical expectations when providing counseling services, while the AMHCA Code of Ethics (2015) and Ethical Standards for School Counselors (ASCA, 2016) provide guidelines that are more specific to the respective settings. This chapter will discuss key ethical and legal issues that are specifically related to counseling children and adolescents.

ETHICAL GUIDELINES

Before we begin, let us take a look at how the three primary ethical guidelines in counseling are designed. The ACA Code of Ethics (2014) contains nine sections that address topics such as the counseling relationship, confidentiality, professional responsibility, professional relationships, assessment, supervision and training, research, technology, and resolving ethical issues. Each section begins with an introduction and is followed by ethical standards that outline professional responsibilities and include directions for fulfilling these responsibilities for professional counselors.

The American Mental Health Counselors Association (AMHCA) provides services for mental health counselors and developed the AMHCA Code of Ethics to help members make ethical decisions, to define ethical behaviors, and to educate members, students, and the public about the standards of care for mental health counselors (AMHCA, 2015). These guidelines are broken down into six sections that focus on commitment to clients, commitment to other professionals, commitment to students, supervisees and employee relationships, commitment to the profession, commitment to the public, and resolution of ethical problems. The standards closely mirror the ACA Code of Ethics, but do have more detail specifically related to mental health counselors working in clinical or private practice settings, such as fees, insurance, and billing.

Finally, the American School Counselor Association serves counselors who are certified or licensed to work in the school setting, primarily focusing on the academic, social/emotional, and career development of students. The Ethical Standards for School Counselors provides guidelines that are specific to working with children, adolescents, and parents in this environment. The document begins with five tenets of professional responsibility that focuses on students' rights 1) to be respected, 2) to receive information and support to move toward self-direction, 3) to understand educational choices, 4) to privacy, and 5) to feel safe (ASCA, 2016). The standards are broken down into seven primary sections, which are then broken down into further sections. Again, the guidelines are similar to the ACA Code of Ethics, but provide much more detail regarding counseling children and adolescents as well as issues that are more specific to the pre-K-through-grade-twelve environment, such as record keeping in a school setting and balancing student confidentiality with parental rights.

While some counselors tend to focus primarily on one set of ethical codes, it is wise to refer to all three ethical guidelines when working with children and adolescents. To help you decipher the guidelines that are specific to children and adolescents, Table 6.1 provides a chart that clearly outlines guidelines related specifically to children and adolescents, and demonstrates the similarities and differences between the ACA, AMHCA, and ASCA. While this chart is not exhaustive of all ethical guidelines (keep in mind that the entire document by ASCA is related to children and adolescents), it will give you an idea of the primary areas of concern that counselors may face when counseling this population.

Table 6.1 Chart comparing and contrasting counseling ethical codes

Topics	2014 ACA Code of Ethics	2015 AMHCA Code of Ethics	2016 Ethical Standards for School Counselors
Counseling relationship	Section A provides ethical guidelines related to client welfare, informed consent, clients served by others, avoiding harm, prohibited and accepted roles relationships, boundaries, serving multiple clients in a relationship, group work, fees and business practices, and termination and referral.	Section I.A, B, and C provides guidelines related to the counseling relationship, such as the counselor-client relationship, counselor process, and counselor responsibility and integrity.	Several guidelines in Section A discuss the counseling relationship, such as responsibilities to students, counseling plans, dual relationships, referrals, group work, and student records.
More specific to children and adolescents	**A.1.b. Records and documentation** Counselors should maintain and protect documentation that is necessary to provide professional services. Documentation should accurately reflect client progress and services provided.	**I.A.2. Confidentiality** Counseling reports and records should be maintained under conditions of security, and provisions are made for their destruction after five years post termination or as specified by state regulations.	**A.8. Student records** Almost identical to the ACA Code of Ethics, except that more detail is provided about records in the school setting. Specifically, the counselor is encouraged to keep sole-possession records or individual student case notes that are separate from students' educational records, and to realize the limits of these records. Additionally, the Standards indicate a "reasonable" timeline should be set for purging sole-possession records.
	A.1.c. Counseling plans Counselors should devise counseling plans that offer reasonable promise of success and are developmentally appropriate.	**B.1. Counseling plans** This section discusses counseling plans but does not have language specific to children or adolescents.	**A.3. Academic, career/college/post-secondary access and personal/social counseling plans** School counselors should provide students with a comprehensive school counseling program based on the ASCA National Model to develop personal/social, academic, and career goals.
	A.2.c. Developmental and cultural sensitivity Counselors should use developmentally appropriate language when communicating with clients.	Developmentally appropriate language is not specifically addressed in regards to the counseling relationship.	Developmentally appropriate language is not specifically addressed in regards to the counseling relationship in the Ethical Standards for School Counselors.
	A.2.d. Inability to give consent Counselors should seek the assent of children/adolescents and include them in decision making as much as appropriate.	**I.B.2. Informed consent** When a client is a minor, mental health counselors act in the client's best interest. Parents and legal guardians are informed about the confidential nature of the counseling relationship, and counselors strive to establish collaborative relationships with parents/guardians to best serve their minor clients.	**A.2. Confidentiality** In regards to obtaining assent, school counselors should inform individual students of the purposes, goals, and techniques of counseling, as well as the limits of confidentiality in a developmentally appropriate manner. These Standards further explain that while every attempt is made to obtain informed consent it is not always possible and when needed will make counseling decisions on students' behalf.

Table 6.1 continued

Topics	2014 ACA Code of Ethics	2015 AMHCA Code of Ethics	2016 Ethical Standards for School Counselors
Confidentiality and privacy	Section B provides ethical guidelines related to respecting client rights, exceptions to confidentially and privacy, information shared with other, groups and families, clients lacking capacity to give informed consent, records and documentation, and case consultation.	Section I.A and B provides guidelines related to confidentiality and privacy.	Guidelines in Section A, B, and C discuss issues surrounding confidentiality and privacy, such as danger to self/others, student records, parent rights, responsibilities, and confidentiality, and sharing information with other professionals.
More specific to children and adolescents	**B.2.a. Serious and foreseeable harm and legal requirements** The general requirements of confidentiality do not apply when disclosure is necessary to protect clients or identified others from harm.	**I.A.2. Confidentiality** If a client has a communicable or life threatening illness (that is verified by a medical provider), the counselor may justify disclosing information to an identifiable third party. **I.B.5 Termination and referral** Counselors should take steps to secure a safety plan if clients are at risk of being harmed or are suicidal.	**A.7. Danger to self or others** Counselors should inform parents/guardians and/or appropriate authorities when a student poses a danger to self or others. This is to be done after careful deliberation and consultation with other counseling professionals.
	B.2.c. Release of confidential information Counselors should seek permission from the appropriate third party (parent/guardian) before disclosing information and should explain to the child/adolescent within their level of understanding about the release.	**I.A.2. Confidentiality** Information in a client's record belongs to the client and may not be shared without a formal release of information.	**A.2.Confidentiality** School counselors can request of the court to not require disclosure if the information could potentially harm the student or counseling relationship. Student records and personal data should be protected in accordance with state laws, school policies, and the Family Educational Rights and Privacy Act (FERPA). Electronically transmitted data should be treated with the same care as traditional student records. **A.5. Appropriate referrals** The school counselor should request that the student and/or parents/guardians sign a release of information when attempting to develop a collaborative relationship with other service providers. **C.2. Sharing information with other professionals** School counselors should understand the "Release of information" process and parental rights when establishing a collaborative relationship with other professionals.

Topics	2014 ACA Code of Ethics	2015 AMHCA Code of Ethics	2016 Ethical Standards for School Counselors
	B.5.b. Responsibility to parents and legal guardians Counselors should inform parents/legal guardians about the role of counselors and the confidential nature of the counseling relationship; however, counselors should respect the inherent rights and responsibilities of parents/guardians regarding the welfare of their children according to law. Counselors should work to establish, as appropriate, collaborative relationships with parents/guardians to best serve clients.	**I.A.2. Counselor–client relationship** Parents and guardians have legal access to client information in the case where primary clients are minors. Where appropriate, a parent(s) or guardian(s) may be included in the counseling process; however, mental health counselors must take measures to safeguard client confidentiality within legal limits.	**A.2. Confidentiality** The primary obligation for confidentiality is to the students; however, school counselors must balance this obligation with an understanding of parents'/guardians' legal and inherent rights. **B.1. Parent rights and responsibilities** School counselors should respect the rights/responsibilities of parents/guardians for the children and strive to establish a collaborative relationship. School counselors should inform all parents of the nature of counseling services that are provided in the school setting. **B.2. Parents/guardians and confidentiality** The school counselor should inform parents/guardians of the counselor's role and the importance of confidentiality between the student and counselor. Counselors should provide parents/guardians with accurate, comprehensive and relevant information in an objective and caring manner while still maintaining ethical responsibilities to the student.
	B.6.a. Creating and maintaining records and documentation Counselors should maintain and protect documentation that is necessary to provide professional services.	**I.A.2. Confidentiality** Counseling reports and records should be maintained under conditions of security, and provisions are made for their destruction after five (5) years post-termination or as specified by state regulations.	**A.8. Student records** School counselors should recognize the limits of sole-possession records and realize that these records could be subpoenaed and/or made educational records when they are shared, accessible to others in either verbal or written form, or include information other than professional opinion or personal observations.

Table 6.1 continued

Topics	2014 ACA Code of Ethics	2015 AMHCA Code of Ethics	2016 Ethical Standards for School Counselors
Professional responsibility	Section C provides ethical guidelines related to knowledge of and compliance with standards, professional competence, advertising and soliciting clients, professional qualifications, public responsibility, treatment modalities, and responsibility to other professionals.	Section I.C. specifically address the counselor's responsibility, including competence, non-discrimination, and conflict of interest.	Guidelines in Sections D, E, and F discuss issues related to the school counselor's responsibility to the school, community, and families, self, and to the profession.
More specific to children and adolescents	**C.2.a. Boundaries of competence** Counselors should practice within their boundaries of competence, based on education, training, supervised experience, state and national credentials, and professional experience. Counselors who work with children/adolescents should have training specific to this population.	**I.C.1. Competence** Mental health counselors should recognize the boundaries of their particular competencies, the limitations of their expertise, and only provide services for which they are qualified by education, training, or expertise. This section provides additional information related to multiple issues of competency.	**E.1. Professional competence** The school counselor should function within the boundaries of his/her professional competence and accept responsibility for the consequences of their actions. Guidelines also encourage counselors to practice wellness, stay abreast of current research, attend professional developmental opportunities, and maintain membership in professional associations.
Relationships with other professionals	Section D provides ethical guidelines related to relationships with colleagues, employers, and employees and provision of consultation services.	Section I.F., II, III all discuss issues related to relationships with other professionals, including colleagues, students, employees, and supervisees.	Sections C and F provide guidelines related to responsibilities to the profession and other professionals.
Evaluation, assessment, and interpretation	Section E provides ethical guidelines related to competent use and interpretation of instruments, informed consent related to assessment, release of data, diagnosis, selecting instruments, conditions of assessment administration, diversity in assessment, scoring and interpretation, assessment security, outdated instruments/ results, assessment construction, and forensic evaluation.	Section I.D. specifically addresses assessment and diagnosis, including selection and administration of instruments, interpretation and reporting of results, competence, and forensic activity.	Section A.9 addresses evaluation, assessment, and interpretation guidelines for the school counselor. These guidelines specifically address the consideration of the developmental level and using language that a child/adolescent can understand.

Topics	2014 ACA Code of Ethics	2015 AMHCA Code of Ethics	2016 Ethical Standards for School Counselors
More specific to children and adolescents	**E.13.b. Consent for evaluation** When children are being evaluated, counselors must obtain written consent from a parent/guardian.	Consent for evaluation is not specifically addressed.	Consent for evaluation is not specifically addressed.
	Developmental level and language is not specifically addressed.	Developmental level and language is not specifically addressed.	**A.9. Evaluation, assessment and interpretation** The school counselor should consider the developmental age, language skills and level of competence of the student before giving an assessment. When discussing assessments with students, school counselors should use language that the student can understand.
Supervision, training, and teaching	Section F provides ethical guidelines related to counselor supervision and client welfare, counselor supervision competence, supervisory relationship, supervisor responsibilities, student/supervisee responsibilities, supervision evaluation, remediation, and endorsement, responsibilities of counselor educators, student welfare, student evaluation and remediation, roles/relationships between counselor educators and students, and diversity competence in counselor education/training programs.	Section III specifically addresses guidelines regarding relationships with students, supervisees, and employees. Guidelines are also provided that are specific to the clinical supervision contract.	Section F provides guidelines related to supervision of school counselors during their practicum and internship experiences, while Section A. 11 discusses school counselors as supervisors of a student peer support program.
Research and publication	Section G provides ethical guidelines related to research responsibilities, rights of research participants, managing and maintaining boundaries, reporting results, and publications/presentations.	Section IV.B. provides guidelines related to research and publication.	Section F provides guidelines regarding conducting appropriate research and reporting findings
More specific to children and adolescents	No guidelines specific to children/adolescents.	No guidelines specific to children/adolescents.	**F.1 Professionalism** The school counselor should seek parent/guardian consent before conducting any research.

Table 6.1 continued

Topics	2014 ACA Code of Ethics	2015 AMHCA Code of Ethics	2016 Ethical Standards for School Counselors
Distance counseling, technology, and social media	Section H provides ethical guidelines related to knowledge and legal considerations, informed consent and security, distance counseling relationship, records and web maintenance, and social media.	Section I.B.6 provides guidelines related to telehealth, distance counseling, and the use of social media.	Section A.10 specifically addresses technology guidelines related to school counselors and includes guidelines related to cyberbullying.
Resolving ethical issues	Section I provides ethical guidelines related to standards and the law, suspected violations, and cooperation with ethics committees.	Section VI provides guidelines regarding the resolution of ethical problems and encourages counselors to use a commonly recognized procedure for ethical decision-making.	Section G provides guidelines for reporting ethical violations, work policies that do not reflect ethical standards, and ethical decision making. Specifically, the model Solutions to Ethical Problems in Schools (STEPS; Stone, 2001) is provided as an example for an ethical decision-making model.

As you can see, the ethical codes provided by ACA, AMHCA, and ASCA are quite helpful in giving us direction on providing counseling services, documenting those services, and negotiating the right to confidentiality for children and adolescents in diverse settings. In the next few sections, we will review some of these primary areas that are specifically related to counseling children and adolescents. These sections will include discussions of the profession's ethical guidelines as well as any legal implications when appropriate. Specifically, we will address counselor competency, informed consent/assent, confidentiality, records, and parents' rights.

Counselor Competency

Counselor competency refers to being accomplished in a specific area of counseling. To exhibit competency, the counselor should be able to demonstrate significant training, education, and experience in the specified area. Strategies for counseling children and adolescents are significantly different from those used with adults; therefore, it is critical that counselors receive additional training and experience that is specific to this population. The same techniques used with a 35-year-old adult simply cannot be used with a 5-year-old child or even a 16-year-old adolescent. Counselors interested in working with children and adolescents should attend professional workshops, read literature related to this population, and participate in professional organizations based on services provided for children and adolescents. In fact, ethical guidelines are very clear that counselors should practice within their boundaries of competence, based on education, training, supervised experience, credentials, and professional experience. A counselor who works with children and adolescents should have education and experiences directly related to working with this population.

Informed Consent/Assent

Informed consent is a process that involves helping clients understand their rights to receive or refuse counseling services, to understand what counseling involves, and to comprehend the possible consequences of involvement. First developed in the medical field, informed consent is a fundamental part of counseling and should be seen as a process that continues throughout the counseling relationship rather than a one-time event (ACA, 2014).

Informed consent typically includes the following information:

1. information about counselor, such as name, title, degree, licensure, address, phone number;
2. confidentiality policy, including verbal communication, records, and exceptions;
3. emergency policies, including directions for what to do in case of an emergency; and
4. financial responsibilities that includes the fee and how it is collected.

The counselor may also wish to request permission to coordinate their treatment with other healthcare providers, which would require an additional signature on a separate document or could be included as part of the informed consent document. Further, parents should receive a Notice of Privacy Practices to be compliant with HIPPA regulations. It is important to note, that in the case of a school counselor, all of these sections may not be necessary due to the settings in which students are automatically opted into services and programming.

When counseling children and adolescents, the process of informed consent can be complicated because guardians or parents must be involved in the process. Ethical guidelines state that counselors seek the assent or consent of the clients in which they serve. According to the ACA Code of Ethics (2014), even if children are not able to provide consent/assent, they should be part of the decision-making process as much as possible. The Ethical Standards for School Counselors (2010) goes into much more detail in regards to working with children. School counselors should inform students about the purpose, goals, and techniques of counseling, and discuss the limits of confidentiality in developmentally appropriate language. The school setting is very different from the private setting, so the standards also address that informed consent may not always be possible, and when this occurs the counselor will make decisions in the child's best interest. For example, if a child or adolescent has a very damaged relationship with the parent or guardian, then obtaining informed consent from the parent may be detrimental to the student. Or perhaps a child has a parent who is uninvolved and simply getting the parent to provide consent has proven unsuccessful. Counseling the child without parental consent in this scenario would be in the child's best interest rather than not providing services at all.

Confidentiality

Confidentiality is critical to the counseling relationship and is the foundation of all counseling work that occurs (ACA, 2014). According to the ACA, AMHCA, and ASCA, confidentiality is given to all clients regardless of age. However, when children are clients, confidentiality becomes complicated. To begin, let's review the general requirements and exceptions to confidentiality and then we will discuss the role of parents.

The expectation is that confidentiality (the promise to keep what is said private) is an ethical standard set by the profession while *privileged communication* is granted by law and refers to the legal rights of the client to prevent disclosure of information. In the case of court, though, a counselor can request that the communication be considered privileged if he or she believes it is in the best interest of the client and disclosing the information would cause more harm than good to the client. It is, however, up to the judge to determine if the communication is privileged or not.

But first, let us talk about confidentiality and its limits. Confidentiality cannot be maintained if the counselor believes that the child or adolescent is a threat to him or herself or others, if the child is being abused, or if a court orders a counselor to testify.

Duty to warn refers to the responsibility of the counselor to inform authorities or a third party if a client poses a threat to him/herself or to someone else. While the general rule is that counselor–client communication is protected and confidential, this is one of the exceptions. The critical element of duty to warn comes from the legal case of Tarasoff I (1974) and Tarasoff (1976). The event occurred during a psychotherapy session at the University of California at Berkeley. A student, Prosenjit Poddar, stated in the session his desire to kill his girlfriend, Tatiana Tarasoff. After asking some probing questions, the therapist discovered that Poddar had not only a desire but a detailed plan on how he would create the crime. The therapist warned the campus police and his supervisor but failed to inform the intended victim, Tarasoff. After the murder plot was carried out, the subsequent legal proceedings found the therapist was negligent for failure to inform. As a result, when a counselor has serious concern that a client may harm someone else, the counselor is legally required to warn the identified victim and/or a third party about the imminent danger. Therefore, duty to warn is now a concrete element of counseling requiring that confidentiality must be broken when a person is in need of protection.

Ethical guidelines also address limits to confidentiality. According to the ACA Code of Ethics (2014), the requirements of confidentiality do not apply when a client or other identified person needs protection from harm. AMCHA further states that if a person has a communicable or life-threatening illness, then the counselor may disclose this information to a third party if the client's partner is in danger of contracting the illness without his or her knowledge. The Ethical Standards for School Counselors (2010) state that school counselors should contact parents/guardians as well as authorities when needed if a child may be in harm. If a client is deemed to present a serious danger, then the counselor must use reasonable care to protect the client or the intended victim against the danger.

Because of this breach in confidentiality, it is critical that counselors elicit informed consent from their clients at the beginning of counseling so that they understand when confidentiality must be broken. Further, it is often difficult to predict the actions of a client. While you do not want to over-predict violent behavior, counselors must be diligent when it comes to protecting children from abuse and clients harming from themselves or others.

Before breaking confidentiality, counselors should consult with colleagues and understand their state's legal requirements when it comes to duty to warn. A great website for state information can be found at http://www.ncsl.org/research/health/mental-health-professionals-duty-to-warn.aspx (National Conference of State Legislatures, 2016).

Another consideration more specific to school counselors is that confidentiality is often much harder to maintain in a school setting where collaboration among educators in the building is the norm. Because school counselors manage multiple relationships with various parties, a thorough understanding of confidentiality is essential as well as setting clear boundaries with other educational partners. When a school counselor practices confidentiality, he or she helps build trust not only among clients but among school personnel.

Records

Another issue that is somewhat related to confidentiality is record-keeping. In order to provide the best services for clients, counselors should maintain and protect appropriate documentation related to client progress and services provided by the counselor. According to AMHCA, these records should be destroyed after five years post-termination or as specified by state regulations. The school setting is somewhat different and more detailed direction is provided by ASCA. For example, the Family Education Rights and Privacy Act (FERPA) is federal legislation that dictates how educational records are shared with parents or guardians. However, one of the five categories that are exempt from the definition of education records under FERPA are records made by school counselors that are kept in the sole possession of the author of the records and not accessible to any other person. ASCA encourages school counselors to keep *sole-possession records* or individual student case notes that are separate from students' educational records (ASCA, 2016). The records are not kept in the cumulative record and therefore are not available to others who might have access to those records. Sole-possession records are not considered educational if the records are: (a) a memory aid, (b) not accessible or shared with anyone else (written or verbally), (c) a private note created solely by the counselor, and (d) includes only observations and professional opinions. If case notes do not meet all four of these criteria, then the school counselor can legally be required to provide them to the parent under FERPA. For example, school counselors cannot record details of the session and must simply write observations and opinions. Keep in mind, though, that in most states these records can still be subpoenaed. ASCA also states that sole-possession records should be destroyed within a "reasonable" time.

Now that you have a pretty good understanding of the many aspects of confidentiality and the limits of confidentiality, let us take a look at the complicated nature of the parent/child/counselor relationship and confidentiality struggles that can emerge.

Parents' Rights

Conflict often arises in regards to parents' rights and confidentiality when counseling children. Ethical standards in counseling have consistently demonstrated that clients should be respected and matters should remain confidential, with the exception of harm to self or others or court orders. However, counseling minors provides challenges in regards to who has the right to information—the child (client) or the parent. According to the ethical guidelines by the ACA (2014), AMHCA (2015), and ASCA (2016), counselors should discuss the importance of the role of counselor, the issues of confidentiality, and the delicate nature of the counseling relationship with parents. Ultimately, however, the ethical guidelines state that counselors must respect that parents have certain inherent rights and responsibilities according to the law.

Historically, parents or legal guardians have control over the legal rights of children. Laws are beginning to shift towards protecting the confidentiality rights of minors, though. In a precedent-setting 2005 ruling by the New Hampshire Supreme Court, "In the Matter of Kathleen Quigley Berg and Eugene E. Berg," the court ruled that parents of minors do not have an absolute right to the counseling records of their child, or the exclusive right to assert or waive the therapist–client privilege on this child's behalf. The court ruled that it is up to the trial court to determine whether an assertion or waiver of the privilege is in the child's best interest. In other words, the court decision prevented the counselor from releasing a minor's records when the parents disagreed about whether privileged communication should be waived. Therefore, a counselor should wait until the court provides an order to disclose confidential records of a child.

The New Hampshire Supreme Court's ruling is also reflected in several other court rulings. The Iowa Supreme Court ruled that mental health professionals can refuse to give access to mental health records of children to parents when it is not in the child's best interest (Harder v. Anderson et al., 2008). The court decision noted that release of records could potentially cause irreparable harm to the therapeutic relationship. State courts in California, Florida, Maryland, Massachusetts, and Oklahoma have also seen similar cases.

ACA, AMHCA, and ASCA all assert that counselors should work to establish a collaborative relationship with parents or guardians as much as appropriate. This is the first step in helping parents understand that counselors are working in the child's best interests. When requested, though, counselors can often simply provide parents with an overview of counseling services that is accurate in an objective and caring manner while still maintaining ethical responsibilities to the child. For example, simply saying that you have been working with the child to help him or her improve behavior and grades in class is often enough for parents. If more information is desired, then you could indicate what strategies you are working on to help the child improve. This information would not disclose any confidential information to the parent and should not damage the relationship that you have developed with the child.

So far, we have examined both ethical and legal guidelines related to counselor competency when working with children and adolescents, getting informed consent/assent, navigating child confidentiality versus parents' rights, and record keeping in a clinical mental health setting compared to a school setting. However, simple knowledge of these will not suffice. As a professional counselor, you must understand that you will be faced with ethical dilemmas throughout your entire career, and that issues are rarely very clear. To help you with this, numerous professionals have developed ethical decision-making models to guide you through the process. Let us take a look at a few of the more prominent ones.

Ethical Decision-Making Models

Ethical decision-making models provide a framework to help counselors closely examine the ethical dilemma that is being faced, the possible course of action that could be pursued, and the consequences of those choices. When used appropriately, these models help counselors produce rational, practical, and consistent ethical decisions. While there are several ethical decision-making models in the literature, the most prominent models include Kitchener's principle model (1984), Rest's four-component model (1994), the social constructivist model (Cottone, 2001, 2004), and the social justice model (Counselors for Social Justice, 2011).

Kitchener's principle model, sometimes referred to as rational model (1984), is perhaps the most well-known ethical decision-making model. Beginning in the field of psychiatry, the premise of this model is that professionals cannot simply rely on personal value judgments, but must have clear ethical guidelines for decision making. According to Kitchener, counselors may better be able to understand ethical dilemmas when examining five moral principles: (a) autonomy, (b) justice, (c) beneficence, (d) nonmaleficence, and (e) fidelity. To encourage client *autonomy*, counselors can encourage clients to make their own decisions and act on their own beliefs as appropriate. *Nonmaleficence* and *beneficence* refer to the counselor's responsibility to act in the client's best interest. Sometimes this best interest may result in treating the client differently; however, this is when the principle of *justice* should be considered. If this client or dilemma needs to be treated differently from other cases, then the counselor must be able to provide a rationale for treating this situation differently. The final principle, *fidelity*, involves the idea of loyalty. Clients must be able to trust their counselor and trust that their counselor will remain loyal to them if growth is to occur.

Rest's four-component model (1994) has been identified as one of the most empirically based approaches for moral development. This model includes four components: (a) moral sensitivity, (b) moral judgment, (c) moral motivation, and (d) moral character (Johnson, 2012). *Moral sensitivity* is simply recognizing that there is indeed an ethical dilemma. Once an ethical problem has been recognized, the counselor must then choose a course of action. At this point, counselors often refer back to their own *moral judgments* about what is right and wrong when determining the best course of action. However, sometimes the "right thing" to do can often be the toughest. For example, perhaps the "right thing" to do is report a child abuse claim; however, your supervisor has told you specifically not to report the case because he is familiar with the family and knows that the child is lying. In this situation, the third component of Rest's model comes into play: *Moral motivation*, or the ability or willingness of a counselor to follow through on a course of action. As in the previous situation, moral values may sometimes interfere with other concerns, such as job security. However, if a counselor determines that he or she will report the child abuse concerns despite a supervisor's directives, then, the counselor is displaying the final component of Rest's model: *Moral character*, or the ability of the counselor to execute the plan despite obstacles.

The social constructivist model of ethical decision-making takes all ethical decisions and views them in a social context (Cottone, 2001, 2004). This model views ethical dilemmas as opportunities and places the ethical decision-making process out in the open to create dialogue between the client and the professional. This model involves engaging all parties involved through open discussions, examining the nature of the relationship, consulting colleagues or literature, and responding in a way that offers an acceptable consensus of all parties.

Social justice advocates have questioned the use and cultural sensitivity of the traditional models of ethical decision-making. The guiding principles of the social justice model include (a) social justice, (b) social action, (c) eradication of all forms of abuse and oppression, (d) dignity and worth of all persons, (e) embracing diversity, and (f) integrity and competence. (Counselors for Social Justice, 2011). This model advocates that counselors should focus their work towards being aware of historical, social, and political inequities that impact clients, confront issues of social injustice experienced by clients, and work to eliminate forms of oppression through advocacy efforts. The fourth principle of this model recognizes that counselor's own worldview and cultural identity are impacted by various social–cultural–contextual factors and that we should value and respect all people. The fifth principle, embracing diversity, addresses the importance of counselors to commit themselves to lifelong learning about various cultures and communities and to overcome their own personal biases. Finally, integrity and competence, address the need to not go beyond a counselor's training and to continuously seek professional development opportunities related to social justice issues. When counselors are faced with ethical dilemmas, the Social Justice model encourages us to view the dilemma through the lens of social justice. Table 6.2 provides an overview of these models.

The models in Table 6.2 apply to counselors in all settings; however, school counselors in particular are often encouraged to use Carolyn Stone's STEPS ethical decision-making model (2001). This model consists of nine steps that focuses on defining the problem applying the ACA and ASCA code of ethics and the law, considering the chronological and developmental levels of the child as well as the setting, parental rights, and minors' rights, and applying the moral principles. After these considerations, Stone encourages school counselors to determine the potential course of action as well as the potential consequences, to then evaluate the preferred course of action, consult with colleagues, and, finally, implement the decision.

Table 6.2 Ethical decision-making models

Kitchener's Principle Model	Examines the five moral principles of 1. autonomy 2. justice 3. beneficence 4. nonmaleficence 5. fidelity
Rest's Four-Component Model	Examines the four components of 1. moral sensitivity 2. moral judgment 3. moral motivation 4. moral character
Social Constructive Model	Engages all parties involved through 1. discussing issue openly 2. examining the relationship 3. consulting colleagues or literature 4. offering an acceptable consensus of all parties involved
Social Justice Model	Focuses work towards being aware of 1. social justice concerns 2. social action needed 3. eradication of all forms of abuse and oppression 4. dignity and worth of all persons 5. embracing diversity 6. integrity and competence

Regardless of the counseling setting that you work in, or the specific ethical decision-making model that you follow, responsible practice requires that we all (a) base our actions on informed, practical, and responsible judgment, (b) consult with colleagues and seek supervision, (c) keep our knowledge and skills current, (d) engage in constant self-examination, and (e) remain open (Corey, Corey, and Haynes, 2014). We have discussed the several models of ethical decision-making, including Kitchener's principle model, Rest's four-component model, the social constructivist model, the social justice model, and the STEP model. While these models all differ in their underlying approach to decision making, they all possess similar steps to follow when analyzing a possible ethical dilemma, such as identifying the problem, applying an ethical code, determining the nature of the dilemma, identifying potential courses of action and consequences, and finally selecting and implementing the course of action.

DECISION MAKING IN PRACTICE

Now that we have provided you with an overview of ethical standards in counseling, legal considerations, and ethical decision-making models, let us now turn to some practical applications. Consider the following two case studies and work through them using the guidelines discussed within the chapter. See if you come to the same conclusion as we do.

Case Study: Eva

The following is a school-setting case study.

Eva, a 10-year-old girl, was recommended to the school counselor—you—by her teacher because of declining grades and sudden outbursts in class. According to the teacher, Eva's behavior has always been positive and her grades have been good. After meeting with the school counselor for a few sessions, Eva reveals that her parents are going through a divorce. The school counselor works with her on numerous issues related to her struggles with the divorce. Eva's mom has now requested a conference with you to discuss what Eva has talked about during counseling and wants a copy of your notes. First, do you meet with the parent? If so, what do you tell her during the conference? Do you give her your notes?

Response

It is important to develop a collaborative relationship with parents at the very beginning of the counseling relationship, if at all possible. Ideally, the school counselor here would have reached out to the parents at the onset of counseling to begin a collaborative relationship to help Eva improve her grades and decrease her outbursts in class, which were the initial concerns of the teacher. This beginning contact helps set the tone that the counselor is partnering with the parent to help the child. Now that counseling has progressed, the true issue is the parents' divorce, which can often complicate matters. In the example above, the counselor should absolutely meet with the parent. However, it will be important to consider whether or not violating confidentiality will harm the relationship that Eva has with the counselor. I would argue that in this case it is in Eva's best interest to keep the information confidential. To honor the relationship with Eva, the counselor can discuss her role in helping Eva process the divorce, the issues of confidentiality, and the delicate nature of the counseling relationship with the parent. Hopefully this will satisfy the parental request. The counselor should not give the parent his or her notes, if they are sole-possession notes. If the parent pursues this issue, then the counselor can clarify the exception to FERPA.

Case Study: Alex

This second case study focuses on a clinical mental health setting.

Alex, a 6-year-old boy, has been coming to you for about six weeks. His parents brought him to counseling because he was having significant behavior problems at school and at home. In the initial meeting with parents, they described Alex as being constantly defiant, always yelling, and destructive with toys. They do not know what to do with him and view him as a bad kid. The father is a prominent member of the community and the mother is involved in community work with the local churches. In your work with Alex, you notice aggressive tendencies and underlying anger. As you begin to use play therapy techniques, Alex begins to reveal possible abuse that is occurring in the home. As you pursue this, Alex reveals that his parents lock him in the closet, withhold meals from him, and spank him with socks with rocks in them. You wonder if you should try to help them with disciplinary strategies first or if you should report the abuse to authorities. If you report the abuse, then you are fairly certain that the parents will know that it was you and will stop bringing Alex to counseling. You are also very concerned with how you will be viewed in the community. After all, both parents are well respected.

Response

For most counselors, the initial response is that of course you would report the suspected abuse. However, this situation is complicated due to your fear of continuing to help Alex as well as your own personal fears of your reputation as a counselor within the community. Let us first look at the fear of not being able to work with Alex. When making an ethical decision, you must consider the best interest of the child, but you must also consider the laws of your state. As a counselor, you are a mandated reporter of child abuse, which means that you must ultimately report any suspected child abuse. If we go back to our initial counseling relationship, hopefully, you have established a collaborative, trusting relationship with the parents. If this relationship is present, then perhaps you will be able to extend that relationship by offering to work with them on their parenting skills and/or other issues that is causing the abusive behavior. Furthermore, you must discuss your breach of confidentiality with Alex. Alex needs to understand that you will tell someone about the abuse for his own protection and that you are doing this to protect him. Alex needs to understand that as his counselor you are not abandoning him; instead, you are seeking additional help for him.

As far as your own concern about your reputation within the community, consider the components of moral development by Rest (1994), specifically moral motivation. This is a clear example of determining if you have the moral motivation to complete an action (in the best interest of the client) despite the fact that it may cause harm to you personally. Ultimately, your reputation with these parents is not important—your commitment to your client and his welfare is the most important aspect of the counseling relationship. Perhaps your determination will show the community that, despite how others perceive adults in the community, you are a person of integrity and will do what's in your client's best interest … and who wouldn't want a counselor like that?

CHAPTER SUMMARY

We have discussed many issues related to ethical and legal considerations when counseling children and adolescents. Hopefully you have gained a greater insight to the specific needs of this population regardless of your future work setting. Specifically, we have discussed the following:

- The core professional values of the counseling profession include improving human development throughout life, supporting diversity, fostering social justice, protecting the counselor–client relationship, and providing services in a competent and ethical manner.
- The principles that guide our behaviors as counselors include autonomy, nonmaleficence, beneficence, justice, fidelity, and veracity.
- Ethical guidelines are very clear that counselors should practice within their boundaries of competence, based on education, training, supervised experience, credentials, and professional experience. A counselor who works with children and adolescents should have education and experiences directly related to working with this population.
- When counseling children and adolescents, the process of informed consent can be complicated because guardians or parents must be involved in the process. Ethical guidelines insist that counselors seek the assent or consent of the clients in which they serve. Even if children are not able to provide consent/assent, they should be part of the decision-making process as much as possible.
- Confidentiality is an ethical standard set by the profession, while privileged communication is granted by law.
- Confidentiality cannot be maintained if the counselor believes that the child or adolescent is a threat to him or herself or others, if the child is being abused, or if a court orders a counselor to testify.
- Counselors should maintain and protect appropriate documentation related to client progress and services provided by the counselor. School counselors, in particular, should keep sole-possession records or individual student case notes that are separate from students' educational records.
- Counseling minors provides challenges in regards to who has the right to information: The child (client) or the parent. According to the ethical guidelines by the ACA (2014), AMHCA (2015), and ASCA (2016), counselors should discuss the importance of the role of counselor, the issues of confidentiality, and the delicate nature of the counseling relationship with parents. Legally, the court has upheld that parents of minors do not have an absolute right to the counseling records of their child, or the exclusive right to assert or waive the therapist–client privilege on this child's behalf. In other words, the court can refuse to grant access to mental health records of children to parents when it is not in the child's best interest
- Ethical decision-making models provide a framework to help us closely examine the ethical dilemma that we are facing, the possible course of action that we could pursue, and then the consequences of those choices. When used appropriately, these models help us to produce rational, practical, and consistent ethical decisions. We discussed five models: Kitchener's Principle Model, Rest's Four-Component Model, the Social Constructivist Model, the Social Justice Model, and STEPS (specifically recommended for the school setting).

Suggested Readings

Herlihy, B. and Corey, G. (2015). *ACA ethical standards casebook.* Alexandria, VA: American Counseling Association.

Hermann, M. A., Remley, Jr., T. P., and Huey, W. C. (2010). *Ethical and legal issues in school counseling,* 3rd ed. Alexandria, VA: American School Counselor Association.

Loue, S. (2015). *Ethical issues in sandplay therapy practice and research.* New York: Springer.

National Conference of State Legislatures. (2016). Mental health professionals' duty to warn. Retrieved from http://www.ncsl.org/research/health/mental-health-professionals-duty-to-warn.aspx

Remley, Jr., T. P. and Herlihy, B. P. (2015). *Ethical, legal, and professional issues in counseling,* 5th ed. New York: Pearson.

Sartor, T. A., McHenry, B. and McHenry, J. (ed.) (2016). *Ethical and legal issues in counseling children and adolescents.* New York: Routledge.

Welfel, E. R. (2015). *Ethics in counseling and psychotherapy.* Salt Lake City, UT: Brooks Cole.

Glossary

Autonomy: Encouraging the right to control one's own direction in life
Beneficence: Working for the good of a person as well as for society
Confidentiality: An ethical standard set by the profession; the promise to keep what is said private
Counselor competency: Being accomplished in a specific area of counseling
Duty to warn: The responsibility of the counselor to inform authorities or a third party if a client poses a threat to him or herself or to someone else
Ethical decision-making models: Provide counselors with a general framework to help us examine the dilemma itself, possible courses of action, and consequences of those actions
Family Education Rights and Privacy Act (FERPA): Federal legislation that dictates how educational records are shared with parents or guardians
Fidelity: Honoring commitments
Informed consent: A process that involves helping the client understand his or her right to receive or refuse counseling services, to understand what counseling involves, and to comprehend the possible consequences of involvement
Justice: Fostering fairness and equality
Moral character: The ability of the counselor to execute the plan despite obstacles
Moral judgment: Determining what is right and wrong
Moral motivation: The level of commitment of a counselor to follow-through on the course of action
Moral sensitivity: Recognizing that there is indeed an ethical dilemma
Nonmaleficence: Avoiding actions that could cause harm
Privileged communication: Granted by law; the legal rights of the client to prevent disclosure of information
Sole-possession records: Individual student case notes that are separate from students' educational records. The records are not kept in the cumulative record and therefore are not available to others who might have access to those records. Sole possession records are not considered educational if the records are: (a) a memory aid, (b) not accessible or shared with anyone else (written or verbally), (c) a private note created solely by the counselor, and (d) includes only observations and professional opinions
Veracity: Being truthful

References

American Counseling Association (2014). *2014 Code of ethics.* Alexandria, VA: Author.

American Mental Health Counselors Association (2015). *AMHCA code of ethics.* Retrieved from http://c.ymcdn.com/sites/www.amhca.org/resource/resmgr/Media/ ethics2015FINAL.pdf

American School Counselor Association (2016). *ASCA ethical standards for school counselors.* Retrieved from https://www.schoolcounselor.org/asca/media/asca/Ethics/ EthicalStandards2016.pdf

Corey, G., Corey, M. A. and Haynes, R. (2014). *Ethics in action*, 3rd ed. Stamford, CT: Cengage Learning.

Cottone, R. R. (2001). A social constructivism model of ethical decision making in counseling. *Journal of Counseling and Development, 79*, 39–45.

Cottone, R. R. (2004). Displacing the psychology of the individual in ethical decision-making: The social constructivist model. *Canadian Journal of Counselling 38*, 5–13.

Counselors for Social Justice (2011). The Counselors for Social Justice (CSJ) code of ethics. *Journal for Social Action in Counseling and Psychology 3* (2), 1–21.

Harder v. Anderson, Arnold, Dickey, Jensen, Gullickson, Sanger, and Pini (2009). Retrieved from http://caselaw.findlaw.com/ia-supreme-court/1073979.html

In the matter of Kathleen Quigley Berg and Eugene E. Berg. (2005). Retrieved from http://www.courts.state.nh.us/supreme/opinions/2005/berg112.htm

Johnson, C. E. (2012). *Organizational ethics: A practical approach*, 2nd ed. Thousand Oaks, CA: Sage Publications.

Kitchener, K. S. (1984). Intuition, critical evaluation and ethical principles: The foundation for ethical decisions in counseling psychology. *Counseling Psychologist 12* (3), 43–55.

Milgram, S. (1963). Behavioral study of obedience. *The Journal of Abnormal and Social Psychology 67* (4), 371–378.

Rest, J. R. and Narvaez, D. (eds.) (1994). *Moral development in the professions: Psychology and applied ethics*. Hillside, NJ: Lawrence Erlbaum.

Tarasoff v. Regents of the University of California, 118 Cal. Rptr. 129, 529 P.2D.533 (Cal. 1974)

Tarasoff v. Regents of the University of California, 113 Cal. Rptr. 14, 551 P.2d334 (Cal. 1976)

PART III

Counseling Children and Adolescents in School and Clinical Mental Health Settings

CHAPTER 7

Counseling Children and Adolescents in School Settings

Emily Goodman-Scott, Blaire Cholewa, Christina Koch Burkhardt, and Melanie Burgess[1]

Step with care and great tact, and remember that life's a great balancing act. You're off to great places! Today is your day! Your mountain is waiting, so get on your way!

Dr. Seuss

CHAPTER OBJECTIVES

After reading this chapter, students will have a greater understanding of:

- the brief history of the school counseling profession and current trends;
- background information on comprehensive school counseling programs, including direct and indirect student services and accountability;
- the school counselor's role in crisis;
- school counselors' role as part of a multi-tiered system of supports;
- the unique roles of school counselors at each of the three levels—elementary, middle and high school; and
- setting-specific school counseling strengths and challenges.

INTRODUCTION

Imagine a career where you can assist students prepare for and get into college, provide resources to a family coping with domestic violence, collaborate with a school leadership team regarding school-wide discipline trends, support a student whose parents are divorcing, run a social skills counseling group for students who struggle to make friends, consult with a teacher regarding students' academics, and create a data report demonstrating the results of your school-wide bullying prevention program. These are some of the many roles of a professional school counselor. According to the American School Counselor Association (n.d.),

school counselors are certified/licensed educators with a minimum of a master's degree in school counseling, making them uniquely qualified to address all students' academic, career and social/emotional development

needs by designing, implementing, evaluating and enhancing a comprehensive school counseling program that promotes and enhances student
success. School counselors are employed in elementary, middle/junior
high and high schools; in district supervisory positions; and counselor
education positions.

Most states license or certify school counselors to work at the K−12 level,
however some licenses/certificates can be more specific, such as K−8, or
9−12. Before the chapter continues, the four chapter authors would like to
introduce themselves and describe their relationship with school counseling.

*Greetings readers! My name is Emily Goodman-Scott and I am an assistant
professor at Old Dominion University in Norfolk, Virginia, as well as the school
counseling coordinator of our master's program. Before entering academia, I
was a special education teacher, an elementary school counselor, and a
mental health counselor serving youth and adults. I still very much consider
myself a school counselor, and love serving the profession in a new way:
Preparing the future generation of school counselors, and helping to shape
the profession through teaching, leadership, scholarship, and service. As an
elementary school counselor, I was struck by four things. First, children are
remarkably resilient; I learned a tremendous amount about the human spirit,
curiosity, love, and fun from the youth and family I served. Next, I love school
counseling because of the potential to have a systemic impact. Not only do
we serve students individually, but we work with their families and the entire
school community utilizing a systemic lens. We have the ability to make a
difference on so many levels. Third, in order to join with a school community,
we need to be culturally alert to the backgrounds and identities of the individuals, families, and community we serve, as well as aware of inequities and
barriers that may hinder students from succeeding. Lastly, although we
school counselors know we make a difference, it is almost equally important
that we show how our work impacts students and schools. We need to be
accountable advocates, and leaders.*

*Hi all. My name is Blaire Cholewa and I am an assistant professor in the
Counselor Education program at the University of Virginia, in Charlottesville,
Virginia. It is such a privilege to work alongside school counselors in training.
There is something truly special about working in schools and having access
to so many students, not to mention the opportunity to observe students,
consult with teachers, and collaborate with caregivers. Thus, I find such joy in
preparing trainees to be effective counselors, leaders, advocates, and systems
change agents who promote equity. School counselors can help transform
students' school experiences, particularly those in marginalized groups, and I
love that I can help equip school counselors with the cultural competence,
knowledge, and skills to do so.*

*Hello! My name is Christina Koch Burkhardt and I am a high school counselor
in Virginia. Before entering the school counseling profession, I studied psychology and coordinated research studies within the fields of child development
and education. Whether I am working individually with a student, presenting to*

a class, consulting with families, collaborating with my school's administration, or serving on my school's leadership team, I am committed to promoting equity and access to opportunities and academic success for all students. I recognize the unique needs and strengths of each student I serve, and work to ensure that all students have accessible plans for their lives after high school. I am particularly passionate about increasing access to post-secondary education among low-income and prospective first-generation college students as well as utilizing both data-driven practices and technology to enhance school counseling programs.

Being a school counselor has afforded me the opportunity to work in a career that combines my passions for advocacy and research. While I can individually see change within my students, I find it particularly meaningful to present reports to my principal and community stakeholders in support of the services my school counseling team provides as well as in support of the profession of school counseling as a whole.

Hi there! My name is Melanie Burgess. I am a doctoral student in Old Dominion University's Counselor Education and Supervision program, and I graduated from ODU's master's program with a concentration in school counseling. I started my master's program assuming I would study mental health counseling; however, I became in awe of the influential role school counselors have in the lives of children and adolescents, and quickly changed tracks. Throughout my time in the master's program, I developed a strong passion for data-driven counseling, multicultural competence, and professional development. It is inspiring to me that school counselors can use data to drive their decisions, goals, and comprehensive school counseling program; legitimize their work by showing their positive impact on students; advocate for systemic change where inequities and barriers to learning are present; and maximize effectiveness through selecting evidence-based practices! I hope to one day share my passion for infusing data and multicultural competency into school counseling programs, as well as assist school-counselors-in-training to embrace becoming lifelong learners in our exciting and evolving field.

Now that the authors have been introduced, the profession of school counseling will now be discussed.

Reflection Question

Think back to your experiences in school K-12. What experiences did you have with school counselors? What memories do you have of your elementary, middle, and high school counselors? What did they do?

Exercise 7.1

THE HISTORY OF SCHOOL COUNSELING: MAKING OUR PROFESSION

School counseling has a rich and varied history, often responding to the ebbs and flows of cultural trends in the U.S. and its education system. According to Galassi and Akos (2012) "school counseling in the United States has both responded to and reflected national trends and challenges" (p. 50). In order to see where school counseling is today, it is important to look at where the profession has been.

School counseling began during the late nineteenth and early twentieth centuries in response to the U.S.'s transition from an agricultural to an industrial economy, which included the need to place individuals in jobs. Hence this era was the start of the vocational guidance movement; school counselors, then called guidance officers or guidance counselors, focused on placing students in post-school employment based on their interests and abilities (Gysbers and Henderson, 2012). The prioritization of vocational counseling and employment would ebb and flow over the next 90 years. Then, during the 1920s and 1930s, the school counseling field expanded to focus on the diagnostic, clinical, and educational aspects of counseling (Gysbers and Henderson, 2012) as well as increasing focus on children's development (Lambie and Williamson, 2004). School counselors wondered how to best define themselves: Were they vocational counselors or mental health counselors?

Due to high rates of unemployment during the Great Depression of the 1930s as well as a need to serve World War II veterans in the 1940s, vocational counseling and employment regained prominence. Carl Rogers' humanistic counseling gained popularity in the 1940s, which led to less directional counseling and greater value on the mutual relationship between counselor and client, or student (Lambie and Williamson, 2004). This was followed in the 1950s by the creation of several professional counseling organizations, including what is currently known as the American Counseling Association and the American School Counselor Association, as well as the development of ethical counseling standards (Lambie and Williamson, 2004). With the advent of the 'Space Race', education heavily focused on math and science in order to prepare students for careers in technology, as is was evident in the 1958 National Defense Education Act (Gysbers and Henderson, 2012), which prioritized vocational counseling and assessment. Further, during this time, school counselors often engaged in administrative tasks such as scheduling and utilized a directive and individually focused approach to school counseling (Lambie and Williamson, 2004).

Due to an increasingly diverse population and the Civil Rights Movement, the 1960s and 1970s resulted in school counselors serving students from a range of backgrounds and prioritizing multicultural counseling. School counseling continued to wrestle with their professional identity: Did they align most with educators or psychologists? Also, school counseling interventions became increasingly focused on measurable and developmentally appropriate interventions. School counselors provided services such as individual and group counseling, appraisal, consultation, and vocational placement (Gysbers and Henderson, 2012). However, the passing of the 1965 Elementary and

Secondary Education Act brought about a renewed emphasis on vocation (Lambie and Williamson, 2004) and prioritized allocating greater resources to students in underserved communities. Also, during this time, the initial seeds of comprehensive school counseling programs were first planted and began to take root. These will be discussed shortly.

During the 1970s, education budgets were tight, student enrollment was down, and some school counseling jobs were eliminated. Consequently, school counselors performed clerical and administrative tasks in order to maintain employment (Lambie and Williamson, 2004). School counselors assisted with the prevention efforts of the 1980s (i.e. DARE, a substance abuse prevention program). During this decade the Carl D. Perkins Act began funding career and technology education in the schools, and thus the focus of school counseling again returned to vocation and career counseling.

RECENT TRENDS IN EDUCATION

Educational trends from the last couple of decades have particularly impacted today's school counseling. Thus, authors will provide greater detail regarding recent educational trends and descriptions of the current status of school counseling. In the 1990s and 2000s, national education focused on accountability and closing the achievement gap for all students, especially students who came from communities with low income, students of color, and students who struggled academically and behaviorally. The No Child Left Behind Act of 2001 (NCLB) mandated an increased focus on accountability in education, having highly qualified teachers, ensuring every student met certain competencies and standards, and the use of standards-based testing to document results. The aim of NCLB was to ensure schools with underserved populations and poor test scores were succeeding academically and that their students' achievement gap decreased. However, these were the schools that typically struggled most under NCLB, due to their lack of resources and high needs of the population. In late 2015, the Every Student Succeeds Act (ESSA) was signed to replace NCLB. This new ESSA responds to concerns with NCLB, continuing with the aim to serve all students, especially underserved students, decreasing standardized testing, and placing greater decision-making at the state-level to ensure schools are meeting academic standards. Further, in recent years, College and Career Readiness has once again become an educational focus, encouraging all students to graduate from high school and successfully transition into education, training, and careers. These recent trends in accountability and College and Career Readiness have certainly shaped school counseling over the past 25 years.

Let's take a closer look at present-day school counseling.

School Counseling Today: Recent Trends

The late 1990s and early 2000s were an exciting time in school counseling! As a result of educational reform over the last 20 years, several school counseling leaders and organizations such as the Education Trust and the

American School Counselor Association (ASCA) have called for school counselors to be integral members in K-12 education. This includes showing that they are central to schools' missions to close the achievement gap, help every student succeed, and support the accountability movement in education. These professional organizations have worked hard to develop a national vision for school counseling.

The Education Trust was a national non-profit organization that promoted closing the achievement gap and academic success for all students, particularly students of color and from low-income homes (Education Trust, 2016). In 1996, the Education Trust developed the *Transforming School Counseling Initiative*, which created a school counseling vision focusing on leadership, advocacy, systemic change, and collaboration and teaming (Martin, 2015). ASCA is an organization of approximately 30,000 members that serves school counselors from around the world through providing resources, advocacy, and promoting a uniform vision of school counseling (ASCA, 2016). In 1997, ASCA published the National Standards for School Counseling Programs (the National Standards), a document listing the attitudes, knowledge, and skills that students should have as a result of participating in a school counseling program (ASCA, 2004). In 2003, ASCA unveiled the ASCA National Model, a comprehensive school counseling program based on the ASCA National Standards, other comprehensive school counseling models, and the Transforming School Counseling Initiative (ASCA, 2012; Dahir, 2001; Gysbers and Henderson, 2012; Martin, 2002). The National Model was updated in 2005 and 2012.

Over the past century there has been tremendous change in the school counseling field, as well as school counselors' corresponding roles and job activities (Gysbers and Henderson, 2012; Lambie and Williamson, 2004). School counseling has gone through many phases, including emphases on vocational guidance and career, mental health, assessment, person-centered and multicultural counseling, prevention, and closing the achievement gap and educational accountability. According to Lambie and Williamson (2004), school counseling has expanded during the last century to include more and more roles and a broader professional identity with each passing decade. At the same time, these changes to the school counseling professional identity and job responsibilities have led to confusion and ambiguity over the role of the school counselor. School counselors and stakeholders such as school administrators, teachers, parents/guardians and students have been left asking what school counselors *do*? As a result, in the last couple decades, professional organizations have focused on clearly defining the role of the school counselor. Comprehensive school counseling programs, such as the ASCA National Model (2012) have helped operationalize the role of the school counselor.

Now, comprehensive school counseling programs, including the ASCA National Model, will be discussed in greater depth.

COMPREHENSIVE SCHOOL COUNSELING PROGRAMS

During the 1960s and 1970s, school counseling leaders recognized the need for school counseling services to be implemented as a program or a set of services rather than a number of separate tasks. During this time, several states began implementing state models of comprehensive school counseling programs (ASCA, 2012). Comprehensive school counseling has become increasingly popular during the last 10 to 15 years, which many attribute to the development of the ASCA National Model, a popular comprehensive program.

Comprehensive school counseling programs:

- are frameworks that can be individualized based on each schools' needs;
- are developmentally appropriate based on the student population;
- are data-driven, demonstrating the impact the school counseling program and school counselor have on students, stakeholders, and the school;
- are run by a school counselor; and
- meet students' academic, career, and social/emotional development (Gysbers and Henderson, 2012).

Further, researchers have reported benefits to implementing a comprehensive school counseling program, including higher student achievement, attendance and graduation rates, as well as lowering student indiscipline (Carey, Harrington, Martin, and Hoffman, 2012; Carey, Harrington, Martin, and Stevenson, 2012; Sink, Akos, Turnbull, and Mvududu, 2008; Sink and Stroh, 2003). Through comprehensive school counseling programs, school counselors offer a number of services to serve students directly and indirectly and are school leaders and advocates for systemic change and collaboration (ASCA, 2012). No longer should school counselors solely provide career guidance services, or primarily run a mental health clinic from their office. Rather, through a comprehensive school counseling program, school counselors are a part of something larger. They can demonstrate that they are an integral part of the school's mission, and that students are different as a result of the school counseling program (ASCA, 2012). The ASCA National Model provides a road map for implementing a comprehensive school counseling program, which will now be discussed, and will serve as a framework for describing the role of the school counselor throughout this chapter.

The ASCA National Model

The ASCA National Model is based on over 50 years of research, theory, and practice, and has assisted school counselors and stakeholders to define and promote a consistent professional vision and mission (ASCA, 2004; 2012).

Through the National Model (see Figure 7.1), ASCA strives to provide one vision and one voice to school counselors, unifying the profession through a common professional identity. The National Model is based on the ASCA Standards for Students and suggests school counselors serve students in three domains: Academic, career, and social/emotional development. Additionally, the model has four overarching themes describing school counselors' roles regarding leadership, advocacy, systemic change, and collaboration. Lastly, the implementation of the model is described by four components: Foundation, management, delivery, and accountability (ASCA, 2012). Through implementing the ASCA National Model, school counselors demonstrate their impact on student achievement as well as their centrality to

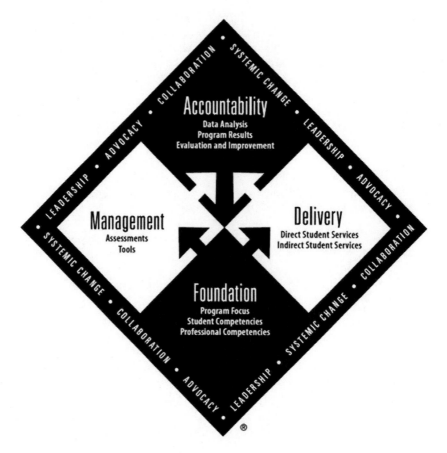

Figure 7.1 ASCA National Model: A framework for school counseling programs

Source: American School Counselor Association (2012). Printed with permission.

the school's mission. Further, through the National Model, school counselors serve students directly and indirectly, which should account for approximately 80 per cent of their time. Let's take a closer look at each of these aspects of the ASCA National Model, and thus school counselors' roles in the schools.

ASCA Standards for Students

To elaborate on the previous description, ASCA published the first iteration of its National Standards in 1997 in order to describe how students should be impacted as a result of participating in a comprehensive school counseling program. The National Standards consisted of competencies and indicators representing the knowledge, attitudes, and skills that students should develop in order to demonstrate academic, career, and personal/social success in pre-K-12 schools and beyond. *ASCA mindsets and behaviors for student success: K–12 college- and career-readiness standards for every student*, a revision that took place in 2014, represents the current standards that guide the development of comprehensive school counseling programs.

ASCA mindsets and behaviors (2014a) is organized by two main categories—the Mindsets category, representing 6 attitudes and beliefs that students hold about themselves, and the Behaviors category, representing a total of 29 learning strategies, self-management skills, and social skills that one would expect students to display as a result of participating in a comprehensive school counseling program. Rather than being tied to a specific domain, each of the 35 standards can be applied to each of the 3 domains: Academic, career, and social/emotional.

School counselors can measure students' progress in developing the mindsets and behaviors standards by evaluating how students demonstrate specific competencies. In contrast with earlier iterations, the competencies in the Mindsets and Behaviors are aligned both to specific grade ranges and curriculum standards (i.e. Common Core or other state-specific standards). Further, rather than being static, the competencies are housed in an online database that is continually developed through submissions from school counselors. For more information, please see the resources listed at the end of this chapter. Next, the authors will discuss the three domains in which school counselors focus their time and energy: Academic, career, and social/emotional.

Domains: Academic, Career, and Social/Emotional

School counselors are called to serve students in three domains, academic, career, and social/emotional.

Academic Development

ASCA charges school counselors with utilizing evidence-based practices to support all students' academic achievement and learning (ASCA, 2014a). School counselors' work in this area is becoming increasingly important as society emphasizes indicators of academic progress and standardized test scores to allocate funding for schools. Additionally, a student's academic performance can impact their access to post-secondary plans of attending college, training programs, or entering the workforce. Thus, it is essential that school counselors demonstrate effective work within this academic domain, supporting students with the post-secondary transition, and demonstrating how students' benefit academically from working with a school counselor. School counselors can track academic outcome data (e.g. GPA/grades, homework completion rates, test scores, attendance rates, etc.) to provide evidence for students' academic growth.

While teachers provide academic instruction that is tied to specific subjects and state standards, school counselors are uniquely positioned to encourage a broader sense of academic growth and the development of students' academic self-concept (Ziomek-Daigle, 2016), which can span academic subjects and disciplines. For example, while a teacher may teach students about a particular geometric concept, school counselors can help students develop academic grit (i.e. perseverance toward obtaining an academic goal), develop effective study skills, or teach students about different learning styles so that students can identify how they learn best.

In their large-scale literature review, Farrington et al. (2012) outlined five categories of non-cognitive factors that impact a student's academic performance: Academic behaviors (e.g. engagement, organization, attendance), academic perseverance (e.g. displaying grit, self-discipline, etc.), academic mindsets (e.g. positive beliefs and attitudes that students hold about school and about themselves as learners), learning strategies (e.g. study skills, goal-setting, etc.), and social skills (e.g. skills to engage positively with peers and with school staff). School counselors are in a prime position to help students develop skills within each of these domains, which in turn encourages positive academic performance.

Academic skills become increasingly important for students as they progress toward high school graduation. Students' academic record can impact access to various post-secondary pathways such as admittance to college, and having the necessary skills and work ethic to be successful in jobs and careers. Additionally, these skills translate into work habits that are beneficial to students in education, training, and work settings.

School counselors can facilitate the development of students' academic skills through the delivery of the school counseling core curriculum (i.e. classroom guidance programming) to the whole school, as well as to targeted individual students or groups of students that have been identified as needing additional supports. School counselors also assist students and families navigate a plethora of educational resources (e.g. tutoring services or test preparation programs), and make referrals for and serve on student support teams that connect students with additional resources (i.e. special education supports, remedial services, etc.).

Career Development

ASCA encourages school counselors to "help students 1) understand the connection between school and the world of work and 2) plan for and make a successful transition from school to postsecondary education and/or the world of work and from job to job across the lifespan" (ASCA, 2014a, p.1). The connection between school and the world of work is crucial, as many of the skills developed in school directly relate to skills needed in the working world.

For example, Carnevale, Smith and Strohl (2013) found that critical thinking skills and mathematical knowledge have high degrees of importance for 96 and 70 per cent of occupations in the U.S., respectively. Further, oral comprehension, oral expression, written comprehension, problem-sensitivity, deductive reasoning, and written expression are the abilities most highly valued within the U.S economy as of 2010. As such, it is critical that school counselors help students develop the skills necessary to be competitive for the pursuit of higher education or within the world of work.

Additionally, school counselors are prepared to help students plan for and transition to post-secondary education, training programs, and the world of work. President Obama and the White House challenged all young adults to pursue at least one year of higher education or post-secondary training beyond high school by the year 2020 (The White House, n.d.). Carnevale, Smith, and Strohl (2013) project that by 2020 65 per cent of the jobs in the U.S will require either higher education or post-secondary training beyond high school (35 per cent of which will require at least a bachelor's degree, and 30 per cent will require at least some college or an associate's degree). Education and training requirements have increased over time; in 1973 only 28 per cent of jobs required some kind of post-secondary education or training, but by 2010 that percentage had increased to 59 (Carnevale, Smith, and Strohl, 2013). As such, it is increasingly important that school counselors help prepare students to be ready for college and post-secondary training programs.

Counseling for college and/or career readiness is a PK–12 endeavor. At the elementary level, college and career awareness is highlighted so that students can begin to understand what lies beyond high school and begin understanding the differences between a job and a career. In middle school, students begin to explore different career pathways and begin identifying their interests, skills, and talents. Career and college fairs can help them make connections between academic performance and access to plans beyond high school. This is continued into the high school level and additional emphasis is placed upon planning for life beyond high school and identifying a pathway that meets students' goals, needs, and interests. School counselors can work with students to develop resumes, cover letters, and learn interviewing skills as well as completing college applications.

The National Office of School Counselor Advocacy (NOSCA; 2010) has identified Eight Components of College and Career Readiness Counseling. These components include eight comprehensive steps that school counselors can take to ensure that their school counseling programs adequately meet the college and career advising needs of all students and especially in support of students who are underrepresented and/or have less access to higher education social capital. Please see Table 7.1 for more information.

Social/Emotional Development

"Social–Emotional Learning (SEL) is the process through which children and adults acquire and effectively apply the knowledge, attitudes, and skills necessary to understand and manage emotions, set and achieve positive goals, feel and show empathy for others, establish and maintain positive relationships, and make responsible decisions" (Collaborative for Academic, Social, and Emotional Learning, n.d. para. 1). The social/emotional domain, referred to as the personal/social domain in earlier iterations of the ASCA Standards, is one of the three domains of the ASCA National Model. School counselors play a critical role in helping students develop social/emotional skills, which can have positive effects on students' academic and social development. Social skills (e.g. interpersonal skills, empathy, cooperation, assertion, and responsibility) impact the behaviors students exhibit in school, which directly impacts a student's overall performance in school (Farrington et al., 2012).

Stressors such as family divorce, relationships with peers and dealing with physical health concerns represent just a few of the many situations that students may encounter that impact their academic and behavioral functioning.

Table 7.1 The eight components of college and career readiness counseling

---

1. **College aspirations**: Building a college-going culture K-12, including the persistence skills to meet challenges and build competencies necessary to enroll in and graduate from college/career/ technical programs.
2. **Academic planning for college and career readiness**: Promoting K-12 preparation for all students, including planning and successful learning in challenging courses for college and career success.
3. **Enrichment and extracurricular engagement**: Increasing school engagement K-12 for every student with varied extracurricular and enrichment experiences that include development of interests, talents, and leadership.
4. **College and career exploration and selection processes**: Providing early and regular information and experiences allowing every student to make informed college/technical school and career choices.
5. **College and career assessments**: Preparing for and participating successfully in multiple career and college assessments.
6. **College affordability planning**: Ensuring students and families receive early and accurate information about the cost of college and postsecondary education, payment options, and the process for successful financial aid and scholarships with minimal or no debt.
7. **College and career admissions processes**: Ensuring students and families have early and accurate information on career and college admissions requirements and application procedures.
8. **Transition from high school graduation to college enrollment**: Helping students successfully transition from high school to college with school and community resources to challenge barriers to enrollment.

Source: NOSCA, 2010.

School counselors can help students cope with these situations, and are also trained to make referrals for longer-term counseling or mental health resources as needed. In these ways, school counselors are able to promote students' academic success by helping them address the personal or emotional situations impacting their ability to learn and thrive academically in school.

Mental health.   Mental health concerns impact many children on a daily basis and can influence students' ability to partake fully in their education. Merikangas et al. (2010) cite 46 per cent of youth, aged 13–18, being diagnosed with a mental health disorder, with over 20 per cent having a very disabling mental disorder. Anxiety and mood disorders are commonly experienced by children and adolescents. In fact, one in four youth experience an anxiety disorder, and nearly 6 per cent experience a severe anxiety disorder. Further, the lifetime prevalence of a mood disorder (depression, dysthymia, and/or bipolar) is 14 per cent, and nearly 5 per cent of children experience a severe mood disorder (Merikangas et al., 2010). School counselors' unique training and skill set allow them to identify mental health concerns and provide both students and their families with information, referrals, and support. While school counselors can serve as valuable support systems for students while in school, they often make referrals for longer-term counseling or mental health resources as needed rather than serving as the student's primary provider of mental health care.

Bullying and overall school climate. According to the National Crime Victimization survey (National Center for Education Statistics [NCES], 2015), over 20 per cent of students reported having been bullied at school, and nearly

7 per cent of students reported being victims of cyber-bullying. Those who reported being victims of bullying and/or cyber-bullying reported fearing an attack or harm, engaging in avoidance behaviors (i.e., skipping school, skipping class, avoiding school activities, avoiding a specific place at school), engaging in a physical fight, and/or carrying a weapon to school for protection (NCES, 2015).

Students who bully have an increased risk for poor academic functioning, substance use, mental health concerns, and behavior problems. Students who are bullied are at greater risk of poor school adjustment, negative health effects, sleep difficulties, and mental health problems such as anxiety and depression (Center for Disease Control, National Center for Injury Prevention and Control, 2015). School counselors can provide counseling and support to both those who bully and those who are bullied, as well as promote positive school climate and prevent issues by conducting school-wide SEL lessons as well as by assisting school administrators develop school-wide policies in support of positive climates and reduction of violence and bullying (Young et al., 2009). Further, school counselors coordinate school-wide initiatives and anti-bullying campaigns, as well as conduct classroom-counseling lessons to prevent bullying and equip students with information regarding how to identify bullying, and, when appropriate, intervene when they see peers being bullied.

The role of school counselors is multifaceted, in order to accommodate the academic, career and social/emotional needs of all students within the school population. While school counselors work within each of the three domains—academic, career, and social/emotional—the information described in this section clearly shows the overlap and relationship among the three domains. Rather than working within the three domains in isolation, school counselors coordinate and implement comprehensive school counseling programs that bridge connections between each of the three domains, meeting students' needs in all three arenas.

Next, the themes found in the ASCA National Model: Leadership, collaboration, advocacy, and systemic change will be outlined.

Themes: Leadership, Collaboration, Advocacy, and Systemic Change

The ASCA National Model (2012) lists four intertwined themes that are integral in school counselors' role implementing a comprehensive school counseling program, closing the student achievement gap, and serving students and stakeholders: Leadership, collaboration, advocacy, and systemic change.

Leadership

Leadership includes "the activities of professional school counselor within the school and beyond to enact system-wide changes to facilitate student success" (Erford, 2015c, p. 30). School counselors are leaders in myriad ways.

Scenario

As a high school counselor, you are responsible for speaking to the freshman class and their parents during Back to School Night. Think of services you can provide for these students and their parents, not only to prepare for the upcoming school year but for life after graduation. Keep the three domains (academic, career, and social/emotional) in mind as you brainstorm ideas.

Leadership activities can include meeting the school's mission and helping students achieve in academic, career, and social/emotional domains, through both direct and indirect student services (ASCA, 2012; Erford, 2015c). Also, as a school leader, school counselors run a comprehensive school counseling program, make data-driven decisions impacting the entire school, and engage in prevention, systemic change, advocacy, and collaboration. According to a study by Young and Bryan (2015), school counselors and school counseling supervisors identified performing specific leadership behaviors:

1. **Interpersonal influence**: Influencing school stakeholders to have a shared vision and ideas, developing relationships with stakeholders, understanding the school climate, and sharing common goals;
2. **Systemic collaboration**: Partnering with stakeholders to enact change in the school systemically, including developing new programs and goals;
3. **Resourceful problem solving**: Utilizing creative methods for solving problems, advocating for change, and obtaining related resources;
4. **Professional efficacy**: School counselors' self-confidence and perceptions of themselves as leaders; and
5. **Social justice advocacy**: Leading through advocating for students, as well as challenging inequalities and the status quo.

Collaboration

According to the ASCA National Model (2012), school counselors do not work in a vacuum—rather, they collaborate with all members of the school community, including students, parents and guardians, teachers, administrators and school staff, as well as school and community leaders. School counselors partner with these named stakeholders toward common goals: To share resources, responsibilities and expertise; and build a sense of community (ASCA, 2012). An example of collaboration is school counselor's work on multidisciplinary teams, such as child study or student support teams. On such teams school counselors work closely with stakeholders to problem solve and create opportunities for enhanced student success. School counselors bring a distinct perspective based on their preparation in human development, social and cultural diversity, and counseling theories. Further, school counselors often collaborate with stakeholders through collaborative consultation, in which the school counselor works with the stakeholder directly, such as a teacher or parent, with the goal of positively impacting the student. In a study by Cholewa, Goodman-Scott, Thomas, and Cook (in review), elementary school teachers were interviewed regarding their consultation practices with school counselors. Teachers reported that school counselors collaboratively consulted to provide background information on students and families as well as share their knowledge on social/emotional topics and youth development. Further, school counselors consult on the topic of social/emotional topics and student behavior (Cholewa et al., in review) and student academics (Sink, 2008). Thus, collaboration is one tool school counselors use to serve students and the school community.

Advocacy

In the last several decades, strides have been made to desegregate schools and provide equity for all students, yet there still exists substantial inequalities in educational resources and opportunities for all students, particularly for students of color and those from low-income backgrounds (Grothaus and Johnson, 2012). In 2013, 21 per cent of school-age children lived in families below the poverty threshold (Kena et al., 2015). Poverty is associated with a number of other risk factors, including instability in food, housing, and healthcare, increased youth aggression and lower academics, and youth living in homes with higher rates of substance and physical abuse (Brown-Chidsey and Bickford, 2016; Wight et al., 2011). In addition to the rates of poverty, disproportionality exists in student academic achievement (Kena et al., 2015) and school discipline practices (Noltemeyer, Marie, Mcloughlin, and Vanderwood, 2015). Thus, there exists a need to promote equity for all students. According to Grothaus and Johnson (2012), equity means "providing the educational resources students need to be successful in the academic, career and personal/social domains" (p. 6).

School counselors are essential figures who can advocate to promote equity for students to achieve in the academic, career, and social/emotional domains. This is accomplished through a variety of interventions, ranging from direct student service to advocating systemically within the school, community, and even at the state and national level (ASCA, 2012). Further, school counselors advocate and raise awareness to support cultural diversity and social justice as well as a welcoming environment for all students. The importance of advocacy within the counseling profession is so integral that the ASCA Ethical Standards (2010b) describe school counselors' ethical responsibility regarding advocacy and social justice. Specifically, the standards relate to their cultural competence (E.2.a), their advocacy for equitable policies and practices (E.2.d), and working to closing achievement and opportunity gaps (E.2.g).

Someone may ask, "But what does this look like?" For example, school counselors may review school and staff policies as well as curriculum content (such as the use of language, religious holidays, family composition, etc.) to ensure it is culturally appropriate and representative of the community. Also, school counselors can examine student outcome data, including academic, attendance, and behavior data, in order to investigate equitable use of resources and staff practices, such as discipline referrals. Thus, school counselors advocate to remove barriers to student success (Grothaus and Johnson, 2012). As an advocate, school counselors also work toward social justice and cultural competence to serve students and stakeholders.

Systemic Change

Imagine throwing a rock into a pond. The rippling effect of the sinking rock impacts the whole body of water. One small change can impact an entire system. Similarly, according to ASCA (2012), "schools are a system, just like a family is a system. When an event occurs that makes an impact on one member of the family or part of the system, it affects other, if not all other, parts of the system" (p. 8). School counselors have a different perspective from many other school personnel, as they view the school as a whole, or a system, rather than as classes or students. School counselors use leadership, collaboration, advocacy, and data to determine student and school needs and address those needs, removing systemic barriers to student success. For example, school counselors investigate whether there is a systemic pattern to student absences, academics, and behaviors. They ask what preventions and interventions can be implemented systemically throughout the entire school. Further, school counselors understand that students are impacted by their family system, and collaborate with parents and guardians accordingly, such as developing school–family–community partnerships (Bryan and Griffin, 2010). Thus, school counselors use a holistic systemic lens when implementing their school counseling program, acknowledging the systemic factors that impact the school climate, culture, and student and stakeholder successes and challenges (ASCA, 2012; Lee and Goodnough, 2015).

Components

The ASCA National Model is comprised of four components, which are evident in Figure 7.1. First, Foundation is the underpinning of the National Model and includes the program's vision, mission, and goals, as well as school counseling competencies, standards, ethical codes, and so on. Next, the Management System and Accountability components house the data-driven tools for organizing, implementing and evaluating the Model, evaluating the school counselor, and collaborating with stakeholders. Many of these tools will be discussed subsequently in the Data-Driven School section of this chapter. Lastly, the Delivery System is comprised of the direct and indirect student services, which will be discussed subsequently.

Serving Students

Although the school counselor has many responsibilities, driven by implementation of a comprehensive school counseling program, most of his or her time should be spent serving students. According to the ASCA Model (2012), approximately 80 per cent or more of the school counselor's time should be spent either directly or indirectly providing services to students in the academic, career, and social/emotional domains. Examples of direct student services include classroom guidance lessons, group activities such as college and career fairs, advising activities, including creating individual learning plans with students, parents and guardians, individual and group counseling, and crisis response. School counselors also serve students through indirect services, specifically making referrals to other service providers or resources, and consulting and collaborating with stakeholders to indirectly serve students. All direct and indirect services involve serving students, either in a direct, face-to-face capacity or indirectly through stakeholders such as parents, guardians, school staff, and community service providers.

As the ASCA National Model is a framework, school counselors can adapt the framework to best meet the needs of their students and schools. Thus, although school counselors should spend the majority of their time serving students, the amount of time school counselors spend in direct-versus-indirect student services will vary by each school and their needs. Now, let's take a closer look at direct and indirect student services.

Direct Student Services

School Counseling Core Curriculum

School counseling core curriculum includes classroom lessons and group activities. School counselors deliver classroom lessons, previously called guidance lessons or classroom guidance, to students as part of their school counseling curriculum. The school counseling curriculum should be developmentally appropriate, preventative, and systematically provided to every student (ASCA, 2012). Thus, school counselors may benefit from a basic understanding of classroom management strategies. Classroom lessons should be based on standards, such as the ASCA Mindsets and Behaviors (2014a), or state specified school counseling standards. Additionally, school counselors can integrate school counseling standards with academic content standards in a process called standards blending (Schellenberg, 2007). Standards blending provides an avenue to meet school counseling and academic standards simultaneously through their classroom lessons. Many school districts require curricula and schedules for classroom lessons; this varies by district. Classroom lessons are a type of psychoeducational counseling and a strategy to interact with and provide prevention to every student, school-wide.

Group activities are another direct student service that school counselors provide to every student (ASCA, 2012). However, group activities are provided outside of the classroom. For example, school counselors may plan and implement college and career fairs, college visits, and school-wide prevention programs focusing on a range of topics such as leadership, kindness, bullying prevention, etc.

Individual Student Planning

School counselors advise students individually and in small groups, often in collaboration with students' parents and guardians (ASCA, 2012). This process often includes focusing on students' academic and career goals, and transitions. For example, school counselors assist students and develop individual learning plans and graduation plans, which can outline their course enrollment and goals while in the K-12 setting and beyond. Further, school counselors provide advising to assist students in making transitions, such as moving from the elementary to middle school level, or from high school to post-secondary training programs, higher education, or employment. Lastly, appraisals also can be conducted as part of advising, as school counselors provide assessments to determine students' skills, abilities, and achievement (ASCA, 2012).

Individual and Group Counseling

At times, students face challenges that impact their educational experiences, and school counselors can assist students overcome these barriers by conducting short-term individual and small-group counseling (ASCA, 2012). Typically, individual and group counseling is initiated by referrals, including students self-referring for counseling, or referrals by stakeholders such as parents, guardians, teachers, or other school staff. Other times, the school counselor may initiate counseling by informing students and stakeholders of upcoming groups or their availability for individual counseling. In addition, when counseling students, school counselors must describe both confidentiality and the process of counseling to students in a way that is developmentally appropriate (Erford, 2015b). Further, when counseling minors, informed consent from parents and legal guardians is recommended. Next, individual and group counseling will be discussed in greater depth.

Individual Counseling. According to Davis (2015), "the primary goal of individual counseling is to help students, one-on-one, explore issues or situations that are affecting their ability to function inside and outside of school" (p. 115). Thus, students can engage in individual counseling to remove barriers to their academic success, which may include academic and social/emotional topics. Hess, Magnuson, and Beeler (2012) described the process of individual counseling with students. Authors recommend counselors first build rapport, determine a student's presenting concerns, create counseling goals and a related plan to reach the goals, and then terminate. At the same time, children's and adolescents' progression through the stages may be fluid due to their varied developmental stages and the time available for counseling, considering the time constraints of the school setting. The focus and format of individual counseling may vary depending on whether it takes place in an elementary, middle, or high school. However, some common topics include but are not limited to family stressors, student motivation, student–teacher dynamics, peer relationships, anger management/impulse control, anxiety, and transitions.

Group Counseling. There are many benefits to group counseling in the schools. Group counseling is an efficient strategy for providing direct services to students, as school counselors can meet with several students at once. Further, students can benefit by learning from other students in the group, and group counseling can normalize students' struggles, as they recognize that their peers may encounter similar challenges (Davis, 2015). Also, Davis (2015) discussed that school counseling-based group counseling can provide students with skills and support. For example, through group counseling, school counselors can teach strategies and enhance skills, such as study skills, anger management, coping, organization, assertiveness, and social skills. Support groups may include the following topics, to name a few: Divorce and changing families, parental incarceration, moving, grief, and chronic illnesses in the student or family member. In addition, some groups can focus on multiple topics. For example, Steen, Henfield, and Booker (2014) proposed a group counseling model called Achieving Success Everyday (ASE) that integrates both students' academics and personal/social development. The ASE model provides school counselors with a method to help students learn social skills in a group setting as well as assist them with the development of new skills that contribute to academic success, such as paying attention and turning assignments in on time (Steen, Henfield, and Booker, 2014). This model runs in flexible phases rather than standard sessions. These phases include assessment, review, acquaintance, challenge, empowerment and support (Steen et al., 2014). When used to study the resiliency of middle school students, the ASE model was found to improve student GPA as well as help students to develop skills as to remain resilient in the future (Steen et al., 2014).

At the same time, there can be challenges associated with conducting group counseling within a school setting, mainly the bounds to confidentiality and accommodating students' schedules. Although school counselors must describe confidentiality to their group members, confidentiality breeches by students can occur, which could be particularly disconcerting due to group members being part of the larger school community. As a result, school counselors should inform all group members that confidentiality is never guaranteed in a group setting, but relay that it is expected. Further, school counselors must be mindful to screen members for group counseling participation in advance in order to determine if the intervention is appropriate. A second challenge for group counseling, particularly in middle and high school, is identifying a time to meet with the group. The variability in group members' schedules and difficulty of removing students from their academic classes necessitates creativity on the school counselor's part. At times, school counselors may have to advocate to classroom teachers and administrators to allow students to miss class time, should the school counselor believe that group participation will ultimately enhance students' abilities to engage and succeed academically.

Theoretical Approaches. As previously discussed in this book, counselors, including school counselors, can utilize a variety of theoretical orientations when conducting individual and group counseling. Solution-focused counseling is optimal in the schools due to its strength-based approach and brief nature, which limits the time students are removed from classroom instruction (Stone and Dahir, 2016). Behavioral counseling, such as positive reinforcement and behavior modification, be regularly used in schools, especially with younger students. Also, cognitive behavioral counseling can be used to assist students with problem solving. Overall, school counselors may utilize a range of theoretical approaches when counseling students in schools. In addition to the approaches previously listed, school counselors may also use play therapy, person-centered, Adlerian, rational emotive behavior therapy, reality, and existential counseling approaches, as well as motivational interviewing (Stone and Dahir, 2016). For more information on these theoretical approaches to counseling, please see chapter 5.

Next, a school counselor's role in crisis responses will be discussed. This is predominantly a direct student service, but does include indirect student services.

Crisis Response

One of the privileges of being a school counselor is the opportunity to work with students when they are encountering some of the most difficult challenges in their lives, including crises. James and Gilliland (2016) examined existing definitions of crisis and have summarized an individual crisis as "a perception or experiencing of an event or situation as an intolerable difficulty that exceeds the person's current resources and coping mechanisms" (p. 9). Consequently, some of the common individual level crises in K-12 schools might include death and loss, abuse and neglect, parental divorce, homelessness, illness, parental incarceration, pregnancy, substance abuse, mental health problems, and accidents. Additionally, because a crisis is based on one's perceptions, resources, and coping mechanisms, what may be a crisis to one student may cause very little distress to another. Therefore, school counselors may also assist students who are in crisis due to bullying, rejection, or loss of friendships and romantic relationships.

Two individual crises are particularly important to mention: Child abuse and students' suicidal ideation. As mandated reporters, when school counselors suspect or have been notified of instances of child abuse and neglect, they are required to notify the proper authorities. Because state laws and the definition of what constitutes abuse can vary, it is important that school counselors stay current and follow their state's requirements (ASCA, 2015b). Through this process, the school counselor supports the student and his or her family as appropriate, and serves as an advocate for the child (ASCA, 2015b). Another crisis that is pertinent in schools relates to student suicide and suicidal ideation—having thoughts about killing oneself. Given the seriousness of suicidal ideation, school counselors take grave precautions to keep their students safe. This often involves an assessment of the suicide risk of students who are presenting with depressive symptoms, hopelessness and helplessness, or who have conveyed suicidal ideation verbally or through written material (Erford, Lee, and Rock, 2015). As part of their response, school counselors assess the severity and frequency of the suicidal thoughts, the student's plan and its specificity, his or her intended method and its lethality, and his or her timeline (Harrington and Daughhetee, 2014;

Stelmacher, 1995). Further, school counselors notify the parents or guardians of students with suicidal ideation and provide proper referrals to facilitate the wellbeing and safety of the student. School districts often have specific protocol and training for staff members regarding assessing for suicidal ideation and intent.

When serving a student in crisis, school counselors respond utilizing a variety of means, ranging from de-escalation techniques (e.g. grounding, box breathing, mindfulness) to talk-therapy to activities such as sand tray or the creative arts, depending on the needs and developmental level of the student. The goal is to often return the student to a state of normalcy, helping him or her to restore his or her emotional, cognitive, and/or behavioral equilibrium (i.e. equilibrium model) and re-establish coping abilities (James and Gilliland, 2016), while also equipping the student with new strategies. At times, the needs of the student may supersede the brief counseling that a school counselor is able to provide given the number of students he or she serves. Therefore, in such cases, the school counselor would provide a referral for more long-term counseling within the community while continuing to provide in-school support.

In conclusion, in order to serve all students on their caseload, school counselors should directly serve *every* student through classroom guidance lessons, group activities, and advising, and serve students with high needs in time-limited individual and small-group counseling, including crisis response. School counselor-facilitated individual and small-group counseling is time-bound and relatively short-term. In fact, some school districts specify the number of individual and small group counseling sessions allowed for each student (e.g. six to eight sessions). However, it is recommended that any number of sessions be fluid, based on the students' needs, the specific situation, and the school counselors' time. While school counselors are mental health providers trained to conduct counseling, counseling is one aspect (one important aspect!) of a comprehensive school counseling program.

Many students have needs that require longer term and more intensive counseling, such as mental health disorders, substance abuse, trauma, and a host of other serious challenges. In these cases, school counselors should refer students to mental health counseling services outside of the school, which will now be discussed.

Indirect Student Services

In addition to school counselors' provision of invaluable responsive services through their direct work with students, school counselors also provide critical indirect services. Through indirect services, school counselors work with key adult stakeholders—such as parents/guardians, teachers, administrators, school staff, and others—to impact positively students' academic, career, and social/emotional development and to promote equity within schools (ASCA, 2012; Gysbers and Henderson, 2012). Some of the commonly cited indirect services include referrals, collaboration, and consultation (ASCA, 2012; Gysbers and Henderson, 2012).

Referrals

Although school counselors are equipped to provide a variety of responsive services within their role, at times students may need additional support and information. As such, school counselors must be familiar with school and community referral sources to supplement in-school service provision and connect students and their families to additional resources (ASCA, 2012; Gysbers and Henderson, 2012). As previously mentioned, school counselors may refer students to mental health counseling services in the community due to mental health issues including depression and anxiety, abuse, eating disorders, violence, suicidal ideation, and other crises. Often school districts have protocols in place for making mental health counseling referrals, such as providing the contact information of local community service boards and several local mental health professionals. Gysbers and Henderson (2012) listed referral sources such as employment and training programs, vocational rehabilitation, juvenile justice, and other social service agencies. Similarly, ASCA (2012) highlights referral sources such as tutoring for academic support, college planning websites and employment training for career support as well as community agencies that treat mental health issues. Overall, school counselors' knowledge of informational and community resources allows them to assist students and their families effectively and across many different situations and contexts.

Consultation and Collaboration

One cannot underestimate the importance of school counselors working with adults as part of a comprehensive school counseling program. Through consultation and collaboration, school counselors can positively impact students' academic achievement and wellness as well as engender change at the individual, classroom, and school level to promote equity (ASCA, 2012; Erford, 2015a). School counselors recognize the significance of these relationships, as they report that they regularly consult and collaborate with stakeholders, such as teachers, administrators and families (Gibbons, Diambra, and Buchanan, 2010; Goodman-Scott, 2015; Perera-Diltz. Moe, and Mason, 2011).

Engaging Teachers.   Due to high student-to-counselor ratios, school counselors' consultation and collaboration with teachers can be a particularly efficient use of their time (Baker, Robichaud, Dietrich, Wells, and Schreck, 2009; Dinkmeyer, Carlson, and Michel, 2016). For example, by working with one teacher, a school counselor has the potential to impact all of the students within his or her class(es). Some areas of school counselor–teacher consultation and collaboration include helping teachers to contextualize and respond to student behavior, providing strategies to improve relationships with students, and helping teachers be more culturally responsive as well as work more collaboratively with families (Amatea and West-Olatunji; 2007; Brigman, Mullis, Webb, and White, 2005; Dinkmeyer et al., 2016; Warren, 2013). In addition, teachers may consult with the school counselor regarding individual students' academic progress, students' social and emotional concerns, and students' home lives. These consultations and collaborations may consist of a formal scheduled meeting to discuss the issue of concern, but may also consist of a brief conversation in the hallway or unscheduled drop-ins (Cholewa et al., in review). Regardless of the format, the collaborative relationship built between school counselors and teachers can maximize the school counselors' impact and facilitate the development of students.

Engaging Families and Communities. A family's engagement in a child's education is one of the biggest predictors of students' academic success (Choi, Chang, Kim, and Reio, 2014; El Nokali, Bachman, and Votruba-Drzal, 2010; Wilder, 2014). School counselors can play a significant advocacy and leadership role within their schools by facilitating family–school partnerships (Amatea and West-Olatunji, 2007; ASCA, 2010a). One of the ways that school counselors can do this is through the promotion of a school culture that values family–school collaboration. Schools that operate under a collaboration paradigm utilize a strength-based approach, which acknowledges the rich knowledge and insight that families bring to a student's education (Amatea, 2013). This allows for schools and families to view each other as co-experts and for schools to include family's voices in decisions about their students (Amatea, 2013). This is particularly poignant among families of color, of low-income, or who have immigrated to the U.S., as these families have historically had less involvement in their children's education (Holcomb-McCoy, 2010; Suarez-Orozco, Suarez-Orozco, and Todorova, 2010).

School counselors can collaborate with families and communities and promote a collaborative culture in various ways. Counselors can work to build relationships and increase the understanding between schools and families/communities through hosting workshops, conducting home visits, and connecting families with resources (Bryan and Griffin, 2010). They may build partnerships with volunteers, businesses and mentors within the community to provide services and programs for students and families (Bryan and Griffin, 2010). School counselors also take into account the diversity of their students and families and aim to communicate in various languages and through multiple means (Suarez-Orozco, Onaga, and Lardemele, 2010), such as phone calls, letters home, and social media. Also, to accommodate family's schedules, meeting times and locations may need to vary throughout the day and evening, and, if possible, should include childcare options.

School counselors directly serve students through classroom guidance lessons, group activities, individual student planning, individual counseling sessions, group counseling sessions and by assisting during times of crisis. Indirect school counseling services include making necessary referrals to in-school and outside professionals and collaborating with students' teachers, caregivers, and community. By directly and indirectly serving students through multiple means, school counselors work to ensure the success of students by including all stakeholders in the counseling process.

DATA-DRIVEN SCHOOL COUNSELING AND ACCOUNTABILITY

When school counselors utilize data and show results through accountability, they are implementing comprehensive school counseling programs that meet students' needs, address inequities, and have appropriate focus. School counselors have an important and influential role within the school; therefore, by using data to inform their programs, they can positively impact more students and show their results to administration and stakeholders. By using needs assessments, SMART goals, data analysis tools, program evaluation, and counselor evaluation tools, school counselors are maximizing their effectiveness and setting their students up for success!

Case Study: Shelly

Shelly is a second grader in your elementary school. Her teacher refers her to you because she notices that Shelly always eats lunch alone and does not play with her peers during recess. Recently, Shelly has begun to bully her classmates, intimidating them during PE and calling them names.

Process Question

1. What direct and indirect services can you provide to Shelly and possibly her classmates to resolve these issues?

Amidst the many roles and responsibilities of a school counselor, collecting and using data to inform their school's comprehensive counseling program might be easily placed on the back-burner. Data-driven counseling programs can assist school counselors in directing resources and interventions to areas with high needs, help school counselors advocate for their jobs, and enhance their effectiveness (ASCA, 2012; ASCA, 2014b; Ziomek-Daigle, 2016). Accountability is an essential keystone to the ASCA National Model; therefore, an effective, credible, and successful school counseling program is a data-driven and accountability based program (ASCA, 2012; Young and Kaffenberger, 2011). While this sounds fantastic, one may think "But I'm not a highly trained researcher or statistician …!" The great news is that school counselors can maximize their effectiveness with a basic understanding of data practices that will then influence their programs.

Next, the authors will describe the latest trends in data-driven education as well as the need for data within school counseling, types of data, and how to use data.

Why is Data Important?

Recently, schools have placed a higher value on student achievement and accountability for everyone in the school building: Administration, office personnel, teachers, and school counselors. School counselors were not always included in the conversation of school reform, student outcomes, and accountability; however, they are now welcomed into this discussion and serve as influential leaders within schools (Martin, 2015). The latest trend in data-driven education focuses on standardized tests, analyzing school statistics to ensure progress towards positive student outcomes, and evidence-based practices (Dimmitt, Carey, and Hatch, 2007; Executive Office of the President, 2015). With the emergence of the Every Student Succeeds Act, which replaced No Child Left Behind, there are even higher academic standards in place, more accountability for schools with students that fall behind, and less ineffective testing procedures (Executive Office of the President, 2015). In the age of accountability, school counselors are expected to contribute to the educational trend of data-driven and evidence-based practices.

Consider a t-shirt labeled "one size fits all." Does it really fit *everyone* appropriately? Petite individuals may end up drowning in fabric, whereas someone full-figured may find the t-shirt uncomfortable and restrictive. Simply put, "one size fits all" does not meet everyone's requirements. Likewise, each school has a unique population of students with varying needs. One school may have a large military family population, a high dropout rate, a large English as a Second Language (ESL) population, or an advanced academy program. Each school, thus, has varying needs based on the population of students.

For school counselors, meeting the needs of students and demonstrating their program's effectiveness will be an intimidating proposition. Where to start? With a four letter word ... data! Data can help inform school counselors to meet students' needs.

Through the use of data, school counselors can demonstrate how students are different as a result of the school counseling program, determine inequities and barriers to learning, advocate for systemic change, and focus interventions, strategies, and resources where they are needed most (ASCA, 2012; Grothaus and Johnson, 2012; Ziomek-Daigle, 2016). Data-driven practices take the guesswork out of comprehensive school counseling programs. No longer are school counselors making programmatic changes based on gut feelings, then crossing fingers and hoping for improvement. Instead, school counselors are identifying areas of need, making changes to meet the needs of students, and evaluating effectiveness.

Types of Data

So far in this section we have discussed data. But what is data? There are actually three types of data that are particularly relevant to school counselors: Process data, perception data, and outcome data.

Process data is collected through observation of an intervention and provides evidence that an event took place (Hatch, 2013). School counselors may note how many people attended an event, the length of time or frequency of an intervention, or the content covered, such as a classroom lesson on cyber safety, etc.

Table 7.2 Examining three types of data for data-driven school counseling and accountability

	Process Data	Perception Data	Outcome Data
Questions answered	What did you do for whom? How many participants were there? How many times/how long did the intervention occur?	What do individuals think they know or can do? What changed in their attitudes or beliefs? What are their perceived gains in knowledge?	How has the intervention/activity impacted the students? How can students utilize knowledge, attitude, and skills learned to impact their achievement, attendance, and/or behavior?
Examples	Five third-grade girls participated in a weekly self-esteem lunch bunch group that occurred over the span of seven weeks. A classroom of 27 sixth graders engaged in monthly school counseling core curriculum for 45 minutes. 187 juniors attended the annual college and career fair presented by the school counseling department in September.	82% of fifth-grade parents/guardians report that the "Transitioning to Middle School" presentation was beneficial for them and their student. 78% of sixth graders report that there is at least one adult in the building that they feel safe talking to if they need help. 91% of sophomores can identify the early warning signs of dating violence.	Discipline referrals decreased by 64% for those students in the six-week anger management group. 87% of eighth-grade students passed all of their required standardized state tests for this school year. Senior attendance has increased from 86% in the first quarter to 91% in the second quarter.

Perception data measures the students' perceptions (Hatch, 2013), which can be measured by pre- and post-tests, feedback surveys, needs assessments, or program evaluation surveys.

Lastly, outcome data provides information about whether or not an intervention had an impact (Hatch, 2013). Outcome data can be collected from a variety of sources including attendance records, discipline referrals, graduation rates, course enrollment, SAT scores, GPA, standardized test scores, etc.

For information related to the questions each type of data answers and examples of each type of data, see Table 7.2.

Ways to Use Data

Needs Assessment

School counselors use a needs assessment in order to get a clear picture of the current conditions of their school. A needs assessment serves several purposes, as it identifies areas of strength and concern, targets achievement gaps, and informs program goals. Needs assessments can be data-driven or perception-based. Data-driven needs assessments report the actual needs of the school based on the school data profile (Ziomek-Daigle, 2016). The school data profile outlines student outcome data related to achievement, attendance, behavior, safety, testing, and course-taking patterns disaggregated, or broken down by race, ethnicity, gender, ESL, special education placement, giftedness, free–reduced lunch, etc. If school counselors are viewing data that is not already disaggregated, they can use simple tools such as SPSS, Excel, or EZ Analyze to identify achievement gaps (see the Resources section at the end of this chapter for more information). Achievement gaps describe educational disparities between groups of students based on characteristics such as race, ethnicity, gender, and socio-economic status (Holcomb-McCoy, 2007). Through the use of school data profiles, school counselors can disaggregate data to clearly present achievement gaps and engage in data-driven decision making to work towards closing these gaps. (For a sample school data profile, see ASCA, 2012, p. 109.) After reviewing a school data profile, school counselors may be presented with data such as:

- 62 per cent of elementary students identified as low socio-economic status are performing below average for reading scores compared to only 21 per cent of non-low socio-economic status students.
- 23 per cent of females in the sixth grade are failing their math course whereas 13 per cent of males are failing their math course.
- While they represent only 60 per cent of the school demographic, 85 per cent of students taking one or more AP courses identify as White.

Reflection Question

School counselors can use results from the school data profile to inform their program goals. Based on the examples listed above, brainstorm potential goals to address each need. For example, with the data for low minority enrollment in AP courses, a school counselor may set a goal to identify and enroll 15 per cent more minority students in AP courses for the next school year.

Exercise 7.3

School counselors can also use perception-based needs assessments, which survey stakeholders (i.e. parents/guardians, teachers, administrators, staff, community members, etc.) about the perceived needs of students. This data can be collected through surveys, questionnaires, and/or focus groups. This can help school counselors prioritize stakeholder needs and incorporate them into the school counseling program as well (Ziomek-Daigle, 2016). After reviewing a perception-based needs assessment, school counselors may be presented with data such as:

- 31 per cent of parents/guardians reported that their child experienced bullying in the last 3 months
- 40 per cent of parents/guardians of seventh-grade girls express interest in having their student participate in a positive body image group
- 38 per cent of teachers for the junior class express concern in the alcohol/drug habits of their students

Exercise 7.4

Reflection Question

School counselors can use results from the perception-based needs assessment to inform their program goals. For example, on a grade-level school climate survey, 30 per cent of fourth-grade students report bullying on the school bus. Thus, program goals could include (a) informing staff and students of the results of the survey; (b) investigating then implementing evidence-based practices to improve the climate on elementary school buses. Based on the examples listed above, brainstorm potential goals to address needs.

Hopefully, you can see how through needs assessments a new counselor entering a school can quickly become informed of the real and perceived needs of the students and staff. This gives school counselors focus and direction. It also provides school counselors the opportunity to observe inequities within the school. School counselors can observe disparities, whether it is a specific fourth-grade class that is underperforming in math, a subgroup of students that do not have equal access to advanced courses, or a population of students of color that has a high dropout rate. School counselors can identify barriers to learning and take a leadership role by advocating for systemic changes. School counselors can incorporate inequities seen in data into program goals to focus their efforts and resources.

SMART Goals

School counselors diligently work to create informed comprehensive school counseling programs, so setting SMART goals is a great step towards success!

Table 7.3 Defining SMART goals

S	Specific	Goals that are specific have a greater chance of being accomplished. Identify as many specifics as possible to ensure success.
M	Measurable	Determine a concrete measurement that will answer the following question: How will I know when it is accomplished?
A	Attainable	Your goals should make you stretch a bit; however, you don't want to set yourself up for failure by choosing something unattainable.
R	Realistic	Make sure your goals are something that you, your students, and your school are willing and able to work towards.
T	Timely	Set a timeframe to keep everyone accountable and have an endpoint in mind.

Here are several examples of SMART goals:

1. By the end of the school year, second-grade Hispanic students will increase their English performance scores from an average score of 65 (not passing) to an average score of 75 (passing).
2. At the end of the first semester, attendance for ninth–twelfth-grade students identified as English Language Learners will increase from 78 to 85 per cent.

Overall, the SMART goals format is helpful to define program goals and focus, based on data-driven needs. School counselors can make a plan for reaching these goals through Action Plans, and report results through Results Reports, all of which are documents provided by ASCA, as part of implementing a comprehensive school counseling program. School counselors can implement direct and indirect services in an effort to meet their SMART goals. For more help on how to formulate SMART goals, as well as to gain copies of Action Plans and Results Reports worksheets, see the ASCA website (members must log in to access member-only resources).

PROGRAM/COUNSELOR EVALUATION

Using data to drive comprehensive school counseling programs is extremely important; however, the road doesn't stop here. Tracking progress, evaluating effectiveness, and measuring school counselors' competence is equally important. By analyzing data collected throughout the school year, school counselors can make changes, improve upon their programs, and show administrators and stakeholders how students are impacted as a result of their interventions. Therefore, school counselors may collect perception and outcome data before and after classroom guidance lessons or a group counseling intervention to assess the influence of their programming on the student. The ASCA Model provides other tools for school counseling evaluation, including assessing the school counseling program, school counselors' competencies and use of time, and an appraisal for school administrators to conduct when annually evaluating school counselors.

Reflection Question

Looking back at the goals you brainstormed earlier, are they SMART goals? If so, great job! If not, how can you improve your goals and make them specific, measureable, attainable, realistic, and timely? Use the examples above as a guide to rewrite your goals.

Exercise 7.5

Evidence-based practices will be discussed next.

Evidence-Based Practices

While discussing evaluating school counseling programs for effectiveness, it is worth noting that evidence-based practices are an important piece of the puzzle. Evidence-based practices are pre-existing interventions that have already been researched and verified for effectiveness with certain populations (Dimmitt et al., 2007). When using evidence-based practices, school counselors can easily determine intervention effectiveness, as well as determine the population in which to use an intervention or curriculum. Since a comprehensive school counseling program should be data-driven and evidence-based, using interventions that already have a gold seal of approval makes things more manageable.

One example of an evidence-based practice is Student Success Skills, a program used in K-12 settings used to positively impact students' cognitive, social, and self-management skills. Over 9,000 school counselors and teachers have used it and 17 outcome research studies have studied its effectiveness (Student Success Skills, n.d.; Webb and Brigman, 2006). The program has a set of five classroom lessons with eight optional group counseling sessions offered to students needing more support. Each lesson involves reviewing previous goals for growth, learning and practicing new skills, and engaging in reflection on their improvement towards goals (Webb and Brigman, 2006). This program is highly effective in improving students' academic and social competencies.

A comprehensive school counseling program must be data driven, the same as other programs operating within a school. School counselors can use data to drive programs and to effectively meet the needs of the school population. Data also provides focus for the school counseling program and helps school counselors to advocate for their jobs. There are several types of data—process, perception and outcome—that counselors can use to determine the needs of the school, develop SMART goals and evaluate the school counseling program. To determine the most useful counseling services and programs to use, school counselors must implement evidence-based practices, those proven to work with particular populations.

Now, an equally important topic will be discussed—crises in schools.

CRISES IN SCHOOLS: PREPARING AND RESPONDING

Crises can impact an individual, school, community, and even a nation. School counselors are called to prepare for and respond to school-related crises. Stephen Brock (2013) notes, "It is not a question of *if*, but rather of *when* a school will be required to respond to a crisis" (p. 19). Thus, most states require that their K−12 school have an emergency management response plan so that schools are prepared to respond effectively to mitigate the effects of school-wide crises and return to normalcy as soon as possible.

School counselors can integrate their clinical training, knowledge of human development, mental health and cultural competence with their knowledge of their school's culture and student population to aid in the development and implementation of school's emergency management response plan. The school counselor's involvement can ensure that not only are students' physical needs taken into account, but their emotional needs as well. Some crises that require a school-wide response may include student suicide, student or faculty/staff death, natural disasters, or human caused/incidental threats (e.g. bomb threats, gang violence, active shooters) (U.S. Department of Education, 2013). As you can no doubt see, each of these crises require thoughtfully developed plans with assigned roles and responsibilities in order to minimize the chaos and protect the welfare of students and staff.

School counselors play a crucial role during any crisis itself and during the recovery stage of a school-wide crisis. In response to a school-wide crisis, there should be a focus on obtaining the facts, assessing the impact of the crisis on the school, determining who may be most impacted by the crisis, and beginning to implement psychological first aid (PFA—James and Gilliland, 2016). As its name implies, PFA is much like general first aid, and aims to reduce distress and enhance coping and functioning in the immediate aftermath of a crisis (Brymer et al., 2012). Its key components include making contact, ensuring safety and comfort, stabilization, information gathering, providing practical assistance, connecting with social supports, providing information on coping, and linking individuals with services and resources (Brymer et al., 2012). It is within these interactions with students and staff that school counselors' knowledge and skill set become invaluable.

PFA may continue through the crisis response itself and move into the recovery stage. School counselors typically work directly with individual and small groups of students and coordinate interventions services within the school following school-wide crises; however, this is also where their indirect services are highlighted (Erford et al., 2015). In addition to working directly with the students and helping them to cope with recent events, school counselors also consult and collaborate with teachers and administrators regarding how to best communicate with students and identify students in distress. Moreover, they serve as a crucial resource to parents/guardians and work alongside community organizations to provide both students and families with additional support and referrals as necessary. Finally, school counselors can work alongside administrators to conduct debriefings with school personnel to plan for next steps, evaluate the crisis response, and to help personnel emotionally cope with the crisis and response (Brock, 2013).

Schools and districts may choose to utilize school counselors in a variety of ways during a crisis. Ultimately, school counselors should proactively discuss their roles in crises with their supervisors and peers before they are needed. In the event of an actual crisis, school counselors must work collaboratively with school and community stakeholders in the creation of an emergency management response plan and provide affected students with psychological first aid if needed.

Reflection Question

Prior to a crisis, what community stakeholders and agencies should be included in emergency management response planning?

MULTI-TIERED SYSTEM OF SUPPORTS

In this chapter, the authors have described the history of school counseling and school counselors' roles in implementing a comprehensive school counseling program through direct and indirect student services, data and accountability, and crisis response. Now, another lens through which to view the role of the school counselor is offered: A multi-tiered system of supports. Multi-tiered systems is a framework for offering services to students that has been endorsed by the U.S. Department of Education (U.S. Department of Education, 2014) and is widely implemented throughout the country. Multi-tiered systems are three-tiered, systemic approaches to prevention (Brown-Chidsey and Bickford, 2016). Specifically, in viewing the school as a system, it can be anticipated that when implementing universal prevention, including academic, career, and social/emotional core curriculum delivered to all students, approximately 80 per cent of students will be successful with this level of universal prevention, or tier-one supports. However, approximately 20 per cent of students won't have their needs met with only universal prevention and will require more advanced supports. Typically, 15 per cent of students can be successful with tier two, or secondary prevention, which includes small-group interventions. Then, roughly 5 per cent of students with the highest needs will need tertiary, or tier three, prevention in order to be successful in school. Tertiary services are the most intensive and include individualized services. These three tiers are presented as a pyramid, which is often referred to as multi-tiered system of supports (Brown-Chidsey and Bickford, 2016). See figure 7.2 for an example of a multi-tiered system of support.

While many schools and organizations can be described in terms of these three tiers (primary, secondary, and tertiary—80, 15, and 5 per cent respectively), schools with higher needs may have a higher percentage of students in need of secondary and tertiary supports and fewer students successful with only universal prevention. Also, types of multi-tiered systems include response to intervention and positive behavioral interventions and supports, which focus on students' academic and social behaviors (Brown-Chidsey and Bickford, 2016). Multi-tiered system of supports are frameworks that should be individualized to each school, thus culturally responsive to each specific school and its needs (Sugai, O'Keeffe, and Fallon, 2012). Further, services implemented at each level should be evidence-based and driven by data (Office of Special Education Programs, 2010).

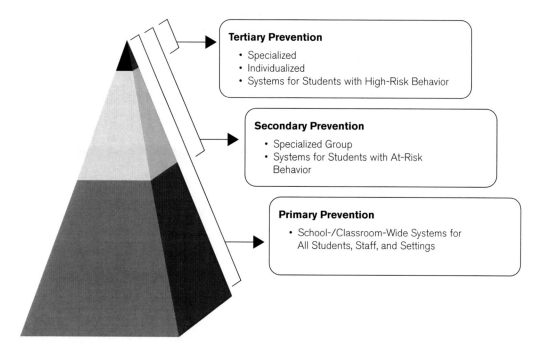

Figure 7.2 Continuum of school-wide instructional and positive behavior support

Source: OSEP Technical Assistance Center for Positive Behavioral Interventions and Support. From http://pbis.org (printed with permission).

Comprehensive school counseling programs such as the ASCA National Model are aligned with a multi-tiered system of supports (ASCA, 2014b; Goodman-Scott, Betters-Bubon, and Donohue, 2016; Ziomek-Daigle, Goodman-Scott, Cavin, and Donohue, 2016)—see Figure 7.3.

These describe school counselors' roles according to the three tiers. For example, school counselors should implement some services for all students (i.e. the universal level), including classroom guidance lessons, group activities, and advising. However, other school counseling services should be reserved for students with elevated needs (i.e. secondary and tertiary levels), including individual and small-group counseling, crisis response, and referrals, as well as consulting and collaborating with stakeholders. Further, data-driven and evidence-based practices should influence services at all three tiers. Thus, a multi-tiered system of supports can be a lens through which school counseling activities are viewed—as providing some services to all students universally, and small-group and individualized services for students with the highest needs. School counselors are particularly unique school-based mental health providers in that they provide services to students at all three tiers.

Now, more information will be provided on school counseling across the three levels: Elementary, middle, and high school.

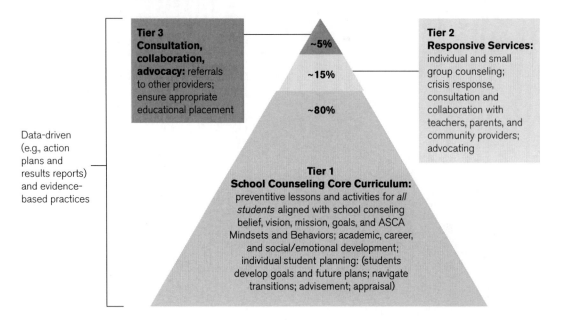

Figure 7.3 Aligning comprehensive school counseling programs/the ASCA National Model with school-wide positive behavior support

Source: Goodman-Scott, Betters-Bubon, and Donohue, 2016 (printed with permission).

SCHOOL COUNSELING BY LEVEL

Elementary School Counseling

What I [Emily] love about elementary school counseling is the opportunity to focus on prevention, having a school-wide emphasis on serving all students through leadership, collaboration, advocacy and systemic change, and working closely with not only the students, but also their parents/guardians and teachers. Children develop tremendously during the elementary years; kindergarteners are in quite a different place from fifth- or sixth-grade students. I found it a privilege to "move up" with my students each year, serving them and their families for consecutive years, developing relationships, and seeing student progress and growth.

School counselors at the elementary level typically have a large caseload. This is often due to elementary schools typically only having one school counselor, with the possibility of another part-time counselor. Therefore, elementary school counselors are charged with the exciting task of developing their own appropriate comprehensive school counseling program, as previously described.

Academically, elementary school students are discovering school routines, school expectations, and how to learn. School counselors can create awareness of learning styles and help students develop their own academic self-concept. School counselors also assist students in learning foundational study skills and organizational skills that will prepare them for a successful future. Collaboration is key at the elementary school level, as school counselors work closely with parents and guardians, faculty, staff, and administration to indirectly serve students, as, typically, young students are highly dependent on the caretakers in their life. Also, school counselors will prepare students for their middle school transition, such as assisting with scheduling middle school courses, the orientation process, and possibly completing recommendation letters for those students applying to middle school academy programs.

The career domain in elementary school is about exploration and exposure. School counselors are charged with promoting awareness of a variety of careers paths and the types of training required for those careers. School counselors also help connect the dots between students' interests, skills, and job roles and responsibilities. Some examples of this might be co-ordinating with parents/guardians and stakeholders to come in and talk about their careers in order to expose elementary school students to the variety of careers available, conducting classroom guidance lessons in which different books are used to showcase professions, or planning field trips out in the community to see some careers in action.

Elementary school counselors are essential in teaching students appropriate social skills, problem-solving strategies, and coping skills. As students learn how to make friends, school counselors can help teach healthy and positive peer relationships. In addition, school counselors assist in creating a positive school climate through bullying awareness and prevention efforts. Furthermore, school counselors may address students' concerns due to early life events or educational barriers. Examples include students needing food bank services, extra supports due to a military parent being deployed, or a call to Child Protective Services due to suspected physical/emotional abuse. School counselors have an influential role at this early point in a child's life. Also, it is important to note that many of the school counseling activities described at the elementary level are also conducted at the middle and high school level. There is tremendous overlap between the job responsibilities at the various school levels, as school counseling is described in a K-12 context.

Middle School Counseling

What I [Blaire] love about counseling at the middle school level is that you are working with students who are really coming into their own in terms of their identity and how they see themselves. Moreover, they are navigating puberty and the "storm and stress" that comes along with that, while working through peer dynamics. Therefore, as a school counselor you never know what is going to come at you next and it keeps you on your toes. You get to play such an integral role in helping students begin to figure out who they are and what they value.

At the middle school level, students are gaining more independence, cultivating interests, and going through a major transitional period. School counselors can provide responsive services and groups covering developmentally appropriate topics related to all three domains. School counselors can also teach students about setting short-term and long-term goals, as well as about organizing and planning to meet these goals. Students are gaining more ownership of their education, and school counselors can empower students and organize academic supports (i.e., peer tutoring programs) to help them succeed. Additionally, school counselors are continuing to meet and collaborate regularly with parents and administrators. As students ready themselves for high school, school counselors can write letters of recommendation for students applying to academies and assist in preparing students and families for the high school transition, including course selection and individual student academic plans.

In the career domain, school counselors help students explore career paths in greater depth, including day-to-day activities, and training/education required for jobs. School counselors can host college and career fairs to expose students to a variety of jobs and areas of employment. During middle school, counselors can also administer and interpret students' career interest inventories and assist in matching students' interests and skills to particular career paths.

Socially and emotionally, middle school can be a very tumultuous time for students. School counselors can help by teaching stress management as it relates to this higher level of school pressure, enhanced focus on peers and peer dynamics, life and body changes, and increased extracurricular activities. School counselors can also work on improving students' conflict-resolution and decision-making skills, while empowering students to gain a greater sense of self-understanding. As students undergo hormonal, bodily, and emotional changes during this time, school counselors can serve as a support and a psycho-educational resource. Further, school counselors can promote healthy student relationships with peers, family, and teachers.

High School Counseling

What I [Christina] love about working as a high school counselor is the ability to support students as they develop increased independence and plan for their lives beyond high school. My relationship with students develops as we work together and they transition into the complex and chaotic world of high school. Over time, my role evolves from directly supporting students and helping them solve problems to serving more as a consultant who assists students with advocating for themselves and achieving their goals on their own as they mature and progress toward adulthood. I find such joy in helping students plan for their futures so that they are equipped with the knowledge, skills, and resources to achieve their post-secondary goals and transition into adulthood.

Counseling at the high school level is both similar and different from counseling at the middle school and elementary school levels. In high school, school counselors work to close achievement gaps and disparities that exist in a school's graduation rate. Increased focus is placed upon the accumulation of high school credits, performance in both academic and career-preparatory curricula, and ensuring that all students remain on track to graduate from high school and have both access to and plans for post-secondary pathways. School counselors can work with their school administration and teachers to ensure that all students have access to college and career readiness curricula that will prepare them for their post-secondary plans.

Counselors in a high school setting must provide additional attention to the demands of the college admissions process. School counselors are often asked to provide letters of recommendation for many (if not all) of their senior students and also provide information, resources, and preparation for any required college entrance examinations (i.e. SAT and ACT). School counselors can help students and their families navigate the complexities of paying for post-secondary education, such as by providing workshops on completing the Free Application for Federal Student Aid, and promoting students to apply for scholarships. Further, as school counselors aim to promote equity, it is particularly important that they engage students from underrepresented groups and their families, as these students may have less access to information needed to facilitate their transition to post-secondary options (Cholewa, Burkhardt, and Hull, 2016).

High school counselors also prepare students for the world of work by helping them craft resumés and cover letters detailing what they have accomplished over their high school years as well as preparing for interviews and applying for jobs. Students can work with their school counselor to identify how their own learning styles and environmental preferences fit with their intended career pathway(s) as well as what education and/or training is required for their career(s) of interest. As students prepare for their careers of interest, school counselors can support students in developing workplace readiness skills and make connections between their performance and behaviors in school and readiness for the world of work, higher education, or training programs. High school counselors work to ensure that all students have a plan for life beyond high school and help students transition into this post-secondary plan.

The social/emotional learning done in elementary and middle school is also continued into high school level. School counselors in high school settings continue to help students develop coping skills and apply decision-making skills necessary for navigating the complexities of adverse life events, relationships, and the transition into adulthood. Adolescence is a time in which students are exposed to novel situations and make new decisions in regards to romantic relationships, friendships, social media, drugs and alcohol, sexual activity, and so on. As students age toward adulthood, school counselors can support students as they develop increased autonomy over their choices and plans for life after high school. Further, school counselors can help students identify family and community resources to utilize beyond high school, which is particularly important for students receiving special education services.

Now that we have examined the roles and responsibilities of school counselors at the three educational levels, three case studies are provided in order to learn more about the realities of school counseling at each stage.

CASE STUDIES: SCHOOL COUNSELING ACROSS THE LEVELS

Case Study: Charlie

The following is an elementary school case study.

Charlie is a second-grade student who lives at home with his mother and grandmother. He has always been described as "quick-tempered" by his mother and teachers. His teacher noted that lately he has been acting out at school by pushing classmates so he can be first in line, refusing to wait his turn in class, and calling other students names when they don't play with him. The school counselor learns that Charlie's mom recently had a baby girl, and although he loves to hold her and read to her Charlie has been receiving less attention from his mother and grandmother lately due to the new baby. He has been getting angry at home, throwing his Lego, slamming his bedroom door, and yelling at his father. Charlie says he doesn't know why he gets so angry at home and at school, but recognizes that he has been getting in trouble more often at school lately, and was recently grounded for two weeks. Charlie's family wants him to make better decisions with his words and actions, but don't have very much time in their daily schedule to work with him. They ask the school counselor if there are any ways to improve Charlie's behavior that will not consume a lot of their time.

Process Questions, Section 1

1. What are the primary concerns for Charlie?
2. What are some ways the school counselor can work with Charlie to improve the situation at school and home?
3. What are some cultural and contextual considerations that need to be addressed?
4. How can the school counselor use data to determine whether the intervention(s) were effective?

Charlie's school counselor decides to complete a baseline evaluation of Charlie's behaviors at school and home. Charlie's negative behaviors, such as name-calling, aggressive acts, and failure to follow rules, are observed and recorded by the school counselor, his teacher, and family in both school and home settings. The school counselor then collaborates with Charlie's family and teachers to better understand the expectations of Charlie in each of these settings. The school counselor decides to create a Social Story with Charlie to explain desired behaviors for school and home.[2]

After collaboration with Charlie, his family, and his teacher, the counselor personalizes Charlie's Social Story for him. In his story, Charlie identifies the triggers for his angry outbursts, lists positive behaviors he can choose instead, and reminds himself of behavioral expectations at home and school. The Social Story is written from Charlie's perspective and he was even able to draw the pictures for his very own book! Copies of the Social Story are given to his teachers, mother, and grandmother, and the school counselor. Charlie reads the book every morning and afternoon, whether with his teacher, school counselor, mother, or grandmother. After three weeks, Charlie is observed again at school and at home to determine whether he has a decrease in negative behaviors. This data shows the effectiveness of the intervention and validates that the school counselor's time spent creating and implementing the Social Story was meaningful.

Process Questions, Section 2

1. What are some other ways you can assist Charlie with his behavioral issues at school and home?

Case Study: Janelle

The second study in this chapter focuses on a middle school case.

Janelle is a sixth grader living as an only child in a single-parent home with her father. Her math teacher reports that Janelle is a very capable student and her math grades have been average all year, but Janelle has recently reached a point where she is giving up. She often states in class that "girls can't do math" and that "there's no point in trying." In P.E., Janelle has been refusing to change into her gym clothes to participate. She has told the gym teacher that she feels "ugly and different from the other girls" due to her physical matura-tion compared to her classmates. Several boys in her class have been calling her names and making fun of her. Other teachers note that Janelle seems anxious, bites her fingers a lot, and seeks a lot of reassurance through asking questions such as "What happens if I fail this grade?" "What if no one wants to sit with me at lunch?"

Janelle's father observes these same behaviors at home. He often hears Janelle putting herself down, criticizing her body, and worrying about her friends and her performance at school. He tries to reassure her, but wonders what the school counselor can do to help. He is concerned about the boys making fun of Janelle and wants to know how the school counselor is involved in the disciplining of these students. He believes that Janelle's self-esteem will improve once she makes more friends, but due to his work schedule he is typically unable to arrange play-dates during the afternoons and weekends.

The school counselor speaks with Janelle and consults with her father and her teachers. Her father shares his frustration regarding the "mean boys picking on Janelle" and says that "something needs to be done." The school counselor clarifies to the father that his role does not involve instituting disciplinary action against the students picking on Janelle. However, the school counselor can certainly advocate for Janelle and ensure faculty are aware that she is being picked on by the boys, informing teachers of the disciplinary protocol in place. Also, the school counselor can meet with the boys and have a proactive discussion with them about respect and appropriate school

Process Questions, Section 1

1. What are the primary concerns for Janelle?
2. What are some ways the school counselor can work with Janelle to improve her situation at school and home?
3. What are some cultural and contextual considerations that need to be addressed?
4. How can the school counselor use data to determine whether the intervention(s) were effective?

behaviors. If, over time, the school counselor determines that this is more of a class-wide issue, a classroom lesson on respect, empathy, and/or accepting differences may be warranted.

The school counselor decided to speak with Janelle about placing her in an afterschool STEM program for girls. This program would provide tutoring, boost Janelle's self-esteem about math, and provide a social outlet for her. This program also breaks down the stigma that girls aren't good at science and math when compared to boys. Janelle would participate in the afterschool program three times per week and take the activity bus home.

The school counselor also decided to start a lunch bunch group of sixth-grade girls that struggle with anxiety and low self-esteem. This seven-week group focuses on building rapport, identifying concerns and worries, teaching coping skills and anxiety reduction, naming positive affirmations for oneself and others, and building up self-esteem through activities/videos. After gaining consent from each parent for the girls to participate in the group, the school counselor gives all the girls an anonymous survey about their anxiety levels, coping skills, and self-esteem. During the last group session, the same anonymous survey is taken to determine whether the group helped increase the students' self-esteem and coping skills and lessen their anxiety.

Process Questions, Section 2

1. What are some other ways you can assist Janelle with her behavioral issues at school and home?

Case Study: Sophia

Sophia is a 16-year-old student in eleventh grade. While she has performed well academically in ninth and tenth grades (receiving grades of As and Bs), her grades recently have dropped to Cs and even a few Ds. Additionally, teachers report that Sophia appears more withdrawn and tired in class, that she's often falling asleep, is neglecting her homework, and appears unprepared for tests and quizzes. She has been absent from school more frequently and just recently quit the school's swim team.

Process Questions, Section 1

1. What are the primary concerns for Sophia?

Sophia's school counselor reaches out to Sophia upon noticing these changes in her grades and after speaking to Sophia's teacher and hearing about her behaviors in class. When speaking with her school counselor, Sophia shares that she has been working longer shifts at her after-school waitressing job in order to make extra money for her family because her father recently lost his job. While she considered attending college when she was younger, Sophia now says that college is not for her because she cannot keep up in school now; further, she reports desiring to work full time upon graduation from high school to support her family. Sophia quit the school swim team to have more time to work after school and because she no longer enjoys the sport. Upon further questioning from her school counselor, Sophia shares that she has been feeling more hopeless and withdrawn over the past few months and wishes that she could just end it all.

Process Questions, Section 2

1. What steps could the school counselor take to support Sophia?
2. Who could the school counselor collaborate with to help support Sophia?
3. What ethical dilemmas might the school counselor encounter as she works with Sophia? How could these be resolved?

Because of Sophia's feelings of hopelessness and comment about "ending it all," the school counselor conducts a suicide assessment. Sophia does not report having any suicidal thoughts or plans. However, she agrees to a safety contract, and with the school counselor's assistance comes up with a plan for how she would remain safe if this changes. The school counselor determines that Sophia could use additional layers of support and encourages Sophia to consider speaking to a counselor or therapist outside of school about her feelings. Sophia is originally disinterested, but is willing to try speaking to a pastoral counselor at her church. Additionally, with Sophia's permission, the school counselor calls Sophia's mother and the three of them meet to discuss Sophia's present concerns, mental health and academic progress. The school counselor also provides recommendations for resources.

Over the next several weeks, the school counselor checks in with Sophia as she arrives at school on the bus. Sophia shares that she has connected with a pastoral counselor and is working on addressing her feelings of depression. The school counselor talks with the pastoral counselor to consult on services after Sophia and her mother sign a waiver giving permission. The school counselor and Sophia arrange to meet weekly during Sophia's lunch period to check in about how she is feeling and about her academic progress. Sophia still feels overwhelmed academically, so the school counselor helps Sophia determine a schedule (in consultation with Sophia's teachers) so that Sophia can catch up on her work over time.

During one of their weekly meetings, Sophia shares with the school counselor that she's unsure of her plans post-graduation. The school counselor arranges for Sophia to take career assessments to help her identify strengths, skills and interests. Sophia is surprised to learn that her answers suggested a career in healthcare. The school counselor and Sophia research various healthcare careers. Sophia is intrigued about the field of nursing, but is intimidated about attending college, as she would be the first in her family to attend. Her biggest concerns are financial, as she is very worried about her family's ability to pay for college. The school counselor provides Sophia and her family with information about financial aid and scholarships and shares information about local colleges that may be a good fit for Sophia's interests and would enable her to live at home and maintain her current employment. Further, the school counselor arranges for Sophia to visit one of the local colleges to talk to a first-year adviser who specializes in supporting first-generation college students.

Attending to Sophia's concerns, mainly creating post-secondary plans, and engaging in pastoral counseling in her church community seem to help Sophia's mental health and thus her school academics and involvement. In the following weeks, Sophia's grades begin to improve, and she has a more positive outlook about her academic and post-secondary plan. She continues to meet with the school counselor regularly to talk about college and has signed up to take a SAT preparation course and the SAT. Because she will be the first in her family to attend college, the school counselor provides extra support to Sophia throughout eleventh grade and during her senior year so that she has the information and preparation to matriculate into college after high school.

Process Questions, Section 3

1. What other ideas could the school counselor implement to help Sophia?

Now that school counseling at the three levels has been discussed, the chapter will wrap up by discussing the strengths and challenges of school counseling.

CONCLUSION

School Counseling Challenges and Strengths

Over the last several years, school counselors have been increasingly recognized as instrumental in students' academic, career, and social/emotional functioning, proving that they make a difference to students and schools. Also, while school counseling professional identity has evolved over the last century, the profession has recently made strides toward a uniform school counseling vision through the creation and implementation of the ASCA National Model and the focus on comprehensive school counseling programs. But while the school counseling profession has changed, grown, and improved over the decades, there is still work to do. First, there is a need to continue to advocate for reduced student caseloads. In order to best serve students, ASCA recommends a 250:1 student-to-school counselor ratio (ASCA, 2012), however the national average is nearly double that: 491:1 (Glander, 2015). In order to best serve students, there must be adequate time in which to do so.

Next, school counseling and comprehensive programs need to be more widespread. For example, nearly half of the states in the U.S. do not mandate school counseling (ASCA, 2015a), and, historically, comprehensive school counseling programs have not been consistently implemented in schools (Burnham and Jackson, 2000; Rayle and Adams, 2007) or across states (Martin, Carey, and DeCoster, 2009; Sink and MacDonald, 1998). Thus, although the school counseling profession has made great strides in recent years to unify the profession and create a central professional identity, more advocacy efforts are needed to support implementing comprehensive school counseling programs.

Additionally, school counselors are typically supervised and evaluated by non-school counselors, including building principals and district-level administrators. These supervisors may not always be familiar with the role of the school counselor. As a result, non-school counseling supervisors may assign non-school counseling job responsibilities, which can detract from school counselors implementing a comprehensive school counseling program and serving students (Clemens, Milsom, and Cashwell, 2009). Thus, school counselors report conducting activities not aligned with comprehensive school counseling programs (Burkard et al., 2012; Goodman-Scott, 2015; Gysbers and Henderson, 2012; Scarborough and Culbreth, 2008). As a result, school counseling job activities can vary between schools, districts, and states, further demonstrating the need for a single vision, voice, and professional identity.

One strategy for combating the assignment of non-school counseling responsibilities is through collaborating with stakeholders, such as school principals and district administrators (Goodman-Scott, 2011). Through collaborating with stakeholders and aligning school counselors' mission, vision, and goals with stakeholders', school counselors can demonstrate that they are central to the school and integral to the school's success. In addition to collaboration, school counselors need to be leaders, advocating systemically for lower caseloads as well as the support, time, and resources to fully implement comprehensive school counseling programs. Further, school counselors can advocate for a release from non-school counseling duties, such as facilitating standardized tests and conducting administrative and disciplinary roles.

School counselors can advocate through lobbying local, state, and national representatives, as well as joining professional counseling organizations that lobby in support of school counselors. Many state school counseling and counseling organizations have paid lobbyists, as does the American School Counselor Association and the American Counseling Association. Thus, being a member of these professional organizations ensures the support of school counseling lobbying efforts.

Although there are challenges, this is also an exciting time for professional school counselors. First, the flagship national organization, the American School Counselor Association, has the energy and strength of approximately 30,000 members. In recent years there has been a tremendous support from former First Lady Michelle Obama. She championed school counseling over the last years of her tenure as First Lady and spoke at the ASCA National Conference, hosted the first-ever School Counselor of the Year Ceremony at the White House, and advocated for school counselors to be active in students' post-secondary transition. Subsequently, school counselors have a unique role as a school-based mental health professional who serves students at all three tiers, offering universal prevention for all students and services for students with elevated needs. In addition, school counselors have the privilege of developing long-lasting relationships with students and families, as they commonly serve students for consecutive years. The professional identity of school counselors is continuing to crystalize as they advocate to be data-driven leaders in schools, implementing comprehensive school counseling programs that are culturally responsive, based on each school's unique needs.

SUMMARY

In this chapter, the authors provided a broad overview of school counseling, including a brief history of the profession and current trends, as well as background information on comprehensive school counseling programs, such as direct and indirect student services and accountability. School counselors' roles in crises and use of multi-tiered system of supports as a framework for understanding their roles were discussed. The chapter concluded by describing the unique roles of school counselors at each of the three educational levels—elementary, middle, and high school—and presented setting-specific school counseling strengths and challenges. Finally, please consider the following quote by Edward Everett Hale:

> I am only one,
> But still I am one.
> I cannot do everything,
> But still I can do something …
> I will not refuse to do the something that I can do.

School counseling is a big job, a tiring job, a meaningful job, a calling. No two days are alike. School counselors have the gift of making a difference to youth, their families, and the school as a whole. And, as Edward Everett Hale said, school counselors have the opportunity to do *something*.

Additional Resources

American School Counselor Association: www.schoolcounselor.org

American School Counselor Association's Ethical Standards for School Counselors: https://www.schoolcounselor.org/asca/media/asca/Ethics/EthicalStandards 2016.pdf

ASCA Mindsets and Behaviors for Student Success: http://www.schoolcounselor.org/ asca/media/asca/home/mindsetsbehaviors.pdf

ASCA Mindsets and Behaviors online database: http://schoolcounselor.org/school-counselors-members/about-asca/mindsets-behaviors

ASCA Mindsets and Behaviors Program Planning Tool: http://schoolcounselor.org/ asca/media/asca/RAMP/M-BProgramPlanningTool.pdf

Evidence-Based School Counseling Conference: http://coehs.nku.edu/centers/ nkcee/center_at_work/profdevinitiatives/EBSCConference.html

EZAnalyze, an excel-based tool for educators: http://www.ezanalyze.com

Social story resources: http://www.friendshipcircle.org/blog/2013/02/11/12-computer-programs-websites-and-apps-for-making-social-stories/

Steen, Henfield, and Booker (2014) proposed a group counseling model that integrated both students' academics and personal/social development, called Achieving Success Everyday

Suggested Readings

American School Counselor Association (2012). *ASCA national model: A framework for school counseling programs*, 3rd ed. Alexandria, VA: Author.

Dimmitt, C., Carey, J. C., Hatch, T. (2007). *Evidence-based school counseling: Making a difference with data-driven practices*. Thousand Oaks, CA: Corwin Press.

Executive Office of the President (2015). Every student succeeds act: A progress report on elementary and secondary education. Retrieved from https://www. whitehouse.gov/sites/whitehouse.gov/files/documents/ESSA_Progress_Report. pdf

Goodman-Scott, E., Betters-Bubon, J., and Donohue, M. (2016). Aligning comprehensive school counseling programs and positive behavioral interventions and supports to maximize school counselors' efforts. *Professional School Counseling* 19 (1), 57–67. doi: 10.5330/1096-2409-19.1.57

Grothaus, T. and Johnson, K. F. (2012). *Making diversity work: Creating culturally competent school counseling programs*. Alexandria, VA: American School Counselor Association.

Gysbers, N. C. and Henderson, P. (2012). *Developing and managing your school guidance and counseling program*, 5th ed. Alexandria, VA: American Counseling Association.

Hatch, T. (2013). *The use of data in school counseling*. Thousand Oaks, CA: Corwin Press.

Holcomb-McCoy, C. (2007). *School counseling to close the achievement gap: A social justice framework for success*. Thousand Oaks, CA: Corwin.

Kaffenberger, C. and Young, A. (2013). *Making DATA work*. Alexandria, VA: American School Counselor Association.

Lambie, G. W. and Williamson, L. L. (2004). The challenge to change from guidance counseling to professional school counseling: A historical proposition. *Professional School Counseling* 8, 134–131.

Shepard, J. M., Shahidullah, J. D., and Carlson, J. S. (2013). *Counseling students in levels 2 and 3: A PBIS/RTI Guide*. Thousand Oaks, CA: Corwin Press.

Glossary

Achievement gap: Educational disparities between groups of students defined by characteristics including race, ethnicity, gender, and socioeconomic status

Direct student services: Providing services to students within the academic, career, and social/emotional domains, such as through classroom guidance lessons, group activities, individual planning, individual and group counseling, and crisis response

Disaggregate: Separating data by identifiers, such as race, ethnicity, gender, special education placement, giftedness, free and reduced lunch, etc.

Indirect student services: School counselors work with key adult stakeholders, such as parents/guardians, teachers, administrators, school staff and more, to positively impact students' academic, career, and social-emotional development and to promote equity within schools or through referrals to other service providers

Individual crisis: Perceiving/experiencing an event or situation to a degree of difficulty that exceeds ones' current resources and coping mechanisms

Interpersonal influence: Influencing school stakeholders to have a shared vision and ideas, developing relationships with stakeholders, understanding the school climate, and sharing common goals

Multi-tiered systems: Three-tiered, systemic approaches to intervention that include tier one, or universal prevention, that is provided to all students; tier two, or secondary prevention, which includes small group interventions, and tier three, or tertiary prevention, which includes individualized interventions and services in order for students to be successful in school

Needs assessment: Data-driven or perception-based assessments that measure the present status of the school and provides information on needed improvement

Outcome data: Data that shows how an intervention/activity impacted students' outcomes, such as attendance, behavior, or achievement

Perception data: Data involving students' knowledge, attitudes, and skills

Process data: Data that describes the process of an event or intervention, such as the number of students involved, the content of material, etc.

Professional efficacy: School counselors' self-confidence and perceptions of themselves as leaders

Psychological first aid: Similar to general first aid, but with the specific aim of reducing distress and enhancing coping and functioning in the immediate aftermath of a crisis

Resourceful problem solving: Utilizing creative methods for solving problems, advocating for change, and obtaining related resources

SMART goals: School counseling goals that are specific, measurable, attainable, reasonable, and timely

Social/emotional learning (SEL): The process through which children and adults acquire and effectively apply the knowledge, attitudes, and skills necessary to understand and manage emotions, set and achieve positive goals, feel and show empathy for others, establish and maintain positive relationships, and make responsible decisions (Collaborative for Academic, Social, and Emotional Learning, n.d. para. 1)

Social justice advocacy: Leading through advocating for students, as well as challenging inequalities and the status quo

Systemic collaboration: Partnering with stakeholders to enact change in the school systemically, including developing new programs and goals

Notes

1   A special thanks to Ms. Stephanie Smith-Durkin for her assistance with this chapter.
2   To learn more about Social Stories, see Goodman-Scott and Carlisle, 2014.

References

Amatea, E. (2013). From separation to collaboration: The changing paradigms of family–school relations. In E. Amatea (ed.), *Building culturally responsive family–school relationships*, 2nd ed. (pp. 27–45). Upper Saddle River, NJ: Pearson.

Amatea, E. and West-Olatunji, C. (2007). Joining the conversation about educating our poorest children: Emerging leadership roles for school counselors in high poverty schools. *Professional School Counseling* 11, 81–89.

American School Counselor Association (2004). *ASCA national standards for students*. Alexandria, VA: Author.

American School Counselor Association (2010a). The school counselor and school–family–community partnerships. Retrieved from https://www.schoolcounselor.org/asca/media/asca/PositionStatements/PS_Partnerships.pdf

American School Counselor Association (2010b). Ethical standards for school counselors. Retrieved from http://www.schoolcounselor.org/asca/media/asca/Resource%20Center/Legal%20and%20Ethical%20Issues/Sample%20Documents/EthicalStandards2010.pdf

American School Counselor Association (2012). *The ASCA national model: A framework for school counseling programs*, 3rd ed. Alexandria, VA: Author.

American School Counselor Association (2014a). *ASCA mindsets and behaviors for student success: K-12 college- and career-readiness standards for every student*. Alexandria, VA: Author.

American School Counselor Association (2014b). The school counselor and multi-tiered system of supports. Retrieved from http://schoolcounselor.org/asca/media/asca/PositionStatements/PS_MultitieredSupportSystem.pdf

American School Counselor Association (2015a). State school counseling mandates and legislation. Retrieved from http://schoolcounselor.org/school-counselors-members/careers-roles/state-school-counseling-mandates-and-legislation

American School Counselor Association (2015b). The school counselor and child abuse and neglect prevention. Retrieved from https://www.schoolcounselor.org/asca/media/asca/PositionStatements/PS_ChildAbuse.pdf

American School Counselor Association (2016). About ASCA. Retrieved from http://www.schoolcounselor.org/school-counselors-members/about-asca-%281%29

American School Counselor Association (n.d.). The role of the school counselor. Retrieved from https://www.schoolcounselor.org/administrators/role-of-the-school-counselor.aspx

Baker, S. B., Robichaud, T. A., Dietrich, V. C. W., Wells, S. C., and Schreck, R. E. (2009). School counselor consultation: A pathway to advocacy, collaboration, and leadership. *Professional School Counseling* 12, 200–206.

Bartlett, J. (1968). *Bartlett's familiar quotations*. New York, NY: Little, Brown, & Co.

Brigman, G., Mullis, F., Webb, L., and White, J. (2005). *School counselor consultation: Skills for working effectively with parents, teachers, and other school personnel*. Hoboken, NJ: Wiley.

Brock, S. (2013). Preparing for the school crisis response. In J. Sandoval (ed.), *Crisis counseling intervention and prevention in the schools* (pp. 19–30). New York, NY: Routledge.

Brown-Chidsey, R. and Bickford, R. (2016). *Practical handbook of multi-tiered systems of support*. New York, NY: The Guilford Press.

Bryan, J. A. and Griffin, D. (2010). A multidimensional study of school–family–community partnership involvement: school, school counselor, and training factors. *Professional School Counseling* 14, 75–86.

Brymer M., Taylor M., Escudero P., Jacobs A., Kronenberg M., Macy R., and Vogel, J. (2012). *Psychological first aid for schools: Field operations guide*, 2nd ed. Los Angeles: National Child Traumatic Stress Network.

Burkard, A. W., Gillen, M., Martinez, M. J., and Skytte, S. L. (2012). Implementation challenges and training needs for comprehensive school counseling programs in Wisconsin high schools. *Professional School Counseling* 16, 136–145. doi: 10.5330/PSC.n.2012-16.136

Burnham, J. J. and Jackson, C. M. (2000). School counselor roles: Discrepancies between actual practice and existing models. *Professional School Counseling* 4, 41–49.

Carey, J., Harrington, K., Martin, I. and Hoffman, D. (2012). A statewide evaluation of the outcomes of the implementation of ASCA national model school counseling programs in rural and suburban Nebraska high schools. *Professional School Counseling* 16, 100–107. doi: 10.5330/PSC.n.2012-16.100

Carey, J., Harrington, K., Martin, I., and Stevenson, D. (2012). A statewide evaluation of the outcomes of the implementation of ASCA national model school counseling programs in Utah high schools. *Professional School Counseling* 16, 89–99. doi: 10.5330/PSC.n.2012-16.89

Carnevale, A. P., Smith, N., and Strohl, J. (2013). Recovery: Job growth and education requirements through 2020. Retrieved from https://cew.georgetown.edu/wp-content/uploads/2014/11/Recovery2020.FR_.Web_.pdf

Center for Disease Control, National Center for Injury Prevention and Control. (2015). Understanding bullying. Retrieved from http://www.cdc.gov/violenceprevention/pdf/bullying_factsheet.pdf

Choi, N., Chang, M., Kim, S., and Reio, T. (2014). A structural model of parent involvement with demographic and academic variables. *Psychology in Schools* 52, 154–167.

Cholewa, B., Burkhardt, C., and Hull, M. (2016). Are school counselors impacting underrepresented students' thinking about post-secondary education? A nationally representative study. *Professional School Counseling* 19, 144–154. doi: 10.5330/1096-2409-19.1.144

Cholewa, B., Goodman-Scott, E., Thomas, A. and Cook, J. (under review). *Teachers' experiences consulting with school counselors: A phenomenological study.*

Clemens, E. V., Milsom, A., and Cashwell, C. C. (2009). Using leader–member exchange theory to examine principal–school counselor relationship, school counselors' roles, job satisfaction, and turnover intentions. *Professional School Counseling* 13, 75–85. doi:10.5330/PSC.n.2010

Collaborative for Academic, Social, and Emotional Learning (n.d.). What is social and emotional learning? Retrieved from http://www.casel.org/social-and-emotional-learning/

Dahir, C. A. (2001). The national standards for school counseling programs: Development and implementation. *Professional School Counseling* 4, 320–327.

Davis, T. E. (2015). *Exploring school counseling: Professional practices and perspectives.* Stamford, CT: Cengage Learning.

Dimmitt, C., Carey, J. C., and Hatch, T. (2007). *Evidence-based school counseling: Making a difference with data-driven practices.* Thousand Oaks, CA: Corwin Press.

Dinkmeyer, J., Carlson, J., and Michel, R. (2016). *Consultation: Creating school-based Interventions*, 4th ed. New York, NY: Routledge.

Education Trust. (2016). Who we are. Retrieved from https://edtrust.org/who-we-are/

El Nokali, N., Bachman, H., and Votruba-Drzal, E. (2010). Parent involvement and children's academic and social development in elementary school. *Child Development* 81, 988–1005.

Erford, B. (2015a). Consultation, collaboration and encouraging parental involvement. In B. Erford (ed.). *Transforming the school counseling profession*, 4th ed. (pp. 303–324). Upper Saddle River, NJ: Pearson.

Erford, B. (2015b). Counseling individuals and groups in schools. In B. Erford (ed.), *Transforming the school counseling profession*, 4th ed. (pp. 279–302). Upper Saddle River, NJ: Pearson.

Erford, B. (2015c). The ASCA National Model: Developing a comprehensive, developmental school counseling program. In B. T. Erford (ed.), *Transforming the school counseling profession*, 4th ed. (pp. 29–44). Boston: Pearson.

Erford, B., Lee, V., and Rock, E. (2015). Systemic approaches to counseling students experiencing complex and specialized problems. In B. Erford (ed.) *Transforming the school counseling profession*, 4th ed. (pp. 325–349). Upper Saddle River, NJ: Pearson.

Executive Office of the President (2015). Every student succeeds act: A progress report on elementary and secondary education. Retrieved from https://www.whitehouse.gov/sites/whitehouse.gov/files/documents/ESSA_Progress_Report.pdf

EZAnalyze (n.d.). Excel-based tools for educators. Retrieved from http://www.ezanalyze.com

Farrington, C. A., Roderick, M., Allensworth, E., Nagaoka, J., Keyes, T. S., Johnson, D. W., and Beechum, N. O. (2012). Teaching adolescents to become learners: The role of noncognitive factors in shaping school performance. A critical literature review. Chicago: University of Chicago Consortium on Chicago School Research. Retrieved from https://consortium.uchicago.edu/sites/default/files/publications/Noncognitive%20Report.pdf

Galassi, J. P. and Akos, P. (2012). Preparing school counselors to promote academic development. *Counselor Education and Supervision* 51, 50–63. doi: 10.1002/j.1556-6978.2012.00004.x

Gibbons, M. M., Diambra, J. F. and Buchanan, D. K. (2010). School counselor perceptions and attitudes about collaboration. *Journal of School Counseling* 8 (34). Retrieved from http://www.jsc.montana.edu/articles/v8n34.pdf

Glander, M. (2015). Documentation to the NCES Common Core of Data State Nonfiscal Survey of Public Elementary/Secondary Education: School Year 2013–14 (NCES 2015-146). U.S. Department of Education. Washington, DC: National Center for Education Statistics. Retrieved from http://nces.ed.gov/pubsearch/pubsinfo.asp?pubid=2015146

Goodman-Scott, E. (2011). School counselors and principals: Creating a powerful partnership. *VSCA Voices* (Fall), 7–8.

Goodman-Scott, E. (2015). School counselors' perceptions of their academic preparedness and job activities. *Counselor Education and Supervision* 54, 57–67.

Goodman-Scott, E., Betters-Bubon, J., and Donohue, M. (2016). Aligning comprehensive school counseling programs and positive behavioral interventions and supports to maximize school counselors' efforts. *Professional School Counseling* 19 (1), 57–67. doi: 10.5330/1096-2409-19.1.57

Goodman-Scott, E. and Carlisle, R. (2014). School counselors' roles in creating and implementing social stories to serve students with autism spectrum disorder. *Professional School Counseling* 18(1), 158–168.

Grothaus, T. and Johnson, K. F. (2012). *Making diversity work: Creating culturally competent school counseling programs*. Alexandria, VA: American School Counselor Association.

Gysbers, N. C. and Henderson, P. (2012). *Developing and managing your school guidance and counseling program*, 5th ed. Alexandria, VA: American Counseling Association.

Harrington, J. and Daughhetee, C. (2014). Risk assessment and intervention: Suicide and homicide. In L. Jackson-Cherry and B. Erford (eds.) *Crisis assessment, intervention and prevention*, 2nd ed. (pp. 85–125). Columbus, OH: Pearson Merrill.

Hess, R. S., Magnuson, S. and Beeler, L. M. (2012). *Counseling children and adolescents in the schools*. Thousand Oaks, CA: Sage.

Holcomb-McCoy, C. (2007). *School counseling to close the achievement gap: A social justice framework for success*. Thousand Oaks, CA: Corwin.

Holcomb-McCoy, C. (2010). Involving low-income parents and parents of color in college readiness activities: An exploratory study. *Professional School Counseling* 14, 115–124.

James, R. K. and Gilliland, B. E. (2016). *Crisis intervention strategies*, 8th ed. Belmont, CA: Cole-Cengage Learning.

Kena, G., Musu-Gillette, L., Robinson, J., Wang, X., Rathbun, A., Zhang, J., Wilkinson-Flicker, S., Barmer, A., and Dunlop Velez, E. (2015). The Condition of Education 2015 (NCES 2015-144). U.S. Department of Education, National Center for Education Statistics. Washington, DC. Retrieved from http://nces.ed.gov/pubsearch

Lambie, G. W. and Williamson, L. L. (2004). The challenge to change from guidance counseling to professional school counseling: A historical proposition. *Professional School Counseling* 8, 134–131.

Lee, V. V. and Goodnough, G. E. (2015). Systemic, data-driven school counseling practice and programming for equity. In B. T. Erford (ed.), *Transforming the school counseling profession*, 4th ed. (pp. 66–91). Boston: Pearson.

Martin, I., Carey, J., and DeCoster, K. (2009). A national study of the current status of state school counseling models. *Professional School Counseling* 12, 378–386. 10.5330/PSC.n.2010-12.378

Martin, P. (2002). Transforming school counseling: A national perspective. *Theory into Practice* 41, 148–153. doi: 10.1207/s15430421tip4103_2

Martin, P. J. (2015). Transformational thinking in today's schools. In B. T. Erford (ed.), *Transforming the school counseling profession*, 4th ed. (pp. 45–65). Boston: Pearson.

Merikangas, K. R., He, J., Burstein, M., Swanson, S. A., Avenevoli, A., Cui, L., and Swendsen, J. (2010). Lifetime prevalence of mental disorders in U.S. adolescents: Results from the national comorbidity study-adolescent supplement (NCS-A). *Journal of the American Academy of Child and Adolescent Psychiatry* 49, 980–989. doi: 10.1016/j.jaac.2010.05.017

National Center for Education Statistics (2015). *Student reports of bullying and cyber-bullying: Results from the 2013 school crimes supplement to the national crime victimization survey*. Retrieved from http://nces.ed.gov/pubs2015/2015056.pdf

National Office for School Counselor Advocacy (NOSCA) (2010*). Eight components of college and career readiness counseling*. Retrieved from https://secure-media.collegeboard.org/digitalServices/pdf/nosca/11b_4416_8_Components_WEB_111107.pdf

Noltemeyer, A. L., Marie, R., Mcloughlin, C., and Vanderwood, M. (2015). Relationship between school suspension and student outcomes: A meta-analysis. *School Psychology Review* 44(2), 224–240.

Office of Special Education Programs, Technical Assistance Center on Positive Behavioral Interventions and Supports, United States Department of Education (2010). *Blueprint and self-assessment: Positive behavioral interventions and supports*. Retrieved from http://www.pbis.org/common/cms/files/pbisresources/SWPBS_ImplementationBlueprint_vSep_23_2010.pdf

Perera-Diltz, D., Moe, J. L., and Mason, K. L. (2011). An exploratory study in school counselor consultation engagement. *Journal of School Counseling* 9 (13). Retrieved from http://www.jsc.montana.edu/articles/v9n13.pdf

Rayle, A. D. and Adams, J. R. (2007). An exploration of 21st-century school counselors' daily work activities. *Journal of School Counseling* 5 (8). Retrieved from http://files.eric.ed.gov/fulltext/EJ901169.pdf

Scarborough, J. L. and Culbreth, J. R. (2008). Examining discrepancies between actual and preferred practice of school counselors. *Journal of Counseling and Development* 86, 446–459. doi:10.1002/j.1556-6678.2008.tb00533.x

Schellenberg, R. C. (2007). Standards blending: Aligning school counseling programs with school academic achievement missions. *Virginia Counselors Journal* 29, 13–20.

Sink, C. A. (2008). Elementary school counselors and teachers: Collaborators for higher student achievement. *Elementary School Journal* 108, 445–458. doi: 10.1086/589473

Sink, C. A. and MacDonald, G. (1998). The status of comprehensive guidance and counseling in the United States. *Professional School Counseling* 2, 88–94.

Sink, C. A. and Stroh, H. R. (2003). Raising achievement test scores of early elementary school students through comprehensive school counseling programs. *Professional School Counseling* 6, 350–364.

Sink, C. A., Akos, P., Turnbull, R. J. and Mvududu, M. (2008). An investigation of comprehensive school counseling programs and academic achievement in Washington state middle schools. *Professional School Counseling* 12, 43–53. doi:10.5330/PSC.n.2010-12.43

Steen, S., Henfield, M. S. and Booker, B. (2014). The achieving success everyday group counseling model: Implications for professional school counselors. *The Journal for Specialist in Group Work* 39, 29–46. doi: 10.1080/01933922.2013.861886

Stelmacher, Z. T. (1995). Assessing suicidal clients. In J. N. Butcher (ed.), *Clinical personality assessment: Practical approaches* (pp. 366–379). New York, NY: Oxford University Press.

Stone, C. B. and Dahir, C. A. (2016). *The transformed school counselor.* Boston, MA: Cengage Learning.

Suárez-Orozco, C., Onaga, M., and Lardemelle, C. D. (2010). Promoting academic engagement among immigrant adolescents through school–family–community collaboration. *Professional School Counseling* 14, 15–26.

Suárez-Orozco, C., Suárez-Orozco, M., and Todorova, I. (2010). *Learning a new land: Immigrant students in American society.* Cambridge, MA: Belknap Press of Harvard University Press.

Sugai, G., O'Keeffe, B. V., and Fallon, L. M. (2012). A contextual consideration of culture and school-wide positive behavior support. *Journal of Positive Behavior Interventions* 14, 197–208. doi: 10.1177/1098300711426334

The White House (n.d.). Higher education. Retrieved from https://www.whitehouse.gov/issues/education/higher-education

U.S. Department of Education. (2014). Guiding principles: A resource guide for implementing school climate and discipline. Retrieved from http://www2.ed.gov/policy/gen/guid/schooldiscipline/guiding-principles.pdf

U.S. Department of Education, Office of Elementary and Secondary Education, Office of Safe and Healthy Students. (2013). Guide for developing high-quality school emergency operations plans. Washington, DC: US Department of Education

Warren, J. M. (2013). School counselor consultation: Teachers' experiences with rational emotive behavior therapy. *Journal of Rational-Emotive and Cognitive-Behavior Therapy* 31, 1–15.

Webb, L. D. and Brigman, G. A. (2006). Student success skills: Tools and strategies for improved academic and social outcomes. *Professional School Counseling* 10 (2), 112–120.

Wight, V. R., Chau, M., and Aratani, Y. (2011). Who are America's poor children? The official story. Retrieved from National Center for Children in Poverty website: http://www.nccp.org/publications/pub_1001.html

Wilder, S. (2014). Effects of parental involvement on academic achievement: A meta-synthesis. *Educational Review* 66 (3), 377–397.

Young, A. and Bryan, J. (2015). The school counselor leadership survey: Instrument development and exploratory factor analysis. *Professional School Counseling* 19 (1), 1–15.

Young, A. and Kaffenberger, C. (2011). The beliefs and practices of school counselors who use data to implement comprehensive school counseling programs. *Professional School Counseling* 15 (2), 67–76.

Young, A., Hardy, V., Hamilton, C., Biernesser, Sun, L.-L., and Niebergall, S. (2009). Empowering students: Using data to transform a bullying prevention and intervention program. *Professional School Counseling* 12 (6), 413–420.

Ziomek-Daigle, J. (2015). *School counseling classroom guidance: Prevention, accountability, and outcomes*. Thousand Oaks, CA: SAGE Publications.

Ziomek-Daigle, J., Goodman-Scott, E., Cavin, J., and Donohue, P. (in press). Integrating multi-tiered systems of support into comprehensive school counseling programs. *The Professional Counselor*.

CHAPTER 8

Counseling Children and Adolescents in Clinical Mental Health Settings

A. Stephen Lenz, Rochelle Cade, Maggie M. Parker, Samantha Klassen, and Claudia Schmidt

I propose a national mental health program to assist in the inauguration of a wholly new emphasis and approach to care for the mentally ill. This approach relies primarily upon the new knowledge and new drugs acquired and developed in recent years which make it possible for most of the mentally ill to be successfully and quickly treated in their own communities and returned to a useful place in society.

John F. Kennedy in his address to U.S. Congress, February 5, 1963

CHAPTER OBJECTIVES

After reviewing this chapter, readers will:

- understand the current state of child and adolescent counseling and the process through which children and adolescents may enter into the counseling relationships
- identify interventions utilized to meet the mental health and developmental needs of children and adolescents, as well as, the wide variety of settings wherein counselors can serve the mental health needs of children and adolescents and the level of care provided within each
- be familiar with the strengths and weaknesses of each setting where children and adolescents receive services
- have a greater understanding of common therapeutic modalities utilized when counseling children and adolescents
- understand how to gather information and formulate accurate conceptualizations of child and adolescent clients and the process of becoming a professional counselor
- understand the differences among options for licensure and credentialing for clinical mental health counselors working with children and adolescents
- recognize and discuss current issues regarding the different settings wherein child and adolescent mental health counseling can occur, as well some of the unique developmental needs of children and adolescents

INTRODUCTION

Clinical mental health counselors provide a core set of services to children and adolescents to promote their optimal development and functioning. The niche settings within which these services are delivered are integral for organizing individuals' attitudes and approaches to coping with adversity that will be called upon across the lifespan. Albeit a prominent professional niche, clinical mental health counseling settings are nuanced in nature because of the many ways in which they contribute to the public behavioral health infrastructure. In this chapter, you will be introduced to counseling children and adolescents in clinical mental health settings, and, specifically, the differences among agencies and activities counselors engage with clients and their families in these respective settings.

EVOLUTION OF COMMUNITY COUNSELING AND MENTAL HEALTH COUNSELING

It can be argued that there are now more community-based resources for treating children and adolescents than at any other time in the history of the United States. The availability of mental health services across the continuum to which children and their families currently have access are products of several socio-political activities that shaped the clinical mental health counseling profession. Most noteworthy among these may be the Community Mental Health Act that was signed into law in 1963. This landmark piece of legislation established and funded a community-based framework for treating individuals with severe mental illness. This alternative was disparate from traditional models of institutionalizing individuals for several years, where they were vulnerable to receiving inhumane treatments and de-socialization. Within this new system, children and adolescents experiencing acute psychiatric crises are treated and stabilized within hospital settings, but then discharged to community-based providers who provide continuing coordination and provision of evidence-supported services. Most often, these community-based providers are represented by a combination of government, county-operated, non-profit, and for-profit organizations, funded through a patchwork of financial sources including local, regional, and federal governmental funds, grants, and private funding.

The Community Mental Health Act (1963) also spurred other important events, one of which was the increased demand for highly qualified service providers who could facilitate increased access to prevention, intervention, and post-intervention care. As a result, educational, training, and licensure standards for clinical mental health counselors (CMHCs) has become relatively standardized, and these professionals have a unique identity within community-based settings where they provide important services to children, adolescents, and families as part of an integrated care team (see Figure 8.1). It is important to note that as a member of the integrated treatment team CMHCs who specialize in working with children and adolescents are the only individuals with counseling as their primary purpose. This is in contrast to other professionals whose education and professional activities are more closely

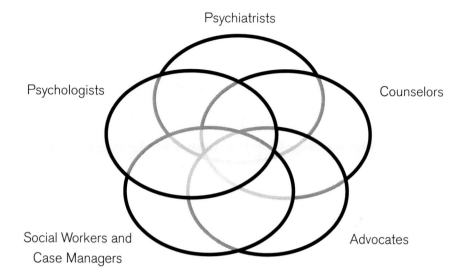

Figure 8.1 Model of integrated care within community mental health agencies

aligned with prescribing, assessment, case management, or systems-based advocacy. Additionally, although CMHCs typically work within care systems that are informed by a medical model of client conceptualization, CMHCs provide services using wellness-focused, developmentally oriented paradigms of care.

Continuum of Care and Service Provision

It is important to consider that the system for child and adolescent care established by the Community Mental Health Act (1963) is contemporarily represented by a continuum of care that allows for different amounts and types of service provision based on the needs of a youth. Within this framework, level of need is most often determined by (a) risk for harm to self or others, (b) psychiatric symptom severity, (c) level of functioning, and (d) degree of access and utilization of resources. With these factors considered, counselors can identify the setting and types of services that will provide stabilization and recovery from psychological distress. To conceptualize this, it is important to consider the broader picture first. As depicted in Figure 8.2, the continuum of care settings can range from very restrictive to being characterized by full autonomy and full hourly contact as needed. It is also important to note that in each setting along the continuum of care there are differences among the core set of services provided to clients.

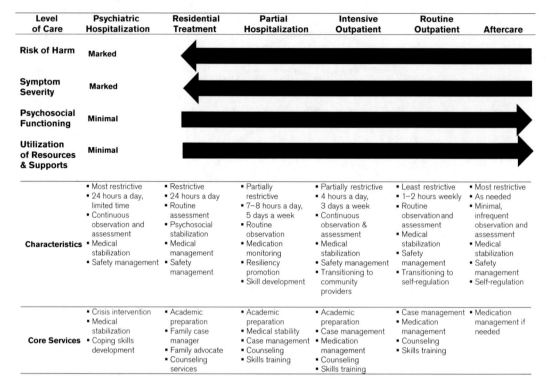

Level of Care	Psychiatric Hospitalization	Residential Treatment	Partial Hospitalization	Intensive Outpatient	Routine Outpatient	Aftercare
Risk of Harm	Marked					
Symptom Severity	Marked					
Psychosocial Functioning	Minimal					
Utilization of Resources & Supports	Minimal					
Characteristics	▪ Most restrictive ▪ 24 hours a day, limited time ▪ Continuous observation and assessment ▪ Medical stabilization ▪ Safety management	▪ Restrictive ▪ 24 hours a day ▪ Routine assessment ▪ Psychosocial stabilization ▪ Medical management ▪ Safety management	▪ Partially restrictive ▪ 7–8 hours a day, 5 days a week ▪ Routine observation ▪ Medication monitoring ▪ Resiliency promotion ▪ Skill development	▪ Partially restrictive ▪ 4 hours a day, 3 days a week ▪ Continuous observation & assessment ▪ Medical stabilization ▪ Safety management ▪ Transitioning to community providers	▪ Least restrictive ▪ 1–2 hours weekly ▪ Routine observation and assessment ▪ Medical stabilization ▪ Safety management ▪ Transitioning to self-regulation	▪ Most restrictive ▪ As needed ▪ Minimal, infrequent observation and assessment ▪ Medical stabilization ▪ Safety management ▪ Self-regulation
Core Services	▪ Crisis intervention ▪ Medical stabilization ▪ Coping skills development	▪ Academic preparation ▪ Family case manager ▪ Family advocate ▪ Counseling services	▪ Academic preparation ▪ Medical stability ▪ Case management ▪ Counseling ▪ Skills training	▪ Academic preparation ▪ Case management ▪ Medication management ▪ Counseling ▪ Skills training	▪ Case management ▪ Medication management ▪ Counseling ▪ Skills training	▪ Medication management if needed

Figure 8.2 Characteristics and core services across levels of care for children and adolescents

MODALITIES OF INTERVENTION AND BEST PRACTICES ACROSS CLINICAL MENTAL HEALTH SETTINGS

Individual Counseling

Between the ages of 4 and 8, children begin to separate more easily from parents; however, relationships remain important and a valuable tool for positive growth (Ray, 2015). During this developmental period, the therapeutic relationship between child and counselor can serve as a tool through which children can promote self-expression, access to the subconscious, indirect teaching, stress inoculation, catharsis, positive affect, and a sense of self (Schaeffer and Drewes, 2009). Therefore, when working with young children, it is prudent to implement play therapy or play-based interventions that draw on this natural means for personal expression and interaction. By contrast, interventions with older children and adolescents characteristically capitalize on cognitive developments that promote a sense of personal accountability, a more defined sense of agency, abstract conceptualization, and application of logical reasoning to problem solving across contexts. Individually, counselors within an agency setting often utilize their personal practice theory when working with clients, though some systems of care may characteristically implement any number of evidence-supportive practices dictated by funding sources or third-party payers. Examples of individual interventions with a strong evidence base for adolescents include cognitive behavior therapy (Hofmann, Asnaani, Vonk, Sawyer, and Fang, 2012), solution-focused brief counseling (De Shazer and Dolan, 2007), and therapeutic psychoeducation (Lukens and McFarlan, 2004).

Group Counseling

As children develop, their focus of relationships shifts from parents to peers, which makes group interventions an effective resource for skill development, socialization, and normalization of experiences with mental health symptoms and developmental issues (Ray, 2016). Groups utilize children's natural developmental tendencies to gravitate towards peers, and thus can promote empowerment regardless of gender, age, presenting concern, family dynamics, or other psychosocial variables. One of the obvious benefits of groups in a community setting is that groups are time effective and allow counselors to provide services to a greater number of clients. Additionally, the group format naturally facilitates trying new behaviors, roles, and perspectives in a relationally safe environment before transferring them into a child's system. Many groups with children and adolescents will focus on activities such as psychoeducation, interpersonal and coping skills acquisition, developmental issues, and a variety of guidance activities related to their treatment goals. It is important to remember that as wonderful as community-based groups can be for supporting development and symptom recovery with children and adolescents, they often require accommodations that take into account short attention spans, limited vocabulary or experience to describe their feelings and experiences, social pressure, lack of control over their environment, and need for structure. Examples of group interventions with a strong evidence base for children and adolescents include psychoeducational groups (Freres, Gillham, Reivich, and Shatté, 2002), social skills groups (Henderson and Thompson, 2016), group play (Ginott, 1961), expressive arts groups (Bratton, Ceballos, and Ferbee, 2009), activity therapy (Zuchelli, 1993), or cognitive behavioral groups (Clark, DeBar, Ludman, Asarnov, and Jaycox, 2002).

Family-Focused Counseling

Children and adolescents spend little time with their counselors. Because of the power of helping relationships and use of evidence-supported interventions, this time is useful, but it may only be a few hours weekly, nonetheless. In between sessions, clients are nested within a family system that influences the arc of physical, relational, spiritual, and moral development. Therefore, one best practice for treating children and adolescents in community settings is always to include important collaterals, which are most frequently going to be close family members such as a parent or sibling. These individuals can support their recovery through reinforcement of skill development and advocacy within the family system. Although the frequency of including the family may range from every few sessions to every session, there is no denying the vital nature of the primary relationship between children and important family members to promote treatment effectiveness (Ray, 2015).

There are myriad family-focused programs that clinicians can utilize within an agency setting. Examples of family-focused interventions with a strong evidence base for children and adolescents include filial therapy (Bratton, Landreth, and Kellum, 2006), parent–child interaction therapy (McNeil and Hembree-Kigin, 2010), functional family therapy (Alexander and Parson, 1982), and multisystemic family therapy (Henggeler, Sheidow, and Lee, 2007). Involving parents in the treatment of adolescents is especially important, despite their developmental desire to separate from their parents (Berk, 2013).

With the passing of the Community Mental Health Act (1963), the mental health treatment of children and adolescents has shifted from long-term institutionalization to short-term hospitalization and transitions to community-based care. Clinical mental health counselors provide unique mental health services tailored to specific subgroups of children and adolescents. Mental health services for children and adolescents include individual, group, and family counseling, and ensure that these utilize developmentally appropriate interventions to meet the unique needs of children and adolescents. Counselors provide these services within a multitude of settings within the public and private sector.

COUNSELING AT CLINICAL MENTAL HEALTH COUNSELING AGENCIES

Clinical mental health agencies are funded by federal, state, and county governments, as well as private and not-for-profit agencies (National Council for Behavioral Health, 2015). Within these agencies, clients typically receive medical and social services, including individual, group, and family counseling. Depending upon the provider agency, some services are free, while others accept private or government-sponsored insurance, allowing individuals to seek services regardless of their financial status (National Council for Behavioral Health, 2015). Oftentimes, these agencies implement some form of integrated care represented by multiple categories of service providers under one roof or as part of a formal collaborative network (see Figure 8.1). From this perspective, having access to psychiatrists, psychiatric nurses, psychologists, professional counselors, case managers, and family advocates contributes to best practice for resource utilization by facilitating access to multiple services at a single site and possibly during a single visit.

Non-profit Agencies

Non-profit mental health agencies provide valuable mental health services to members of the community, thus allowing all individuals to receive mental health services. These services are provided at little to no cost to individuals, as a result of government and private grants. Within non-profit settings, the clientele may present with greater hope for the future and internal locus of control. In addition, clients within a non-profit mental health organization are more likely to have sought services from other professionals (Segal, Hardiman, and Hodges, 2002).

Direct Versus Indirect Services

When conceptualizing the roles and activities of counselors, most people generally envision direct service provision—face-to-face interactions between counselors and clients delivering the individual, group, or family-focused interventions previously discussed. However, there is another class of activities: indirect services, which require considerable time and effort from counselors and may be equally as helpful to clients in supporting their journey to wellbeing and recovery. Indirect services include activities such as training others, monitoring client progress, engaging in or delivering clinical supervision, peer consultation, collaborating with teachers or parents, communicating with stakeholders and third-party payers, developing and modifying materials for client use, advocacy, and reporting. In many mental health agencies, counselors spend a significant amount of time in the provision of indirect services as a member of an integrated treatment team so that clients have access to necessary services and challenges to their progress are mitigated (Waters, 2015).

Strengths of Setting

Working within a community mental health agency can be highly rewarding. A survey of counselors at many non-profit or other community-based agencies revealed a general sense of difference-making associated with providing services to children and adolescents who are experiencing myriad, and often acute, emotional and behavioral difficulties (Waters, 2015). Counselors in these settings feel a sense of accomplishment in assisting children and adolescents who may not be able to receive help elsewhere or are generally underserved by other community resources. From a practical perspective, agency work has some tremendous implications for understanding the continuum of care and establishing a sound foundation of best practices for integral activities such as screening, interviewing, documentation, treatment planning, and liability management. In addition, counselors in agency settings are often compelled to use evidence-supported treatments that are manualized, components-based, and highly efficacious when implemented with fidelity. Also, working within an agency or clinic allows for access to insurance panels, support staff, and group liability coverage that may logistically be quite cumbersome without that available infrastructure. Finally, agency settings often provide a degree of stability through provision of health insurance, medical benefits, a salaried position, set work schedules, and paid leave to a greater degree than many other settings (Zwolinksi and Zwolinski, 2011).

Challenges of Setting

Regardless of setting, there are always challenges when engaging in mental health counseling. Within agency settings, clinicians may become disheartened at the amount of time spent counseling versus case management activities (Waters, 2015). Another significant challenge of working within a community agency is the emotional challenges that one may face as one routinely encounters the struggles of children and adolescents who are typically under-served in many areas of their community (Waters, 2015). Children receiving services within a community mental health center are often accessed by vulnerable populations such as single-parent families, low socio-economic status, and minority groups, and often terminate services prematurely (Ambruster and Fallon, 1994; Hoagwood et al., 2001). Many children seen at community agencies experience extreme hardship and may not have the resources to overcome all of the obstacles they encounter. In addition, families may discontinue services prior to completion of treatment, perhaps attending only one or two sessions (Ambruster and Fallon, 1994; Hoagwood, et al., 2001), which can be extremely disheartening for counselors. Counselors can become frustrated, over-involved, and may experience a sense of helplessness when working with such vulnerable populations. Counselors should ensure that they do not become overburdened and engage in self-care and supervision vital to ensuring that counselors do not experience compassion fatigue. Self-care is essential in any setting and each counselor can determine which outlet or wellness activity will provide the most benefit.

Modalities of Counseling

Agency counselors provide services through a variety of modalities including group, individual, and family counseling, but in most cases specific interventions are determined by clinical directors, in affiliation with mandates for delivering evidence-based practices. Clinicians may provide several groups a day, as well as individual and family services. For example, CMHCs may provide CBT, mindfulness, and activity groups one day and individual solution-focused counseling and child–parent relationship therapy the next. Because services can be billed to outside insurance companies, the services provided may be determined by reimbursement rates. Most of the services provided are evidence-based and manualized, which can provide valuable structure to counselors with large caseloads. Examples of evidenced based services with treatment manuals include The Coping Cat Program (Kendall and Hedtke, 2006), the FRIENDS Program (Barrett, Lowry-Webster, and Turner, 2000), dialectal behavior therapy for adolescents (Rathus and Miller, 2015), Child–Parent Relationship Therapy, and Attachment and Bio-Behavioral Catch-up. Many clinicians appreciate the diversity, the structure, and the multitude of clinical experiences community mental health agencies can provide.

Individual counseling

Relationships are extremely important for children and adolescents and the therapeutic relationship between child and counselor can serve as a valuable tool for children's positive growth. With this in mind, individual services are often goal directed and focused on emotional regulation, identifying alternative cognitions, and modification of behaviors. Within agency settings, counselors may utilize a variety of individual services to address clinical goals such as behavior therapy, cognitive behavior therapy, solution-focused brief counseling, and therapeutic psychoeducation (Lukens and McFarlan, 2004). Incorporating activity therapy and play within the sessions may also help meet the developmental needs of younger clients.

Group Counseling

Group counseling is an effective and developmentally appropriate intervention that utilizes children's natural tendency to socialize. Providing group services for children and adolescents in agency settings can be highly beneficial, and groups can become a source of support and recognition that others with similar backgrounds encounter similar experiences. There are also a number of different types of groups that can be utilized in agency settings, including psychoeducational groups, social skills groups (Henderson and Thompson, 2016), group play (Ginott, 1961), expressive arts groups (Bratton, Ceballos, and Ferbee, 2009; Bratton and Ferebee, 1999), or activity therapy (Zuchelli, 1993). Within an agency setting, children may attend several different types of groups each week, thus strengthening their bonds with others and learning skills in a format that is a source of support and healing.

Family Counseling

There are myriad parent-inclusive programs that clinicians can utilize within an agency setting. Within an agency setting, directors may determine which parent–child interventions should be utilized to meet the identified goals. Involving parents in adolescents' care is equally as important, despite adolescents' developmental desire to separate from their parents (Berk, 2013). Clinicians can engage in individual counseling with adolescents and meet with parents on a bi-weekly or monthly basis. In addition to set parent–child programs, individuals can provide family therapy utilizing different theoretical orientations or a family systems approach.

Counselors at community mental health agencies provide a multitude of services for child and adolescent clients and provide excellent sources of professional development and education for counselors. These services are provided in individual, group, and family counseling formats for several clients daily, thus providing valuable resource for the community. Interventions are often manualized and evidence based in an attempt to ensure quality of care. While the experience is invaluable, counseling within CMHAs can become exhausting and at times overwhelming.

Case Study: Jessica

The following case study relates to a client at a clinical mental health counseling agency.

Jessica, an 8-year-old girl who experienced previous sexual abuse, was referred to counseling after testifying against her perpetrator. Following screening and intake assessment, Jessica was admitted to an intensive outpatient program due to notable impairments in psychosocial functioning and marked difficulties with boundaries and self-esteem. Her father and stepmother reported that she often vacillated between being incredibly angry or deeply sad and the expression of these emotions was bringing into question her personal safety, although no self-injury behaviors were reported.

Jessica was assigned to a case manager, a family advocate, a licensed professional counselor, and scheduled an appointment with the agency's pediatric psychiatrist. As part of the treatment team, the case manager supported her family's needs for linking and referral to community supports. The family advocate supported interactions with the legal system and provided support to Jessica's parents, who were also dealing with the disarray of Jessica's trauma. The psychiatrist evaluated the degree of need for medical stabilization and determined that no medication was necessary. Jessica engaged in group therapies including CBT, group therapy, and mindfulness in addition to individual therapy. Her primary counselor met with Jessica twice per week and met with her father and stepmother bi-weekly to discuss her progress, any concerns, and provide suggestions to assist Jessica while at home. In addition, Jessica met with a psychiatrist bi-monthly to discuss medication concerns and medication management.

Within her individual counseling, Jessica engaged in the same activity each session. During the sessions, the counselor reflected Jessica's feelings and her sense of accomplishment in an effort to develop a sense of competence, increase self-esteem, and foster an internal locus of control. In addition, the counselor discussed boundaries, thoughts, and emotions to educate Jessica on the connections and enable her to better recognize her thoughts and emotions to regulate her behaviors. Within family sessions, the therapist focused on limit setting and recognition of emotions with Jessica's parents in an effort to assist Jessica in understanding appropriate boundaries and assist in the development of an internal locus of control. Within three months of intensive bi-weekly individual sessions, Jessica displayed more confidence in herself. Within group settings, she participated more actively, engaged with other group members, and demonstrated more appropriate boundaries with staff.

COUNSELING AT RESIDENTIAL TREATMENT CENTERS

Counselors generally provide counseling for children and adolescents in the least restrictive environment such as community-based agencies or outpatient settings. However, when the least restrictive resources are not available, not appropriate, or not successful, the best intervention for mental health issues that cannot be treated in the youth's home environment is a facility that has a multidisciplinary treatment team (American Academy of Child and Adolescent Psychiatry, 2010). These facilities are called residential treatment centers (RTCs) and provide a supportive, safe environment for intensive services in which the client resides. The setting is characteristically restrictive and intended to promote psychosocial stabilization, medical management of symptoms, and safety (See Figure 8.2). As part of the RTC experience, clients engage in academic preparation, family case management, counseling service, and family advocacy. The primary referral source to RTC is child welfare services although youth can be referred by representatives from foster care, public schools, or juvenile justice settings (Sternberg, et al., 2013). The length of stay in treatment typically depends on the client's symptom severity, level of potential for harm, treatment needs, and insurance coverage.

Strengths of Setting

There are a number of strengths of residential treatment for youth. Residential care offers opportunities to aid in stabilizing child and family situations and creating the space or sanctuary for stability and solid planning, based on a comprehensive assessment (American Association of Children's Residential Centers, 2009). Counselors in these settings work in a multidisciplinary team and collaborate with other professionals about the progress and treatment of clients. This gives counselors an increased amount of information from diverse perspectives about the client.

Challenges of Setting

Residential treatment also has notable challenges. First, although it can be necessary to remove the youth from his or her home, placement in an RTC disrupts the youth's home environment, daily schedule, and interactions with family and peers. The child or adolescent will need to adjust to the RTC, which includes a loss of autonomy as the facility will have a structured environment and schedule. Second, access to RTCs is determined by the availability of an opening or bed, as opposed to when the youth is in need of the services. Even if space is available, some families without insurance or ability to pay out of pocket may not be able to afford treatment at an RTC, which can be costly. Additionally, the geographic area in which the client and his or her family reside may not have an RTC. A final challenge is a lack of guidelines as to when it is appropriate to refer a youth to residential treatment (American Academy of Child and Adolescent Psychiatry, 2010; Frensch and Cameron, 2002). This is directly related to the final challenge of the setting—that RTCs are sometimes often regarded as a placement of last resort (AACRC, 2009; Frensch and Cameron, 2002). Thus, the referral can be internalized by the client or their family as a failure to respond to previous treatment.

Typical Interventions and Modalities

Counseling services and modalities will vary by residential treatment centers. These variations are related to the treatment focus or specialization of the RTC. For example, an RTC may specialize in the treatment of clients with a diagnosis of substance abuse and therefore its programming would be specific to addiction and dependence. Regardless of the RTC, clients participate in multimodal services including individual, group, and family counseling to address the complex behavioral health needs and to create a partnership with client families.

Individual Counseling

Intensive individual treatment, skill-based, and group/milieu therapy have historically dominated approaches in RTCs (Abramovitz and Bloom, 2003; Lieberman and den Dunnen, 2014). Individual counseling can serve the client in a number of ways. Initially, counseling will typically focus on crisis intervention or stabilization of the client. This can also include addressing specific skills connecting to the precipitating event or behavior leading to residential treatment, such as violent behavior or delinquency. Counseling can shift to adjustment to residential treatment and a safe space for clients to process their thoughts and feelings. Clients often have histories of trauma, trauma exposure, maltreatment, abuse, and neglect, and residential treatment provides a context in which the full impact of trauma can be witnessed (Zelechoski et al., 2013). Thus, counselors adopt a trauma-informed perspective that considers how the residential treatment setting and its operation (i.e. structure, rules, authority) may trigger a traumatized youth. The counselor may utilize a trauma-informed approach such as structured sensory intervention for traumatized children or trauma-focused cognitive behavioral therapy (TF-CBT) to help the client navigate his or her sense of safety within the context of residential treatment.

Group Counseling

Milieu therapy is a commonly used approach that incorporates the treatment environment (i.e. a milieu) and the peer group in treatment. In this approach, clients do not wait for individual counseling for process or reflection and instead use their interactions, activities, and everyday events for therapeutic purposes. Counselors and staff support and reinforce the client as he or she practices new skills such as interpersonal skills or anger regulation. Clients practice these skills within the peer group and safety of the RTC with the goal of internalizing and generalizing them for use upon integration back into their home environments.

Family Counseling

Within an RTC setting, counselors see their clients in the context of a family as opposed to seeing their client in the context of treatment or residential care (Hust and Kuppinger, 2014). This practice also reflects the vision that families have a decision-making role and that every family member can be a valuable partner (Hust and Kuppinger, 2014). Outcome researchers have demonstrated that changes upon discharge depend on family involvement throughout treatment, community support, and a continuum of care such as aftercare services (Hair, 2005). Thus, counselors develop appropriate and meaningful plans with families for aftercare services that anticipate obstacles and challenges, identify and integrate strengths, and utilize community resources to support the client's transition back into the family environment.

Both Residential Treatment Facilities and Clinical Mental Health Agencies provide mental health services for youth who may require intensive therapeutic services. RTFs often serve as a place for children and adolescents to stabilize. Upon stabilization clients often transition to the Clinical Mental Health Agencies where more intensive personal, group, and family therapy can occur. Within each facility, the child is in need of more intensive services than once-weekly individual sessions. In addition, children and youth receiving services within RTFs and CMHAs participate in individual, group, and family counseling weekly and sometimes daily, unlike other treatment locations such as private practice wherein clients receive either individual, group, or family counseling usually once per week.

COUNSELING IN A PRIVATE PRACTICE

Counselors working in a private practice do many of the same activities as those within a community agency with the exception that they are rarely part of an integrated care team and instead rely on release of information contracts to communicate with the client's other providers. Private practitioners can provide individual, family, and group counseling, addiction counseling, or some may expand their service options to business and writing. Private practitioners can utilize their mental health expertise to provide executive coaching or consulting (Harington, 2013), or utilize their expertise within the community by providing workshops, corporate trainings, or even writing blogs on mental health (Shallcross, 2016).

Counselors in private practice hold more flexibility in their treatment approaches than counselors working within an agency or RTC. Counselors may provide mental health services utilizing a multitude of theoretical orientations and serve clients with a variety of mental health needs at varying levels of severity (Harrington, 2013). Those that do not utilize third-party payment options have a much higher degree of freedom to determine which services and interventions to utilize when counseling children and adolescents.

The structure of private practices can differ as well. Some private practitioners become sole practitioners; others decide to join others within group practices, or provide services within physicians' offices or faith-based organizations (Harrington, 2013). Clinicians can also utilize a variety of different legal structures to create their practices, including Limited Liability Corporations (LLCs), independent practice associations, sole proprietorships, independent practice associations, and partner/associates groups to assist in the financial and legal issues that arise within a private practice (Harrington, 2013).

Launching into a successful private practice can be difficult. Clinicians must become aware of business and legal aspects of creating a business, gain familiarity with business law, engage in entrepreneurship, and become familiar and comfortable speaking about money (Shallcross, 2016). In addition, counselors in private practice must also gain clients, thus creating a need to engage in a network of referral sources, and a high degree of self-motivation and flexibility is necessary. When venturing into private practice, it is important to note that while the need for mental health counseling may always be present, due to economic difficulties, increased level of no-shows, decreased payment from managed care companies, and lack of client referrals can create a stressful environment for private counselors (Colburn, 2013). Private practitioners can partner with different community agencies as a referral source for individuals who no longer qualify for more intensive services or provide unique services meeting the needs of community clients, or engage in relationships with professionals in other disciplines such as divorce or family court lawyers (Colburn, 2013). Others may gain training in assessments and provide different learning, development, mental health, or forensic screenings for clients (Colburn, 2013).

Strengths of Setting

One of the most appealing strengths of private practice is the flexibility it allows counselors (Harrington, 2013). Practicing within a private setting can provide high levels of freedom as the clinician is able to make his or her own decisions regarding types of services provided, client loads, the theoretical orientation utilized, and even office location (Harrington, 2013). As the sole owner and practitioner, one can set hours, take vacations or shorten work weeks when needed, and determine how many clients to see per week (Harrington, 2013). Many private practitioners experience a high degree of satisfaction as counselors as a result of the freedom and flexibility provided within private practice. There is some indication this level of satisfaction may lead to lower job-related stress, health concerns, and mental health problems. Being able to choose client caseload size and modality can also lead to fewer instances of burn out.

Challenges of Setting

While private practice can provide immense flexibility for counselors, there can often be some challenging aspects. One of the most prominent disadvantages is the "complete responsibility for all financial matters [including] overhead, insurance policies, furnishings, equipment, continuing education … billing, accounting, administrative work … inconsistent revenue streams, and financial barriers for uninsured or under-resourced clients to access service" (Harrington, 2013, p. 193). For clinicians to be reimbursed by third-party payers for their services, they must first become part of insurance boards, which can be a lengthy and difficult process. Because of the sometimes lengthy process of reimbursement, many counselors identify alternative forms of revenue, or obtain a business loan to meet financial obligations.

In addition, when engaging in a private practice, there is often less support provided, and many private practitioners express a sense of loss or loneliness as a result (Legge, 2014). When in private practice it can be helpful to create consultation or supervision groups to not only discuss clients and provide support, but to also alleviate some of the stress that occurs when holding others' pain in counseling. Carney and Jefferson (2014) noted that consultation is a cornerstone of the profession and is supported by professional organizations as a professional activity aimed to assist counselors in addressing difficult cases and ensuring quality care.

Typical Interventions and Modalities

Working within a private practice, counselors may experience a high degree of freedom in regards to treatment modalities. The counselor is not necessarily required to provide the same services as those within community mental health agencies, and those who work with private pay clients may not have to limit sessions based upon insurance company determinations. Within a private practice, reimbursement for group and family sessions can be difficult, so it may be more financially beneficial to provide individual sessions with parental consultations.

Regardless of the freedom provided in beginning one's own practice, as well as the potential limitations in reimbursement from insurance companies, it is important to recognize the developmental stage of clients when determining which intervention to utilize (Hoagwood Burns, Kiser, Ringeisen, and Shoenwald, 2001).

Individual Counseling

Many counselors in private practice choose to focus on individual counseling with clients. Counselors can choose to incorporate toys, art, or activities in private practice and practice from a variety of theoretical orientations. Each major theory of personality development addresses work with children and adolescents and provides a framework for clinical practice. Practitioners may utilize play therapy, talk therapy, or a combination of both, as well as incorporate activities, expressive arts, music, or bibliotherapy within their sessions if proper training is obtained.

Group Counseling

Within private practice, there is much more freedom to determine which groups one will hold. Within a private practice, the therapist can determine which types of groups to provide, if any. Usually, this is done in conjunction with the community to ensure that the clinician is providing a needed service (Colburn, 2013). A referral source may note that some adoptive parents are struggling with relationship issues and therefore the counselor may create a child–parent relationship therapy group for adoptive parents, or perhaps a school counselor notes a high incidence of drug usage and therefore the counselor creates a substance abuse group.

Family Counseling

A private practitioner can determine how much or how little he or she would like to involve families when focusing on the child. Clinicians who are more focused on family systems may find the best way to help the child is to work with the family unit (Goldenberg and Goldenberg, 2012). Others clinicians may strive to assist the parent–child dyad in an effort to alleviate internalizing or externalizing behaviors and enhance the parent–child relationship. A private practice counselor has the flexibility to choose to limit family therapy to bi-weekly or monthly parent consultations in conjunction with individual counseling (Post, Ceballos, and Penn, 2012). Doing so engages the parents within the process of counseling, provides support for the parents, and allows for the counselor to understand the process of change at home (Cates, Packman, and Margolis, 2006; Landreth, 2012).

Case Study: Danny

The following study is an example of the brief counseling process.

Danny is a 15-year-old girl whose parents contacted a Licensed Professional Counselor (LPC) in private practice following a referral from their primary care physician (PCP) and linking by insurance carrier. Over the phone, the parents tell the LPC briefly that they have become very worried about their daughter, who has been notably down and distant lately and whose grades have begun to suffer, especially since quitting her high school cross country team. The LPC provides brief psychoeducation to the parent, indicating that some mild to moderate mood disturbances can be expected during adolescence and that there are several evidence-supported treatments available to help teens bounce back from developmental challenges.

During the initial meeting with the family and Danny, the LPC learns that during the last four weeks Danny has started to receive failing grades in her coursework and has become increasingly discouraged about her academic achievement, despite having good grades up to this point. The results of her scores on the Symptom Assessment 45 (Strategic Advantage, Inc., 1998) and a clinical interview indicated a moderate degree of despondency, mild anxiety symptoms, decreased interest in school, poor academic performance, irritability with her parents, anger outbursts with her siblings, bouts of crying, general feelings of worthlessness, increased sleeping, low motivation and energy, and decreased appetite. Danny reported no suicidal ideations, plans, intent, or history, and no history of abuse. Her parents indicate that the PCP had prescribed 10mg of Lexapro once daily, which Danny had been taking as prescribed, but had not noticed any major differences.

The LPC assigned Danny a diagnosis of major depressive disorder, single episode, moderate (296.32; F33.1) and developed an initial six-week treatment plan with two goals: (a) increase engagement in pleasant activities and (b) increase positive mood. The LPC designed a six-session protocol based on a brief, evidence-based cognitive behavioral therapy for teenagers. As a part of the intervention protocol, Danny self-monitored her mood and activity level for six weeks, engaged in behavioral planning for being active and doing fun things, and learned and practiced CBT coping skills such as monitoring self-talk, catching her thinking traps, challenging negative beliefs, strategic problem solving, and giving herself credit for her achievements. As a part of the intervention, the LPC provided skills training to Danny's parents so that they could use praise, encourage, and selective attention to reinforce her skill use and general coping. The LPC met with Danny once a week for a 55-minute appointment where 45 minutes was dedicated to educating, modeling, and practicing CBT skills with Danny and the last 10 was intended to educate her parents about what skills/activity planning had been covered and to engage parent support with her action plan for the week.

At her six-weeks review, Danny's SA-45 indicated minimal symptoms of depression or anxiety and review of her mood and activity logs indicated a sustained trend during the previous weeks where she reported feeling quite well and was back doing many activities that she regarded as pleasant and enjoyable. She reflected that although the approach to treatment was brief and not what she had imagined counseling to be like (due to media portrayals), she believed that she had learned a lot of useful activities that she noticed was helping in other aspects of her life apart from just managing her mood. Her parents indicated that they had noticed marked improvements in Danny and that the use of parent skills and emphasis on clear, frequent communications had really supported the overall family unit. During the final meeting, the LPC facilitated the family identifying the differences that their counseling process had made on Danny's functioning and their overall happiness. Additionally, the family identified potential instances when skills may be useful in the short-term and long-term future. Finally, the LPC provided clear instructions for follow up with their PCP, referrals to online and community-based resources, and instructions for making contact with LPC for resuming services if needed.

Working with a private practice provides counselors with an exponentially higher degree of freedom; however, private practitioners also hold a high degree of responsibility. In an effort to maintain a steady client load and establish professional relationships, private practitioners may form partnerships with other clinicians, or community members. Consultation is a vital activity, especially for private practitioners who often do not have the collegial support provided within RTFs and CMHAs. Consultation and supervision groups can assist counselors in maintaining an ethical practice and provide professional support in what can be a lonely position (Carney and Jefferson, 2014).

COUNSELING AT SHELTERS AND SAFE SLEEPING RESIDENCES

Homeless shelters and safe sleeping residences are facilities that offer a temporary safe living environment for children and adults. Some of the shelters serve specific populations: victims of domestic violence, victims of sex trafficking, homeless youth, individuals with co-occurring disorders (COD), and individuals with severe mental illness who are homeless and their families.

Approximately 7.4 per cent of the general U.S. population will be homeless at some point with 23 per cent being diagnosed with a mental illness and 30 per cent having a substance abuse disorder (Congressional Research Service, 2005; Tompsett, Toro, Guzicki, Manrique, and Zatakia, 2006). In 2007, the United States Department of Housing and Urban Development reported that 1.35 million children were considered homeless.

The primary focus of most shelters is the safety of the children and individuals they serve (Poole, Beran, Thurston, 2008). The direct care staff and counselors provide day-to-day support, case management, and psychotherapy. The facilities will offer services according to the program requirements of the facility, with an emphasis on life skills, job training, support groups, group therapy, individual counseling, linking to resources and housing, and education regarding access to governmental programs (Sun, 2012).

McBride (2012) conducted a phenomenological study with 11 homeless individuals to identify what their needs were and made suggestions for counselors. McBride (2012) found numerous areas of need, including safety, employment, social skills, and positive coping. Surprisingly, the researchers found this population is inundated with programs, but often they are not specific enough for their needs (McBride, 2012). The need for mental health counseling is important, but McBride (2012) noted most homeless shelters only offer counseling for substance abuse and transition from prison to community living. Substance abuse counseling is beneficial for those who need services, but those who have other mental health needs will not have counseling services available to them. McBride (2012) stated counselors need to be familiar with the various community services programs and services available for this population. This will allow the counselor to connect better with homeless individuals and support them in the most appropriate way. Counselors should also have some education in career counseling or be aware of employment opportunities, as a lack of employment was identified as one of the highest needs for this population (McBride, 2012). Having counselors with an ability to identify appropriate job placement for homeless men and women can result in long-term benefits for them.

Strengths of Setting

Despite the lack of funding or funding cuts, places like the Salvation Army, Union Mission, and Goodwill have been serving this population for years (McBride, 2012). There are numerous national, state, and community programs being offered at the various homeless shelters across the country. An individual can receive multiple services in one place, which is a benefit considering lack of transportation is often identified as a barrier for services and employment (McBride, 2012). Receiving multiple services at one site allows for easier access to counseling services through shelter-based collaborative mental health care arrangements or collaborative health care models (Stergiopoulos et al., 2015).

Challenges of Setting

Shelters can provide much-needed services and a place to live; however, there are rules and requirements that must be followed as a result of funding or policy (McBride, 2012). For some individuals and families, this poses a problem. There can be concerns regarding trust and confidentiality for this population when seeking help. Living in shelters leads to a lack of privacy, which causes difficulty with building rapport for counselors. Homeless shelters can sometimes require disclosure of personal information by the counselor that prevents the homeless individual or family from utilizing the services offered (Poole et al., 2008; McBride, 2012). Counselors and staff within the shelters are often mandated reporters of abuse, which includes neglect, physical, and sexual abuse. Homeless parents with children may have challenges accepting counseling services for their children, due to a fear of state child protection agencies being contacted and getting involved (Poole et al., 2008; Brinamen et al., 2012).

Typical Interventions and Modalities

Individual Counseling

Motivational interviewing can be beneficial for counselors working in shelter settings. The use of motivational interviewing can help counselors facilitate change by educating the client about his or her mental health needs and exploring his or her commitment to change (Sun, 2012). Motivational interviewing (MI)/motivational enhancement therapy (MET) produces some evidence of decreasing substance use and psychiatric symptoms and increasing treatment engagement during the short-term services among individuals with CODs (Cleary, Hunt, Matheson, and Walter, 2009). For example, researchers conducted several randomized control trials comparing MI with other alternative educational treatment interventions, and found MI was more likely to reduce substance use and psychiatric symptoms (Cleary et al., 2009; Graber, Moyer, Griffith, Guajardo, and Tonnigan, 2003). Psychoeducation is an important service to increase understanding of mental illness and medication needed to manage symptoms (Sun, 2012). The combination of MI/MET with psychoeducation can improve an individual's level of functioning. Counseling techniques that are brief will be most helpful when working with a transient population. Incorporating solution-focused brief therapy techniques can be helpful by exploring with individuals how they would like their lives to be as a result of therapy, and by examining the skills and resources they have for getting there (de Shazer, Dolan, Korman, Trepper, McCollum, and Berg, 2006).

Incorporating strategies from reality therapy, looking at the client's quality world and identifying his or her wants and needs could be beneficial in helping this population work towards behaviors that they choose to assist them in obtaining their personal goals (Wubbolding, 2011). Cognitive behavioral approaches can be helpful by assisting them with identifying their triggers and learning positive coping strategies in order to reduce negative coping habits

(Sun, 2012). Working with this population to correct maladaptive thinking and exploring their core beliefs can help facilitate change.

Group Counseling

Group work in shelters can be helpful for all ages, and for counselors working in shelters it is important to offer group work for children. Jaffe, Wolf and Wilson (1990) stated how group work is usually the first time children are able to express what they are experiencing with their families. The development of appropriate skills and new behaviors can be learned while attending group (Poole et al., 2008). Programs like the Manual for a Group Program for Children Exposed to Wife Abuse for children 8–13 years old demonstrated effectiveness in attitudinal changes (Poole et al., 2008). The program focuses on adjustment, attitudes towards violence, and appropriate behaviors of a responsible adult. Although researchers examining the effectiveness of this program had a small sample, the program showed promise with children.

When working with adults in shelters, providing group work that incorporates various needs can be utilized. Group work that involves psychoeducation and counseling that focuses on substance abuse and mental health is recommended (Sun, 2012). In a quasi-experimental study examining the effectiveness of a specialized 12-step group called Double Trouble in Recovery, Magura (2008) found that attendees reported significantly fewer days of alcohol and other drug use than did comparison groups without the specialized 12-step group exposure. This supports previous findings by Bogenschutz (2005, 2007) and Magura, Laudet, Mahmood, Rosenblum and Knight (2002) on the effectiveness of 12-step specialized groups in shelters for this population.

Family Counseling

A homeless mother's mental health and parenting are closely linked to her child's adjustment (Gewirtz, DeGarmo, Plowman, August, and Realmuto, 2009). Working with families who are homeless through various services that include parenting training and family counseling can be beneficial. Nurturing Parenting is a family-based program developed by Dr. Stephen Bavolek and has been used with underserved populations involved with state child protection agencies (Cowen, 2001). Programs are usually 15 to 45 sessions that focus on prevention and intervention of child abuse and neglect (Cowen, 2001). Two studies using Nurturing Parenting programs found positive changes in child rearing and parenting skills along with a decrease in familial conflict (Bavoleck, Comstock, and McLaughlin, 1990; Cowen, 2001). There were also improvements in family cohesion, independence, and achievement (Bavoleck et al., 1990). A Nurturing program can be effective for counselors who work with families in shelters that might need parenting skills and support that will help increase familial bonds while going through the challenges of being displaced.

There are other programs that can be used with homeless families or families living in shelters that provide training and support. Fraenkel and his team developed a multiple family discussion group program (Holtrop, McNeil, and McWey, 2015) that integrates collaboration and narrative practices through experiential activities and group discussions. Fraenkel and Shannon (2009) state the program is designed to empower displaced or homeless families by escaping problem-saturated stories and emphasizing strengths and coping strategies while working towards their preferred future. Fraenkel (2005) stated the program has seen promising results, including increased participation with services, positive behavioral changes in children, and positive changes with adult employment.

Counseling within a shelter setting is slightly different from other mental health settings as services are not as focused on deep psychological change, but rather on the importance of stabilization and relevant assistance. Providing career counseling, motivational interviewing/counseling, group psycho-education, and family support can be extremely beneficial when working with children and adolescents within a shelter. Counselors need to be aware of the limitations of confidentiality and how individuals may avoid full disclosure or engaging in counseling out of fear of potentially becoming involved with state protection agencies.

COUNSELING AT HOSPITALS, INPATIENT CARE, AND MEDICAL SETTINGS

Mental health services in both acute psychiatric hospitals and inpatient settings are on the rise. Acute psychiatric hospitals have an average stay of between 5 and 7 days, and inpatient treatment can be of an average 30 days or more (Balkin and Roland, 2007). Counselors in these settings have a limited amount of time to work with clients, so their primary focus is medical stabilization. Clients are typically admitted for decompensation, self-harming behaviors, suicidal ideations, and attempted suicide (Balkin and Roland, 2007). As a part of the treatment team, counselors work with psychiatric staff to ensure the safety of the child; therefore decreasing self-harming behaviors, developing a treatment plan, the use of assessments, and linking the client to community resources is key (Tubman, Montgomery and Wagener, 2007). The work of the clinician can be difficult within the time constraint of the acute psychiatric setting. Building the therapeutic alliance and collaborating to establish a goal for treatment with a crisis stabilization treatment plan is perplexing to say the least. Balkin and Roland (2007) proposed a model to re-conceptualize stabilization while working with adolescents: "The model includes a three step goal attainment process: (a) The client identified the problem(s) that resulted in being hospitalized, (b) the client processed relevant coping skills to identified problem(s), and (c) the client committed to follow up" (Balkin and Roland, 2007, p. 64). The same process can be utilized with adults in these settings. Discharge from acute settings is driven by symptom management. As managed care companies or third-party payers focus on stabilization as the management of symptoms, clients will need goal-driven coping and self-regulating strategies to help them achieve stabilization (Balkin and Roland, 2007).

Cancer Patients Services

As counseling interventions become more prevalent, increasing attention is being paid to the co-occurring psychiatric systems that these patients experience. (Serfaty et al., 2016). Walker et al. (2014) stated approximately 10 per cent of all patients diagnosed with cancer are simultaneously diagnosed with depression. Mitchell et al. (2011) found depression in patients with advanced cancer may have rates as high as 21 per cent. Clinicians must be cognizant of their physical health problems, life stressors, and the increasing need to communicate openly with their family and support systems. "Patients with advanced cancer may struggle with positive coping due to the increase in cancer treatments as their health may be deteriorating" (Serfaty, 2016, p. 5).

The use of an integrated holistic approach can be helpful in addressing treatments for psychological and emotional symptoms as well as physical problems, including the management of symptoms such as pain, nausea and fatigue that are common as health deteriorates (Serfaty et al., 2016). The use of therapeutic interventions like CBT may improve the experience not only for those individuals facing advanced cancer but also for their family members and those close to them. It is possible to treat depression effectively and cognitive behavioral therapy (CBT) approaches show promise with this population (Serfaty et al., 2016).

Hospice Services

Hospice care is a team approach to delivering services needed by an individual with a limited life expectancy and his or her support system (National Hospice and Palliative Care Organization [NHPCO], 2011). Providing services and support for individuals and their families that are receiving hospice care is a necessary aspect of counseling. Providing counseling services to a hospice patient and family can be a challenge for any clinician in the field, regardless of experience. The services provided are there to support the individual and their loved ones through one of the most difficult times in life.

While counseling hospice patients, it is imperative to be sensitive to the whole person. It is easy to focus on the immediate physical or medical needs, but counselors must attend to the emotional needs of the individual (Crawford, 2014). Counselors or hospice workers who ignore or avoid patient fears, moods, or attitudes can cause feelings of rejection that may escalate feelings of anxiety, magnify fears, or underscore depression (Crawford, 2004). Hospice patients need to be supported and counselors should encourage acceptance and self-affirmations rather than focus on regrets or denial of self. Through hospice care, services provided are individualized to the end-of-life experience of the patient. Counseling is vital for all involved and providing support during the end-of-life process allows the individual to explore life's accomplishments and identify all of life's successes. It also allows his or her family and loved ones to have the support they need while spending the final days as a family.

Counselors may find assessments can be a great tool to assist the counselor and client in identifying areas of need. The use of a mental status exam can provide a framework for the counselor to use to evaluate the whole person (Crawford, 2004). This will lay the groundwork for the counselor. A mental status exam will also compliment the team approach used in hospice care. Establishing the goals for the counseling services should include individual and family counseling services. Serfaty et al. (2016) reported evidence from qualitative studies that support the use of cognitive behavioral therapy with patients utilizing hospice care services.

Counselors within hospital settings can counsel individuals who are experiencing acute psychiatric crisis or crises related to physical health issues such as cancer. The mental health needs of individuals experiencing acute physical health crises are becoming more recognized within the field of counseling. As a result, counselors are increasingly providing mental health services within hospital and hospice settings. Within these settings, counselors can assist both clients and their family and friends through allowing a safe space for mourning, better understanding the meaning and reality of their diagnoses, as well as serving as a point of hope and encouragement.

CHILD AND ADOLESCENT SPECIALTIES ACROSS SETTINGS

Career Counseling

Counselors across settings may be called to assist children and adolescents in exploring future career options and creating vocational plans based on their individual interests, aptitudes, and values. Three examples of career development frameworks that are particularly relevant to working with children and adolescents include the Integrative Contextual Model of career development (ICM), Person–Environment (P x E) Fit model of career exploration, and Life-Design model. These three examples of career development theories may be used to structure the career counseling process with adolescents (Lapan, 2004; Chartrand, 1991; Savickas, 2001).

Regardless of the theoretical paradigm utilized, career counseling interventions often include the use of specialized curricular programming, career inventory assessment, lectures on career development from field experts, guidance in obtaining mentoring in occupations of interest, and assistance in facilitating job shadowing opportunities. Children and adolescents who receive career counseling interventions demonstrate maturation in career development skills, increased confidence, and greater academic success, three components that are essential to facilitating strong career development (Choi, Kim, and Kim, 2015). Computer-assisted career guidance systems (CACGS) may be especially suited for helping youth explore future vocational choices. Beyond these general interventions and techniques, specialized programs have been created to assist diverse groups of adolescents with career development. Programs have been created for adolescents living in inner-city environments (Turner and Conkel, 2010), Native American adolescents (Turner, Trotter, Lapan, Czajka, Yang, and Brissett, 2006), teenagers affected by divorce (Thomas and Gibbons, 2009), gifted girls (Maxwell, 2007), and adolescents with learning disabilities (Biller and Horn, 1991).

Rehabilitative Counseling

According to the National Center for Education Statistics (2016), approximately 6.5 million children ages 3–21 were served under the Individuals with Disabilities Education Act (IDEA) to address concerns with specific learning disabilities, speech or language impairments, autism, intellectual disabilities, developmental delays, emotional disturbances, and health impairments (e.g. hearing, orthopedic, visual, deaf-blindness). Given the large number of children with disabilities in the United States, counselors have an opportunity to impact positively the lives of children with disabilities by working as rehabilitation counselors. Rehabilitation counselors work systematically with healthcare providers, direct support professionals, and family members to assist children and adolescents with physical, mental, developmental, cognitive, and emotional disabilities to maximize life functioning and achieve their individual goals.

Ameratunga, Officer, Temple, and Tin Tin (2009) described disability as "the interaction between the injured child and their environment, encompassing impairments in body functions and structures as well as limitations in activities and participation" (p. 327). The rehabilitative process is designed to help individuals with disabilities reach optimal functioning in their environment by helping them navigate complexities in relationships with their families, friends, peers, schools, and future vocational settings. A unique aspect of rehabilitative counseling with youth includes the goal of helping children develop a sense of autonomy in their care, particularly as they transition from childhood to adolescence, and youth with acquired rather than congenital disabilities may experience additional stressors related to adapting to life with the disability (Ameratung, Officer, Temple, and Tin Tin, 2009).

Rehabilitative counselors assist clients using several different techniques to improve interpersonal, social, and emotional health. Rehabilitative counselors may use assessments and appraisals, diagnosis and treatment planning, career counseling, individual and group counseling to facilitate adjustment to the medical and psychosocial impact of disability, case management, referral, and service coordination, interventions to remove environmental, employment, and attitudinal barriers, and consultation services among parties such as school counselors and educational professionals who are also invested in helping youth maintain optimal functioning despite ability status (Commission on Rehabilitation Counselor Certification, n. d.). Mental health professionals who assist young people with disabilities and their families should utilize strengths-based interventions that help clients access opportunities to build self-esteem, form and maintain social connections with peers, and assist parents in supporting the unique developmental trajectory of youth with disabilities (Antle, 2004).

Substance Abuse and Addiction Counseling

Substance use among adolescents, including the use of alcohol, drugs, and prescription medications, is a major public health concern and a priority for counselors in community-based settings. Adolescents who use drugs and alcohol are likely to experience a more complex set of psychiatric difficulties than those who abstain from use and, compared with adults who use the same substances, fall into patterns of substance abuse and addiction more rapidly (Becker, 2013). According to the National Institute on Drug Abuse's (NIDA) Monitoring the Future survey (2016), adolescents appear to be using alcohol, cigarettes, and many illicit drugs at lower rates than in the past five years; however, for those teens who continue to struggle with substance use, early intervention and treatment is imperative for the remediation and prevention of additional substance use concerns across the lifespan.

Fortunately, a number of evidence-based approaches exist for adolescents with substance use concerns. Individual cognitive behavioral therapy (CBT), group CBT, Brief Strategic Family Therapy (BFST), Functional Family Therapy (FFT), and Multisystemic Therapy (MST) are individual, group, and family-based approaches that have demonstrated the ability to assist adolescents in reducing substance use and related behavioral problems in randomized clinical trials (Waldron and Turner, 2008). Recently, mindfulness-based approaches such as Mode Deactivation Therapy (MDT) have been used to help clients become more aware of their maladaptive thoughts, feelings, and behaviors and reduce the frequency and intensity of substance use (Bayles and Villalobos, 2015). Incarcerated adolescents with significant substance use history described mindfulness meditation training as a strategy for experiencing a natural high and reported other benefits such as increased calmness, relaxation, self-regulation, decision-making abilities, and self-contemplation, improved sleep quality, decreased stress, and an enhanced understanding of cause/effect likely to reduce substance abuse and prevent recidivism in the future (Himelstein, Saul, Garcia-Romeu, and Pinedo, 2014). Some individuals may also benefit from participating in 12-step groups such as Palmer Drug Abuse Program (PDAP), Teen Addiction Anonymous (TAA), and Young Persons Alcoholics Anonymous (YPAA), as those who participate often maintain long-term recovery, particularly when augmented by social support and regular involvement with a religious or spiritual group (Chi, Kaskutas, Sterling, Campbell, and Weisner, 2009; Kelly, Dow, Yeterian, and Kahler, 2010).

Regardless of the treatment modality employed, counselors should be aware of and sensitive to both external and internal barriers to treatment. These concerns may include youth and family conflict, fragmented service delivery systems for those who experience dual diagnoses, issues in funding and financial access to treatment, and teens' refusal to participate in services or stop substance use (Bayles and Villalobos, 2015). Successful treatment also depends on structural factors related to the counselor's setting, and some treatment programs experience barriers to providing quality care due to a lack of family engagement, poor community support and involvement, and gender and other diversity issues (Riekmann, Fussell, Doyle, Ford, Riley, and Henderson, 2011). Factors that may increase the likelihood of success in treatment include the use of evidence-based practices (EBPs), regular attendance and willingness to engage on the client's behalf, staff who are in recovery, an interactive and collaborative relationship with clients and families, and an openness to using new practices to help facilitate client success (Amodeo, Lundgren, Beltrame, Chassler, Cohen, and D'Ippolito, 2013).

Court-Referred Clients

Court-referred clients are those individuals who have been referred to treatment following involvement with the juvenile justice system for a crime, offense, or other violation. Common juvenile offenses include theft or larceny, vandalism, alcohol and drug-related offenses, disorderly conduct, assault or battery, curfew violations, truancy, criminal trespass or mischief, burglary, runaway and resisting arrest, and unauthorized use of a motor vehicle (Global Youth Justice, n.d.). While the juvenile justice system often focuses on using deterrence-oriented and sanction-based programming to prevent recidivism in youth, counselors are in a unique position to help adolescents maintain lasting behavioral changes by encouraging personal growth and development using social skills training (Steinberg, 2009). Antisocial behaviors, poor anger control, and ongoing emotional distress are factors that influence recidivism in youth, and counselors can assist youth in reducing the likelihood of reoffending by using interventions that focus on empathy, anger/impulse control, and positive coping (Balkin, Miller, Ricard, Garcia, and Lancaster, 2011). Group-based psychoeducational approaches with an emphasis on life skills have been used to teach court-referred youth how to identify and cope with feelings, understand and moderate anger triggers, develop healthy coping strategies to manage stress, communicate more effectively with peers and family members, improve self-esteem, and avoid substance abuse (Lancaster, Balkin, Garcia, and Valarezo, 2011).

Counselors assist children and adolescents with a variety of developmental concerns including career choice, acquired disabilities, drug and alcohol abuse, and legal difficulties (Berk, 2016). Vocational or career choice is a major developmental task for children and adolescents (Berk, 2016). Counselors can greatly assist clients with this developmental task through the utilization of career counseling and vocational inventories. As children develop, rehabilitative counselors can provide valuable services and support to facilitate client adjustment to the realities of his or her disabilities and to improve overall wellbeing. As adolescents often begin to take risks and experiment with drugs, alcohol, and risky behaviors, they may become dependent or addicted or involved with the legal system (Berk, 2016). Counselors can also assist child and adolescent clients who may struggle with addictions by utilizing a variety of interventions and understanding the difficulties social environments may present in their ability to remain drug free. In addition, counselors can provide counseling in conjunction with the court system to better equip children and adolescents with social and coping skills to reduce future rates of recidivism.

Case Study: James

The following case study relates to a court-referred client.

After physically assaulting his cousin and subsequent arrest, 13-year-old James was court-referred to counseling as a condition of his juvenile probation. James had never participated in counseling before and was unsure of what to expect from the counselor or the first counseling session. In the first session, James's mother attended and asked a few questions while the counselor discussed the elements of informed consent and what to expect during the intake interview. James watched the counselor carefully as his mother described James's anger outbursts, poor school performance, and problematic peer group. James was annoyed that his mother did so much of the talking and was relieved when the counselor turned to him and asked for his perspective. He was even more relieved when the counselor stopped James's mother from interrupting his description of his anger and how it led to the assault. James was still suspicious of what the counselor would tell his mother about his time in counseling and what the counselor would tell his probation officer about his progress.

Through their subsequent sessions, the counselor continued to establish trust with James. She did this by attempting to truly understand James's experience and remaining honest about the limitation of confidentiality, specifically what would need to be discussed within court. The counselor attempted to honor both the court representatives' goals for counseling while also recognizing James's goals. The counselor was aware of the need to provide clients with accurate informed consent within each session, understanding that this process may need to be discussed throughout James's and her work together. In this effort, the counselor also processed the client's court experiences in addition to recognizing how some of James's maladaptive behaviors served a purpose within his life. Instead of attempting to eliminate those maladaptive behaviors, his counselor attempted to incorporate new, more pro-social behaviors that James could utilize when needed.

ASSESSMENT AND EVALUATION IN CLINICAL MENTAL HEALTH COUNSELING

Intake Interviews

An intake interview is an information-gathering process that occurs at the beginning of the counseling process. The primary purpose of an intake interview is to gather information about the client, his or her presenting problem, and background information relevant to the presenting problem. It is important for the counselor to remember that in addition to gathering information he or she is also engaging the client in the counseling process and building the relationship between client and counselor throughout the intake interview. Counselors need to balance obtaining information from the client while tending to the formation of the therapeutic relationship. If a counselor focuses too much on gathering information, the client can perceive the counselor as interrogative or mechanical. This can decrease the likelihood the client will attend another session. Counselors can explain to clients what questions will be asked and why the counselor will ask these questions before they attempt to gather information about the client. This can be particularly beneficial for clients entering counseling for the first time.

Additionally, counselors need to consider how an intake interview should meet the needs of a child or adolescent. Of importance is the counselor establishing rapport with the child or adolescent client. This is particularly true if a parent or guardian is present in the intake. Although a parent or guardian can provide valuable information and be a resource for both the counselor and client in the course of counseling, the counselor needs to ensure to connect with the child or adolescent client in the intake. Counselors should also consider the cognitive and emotional developmental level of the client and present information consistent with the child or adolescent's level of understanding. These adjustments can include but are not limited to the phrasing of information or questions, altering vocabulary, and limiting the duration of the session. Additionally, counselors can incorporate toys, sandtray, or other expressive arts (Salmon, 2006).

Cultural considerations are another signification component of the intake process. Counselors are aware of how the counselor's cultural, cultural competence, and the client's culture may affect the intake interview, the initial formation, or lack thereof, of the therapeutic alliance. Integrating culture into the intake interview allows the counselor to gain an understanding of the client and is consistent with the American Counseling Association's Code of Ethics (ACA, 2014) and with multicultural competencies (Ratts, Singh, Nassar-McMillan, Butler, and McCullough, 2015). In addition, it is important for the counselor to explore the presenting problem from the context of culture. This includes how the problem is defined or understood, described, measured, treated, and how cultural factors in the environment influence these (Ecklund and Johnson, 2007). A culturally relevant child or adolescent intake, according to Ecklund and Johnson (2007), is rooted in a respectful, sensitive, and integrated interest in the cultural identity, context, and experiences of the client and that this will foster a relationship between counselor and client that is both open to and respectful of diversity.

Collecting a Biopsychosocial History

Intake interviews can provide counselors with important information, but often counselors will need more background information from the client or the client's parents or guardians. When counselors collect more background information, this is called a biopsychosocial history or interview. Counselors can obtain this information from intake paperwork, interviewing the client, and other sources of information such as the client's parent(s)/guardian(s), case manager, school counselor, or client records. The biopsychosocial history gathers a wide range of information about the client and typically includes the following:

1. ***Demographic information.*** This section typically includes the client's name, address, phone number, age, gender, race, parent/guardian information, and identification of an emergency contact person.
2. ***Presenting problem or reason for referral.*** This section includes the client's description of the problem and detailed information about the problem. If the client has been referred by an external source, then this would include the reason the client was referred to counseling by that source.

3. **Family history.** This section includes parents' marital status, number of siblings, residents in household, cultural identity of family, spiritual/religious identity of family, quality of relationships among family members, and abuse, neglect, or violence within the family.

4. **Academic/educational history.** This section includes the client's level of education, learning disabilities, or accommodations in the school environment.

5. **Medical and health history.** This section will include the client's current health status, previous illnesses or diseases, previous hospitalizations or major surgeries, use of prescription medications, use of over the counter medications, and changes in appetite or sleep.

6. **Mental health history.** This section will include the client's previous or current mental health diagnoses, family history of mental health history, suicidal ideation or attempts, family history of suicide, substance use and abuse history, and previous participation in counseling or psychiatric services.

7. **Other relevant information.** Clients may have something that is of particular importance or significance to share that does not clearly fall into a previous section. Or, a counselor's setting may ask for particular information that is not categorized under one of the previous sections, such as any potential disabilities, current living situation, past or current drug/alcohol abuse, and any involvement with the court system in addition to identified strengths and areas of interest.

Counselors can easily become focused on the client's problems, deficits, or pathology and overlook or fail to inquire about a client's strengths, resources, and areas of wellness. An adolescent client may have been nominated for a gifted and talented program in school, have a positive peer group, and enjoy golf as a school sport and leisure activity, and these would be important to know from the interview.

The information gathered in an initial interview and biopsychosocial history may vary somewhat depending on the counselor's setting. Certain settings may include other sections or explore a particular section in more detail. In a correctional setting, the counselor will likely include a criminal history as a section in the biopsychosocial history. This would include the client's history of citations, warrants, arrests, criminal or civil proceedings and dispositions, and probation terms or requirements.

Mental Status Exam

A mental status exam or mental status examination (MSE) is also a common part of the intake and interview process. It is a structured method used to assess the client's mental state and behavior at the time of the interview. Counselors can administer the MSE again during the course of counseling to measure client changes over time. The MSE can be brief or more comprehensive depending on the clinical setting. In addition, the MSE can be used by other professionals, such as primary care physicians, to refer the client for further evaluation or referral to a mental health professional (Snyderman and

Rovner, 2009). There are different versions of the mental status exam, but domains typically covered include appearance, behavior, affect/mood, speech/language, thought process, memory, intellectual functioning, and insight/judgment. Counselors complete the MSE through observation of the client, obtaining information from the client through an interview, or formal assessment measures discussed below.

Psychological Assessments

Assessment is a broad term that is often used interchangeably with other terms like appraisal, evaluation, or test. Assessment refers to a systematic process of collecting data that integrates test information with other sources of data. The process includes the counselor identifying a need for an assessment, introducing the assessment and its purpose to the client, administering and scoring the assessment, interpreting the assessment results with the client, and using the results to inform the counseling process. The term assessment can also refer to a measure that is used in the assessment process. An example of a measure is the Child and Adolescent Needs and Strengths (CANS). Although assessments can provide valuable information, counselors do not rely on a single score to make clinical decisions. Counselors rely on multiple sources of data such as client self-reported information from the intake interview, biopsychosocial history, mental status exam, client records, and along with assessment data to inform the counselor's case conceptualization, treatment plan, and diagnosis. Counselors select assessments that have a therapeutic purpose, are appropriate for the client, cross-culturally fair, and those that have sound psychometric properties.

DOCUMENTATION OF COUNSELING ACTIVITIES

Documentation refers to any written, digital, audio, visual, or artistic record of the work within the counseling relationship between the counselor and the client (Mitchell, 2007). The process of documenting services can vary dramatically depending on the setting in which the counselor works, and the types of records available to guide treatment may also be very different. For example, the amount and types of information available to a therapist working in a behavioral health hospital may be dramatically different from the types of information available in private practice or community-based settings. Regardless of the setting or availability of records, keeping clear, timely records is essential in the era of managed care.

Progress Notes Versus Psychotherapy Notes

Progress notes contain information related to the provision of counseling services for the purpose of treatment reimbursement. Some common types of progress notes include SOAP notes (i.e. subjective information, objective information, assessment, plan) and DAP notes (description of session, assessment of client and progress, plan). While information may be more or less detailed depending on the setting in which the counselor works and the process of obtaining reimbursement for services provided, progress notes typically include (Mitchell, 2007):

- type of service
- date of service, including exact session start and stop times
- nature of interventions provided (e.g., specific treatment modalities used)
- client progress in relationship to overall treatment goals
- clinical observations or brief mental status examination
- risk assessment (e.g. suicidal/homicidal ideation, self-harming behaviors)
- potential protective factors (e.g. family support, friendships, spiritual/religious beliefs)
- consultations with, or referrals to, other professionals
- name and credentials of the service provider

While progress notes are necessary for documenting treatment and obtaining reimbursement, many practitioners also choose to keep psychotherapy notes. Psychotherapy notes are kept separate from the rest of the client's record and generally contain information related to specific conversational processes and the therapist's hypotheses or hunches about client behavior. These notes are protected under the Health Insurance Portability and Accountability Act (HIPAA) and, if records are subpoenaed, are generally not admissible in a court of law without express authorization by the client or his or her legal guardian (Clay, 2007).

Managing Records

The American Counseling Association (ACA)'s Code of Ethics (2014) section A.1.b. outlined the need for counselors to "create, safeguard, and maintain documentation necessary for rendering of professional services" using "sufficient and timely documentation to facilitate the delivery and continuity of services" (p. 4). Improvements in technology and the creation of cloud-based records management systems has led to a movement away from traditional paper records to web-based management. A number of online record management systems exist to help practitioners manage records, track client progress, and quantify clinical outcomes. While the method of keeping and storing records will depend considerably on the clinician's work site, practitioners should ensure that the record management system they use is safe, secure, encrypted, and meets HIPAA guidelines to protect client confidentiality and safeguard against unwarranted disclosures of protected healthcare information.

Managed Care and Third-Party Reimbursement

Managed care organizations (MCOs) add an additional layer to the process of documentation and service provision. MCOs often impose limitations on treatment and mandate a predetermined session allotment for each client, necessitating a utilization review (UR) to evaluate treatment necessity, the appropriateness of the interventions used by the counselor, and the effectiveness of therapy based on some objective measure of client progress (Daniels, 2001). Reimbursement by third-party payers largely depends on the number of sessions approved or budgeted based on the type of billing completed. For private healthcare settings, peer-to-peer consultation may be required in order to justify adding additional sessions if sufficient client progress has not been made in the original time allotted. Considering the additional complications sometimes involved with billing MCOs, keeping clear, concise, and sufficiently detailed progress notes is especially important.

When providing counseling services, it is important to gather a broad and as accurate as possible understanding of the client. Intake interviews provide counselors with an understanding of the client's perspective of his or her experiences, history, and reasons for attending counseling. Mental status exams allow for focused clinical observations of a client's demeanor and presentation in counseling and assessments allow for a more structured and measured approach to understanding a client. Each of these is utilized in conjunction to allow for a more complete conceptualization of the client's current needs. To maintain accurate conceptualizations of clients and ensure quality of care, counselors are expected to maintain accurate records of their sessions with clients. Counselors utilizing managed care or third-party reimbursement are also expected to maintain communication with MCO's regarding client goals and progress towards those goals.

CREDENTIALING AND CONTINUING EDUCATION

Licensure

A license is a state government-sanctioned credential granted by a state regulatory board. The license permits an individual to practice independently or to practice under the supervision of a licensed counselor in that particular state. Licensed counselors are regulated by federal and state laws that restrict or regulate the title of licensed counselor, define the scope of practice of counselors, and protect the public.

The requirements for state licensure as a counselor vary by state, but all states will have an application for licensure that documents educational standards or degree requirements, a supervised clinical experience, and an examination. Some states have a single license for professional counselors; other states have a two-tiered licensure system. Examples of titles and acronyms of states licenses include Licensed Professional Counselor (LPC), Licensed Clinical Professional Counselor (LCPC), and Licensed Mental Health Counselor (LMHC).

Certification

Certification is a credential awarded by a professional organization or association to individuals that have met the requirements for the certification. A counselor may pursue certification as a means to document and market professional competence or a particular counseling specialization. Organizations or associations that award the credential frequently maintain a registry of individuals that have been certified. These lists can be made available to potential clients, other clinicians, insurance panels, organizations, and researchers. The National Board for Certified Counselors (NBCC) is an example of an organization that offers certification of professional counselors. Its credential is the NCC, which stands for National Certified Counselor. Additionally, NBCC offers specialty certifications including one for clinical mental health.

In addition to licensure and certifications, counselors can become members of professional associations. Counselors join professional associations for a variety of reasons, including professional identity, commonality in counseling or research interests, networking, and continuing education opportunities. Membership in a professional association also includes specific benefits only available to members. Access to publications like newsletters and the association's journal, employment postings, and legal consultation are examples of member benefits. The American Counseling Association (ACA) and a division of ACA, the American Mental Health Counselors Association (AMHCA), are examples of counseling associations in which a clinical mental health counselor can become involved and join. It is common for associations to offer a discounted membership rate for students or new professionals to become involved in professional associations.

Continuing Education

Counselors continue to learn and pursue new knowledge and skills throughout their careers. There are a variety of ways in which counselors can continue their education, develop, or enhance their counseling skills, and pursue interests in a counseling specialty, diagnosis, or client population. Counselors are required to complete a specified number of continuing education hours or units, commonly called CEUs, to maintain a license or certification. CEUs can be obtained through attendance at national, regional, and state conferences. Workshops, professional trainings, or webinars are also sources of CEUs that counselors can find at the local level through community agencies or organizations.

In order to provide clinical services, it is vital that counselors become licensed within their state. Licensure requirements may vary by state, but all include an application and education, experience, and supervisory prerequisites necessary to become fully licensed. Counselors can also become credentialed in a specialty or as an NCC, and this credentialing is often optional, though it can assist in meeting one's professional goals. In order to maintain one's license and credentialing, counselors must engage in continuing education to ensure that they are aware of new innovations in the field, current ethical codes and issues, and best practices within counseling.

SUMMARY

This chapter reviewed the role of counselors who provide a core set of services to children and adolescents in an effort to promote their optimal development and functioning. It has described the concept of an integrated care team, the continuum of service provision, and the many settings within which counselors' work. Additionally, individual, group, and family-focused interventions and some of the critical activities child and adolescent counselors engage in across settings has been described. Finally, there are some resources identified below that can support your practice and collaborations.

Additional Resources

Kaiser Permanente Center for Health Research: https://research.kpchr.org/Research/Research-Areas/Mental-Health/Youth-Depression-Programs#Downloads
National Registry of Evidence-Based Practices for Children and Adolescence: http://nrepp.samhsa.gov
The Evidence-Based Practice for Children and Adolescents Report: https://www.apa.org/practice/resources/evidence/children-report.pdf
The National Child Traumatic Stress Network: http://www.nctsn.org/

Suggested Readings

Peer-Reviewed Journals

Journal of Child and Adolescent Counseling: http://www.tandfonline.com/loi/ucac20#.V3gV8vkrLIU
Journal of Child and Adolescent Mental Health: http://www.tandfonline.com/toc/rcmh20/current
Journal of Child Psychotherapy: http://www.tandfonline.com/toc/rjcp20/current
International Journal of Play Therapy: http://www.apa.org/pubs/journals/pla/

Books

Cohen, J. A., Mannarino, A. P., and Deblinger, E. (2006). *Treating trauma and traumatic grief in children and adolescents*. New York, NY: The Guilford Press.
Corcoran, J. (2010). *Mental health treatment for children and adolescents*. Oxford: Oxford University Press.
Flamez, B. and Sheperis, C. (2015). *Diagnosing and treating children and adolescents: A guide for mental health professionals*. Hoboken, NJ: John Wiley & Sons.
National Institute of Mental Health (2009). *Treatment of children with mental illness: Frequently asked questions about the treatment of illness in children*. Bethesda, MD: Author. Retrieved from http://www.nimh.nih.gov/health/publications/index.shtml

Glossary

Biopsychosocial history: Includes the client's demographic information, presenting problem or reason for referral, family history, academic/educational history, medical and health history, mental health history, and any other relevant information that does not clearly fall into an aforementioned category

Certification: A credential awarded by a professional organization or association to individuals that have met requirements for the certification

Continuum of care: The amount and types of services provided to youths based on their risk for harm to self and others, psychiatric symptom severity, level of functioning, and degree of access and utilization of resources

Direct services: Face-to-face interactions between clients and counselors delivering individual, group, or family-focused interventions

Documentation: Any written, digital, audio, visual, or artistic record of the work within the counseling relationship between the counselor and the client

Indirect services: Activities such as training others, monitoring client progress, engaging in or delivering clinical supervision, peer consultation, collaborating with teachers or parents, communicating with stakeholders and third party payers, developing and modifying materials for client use, advocacy, and reporting

Intake interview: A process that occurs at the beginning of the counseling relationship intended to gather information about the client, his or her presenting problem, and background information relevant to the presenting problem

Integrated care: Occurs when multiple categories of service providers (e.g. psychiatrists, psychiatric nurses, psychologists, professional counselors, case managers, and family advocates) form a collaborative network, thereby improving resource utilization and facilitating access to multiple services at a single sit and possibly during a single visit

Licensure: A state government-sanctioned credential granted by a state regulatory board, which permits an individual to practice independently or to practice under the supervision of a licensed counselor in a particular state

Mental status exam: A structured method utilized to assess the client's mental state and behavior at the time of the interview, often including domains such as appearance, behavior, affect/mood, speech/language, thought process, memory, intellectual functioning, and insight/judgment

Progress notes: Notes that contain information related to the provision of counseling services for the purpose of treatment reimbursement, typically including the type of service, date of service, nature of interventions provided, client progress in relationship to overall treatment goals, clinical observations, risk assessment, protective factors, consultations with or referrals to other professionals, and the name and credentials of the service provider

Psychotherapy notes: Notes kept separate from the client's record, generally containing information related to the specific conversational processes and the therapist's hypotheses or hunches about client behavior

Rehabilitation counselors: Licensed professionals who systematically work with healthcare providers, direct support professionals, and family members to assist children and adolescents with physical, mental, developmental, cognitive, and emotional disabilities maximize life functioning and achieve their individual goals

References

Abramovitz, R. and Bloom, S. L. (2003). Creating sanctuary in residential treatment for youth: From the "well-ordered asylum" to a "living-learning environment." *Psychiatric Quarterly* 84, 119–135.

Alexander, J. and Parsons, B. V. (1982). *Functional family therapy.* Monterey, CA: Brooks & Cole.

American Academy of Child and Adolescent Psychiatry (2010). *Principles of care for treatment of children and adolescents with mental illnesses in residential treatment centers.* Washington, DC: Author.

American Association of Children's Residential Centers (2009). Redefining the role of residential treatment. *Residential Treatment for Children and Youth* 26, 226–229.

American Counseling Association (2014). *Code of ethics.* Alexandria, VA: Author.

Barrett, P. M., Lowry-Webster, H., and Turner, C. (2000). *FRIENDS program for children: Group leaders manual.* Brisbane: Australian Academic Press.

Bates, B. C., English, D. J., and Kouidou-Giles, S. (1997). Residential treatment and its alternatives: A review of the literature. *Child and Youth Care Forum* 26 (1), 7–51.

Bratton, S., Landreth, G., Kellum, T., and Blackard, S. R. (2006). *Child–parent relationship therapy (CPRT) treatment manual: A 10-session filial therapy model for training parents.* New York, NY: Routledge.

Carney, J. M. and Jefferson, J. F. (2014). Consultation for mental health counselors: Opportunities and guidelines for private practice. *Journal of Mental Health Counseling* 36 (4), 302–314.

Clark, G., DeBar, L., Ludman, E., Asarnov, J., and Jaycox, L. (2002). *Steady project intervention manual: Collaborative care, cognitive-behavioral program for depressed youth in a primary care setting.* Portland, OR: Kaiser Permanente Center for Health Research.

Colburn, A. A. N. (2013). Endless possibilities: Diversifying service options in private practice. *Journal of Mental Health Counseling* 35 (3), 198–210.

Community Mental Health Act, 42 U.S.C. (1963).

Ecklund, K. and Johnson, W. B. (2007). Toward cultural competence in child intake assessments. *Professional Psychology: Research and Practice* 38, 356–362.

Frensch, K. M. and Cameron, G. (2002). Treatment of choice or a last resort? A review of residential mental health placements for children and youth. *Child and Youth Care Forum* 31, 307–339.

Freres, D. R., Gillham, J. E., Reivich, K., and Shatté, A. J. (2002). Preventing depressive symptoms in middle school students: The Penn Resiliency Program. *International Journal of Emergency Medicine* 4, 31–40.

Hair, H. J. (2005). Outcomes for children and adolescents after residential treatment: A review of research from 1993 to 2003. *Journal of Child and Family Studies* 14, 551–575.

Harrington, J. A. (2013). Contemporary issues in private practice: Spotlight on the self-employed mental health counselor. *Journal of Mental Health Counseling* 35, 189–197.

Henggeler, S. W., Sheidow, A. J., and Lee, T. (2007). Multisystemic treatment (MST) of serious clinical problems in youths and their families. In D. W. Springer and A. R. Roberts (eds.), *Handbook of forensic mental health with victims and offenders: Assessment, treatment, and research* (pp. 315–345). New York, NY: Springer Publishing.

Hofmann, S. G., Asnaani, A., Vonk, I. J., Sawyer, A. T., and Fang, A. (2012). The efficacy of cognitive behavioral therapy: A review of meta-analyses. *Cognitive Therapy and Research* 36, 427–440.

Hust, J. A. and Kuppinger, A. (2014). Moving toward family-driven care in residential. In G. M. Blau, B. Caldwell, and R. E. Lieberman (eds.), *Residential interventions for children, adolescents, and families: A best practices approach* (pp. 15–33). New York, NY: Taylor & Francis.

Kendall, P. C. and Hedtke, K. (2006). *Cognitive-behavioral therapy for anxious children: Therapist manual,* 3rd ed. Ardmore, PA: Workbook Publishing.

Kennedy, John F. (1963). "Special Message to the Congress on Mental Illness and Mental Retardation." Retrieved from http://www.presidency.ucsb.edu/ws/?pid=9546

Lieberman, R. E. and den Dunnen, W. (2014). Residential interventions: A historical perspective. In G. M. Blau, B. Caldwell, and R. E. Lieberman (eds.), *Residential interventions for children, adolescents, and families: A best practices approach* (pp. 8–14). New York, NY: Taylor & Francis.

McNeil, C. and Hembree-Kigin, T. (2010). *Parent–child interaction therapy*, 2nd ed. New York, NY: Springer.

Rathus, J. H. and Miller, A. L. (2015). *DBT skills manual for adolescents*. New York, NY: Guilford Press.

Ratts, M. J., Singh, A. A., Nassar-McMillan, S. N., Butler, K., and McCullough, J. R. (2015). *Multicultural and social justice counseling competencies*. Alexandria, VA: American Counseling Association.

Salmon, K. (2006). Toys in clinical interviews with children: Review and implications for practice. *Clinical Psychologist* 10, 54–59.

Schaefer, C. E. and Drewes, A. A. (2009). The therapeutic powers of play and play therapy. In A. A. Drewes (ed.), *Blending play therapy with cognitive behavioral therapy: Evidence based and other effective treatments and techniques* (pp. 3–16). Hoboken, NJ: John Wiley & Sons.

Snyderman, D. and Rovner, B. W. (2009). Mental status examination in primary care: A review. *American Family Physician* 80, 809–814.

Sternberg, N., Thompson, R. W., Smith, G., Klee, S., Cubellis, L., Davidowitz, J., Muirhead, J., and Schnur, E. (2013). Outcomes in children's residential treatment centers: A national survey 2010. *Residential Treatment for Children and Youth* 30, 93–118.

Trzepacz, P. T. and Baker, R. W. (1993). *The psychiatric mental status examination*. New York, NY: Oxford University Press.

Zelechoski, A. D., Sharman, R. Beserra, K., Miguel, J. L., DeMarco, M., and Spinazzola, J. (2013). Traumatized youth in residential treatment settings: Prevalence, clinical presentation, treatment, and policy implications. *Journal of Family Violence* 28, 639–652.

PART IV

Assessment, Diagnosis, and Treatment of Children and Adolescents in School and Clinical Mental Health Settings

CHAPTER 9

Appraisal and Assessment Techniques Specific to Children and Adolescents

Jacqueline M. Swank and Patrick R. Mullen

Everything that can be counted does not necessarily count; everything that counts cannot necessarily be counted.

Albert Einstein

CHAPTER OBJECTIVES

After reading this chapter, you should be able to:

■ differentiate between the assessment purposes
■ explain the methods of assessment
■ explain the assessment process (selecting, administering, scoring, interpreting, communicating results)
■ evaluate assessments to determine appropriateness for a child or adolescent

---

INTRODUCTION

From the moment a counselor picks up a file, engages in a conversation about a child, or meets a child for the first time, he or she begins to gather information about the child. Through the process of gathering information from multiple sources (child, parent, teacher, education or treatment file), using a variety of methods (interviews, tests, observation), the counselor is engaging in the assessment process. This chapter focuses on key aspects of the assessment process with children and adolescents, including the basic components of the assessment process and types of assessments used with this population. For the purposes of this chapter, the term child(ren) will be used to describe both children and adolescents, unless otherwise noted by the authors.

LAWS, COURT DECISIONS, AND ETHICS REGARDING ASSESSMENT PRACTICES WITH CHILDREN AND ADOLESCENTS

When engaging in the assessment process, it is important to think about legal and ethical considerations that are applicable to this process. There are key laws and court decisions that guide counselors' use of assessments with children and adolescents. Table 9.1 presents the various federal law and court rulings that are associated with the use of tests and assessments with children and adolescents. In addition to these laws, counselors must become acquainted with their state's unique laws regarding assessment. It is the counselor's responsibility to develop a thorough understanding of his or her state's laws regarding assessment.

In regards to ethics, the American Counseling Association (ACA) 2014 *Code of Ethics* encompasses an entire section (Section E: Evaluation, Assessment, and Interpretation) devoted to the assessment process. Specifically related to interpreting and reporting assessment results, the Code states that counselors will acknowledge reservations regarding questionable psychometric properties of an assessment or use of an assessment that was normed with a group outside of the client's group. The counselor also uses caution to not extend the interpretation of the results beyond their intended purpose.

Table 9.1 Laws and court rulings related to administering assessments to children and adolescents

Law	Brief Description in Relationship to Testing with Children and Youth
Civil Rights Act, Title VII (1964, 1972, 1978, and 1991)	Employment testing cannot discriminate based on grounds of race, gender, age, pregnancy, national origin, or religion.
Family Educational Rights and Privacy Act of 1974 (FERPA)	Student records, including test information, must remain secure and private from individuals who do not have the right to view the results. Support student and parental rights to have access to student records.
Education of All Handicapped Children Act of 1975 (EAHC; Public Law, 94–142, Individuals with Disabilities Education Improvement Act of 2004 (IDEA, Public Law, 99–457; amendment of Pub. L., 94–142)	The Education of All Handicapped Children Act (1975) requires that parents provide consent prior to the assessment of student's abilities to qualify for exceptional education needs and an individualized education plan. The Individuals with Disabilities Education Improvement Act (IDEA, 2004) reauthorized and renamed the Education of All Handicapped Children Act. In addition, it removed the requirement of the ability–achievement discrepancy model and started to mandate the use of scientific assessments along with the use of instructional and behavioral interventions to determine whether students have specific learning disabilities. IDEA promoted the use of Response to Intervention or RTI.
Vocational Education Act of 1984 (Public Law, 98–524)	The Vocational Education Act, commonly called the Carl D. Perkins Vocational and Technical Education Act, was reauthorized in 2006. Disadvantaged individuals are entitled to federally funded career and technical education that has a focus on achievement and a preparation for work and post K-12 education opportunities. The reauthorization of this act strengthens the connection between K-12 and post K-12 education and enhanced accountability at the state and local levels.
Education of the Handicapped Act of 1990 (Pub. L., 101–476)	Any student with an identified disability has the right to obtain support to move from school into continuing education, rehabilitation, vocational, or adult services.

Americans with Disabilities Act of 1990 (ADA)	The assessments that employers use during screening and selections processes to assess ability must be accurate and cannot be affected by a person's disability. A person with a disability has a right to appropriate testing accommodations.
Health Insurance Portability and Accountability Act (HIPPA) of 1996	Client records, including test information, are required to be secure and private, and must be made available to the client. Third-party stakeholders must provide consent before obtaining access to client's records.
No Child Left Behind Act of 2001	Requires that states examine students' math and reading skills continuously to ensure quality education is taking place. Schools and their personnel are responsible and accountable for the progress students make and their test scores.

Judicial Decision	*Brief Description in Relationship to Testing with Children and Youth*
Larry P. v. Riles (1974, 1979, 1984)	Decided that racial bias in intelligence tests disadvantaged African American students and placed inaccurately high numbers of them in special education coursework. Put increased attention on the use of multiple assessments and development of culture fair assessments. Requires counselors to provide proper documentation before placing students in special education services.
Diana v. California State Board of Education (1973, 1984)	Students in schools should have access to tests in their native language in addition to English. Clients should have access to tests in their native language in addition to English.
Sharif v. New York State Educational Development (1989)	Individuals that work in New York schools are not permitted to solely use SAT score for making decisions regarding scholarships.
Bakke v. California (1978)	The use of racial quota systems for minority group admissions into colleges and universities is not permissible.
Golden Rule Insurance Company v. Richard Mathias (1984)	A case settled out of court that required Educational Testing Service (ETS) to use test items that the percentage of correct answers for all examinees is at minimum 40 per cent and consider items biased if there is a difference in the percentage correct between white and African American examinees who responded to the items if it exceeds 15 per cent.

Sources: Drummond and Jones (2016) and Hays (2013).

PURPOSES OF ASSESSMENT

When engaging in an assessment process, it is important to consider the reason for the process. What do you want to know? Having a clear purpose and intent of the assessment process will assist the counselor in determining what assessment procedures to use with children. There are four overarching purposes for assessment—screening, identifying and diagnosing, intervention planning, and evaluating interventions—identified through the literature by Drummond, Sheperis, and Jones (2016).

Screening

The screening process is designed to provide preliminary information to determine the level of risk for specific mental health concerns and the need for further assessment and counseling services. A screening questionnaire is brief and the counselor may administer it to a group of children or an individual child to determine the need of services. The counselor may also use this information to determine the level of services (i.e., outpatient, inpatient) and frequency of sessions. In considering the need for services, a school counselor may administer a screening questionnaire or needs survey to a group of children to determine the level of risk for test anxiety and use this data to assist in the decision-making process of selecting children to participate in a small group. Additionally, a mental health counselor may administer a screening instrument to an individual child to make decisions about further assessment for diagnosis. A screening questionnaire is not designed for diagnosing.

Identifying and Diagnosing

Beyond the initial screening process, counselors may engage in a more comprehensive assessment process to identify problems and diagnose mental disorders. Regarding school counseling, the Individuals with Disabilities Education Improvement Act (IDEA, 2004) mandates that schools identify and serve children with social, emotional, and behavioral problems. Although school counselors do not diagnose mental disorders in school settings, school counselors are involved in the Response to Intervention (RTI) process, and therefore have a role in identifying specific problems or concerns that are interfering with the learning process. Within clinical mental health settings, counselors are often required to diagnose mental disorders classified within the Diagnostic and Statistical Manual of Mental Disorders (DSM-5; American Psychiatric Association [APA], 2013). Therefore, counselors in clinical settings may administer an assessment or a battery of assessments (multiple assessments) to assist with the diagnosis process.

Intervention Planning

After identifying the areas of concern and determining a diagnosis (if necessary), the counselor then, while collaborating with the child, has to make decisions about what interventions to integrate in counseling. In making this decision, the counselor may consider information gathered about the child's history of counseling and the success of previous counseling interventions. Additionally, the counselor may observe the child's interactions within the classroom, as well as with the parents, to determine what strategies (i.e. behavioral) are being used by these individuals and what therapeutic interventions to focus on during counseling. The counselor may also gather information about the child's strengths and consider strategies to integrate these strengths within the counseling process. For example, a counselor may choose to integrate expressive arts into counseling sessions with a child who enjoys art.

Evaluating Interventions

After developing and implementing counseling interventions, the counselor then seeks to evaluate the effectiveness of the intervention. The evaluation process includes assessing progress, as well as the outcome of the intervention. In evaluating the effectiveness of interventions, it is helpful to have assessment data from the initial session or prior to beginning an intervention (baseline data) to compare this data to subsequent data that is gathered throughout the counseling process and at the end of counseling. Progress evaluation specifically focuses on assessing how the client is doing throughout the counseling process. For example, a school counselor facilitating an eight-session small group on social skills may observe the children in their classrooms following the fourth session to identify improvements and continued areas for growth and then use this information to guide interventions in the remaining four sessions. Similarly, a counselor in a clinical setting working with an adolescent who is experiencing depression, as well as having poor relationships with her parents and peers, may administer a formal assessment to the child (i.e. Youth-Outcome Questionnaire-Self Report; Y-OQ-SR 2.0; Wells, Burlingame, Rose, and Lambert, 2005) after six sessions and compare the results to the assessment results from the first administration of the assessment during the first session to assess progress. Outcome evaluation involves assessing the area of focus after the intervention is completed (end of counseling). In the school example provided, this may involve classroom observations following the last group session (session 8). For the clinical setting example, this would involve administering the formal assessment (i.e. Y-OQ-SR 2.0) during the last counseling session.

Think about a client concern that is of interest to you for your specific setting (clinical mental health, school) and imagine working with a child or adolescent or group of children or adolescents experiencing that concern (academic problems, anxiety, depression, poor peer interactions, aggressive behavior). How would you assess the level of the concern and evaluate progress and the outcome of the intervention?

Exercise 9.1

METHODS OF ASSESSMENT

There are three main methods of assessment outlined in the assessment literature: (a) tests, (b) interviews, and (c) observations. Additionally, each of the assessment methods can be either formal (standardized or structured) or informal (unstructured). Formal assessments (i.e. standardized tests, structured interviews, formal observations) are developed through a rigorous process and include examining the psychometric properties (reliability and validity [discussed later in the chapter]) of the instrument. In contrast, informal assessments (i.e., non-standardized tests [e.g. checklists, questionnaires], unstructured interviews, informal observations) are developed without examining the psychometric properties. Furthermore, the counselor may use the methods of assessment with the child and/ or other individuals involved in the child's life (i.e. parents/ guardians, teachers) to gather data about the child.

Tests

Tests measure a vast array of topics and are designed using a variety of formats. Tests may include selected responses (e.g. multiple choice, true/false) and constructed responses (e.g. sentence completion, short answer, drawings, verbal responses [pronouncing a word]). Additionally, an individual may administer a test individually or in a group. Tests may also be self-administered (test takers read the test and answers the questions on their own). Furthermore, an individual may take a test on paper or on the computer, and tests may also be internet-based. Standardized tests are often available for purchase through a publishing company. In contrast, counselors may develop their own tests without going through the standardization process (non-standardized tests). For example, in assessing for depression, a counselor in a clinical mental health setting may administer a standardized test (e.g. Children's Depression Inventory-2 [CDI-2]; Kovacs, 2010; Reynolds Adolescent Depression Inventory-2 [RADS-2]; Reynolds, 1987) or create a non-standardized test (e.g. a checklist of symptoms based on the diagnostic criteria in the DSM-5 mood thermometer for the child to record how he or she is feeling). A school counselor may administer the Children's Academic Intrinsic Motivation Inventory (CAIMI; Gottfried, 1986) to assess formally academic motivation, or informally ask a child about specific classes and have him or her respond with a "thumbs up" for a class he or she likes and a "thumbs down" for a disliked class, along with further discussion about specific classes. Thus, counselors have a vast selection of tests to choose from that encompass a variety of formats.

Interviews

The interview process generally involves a verbal interaction between the counselor and the child, or other individual providing information about the child (i.e. parent/guardian, teacher). There are three general types of interviews: (a) structured, (b) semi-structured, and (c) unstructured. Structured interviews are standardized and involve a specific list of questions that are read in a specific order without varying from the format. There is limited flexibility in conducting a structured interview. A semi-structured interview, like a structured interview, contains a list of questions; however, within a semi-structured interview, the counselor can ask follow-up questions to gather additional information. The semi-structured format continues to provide some structure while also allowing for some flexibility. The final interview format, unstructured interview, allows for the greatest amount of flexibility. Within the unstructured format, the counselor may ask questions to gather information in a list of domains; however, there is not a predetermined list of questions that the counselor must ask and there is not a specified order for gathering information.

Observations

An observation is an assessment method that involves watching an individual or a group of individuals to obtain information about behavior. Observing behavior may involve a variety of components including (a) counting (tallying) the number of times a behavior occurs during a specified time, (b) recording the duration of time that the behavior occurs, or (c) rating the intensity of a behavior. Formal observations involve the use of a standardized observation instrument/protocol with a specific list of behaviors to observe and instructions regarding how to record the observations. Additionally, trained raters conduct formal observations. The Direct Observation Form (DOF; McConaughy and Achenbach, 2009) is an example of a formal observation instrument that involves observations of children in the classroom or during recess. In contrast, an informal observation is less structured and may involve taking notes while observing a child, without designating specific behaviors to observe, recording the data in a specific format, or receiving training on how to conduct the observation.

In a small group, develop an observation protocol to use in observing a child or adolescent in a classroom. What behaviors would you want to observe? How would you record data (counting the number of occurrences, duration, intensity)?

Exercise 9.2

ASSESSMENT PROCESS

The assessment process involves five overall steps. First, based on the purpose of the assessment, the counselor decides what assessments to use for collecting information. Next, the counselor administers the assessments. The third step involves scoring the assessments. Then, the counselor interprets the scores to make meaning of the assessment information. Finally, the counselor communicates the assessment results to the child and parent/guardian during feedback sessions. The information is shared with other stakeholders (e.g. a teacher) as appropriate and with the permission of the parent/guardian.

Selecting Assessments

After the purpose of the assessment is determined, the counselor then decides what assessments to use to gather information. Counselors may use a variety of sources to identify potential instruments, including assessment publishers' websites and catalogs (e.g. Mind Garden, Multi-Health Systems, Pearson Assessments, Psychological Assessment Resources [PAR], Western Psychological Services [WPS]), assessment manuals, counseling articles, internet searches, electronic databases [e.g. Mental Measurements Yearbook]). The decision about what specific assessments to use, specifically related to the selection of formal assessment, involves considering if the instrument is appropriate for the child (similar demographics of the child with the norming group). There are also practical considerations that may factor into the selection process (e.g. cost, administrating time, ease of scoring and interpreting the results). Additionally, counselors should only select assessments within their competency level. Many assessment publishing companies follow a qualification-level system to determine competency for the user (person administering, scoring, and interpreting the results; or overseeing this process if training others to help with administering and scoring who have less training). The system includes A, B, and C levels. Level A assessments require no specific qualification for the user. Level B requires a master's-level degree in the helping profession (e.g. counseling, education, psychology), licensure, certification, or membership in an approved organization in the helping profession, and training in administering, scoring, and interpreting clinical assessments. Level C requires a doctoral degree in the helping profession, licensure, certification, or membership in an approved organization in the helping profession, and training in the specific area of the assessment.

Selecting a test also requires counselors to have knowledge about the reliability and validity of an instrument, as it allows them to determine the appropriateness of the test. Information about the psychometrics of a test should be provided by the publisher and is often part of the test manual. Counselors should become especially familiar with tests that they give or receive regularly at their site. Another consideration is that counselors take the actual tests they administer. By taking the test, the counselor can learn more about the test-taking processes, the instructions, and working difficulties and other aspects of the test itself.

Reliability

The term reliability represents consistency and dependability of scores on a test (Gall, Gall, and Borg, 2007). The aim of reliability is to have a person score in the same way (consistently) if he or she were to take the test more than one time. Nonetheless, every time an individual takes a test, there is likely error that causes his or her scores to vary to some degree. The presence of error may cause the scores to vary across multiple testings. Some examples of sources of error across multiple testing periods are test-taker issues (e.g., anxiety, poor sleep, disengagement), environmental issues (e.g., a novel or distracting setting, noisy room, presence of others in the room), or instrument issues (e.g., items are worded unclearly, length of the test, unclear instructions). Reliability of a test can be calculated through different methods, including inter-rater (or inter-observer) reliability, internal consistency, test-retest reliability, and parallel form reliability. Reliability is an important aspect of determining the appropriateness of an instrument and the test publisher has the responsibility to provide evidence that a test is reliable and appropriate for the specified population.

Validity

Where reliability relates to the consistency of score over multiple test administrations, validity is the accuracy for which an instrument represents a construct. In other words, validity addresses whether or not a test measures the constructs it is said to measure. Further, validity relates to the usefulness and meaningfulness of the inferences or conclusions one can draw from the results of an instrument (Gall et al., 2007). Undoubtedly, counselors should be rigorous in identifying a test that intentionally measures the construct being examined. For example, a counselor trying to measure a student's test anxiety would not want to use a career values inventory, as it does not measure the desired construct. Similarly, a counselor would not want to use the Beck Depression Inventory II, a measure designed for individuals aged 13 and older, with a 7-year-old client because it was not intended for that population of test-taker. Counselors should consider the validity of a test for the construct that they are seeking to measure and the population of the clients they are serving. There are several types of validity, which include content validity, criterion validity, construct validity, and face validity. Within criterion validity, there is concurrent and predictive validity. Also, construct validity includes convergent and discriminant validity.

Administering Assessments

After selecting the assessment, the counselor administers the assessment to the child. When administering formal assessments, it is crucial that the counselor is familiar with the assessment and follows the procedures for administering the assessment. The counselor should only make modifications to accommodate for disabilities or exceptionalities and these accommodations should only be made after consulting with the manual to determine if the modifications will compromise the integrity of the assessment. It is also important that the directions for the assessment are clearly followed. For example, if the assessment is designed to focus on behavior during the past six months (e.g., Youth Self-Report [YSR]; Achenbach and Rescorla, 2001), it is important that the

Table 9.2 Types of evidence for validity

Type of Evidence	Description
Content validity	The evidence for the validity of a test is determined by how well the items on the test represent the construct under examination. Content validity can be established through the use of a panel of expert judges, a table or specifications or test blueprint, and the analysis of the response process.
Criterion-related validity	The evidence for the validity of a test is determined by the relationship between scores on a test (or subtest scores) and some external variables that should relate to the construct being measured. Criterion-related validity can be established by examining the correlations between test scores and scores on a test that is similar or different.
Concurrent validity	A form of criterion-related validity in which the scores on a test are related to the scores from an established or validated test that measures a related construct.
Predictive validity	A form of criterion-related validity in which the scores on a test are able to predict an outcome that is theoretically appropriate.
Construct validity	The evidence for the validity of a test is determined by the degree to which inferences can appropriately be made based on the test scores and the theoretical construct they theoretically measure. Construct validity can be established through factor analysis, evidence of homogeneity, convergent and discriminate validity, and group differentiation studies.
Convergent validity	A form of construct validity in which the scores on two separate tests (or subtest scores) that should correspond to one another are in fact related (i.e., measure the same construct).
Discriminant validity	A form of construct validity in which the scores on two separate tests (or subtest scores) that should be different are in fact dissimilar from one another (i.e., measure different constructs).
Face validity	The evidence for the validity of a test is determined by the appearance of a test. Face validity alone is not a sufficient source of validity.

child knows to complete the assessment related to what has occurred during that timeframe. In conducting an observation, the directions would apply to the observer. For example, the directions for the DOF (Direct Observation Form) state that information is collected during a 10-minute observation, therefore, it is important that the observation is 10 minutes in duration. Another consideration during the administration process is the assessment environment (i.e. noise, lighting, seating). Thus, the counselor attempts to promote a positive environment for the assessment process.

Scoring Assessments

Once the assessment information is gathered, the next step involves scoring the assessment. Some assessment data may not require scoring; however, tests and formal observations will generally require scoring. In scoring formal assessments, counselors should review the manual to ensure that they are following the scoring procedures correctly. The scoring process may involve transferring the data to another form or entering it into a software program. It is crucial that data are entered correctly to ensure accurate scoring; therefore checking the entry for mistakes is a necessary component of scoring assessments. The scoring process may also include conducting calculations and the counselor should also check the calculations for mistakes. Furthermore, some assessments have a computer software program that scores the assessment after the data is entered in the program.

Interpreting Assessments Results

After the assessment is scored, the counselor then interprets the assessment results. The assessment may have a variety of scores that require interpretation (i.e. age equivalent, grade equivalent, percentile rank, standard score). See Table 9.3. Specifically, when using norm-referenced tests, the individual's score is compared to a group of people who took the test when it was standardized (norm group).

   The interpretation of the scores may also require reviewing the technical manual for the assessment. The counselor may record the interpretation of results in an assessment report. Additionally, the counselor will use this information to communicate the assessment results to the child, parent/guardian,

Table 9.3 Types of assessment results scores

Terminology	Definition	Example
Age equivalent	Age at which the average individual's performance in the norm group is equivalent to the performance of the individual who you gave the test to in years and months	6-2 means that the individual is performing similarly to children who are 6 years old and 2 months
Grade equivalent	The grade level at which the average individual's performance in the norm group is similar to the performance of the individual who you gave the test to in grade level and months	7.5 means that the individual is performing similarly to children who are in the fifth month of seventh grade
Percentile rank	Rank of the individual's performance compared to others	45th percentile means that the individual scored equal to or better than 45 per cent of the other individuals who took the test
Raw score	Sum of responses on the test	
Standard score	Individual's score related to a normal distribution of scores	A score of 113 on a test with a mean of 100 and standard deviation of 15 would be interpreted as follows—the child scored slightly less than one standard deviation above the mean

and possibly other stakeholders. Therefore, it is crucial for the counselor to have a clear understanding of what the assessment results mean for the client, interpreting them accurately.

Communicating Assessment Results

In working with children and adolescents, it is crucial to communicate the assessment results to the child and the caregiver. This is important because the child and/or caregiver may provide information that helps further explain the results (e.g. not understanding specific items, factors that may have influenced responses [temperature of the room, noises or other distractions], results that yield a flat profile [results are similar across the assessment without having scores that are significantly higher or lower (Drummond et al., 2016)]). Additionally, failure to communicate the results may lead to the child or caregiver questioning the purpose of the assessment and viewing it as a waste of time or perceiving the lack of information as an attempt to hide the results from them. A child or caregiver may also assume that the lack of information means the results were negative, which may create unnecessary anxiety and concern among the child and/or the caregiver. Likewise, sharing information with only the caregiver may negatively influence the relationship between the counselor and the child because the child may view it as the counselor and caregiver keeping a secret. Some key areas to consider in communicating assessment results are (a) language, (b) timing, (c) amount of information, and (d) approach.

Language

In regards to language, the counselor will want to ensure that the language used is developmentally appropriate. Therefore, communicating the results with the child may be different from communication with the caregiver. Also, in regards to language, it is important to not use technical terms (e.g. standard score, percentile ranks) that may not be understood by the child or caregiver and to provide an explanation of the terms if they are important in understanding the results—using technical language that is not understood may overwhelm the child or caregiver. A counselor should consider whether the technical terms are needed to understand the results and how they will be used in working with the child and caregiver. Additionally, the counselor should avoid language associated with pathology, such as referring to the child's behavior as abnormal (Drummond et al., 2016).

Timing

Timing is another factor to consider. The counselor should ensure that the results are discussed in a timely manner. This may occur in the session following that when the assessments were administered; however, additional time may be required in some instances to score and interpret the assessments to provide a clear and accurate report to the child and caregiver. Following the completion of the assessments, the counselor can communicate to the child and caregiver when the feedback session will be held to discuss the results. This promotes open communication between the counselor and the child and caregiver.

Information to Share

A third area to consider is the amount of information to share with the child and the caregiver. The counselor will want to discuss each assessment briefly; however, the counselor may choose to highlight a few strengths and areas of greatest concern when discussing the results without reviewing every area of every assessment. This will vary depending on the number of assessments and the complexity of the assessment(s). The counselor strives to find a balance between informing the child and caregiver while being cautious not to overwhelm them.

Approach

A final area to consider is the approach used to communicate the assessment results. Many people are visual learners and so the inclusion of a visual may help communicate the assessment results. This may include a table or graph, and it may differ for a child and a caregiver. For example, a counselor may use a bar graph to display data for a parent/guardian or an adolescent and use different smiley faces and a variety of colors with children. Thus, the counselor strives to communicate the results to the child and caregiver in a client-friendly manner that will facilitate understanding.

This section of the chapter has focused on the five steps of the assessment process and the various aspects of each of these steps, including:

- selecting the assessments to administer that includes a review of the psychometric properties (e.g., reliability and validity) of the assessment
- administering assessments
- scoring assessments
- interpreting assessments that may involve explaining a variety of data (e.g., age equivalent, grade equivalent, percentile rank, standard score)
- communicating results to others (i.e., child, parent/ guardian, other stakeholders)

The next section focuses on categorizing assessments within five areas: (a) ability, (b) career, (c) intelligence, (d) behavioral, and (e) personality.

ASSESSMENT OF ABILITY

Achievement Tests

Achievement tests measure the *knowledge* or information an individual has acquired at the time of testing (Drummond et al., 2016; Hays, 2013). Typically, achievement tests measure the knowledge that an individual has learned and developed over the course of instruction or training. Educational environments (e.g., K-12 schools; higher education) commonly use achievement testing to assess student learning; however, achievement tests can be used in clinical and career settings as well. Further, achievement tests are regularly used for placement, selection, classification, and instructional reasons. The types of test used for examining achievement range from teacher-created criterion-referenced tests (e.g., a test made by a teacher for a lesson or class topic) to standardized normed-reference tests (e.g., a Stanford Achievement Tests). Across all types, the aim is to measure the knowledge a client poses for a given subject area.

Achievement tests include the use of survey batteries and diagnostic tests. *Survey batteries* are measures that include a collection of tests intended to measure one's knowledge spanning several content areas (e.g., Iowa Test of Basic Skills [ITBS]). Survey batteries are often used to measure the student's progress across grade levels and educational pathways. Additionally, survey batteries are commonly administered in a group format and norm-referenced. On the other hand, *diagnostic tests* are intended to examine specific learning difficulties or disabilities for a targeted academic area (e.g., Woodcock Johnson IV – Tests of Achievement). Diagnostic tests are commonly administered on an individual basis but are still norm-referenced. While survey batteries measure broad topics and do not go into great depth for a single area, diagnostic tests provide a detailed examination of an individual's competency for a specified area. Peterson, Lomas, Neukrug, and Bonner (2014) found that the *Wide Range Achievement Test* is one the most commonly used achievement tests, as noted by a sample of counselors in the United States, shortly followed by the Woodcock Johnson Tests of Achievement and Wechsler Individual Achievement Test. Table 9.4 provides some examples of commonly used survey batteries and diagnostic tests.

High-Stakes Testing

The expression *high-stakes testing* refers to any test that is used for important decision-making situations (i.e. accountability, funding, and mobility) and aids educational stakeholders in allocating resources. In other words, high-stakes testing is when there are significant consequences based on the outcomes of students' test results. High-stakes testing dates as far back as the 1960s with the Elementary and Secondary Education Act (ESEA) of 1965 and is more recently associated with the No Child Left Behind Act of 2001 (2002; Duffy et al., 2008). High-stakes testing may also be referred to as *accountability testing*, as educational stakeholders (e.g., students' teachers and/or administrators) are often responsible for the results. For example, if a school does well

Table 9.4 Examples of achievement tests for children and adolescents

Assessment	Grade Levels	Areas Assessed/Description
Common Achievement Batteries		
Stanford Achievement Test (SAT)	Elementary and Secondary levels	Spelling, writing, reading comprehension, science, and mathematics
Metropolitan Achievement Test (MAT)	K-12	Language arts, mathematics, science, and social studies
Iowa Test of Basic Skills	K-12	Language skills, mathematics, social studies, science, and study skills
TerraNova, Third Edition	K-12	Reading, mathematics, language arts, science, and social studies
Common Individual Diagnostic Tests		
Key Math Diagnostics Test	K-12	Measures essential skills and concepts in mathematics
Woodcock Johnson IV—Tests of Achievement	K-12 (ages 4–21)	Reading skills and ability, mathematics, writing, and academic skill
Wide Range Achievement Test 4	K-12 (ages 5–94)	Reading, spelling and mathematics
Peabody Individual Achievement Test–Revised	K-12	Reading recognition and comprehension, spelling, written expression, and mathematics
Kaufman Test of Educational Achievement Test	K-12 (ages 5–85)	Measures in-depth examination of key academic skills

on a high-stakes test, it may get increased funds, while a school that performs poorly may lose funding. Another example is if students perform well on a high-stakes test they can move to the next grade level, but if they do poorly then they may have to be retained a year.

High-stakes testing developed due to policymakers and public dissatisfaction with school performance and resulted in *standards-based reform*—the idea that goals or standards should be created for a school and teachers and administrators are held accountable for achieving the goals. High-stakes testing, often incorporating the use of achievement tests, is a method to measure the standards set for schools, and a determination is made on whether the standard was met or not. The aim of high stakes testing is also to ensure that students acquire vital topics and skills that are a part of the state curriculum. In addition, high-stakes testing was intended to create ways for students that were "left behind" to have access to educational resources that were equitable for all students. As Madaus and Russell (2010–2011) discuss, testing serves to monitor students' progress and to be an agent of change in regards to the content that is being taught. Madaus and Russell further note some of the negative consequences of high-stakes testing, including: (a) narrowed curriculum focus, (b) less time spent on topics not being tested (e.g., art and music), (c) curriculum changes in kindergarten and preschool, (d) corruption of the test results, (e) cheating, (f) a focus on students that are going to succeed versus students that need more attention, (g) student repeating grade levels, (h) dropout, and (i) anxiety and stress due to testing.

Counselors that work with students that undergo high-stakes testing, whether as a school counselor or mental health counselor, should consider several issues. First, students may experience elevated stress and anxiety that could be a focus of counseling such as mindfulness, coping skills for stress, or approaches to study and prepare for testing. Similarly, teachers and administers feel pressure for students to perform. Therefore, counselors can plan groups or school-wide initiatives to support the wellbeing of these different stakeholders (e.g., Thompson, Robertson, Curtis, and Frick, 2013). Counselors can be familiar with the testing procedures and score results, and as a result be a resource for students and parents as they receive the results. Oftentimes, testing procedures and results can be complex and hard to follow. As such, counselors can be allies with families and help them have a clear understanding about what the results mean. A last consideration for counselors is to prepare resources or access to resources for students and families to use in preparation for high-stakes testing. Resources (e.g. tutoring, support groups, advocacy strategies for students) can help families prepare and respond to periods of testing. Counselors have the skills and competencies in understanding assessment and providing helpful support to prepare students and their families for high-stakes testing.

Aptitude Tests

Aptitude tests measure the potential that students have to learn or acquire knowledge or skill in a given area (Drummond et al., 2016; Hays, 2013). That is, aptitude tests measure how well students are likely to perform in the future in a given area, given their scores on the test. Aptitude tests are normally used for prediction purposes. In relationship to working with youth, aptitude testing is uniquely important for higher education, professional schools (e.g., training for a specific trade or discipline such as hair stylist, mechanic, or IT specialist), and college admissions. The *SAT Reasoning Test* (www.collegereadiness.collegeboard.org) is a popular aptitude test that high school students complete as they are applying and considering undergraduate college careers. The *SAT Reasoning Test* is used by college admissions as a way to examine the likelihood that the students will be successful when they participate in college coursework. On the other hand, the Preliminary SAT/National Merit Scholarship Qualifying Test (PSAT/NMSQT) is similar and often used to prepare for the SAT. However, the PSAT/NMSQT can also be used to help students during the college decision-making process and is the initial qualifying step for National Merit Scholarships. A second commonly used aptitude test used for college admissions is the *ACT* (www.act.org). The ACT was first called American College Testing and was based on the Iowa Test of Educational Development. The ACT is more common in the midwestern part of the United States; however, most colleges will accept both the ACT and SAT. Aptitude tests also apply to graduate and professional schools (e.g., the Graduate

Record Exam [GRE], Milers Analogies Test [MAT], and Medical College Admissions Test [MCAT]). The SAT and ACT both ranked high in Peterson et al.'s (2014) study of assessments commonly used by counselors, which demonstrates their popularity in the counseling field.

ASSESSMENT USED IN CAREER COUNSELING

Careers and work is a large part of an adult's life and career assessment is a vital aspect of career planning. For young people, careers and job decision-making are likely seen as distant events or goals. One consideration for counselors working with children and adolescents is to help these youth recognize the trajectory or pathway to a post-school career and to help them to acknowledge that their academic and personal experiences today inform their initial career paths. Also, counselors should consider the developmental perspective of children and adolescents and recognize when specific assessment activities are appropriate. Career assessment is a process that aims to help young people make decisions about their career direction and can range from experiential activities (e.g., Holland's Party Game) to standardized and formal assessments (e.g., Strong Interest Inventory). Counselors should tailor the activities to the developmental and academic needs of their clients and their goals in career counseling.

Within career counseling, there are several constructs measured by assessments, including: (a) interests, (b) values, (c) personality, (d) ability and skills, (e) career development/readiness, and (f) standardized assessment programs. Zunker (2016) reported that academic achievement tests are also useful in career counseling, and we discuss these tests in an earlier section of this chapter. Additionally, Peterson et al. (2014) found that the *Strong Interest Inventory* was ranked as the most commonly used career assessment, closely followed by the *Self-Directed Search*, *Occupational Information Network* (O*Net), and *Values Scale*. Table 9.5 lists some commonly used standardized assessments by the type of construct they measure. Counselors seeking to use a standardized assessment should consider their aim or goal for using the test (e.g., to learn about a student's career interests) and then identify which test would match the resources and needs of the client.

For many counselors, the cost of assessments is a challenge; this is especially true for school counselors. However, many states offer a standardized career assessment system. For example, Florida residents can access Employ Florida Marketplace and complete several interest and skills assessments. In North Carolina, residents can access the College Foundation of North Carolina's website (www.cfnc.org) and take a series of assessments (i.e. interests, skills, and values). Many of these programs include career and college planning tools. Other states have similar programs that counselors can utilize for their work with clients. Counselors can check with their state's department of education (DOE) or employment support programs to see if they provide similar tools for career assessment. In addition, Occupational Information Network (O*Net) (www.onetonline.org) has several assessment tools (e.g., interest profiler and career exploration/information) available for free in the My Next Move section of the website. A notable resource on O*Net

Table 9.5 Examples of standardized assessments commonly used for career assessment

Career Assessment	Type of Assessment
Career Beliefs Inventory	Career beliefs
Career Thoughts Inventory	Career beliefs
My Vocational Situation	Career beliefs
Self-Directed Search	Interest
Strong Interest Inventory	Interest
Campbell Interest and Skills Survey	Interest
Childhood Career Development Scale	Interest
Super's Work Values Inventory	Values
Rokeach Values Survey	Values
Myers-Briggs Type Indicator	Personality
California Test of Personality	Personality
Minnesota Counseling Inventory	Personality
Differential Aptitude Test	Ability and skills
Armed Services Vocational Aptitude Battery	Ability and skills
The General Aptitude Test Battery	Ability and skills
Ability Explorer	Ability and skills
Career Maturity Inventory	Career development/readiness
Career Development Inventory	Career development/readiness
Occupational Information Network (O*Net)	Standardized assessment programs
Kuder Career Planning System	Standardized assessment programs
Career Occupational Preferences System	Standardized assessment programs
ACT WorkKeys	Standardized assessment programs

is the Mi Próximo Paso section, which is the same resource as My Next Move, but written and designed for Spanish-speaking users. Counselors can use any of these systems to assess the career interests of children and adolescents.

Qualitative assessments, often times informal and unstandardized, can also be useful tools for counselors seeking to explore career-related issues with children and adolescents. Counselors may use qualitative assessments as the sole form of assessment or in conjunction with other assessments (i.e. interview, self-report of ability/interests/values, behavioral observation, or other assessment activities related to career issues). Okocha (1998) noted four qualitative career assessments that counselors may find useful, including career genograms, lifeline activity, Super et al.'s (1992) life career rainbow, and a life career assessment interview. Career genograms are a qualitative activity used to explore career patterns within the family (Gibson, 2005). Career genograms help clients to recognize patterns of the careers family members chose, their educational background, and their career values and interests. Along with creating a three-generational (or more) pictorial graph of their family, the client can engage in a dialogue with the counselor about his or her impressions and reflections on his or her family's career history. Furthermore, career lifelines help clients explore past life experiences that shape their career interests and trajectories (Brott, 2001).

Super's (1992) life career rainbow is an activity in which clients depict, in graphical form, how nine life roles are noticeable across their life from birth to death. The activities require clients to draw each of their current and ideal life roles and the barriers to achieving these roles that are present. Okocha (1998) provided a graph to demonstrate this activity by showing two pie charts depicting current and preferred percentage of time given to the individual's life roles. The fourth qualitative assessment, noted by Okocha, is the life career assessment, which is a structured interview protocol originally developed by Gysbers and Moore (1987). In administering the life career assessment, counselors ask and explore the following four areas: (a) career assessment (e.g., work experience, volunteer experience, education, training, and leisure activities), (b) typical day (e.g., personal style of the client), (c) strengths and obstacles (e.g., identify barriers in the career planning process and strengths used), and (d) summary of the themes, interests, and skills. Counselors interested in learning more about these qualitative methods of career assessment are encouraged to read Okocha's article.

Another example of a qualitative assessment for career exploration is a *card-sort activity*. A card-sort activity (Osborn and Bethell, 2009; Peterson, 1998) for occupational skills involves having a client sort job titles into piles based on their similarity. Then, the client compares the jobs in each of the piles and label them. As a part of the process, the client can identify the characteristics of each pile and note which of the piles is most aligned with his or her own desires and skills. A similar adaptation of a card-sort activity is to list a series of work-related values on a set of cards. On one side of the card a value is named and the other side includes the definition of the value. The client can then rank the values he or she believes to be most important. Then, the counselor and client can discuss the identified work values in relationship to potential jobs or careers. In either case, card-sort activities require the client to articulate preferences or knowledge about him or herself. In doing so, the individual is able to reduce the number of career related topics/issues for consideration and planning.

ASSESSMENT OF INTELLIGENCE

There is a vast array of definitions for intelligence and many theorists have proposed different ways to conceptualize the construct of intelligence. Scholars disagree on whether there is one general intellectual ability, several intellectual abilities, or multiple intelligences that are separate from each other. Nonetheless, many scholars generally agree that intelligence includes the development of cognitive abilities (i.e. acquiring knowledge, reasoning, problem-solving), and therefore intelligence tests may focus on measuring a variety of cognitive abilities (Drummond et al., 2016).

There are numerous intelligence tests that professionals may use to assess for intelligence. The Individuals with Disabilities Education Improvement Act (IDEA, 2004) requires the use of intelligence tests to assess for intellectual disabilities, and professionals may also use them to assess for specific learning disabilities, or giftedness (Kranzler and Floyd, 2013). Some intelligence tests are designed for individual administration while others are designed for group administration. Additionally, there are non-verbal intelligence tests designed for individuals who may have difficulty with the verbal tests, such as individuals with language or hearing problems. Nonverbal intelligence tests require no verbal instructions from the individual administering the test and all test-taker responses are nonverbal. There are also brief intelligence tests that are typically used for screening purposes. Most intelligence tests require a "C"-level qualification of the administrator. However, the Kauffman Brief Intelligence Test (KBIT-2; Kauffman and Kauffman, 2004b) is an example of a brief intelligence test that level "B" users would be qualified to administer. Although counselors will not administer most intelligence tests, children or caregivers may ask them to interpret the scores on the assessment. Therefore, it is important that counselors have an understanding of scoring terms. Table 9.6 provides a list of well-known individual, group, non-verbal, and brief intelligence tests.

Behavioral Assessment

Behavioral assessments focus on the measurement of observable behavior. This is distinguished from personality assessments that focus on traits. Frick, Barry, and Kamphaus (2010) describe three characteristics of behavioral assessments that distinguish them from personality trait assessments. First, behavioral assessments are grounded in behavioral theory and the concept of operant conditioning. Second, behavioral assessments are more distinguishable from medical-model assessments by focusing on the measurement of symptoms and behaviors instead of focusing on the underlying conditions or causes. Finally, behavioral assessments focus on measuring specific behaviors instead of measuring several behaviors that are then grouped together to form a scale. Although the traditional measurement of behaviors and traits are different, Frick and colleagues (2010) acknowledged that some scholars (i.e. Achenbach, Conners) have classified behaviors into dimensions of behaviors that may not be distinguishable from assessments that focus on measuring personality traits. We present some examples of structured behavioral assessments within Table 9.7.

Table 9.6 Examples of individual, group, nonverbal, and brief intelligence tests for children and adolescents

Individual Tests	Age	Areas Assessed
Cognitive Assessment System (CAS-2)	5–18	full scale (standard or battery)—planning, attention, simultaneous, and successive processes
Differential Abilities Scales (DAS-II) (3 scales)		
Lower-Level Early Years Battery	2:6–3:5	general conceptual ability—verbal, nonverbal
Upper-Level Early Years Battery	3:6–7	general conceptual ability—verbal, nonverbal, spatial, processing speed (5+), working memory (5+)
School-Age Battery	7–18	general conceptual ability—verbal, nonverbal, spatial, processing speed, working memory
Kauffman Assessment Battery for Children (KABC-2)	3–18	fluid crystalized or mental processing—crystalized IQ, fluid IQ, long-term retrieval, short-term memory, visual–spatial
Reynolds Intelligence Assessment Scales (RIAS-2)	3–94	composite IQ—verbal IQ, nonverbal IQ, composite memory, speeded processing
Stanford-Binet Intelligence Scales (SB5)	2–90	full scale, verbal, nonverbal—fluid reasoning, knowledge, quantitative reasoning, visual–spatial processing, working memory
Wechsler Scales (2 of 3 scales for children)		
Wechsler Preschool and Primary Scale of Intelligence (WPPSI-IV)	2:6–7:7	full scale—verbal comprehension, visual–spatial, working memory, fluid reasoning (4+), processing speed (4+)
Wechsler Intelligence Scale for Children (WISC-V)	6–17	full scale—verbal comprehension, visual–spatial, working memory, fluid reasoning, processing speed
Woodcock-Johnson IV Test of Cognitive Abilities (WJ-IV)	2–90+	general intellectual ability (extended or standard)—comprehension–knowledge, long-term retrieval, visual–spatial thinking, auditory processing, fluid reasoning, short-term memory
Group Tests		
Cognitive Abilities Test (CogAT)	K-12	composite—verbal, nonverbal, quantitative
Otis-Lennon School Ability Test (OLSAT-8)	K-12	overall school ability—verbal, nonverbal, quantitative
Nonverbal Tests		
Leiter International Performance Scale (Leiter-3)	3–75+	nonverbal IQ—nonverbal memory, processing speed, social–emotional examiner rating scales
Universal Nonverbal Intelligence Test (UNIT-2)	5–22	full scale, abbreviated, standard with memory, standard without memory—memory, reasoning, quantitative
Wechsler Nonverbal Scale of Ability (WNV)	4 – 22	full scale
Brief Tests		
Kauffman Brief Intelligence Test (KBIT-2)	4–90	intelligence composite—verbal, nonverbal
Wechsler Abbreviated Scale of Intelligence (WASI-2)	6–90	full scale-4, full scale-2—verbal comprehension, perceptual reasoning
Wide Range Intelligence Test (WRIT)	4–86	general IQ, verbal IQ, visual IQ

PERSONALITY ASSESSMENT

Similar to the construct of intelligence, there is a vast array of definitions and theories to explain the construct of personality. Personality is an "individual's stable tendencies to think, feel, and act in particular ways" (Donnellan and Robins, 2012, p. 68). Personality assessments are methods used to assess these individual differences or traits. Personality assessments include (a) standardized (objective) assessments and (b) projective techniques. These assessments may also focus on either pathological or non-pathological aspects of personality.

Structured Personality Assessments

Structured or objective personality assessments generally encompass a selected-response format or rating scale. The selected-response format offers a relatively quick response as well as scoring time. There is a vast array of structured personality assessments that encompass either a broad or narrow focus. Personality assessments with a broad focus assess multiple aspects of personality, while assessments with a narrow focus may assess specific symptoms or behaviors. Personality assessments may also measure positive aspects of personality (e.g. self-esteem). Table 9.7 presents a list of well-known structured behavioral and personality assessments for children and adolescents.

Table 9.7 Examples of behavioral and personality assessments for children and adolescents

Assessment	Age	Areas Assessed	Qualification
Achenbach			
Child Behavior Checklist (CBCL) (parent ratings)			B
Child Behavior Checklist (CBCL) Preschool	1:6–5	7 syndrome scales; internalizing, externalizing, and total problems; 5 DSM oriented scales, language development	B
Child Behavior Checklist (CBCL) School Age	6–18	3 competence scales and total competence; 8 syndrome scales; internalizing, externalizing, and total problems; 6 DSM oriented scales; 3 other problem scales	B
Teacher Report Form (TRF) (teacher ratings)			B
Caregiver–Teacher Report Form (CTRF)	1:6–5	6 syndrome scales; internalizing, externalizing, and total problems; 5 DSM oriented scales	B
Teacher Report Form (TRF) School Age	6–18	same scales as CBCL-school age, except for no competence scales, 5 adaptive functioning scales, and total functioning	B

Assessment	Age	Areas Assessed	Qualification
Youth Self-Report (YSR)	11–18	same scales as CBCL-school age, except for 2 other problem scales, and positive qualities	B
Brief Problem Monitor (BPM) (brief forms for progress monitoring for BCL-school age, TRF-school age and YSR)	6–18 11–18 (YSR)	internalizing, externalizing, attention, and total problems	B
Direct Observation Form (DOF)-classroom	6–11	classroom observation—six problem areas, total problems, on task behavior	B
Direct Observation Form (DOF)-recess	6–11	recess observation—aggressive behavior, total problems	B
Test Observation Form (TOF)	2–18	5 syndrome scales; internalizing, externalizing, and total problems; attention deficit/hyperactivity problems scale	B
Behavior Assessment System for Children (BASC-3)			
BASC Parent Rating Scales (BASC-3 PRS)		7 content scales and 4 composite scales on all PRS forms	B
BASC-3 PRS-P (preschool)	2–5	8 clinical scales, 4 adaptive scales, 2 clinical indexes	B
BASC-3 PRS-C (child)	6–11	9 clinical scales, 5 adaptive scales, 4 clinical indexes	B
BASC-3 PRS-A (adolescent)	12–21	9 clinical scales, 5 adaptive scales, 4 clinical indexes	B
BASC Teacher Rating Scales (BASC-3 TRS)		7 content scales on all PRS forms	B
BASC-3 TRS-P (preschool)	2–5	8 clinical scales, 3 adaptive scales, 4 composite scales, 2 clinical indexes	B
BASC-3 TRS-C (child)	6–11	10 clinical scales, 5 adaptive scales, 5 composite scales, 4 clinical indexes	B
BASC-3 TRS-A (adolescent)	12–21	10 clinical scales, 5 adaptive scales, 5 composite scales, 4 clinical indexes	B
BASC-3 Student Observation System (BASC-3 SOS)	school ages	classroom observation—adaptive behaviors and maladaptive behaviors	B
BASC-3 Self-Report of Personality (SRP)			B

Table 9.7 continued

Assessment	Age	Areas Assessed	Qualification
BASC-3 SRP-I (interview)	6–7	total score	B
BASC-3 SRP-C (children)	8–11	10 clinical scales, 4 adaptive scales, 5 composite scales	B
BASC-3 SRP-A (adolescents)	12–21	12 clinical scales, 4 adaptive scales, 4 content scales, 5 composite scales, 1 clinical index	B
BASC-3 SRP-COL (college)	18–25	12 clinical scales, 4 adaptive scales, 4 content scales, 4 composite scales, 1 clinical index	B
Lachar et al.			
Personality Inventory for Children-2 (PIC-2) (parent rating)	5–19	9 adjustment scales, validity response scales	C
Student Behavior Survey (SBS) (teacher rating)	K-12	academic resources, adjustment problems, disruptive behavior	C
Personality Inventory for Youth (PIY) (self-report)	9–19	9 clinical scales, 4 validity scales	C
Minnesota Multiphasic Personality Inventory-Adolescent (MMPI-A)	14–18	10 clinical scales, 15 content scales, 11 supplementary scales, 8 validity scales	C
Myers-Briggs Type Indicator (MBTI) Form M	14–adult	generates 4 letter code representing one of 16 personality types	C
Youth Outcome Questionnaire (Y-OQ) 2.01 (parent rating)	4–11	64 items, 6 subscales, measures treatment progress	B
Youth Outcome Questionnaire (Y-OQ) SR 2.0 (youth self-report)	12–17	64 items, total score, 6 subscales	B
Youth Outcome Questionnaire (Y-OQ) 30.2 PR and SR (parent and self-report versions)		brief versions, 30 items, total score	B

Projective Techniques

Projective techniques encompass an open-ended response format, which results in more subjective interpretations. This response format generally requires more time for an individual to take the assessment and for the professional to score the assessment compared to administration and scoring time for a structured personality assessment. However, the open-ended response format provides an opportunity for individuals to disclose information about themselves that may not be revealed in a structured personality assessment. Advanced training is needed to score and interpret projective assessments and counselors should also consult their state laws regarding the use of these assessments. Controversy exists regarding the use of projective techniques due to the challenges associated with objectivity and standardization of these assessments. There is a variety of projective techniques that include drawing techniques, inkblot techniques, projective questions and sentence completion, and thematic storytelling.

Drawing Techniques

A counselor may use drawing techniques with children of various ages, including young children who may have difficulty with verbal expression. Children often enjoy drawing and the counselor may provide a variety of drawing materials (i.e. crayons, markers, colored pencils) to facilitate this assessment process. One drawing technique is Draw-a-Person (DAP; Machover, 1949), which involves the child drawing a picture of a whole person and then giving the child another sheet of paper and asking him or her to draw a person of the opposite sex. The counselor then asks the child open-ended questions about the drawing (e.g. How is the person feeling? What is the person doing?). Koppitz (1968) discussed three areas to focus on for interpreting the drawing in the DAP: (a) how is the figure drawn, (b) who is the person in the drawing, (c) what is being expressed in the drawing. Another projective drawing technique is House–Tree–Person (HTP; Buck, 1948), which involves asking the child to draw a house, tree, and a person on separate sheets of paper. Typically, the house represents home life and family relationships, the tree represents the inner strengths and weaknesses and relationship with the environment (unconscious level), and the person represents how the person feels about him or herself (self-concept) at the conscious level (Frick et al., 2010).

The counselor may also have the child include drawings of others to reveal information about a child's personality. Kinetic family drawings (KFD; Burns and Kaufman, 1970) involves the counselor asking the child to draw a picture of everyone in the family, including the child him or herself, doing something. The counselor processes the drawing with the child by asking open-ended questions about the people in the drawing and what they are doing. Additionally, the counselor may use a kinetic school drawing (KSD; Prout and Phillips, 1974), which involves asking the child to draw a picture of him or herself, teacher, and one or two friends, with everyone doing something. Thus, the counselor may use a variety of prompts in using drawings for assessment purposes. There are numerous books that scholars have written about interpreting children's drawings; however, it is important to use caution when interpreting drawings and to use this as one piece of assessment data along with other types.

Inkblot Techniques

The inkblot technique involves the child looking at an inkblot and describing what he or she sees in the inkblot. The Rorschach is a well-known inkblot technique that includes a series of 10 inkblot cards. The Rorschach Comprehensive System (Exner, 1974) is commonly used for administering, coding, and interpreting the Rorschach. Another inkblot technique is the Holtzman Inkblot Technique (HIT; Holtzman, 1961), which includes 45 inkblots in a variety of different formats (i.e. color, visual texture). The HIT is designed for children aged 5 and above and requires a "C"-level qualification.

Projective Questions and Sentence Completion

Projective questions encompass the counselor asking the child a question and the child providing a verbal or written response that reveals aspects of the child's personality. Some example of projective questions are: (a) If you had three wishes, what would you wish for? and (b) If you could wave a magic wand and change something in your life, what would it be? Sentence completion involves a list of sentence stems (i.e. I wish … I feel …) and the child provides a verbal or written response to complete the sentence. The Rotter Incomplete Sentence Blank-2 (RISB-2; Rotter and Rafferty, 1992) is a well-known 40-item sentence completion test designed for individuals in high school through adulthood (there are three versions—high school, college, adult). The counselor can also use story completion with children, which involves the counselor beginning a story and then asking the child what will happen next.

Thematic Storytelling

In thematic storytelling, the professional shows a child a picture and asks the child to tell a story about the picture, which may include what is currently happing in the picture, what happened before the scene in the picture, and what will happen next. The professional may also ask the child to describe what the characters in the picture might be saying and feeling. Some examples of thematic storytelling assessments include the Thematic Appreciation Test (TAT; Murray, 1943), Children's Appreciation Test (CAT; Bellak and Bellak, 1949), Children's Appreciation Test-Humans (CAT-H; Bellak and Bellak, 1949), Children's Appreciation Test-Supplement (CAT-S; Bellak and Bellak, 1949), Roberts Appreciation Test for Children (RATC; Roberts and Gruber, 2005), and Tell Me A Story (TEMAS; Constantino, Malgady, and Rogler, 1988). See Table 9.8.

Table 9.8 Thematic storytelling assessments

Assessment	Age	Areas Assessed/Description	Qualification
Thematic Appreciation Test (TAT)	5–79	31 pictures (subsets for girls, boys, men, and women); reveals individual's emotions, conflicts, and drives	C
Children's Appreciation Test (CAT)	3–10	10 animal pictures in a social context (e.g. child in conflict, identities, roles, family structures, interpersonal interaction)	C
Human pictures (CAT-H)	3–10	10 human pictures addressing social context	C
Supplement (CAT-S)	3–10	10 animal pictures that focus on common family situations	C
Roberts Appreciation Test for Children (RATC-2)	6–18	16 pictures in 3 versions (black, Hispanic, white children); scales include theme overview, available resources, problem identification, resolution, emotion, outcome, and unusual or atypical responses	C
Tell Me A Story (TEMAS)	5–18	23 stimulus cards in 2 versions (minority, non-minority); designed for inner-city children and adolescents; measures 9 personality, 18 cognitive, and 7 affective functions	C

Table 9.9 Additional assessments

Assessment	Age	Areas Assessed/Description	Setting	Qualification
Self-Esteem				
Piers-Harris 2 Children's Self Concept Scale	7–18	self-concept	both	B
Anxiety				
Multidimensional Anxiety Scale for Children (MASC-2)	8–19	identify anxiety symptoms	clinical	B
Depression				
Children's Depression Inventory (CDI-2)	7–17	identify depressive symptoms	clinical	B
Reynold's Adolescent Depression Scale (RADS-2)	11–20	identify depressive symptoms	clinical	B
Reynold's Child Depression Scale (RCDS-2)	7–13	identify depressive symptoms	clinical	B

Table 9.9 continued

Trauma

Trauma Symptom Checklist for Children	8–16	acute and chronic posttraumatic symptoms	clinical	B
Trauma Symptom Checklist for Young Children	3–12	acute and chronic posttraumatic symptomology	clinical	B

School Motivation

Children's Academic Intrinsic Motivation Inventory (CAIMI)	9–14	motivation for learning in general and in specific areas	school	B
School Motivation and Learning Strategies Inventory (SMALSI)	8–18	identify poor learning strategies that affect academic performance	school	B

Miscellaneous

Beck Youth Inventories (BYI-II)	7–18	5 inventories of 20 questions each (anger, anxiety, depression, disruptive behavior, self-concept)	clinical	B
Screening Assessment for Gifted Elementary and Middle School Students (SAGES-2)	5–14	mathematics/science, language arts/social studies, reasoning	school	B
Five Factor Wellness Inventory (FFWEL-E)	third grade and up	wellness	both	B
Five Factor Wellness Inventory (FFWEL-T)	sixth grade and up	wellness	both	B
Suicidal Ideation Questionnaire (SIQ)	12–18	screen for suicidal ideation	both	B

In summary, the authors discussed five general categories of assessments related to children and adolescents and provided examples of assessments in each area. Although counselors may not administer assessments in each of these areas, the assessment data may be presented in a client's file, and therefore it is important that counselors have a basic understanding of each of these five categories:

- ability tests
- career assessments
- intelligence tests
- behavioral assessments
- personality assessments

The final section of this chapter focuses on two case studies. The first focuses on counselors using achievement assessments in a school setting and the second relates to counselors using behavioral assessments in a clinical mental health setting.

Case Study: Ryan

This case study focuses on a counselor using achievement assessments in a school setting.

Ryan is in the Fall semester of his junior year at Brookshire High School and is preparing to take the SAT. Ryan has asked for help to prepare for the test and remembers taking the PSAT in his sophomore year. He asked for his parents to join the meeting to help him develop a plan to study for the test. Ryan and his parents meet with his school counselor, Ms. Markus, after school. At the start of the meeting, Ms. Markus described the purpose of the PSAT and common terminology associated with the test. She noted the similarities between the PSAT and the SAT and remarked that it is the initial step for National Merit Scholarships. Also, Ms. Markus gave Ryan's parents a copy of the PSAT report and the link to the college board website that contains more information about the test. Ms. Markus inquired about the family's prior knowledge about the PSAT and then discussed additional aspects of the test. Ms. Markus devoted sufficient time to helping the family understand the meaning of the PSAT and the associated processes prior to reviewing the results.

After Ms. Markus answered the family's questions, she reviewed the scores (total score and section scores) Ryan received on his PSAT during his sophomore year with the family. During the review, they discovered that Ryan performed particularly well on the math section, with a score of 700. However, the reading and writing score was 280, which is low, and needs strengthening. They further examined the reading and writing scores and discovered that Ryan performed well on the Reading section with a score of 35, but performed poorly on the Written and Language sections with a score of 14. After reviewing the results with Ryan, Ms. Markus processed his thoughts and reactions to the results to assign meaning to this new information. Then, Ms. Markus sought Ryan's ideas about ways to move forward with the support of his parents. As a result, Ryan decided to continue studying across all areas of the SAT, and to seek additional support on the writing section of the test. Next, Ryan developed a plan that included seeking extra help from his language arts teacher, enrolling in a creative writing class for the spring semester, and working with a writing tutor. The counselor asked Ryan and his parents to meet with her again at the end of the Spring semester to discuss his progress and modify the plan if necessary.

Case Study: Mark

This second case study relates to clinical mental health involving behavioral assessment.

Sarah is a mental health counselor who works for a community mental health agency that provides counseling for children and adolescents and their families. Mark is an 11-year-old in sixth grade who was referred to the counseling agency for disruptive behavior at school, including aggressive behaviors towards his peers and difficulty following directions and redirection from teachers. The referral indicated that Mark had the most difficulty in math class and had received several discipline referrals from his math teacher. Sarah was giving the referral and met with Mark and his parents. Mark's parents reported that Mark is an only child, has only a few friends, and struggles with interacting with his peers. They also reported that they have some problems with Mark following directions at home, but they can tolerate his behavior.

Sarah asked Mark's parents to sign a release of information to talk with the school and she contacted the school counselor and the math teacher at the school to obtain more information and to arrange a visit to the school to observe Mark's behavior in the classroom. During the school visit, Sarah met with the school counselor and the math teacher and also observed in the math classroom. She used an informal narrative to collect information during the classroom observation, emphasizing what occurred prior to Mark becoming aggressive, how the teacher responded to his behavior, and how Mark responded to the teacher. Sarah also observed Mark for a short time in science class for comparison. Additionally, Sarah asked Mark to complete the Youth Self-Report (YSR), his parents to complete the Child Behavior Checklist (CBCL), and the teacher to complete the Teacher's Report Form (TRF). The data from the TRF and CBCL were similar; however, the parents reported the problems being less severe than the teacher. Mark's own assessment of his behavior showed only slight concerns. Sarah discussed the data with Mark and his parents separately. Mark stated that math was stupid and that his math teacher just didn't like him. Sarah discussed with Mark that her observation of his behavior in science and his parents' report showed similar concerns with a lower level of severity. Mark stated that he had met with the school counselor a few times, but that it didn't fix anything because his math teacher was still "on his case" all the time and nothing he did helped.

Despite some reluctance, Mark agreed to meet with Sarah once a week to "try out" counseling with her. On a weekly basis, Sarah had Mark, his parents, and the teacher complete the BPM (Brief Problem Monitor) to monitor his progress. She also remained in contact with the school counselor about discipline referrals. In the first two weeks of counseling, Mark's score showed significant improvement on the BPM; however, this was inconsistent with scores from his parents and the teacher. Sarah processed this information with Mark and he acknowledged that he thought if he showed improvement on the report that he completed that he wouldn't have to come back to counseling. After further discussion, Mark agreed to continue attending counseling and gradually he showed progress on the reports from his parents, teacher, and his own report. The reports provided clear data for Mark to see his progress, along with a decrease in referrals, and improved grades.

SUMMARY

Assessment is a crucial aspect in working with children and adolescents in both the clinical metal health and school settings. This chapter has focused on discussing the purposes, methods, and categories of assessment. The authors presented form ethical and legal information related to the use of assessments with children and adolescents. Additionally, the authors discussed the steps in the assessment process. Moreover, the authors presented information about test reliability and validity. Finally, the authors highlighted well-known assessments in each of the five assessment categories, presented in the chapter, and provided some case studies to illustrate the use of tests with children and adolescents. Key points that arose were:

- Counselors engage in the assessment process for four primary purposes: (a) screening, (b) identifying and diagnosing, (c) intervention planning, and (d) evaluating interventions (progress and outcome).
- Counselors collect information through three primary methods: (a) tests, (b) interviews, and (c) observations.
- The assessment process involves five steps: (a) selecting, (b) administering, (c) scoring, (d) interpreting, and (e) communication results.
- Data may come from multiple sources (e.g., child, parent/guardian, teacher, treatment file, school record).
- Categories of assessments include ability, career, intelligence, behavior, and personality.

Additional Resources

American Educational Research Association (AERA), American Psychological Association (APA), and National Council on Measurement in Education (NCME). (2014). *Standards for educational and psychological testing*. Washington, DC: Authors.
Association for Assessment and Research in Counseling (AARC): http://aarc-counseling.org/
The National Child Traumatic Stress Network Measures Review Database: http://www.nctsn.org/resources/online-research/measures-review

Assessment Publishers

College Board: www.collegereadiness.collegeboard.org
Mind Garden Assessment: www.mindgarden.com
Multi-Health Systems (MHS): www.mhs.com
Pearson Assessment: http://www.pearsonclinical.com
Psychological Assessment Resources (PAR): www.parinc.com
Western Psychological Services (WPS): wpspublish.com

Suggested Readings

Connors, E. H., Arora, P., Curtis, L., and Stephan, S. H. (2015). Evidence-based assessment in school mental health. *Cognitive and Behavioral Practice* 22, 60–73.
Frick, P. J., Barry, C. T., and Kamphaus, K. W. (2010). *Clinical assessment of child and adolescent personality and behavior*, 3rd ed. New York, NY: Springer.
Jensen-Doss, A. and Hawley, K. M. (2010). Understanding barriers to evidence-based assessment: Clinician attitudes toward standardized assessment tools. *Journal of Clinical Child and Adolescent Psychology* 39, 885–896. doi:10.1080/15374416.2010.517169
Klepsch, M. and Logie, L. (1982). *Children draw and tell: An introduction to the projective uses of children's human figure drawings*. New York, NY: Brunner/Mazel.
McLeod, B. D., Jensen-Doss, A., and Ollendick, T. H. (eds.) (2013). *Diagnostic and behavioral assessment in children and adolescents: A clinical guide*. New York, NY: The Guilford Press.

Nickerson, A. B. and Fishman, C. E. (2013). Promoting mental health and resilience through strength-based assessment in US schools. *Educational and Child Psychology* 30, 7–17.

Substance Abuse and Mental Health Services Administration (2011). *Identifying mental health and substance use problems of children and adolescents: A guide for child-serving organizations* (HHS Publication No. SMA 12-4670). Rockville, MD: Author. Retrieved from http://store.samhsa.gov/shin/content//SMA12-4700/SMA12-4700.pdf

Woolford, J., Patterson, T., Macleod, E., Hobbs, L., and Hayne, H. (2015). Drawing helps children to talk about their presenting problems during a mental health assessment. *Clinical Child Psychology and Psychiatry* 20, 68–83. doi:10.1177/1359104513496261

Glossary

Achievement test: Measures the *knowledge* or information an individual has acquired at the time of testing (Drummond et al., 2016; Hays, 2013)

Age equivalent: Age at which the average individual's performance in the norm group is equivalent to the performance of the individual who you gave the test to in years and months

Aptitude test: Measures the potential that students have to learn or acquire knowledge or skill in a given area (Drummond et al., 2016; Hays, 2013)

Behavioral assessments: Measures observable behavior

Formal assessment: Assessment (i.e. standardized tests, structured interviews, formal observations) developed through a rigorous process that includes examining the psychometric properties (e.g., reliability and validity) of the instrument

Grade equivalent: The grade level at which the average individual's performance in the norm group is similar to the performance of the individual who you gave the test to in grade level and months

High-stakes test: A test that is used for important decision-making situations (i.e. accountability, funding, and mobility) and aids educational stakeholders in allocating resources

Informal assessment: Assessment (e.g., nonstandardized tests [i.e. checklists, questionnaires] unstructured interviews, informal observations) developed without examining the psychometric properties

Intelligence test: Typically focused on measuring cognitive abilities (i.e., acquiring knowledge, reasoning, problem-solving) (Drummond et al., 2016)

Norm-referenced test: An individual's score is compared to a group of people who took the test when it was standardized (norm group)

Outcome evaluation: Assessing the area of focus after the intervention is completed (end of counseling) to determine the effectiveness of the intervention

Percentile rank: Rank of the individual's performance compared to others

Personality: An "individual's stable tendencies to think, feel, and act in particular ways" (Donnellan and Robins, 2012, p. 68)

Personality assessment: Measures individual differences or personality traits

Progress evaluation: Assessing how the client is doing (progress) throughout the counseling process

Raw score: Sum of responses on the test

Reliability: Consistency and dependability of scores on a test (Gall, Gall, and Borg, 2007)

Standard score: Individual's score related to a normal distribution of scores

Validity: Accuracy for which an instrument represents a construct; whether or not a test measures the constructs it is said to measure

References

Achenbach, T. M. and Rescorla, L. A. (2001). *Manual for the ASEBA school-age forms and profiles*. Burlington, VT: University of Vermont, Research Center for Children, Youth, and Families.

American Counseling Association (2014). *Code of ethics*. Alexandria, VA: Author.

American Psychiatric Association (2013). *Diagnostic and statistical manual of mental disorders*, 5th ed. Arlington, VA: Author.

Beck, J. S., Beck, A. T., and Jolly, J. B. (2005). *Beck Youth Inventories, Second Edition (BYI-II)*. San Antonio, TX: Pearson Assessments.

Bellak, L. and Bellak, S. S. (1949). *Children's Appreciation Test (CAT)*. Englewood, NJ: CPS Publishing.

Bracken, B. A. and McCallum, R. S. (2016). *Universal Nonverbal Intelligence Test, Second Edition (UNIT-2)*. Austin, TX: PRO-ED.

Briere, J. (1996). *Trauma Symptom Checklist for Children (TSCC)*. Lutz, FL: Psychological Assessment Resources.

Briere, J. (2005). *Trauma Symptom Checklist for Young Children (TSCYC)*. Lutz, FL: Psychological Assessment Resources.

Briggs, K. C., Myers Briggs, I., McCaulley, M. H., Quenk, N. L., and Hammer, A. L. (1998). *Myers-Briggs Type Indicator (MBTI), Form M*. Sunnyvale, CA: CPP.

Brott, P. E. (2001). The storied approach: A postmodern perspective for career counseling. *The Career Development Quarterly* 49(4), 304–313.

Buck, J. N. (1948). The H-T-P test. *Journal of Clinical Psychology* 4, 151–159. doi: 10.1002/1097-4679(194804)4:2%3C151::AID-JCLP2270040203%3E3.0. CO;2-0

Burlingame, G. M. and Lambert, M. J. (2005). *Youth Outcome Questionnaire (Y-OQ 2.01)*. Salt Lake City, UT: OQ Measures.

Burlingame, G. M., Wells, M. G., and Lambert, M. J. (2002). *Youth Outcome Questionnaire (Y-OQ 30.2 PR/SR)*. Salt Lake City, UT: OQ Measures.

Burns, R. C. and Kaufman, S. H. (1970). *Kinetic family drawings (K-F-D)*. New York, NY: Brunner-Mazel.

Butcher, J. N., Williams, C. L., Graham, J. R., Kaemmer, B., Archer, R. P., Tellegen, A., and Ben-Porath, Y. S. (1992). *Minnesota Multiphasic Personality Inventory-Adolescent (MMPI-A)*. Minneapolis, MN: University of Minnesota Press.

Constantino, G., Malgady, R., and Rogler, L. (1988). *Tell-Me-A-Story (TEMAS)*. Los Angeles, CA: Western Psychological Services. Retrieved from http://temastest.com/

Council for Accreditation of Counseling and Related Educational Programs (2016). 2016 standards. Retrieved from http://www.cacrep.org/wp-content/uploads/2016/02/2016-Standards-with-Glossary-rev-2.2016.pdf

Donnellan, M. B. and Robins, R. W. (2012). Personality development. In V. S. Ramachandran (ed.), *Encyclopedia of Human Behavior*, vol. 3, 2nd ed. (pp. 62–73). Burlington, MA: Elsevier.

Drummond, R. J., Sheperis, C. J. and Jones, K. D. (2016). *Assessment procedures for counselors and helping professionals*, 8th ed. Boston, MA: Pearson.

Duffy, M., Giordano, V. A., Farrell, J. B., Paneque, O. M., and Crump, G. B. (2009). No Child Left Behind: Values and research issues in high-stakes assessments. *Counseling and Values* 53 (1), 53–66.

Elliott, C. D. (2007). *Differential ability scales, second edition (DAS-II)*. San Antonio, TX: Harcourt Assessment.

Exner, J. E. (1974). *The Rorschach: A comprehensive system*, vol. 1. New York, NY: Wiley.

Frick, P. J., Barry, C. T., and Kamphaus, K. W. (2010). *Clinical assessment of child and adolescent personality and behavior*, 3rd ed. New York, NY: Springer.

Gibson, D. M. (2005). The use of genograms in career counseling with elementary, middle, and high school students. *The Career Development Quarterly* 53 (4), 353–362.

Glutting, J. J., Adams, W., and Sheslow, D. (2000) *Wide Range Intelligence Test (WRIT)*. Wilmington, DE: Wide Range.

Gottfried, A. (1986). *Children's Academic Intrinsic Motivation Inventory (CAIMI)*. Lutz, FL: Psychological Assessment Resources.

Gysbers, N. C. and Moore, E. J. (1987). *Career counseling: Skills and techniques for practitioners*. Englewood Cliffs, NJ: Prentice-Hall.

Holtzman, W. H. (1961). *Holtzman inkblot technique*. New York, NY: The Psychological Corporation.

Individuals with Disabilities Education Improvement Act. (IDEA, 2004).

Kaufman, A. S. and Kaufman, N. L. (2004a). *Kaufman Assessment Battery for Children, second edition (KABC-2)*. Circle Pines, MN: American Guidance Service.

Kaufman, A. S. and Kaufman, N. L. (2004b). *Kaufman Brief Intelligence Test, second edition (KBIT-2)*. Bloomington, MN: Pearson.

Koppitz, E. M. (1968). *Psychological evaluation of children's human figure drawings*. New York, NY: Grune & Statton.

Kovacs, M. (2010). *Children's Depression Inventory, second edition (CDI-2)*. North Tonawanda, NY: Multi-Health Systems.

Kranzler, J. H. and Floyd, R. J. (2013). *Assessing intelligence in children and adolescents: A practical guide*. New York, NY: Guilford Press.

Lachar, D. and Gruber, C. P. (1995). *Personality Inventory for Youth (PIY)*. Torrance, CA: Western Psychological Services.

Lachar, D. and Gruber, C. P. (2002). *Personality Inventory for Children, second edition (PIC-2)*. Torrance, CA: Western Psychological Services.

Lachar, D., Wingenfeld, S. A., Kline, R. B., and Gruber, C. P. (2000). *Student Behavior Survey (SBS)*. Torrance, CA: Western Psychological Services.

Lohman, D. F. and Hagen, E. (2001). *Cognitive Abilities Test (CogAT)*. Itasca, IL: Riverside.

Machover, K. (1949). *Personality projection in the drawing of the human figure*. Springfield, IL: Thomas.

Madaus, G. and Russell, M. (2010-2011). Paradoxes of high-stakes testing. *The Journal of Education* 190 (1/2), 21–30.

March, J. S. (2013). *Multidimensional Anxiety Scale for Children, Second Edition (MASC-2)*. North Tonawanda, NY: Multi-Health Systems.

McConaughy, S. H. and Achenbach, T. M. (2004). *Manual for the Test Observation Form for ages 2–18*. Burlington, VT: University of Vermont, Center for Children, Youth, and Families.

McConaughy, S. H. and Achenbach, T. M. (2009). *Manual for the ASEBA Direct Observation Form*. Burlington, VT: University of Vermont, Research Center for Children and Families.

Murray, H. A. (1943). *Thematic Appreciation Test (TAT)*. Cambridge, MA: Harvard University Press.

Myers, J. E. and Sweeney, T. J. (2014). *Five Factor Wellness Inventory (FFWEL)*. Menlo Park, CA: Mind Garden.

Naglieri, J. A. and Das, J. P. (2014). *Cognitive Assessment System, Second Edition (CAS-2)*. Austin, TX: PRO-ED.

No Child Left Behind Act of 2001, Pub. L. No. 107–110, 20 U.S.C. 6301 et seq. (2002).

Osborn, D. S. and Bethell, D. S. (2009). Using card sort in career assessment. *Career Planning and Adult Development Journal* 25 (4), 101–114.

Otis, A. and Lennon, R. (2003). *Otis–Lennon School Ability Test, Eighth Edition (OLSAT8)*. San Antonio, TX: Pearson Assessments.

Peterson, C. H., Lomas, G. I., Neukrug, E. S., and Bonner, M. W. (2014). Assessment use by counselors in the United States: Implications for policy and practice. *Journal of Counseling and Development* 92 (1), 90–98.

Peterson, G. W. (1998). Using a vocational card sort as an assessment of occupational knowledge. *Journal of Career Assessment* 6 (1), 49–67.

Piers, E. V., Harris, D. B., and Herzberg, D. S. (2002). *Piers–Harris Children's Self-Concept Scale, Second Edition (Piers Harris-2)*. Torrance, CA: Western Psychological Services.

Prout, H. T. and Phillips, P. D. (1974). A clinical note: The kinetic school drawing. *Psychology in the Schools* 11, 303–306. doi:10.1002/1520-6807 (197407)11:3<303::AID-PITS2310110311>3.0.CO;2-Y

Reynolds, C. R. and Kamphaus, R. W. (2003). *Reynolds Intellectual Assessment Scales (RIAS)*. Lutz, FL: Psychological Assessment Resources.

Reynolds, C. R. and Kamphaus, R. W. (2015). *Behavior Assessment System for Children, Third Edition (BASC-3)*. San Antonio, TX: Pearson Assessments.

Reynolds W. M. (1987). *Reynolds Adolescent Depression Scale, Second Edition (RADS-2)*. Lutz, FL: Psychological Assessment Resources.

Reynolds W. M. (1988). *Suicidal Ideation Questionnaire (SIQ)*. Lutz, FL: Psychological Assessment Resources.

Reynolds W. M. (2010). *Reynolds Child Depression Scale, Second Edition (RCDS-2)*. Lutz, FL: Psychological Assessment Resources.

Roberts, G. E. and Gruber, C. (2005). *Roberts Appreciation Test for Children, Second Edition (RATC-2)*. Torrance, CA: Western Psychological Services.

Roid, G. H. (2003). *Stanford–Binet Intelligence Scales, Fifth Edition (SB5)*. Itasca, IL: Riverside.

Roid, G. H., Miller, L. J., Pomplum, M., and Koch, C. (2013). *Leiter International Performance Scale, Third Edition (Leiter-3)*. Wood Dale, IL: Stoelting.

Rotter, J. B., Lah, M. I., and Rafferty, J. E. (1992). *Rotter Incomplete Sentence Blank, Second Edition (RISB-2)*. San Antonio, TX: Pearson Assessments.

Schrank, F. A., McGrew, K. S., Mather, K., Wendling, B. J., and Dailey, D. (2014). *Woodcock–Johnson IV (WJ-IV)*. Rolling Meadows, IL: Houghton Mifflin Harcourt.

Stroud, K. C. and Reynolds, C. R. (2006). *School Motivation and Learning Strategies Inventory (SMALSI)*. Torrance, CA: Western Psychological Services.

Super, D. E., Osborne, W. L., Walsh, D. J., Brown, S. D., and Niles, S. G. (1992). Developmental career assessment and counseling: The C-DAC model. *Journal of Counseling and Development* 71 (1), 74–80.

Thompson, E. H., Robertson, P., Curtis, R., and Frick, M. (2013). Students with anxiety: Implications for professional school counselors. *Professional School Counseling* 16 (4), 222–234.

Wechsler, D. (2011). *Wechsler Abbreviated Scale of Intelligence, Second Edition (WASI-2)*. San Antonio, TX: Pearson Assessments.

Wechsler, D. (2012). *Wechsler Preschool and Primary Scale of Intelligence, Fourth Edition (WPPSI-IV)*. San Antonio, TX: Pearson Assessments.

Wechsler, D. (2014). *Wechsler Intelligence Scale for Children, Fifth Edition (WISC-V)*. San Antonio, TX: Pearson Assessments.

Wechsler, D. and Naglieri, J. A. (2006). *Wechsler Nonverbal Scale of Ability (WNV)*. San Antonio, TX: Pearson Assessments.

Wells, M. G., Burlingame, G. M., Rose, P. M., and Lambert, M. J. (2005). *Youth Outcome Questionnaire-Self Report (Y-OQ-SR-2.0)*. Salt Lake City, UT: OQ Measures.

Zunker, V. G. (2016). *Career counseling: A holistic approach*, 9th ed. Belmont, CA: Brooks/Cole-Thomson.

CHAPTER 10

Diagnosis and Treatment of Children and Adolescents

Mood, Anxiety, Trauma- and Stressor-Related, and Disruptive Behavior Disorders

Casey A. Barrio Minton, Carrie A. Wachter Morris, and Sharon L. Bruner

Half of all lifetime cases of mental illness begin by age 14.

National Institute of Mental Health

CHAPTER OBJECTIVES

After reading this chapter, counselor trainees will be able to:

- differentiate between typical and atypical development (CACREP 2016 2.F.3.c, 2.F.3.e)
- identify considerations for conducting clinical interviews with youth (CACREP 2016 2.F.7.b, 5.C.3.a)
- recognize symptoms of the most common DSM-5 disorders in youth (CACREP 2016 5.C.2.d, 5.G.2.g)
- identify treatment implications for the most common DSM-5 disorders in youth (CACREP 2016 2.F.5.h, 2.F.5.j, 5.C.2.b, 5.C.3.b, 5.F.3.f)

INTRODUCTION

Note: In this chapter, the word "youth" refers generally to children and adolescents. "Children" refers to individuals in early, middle, or late childhood, up to age 12 or 13. "Adolescents" refers to individuals from age 13 to late teens or early 20s.

Counselors in clinical mental health and school counseling settings will frequently encounter youth who are experiencing a range of difficulties, some of which will be developmentally typical and some of which will be atypical, qualifying for a diagnosis in the *Diagnostic and Statistical Manual of Mental Disorders* (*DSM-5*) (American Psychiatric Association [APA], 2013). In this chapter, you will learn about characteristics of typical and atypical development and procedures for clinical interviewing.

Next, the authors will focus attention on the disorders most commonly diagnosed by counselors who work with children and adolescents:

- anxiety disorders
- depressive disorders
- trauma- and stressor-related disorders
- disruptive behavior and conduct disorders

Neurobiological considerations and medication management options for each category of disorder will be further discussed.

TYPICAL AND ATYPICAL DEVELOPMENT

Although many adults like to think of childhood as a carefree time filled with fascinating growth and development, childhood is anything but carefree for the 13–20 per cent of youth in the U.S. who experience mental, emotional, or behavioral disorders in any given year (Centers for Disease Control [CDC], 2013). In fact, there is some evidence that children are much more frequently diagnosed with mental disorders than ever before, and these diagnoses are associated with rapid increases in use of psychotropic medications. Researchers are uncertain whether these increases are associated with more disturbance in youth (CDC, 2013); adults may be more sensitive to youths' experience or have unrealistic expectations for how youth should think, feel, and behave.

Humans face a myriad of physical, cognitive, emotional, and social developmental tasks, and those who study human development know that typical developmental transitions may be anything but smooth. Child development experts tell us to expect stormy and smooth cycles and spirals as children navigate different developmental tasks (The Center for Parenting Education, 2016). Certainly, parents of young children will tell you there will be weeks and months when children have problems with sleeping, eating, and mood, and there will be times that children wake up from these stormy periods looking "older" or "bigger" and possessing new language, social, or motor skills. Adolescence is second only to infancy in terms of speed of development, and developmental experts have conceptualized this adolescence as a period of storm and stress in which adults might expect moodiness, experimentation, and limit testing as a part of normative behavior (Broderick and Blewitt, 2015).

How, then, can counselors differentiate between typical and atypical development? At what point might a young person's moodiness be a normal, natural part of his or her body and mind maturing? At what point might that moodiness cross the line into a disorder in need of treatment? When is testing boundaries at home and school and getting into scuffles with peers a normal part of development? And, when do these behaviors indicate the clinically significant distress or impairment associated with mental disorders? What of diagnostic criteria that ask mental health professionals to differentiate concerns from what would be expected given developmental, social, and cultural context? How can professional counselors embody a professional identity involving wellness and optimal development while also keeping sight of the fact that about half of all mental illness emerges by early adolescence (CDC, 2013)?

Continuing to study human development will help counselors have a strong foundation for differentiating typical and atypical development. Similarly, examining social and cultural diversity and committing to developing cultural self-awareness will be helpful for discerning when youth are engaging in typical developmental processes (however unpleasant they may be in that moment) and when they may benefit from more specialized intervention.

"Clinically significant distress or impairment in social, occupational, or other important areas for functioning" is a diagnostic criterion for nearly every disorder in the *DSM-5* (APA, 2013). When working with youth, it is important to consider this criterion carefully. What is an "appropriate" level of distress for children and youth who, developmentally speaking, experience their feelings much more strongly than adults and who, developmentally speaking, have not yet developed parts of the brain needed for impulse control and perspective taking? What are the social and occupational areas of functioning important for youth? Does a disturbance impact school functioning or performance? What level of conflict might we expect in relationships with caregivers and peers? When is challenging boundaries at home and school developmentally typical, and when is it impairing? Throughout the majority of this chapter, the authors will present snapshots of disorders youth may experience. Diagnostic criteria for distress or impairment will not be repeated because this is a hallmark of all mental disorders. Key experiences or themes related to the disorder will be presented, and specific impacts of the disorder on a youth's life will be included.

Counselors should render diagnoses with careful attention to potential impacts on youth and their families. On the positive side, providing a diagnosis might allow youth and their families to name or label an experience that has been distressing for them. From a practical standpoint, a diagnosis often serves as a gateway to counseling, medication, and supportive services. Some individuals who have been isolated by nature of their mental illness may find that having a diagnosis helps them to access online or in-person communities of others who have similar struggles. Similarly, counselors who have a name for concerns experienced from clients can access literature and treatment recommendations specific to that concern. Doing so may help counselors to be more thorough in their assessment and intentional in their treatment planning.

The first author recalls a time when a parent cried tears of relief when discussing a potential diagnosis of Attention Deficit/Hyperactivity Disorder (ADHD). The parent had been infinitely frustrated by her child's behavior and began to believe that he was perhaps even "afflicted by the devil." When they sat together and read descriptions of ADHD, the mother teared up and asked "Others go through this too?" and then "So, you can help him?"

Diagnosis can also have negative impacts on clients and client systems. Some individuals may find naming symptoms to be discouraging and resign themselves to the fact that they are "sick" or "bad," perhaps creating a self-fulfilling prophecy. The stigma of mental illness remains strong in many communities, and it is possible that labeling may be particularly difficult for some youth and their families, resulting in shame and isolation. Further, some individuals may use diagnostic labels as "reasons" or "excuses" for inappropriate behaviors, reducing their sense of agency. Caregivers might set low expectations for youth based on diagnoses. For example, a child might announce "My conduct disorder made me do it!" or a parent might insist his or her child is not responsible for bullying due to the conduct disorder. Other times, teachers may only expect the worst of students or see the child as her diagnosis (e.g., "the OCD-kid") rather than as a unique child who happens to have a mental disorder. Finally, it is important to remember that the *DSM-5* is a historical and cultural artifact; it is imperfect in creation and has had a history of cultural bias and stigma. Consumers must remain alert to cultural bias in diagnostic criteria and our application of criteria, especially for the most vulnerable of clients (Miller and Prosek, 2013).

Consistent with the American Counseling Association (ACA) *Code of Ethics* (2014), counselors must take great care to ensure diagnoses, and the methods used to obtain them, are accurate, culturally sensitive, and developmentally appropriate. Because diagnoses are permanent elements of a client's historical medical record, counselors must consider long-term impacts on youth. Although it is never appropriate to alter or falsify a diagnosis, counselors can decide to refrain from diagnosing if they believe the diagnosis may be harmful to the client. In some cases, counselors will determine that the concern, while problematic, does not meet criteria for mental disorder diagnosis and, instead, may assign a descriptive code (known as z-code) to capture the content of the concern (e.g., Z60.4 Social Exclusion or Rejection or Z63.5 Disruption of Family by Separation or Divorce). In any case, honest, open communication with client systems is best practice when navigating the diagnostic process.

- A substantial portion of youth experience mental illness, and most mental illness emerges by the end of adolescence.
- Knowledge of human development is essential for understanding the wide range of thoughts, feelings, and behaviors youth may bring to counseling.
- Professional counselors need to use clinical judgement to determine whether concerns are normal or abnormal given youths' social, cultural, and developmental context.
- Even when presenting with normal or typical concerns, youth may still benefit from counseling.

Brainstorm Activity

Brainstorm as many benefits and drawbacks to diagnosis as you can. Then, identify the three greatest benefits and drawbacks. For each drawback, think of strategies you can use to minimize impact or risk.

Exercise 10.1

THE CLINICAL INTERVIEW

There are a number of resources available to assist counselors in conducting clinical interviews and navigating the diagnoses explored in the remainder of this chapter and Chapter 11. Although somewhat ideal, the best assessment techniques involve multiple informants and multiple methods. Consider, for example, the following individuals or sources who may be able to give voice to youths' experiences, performance, and impacts:

- youths themselves
- parents or caregivers
- teachers
- coaches
- peers
- academic records
- law enforcement or court records
- medical personnel or records

Counselors must balance time demands, privacy, and context when choosing whom to involve in assessment procedures. Counselors in clinical mental health counseling settings, for example, will likely have ready access to parents or caregivers. They may also coordinate care with medical personnel or serve youth referred through courts; however, they may not reach out to school personnel unless there is good reason to do so. School counselors, on the other hand, may become aware of concerns from teachers, coaches, or peers, and they may have ready access to academic records. They may or may not reach outside the school district to serve students.

When deciding whom to include in assessment activities, counselors should also consider carefully *how* they wish to include these individuals. For example, it may not be wise for a child to witness parents and counselors talking about her behaviors, family history, and current family stressors. Counselors may conduct initial interviews with parents, allowing them an opportunity to share their concerns openly, vent if needed, and develop faith in the counseling process. An adolescent, however, may become highly suspicious of closed-door conversations and may refuse to participate or provide accurate information in the presence of caregivers. In this case, it may be best to respect the adolescent's autonomy by interviewing him or her first (Woo and Keatinge, 2016).

Regardless of resources and process, the clinical interview is likely the most common and critical element of the assessment process. Strong clinical interviews should involve youth as much as seems appropriate for the context. Woo and Keatinge (2016, p. 24) recommended attending to the following factors:

- identifying information
- chief complaint and presenting problem(s)
- history of the presenting problem(s)
- psychiatric and psychological history
- medical history
- cultural formulation and sense of identity
- family, developmental, and social history
- educational and occupational history
- legal history
- resilience, strengths, competence, and challenges

You may use the mnemonic CLIENTS to assess the presenting problem (Woo and Keatinge, 2016). This involves asking clients to talk about **cause** of problem, **length** of concern, **impairment** or consequences of the problem,

emotional impact of the problem, what others have **noticed**, what the client or system has **tried** to help the problem, and how life would be different if the problem **stopped**. Counselors should include careful attention to impact on functioning. Functioning at home includes attention to relationships with parents, siblings, and engagements in chores and activities of daily living. Functioning at school includes academic performance, behavior in the classroom, relationships with teachers, and relationships with peers. Functioning in the community includes elements such as peer relationships, relationships with neighbors, extracurricular involvement, and legal involvement.

Although it is beyond the scope of this chapter, counselors may use formal measures to screen for and further explore specific concerns. The *DSM-5* (APA, 2013) provides a *Level 1 Cross-Cutting Symptom Measure* that may be completed by parents on behalf of youth aged 6–17 and a self-report measure appropriate for adolescents aged 11–17. The measure includes 25 questions that screen for the presence of a broad range of symptoms including somatic, sleep, inattention, depression, anger, irritability, mania, anxiety, psychosis, repetitive thoughts and behaviors, substance use, and suicidal ideation/suicide attempts. APA also provides semi-structured interview protocols to use for collecting information about children's background and home environments. Counselors can download the measures and instructions at www.psychiatry. org. Counselors also may consider well-validated general assessment instruments such as the Achenbach System of Empirically Based Assessment (www.aseba.org) as a part of standardized practice. Finally, professionals may choose to use assessments designed to assess for specific concerns such as development, depression, anxiety, attention, or trauma. In each case, it is critical that counselors have appropriate training to use the assessment tools, select tools relevant for youths' developmental and cultural context, and interpret assessments with care (ACA, 2014).

- The best assessment includes formal and informal measures, interviews, and multiple informants.
- Counselors have to balance ideal assessment practices with the realities of counseling in their specific settings.
- There are many resources for developing skills in clinical interviewing and assessment.

ANXIETY DISORDERS

Anxiety disorders appear to be the most common mental disorder (Merikangas et al., 2010), leading some professionals to consider anxiety disorders the "common cold" of mental disorders. Conservative estimates indicate that about 4–5 per cent of youth experience anxiety disorders at any given time (CDC, 2013), and rates of diagnoses seem to go up with age, education, and income. Up to one-third of adolescents meet criteria for an anxiety disorder at some point (Merikangas et al., 2010).

Anxiety disorders include elements of *fear* (i.e. "emotional response to real or perceived imminent threat") and *anxiety* (i.e. "anticipation of future threat") (APA, 2013, p. 189). We experience fear and anxiety both physiologically (e.g., sweaty hands, racing heart, tremors, faster breathing, digestive upset) and cognitively (e.g., specific thoughts or inability to think). Although fear and anxiety are a natural part of the human condition, anxiety disorders involve persistent difficulties navigating daily life. For example, it is typical and natural for an adolescent to fear public humiliation or embarrassment, perhaps even refusing to go to school the day after an embarrassing incident such as having one's crush revealed to a group of peers. However, adolescents who refuse school completely and risk academic failure because they fear a teacher will call on them are experiencing anxiety beyond what is developmentally typical.

Diagnosis

Youth may experience a number of anxiety disorders. In this section, Separation Anxiety Disorder, Selective Mutism, Specific Phobia, Social Anxiety Disorder, Panic Disorder, Agoraphobia, and Generalized Anxiety Disorder are explored.

Separation Anxiety Disorder

Separation Anxiety Disorder is the most common of all anxiety disorders in youth, impacting about 4 per cent of children and 1.6 per cent of adults (APA, 2013). Characterized by at least one month during which the youth has excessive difficulty separating from caregivers, separation anxiety involves a variety of symptoms including distress at separation (or even the thought of separation), excessive worry about loss of attachment figures and possible harm that could come to them, activity refusal out of fear of separation, sleep difficulties (including nightmares), and physical complaints (APA, 2013). Because of these experiences, individuals with separation anxiety live in fear of separation and may restrict their activities, refusing to go to school or spend time with peers. Because children may not have the words to express their fears, adults may understand a child's fears only through observing a pattern of clinging or physical complaints.

Separation anxiety may begin as early as preschool age, is most common in childhood, and becomes less common in adolescence. Counselors may struggle to differentiate developmentally typical and atypical separation anxiety. It is natural for young children to seek comfort and refuge in their caregivers, and it is also typical to have waves of anxiety related to transitions such as starting a new school or having a change in caregiver. Similarly, cultural expectations for attachment vary greatly, with adults and children in some cultures rarely separating for much of childhood.

Selective Mutism

Although relatively rare as a mental disorder, Selective Mutism (sometimes called Elective Mutism) is most common in preschool aged children and involves "consistent failure to speak in specific social situations in which there is an expectation for speaking (e.g., at school) despite speaking in other situations" (APA, 2013, p. 195). This failure to speak lasts at least a month and is not related to language difference or ability to speak as might be seen in neurodevelopmental or communication disorders (discussed in Chapter 11).

Selective Mutism seems to be related to social anxiety. Children are able to speak with individuals with whom they have emotionally close relationships but may struggle with speaking when outside the home or in the presence of less familiar adults or peers. All youth may struggle in novel or threatening situations; for this reason, APA (2013) advises against considering a diagnosis of Selective Mutism during the first month of school.

Specific Phobia

Specific Phobias involve recurrent, intense fear or anxiety focused on an object or situation (e.g., getting a shot at the doctor's office, encountering dogs). To qualify for a diagnosis, reaction to the feared object or situation must be immediate, severe, and "out of proportion to the actual danger posed by the specific object or situation and to the sociocultural context" (APA, 2013, p. 197). The phobia must last at least six months, cause problems in functioning, and not be directly related to triggers for other diagnoses (e.g., reminder of traumatic event, separation from caregivers, or public speaking or humiliation).

According to the *DSM-5* (APA, 2013), approximately 5 per cent of children and 16 per cent of adolescents meet criteria for a specific phobia in a given year, and specific phobia is most likely to appear in mid–late childhood, especially for phobias related to animals, natural environment, and blood or injection (Woo and Keatinge, 2016). Because young children may not have the skills to give voice to their fears or the freedom to navigate life around their fears, they may show adults their fears through freezing or tantruming. As with other anxiety disorders, it is quite typical for children to experience intense, transient fears to new situations and events, and diagnosis will not be appropriate in all cases. Specific Phobia should only be considered for diagnosis on basis of time, intensity, and impact on daily functioning.

Social Anxiety Disorder

Social Anxiety Disorder is characterized by intense fear and anxiety related to social situations in which one may be judged or evaluated negatively (APA, 2013). The fears might be related to specific types of social situations, observations, or performances. To qualify for a diagnosis, children must experience anxiety in peer situations rather than only experience social anxiety with adults. Children may fear a variety of situations including reading in front of the class, athletic or musical performances, or starting conversations (Woo and Keatinge, 2016).

One of the most common anxiety disorders, Social Anxiety Disorder often begins by early adolescence and occurs in about 7 per cent of youth and adults. *DSM-5* (APA, 2013) criteria for Social Anxiety Disorder include fear and anxiety specific to social situations, a sense that one will be humiliated or embarrassed in social situations, persistence of anxiety in social situations, and avoidance or endurance of social situations with intense fear. Counselors must determine that the fear is "out of proportion to the actual threat posed by the social situation and to the sociocultural context" (p. 203), lasts at least six months, and causes problems in functioning. Counselors who consider a diagnosis of Social Anxiety Disorder in young people should consider carefully their assumptions regarding what is typical especially as it is developmentally expected that many adolescents will navigate life believing they have an imaginary audience. Additionally, individuals who are experiencing puberty, especially those who may be off-time from their peers, may be particularly vulnerable to scrutiny and shame (Broderick and Blewitt, 2015).

Panic Disorder

Panic attacks are brief experiences in which an individual experiences "an abrupt surge of intense fear or intense discomfort" involving a range of physical and cognitive symptoms (APA, 2013, p. 208). Panic attacks may be a feature of many mental disorders and are not, by themselves, cause for diagnosis of mental disorder. Panic Disorder involves recurrent patterns of panic attacks coupled with worry about having more attacks and/or adjustment in behavior related to them. Rare in children, approximately 2–3 per cent of adolescents and adults experience panic disorder. Still, youth may experience panic attacks related to other fears and triggers (e.g., the thought of speaking in public or separation from a caregiver).

Agoraphobia

Agoraphobia involves fear or anxiety related to situational factors including public transportation, open or enclosed places, lines, or being outside of the home alone (APA, 2013). In Agoraphobia, one worries that he or she would not be able to escape or get necessary help if needed. As with other anxiety disorders, these fears or anxieties must be greater than what would be expected for one's context, persist for at least six months, and result in severe distress or changes in behavior. Childhood Agoraphobia appears to be quite rare, and prevalence in adolescents and adults is about 1.7 per cent per year.

Generalized Anxiety Disorder (GAD)

GAD seems to be a lifelong condition, with most adults noting that they have struggled with fear and apprehension their entire lives. Still, the APA (2013) notes that GAD does not often appear prior to adolescence, and less than 1 per cent of adolescents meet criteria for this disorder. Counselors who are considering a GAD diagnosis in youth should also consider developmental transitions and environmental stressors that may be contributing to anxiety.

Table 10.1 Summary of anxiety disorders

Disorder	Summary
Separation Anxiety Disorder	One or more months of developmentally inappropriate difficulty separating from caregivers
Selective Mutism	One or more months of refusing to speak in some, but not all, social circumstances
Specific Phobia	Six or more months of intense fear or anxiety focused on a specific object or situation
Social Anxiety Disorder	Six or more months of intense fear and anxiety related to social situations in which one may be judged or evaluated negatively
Panic Disorder	Recurrent, unexpected panic attacks resulting in at least a month of excessive worry or behavioral change
Agoraphobia	Six or more months of intense fear or anxiety regarding being in places or situations from which escape or help would not be possible
Generalized Anxiety Disorder	Six or more months of worry and apprehension regarding a broad range of concerns and resulting in physical or mental health concerns

Treatment

Anxiety disorders can cause significant impairment in many settings and be especially problematic in educational settings. For all anxiety disorders in youth, typical treatment consists of a combination of cognitive, behavioral, and parenting interventions. Primary treatment for Separation Anxiety Disorder and Selective Mutism typically involves individual, group, or family counseling; on rare occasions, treatment may include medication (Sharkey and McNicholas, 2008). Other anxiety disorders may more often be treated with medication (Fisher, Tobkes, Kotcher, and Masia-Warner, 2006). These interventions are designed to increase the desired behavior (e.g., navigating triggers of anxiety appropriately) while decreasing problematic behaviors or impacts (e.g., school refusal or clinging behavior).

Behavioral interventions for anxiety disorders vary slightly based on the diagnosis, but may include positive reinforcement, systematic desensitization, social skills training, and modeling (Fisher et al., 2006; Woo and Keatinge, 2016). Social skills training can help youth with Separation Anxiety Disorder, Selective Mutism, or Social Anxiety Disorder develop confidence and skills to function in required settings. Systematic desensitization may help to slowly decrease feared stimuli and allow children to overcome Specific Phobias. By developing coping skills, youth can feel more confident when confronted with anxiety-producing stimuli.

Although cognitive interventions may not be appropriate for young children, cognitive interventions may help adolescents develop relaxation skills, identify and challenge thoughts, focus on positive thoughts and emotions, and develop coping plans. By employing these strategies in conjunction with exposure-based interventions mentioned above, youth can learn to manage their anxious thoughts and feelings, function in multiple settings, and develop positive relationships with peers and family (Davis, Ollendick, and Ost, 2009).

Research on the impact of parent involvement in the treatment of child anxiety has mixed results (Choate, Pincus, Eyeberg, and Barlow, 2006; Thulin, Svirsky, Serlachius, Andersson, and Ost, 2014). For some children with anxiety disorders, parents may be the primary interventionists that aid them in implementing strategies learned in counseling. Counselors should consider working closely with parents to ensure understanding and ability to implement behavior modification strategies (Drake and Ginsburg, 2012). In addition, parents should be able to assist youth in implementing cognitive strategies to cope with anxiety. When parents struggle with their own anxiety, counselors might recommend they seek their own counseling service as well (Fisher et al., 2006).

Case Study: Jeffrey

Jeffrey is a 5-year-old boy who recently started Kindergarten. Although Jeffrey only began school a little over a month ago, he has already been absent six times and tardy an additional six times. The social worker at Jeffrey's school contacted his mother due to excessive absences. Jeffrey's mother reports that he has trouble going to sleep at night because he worries about going to school the next day. In the mornings, Jeffrey is tearful and clingy and refuses to get ready for school. Jeffrey's mother reports that he is often late because it takes her at least an hour, sometimes two hours, to help him prepare for school.

Jeffrey's teachers report significant trouble in the morning after Jeffrey is dropped off. He often reports feeling sick and begs to visit the school nurse. Recently, Jeffrey has struggled when his parents leave him for short periods of time at church and home. Jeffrey's mother reports that he had some problems when they placed him in daycare for a short time at age 3, but never to the same extent. Ultimately, Jeffrey's mother sought treatment with a local counselor.

The counselor begins with a thorough assessment of Jeffrey's behavioral, cognitive, and emotional symptoms. In addition, the counselor seeks to better understand environmental and cultural considerations that are impacting Jeffrey's behavior. It quickly becomes clear that Jeffrey meets criteria for Separation Anxiety Disorder. The counselor begins treatment by visiting with Jeffrey's parents about the nature of the disorder and ways they can be helpful to Jeffrey. Treatment for Jeffrey includes a need for cooperation between the parents, school, and counselor. Using cognitive and behavioral techniques, the counselor helps Jeffrey's parents to develop a system for slowly building Jeffrey's confidence in being separated from his parents. Jeffrey is rewarded for small progress in the evenings and mornings. Slowly, Jeffrey spends less time crying in the mornings and is able to fall asleep more quickly at night. Jeffrey and his parents practice breathing and relaxation techniques to aid him in falling asleep and work to increase focus on positive thoughts and emotions in the morning.

Process Questions

1. To what degree are Jeffrey's symptoms normal for his cultural and developmental context?
2. What are the pros and cons of assigning this diagnosis for Jeffrey?
3. Considering your role as a counselor, how would you see yourself working with Jeffrey? His parents? His teachers?

Anxiety disorders are the most common disorders and feature intense fear or apprehension. The experience of anxiety may be the same even if the trigger or circumstance in which it is experienced (e.g., separation from caregiver, social situation, fear of injection, broad range of concerns) is different. Cognitive, behavioral, and parenting interventions are the most common treatments for anxiety; some youth may benefit from medication to assist in managing anxiety.

DEPRESSIVE DISORDERS

Depressive disorders are among the most common mental disorders in the U.S., and about 4 per cent of youth have received diagnoses of depression (CDC, 2013). These rates vary significantly with age; roughly 10 per cent of adolescents report meeting criteria for major depressive episodes in the past year, with about 6.7 per cent experiencing depression at any given time. Girls appear to be at greater risk of depression, and individuals with higher incomes and education are more likely to be diagnosed with depression. The cause of these differences is unknown (CDC, 2013). It could be that some groups are at greater risk of having problems with mood and/or some youth may be more likely to report concerns and receive help compared to less-privileged peers.

When considering a diagnosis of a depressive disorder, it is important to differentiate from normal sadness and developmental angst, especially as over one-third of high school-aged girls reported feeling "so sad or hopeless almost every day for 2 weeks or more in a row that you stopped doing some usual activities" (CDC, 2013, p. 12). It is also important to remember that depression may look different in youth than it does in adults (APA, 2013; Carr, 2008). For example, children may act out or appear irritable rather than appearing sad. Adults may struggle to determine whether changes in appetite are related to growth spurts, pickiness, or depression. Some youth will report vague physical symptoms such as stomachaches and headaches, which may or may not be related to depressive disorders. Preschoolers may not talk about mood; however, adults may notice depressive themes in their play or artwork. Similarly, many of the diagnostic symptoms of depression discussed below (e.g., loss of interest/pleasure, hopelessness, social withdrawal) emerge with age (Carr, 2008).

Diagnosis

Counselors should be aware of four depressive disorders in youth: Disruptive Mood Dysregulation Disorder, Major Depressive Disorder, Persistent Depressive Disorder, and Premenstrual Dysphoric Disorder. Each are summarized in the following paragraphs.

Disruptive Mood Dysregulation Disorder (DMDD)

DMDD is a new mental disorder introduced in the *DSM-5* (APA, 2013). This disorder was created in response to the seemingly exponential increase in childhood bipolar disorder among youth. In particular, researchers noticed that most children who were diagnosed with bipolar disorder did not have discrete episodes of mania (Roy, Lopes, and Klein, 2014). Rather, their behavior problems were interspersed with ongoing irritability. These behavior problems were often treated with powerful medications such as mood stabilizers and antipsychotics, and desperate parents sometimes resigned themselves to what seemed the inevitable "reality" of lifelong management of Bipolar Disorder.

The criteria for DMDD are quite stringent. To receive this diagnosis, a youth must have over a year's history of "severe recurrent temper outbursts manifested verbally (e.g., verbal rages) and/or behaviorally (e.g., physical aggression toward people or property) that are grossly out of proportion in intensity or duration to the situation or provocation" (APA, 2013, p. 156). In addition to temper outbursts at least three times a week and being out of proportion to what one would expect for one's developmental level, the youth must also have persistent irritable or angry moods between outbursts. Additional diagnostic criteria note that DMDD may not be diagnosed prior to age 6, symptoms must begin by age 10, and concerns must happen in at least two different settings such as school and home. Additional diagnostic criteria help counselors ensure the disorder is not better accounted for by other disorders such as Oppositional Defiant Disorder, Intermittent Explosive Disorder, Conduct Disorder, or Substance Use Disorders.

Major Depressive Disorder (MDD)

MDD involves experiences of five or more symptoms within a two-week period. In addition to depressed mood or loss of interest or pleasure nearly all day every day, depression may involve problems with eating (including not growing as expected), sleep disturbance, motor agitation or retardation, low energy, feeling worthless, difficulty concentrating, and thoughts of death or suicide (APA, 2013). Younger children who experience MDD may have fewer symptoms than adolescents or adults (Carr, 2008), perhaps because they do not have the words to express their internal experiences.

MDD is more common in females than males, a sex difference that tends to begin around puberty and continue into adulthood. As with other mood disorders, MDD is likely the result of interplay between unique individual factors, including genetic predisposition and environmental factors or stressors, especially as those factors compound. Some youth may experience MDD in response to a major stressor or life event, and they may recover from the experience never to experience depression again. Others may find managing their MDD to be a lifelong challenge.

Persistent Depressive Disorder

Previously known as Dysthymia, Persistent Depressive Disorder involves long-term experiences with depression. Because depression may look different in youth than it does in adults, the APA (2013) allows diagnosis of Persistent Depressive Disorder based on a one-year history of irritable or depressed mood rather than the two years required for adults. In addition, the youth must experience two or more related symptoms without substantial relief over time. Similar to those of MDD, symptoms include problems with appetite, sleep, fatigue, self-esteem, concentration, and hopelessness. In some cases, initial experiences with milder symptoms progress into Major Depressive Episodes, an experience sometimes called "double depression."

Dysthymia is believed to impact up to 4.6 per cent of children and 8 per cent of adolescents (Nobile, Cataldo, Marino, and Molteni, 2003). On the surface, symptoms of Persistent Depressive Disorder appear less severe than those of MDD; however, children who have early onset dysthymia tend to struggle with mood for many years and tend to have poorer educational, social, and mental health outcomes. The seriousness of Persistent Depressive Disorder is highlighted in the fact that up to 19 per cent of adolescents with dysthymia attempt suicide (Nobile et al., 2003).

Premenstrual Dysphoric Disorder (PMDD)

Also new to the *DSM-5*, PMDD involves a strong history of mood fluctuation associated with a female's menstrual cycle. To be diagnosed, a young woman must have at least five symptoms the week before her period starts, improvement at onset of menses, and resolution of symptoms the week after the period concludes (APA, 2013). Symptoms must include at least one of the following: Severe mood swings, irritability or anger, depressed mood, or anxiety or tension. In addition, the young woman may experience decreased interest, difficulty concentrating, fatigue, appetite changes, problems sleeping, a sense of being out of control, or physical concerns. Because demonstrating a cycle is so important to justifying this diagnosis, the diagnosis must be made based on at least two months of daily ratings of mood and related symptoms. Counselors or physicians may ask clients to complete these ratings using paper questionnaires or a free app such as Period Tracker.

It is important to distinguish between normal hormonal fluctuation, Premenstrual Syndrome (PMS), and PMDD. There is wide variation in reports of PMS in adolescent girls, with researchers noting moderate to severe symptoms in 14–88 per cent of the population (Claman and Miller, 2006). It is likely safe to say that about 40 per cent of women are disturbed enough by monthly physical or emotional changes to warrant a medical diagnosis of PMS.

Table 10.2 Summary of depressive disorders

Disorder	Summary
Disruptive Mood Dysregulation Disorder	At least one year of severe, recurrent temper outbursts coupled with persistently irritable mood that causes disruption in at least two settings
Major Depressive Disorder	Two or more weeks in which a youth experiences an array of depressive symptoms
Persistent Depressive Disorder	At least one year of persistently depressed or irritable mood; symptoms may vary in intensity but are present across time
Premenstrual Dysphoric Disorder	Intense pattern of cognitive, emotional, and behavioral symptoms that are clearly linked to a woman's menstrual cycle

Still, only 3–5 per cent of menstruating women have symptoms severe enough to warrant a PMDD diagnosis. Counselors considering this diagnosis should be careful to gather information about symptoms experienced, associated history (including experiences of trauma), and ways in which the symptoms impact one's functioning at home, school, and with peers.

Treatment

Treatment for depression varies depending on the developmental level of the youth and the nature of the depression. Counselors should base treatment plans on careful assessment. This assessment should include the nature of the experience with mental health concerns; presence of suicidal thoughts; functioning at home, school, and with peers; and environmental supports and stressors. Counselors should include both youth and caregivers in the assessment and treatment planning process. Some medical conditions initially appear as depression. If the family has not already consulted with a physician, a recommendation to do so would be helpful, especially for cases of depression that appear severe, may have a hormonal link, or are ongoing.

General treatment recommendations for youth depression include cognitive behavioral therapy (CBT), interpersonal therapy (IPT), family therapy, and medication (Carr, 2008). A systematic review and network meta-analysis of 52 randomized studies regarding treatment of youth with depression revealed that cognitive behavioral therapy (CBT) and interpersonal therapy (IPT) appeared most effective than any other treatment modality (e.g., supportive therapy, play therapy, family therapy, problem-solving therapy), and those who engaged in interpersonal therapy seemed to have the best results at follow-up (Zhou et al., 2015). In contrast, those who examined systematic studies specific to children with depression were unable to determine that CBT was any better than no treatment at all (Forti-Buratti, Saikia, Wilkinson, and Ramchandani, 2016), perhaps because young children do not have the developmental skills to participate in CBT.

In general, earlier onset of depression is associated with longer and more persistent concerns with mental illness, peer functioning, and educational attainment (Forti-Buratti et al., 2016), thus indicating a need to attend to both the symptoms of the depression and the systemic impact on youth and their families. Researchers have also noted a number of factors that appear to protect against depression. Counselors who work with adolescents at risk of depression might help them refrain from substance use, ensure adequate nutrition, practice healthy sleep habits, and develop coping skills (Carines, Yap, Pilkington, and Jorm, 2014). Further, counselors can help parents explore when medication may be appropriate for their children, communicate with physicians regarding choices, and monitor for side effects, especially given the FDA's controversial black box warning regarding a connection between selective serotonin reuptake inhibitor (SSRI) use and suicidal behaviors in young people (Woo and Keatinge, 2016).

Treatment recommendations for Persistent Depressive Disorder mirror general recommendations for youth depression. "As children with dysthymia often have multiple problems, interventions should involve multiple levels and measures: individual psychotherapy, family therapy/education and pharmacological treatment" (Nobile et al., 2003). CBT and IPT are recommended for mild to moderate cases of persistent depression. Youth who have severe depressive symptoms and those with major impairment in functioning may benefit from medications such as SSRIs. Given the ongoing nature of Persistent Depressive Disorders, counselors should take special care to provide support to caregivers and include attention to psychosocial functioning, including relationships with peers.

Treatment of DMDD often involves individual management of the two characteristic symptoms of the disorder: Aggression/temper and chronic irritability (Tourian et al., 2015).

Experts recommend providing parental support for younger children with DMDD and individual CBT for adolescents who have DMDD (Roy et al., 2014). Some psychiatrists believe stimulant treatments are helpful for managing aggression in some children with DMDD, especially when those children also have ADHD. In some cases, psychiatrists will treat DMDD with atypical antipsychotics. Although traditionally used to manage problems with temper or rage in youth, mood stabilizers are not believed to be as effective in treating DMDD (Roy et al., 2014; Tourian et al., 2015).

Treatment recommendations for PMDD are also quite specialized. First-line medical recommendations include non-prescription therapies such as calcium supplementation, nutrition intervention (e.g., decreasing sodium, sugar, and caffeine), exercise, and stress management (Claman and Miller, 2006; Rapkin, 2003). When first line recommendations are not effective, physicians might consider prescribing oral contraceptives or SSRIs to be taken on an intermittent basis. Although counselors are not qualified to make medical recommendations, counselors can help clients understand the nature of PMDD, communicate with their physicians, navigate lifestyle considerations, develop coping skills, and engage in stress management.

Case Study: Lashonda

Lashonda is a 16-year-old African American female who lives with her mother and younger sister and is in the tenth grade. She is currently earning low Bs in her courses and does not engage in any extracurricular activities. She attends school each day, comes directly home, and closes herself in her room, asking for "solitude." On weekends, Lashonda stays in bed most of the day, saying she does not "have the energy to deal" and "needs more sleep."

Lashonda's English teacher approaches the school counselor for consultation after becoming concerned regarding the increasingly dark nature of Lashonda's writing, including a recent story that featured a young girl and alluded to thoughts of suicide. The school counselor requested a visit with Lashonda and, concerned regarding her seeming lack of care and connection, reached out to Lashonda's mother.

Lashonda's mother reported that she has struggled to know whether Lashonda's attitude is typical for "girls her age." She reported that Lashonda was a bright and precocious child, earning straight As, loving soccer, and doting on her sister until the eighth grade. After she "got her cycle" Lashonda became increasingly moody and withdrawn. Last year, she stopped interacting with her sister, dropped out of soccer, and was doing the bare minimum to keep up with her courses. Lashonda's mother also noted that she did not seem interested in spending time with friends and responded to inquiries about her life with anger and irritability. Together, the school counselor and Lashonda's mother decided it was time for a serious conversation.

Process Questions

1. What developmental, gender, and cultural elements might be at play for Lashonda?
2. Based on information provided, what is the most likely diagnosis for Lashonda? What additional information would you need to confirm this diagnosis?
3. Given what you know about depression, how would you approach treatment with Lashonda?
4. What additional or adjunct services might Lashonda need?

Depressive disorders involve anywhere from two weeks to a year or more of disturbance in mood. A wide variety of factors, including genetic and biological, appear to contribute to depressive disorders. Young children express their depression differently than adolescents. CBT, IPT, family therapy, and medication are the most common treatments for depression; however, they may not be as effective with younger children. Girls with PMDD are in need of medical consultation.

TRAUMA- AND STRESSOR-RELATED DISORDERS

Trauma- and Stressor-Related Disorders are unique in that they are all associated with external events that impact an individual's mental health. Unfortunately, experiences of trauma are anything but rare. Up to three-quarters of individuals have experienced trauma at some time or another (Woo and Keatinge, 2016). Youth report experiencing a range of traumatic events with the most frequent traumas including witnessing community violence, media violence, and separation and loss (Taylor and Weems, 2009). Traumatic events also vary by age and gender with adolescents, for example, at greater risk of automobile accidents and females at greater risk of physical trauma.

Early experiences of trauma may have lifelong effects on our brains and bodies, especially when not buffered in the context of supportive caregiving relationships (CDC, 2016). Adverse Childhood Experiences (ACEs) include a wide range of traumas including abuse, household challenges (e.g., witnessing partner violence, separation or divorce, parental mental health and substance concerns), and neglect. About two of three youth experience at least one ACE, and one of five youth experience three or more ACEs. The research is very clear: As number of ACEs increases, so do risk for medical problems, poor health practices, and low educational and occupational achievement in adulthood. Researchers believe these outcomes are related to the cumulative impact of stress and trauma on the developing brain.

It may be typical to respond to developmental changes or challenges with distressing emotions or behaviors, and many youth who experience traumas and adverse experiences are resilient. Still, some youth have difficulty in functioning related to the severity of trauma and/or their responses to the stressor. Regardless of whether we consider the response typical or atypical, timely and appropriate support can be critical for promoting long-term wellbeing.

Diagnosis

The *DSM-5* presents a wide range of disorders specific to trauma and stressors. In this section, we explore Reactive Attachment Disorder (RAD), Disinhibited Social Engagement Disorder (DESD), Posttraumatic Stress Disorder (PTSD), Acute Stress Disorder, and Adjustment Disorders.

Reactive Attachment Disorder (RAD)

RAD is diagnosed when an infant or young child experiences extreme neglect, abuse, or instability in primary caregivers and, as a result, has difficulty forming appropriate attachment with adults. Children with RAD may be described as "inhibited" and "emotionally withdrawn" from adult caregivers (APA, 2013, p. 265). They do not seek or respond to comfort, have limited emotional responsiveness, and may not experience positive emotions. Contrary to neurodevelopmental disorders such as Autism Spectrum Disorder where individuals may struggle to form attachments with others (see Chapter 11), it is believed that the lack of appropriate care causes this pattern of behavior. To be diagnosed with RAD, there must be evidence of attachment concerns prior to age 5, and the child must have a developmental age of at least 9 months, the age by which infants form selective attachments.

Although individuals may experience disturbance or fluctuation in attachment styles, the *DSM-5* (APA, 2013) notes that true diagnosis of RAD is quite rare, occurring in only one of ten children who experience severe neglect. Although serious, it is important to note that experts believe even those with difficult beginnings in life may form selective attachments provided quality care and stable, enriching environments over time.

Disinhibited Social Engagement Disorder (DSED)

Like RAD, DSED is only diagnosed in individuals who have experienced early, extreme neglect, abuse, or instability of caregivers (APA, 2013). Individuals with DSED show their distress through disinhibited externalizing behaviors. In short, children struggle with appropriate boundaries and tend to be quite active and overly familiar with adults, including those who are not known to them. Like RAD, DSED is only diagnosed among children who have a developmental age that would allow them to form selective attachments with adults. DSED is rare and occurs in one in five children who experience extreme neglect.

Posttraumatic Stress Disorder (PTSD)

PTSD involves a combination of affective, behavioral, and cognitive symptoms following exposure to a traumatic event or severe stressor. The DSM-5 (APA, 2013) includes two criteria sets for PTSD: One for children younger than six years of age and one for older children, adolescents, and adults. The traumatic or qualifying event must meet the following criterion:

A. Exposure to actual or threatened death, serious injury, or sexual violence in one (or more) of the following ways:

1. Directly experiencing the traumatic event(s).
2. Witnessing, in person, the event(s) as it occurred to others.
3. Learning the traumatic event(s) occurred to a close family member or close friend. In cases of actual or threatened death of a family member or friend, the event(s) must have been violent or accidental.
4. Experiencing repeated or extreme exposure to aversive details of the traumatic event(s) (e.g., first responders collecting human remains; police officers repeatedly exposed to details of child abuse).

Note that Criterion A4 does not apply to exposure through electronic media, television, movies, or pictures, unless this exposure is work related (APA, 2013, p. 271). In very young children, Criterion A4 includes specific language around witnessing trauma occurring to primary caregivers or learning of death or injury of caregivers.

Following exposure to the traumatic event, individuals who have PTSD experience a month or more of four distinct types of symptoms:

■ intrusive—memories, dreams, flashbacks, or distress at cues
■ avoidance—avoiding memories or external reminders
■ cognition and mood—inability to remember, negative beliefs, blaming, negative emotional state, loss of interest, detachment, or inability to experience positive emotions

■ arousal and reactivity—irritable/angry behavior, reckless behavior, hypervigilance, startle response, impaired concentration, and sleep disturbance

PTSD criteria specific to children 6 years and younger are simplified and recognize that young children may not be able to give voice to their internal experiences. For this reason, the number of symptoms needed to make a diagnosis is lower. Symptom clusters include intrusion, avoidance or alteration in cognitions, and arousal and reactivity.

It is important to note that children may not have the language and cognitive structures needed to voice their experiences as adolescents or adults may share (Woo and Keatinge, 2016). Rather, counselors may look to children's play for cues regarding how they are experiencing their trauma. We may see signs of trauma in repetitive play, drawings, or trauma-specific reenactment. Similarly, children may have difficulty with sleep, but not be able to recall content of nightmares or memories.

Acute Stress Disorder

Like PTSD, Acute Stress Disorder occurs following exposure to a traumatic event as described in Criterion A above. Unlike PTSD, Acute Stress Disorder is diagnosed in the days or weeks following the trauma. Because it is quite normal to experience distress following a trauma, this disorder requires the presence of at least nine symptoms across five categories: Intrusion, negative mood, dissociation, avoidance, and arousal (APA, 2013). After a period of one month, counselors should consider PTSD instead of ASD.

Individuals who are considering a diagnosis of ASD must take into account intensity of symptoms following the stressor and degree of impact on the person's life. Although we believe it is important to avoid pathologizing typical responses to atypical events, about one-half of individuals who experience ASD go on to develop PTSD. Counselors who can identify those struggling in early days and weeks following a stressor may be able to provide assistance that protects against long-term struggles.

Adjustment Disorders

Most simply, Adjustment Disorder includes emotional or behavioral symptoms within three months of onset of a stressor (APA, 2013). Because it is part of the human condition to experience distress following a stressor, a counselor must be able to justify the response as either out of proportion to the nature of the trigger given one's social and cultural context and/or as causing substantial difficulty in functioning. Counselors must also note whether the symptoms involve depressed mood, anxiety, mixed anxiety and depressed mood, conduct, or mixed emotions and conduct. The *DSM-5* notes that symptoms should resolve within six months of the "stressor or its consequences" (p. 287).

When diagnosing adjustment disorders, counselors should consider what one believes to be a developmentally typical response to a stressor or trigger.

Table 10.3 Summary of trauma- and stressor-related disorders

Disorder	Summary
Reactive Attachment Disorder	A pattern of severely inhibited or emotionally withdrawn interaction with caregivers and social and emotional disturbance following severe neglect
Disinhibited Social Engagement Disorder	A pattern of severely disinhibited behavior in social situations following severe neglect
Posttraumatic Stress Disorder	One or more months of symptoms following exposure to one or more traumatic events; symptoms include intrusion, avoidance, negative alterations in cognitions and mood, and arousal and reactivity
Acute Stress Disorder	Nine or more symptoms lasting up to one month following exposure to a traumatic event
Adjustment Disorders	Emotional or behavioral symptoms that begin within three months of a stressor and are out of proportion to the stressor or cause substantial impairment in functioning

For example, what would be a typical response for a young adolescent whose parents divorced? What if this divorce was followed by a move from a single-family home in a community where she lived her entire life to an apartment in an unfamiliar community where she had to share a room with two younger siblings? What level of distress would be "out of proportion to the severity or intensity of the stressor" (APA, 2013, p. 286) if she also had to discontinue her favorite activity, volleyball, to babysit her siblings after school while her mother worked a second job? Additionally, counselors should carefully rule out the possibility of Acute Stress Disorder, PTSD, or worsening of other mental health conditions such as anxiety, depression, and disruptive behavior disorders.

Treatment

Treatment for Trauma and Stressor-Related Disorders frequently addresses cognitive, behavioral, and emotional aspects of the youth's experience. Youth experiencing trauma or extreme stress may find it difficult to continue in academic and social roles. As further discussed below, trauma treatment should include attention to coping and address environmental factors that might be contributing to the concern.

Children exposed to significant abuse and neglect in their primary caregiving setting who demonstrate externalizing or internalizing behaviors may qualify for a RAD or DSED diagnosis. The introduction of a healthy caregiving environment can significantly decrease symptoms of both disorders. In addition, interventions designed to assist in healthy attachment and develop appropriate boundary setting behaviors may decrease problematic behaviors (Zeanah and Gleason, 2015). Evidence-based counseling approaches for responding to attachment concerns in adoptive families include Dyadic Developmental Psychotherapy, Parent–Child Interaction Therapy, and Child–Parent Relationship Therapy (Carnes-Holt, 2015). Healing from RAD and DSED is most likely to come in the context of months and years of predictable, stable, and nurturing support from securely attached caregivers. Given the intensity of such a task, caregivers may also benefit from ongoing counseling and support.

Treatment for PTSD and ASD may include use of Cognitive Based Therapies, Exposure-Based Therapies, Eye Movement Desensitization and Reprocessing (EMDR), Stress Inoculation Training, and, at times, pharmacological treatment (Perrin, Smith, and Yule, 2000). As with other approaches, play-based treatment and parental support are likely most appropriate with the youngest clients (Lenz and Klasson, 2016). Trauma-Focused Cognitive Behavioral Therapy (TF-CBT) is one of the most common and highly supported interventions for PTSD in youth and addresses all three facets of stress reactions (Smith et al., 2013). TF-CBT encourages youth to develop coping skills necessary for dealing with the trauma, helps youth construct a trauma narrative, and provides parenting support to caregivers. TF-CBT can be implemented in school or community settings with high success.[1]

There is limited literature regarding treatment of Adjustment Disorders; however, counselors might consider implications related to the mood, anxiety, or behavioral concerns experienced by the youth (Kress, Hartwig Moorhead, and Zoldan, 2015). In many cases, brief counseling may be helpful for providing a safe place for processing regarding the stressor and developing coping skills to navigate the new task. Counselors may provide psychoeducation to youth and their families about healthy coping. In some cases, group counseling specific to the stressor (e.g., children coping with divorce, grief) may be quite helpful for reducing isolation and developing skills for navigating change.

Case Study: Amber

Amber, a 17-year-old female, was involved in a serious car accident with three of her best friends over spring break. Amber was riding in the passenger's seat of her best friend's car when a car came over the dividing line and hit them head on. Amber and her friends were extracted from the car and rushed to the hospital where two of her friends later died. Amber suffered significant injuries but survived.

After returning to school, Amber struggles to focus during class and frequently asks to be dismissed because she is not "feeling well." Amber struggles to focus on her homework and frequently does not complete assignments. Amber's grades have dropped significantly, and she is at risk for failing several classes.

Amber's parents frequently hear her crying at night and often rush to her bedside when she wakes up screaming from nightmares. Amber tells her parents that she wishes she had not ever suggested the trip to Florida. She often blames herself for suggesting the trip, because without the trip there would have been no car accident. Amber refuses to spend time with her previous friends, eats lunch alone, and spends most of her time at home in her room. She refuses to talk about the car wreck and frequently gets angry when others attempt to bring it up. Amber's parents initially thought she was experiencing a normal response to the trauma; however, three months after the accident, Amber seems to be struggling more than in the initial weeks following it, and her parents become more concerned.

Process Questions

1. Based on information provided, what is the most likely diagnosis for Amber? What additional information would you need to confirm this diagnosis?
2. Given what you know about trauma, how would you approach treatment with Amber? How would you advise her parents to help her?
3. What additional or adjunct services might Amber need?

Trauma- and stressor-related disorders involve cognitive, emotional, and behavioral responses to difficult events. Counselors should take care not to pathologize culturally and developmentally expected responses to traumas and stressors. Even those who are experiencing expected responses to traumas and stressors may benefit from proactive support. Treatment for RAD and DESD includes providing a healthy caregiving environment as well as family-based counseling interventions. TF-CBT is considered one of the most supported treatments for trauma in youth.

DISRUPTIVE, IMPULSE-CONTROL, AND CONDUCT DISORDERS

Disruptive disorders are quite common among youth, as is it common for youth to have developmentally normal variation with risk-taking and limit testing. Disorders in this section all involve violating rights of others or conflicting with authority or sociocultural norms. Nearly 5 per cent of parents indicate that their child has a history of a disorder such as oppositional defiant disorder (ODD) or conduct disorder (CD) (CDC, 2013), and up to one in five adolescents show signs of disruptive behavior disorders at some time (Merikangas et al., 2010).

These disorders are diagnosed nearly twice as often among boys compared to girls and increase with age, peaking in adolescence. Risk factors for disruptive behavior disorders are multidimensional and include biological (family history of Antisocial Personality Disorder, birth complications), individual temperament, abuse, low intelligence, academic difficulty, disruptive peer relationships, lack of parental supervision and warmth, lower SES, poorer schools, crime-rich neighborhoods, and involvement with deviant peer groups (Woo and Keatinge, 2016). Protective factors include being female, high intelligence, parental warmth and supervision, connection with others who have prosocial norms, and involvement in extracurricular activities.

Diagnosis

This section of the *DSM-5* includes five disorders: Oppositional Defiant Disorder, Intermittent Explosive Disorder, Conduct Disorder, Pyromania, and Kleptomania.

Oppositional Defiant Disorder (ODD)

ODD involves "a pattern of angry/irritable mood, argumentative/defiant behavior, or vindictiveness lasting at least 6 months" (APA, 2013, p. 462) and involves at least four symptoms. Symptoms of angry/irritable mood include losing temper, being easily annoyed, and acting angry and resentful. Argumentative/defiant behavior includes arguing with adults, defying rules or adults, deliberately annoying others, and blaming others for own mistakes. Finally, vindictiveness is operationalized as being spiteful or vindictive at least twice in a six-month period.

As you read through these symptoms, you might note that a number of these appear to be "par for the course" for some children and adolescents. Indeed, those who created ODD require that the symptoms be present with at least one person who is not a sibling, perhaps because a degree of sibling conflict is normal and to be expected. The *DSM-5* includes strong cautions that one must consider frequency, intensity, and duration of the behavior in light of what one might expect for a child of same developmental level, gender, and culture. Generally, ODD is considered mild if it only happens in one setting (e.g., school), moderate if it happens in two settings (e.g., school and home), and severe if it happens in three or more settings (e.g., school, home, neighbor-hood) (APA, 2013).

Depending on how it is assessed, ODD may occur in up to 10 per cent of the population. First signs of ODD may be present as early as preschool, and nearly all cases develop by early adolescence. Many youth who have ODD also have ADHD, perhaps due to "shared temperamental risk factors" (APA, 2013, p. 466). About one-quarter of youth who experience ODD go on to develop Conduct Disorder (APA, 2013; Woo and Keatinge, 2016).

Intermittent Explosive Disorder (IED)

Whereas ODD involves ongoing disruption in mood and behavior, IED involves "impulsive (or anger-based) aggressive outbursts ... [with] ... little or no prodromal period" (APA, 2013, p. 466). Aggressive outbursts may be more frequent (i.e. at least twice weekly for at least three months) verbal and/or physical outbursts without substantial injury or damage. These outbursts may also be less frequent (i.e. three in one year), but involve harm to people, animals, or property. Mental health professionals who diagnose IED must determine that the outbursts are disproportionate for the situation, not premeditated or for tangible gain, and have problematic consequences to relationships, functioning, or financial/legal status.

Because a degree of impulsive temper tantrums and aggression is somewhat typical in early childhood, IED cannot be diagnosed until a youth is at a chronological and developmental age of at least six years. IED can be diagnosed alongside other disorders such as ADHD, conduct disorder (discussed next), and ODD if the outbursts are particularly problematic. As with many other disorders we have discussed in this chapter, signs of IED tend to be present by late childhood or early adolescence and exist on a continuum of normal in which some youth will struggle with impulse control and frustration tolerance.

Conduct Disorder (CD)

CD is "a repetitive and persistent pattern of behavior in which the basic rights of others or major age-appropriate societal norms or rules are violated" (APA, 2013, p. 469). For an official diagnosis of CD, an individual must have three symptoms in the last year, at least one of which has occurred in the last six months. There are four main categories of symptoms:

- aggression to people and animals—bullying, threatening, or intimidating others; initiating physical fights; using a weapon with potential for serious harm; physical cruelty to people; physical cruelty to animals; stealing while confronting a victim; and forcing sexual activity
- destruction of property—deliberate fire-setting and deliberate destruction other than fire setting
- deceitfulness or theft—breaking into others' property; lying or conning; stealing valuable items without confronting victim
- serious violations of rules—staying out overnight without permission (before age 13), running away at least twice, truancy (before age 13)

CD involves a very broad range of symptoms and has equally broad impact on youth and their families. One youth with CD may leave home for a week, skip school, and shoplift frequently, showing genuine remorse when caught. Another youth with CD may torture the neighbor's cat, set fire to his home, and threaten to kill his younger sister in her sleep, only showing superficial remorse in attempts to convince adults of his need for freedom. The severity of CD ranges from mild (for few symptoms with minimal impact on others) to severe (for multiple symptoms and/or considerable harm to others). In all, CD occurs in up to 10 per cent of the population and seems to be more common among males compared to females (APA, 2013).

The *DSM-5* (APA, 2013) allows counselors to note childhood-onset (i.e. prior to age 10) or adolescent-onset (i.e. no signs prior to age 10) and whether the individual has *limited prosocial emotions*. Limited prosocial emotions involve at least two of the following: lack of remorse or guilt, lack of empathy (callousness), lack of concern about performance, and shallow/deficient affect. In general, those who develop CD earlier in life and show limited prosocial emotions have much poorer outcomes, often developing criminal behavior, substance use disorders, or Antisocial Personality Disorder (Woo and Keatinge, 2016). Those who develop CD in adolescence have healthy peer relationships, and do not show problems with prosocial emotions often recover fully and function well as adults. Given the nature of CD, including deception to others, it is important that mental health professionals consider both youth reports and those from caregivers (e.g., teachers, parents) familiar with the youth.

Pyromania

Pyromania is a very rare disorder involving repeated, deliberate fire-setting in context of fascination with the fire-setting process (APA, 2013). The fire-setting behavior occurs within a cycle of tension prior to the event and pleasure associated with the fire-setting. Those with pyromania do so for the pleasure of the specific fire-setting experience; the fire-setting is not for gain, to hide activity, or to enact revenge. Although 40 per cent of arson cases involve youth (APA, 2013), most youth who set fires do so in the context of other mental disorders such as CD.

Kleptomania

Kleptomania is also a very rare disorder involving "recurrent failure to resist impulses to steal objects that are not needed for personal use or for their monetary value" (APA, 2013, p. 478). Like Pyromania, Kleptomania is more about the process of stealing than the outcome, including building tension prior to stealing and pleasure or relief at time of the theft. Kleptomania is not associated with ordinary theft in which one steals out of desire to use or sell the object, gain status among peers, or rebel against adults. As with Pyromania, most youth who engage in stealing will do so in the context of normal developmental experimentation or another disorder such as CD, eating disorder (e.g., to obtain laxative or diuretics), or substance use (e.g., to obtain the substance).

Treatment

Although treatment for Disruptive, Impulse-Control, and Conduct Disorders are similar, often combining family-based therapy, CBT, and social skills training, there are some differences that should be noted. It is vital that counselors consider a youth's unique developmental and contextual considerations when crafting effective treatment plans.

Table 10.4 Summary of disruptive, impulse control, and conduct disorders

Disorder	Summary
Oppositional Defiant Disorder	Six or more months of developmentally and culturally inappropriate angry/irritable mood, argumentative/defiant behavior, and/or vindictiveness
Intermittent Explosive Disorder	Pattern of verbal and/or behavioral outbursts that are out of proportion to context and not premeditated
Conduct Disorder	Pattern of behavior in which one violates the rights of others or conflicts with norms or rules, requiring at least three symptoms over one year and one symptom in the last six months
Pyromania	Deliberate fire-setting related to cycle of tension and relief
Kleptomania	Stealing related to cycle of tension and relief rather than gain

Treatment for ODD most commonly calls for a combination of parent training programs, family therapy, cognitive problem-solving skills training, social skills training, and school-based programming (American Academy of Child and Adolescent Psychiatry [AACAP], 2009). Parent training programs help parents learn how to better reinforce positive behavior and consistently apply discipline. Cognitive problem-solving skills training helps adolescents decide how to respond to stress and problems. Social-skills programs prepare children and adolescents to interact appropriately with peers. Most frequently, social-skills programs are implemented in schools or other settings in which target students would typically interact with peers. Medication, if prescribed at all, is typically used to control symptoms of a comorbid disorder and is not used as a stand-alone treatment for ODD (AACAP, 2009).

There is limited research on IED, but the existing research suggests CBT as a primary method of approaching treatment (Adamson, Campbell, and Kress, 2015). Cognitive-behavioral approaches may include helping children and adolescents recognize their triggers and use relaxation strategies when experiencing rage. Although medication is not typically used as a primary treatment of IED, it may be used in conjunction with other treatments to help stabilize mood or reduce irritability.

Treatment for CD includes systematic attention to multiple types of interventions. These include Multisystemic Therapy (Henggeler, Cunningham, Schoenwalk, Borduin, and Rowland, 2009) as well as behavioral and cognitive-behavioral interventions (e.g., contingency management programs, parent management training, and cognitive–behavioral skills training) (Frick 2001). There are no medications to treat CD, but youth may benefit from medication if they also have co-occurring ADHD (Gillen, Rose, and Schwarze, 2014).

Pyromania and Kleptomania are relatively rare disorders and there is limited attention in the literature regarding their treatment. There is some focus on CBT as having promise for identifying triggers and learning to resist impulses to steal and set fires (Grant and Kim, 2007; Mayo Clinic, 2014). The pyromania literature includes some initial discussion of medication management (Burton, McNiel, and Binder, 2012), and medications may be used to treat co-occurring disorders (Mayo Clinic, 2014).

Case Study: Jenny

Jenny is a third-grade student of above-average intelligence. Although she has a stable peer group and usually performs well at school, sometimes she is prone to fits of rage that come on without warning and are incredibly disruptive and potentially dangerous to those around her. In the previous six months, she has had four of these outbursts, one of which involved throwing her dining room chair through the living room window. Three outbursts have been at home and one has been at school, where she was sent to the principal's office for screaming profanities at a classmate and teacher. When she arrived at the principal's office, she continued to rage; she was sent to in-school suspension (ISS) for the remainder of the day. At home, her siblings have started doing anything that Jenny says, in part, it seems, to avoid setting her off. Her parents are at a loss for what to do. They have stated that once she calms down, Jenny shows remorse for her behavior and attempts to make amends, but in the moment she seems to have no control over her anger.

Process Questions

1. Based on information provided, what is the most likely diagnosis for Jenny? What additional information would you need to confirm this diagnosis?
2. How might your assumptions regarding gender and culture influence (or not influence) your diagnosis?
3. Given what you know about disruptive behavior disorders, how would you approach treatment with Jenny?
4. How would you advise her teachers to respond to her outbursts?

Disruptive behavior disorders are quite common in youth and vary with age and gender. Counselors should carefully consider cultural, developmental, and situational context before diagnosing disruptive behavior disorders. Treatment recommendations vary by disorder and developmental age and most often involve family-based therapy, CBT, parenting interventions, and social skills training.

SUMMARY

Counselors will have opportunities to serve youth who experience a wide range of mental health concerns. Diagnosing these concerns requires the ability to understand behavioral, cognitive, and affective experiences in developmental and sociocultural context. Unless counselors are working in specialized treatment settings (e.g., substance abuse services or an eating disorder clinic), anxiety, depressive, trauma- and stressor-related, and disruptive behavior disorders will more commonly be diagnosed. In Chapter 11, readers will have the opportunities to learn about additional disorders that are often diagnosed and treated in an interdisciplinary manner.

Additional Resources

Adverse Childhood Experiences: http://www.cdc.gov/violenceprevention/acestudy
American Academy of Child and Adolescent Psychiatry: www.aacap.org
American Counseling Association Practice Brief Series: https://www.counseling.org/knowledge-center/practice-briefs
DSM-5 Online Assessment Measures: www.psychiatry.org
Substance Abuse and Mental Health Services Administration Evidence-Based Practices KITS: http://store.samhsa.gov/list/series?name=Evidence-Based-Practices-KITs
Substance Abuse and Mental Health Services Administration National Registry of Evidence-Based Programs and Practices: http://www.samhsa.gov/nrepp
Trauma-Focused CBT Training Module: https://tfcbt.musc.edu/

Suggested Readings

American Psychiatric Association (2013). *Diagnostic and statistical manual of mental disorders*, 5th ed. Alexandria, VA: Author.

Cairns, K. E., Yap, M. B. H., Pilkington, P. D., and Jorm, A. F. (2014). Risk and protective factors for depression that adolescents can modify: a systematic review and meta-analysis of longitudinal studies. *Journal of Affective Disorders* 169, 61–75. doi: 10.1016/j.jad.2014.08.006

Centers for Disease Control and Prevention. (2013, May). Mental health surveillance among children—United States, 2005–2011. *Morbidity and Mortality Weekly Report* 62 (2). Retrieved from http://www.cdc.gov/mmwr/pdf/other/su6202.pdf

Drake, K. L. and Ginsburg, G. S. (2012). Family factors in the development, treatment, and prevention of childhood anxiety disorders. *Clinical Child and Family Psychology Review* 15 (2), 144–162.

Fisher, P. H., Tobkes, J. L., Kotcher, L., and Masia-Warner, C. (2006). Psychosocial and pharmacological treatment for pediatric anxiety disorders. *Expert Review of Neurotherapeutics* 6, 1707–1719.

Roy, A. K., Lopes, V., and Klein, R. G. (2014). Disruptive mood dysregulation disorder: A new diagnostic approach to chronic irritability in youth. *American Journal of Psychiatry* 171, 918–924.

Smith, P., Perrin, S., Dalgleish, T., Meiser-Stedman, R., Clark, D. M., and Yule, W. (2013). Treatment of posttraumatic stress disorder in children and adolescents. *Current Opinion in Psychiatry* 26, 66–72.

Woo, S. M. and Keatinge, C. (2016). *Diagnosis and treatment of mental disorders across the lifespan*, 2nd ed. Hoboken, NJ: Wiley.

Zhou, X., Hetrick, S. E., Cuijpers, P., Qin, B., Barth, J., Whittington, C. J. and Zhang, Y. (2015). Comparative efficacy and acceptability of psychotherapies for depression in children and adolescents: A systematic review and network meta-analysis. *World Psychiatry* 14 (2), 207–222. doi: 10.1002/wps.20217

Glossary

Adjustment disorder: A mental disorder in which an individual experiences changes in anxiety, mood, and/or conduct that impair functioning following onset of a stressor

Anxiety disorders: A group of mental disorders involving elements of *fear* (i.e. "emotional response to real or perceived imminent threat") and *anxiety* (i.e. "anticipation of future threat") (APA, 2013, p. 189)

Clinical assessment: A process, using formal and/or informal measures, interviews, and/or informants to derive a client diagnosis and inform a treatment plan

Cognitive behavioral therapy: An evidence-based counseling approach focused on understanding the impact of thoughts on behaviors and feelings

Conduct disorder: A "repetitive and persistent pattern of behavior in which the basic rights of others or major age-appropriate societal norms or rules are violated" (APA, 2013, p. 469)

Disruptive mood dysregulation disorder: A mental disorder featuring severe, recurrent temper outbursts and persistent irritable or angry moods among youth

Major depressive disorder: A mental disorder focused on depressed mood or loss of interest or pleasure and including at least five symptoms experienced most of the day over a two-week period

Oppositional defiant disorder: A mental disorder characterized by "a pattern of angry/irritable mood, argumentative/defiant behavior, or vindictiveness lasting at least 6 months" (APA, 2013, p. 462)
Posttraumatic stress disorder: A mental disorder involving a combination of affective, behavioral, and cognitive symptoms following exposure to a traumatic event or severe stressor
Selective serotonin reuptake inhibitors: A class of psychotropic medication typically used to treat depression and anxiety
Trauma-focused cognitive behavioral therapy: An evidence-based intervention focused on assisting youth and their parents to develop coping skills and cognitive frameworks for resolving trauma

Note

1   You can learn more about TF-CBT by completing free training here: https://tfcbt. musc.edu/.

References

Adamson, N. A., Campbell, E. C., and Kress, V. E. (2015). Disruptive, impulse-control, and conduct disorders, and elimination disorders. In V. E. Kress and M. J. Paylo, *Treating those with mental disorders: A comprehensive approach to case conceptualization and treatment* (pp. 384–420). Upper Saddle River, NJ: Pearson.

American Academy of Child and Adolescent Psychiatry (2009). ODD: A guide for families. Retrieved from https://www.aacap.org/App_Themes/AACAP/docs/ resource_centers/odd/odd_resource_center_odd_guide.pdf

American Counseling Association (2014). *Code of ethics.* Alexandria, VA: Author. Retrieved from https://www.counseling.org/resources/aca-code-of-ethics.pdf

American Psychiatric Association (2013). *Diagnostic and statistical manual of mental disorders*, 5th ed. Alexandria, VA: Author.

Broderick, P. C. and Blewitt, P. (2015). *The life span: Human development for helping professionals*, 4th ed. Upper Saddle River, NJ: Pearson.

Burton, P. R. S., McNiel, D. E., and Binder, R. L. (2012). Firesetting, arson, pyromania, and the forensic mental health expert. *Journal of the American Academy of Psychiatry and the Law* 40, 355–365.

Cairns, K. E., Yap, M. B. H., Pilkington, P. D., and Jorm, A. F. (2014). Risk and protective factors for depression that adolescents can modify: a systematic review and meta-analysis of longitudinal studies. *Journal of Affective Disorders* 169, 61–75. doi: 10.1016/j.jad.2014.08.006

Carnes-Holt, K. (2015, February). *Attachment concerns within adoptive families.* Retrieved from https://www.counseling.org/docs/default-source/practice-briefs/ adoption.pdf

Carr, A. (2008). Depression in young people: Description, assessment and evidence-based treatment. *Developmental Neurorehabilitation* 11, 3–15. Doi: 10.1080/ 17518420701536095

Center for Parenting Education (2016). *Child development.* Retrieved from http:// centerforparentingeducation.org/library-of-articles/child-development/

Centers for Disease Control and Prevention (2013, May). Mental health surveillance among Children—United States, 2005–2011. *Morbidity and Mortality Weekly Report* 62(2). Retrieved from http://www.cdc.gov/mmwr/pdf/other/su6202.pdf

Centers for Disease Control and Prevention (2016). About adverse childhood experiences. Retrieved from http://www.cdc.gov/violenceprevention/acestudy/about_ace.html

Choate, M. L., Pincus, D. B., Eyberg, S. M., and Barlow, D. H. (2006). Parent–child interaction therapy for treatment of separation anxiety disorder in young children: A pilot study. *Cognitive and Behavioral Practice* 12, 126–135.

Claman, F. and Miller, T. (2006). Premenstrual syndrome and premenstrual dysphoric disorder in adolescence. *Journal of Pediatric Health Care* 20 (5), 329–333.

Davis, T. E., Ollendick, T. H., and Öst, L. G. (2009). Intensive treatment of specific phobias in children and adolescents. *Cognitive and Behavioral Practice* 16, 294–303.

Drake, K. L. and Ginsburg, G. S. (2012). Family factors in the development, treatment, and prevention of childhood anxiety disorders. *Clinical Child and Family Psychology Review* 15 (2), 144–162.

Fisher, P. H., Tobkes, J. L., Kotcher, L., and Masia-Warner, C. (2006). Psychosocial and pharmacological treatment for pediatric anxiety disorders. *Expert Review of Neurotherapeutics* 6, 1707–1719.

Forti-Buratti, M. A., Saikia, R., Wilkinson, E. L., and Ramchandani, P. G. (2016). Psychological treatments for depression in pre-adolescent children (12 years and younger): Systematic review and meta-analysis of randomised controlled trials. *European Child and Adolescent Psychiatry* 1–10.

Frick, P. J. (2001). Effective interventions for children and adolescents with conduct disorder. *Canadian Journal of Psychiatry* 46, 597–608. Retrieved from http://www.ncbi.nlm.nih.gov/pubmed/11582820

Gillen, M., Rose, E., and Schwarz, J. (2014). *Conduct disorder*. Retrieved from https://www.counseling.org/docs/default-source/practice-briefs/conduct-disorder.pdf?sfvrsn=7

Grant, J. E. and Kim, S. W. (2007). Clinical characteristics and psychiatric co-morbidity of pyromania. *Journal of Clinical Psychiatry* 68, 1717–1722.

Henggeler, S. W., Cunningham, P. B., Schoenwalk, S. K., Borduin, C. M., and Rowland, M. D. (2009). *Multisystemic therapy for antisocial behavior in children and adolescents*, 2nd ed. New York, NY: Guilford.

Kress, V. E., Hartwig Moorhead, H., and Zoldan, C. A. (2015). Trauma- and stressor-related disorders. In V. E. Kress and M. J. Paylo, *Treating those with mental disorders: A comprehensive approach to case conceptualization and treatment* (pp. 194–224). Upper Saddle River, NJ: Pearson.

Lenz, A. S. and Klassen, S. (2016, May). *Posttraumatic stress disorder in youth*. Retrieved from https://www.counseling.org/docs/default-source/practice-briefs/posttraumatic-stress-disorder-in-youth.pdf?sfvrsn=4

Mayo Clinic (2014). *Kleptomania*. Retrieved from http://www.mayoclinic.org/diseases-conditions/kleptomania/

Merikangas, K. R., He, J. P., Burstein, M., Swanson, S. A., Avenevoli, S., Cui, L., Benjet, C., Georgiades, K., and Swendsen, J. (2010). Lifetime prevalence of mental disorders in U.S. adolescents: Results from the National Comorbidity Survey Replication–Adolescent Supplement (NCS-A). *Journal of the American Academy of Child and Adolescent Psychiatry* 49, 980–989. doi: 10.1016/j.jaac.2010.06.017

Miller, E. and Prosek, E. A. (2013). Trends and implications of proposed changes to the DSM-5 for vulnerable populations. *Journal of Counseling and Development* 91, 359–366. doi: 10.1002/j.1556-6676.2013.00106.x

Nobile, M., Cataldo, G. M., Marino, C., and Molteni, M. (2003). Diagnosis and treatment of dysthymia in children and adolescents. *CNS Drugs* 17, 927–946.

Perrin, S., Smith, P., and Yule, W. (2000). Practitioner review: the assessment and treatment of post-traumatic stress disorder in children and adolescents. *Journal of Child Psychology and Psychiatry* 41 (3), 277–289.

Rapkin, A. (2003). A review of treatment of premenstrual syndrome and premenstrual dysphoric disorder. *Psychoneuroendocrinology* 28, 39–53.

Roy, A. K., Lopes, V., and Klein, R. G. (2014). Disruptive mood dysregulation disorder: A new diagnostic approach to chronic irritability in youth. *American Journal of Psychiatry* 171, 918–924.

Sharkey, L. and McNicholas, F. (2008). "More than 100 years of silence": Elective mutism. *European Child and Adolescent Psychiatry* 17, 255–263.

Smith, P., Perrin, S., Dalgleish, T., Meiser-Stedman, R., Clark, D. M., and Yule, W. (2013). Treatment of posttraumatic stress disorder in children and adolescents. *Current Opinion in Psychiatry* 26, 66–72.

Taylor, L. K. and Weems, C. F. (2009). What do youth report as a traumatic event? Toward a developmentally informed classification of traumatic stressors. *Psychological Trauma* 1, 91–106. doi: 10.1037/a0016012

Thulin, U., Svirsky, L., Serlachius, E., Andersson, G., and Öst, L. G. (2014). The effect of parent involvement in the treatment of anxiety disorders in children: a meta-analysis. *Cognitive Behaviour Therapy* 43, 185–200.

Tourian, L., LeBoeuf, A., Breton, J. J., Cohen, D., Gignac, M., Labelle, R. and Renaud, J. (2015). Treatment options for the cardinal symptoms of disruptive mood dysregulation disorder. *Journal of the Canadian Academy of Child and Adolescent Psychiatry* 24 (1), 41.

Woo, S. M. and Keatinge, C. (2016). *Diagnosis and treatment of mental disorders across the lifespan*, 2nd ed. Hoboken, NJ: Wiley.

Zeanah, C. H. and Gleason, M. M. (2015). Annual research review: attachment disorders in early Childhood: clinical presentation, causes, correlates, and treatment. *Journal of Child Psychology and Psychiatry* 56, 207–222.

Zhou, X., Hetrick, S. E., Cuijpers, P., Qin, B., Barth, J., Whittington, C. J., and Zhang, Y. (2015). Comparative efficacy and acceptability of psychotherapies for depression in children and adolescents: A systematic review and network meta-analysis. *World Psychiatry* 14 (2), 207–222. doi: 10.1002/wps.20217

CHAPTER 11

Diagnosis and Treatment of Children and Adolescents

Neurodevelopmental, Substance-Related, and Other Specialized Disorders

Casey A. Barrio Minton, Sharon M. Bruner, and Carrie A. Wachter Morris

> I never treat what I diagnose ... to do so would be akin to eating the cookbook rather than the meal.
>
> Ronald Amundson

CHAPTER OBJECTIVES

After reading this chapter, counselor trainees will be able to

- identify key characteristics of neurodevelopmental disorders in youth (CACREP 2016 5.C.2.d, 5.C.2.g, 5.G.2.g)
- recognize symptoms of a broad range of DSM-5 disorders after diagnosed and/or treated by other professionals (CACREP 2016 5.C.2.d, 5.G.2.g)
- identify signs and symptoms of youth substance abuse (CACREP 2016 5.C.B.e, 5.G.2.i)
- consider indications that youth may need referral to specialized mental health and medical professionals (CACREP 2016 5.C.2.h, 5.C.3.d, 5.G.2.d, 5.G.2.k)
- identify treatment implications for youth and families experiencing a broad range of DSM-5 disorders (CACREP 2016 2.F.5.h, 2.F.5.j, 5.C.2.b, 5.C.3.b, 5.C.3.e, 5.F.3.f)

INTRODUCTION

Note: In this chapter, the word "youth" refers generally to children and adolescents. "Children" refers to individuals in early, middle, or late childhood, up to age 12 or 13. "Adolescents" refers to individuals from age 13 to late teens or early 20s.

Counselors in clinical mental health and school settings should be familiar with a wide range of mental disorders. In some cases, counselors will recognize signs of disorders and refer youth for further assessment and specialized treatment. In other cases, counselors will bring their unique skills and perspectives to an inter-disciplinary team that provides services to youth and their families.

The disorders discussed in this chapter may begin as early as birth and may be particularly relevant for children and adolescents. Some disorders covered in this chapter are primarily found in adults; however, signs of the concern may begin earlier in life. In this chapter, you will learn general characteristics and treatment recommendations regarding:

- Neurodevelopmental Disorders
- Schizophrenia Spectrum and Other Psychotic Disorders
- Bipolar and Related Disorders
- Obsessive–Compulsive and Related Disorders
- Substance-Related and Addictive Disorders
- Feeding and Eating Disorders
- Elimination Disorders
- Sleep–Wake Disorders
- Gender Dysphoria

NEURODEVELOPMENTAL DISORDERS

Neurodevelopmental Disorders include a broad range of concerns that manifest early in life and are largely believed to be based in the developing brain. Some neurodevelopmental disorders, such as Intellectual Disability and Autism Spectrum Disorder, may have profound and pervasive impact on youths' development and needs. Others, such as specific learning or communication disorders, may impact more specific areas of functioning, sometimes for a limited time.

Generally, disorders highlighted in this section will be evaluated and diagnosed by professionals, such as educational diagnosticians and school psychologists, who have specialty expertise in assessment procedures. Still, counselors who work with youth need to be able to recognize signs of neurodevelopmental disorders, make appropriate referrals, and work with youth, teachers, and families to promote and support holistic development. Counselors should be familiar with typical and atypical development in early childhood so they can identify when youth may benefit from more focused assessment. The following resource provides detailed charts and checklists regarding expected range of fine motor, gross motor, phonological awareness, play and social skills, self-care, sensory processing, speech sounds, language, and written communication development by age group: http://www.childdevelopment.com.au/home/170. You may find this website particularly helpful for refreshing your understanding of typical child development.

Diagnosis

There are multiple subcategories of Neurodevelopmental Disorders. In the following pages, we provide an overview of Intellectual Disabilities, Communication Disorders, Attention-Deficit/Hyperactivity Disorder, Specific Learning Disorder, and Motor Disorders.

Intellectual Disabilities (ID)

ID, known as Mental Retardation prior to Public Law 111-256 (Rosa's Law), involve deficits in intellectual and adaptive functioning apparent early in development. Individuals with ID struggle with intellectual functions involving "reasoning, problem solving, planning, abstract thinking, judgment, learning from instruction and experience, and practical understanding" (American Psychiatric Association [APA], 2013, p. 37). These difficulties are apparent through formal intelligence testing (IQ scores) that have been designed with attention to development, cultural, and context of the individual. In addition, individuals with ID must show difficulties in adaptive functioning, defined as "how well a person meets community standards of personal independence and social responsibility, in comparison to others of similar age and sociocultural background" (APA, 2013, p. 37). As with IQ, adaptive functioning can be assessed via standardized tests and interviews with individuals and their caregivers.

There are limitations to using IQ tests as sole indicators of ID. Professionals who diagnose ID must consider IQ tests in conjunction with an individual's conceptual, social, and practical functioning. The *DSM-5* (APA, 2013) provides extensive descriptions regarding mild, moderate, severe, and profound impacts in each of these domains. For example, individuals who have mild ID may not show difficulty with conceptual domains until they enter school, and adults may be able to function academically and solve concrete problems with appropriate supports. Those with mild ID may be able to function in a number of social domains, although they may appear immature and struggle with emotion regulation at times. Practically speaking, persons with mild ID may be able to take care of most activities of daily living; however, they may need additional support navigating complex or poorly identified situations. In contrast, individuals with severe ID may not learn to read or write, have limited spoken language (e.g., uses and understands only words or phrases), and need extensive support for all activities of daily living from a very young age.

Communication Disorders

The *DSM-5* includes several Communication Disorders impacting speech (i.e. sounds, articulation), language (i.e. use of spoken or written words), and communication (i.e. verbal and nonverbal behavior) (APA, 2013). There is a very wide range of typical communication development. Specialists assess communication disorders via formal standardized measures; these measures, however, need to include special attention to the client's sociocultural context. Certainly, youth who are operating in a second (or third) language may not appear "typical" in speech or language. Similarly, culture can have a profound impact on the types of verbal and nonverbal behavior considered appropriate for individuals of all ages. You may find this resource helpful for understanding expected speech and language milestones: https://www.nidcd.nih.gov/health/speech-and-language.

The *DSM-5* includes four types of Communication Disorders: Language Disorder, Speech Sound Disorder, Childhood-Onset Fluency Disorder (Stuttering), and Social (Pragmatic) Communication Disorder. Language

Disorder involves "persistent difficulties in the acquisition and use of language across modalities (i.e., spoken, written, sign language, or other) due to deficits in comprehension or production" (APA, 2013, p, 42). Language Disorder involves problems with vocabulary, sentence structure, and discourse and must be below expectation for developmental level and not related to a more global neurodevelopmental disorder. In general, Language Disorder may include difficulty with expressing oneself and/or understanding others.

Speech Sound Disorder includes difficulty articulating or producing sounds in ways that can be understood by others (APA, 2013). As with the other Communication Disorders, Speech Sound Disorder must cause difficulty in functioning, not be related to a specific medical condition, and be markedly off-course in terms of overall development. An understanding of normal speech development is important when considering Speech Sound Disorder. A general guideline shared with parents is that one familiar with a child can expect to understand up to 50 per cent of communication by age 2, 75 per cent of communication by age 3, and nearly all communication by age 4. Still, children may struggle with specific sounds and pronunciation for much of elementary school.

Childhood-Onset Fluency Disorder, or stuttering, involves difficulty in fluency and timing of speech. In this case, youth may have an understanding of the words but will struggle to express themselves, thus invoking anxiety about performance and communication with others (APA, 2013). In some ways, the anxiety related to stuttering may cause more distress or difficulty in school or social situations than the stuttering itself. Most stuttering begins by early elementary school and resolves by adolescence or adulthood.

Finally, Social (Pragmatic) Communication Disorder was introduced in the DSM-5 to describe the experiences of individuals who have problems related to social communication. Youth may be able to understand and produce speech and language technically, but they struggle with social norms and expectations related to verbal and nonverbal communication. Diagnostic criteria include difficulties related to communication for social purposes (e.g., greeting), matching communication to context (e.g., classroom vs. playground), and following "rules" for conversation and storytelling (APA, 2013). Again, these concerns need to be beyond those expected for one's developmental level and not related to broader developmental concerns.

Autism Spectrum Disorder (ASD)

ASD represents a spectrum of neurodevelopmental disorders in which individuals struggle with both social communication and restricted, repetitive behaviors. Concerns with social communication may appear much as they do in Social Communication Disorder; however, the concerns may also be broader and involve social–emotional reciprocity, nonverbal communication, and navigating social relationships. Restricted, repetitive behaviors, interests, or activities include stereotyped motor movements, insistence of sameness, fixated interests, and over- or under-reactivity to sensory input (APA, 2013). As with ID, there is a very broad range of severity within ASD. In mild cases, individuals may need some guidance navigating social relationships and appear odd or inflexible in their daily activities (these individuals may have previously received diagnoses of Asperger's Disorder). In severe cases, youth may require constant support or supervision, perhaps not able to speak or navigate basic activities of daily living.

Approximately 1 per cent of children in the U.S. carry a diagnosis of ASD (CDC, 2013). Wide variation in rates of diagnoses has been subject to much discussion regarding overdiagnosis, recent trends, and methods for supporting individuals who show this concern. Boys with ASD outnumber girls with ASD by 3.4 to 4.5 times.

Attention-Deficit/Hyperactivity Disorder (ADHD)

By definition, ADHD emerges prior to age 12 and influences one's experiences in multiple areas of life. There are two major types of ADHD: Inattentive and hyperactive/impulsive. Many children experience both subtypes. To qualify for a diagnosis, one must have at least six symptoms of inattention and/or at least six symptoms of hyperactivity/impulsivity that last for at least six months (APA, 2013). Symptoms of inattention include: Difficulty with attention to detail, difficulty sustaining attention, not listening when spoken to directly, not following through with instructions or tasks, difficulty organizing tasks, difficulty with tasks requiring sustained attention, losing things frequently, being easily distracted, and forgetting things. Symptoms of hyperactivity/impulsivity include: Fidgeting or squirming, leaving seat, running or climbing inappropriately, difficulty with quiet activities, being "on the go" or "driven by a motor," talking excessively, blurting answers, difficulty waiting turn, and interrupting or intruding on others (p. 60).

ADHD is one of the most common mental disorders among youth, with approximately 8.5 per cent of parents indicating their youth has received this diagnosis (CDC, 2013), and prevalence studies producing ranges from as low as 1.4 per cent to more than 10 per cent depending on methodology (Woo and Keatinge, 2016). Although some scholars proposed that many children outgrow ADHD, research does not seem to support this claim. Rather, most children who have ADHD will *experience* ADHD in adolescence and into adulthood. However, they may not *express* their symptoms in the same manner as they mature. Rather than falling or jumping out of one's seat repeatedly, for example, a teenager may fidget with a ring to cope with his or her own internal sense of restlessness.

ADHD appears at least twice as common in boys than girls, although some wonder whether girls may simply express their symptoms in ways that are not as troublesome to adults (e.g., inattentiveness). When considering a diagnosis of ADHD, it is important to consider developmental and situational factors at play. As children attend schools in which playtime is reduced and time in seat is increased, it is quite possible that children are asked to be doing things their bodies and minds are not able to do. Similarly, many experts are concerned that ADHD is overdiagnosed and children are medicated simply for being children. Such critiques are valid in some cases; however, sweeping overgeneralizations may result in lack of appropriate care for children who truly struggle with ADHD.

Specific Learning Disorder

Specific Learning Disorders are diagnosed when youth have academic difficulties that appear disproportionate to their overall capacity for performance. Potential areas of difficulty include reading, written expression, and mathematics (APA, 2013). Those who struggle in reading may have difficulty with word reading, rate or fluency (i.e. dyslexia), or comprehension. Those who have difficulty with written expression may struggle with spelling, grammar and punctuation, or clarity and organization. In mathematics, individuals may have trouble with number sense, memorization of facts, calculation, or reasoning.

Specific Learning Disorders appear in about 5–15 per cent of school-aged children (APA, 2013) and may become apparent at different times in development, depending on the nature and pervasiveness of concerns. In some cases, adults may struggle to detect the Specific Learning Disorder because a child's behavior (e.g., refusing to do tasks, insisting one does not like the teacher) masks the problem. If one suspects a Specific Learning Disorder, he or she should refer the child for comprehensive academic testing to better understand the concern and potential accommodations that may support learning.

Motor Disorders

Motor Disorders comprise a cluster of disorders in which individuals have difficulty controlling or struggle to control specific motor skills. These include Developmental Coordination Disorder, Stereotypic Movement Disorder, and Tic Disorders.

Developmental Coordination Disorder is diagnosed when a youth is unable to coordinate gross and/or fine motor skills expected for his or her developmental level. The child may appear clumsy, or take a good deal of time and effort to perform a range of motor tasks such as writing, drawing, or playing sports (APA, 2013). As with other neurodevelopmental disorders, the concern needs to cause difficulty in functioning, begin early, and be well beyond what one would expect at that developmental level. For example, one would expect a young child to need help getting dressed, but most elementary school children should be able to operate zippers.

Stereotypic Movement Disorder involves "repetitive, seemingly driven, and apparently purposeless motor behaviors (e.g., hand shaking or waving, body rocking, head banging, self-biting, hitting own body)" (APA, 2013, p. 77). These behaviors begin early in development, often result in self-injury, and are commonly associated with other neurodevelopmental conditions such as ID. The stereotypic behaviors may worsen during times of stress.

Tic Disorders are those in which individuals have persistent problems with motor or vocal tics. Tics are "sudden, rapid, recurrent, nonrhythmic motor movements or vocalizations" (APA, 2013, p. 82) and can be simple or complex. The DSM-5 provides examples as follows:

- simple motor—blinking, shrugging, straightening arms and legs
- simple vocal—clearing throat, sniffing, grunting

- ■ complex motor—combining simple motor tics, gesturing, imitating
- ■ complex vocal—repeating sounds or phrases, blurting obscenities

By definition, Tourette's Disorder begins in childhood or adolescence. Youth who have Tourette's Disorder have multiple motor and vocal tics at some point during a period of at least a year. Persistent (Chronic) Motor or Vocal Tic Disorder is diagnosed when one has motor *or* vocal tics, not both, for at least a period of a year. Finally, Provisional Tic Disorder is reserved for cases of motor or vocal tics that have not lasted at least a year.

Table 11.1 Summary of neurodevelopmental disorders

Disorder	Summary
Intellectual Disabilities	Deficits in intellectual (e.g., reasoning, problem solving, abstracting thinking) and adaptive functioning (e.g., activities of daily living, independence, social responsibility) apparent early in development
Language Disorder	"Persistent difficulties in the acquisition and use of language across modalities (i.e., spoken, written, sign language, or other) due to deficits in comprehension or production" (APA, 2013, p, 42)
Speech Sound Disorder	Difficulty articulating or producing sounds in ways that can be understood by others
Childhood-Onset Fluency Disorder	Difficulty in fluency and timing of speech despite successful language acquisition and understanding
Social (Pragmatic) Communication Disorder	Difficulties related to communication for social purposes, matching communication to context, and following "rules" for conversation and storytelling
Autism Spectrum Disorder	Spectrum of neurodevelopmental disorders in which individual struggles with both social communication and restricted, repetitive behaviors
Attention-Deficit/ Hyperactivity Disorder	At least six symptoms of inattention and/or at least six symptoms of hyperactivity/impulsivity that last for at least six months and impair functioning in multiple settings
Specific Learning Disorder	Academic difficulties in reading, written expression, and/or mathematics that appear disproportionate to youth's overall capacity for performance
Developmental Coordination Disorder	Inability to coordinate gross and/or fine motor skills expected for a youth's developmental level
Stereotypic Movement Disorder	"Repetitive, seemingly driven, and apparently purposeless motor behaviors (e.g., hand shaking or waving, body rocking, head banging, self-biting, hitting own body)" (APA, 2013, p. 77)
Tourette's Disorder	Multiple motor and vocal tics at some point during a period of at least a year
Persistent (Chronic) Motor or Vocal Tic Disorder	Motor *or* vocal tics (not both) for at least a period of a year
Provisional Tic Disorder	Motor or vocal tics that have not lasted at least a year

Often beginning during or before elementary school, tic disorders such as Tourette's Syndrome impact about 0.3 per cent of the population (CDC, 2013). Tic Disorders are more common in boys, seem to be at their worst by late childhood, and will often improve during adulthood (APA, 2013). Although tics may not interfere with many aspects of functioning, those who experience them may struggle with social isolation or embarrassment, especially as they may be bullied at school or withdraw from situations in which others will notice them.

Treatment

The diagnosis of Neurodevelopmental Disorders requires specialized assessments that must be completed by a qualified practitioner, typically a psychologist, psychiatrist, or educational diagnostician. A multidisciplinary team that might include caregivers, teachers, mental health providers, and medical providers can provide a holistic picture of symptoms and contribute to an accurate diagnosis. Due to a high level of comorbidity, assessment for neurodevelopmental disorders should also include attention to symptoms of other physical or mental health disorders.

Depending on the nature of the concern and the extent of impact, a wide variety of professionals may participate in treatment of Neurodevelopmental Disorders to address speech, physical, learning, and/or motor implications of these disorders. Collaborating with school personnel in treatment of neurodevelopmental disorders is an important part of supporting youth in those settings; however, some families will also access care outside the schools. Examples of specialized care providers include Speech–Language Pathologists, Occupational Therapists, Reading Specialists, Physical Therapists, Applied Behavioral Analysis (ABA) Therapists, case managers, and social workers. Counselors can collaborate with other providers to address comorbid mental health issues while also helping youth manage the social and emotional impact of these disorders. In addition, counselors can assist with supporting caregivers as they implement behavioral and cognitive strategies with youth.

ASD interventions are frequently implemented by individuals with specialized training. ABA can assist families with targeting specific problematic behaviors (Lindgren and Doobay, 2011). ABA interventions frequently used to treat ASD include discrete trial training, functional communication training, and pivotal response training. In addition to ABA, social skills training and Cognitive Behavioral Therapy (CBT) can be helpful for youth with ASD. Social skills training can target frequently problematic social behaviors commonly found in individuals with ASD, including lack of eye contact and communication difficulties. CBT can help some youth develop self-monitoring skills and reward their own behaviors.

Assessment for ADHD requires significant collaboration between school personnel, caregivers, mental health providers, and medical providers. Assessment should include attention to other frequently comorbid disorders, including behavioral, neurodevelopmental, and physical disorders. Behavioral management training interventions including behavioral classroom management, behavioral peer intervention, and organization training are well-established treatments for ADHD (Evans, Owens, and Bunford, 2014). Neurofeedback training has shown promise in the treatment of ADHD. In school-aged children and adolescents, medication in combination with behavioral therapy is often recommended to treat ADHD. According to the American Academy of Pediatrics (2011), stimulants, atomoxetine extended-release guanfacine, and extended release clonidine have all demonstrated effectiveness with children and adolescents. Medication is not recommended for preschool-aged children unless behavioral interventions are ineffective.

Psychosocial intervention for tic disorders includes habit reversal therapy, comprehensive behavioral intervention, and CBT. In addition, psychoeducation and contingency management can increase positive effects of these interventions (Bennet, Keller, and Walkup, 2013; Theule, Ward, Cheung, and Lee, 2015). For moderate to severe tics, pharmacological treatment may help to improve quality of life. Medications for tic disorders include a-2 agonists and some antipsychotic medications, all of which require special monitoring for side effects (Murphy, Lewin, Storch, and Stock, 2013). Medication should be used in combination with other interventions, and counselors can pay special attention to the social and emotional experiences of clients with tic disorders.

Case Study: Micah

Micah is a first-grade student who is struggling socially and academically. Although he appears to be of average intelligence, he becomes easily fixated on topics of interest to him. If there is an unexpected deviation in his normal routine, Micah is nearly inconsolable. He will repeatedly bang his head on any nearby object while yelling. He will continue banging his head until physically restrained, and he seems oblivious to the pain it should cause, even if his head bleeds. Despite an apparent lack of sensitivity to pain, Micah is very picky about how clothing needs to feel. For example, he will only wear a specific type of socks that do not have a seam in the toes and refuses to wear t-shirts that have tags on the neck. Trying to get Micah to wear either of these types of clothing results in him throwing himself on the floor and screaming.

Micah has difficulty relating to other children and adults. He often has a flat affect, and does not typically smile or make eye contact. His teachers and parents have tried to get him to engage with and play with other children, but Micah is usually not interested. If other children or adults try to speak with Micah or play a game with him, he either does not respond at all, or responds in a way that is atypical. For example, Micah may turn the conversation to his favorite topic, dinosaurs, and talk in a monotone voice about whichever dinosaur is his favorite at that moment.

Process Questions

1. What are your primary concerns regarding Micah's behaviors?
2. Which neurodevelopmental disorders seem most likely given Micah's presentation?
3. As a school counselor, how would you see your role working with Micah, his family, and his teachers?
4. As a clinical mental health counselor, how would you envision working with Micah and his system?

Neurodevelopmental disorders have a biological/neurological basis and often begin early in life. Neurodevelopmental disorders should be assessed and diagnosed with individuals who have specialty training and expertise (e.g., psychologists, psychiatrists, and educational diagnosticians). Treatment for neurodevelopmental disorders most often includes engagement with allied health and mental health professionals; professional counselors may serve an important role on interdisciplinary treatment teams. Professional counselors may help youth and families impacted by neurodevelopmental disorders cope with the impact of the experience, navigate developmental transitions, and attend to holistic wellness.

SCHIZOPHRENIA SPECTRUM AND OTHER PSYCHOTIC DISORDERS

For many, Schizophrenia is a pervasive, lifelong disorder, and it is believed to be genetic and physiological in nature. Although most individuals do not develop active symptoms of schizophrenia until early adulthood and onset of schizophrenia in childhood is quite rare (0.14 in 1000, 50 times less than in adults), researchers are working to identify early indicators that could be associated with later onset of schizophrenia (Tiffin and Welch, 2013; Woo and Keatinge, 2016). Predictors of positive outcomes in schizophrenia include female, good premorbid functioning, higher IQ, sudden onset, mood symptoms, positive symptoms, family support, and early and available treatment. In contrast, those with poor lifelong functioning, early or slowly progressive onset, family disruption, and lack of emotionality may have poorer long-term outcomes.

Diagnosis

The *DSM-5* (APA, 2013) includes a number of disorders on the Schizophrenia Spectrum. These disorders include ways to capture experiences of those who have symptoms for less than a month (Brief Psychotic Disorder), one to six months (Schiozphreniform Disorder), and more than six months (Schizophrenia). Delusional Disorder accounts for experiences of those who have delusions in the absence of other psychotic symptoms, and Schizoaffective Disorder attends to those who have overlapping mood disruption and psychosis.

Individuals who have Schizophrenia have two or more characteristic symptoms during a one-month period. Characteristic symptoms (APA, 2013) include

- delusions—strongly held beliefs that are not considered culturally appropriate and do not change, even with evidence to the contrary
- hallucinations—hearing, seeing, tasting, smelling, feeling experiences that are not present
- disorganized speech—switching topics, making loose connections, incoherence
- disorganized behavior—agitation, rigidity, stupor, stereotyped movements
- negative symptoms—diminished emotional expression and avolition, including difficulty in initiating purposeful activities

In addition to experiencing at least one month in which two characteristic symptoms are present, those with Schizophrenia have substantial decreases in multiple areas of functioning. Young people with Schizophrenia may not regress, but they may not make expected developmental gains. These concerns must go on for at least six months. Professionals who diagnose Schizophrenia must take special care to ensure symptoms are not related to neurodevelopmental concerns such as ASD (which may account for negative symptoms and disorganized behavior), mood disturbances including Bipolar Disorder, substance use, or medical conditions.

Schizophrenia rarely begins earlier than adolescence (APA, 2013), and most individuals will have first active signs of Schizophrenia sometime in their 20s (early–mid-20s for males, late 20s for females). Early-onset Schizophrenia is remarkably similar to later-onset Schizophrenia; however, those who develop signs of Schizophrenia earlier in life have poorer outcomes, perhaps due to genetic strength or predisposition of concerns (Lachman, 2014; Woo and Keatinge, 2016).

Treatment

Rapid entry into appropriate services is one of the few prognostic indicators that may be within mental health providers' control. There is an emerging body of literature regarding appropriate responses to first episode psychosis, and emerging evidence indicates that those who participate in focused interventions have substantially higher remission rates (95 per cent) compared to those who engaged in medication only (59 per cent) (Valencia, Juarez, and Orega, 2012). Focused interventions include medication management, psychoeducation, family support, and case management beginning with the very first signs of psychosis. Most simply, timely identification and treatment is essential with early onset Schizophrenia (Lachman, 2014).

There are generally three phases of Schizophrenia treatment (APA, 2004). During initial onset or *acute phase* of psychosis, professionals will focus on medication management and ensuring immediate safety. In the months that follow, individuals will enter the *stabilization phase* in which they focus on stress management and creating lifestyle and environmental supports associated with long-term success. *Stable phase* treatments include continued psychosocial interventions such as psychoeducation, skills training, and family therapy.

When counselors work with youth who are experiencing psychosis, they should do so as part of an interdisciplinary team that includes a child and adolescent psychiatrist, case manager, and education personnel. Together, these individuals will provide the pillars of treatment for Schizophrenia: Medication, psychosocial interventions to promote coping and reduce relapse, and vocational rehabilitation (Rossler, 2011). Unfortunately, research is limited regarding efficacy of treatments in youth with psychosis (Stafford et al., 2015). First-line medication treatments include atypical antipsychotics; however, psychiatrists may also utilize antidepressants, anxiolytics, and mood stabilizing drugs (Schizophrenia Medications, 2013). Counselors may provide psychosocial interventions in which they help youth and their families understand how lifestyle changes and development of coping skills may support their long-term wellbeing.

- Childhood onset Schizophrenia is very rare; however, some individuals may experience first onset of psychosis in adolescence.
- Schizophrenia spectrum disorders include experiences with a range of symptoms including delusions, hallucinations, disorganized speech, disorganized behavior, and negative symptoms.
- Early, focused prevision of medication, psychoeducation, family support, and case management services can make a positive impact in long-term prognosis and adaptive functioning.

BIPOLAR AND RELATED DISORDERS

Bipolar Disorders are considered serious mental illness, have genetic and physiological basis, and may require lifelong management. In recent years, the mental health community has seen an exponential increase in the number of childhood Bipolar Disorder diagnoses. There is considerable agreement that clinicians may have been overzealous in assigning Bipolar Disorder diagnoses for children who had significant problems with mood and behavior (Youngstrom, Findling, Kogos, Youngstrom, and Calabrese, 2005) (see Disruptive Mood Dysregulation Disorder in Chapter 10). In reality, Bipolar Disorders are quite rare in children. In this section, we explore criteria for Bipolar Disorder, provide treatment implications, and illustrate via a vignette.

Diagnosis

To understand Bipolar Disorders, one must understand three distinct types of mood episodes: Manic, hypomanic, and depressive. A **manic episode** involves

> a distinct period of abnormally and persistently elevated, expansive, or irritable mood and abnormally and persistently increased goal-directed

activity or energy, lasting at least 1 week and present most of the day, nearly every day (or any duration if hospitalization is necessary).

(APA, 2013, p. 124)

This mood alteration involves a number of changes including those in self-esteem, need for sleep, talkativeness, flight of ideas, distractibility, goal-directed activity, psychomotor activity, and involvement in high-risk activities. Together, the symptoms are severe enough that one cannot function in daily tasks, may need supervision or hospitalization to prevent harm to self or others, and may even experience symptoms of psychosis.

Hypomanic episodes are quite similar to manic episodes; however, they are less severe in nature. Specifically, hypomanic episodes may last as little as four days; although symptoms are parallel, they are not severe enough to cause major problems in functioning, present danger to self or others, or require hospitalization. Because mood fluctuations are sometimes extreme in youth (e.g., excitement about an upcoming event, high energy, seemingly little need for sleep), it may be particularly difficult to distinguish between developmentally normal mood fluctuations and hypomanic episodes.

Finally, *major depressive episodes* involve a period of at least two weeks in which the person experiences depressed or irritable mood and/or loss of interest in pleasure. As described in Chapter 10, these symptoms are accompanied by changes in appetite/weight, changes in sleep, psychomotor agitation or retardation, loss of energy, feelings of worthlessness or guilt, problems with concentration, and/or thoughts of death or suicide.

Although individuals with Bipolar I Disorder usually also experience hypomanic or major depressive episodes, the only distinguishing feature for Bipolar I Disorder is history of a manic episode. The *DSM-5* (APA, 2013) notes that the average age of first mood episode is 18, meaning that about half of people with Bipolar I Disorder will experience their first manic, hypomanic, or depressive episode in adolescence.

Bipolar II Disorder is diagnosed for individuals who have a history of both major depressive and hypomanic episodes but have not ever had a full-blown manic episode (APA, 2013). Bipolar II Disorder tends to develop in early adulthood, and it is not often diagnosed in childhood. When considering this diagnosis in youth, it is very important to consider developmental and cultural norms for both mood and behavior. Similarly, one must consider whether irritability is episodic (i.e., happens in distinct shifts) or non-episodic. Non-episodic irritability is more likely to be associated with anxiety or depressive disorders, including Disruptive Mood Dysregulation Disorder (APA, 2013).

Cyclothymic Disorder is diagnosed for youth who have at least a one-year history of distinct mood fluctuations that do not fully meet criteria for depressive and hypomanic episodes described above. These hypomanic and depressive symptoms are present at least half the time and present disturbance in functioning (APA, 2013). Cyclothymic disorder tends to begin in adolescence or early adulthood and is associated with persistent problems over time.

Table 11.2 Summary of bipolar disorders and differential diagnoses

Disorder	Summary
Bipolar I Disorder	Any history of a manic episode; the individual may also have a history of hypomanic and/or depressive episodes
Bipolar II Disorder	History of at least one major depressive episode and at least one hypomanic episode; the individual may not have any history of manic episodes
Cyclothymic Disorder	At least one year of fluctuating hypomanic and depressive symptoms that do not meet criteria for depressive, manic, or hypomanic episodes
Major Depressive Disorder	Presence of major depressive episodes in absence of manic or hypomanic episodes
Disruptive Mood Dysregulation Disorder	At least one year of severe, recurrent, non-episodic temper outbursts coupled with persistently irritable mood that causes disruption in at least two settings

Treatment

Accurate assessment is critical in treatment of pediatric bipolar disorder (Youngstrom et al., 2005). This assessment should be comprehensive in nature and include input from caregivers and teachers. Given frequent misdiagnosis of this disorder, mental health professionals should pay careful attention to nature of mood episodes as well as co-occurring medical problems and medications, ADHD, and disruptive behavior disorders.

Treatment for Bipolar Disorders in youth is similar in many ways to the treatment that adults receive, with psychopharmaceutical prescriptions (particularly mood stabilizers, atypical antipsychotics, and sometimes antidepressants, often in combination) a primary source of treatment (Jairam, Prabhuswamy, and Dullur, 2011; Moreno et al., 2007). Unfortunately, finding the right combination of medications may take months or years. If a manic or major depressive episode is severe, it may warrant hospitalization to help prevent harm to self or others and allow for stabilization.

Talk therapy is also recommended in combination with medication, with CBT, social skills training, family therapy, and psychoeducation (Apps, Winkler, and Jandrisevits, 2008). Counselors can help youth and their families process the meaning diagnoses hold for them, including working through stigma or hopelessness families may feel at the prospect of lifelong management of mental health concerns. Similarly, counselors can help youth and families identify triggers for episodes; ensure a warm stable environment, and engage in wellness activities (e.g., appropriate nutrition, adequate sleep, stress management) that may help to moderate frequency and intensity of episodes (Woo and Keatinge, 2016).

Case Study: Kelsey

Kelsey is an 18-year-old whose parents divorced when she was 15. Her parents' relationship had been marked by ongoing emotional abuse between both parents and some instances of violence perpetuated by Kelsey's father against her mother. After the divorce Kelsey was perpetually sullen and made two suicide attempts. Given the recent divorce and family trauma, most of this was explained away as a response to her family situation.

Kelsey moved out of the house after she graduated high school to live with some friends while she attended a local community college. One day, her roommates came home to find Kelsey giddily painting a mural on the living room wall. She was covered in paint and talking about how she had a flash of inspiration that would help her become a great artist. When her roommates attempted to talk her out of continuing to paint, Kelsey became angry at them for trying to steal her ideas. She started throwing anything within reach. Her roommates, stunned, contacted Kelsey's mother, who arrived in time to find Kelsey painting her naked body and then pressing her body against the wall, continuing her painting project.

Process Questions

1. What developmental, gender, and cultural elements might be at play for Kelsey?
2. Based on information provided, what are the three most likely diagnosis for Kelsey? What additional information would you need to confirm this diagnosis?
3. Given what you know about Bipolar Disorders, how would you approach treatment with Kelsey?
4. What additional or adjunct services might Kelsey need?

Bipolar Disorders rarely begin in childhood; however, manic episodes may occur in mid–late adolescents for many individuals with bipolar disorder. Bipolar Disorders involve various constellations of manic, hypomanic, and depressive episodes. Treatment approaches for Bipolar Disorders involve combinations of medication management, psychoeducation, and counseling. Engagement in wellness behaviors may enhance functioning and reduce number of mood episodes.

OBSESSIVE–COMPULSIVE AND RELATED DISORDERS

Although the specific nature of concerns may vary, Obsessive–Compulsive and Related Disorders are unified in that they are associated with repetitive thoughts and/or behaviors.

Obsessions are recurrent and persistent thoughts, urges, or images that are experienced as intrusive and unwanted, whereas *compulsions* are repetitive behaviors or mental acts that an individual feels driven to perform in response to an obsession or according to rules that must be applied rigidly.

(APA, 2013, p. 235)

Several of the disorders we explore in this section are most common in youth, and many begin with early childhood. At the same time, they can be difficult to spot, as children may not have the developmental skills to articulate their thought process or understand the driving forces behind behaviors. As with other disorders, counselors who consider diagnoses of these disorders must decide how to differentiate typical childhood behavior, which can be quite focused, rigid, and rule-oriented at times, with behavior indicative of a mental disorder.

Diagnosis

Obsessive–Compulsive Disorder, Body Dysmorphic Disorder, Trichotillomania, and Excoriation Disorder may begin in childhood or adolescence. We review each disorder below.

Obsessive–Compulsive Disorder (OCD)

To receive a diagnosis of OCD, a youth may experience either obsessions and/or compulsions, and these experiences must take considerable time and/ or energy for the youth, thus interfering with daily activities or, at the least, making daily activities quite difficult (APA, 2013). Youth who have OCD may be preoccupied with washing or checking, worry extensively about germs or harm, repeat words or phrases, and need a great deal of order. For example, they may become exceptionally distressed if objects appear out of order or mismatched. Engaging in the mental ritual or a compulsion helps youth feel temporarily relieved and less anxious.

Nearly a quarter of cases of OCD are present by early adolescence (APA, 2013), and those who develop OCD earlier tend to experience longer life-time problems. Boys tend to develop OCD earlier than girls (Woo and Keatinge, 2016). There is often overlap between OCD and tic disorders, with as many as one-third of people with OCD also having tic disorders. For many, these concerns start together in childhood.

Body Dysmorphic Disorder

Body Dysmorphic Disorder includes obsession, or preoccupation, with "one or more perceived defects or flaws in physical appearance that are not observable or appear slight to others" (APA, 2013, p. 242). In response to this specific type of obsession, individuals either engage in repetitive behaviors or acts focused on appearance and experience distress or impairment. For example, an individual may check the mirror repeatedly, have difficulty making it to school on time because she changes clothes in attempts to hide perceived defects, tan excessively, or spend copious amounts of time engaged in activities to help hide or modify the perceived defect.

Signs of Body Dysmorphic Disorder most often begin in early to mid-adolescence (APA, 2013), just as youth are navigating changes related to puberty and exploring their identities. Although it is developmentally common for adolescents to believe they have an imaginary audience and overestimate others' focus on their appearance and actions, those with Body Dysmorphic Disorder experience these concerns to an extreme degree. In many cases, the concern keeps youth from attending school, spending time with friends, or otherwise engaging in activities of youth.

Trichotillomania (Hair-Pulling Disorder)

Trichotillomania, or Hair-Pulling Disorder, is characterized by obsessions and compulsions related to pulling their own hair (APA, 2013). Individuals with trichotillomania may pull hair from any body region (e.g., scalp, eyebrows, pubic) and have hair loss as a result of their behavior. The hair-pulling behavior is not due to itchiness or discomfort of a medical condition, nor is it an attempt to change one's physical appearance. Rather, pulling may be emotionally related or seem to appear as if it is automatic. Trichotillomania often happens alongside puberty (APA, 2013) and can worsen in rhythm with a woman's menstrual cycle.

Excoriation (Skin-Picking) Disorder

Excoriation, or Skin-Picking Disorder, parallels Trichotillomania in many ways. In this case, individuals experience a loss of control around skin picking, and the skin picking causes damage or lesions. Like hair-pulling, a degree of skin-picking seems to be normal or typical. For example, many of us may be reluctant to admit that we pick at our fingernails, acne, or other skin blemishes, especially when tired or stressed. In the case of Excoriation Disorder; however, the severity and intensity of the picking is concerning. Excoriation disorder often coincides with puberty.

Table 11.3 Summary of obsessive–compulsive and related disorders

Disorder	Summary
Obsessive–Compulsive Disorder	Obsessions and/or compulsions that take considerable time and/or energy, interfering with daily activities or making daily activities difficult
Body Dysmorphic Disorder	Obsession, or preoccupation, with "one or more perceived defects or flaws in physical appearance that are not observable or appear slight to others" (APA, 2013, p. 242)
Trichotillomania (Hair-Pulling Disorder)	Obsessions and compulsions related to pulling their own hair and resulting in bodily harm
Excoriation (Skin-Picking Disorder)	Obsession and compulsions related to skin picking and resulting in damage or lesions

Treatment

As with any disorder, it is important that clinicians reach an accurate assessment in order to determine the best treatment options. In the case of Obsessive–Compulsive and Related Disorders, part of this is determining the function and experience of the behavior (Berman and Abromowitz, 2010). For example, a behavior driven to reduce anxiety or distress would be likely to fall into the arena of an Obsessive–Compulsive and Related Disorder, while a similar behavior may be driven by a medical condition or tic.

Treatment for OC disorders often focuses on cognitive–behavioral strategies, which may be combined with other approaches and medication management. Individual, group, or family-focused CBT results in up to 88 per cent of children diagnosed reaching clinical remission (Barrett, Healy-Farrell, and March, 2004; Freeman et al., 2008; POTS, 2004). A specific type of CBT, Exposure and Response Prevention (ERP), is particularly recommended for OCD (Jacobson, Newman, and Goldfried, 2016) and BDD (Burrows, Slavec, Nangle, and O'Grady, 2013). ERP helps youth face the fears (obsessions) that drive their behaviors (compulsions) while simultaneously refraining from their compulsive or ritualistic behaviors.

In addition to CBT, selective serotonin reuptake inhibitors (SSRIs) may be used to help control symptoms related to OCD. These medications do not "cure" OCD; rather, they help reduce the impact of some OCD symptoms. As with any medication, it is important to be vigilant about potential side effects, as SSRIs have been linked to suicidal behavior in some youth.

Case Study: Will

Will is a fourth grader who has been identified as in the 98th percentile for writing and mathematics. Although he earned top marks on his report card and earned accolades from all his teachers since Kindergarten, Will has failed to complete multiple homework assignments, and his in-class grades have dropped because he has been unable to complete classroom assignments during the allotted times.

Will's teacher has noticed him appearing preoccupied during class, often spending large amounts of time studying the contents of his desk, arranging and rearranging pencils and papers multiple times before he will start on a task. Will will trace and retrace letters until they are formed correctly, wearing down erasers in hours and getting up to use the pencil sharpener multiple times a day. Although he rarely makes a sound, the teacher has seen Will mouthing words while organizing his work. If interrupted, Will often appears distressed, grimacing, clearing his throat, and blinking rapidly until he is able to resume his task. Will's peers have started to comment on his odd behaviors, calling him Wacko-Will, and he has stopped sitting with others during lunch or engaging in recess.

After a particularly difficult day, Will's teacher contacted his mother. Will's mother expressed frustration, noting that the incomplete homework was not for lack of trying. Each evening, Will would sit at the kitchen table for hours past his bedtime, often breaking pencils and reduced to tears when he could not complete a question to his satisfaction. He panicked and tantrummed when his concerned mother insisted he go to bed and try with "fresh eyes" in the morning. Following this conversation, the teacher requested the school counselor visit with Will.

Process Questions

1. What are your primary concerns for Will?
2. As a school counselor, how would you see your role working with Will? How would you advise his teacher? His mother?
3. What additional supports or referrals might Will need?

Obsessions involve unwanted, repetitive, and persistent thoughts, urges, or images. Compulsions involve unwanted, repetitive, and persistent behaviors or mental acts. OCD may involve an array of obsessions and/or compulsions. Body Dysmorphic Disorder involves obsessions and/or compulsions specific to a perceived defect in one's appearance. Trichotillomania and Excoriation involve loss of control around compulsions to pull hair or pick skin, respectively. Treatment for Obsessive–Compulsive and Related Disorders tends to involve cognitive-behavioral strategies in combination with medication management.

SUBSTANCE-RELATED AND ADDICTIVE DISORDERS

Substance use is quite high in the U.S. in general, and experimentation is normative for many adolescents. Over a quarter of adolescents use alcohol in any given year, and nearly one in five report using illicit drugs in any given year (CDC, 2013); these numbers are much higher for older adolescents. Depending on frequency, context, and risk-taking behavior, this use may or may not be of clinical concern. The National Institute on Drug Abuse (NIDA) notes that

> the teenage years are a critical window of vulnerability to substance use disorders, because the brain is still developing and malleable (a property known as neuroplasticity), and some brain areas are less mature than others.
>
> (2014, p. 3)

The pattern of adolescent substance use is somewhat different than adults; cannabis, alcohol, and prescription drugs are the most commonly abused substances (NIDA, 2014). National data indicate 8.3 per cent of adolescents qualified for a substance use disorder (SUD) in the past year with common substances of abuse including alcohol (4.2 per cent), illicit drugs (4.7 per cent), and cigarettes (2.8 per cent) (CDC, 2013).

Risk factors for developing a substance use concern are various and include genetic factors or predispositions, adverse childhood experiences, and impulse control concerns (NIDA, 2014). There is a strong link between age of first use and severity of continued use, with those who begin using alcohol or other drugs earlier developing longer-term concerns. On the other hand, healthy parenting and school environments seem to protect against drug use. The NIDA (2014, p. 3) lists the following risks of repeated substance use in youth:

- school failure
- problems with family and other relationships
- loss of interest in normal healthy activities
- impaired memory
- increased risk of contracting an infectious disease (like HIV or hepatitis c) via risky sexual behavior and sharing contaminated injection equipment
- mental health problems, including substance use disorders of varying severity
- the very real risk of overdose death

Diagnosis

Over 100 pages of the *DSM-5* (APA, 2013) is devoted to Substance-Related and Addictive Disorders. There are three main types of disorders related to substances—use, withdrawal, and intoxication. With a few exceptions, the *DSM-5* presents diagnostic criteria for 10 different classes of substances for each of those types of disorders. In the following pages, we provide an overview regarding general considerations for each type of disorder. We complete this section with attention to process disorders.

Substance Use Disorders (SUDs)

"The essential feature of a substance use disorder is a cluster of cognitive, behavioral, and physiological symptoms indicating that the individual continues using the substance despite significant substance-related problems" (APA, 2013, p. 483). Although the *DSM-5* presents SUDs separately for nine categories of substances, the core criteria are the same. SUDs involve "a problematic pattern of [substance] use leading to clinically significant impairment or distress, as manifested by at least two of the following, occurring within a 12-month period" (APA, 2013, p. 490). The eleven core symptoms cluster into four areas:

- impaired control—using larger amounts or over longer period than intended; desire or difficulty cutting down or controlling use; spending extensive amounts of time obtaining, using, or recovering; and craving the substance
- social impairment—failing to fulfill major role obligations; continuing to use despite problems caused by use; and giving up important activities in favor of use
- risky use—using when physically hazardous (e.g., driving a car) and continuing use despite physical or psychological problems caused by use

■ pharmacological criteria—tolerance (i.e., needing more substance for same effect, having less effect with same amount) and withdrawal (i.e., experiencing symptoms when not using, using substance to avoid symptoms)

The severity of the SUD is related to a number of symptoms and is classified as mild (2–3 symptoms), moderate (4–5 symptoms), or severe (6 or more symptoms). When counselors make SUD diagnoses, they code the disorder by both severity and substance category, for example, "moderate alcohol use disorder" or "severe inhalant use disorder." When individuals meet criteria for multiple SUDs, counselors diagnose all relevant SUDs. It is not uncommon for a youth with a considerable substance use concern to be assigned two or three different SUDs.

Substance Intoxication

Intoxication disorders are a specific type of substance-induced disorder. These are diagnosed based on a series of symptoms that begin shortly after one administers (e.g., eats, drinks, snorts, injects) the substance and lasts while the body metabolizes the substance. Intoxication symptoms are unique to the specific substance and are listed throughout the *DSM-5*. For example, a youth with alcohol intoxication may have slurred speech, impaired coordination, loss of memory, and "pass out." A youth who has had too many energy drinks and is experiencing caffeine intoxication may be restless, speak rapidly, be unable to sleep, have heart palpitations, and run to the bathroom to deal with digestive upset. Like SUDs, substance intoxication disorders include the name of the specific substance of use.

In some cases, substance intoxication simply means one needs to wait until the effects of the substance has passed. In other cases, intoxication might be such that a youth needs immediate medical attention. Regardless, youth who are intoxicated should not be left unattended. Counselors can learn to recognize the signs of substance intoxication by reading the *DSM-5* or pursuing professional resources such as those available via http://www.drugabuse.gov.

Substance Withdrawal

Whereas intoxication involves immediate effects of a substance when entering the body, withdrawal occurs when the body does not receive a substance it is used to having. Many coffee drinkers experience caffeine withdrawal, for example, when morning coffee is not consumed. By mid-afternoon, individuals may have headaches, snap at coworkers, and feel sluggish. Just as individuals may self-medicate this withdrawal syndrome by securing an afternoon cup of coffee, someone who is beginning to experience alcohol withdrawal may drink to ward off shakes or agitation.

Like other mental disorders, withdrawal is uniquely tied to the substance(s) used. You can think of withdrawal symptoms as the opposite of intoxication symptoms. Although alcohol, opiates, and sedatives may have a calming effect during intoxication, withdrawal from them includes agitation or arousal. Amphetamines and cocaine, on the other hand, have a stimulating intoxication, and their withdrawal effects include fatigue, exhaustion, and depression-like symptoms. As with intoxication symptoms, impacts of withdrawal are both physical and psychological. Some withdrawal may be simply unpleasant, and other withdrawal experiences may be life-threatening. You can learn more about withdrawal in the *DSM-5* or via resources such as www.drugabuse.gov.

Process Addictions

Process or behavioral addictions include experiences in which individuals experience a drive or craving to engage in highly rewarding non-drug activities such as gambling, internet use, gaming, or sexual behaviors. Over time, one begins to experience the activity much like a drug. Indeed, emerging research regarding addiction shows that the brains of individuals with process addictions respond to the process much like the brains of individuals with substance use respond to drugs (APA, 2013). As with substance use, engagement in the process over time can have a number of detrimental consequences. For example, a youth may become so engaged in internet gaming that he or she does not eat or sleep, neglects essential hygiene, stops responding to friends other than those with whom he games, and falls out of all his classes.

The only process addiction currently included in the *DSM-5* is gambling disorder (APA, 2013). Gambling disorder includes a persistent, recurrent pattern of gambling in which the person has a number of consequences of use. For example, the person may need to gamble with more money to get the same high, may not be able to control activities, has emotional difficulty stopping gambling, cannot stop thinking about gambling, and has negative consequences at home, school, and work. The developers of the *DSM-5* (APA, 2013) have also proposed criteria for related process addictions such as internet gaming disorder, a situation believed to impact adolescents and young adults.

Table 11.4 Summary of substance use and related disorders

Disorder	Summary
Substance Use Disorders	"A problematic pattern of [substance] use leading to clinically significant impairment or distress" (APA, 2013, p. 490); symptoms may include impaired control, social impairment, risky use, tolerance and/or withdrawal
Substance Intoxication	Substance-specific symptoms that begin shortly after one administers a substance and lasting while the body metabolizes the substance
Substance Withdrawal	Physical and psychological substance-specific symptoms that occur as a result of the body not receiving a substance it is used to receiving
Gambling Disorder	Persistent, recurrent pattern of gambling in which the person has a number of consequences of use

Treatment

Intoxication and withdrawal can pose serious health concerns. Counselors who are concerned about the possibility of intoxication or withdrawal should inform parents or guardians of their concerns. Youth who are under the influence should not be allowed to participate in individual and group counseling; rather, they need to be supervised until the substance is out of their system. In cases of severe intoxication or withdrawal, counselors may call 911, or encourage parents to seek medical guidance. Coordinating care with medical providers to ensure effective management of symptoms is a crucial part of treatment for adolescents with SUDs.

Youth substance use significantly impacts multiple dimensions of development. The NIDA (2014) provided a holistic guide for substance use treatment in adolescence, which includes details on evidence-based treatment. A basic overview of treatment including many of the components listed in those guidelines is provided in this section. Early intervention for youth who show signs of substance use or may be at increased risk can help to decrease later diagnoses. Ideally, intervention would begin even before a youth develops a diagnosable substance use disorder. Family members, medical providers, teachers, and other adults play an important role in recognizing substance use and encouraging youth to engage treatment.

Once in treatment, it is important that youth are assessed for other contributing issues, including mental illness and prior abuse history. Additional assessment should address the environmental and cultural factors that may serve as risk or protective factors for youth during and after treatment. It is important that family or other authority figures are involved in the treatment process (Tanner-Smith, Wilson, and Lipsey, 2012). Family involvement in treatment for adolescents can significantly increase likelihood of positive outcomes. In addition, it is important that cognitive, behavioral and emotional aspects of addictive behaviors are addressed within treatment.

Motivational Enhancement Therapy can help to build motivation for treatment, while other interventions such as cognitive behavior therapy, 12-step groups, and family therapy can help to address multiple dimensions of addiction (NIDA, 2014). Each of these interventions could occur within an inpatient program, intensive outpatient program, partial hospitalization or outpatient program. Each of these settings are commonly used to address youth substance use, with level of care depending on severity of risk and impairment. Unfortunately, many youth and their families will struggle to locate and access appropriate care.

Process addictions can have a negative impact on social functioning and mental health (Ko et al., 2014). Treatment for process addictions may include psychological and pharmacological interventions. Individuals with process addictions may exhibit signs of depression, anxiety, and aggression in addition to being at increased risk for SUDs (Jorgenson, Hsiao, and Yen, 2016). Treatment for process addictions is not as well researched as other addiction treatment, but mirrors treatment for other types of addiction. CBT, reality therapy, family therapy, group therapy, and school-based interventions have all been suggested. Group CBT is currently the most researched and used intervention for process addictions (Winkler, Dorsing, Rief, Shen, and Glombiewski, 2013).

Case Study: Lewis

Lewis is a 12-year-old male recently admitted into a residential treatment center. Lewis's parents have been trying to get treatment for Lewis for the last two years. Despite their best efforts, no outpatient programs have been successful. He was finally admitted to this treatment facility after overdosing at a friend's house on pills that appeared to have been scavenged from a variety of medicine cabinets.

When Lewis began 6th grade two years ago, several of his closest friends were sent to a different middle school. Lewis struggled to make new connections at his school. Several weeks into the school year, Lewis began talking about new friends he was making, and his parents were encouraged that he would have a smooth transition. Slowly, Lewis's behavior began to change. He started withdrawing from his parents, wanting to spend all of his time at friend's houses, bringing home Cs instead of As and Bs. In late November, Lewis's assistant principal called his parents and informed them that Lewis had been suspended for fighting. Over the next months, Lewis received multiple disciplinary actions for fighting, skipping school, and smoking. Lewis's parents grounded him, gave him strict rules, and attempted to talk with him about the consequences of his behavior. Lewis showed little interest.

In February, Lewis was caught bringing marijuana to school and was suspended again. This time, police were called, and Lewis was ordered to complete an intensive outpatient program. Lewis did surprisingly well in the program and appeared to have changed his behavior. Lewis returned to the happy boy they had once known.

Two months after completing treatment, Lewis slowly began to return to his old ways. Lewis began withdrawing from family and returned to his old group of friends. Sometimes, Lewis would stay gone until late into the night without his parents' permission. Lewis's parents learned that he had stolen money from his mother's purse and was using the money they gave him for lunch to purchase drugs. When confronted, Lewis denied that he had taken the money. Additional items began showing up missing from the home including his mother's wedding ring, a family heirloom vase, and his Xbox. Lewis's father searched his room one day while he was at school and found multiple bags of marijuana and related paraphernalia. His parents realized he needed help they were not able to provide on their own, but they didn't know where to start.

Process Questions

1. What are your primary concerns regarding Lewis's behaviors?
2. Which DSM-5 diagnoses seem most likely at this point? What additional information would you need to make your decision?
3. What would be the most important treatment components for Lewis?
4. How could a school counselor support Lewis following his return to school?

Although experimentation with alcohol and other drugs is somewhat normative during adolescence, adolescents are particularly vulnerable to the impacts of substance use on their developing brains. Youth experiencing substance intoxication or withdrawal may need immediate supervision and medical attention to ensure their safety. Recommendations for adolescent substance use treatment highlight the need for early intervention, family involvement in treatment, psychoeducation, individual counseling, and group counseling; 12-step and other self-help groups may be used as an adjunct to treatment.

FEEDING AND EATING DISORDERS

Feeding and Eating Disorders involve disruption in both quality and quantity of food intake. This disorder may impact whether a youth eats (e.g., Avoidant/Restrictive Food Intake Disorder and Anorexia Nervosa), what one eats (e.g., Avoidant/Restrictive Food Intake Disorder and Pica), and the process of eating (e.g., Rumination Disorder, Bulimia Nervosa, Binge Eating Disorder). Although there is variation among specific disorders, eating disorders tend to impact young, European American women disproportionately (Woo and Keatinge, 2016), perhaps due to socio-cultural norms regarding appearance.

As you will read below, feeding and eating disorders can have a profound impact on one's physical health, psychological health, and social relationships. As with other mental disorders, feeding and eating disorders are believed to be related to interactions among genetic factors, brain changes (especially as the disorder progresses), cognitive factors, familial environment, and sociocultural context (Woo and Keatinge, 2016).

Diagnosis

Feeding and eating disorders occur throughout the lifespan. Disorders such as Pica, Rumination Disorder, and Avoidant/Restrictive Food Intake Disorder may begin as early as infancy. Often, Anorexia Nervosa and Bulimia Nervosa begin by adolescence or early adulthood.

Pica

Pica involves the "persistent eating of nonnutritive, nonfood substances over a period of at least 1 month" (APA, 2013, p. 329). Because it is quite normal for infants and toddlers to explore the world with their mouths, this eating must be out of line for what one would expect developmentally, and not a part of a cultural practice.

Pica often begins in childhood, although it may also begin later in life, especially among individuals with other mental health concerns, including intellectual disability (APA, 2013). Individuals who have concerns related to Pica should be referred for medical attention for two reasons. First, craving nonnutritive substances may be related to medical conditions, including vitamin or mineral deficiency. Second, ingestion of nonfood substances may cause medical concerns over time.

Rumination Disorder

Rumination Disorder may also begin as early as infancy. In this disorder, youth repeatedly regurgitate food over a period of at least a month, and the behavior is not related to a medical condition such as reflux (APA, 2013). The *DSM-5* notes that rumination often begins in infants aged 3–12 months. Because regurgitation may be related to a medical condition and can result in malnutrition, it is important that counselors urge parents to work with pediatricians and other medical specialists for appropriate support.

Avoidant/Restrictive Food Intake Disorder

Avoidant/Restrictive Food Intake Disorder may also begin in infancy or early childhood and may have substantial impacts on a child's physical development. This disorder is characterized by lack of interest in or avoidance of food, which causes weight loss, restricted growth, nutritional deficiency, and special feeding care (e.g., supplementation or feeding tubes) (APA, 2013). Infants may appear disinterested in eating, toddlers may reject foods based on color or texture, and children of all ages may engage in power struggles with caregivers related to feeding. The impacts of Avoidant/Restrictive Food Intake Disorder are much more severe than fussy eating experienced by most children at some time or another. As with the other feeding disorders, the disturbance is not the result of a medical condition and requires special management and collaboration with physicians and nutritionists.

Anorexia Nervosa (AN)

AN is characterized by "persistent energy intake restriction; intense fear of gaining weight or of becoming fat, or persistent behavior that interferes with weight gain; and a disturbance in self-perceived weight or shape" (APA, 2013, p. 339). Youth who have anorexia may restrict caloric intake to an extreme degree or engage in binge eating and purging behaviors in which they utilize vomiting, laxatives, diuretics, or enemas in attempts to manage their weight. The severity of AN is calculated with attention to body mass index for one's physical age and with attention to developmental context. Children and early adolescents who experience AN may not have weight loss; rather, they may fail to gain weight and grow as expected. Although dissatisfaction in body image appears normative for many young women in Western cultures, those with AN have even more disturbance in body image.

Although disordered eating is not uncommon in youth, AN is relatively rare, occurring in about 0.4 per cent of young females (APA, 2013). Onset of the disorder usually happens during adolescence or young adulthood and may be associated with developmental transitions such as puberty or leaving home. Youth involved in activities such as gymnastics and ballet seem to be at particular risk for AN. This disorder is much more common in women; however, researchers have documented growth in this disorder among young men (Woo and Keatinge, 2016).

Bulimia Nervosa (BN)

Whereas AN is characterized by restriction and resulting impact on body mass, BN is characterized by episodes of binging and purging. BN is more common than AN, occurring in 1.0–1.5 per cent of young females and often beginning during adolescence or young adulthood (Woo and Keatinge, 2016). Individuals with BN often present with normal weight for their age (APA, 2013). During binge eating episodes, youth may eat large volumes and feel a loss of control over their eating. Following the episodes, they may attempt to purge through use of vomiting, laxative, diuretics, enemas, excessive exercise, or food restriction. When these episodes happen at least weekly for three months and one also reports body image disturbance, a counselor may consider diagnosing BN.

Binge-Eating Disorder (BED)

New to the *DSM-5*, BED is the most common eating disorder (Woo and Keatinge, 2016). BED is characterized by a recurrent cycle of binge eating without inappropriate compensatory behavior. During the binge, individuals feel a loss of control over their behaviors. Following the binge, individuals with BED do not vomit, use medications, fast, or otherwise attempt to compensate for the binge. Like BN, binge eating episodes must happen at least once a week for three months (APA, 2013).

In contrast to AN and BN, prevalence of is more equally balanced by both gender and ethnicity. BED generally begins in early adolescence, and adolescent girls are at three times the risk of adolescent boys (2.3 vs. 0.8 per cent) (Woo and Keatinge, 2016). Individuals who have BED may be of normal weight, overweight, or obese.

Treatment

It is vital that counselors understand medical complications related to Feeding and Eating Disorders. These disorders may cause malnutrition, lead to dangerous electrolyte imbalances, and damage the gastrointestinal system. It is critical that clients receive appropriate medical attention, and treatment will likely involve ongoing collaboration between physicians, nutritional specialists, and mental health professionals.

Pica and Rumination Disorders

Treatment of Pica and Rumination disorders should involve collaboration with medical and nutrition specialists. Use of behaviorally based therapies and development of behavior modification plans to alter eating of non-food items or rumination behaviors are recommended (Barkoukis, Reiss, and Dombeck, 2008a; Barkoukis, Reiss, and Dombeck, 2008b). Children diagnosed with Pica may enjoy both the taste/texture and oral stimulation of the non-food items that they eat; attention should be paid to offering healthy food alternatives and other developmentally appropriate ways for the child to be stimulated. These may include non-oral methods and oral methods of stimulation. In severe cases of Pica or Rumination, hospitalization may be necessary until a child is medically stable.

Avoidant/Restrictive Food Intake Disorder, Anorexia Nervosa, Bulimia Nervosa, and Binge-Eating Disorder

When looking at these four disorders related to eating, it is important to note that there are physical, psychological, social, and cultural factors at play. ARFID, AN, and BN can be particularly damaging or life-threatening if left untreated. For this reason, careful supervision and coordination of care among an array of professionals is necessary. Coordination of care will allow for psychological and physical stabilization while also examining social, emotional, and cultural factors that may also be reinforcing the eating disorders. Inpatient or outpatient care can both be appropriate, based on the level of severity of the disorder and the physical and psychological needs of the client.

Treatments for psychological facets of eating disorders include CBT, interpersonal therapy, dialectic and behavioral therapy, family-based interventions, and medication management (Yager et al., 2012). Youth with BN and BED may learn to identify triggers for binge episodes and focus energies on other ways of coping (Woo and Keatinge, 2016). Although research findings are mixed, family-based treatment appears particularly important for youth with eating disorders, especially as there appears to be a familial link in AN (Couturier, Kimber, and Szatmari, 2013). Counseling interventions are often offered in combination with ongoing attention to dietary needs, physical and medical treatment, and medication for coexisting mood or symptoms.

Case Study: Nikki

Nikki is a seventh-grade student whose weight falls within normal range. She has a stable friend group and is involved in a variety of school activities. One of the activities that she has been a part of for the school year has been the Spirit Club, a group of middle school students involved in fundraising, decorating lockers, and planning school dances. The Spirit Club offers a weekly bake sale that Nikki organizes and runs with a few of her friends. When lunch period is over, Nikki always volunteers to be the one to pack up the food items, in part because she has permission to miss study hall because of her Spirit Club activities.

One Tuesday, Nikki's friend Tara has to go to the locker room to get a permission slip from her gym bag. She enters the locker room to the sound of someone vomiting. She notices that the trash can by the sink has an assortment of empty bags and containers from leftover bake sale items. Tara recognizes Nikki's shoes and tights in the stall. She quietly retrieves her permission slip and heads back to study hall, leaving Nikki in the locker room, unaware.

After stewing about it for a few days, Tara tells her mother what she saw, and Tara's mother reaches out to the school counselor. The school counselor calls Nikki into her office and learns that Nikki has been taking the leftover bake sale items to the locker room and eating them as quickly as possible to avoid detection. Nikki reluctantly shared that she sometimes hoards food in her room and binges when she feels lonely. When asked what she does after she eats all that food, Nikki says she feels guilty and, embarrassed, throws up so she will not "get fatter."

Process Questions

1. What disorder(s) seem most likely given the information you have regarding Nikki's concern? What additional information would you need to make a final diagnosis?
2. Nikki pleads with you not to inform her dad regarding what you have learned. How would you respond?
3. How would you envision working with Nikki?
4. As a school counselor, how could you build attention to eating disorder prevention and early intervention into your comprehensive developmental school counseling program?

While some eating disorders may appear as early as infancy or early childhood (e.g., Pica, Rumination Disorder, Avoidance/Restrictive Intake Disorder), others tend to appear by adolescence (e.g., Anorexia Nervosa, Bulimia Nervosa, Binge-Eating Disorder). Gender differences in eating disorders are likely related to sociocultural norms and values. Eating disorders may present severe threats to physical health and should always include medical assessment. Eating disorder treatment for infants and early childhood often include close medical monitoring and behavioral interventions; in adolescence, treatment may be multimodal and include counseling, family involvement, and medication management.

ELIMINATION DISORDERS

Elimination Disorders are nearly exclusive to childhood and include recurrent difficulty with developmentally appropriate passage of urine or feces. Researchers believe elimination disorders are likely the result of genetics, biology, psychological, and environmental factors (Adamson, Campbell, and Kress, 2015). Although trauma and stressors may not explain all concerns, these disorders are particularly high among individuals who have experienced abuse or neglect (APA, 2013).

Diagnosis

The two elimination disorders include enuresis and encopresis. Each is discussed next.

Enuresis

Enuresis involves recurrent urination in clothing or bedding, and the behavior may be intentional or unintentional (APA, 2013). Because there is wide variation in developmental milestones and young children may regress or cycle back through milestones, this disorder is only diagnosed in individuals who are at chronological and developmental age of at least 5 years. The behavior must also happen at least twice weekly for three months and cannot be related to a medical condition or concern. A counselor may make an Enuresis diagnosis for less frequent concerns if the concerns result in substantial distress or impairment. For example, if a child refuses to go to school or participate in peer activities out of a fear of wetting himself, a diagnosis might be warranted even if the frequency criterion is not met.

Enuresis is not uncommon among young children. The DSM-5 notes a prevalence of 5–10 per cent in 5-year-olds and 3–5 per cent in 10-year-olds. Enuresis may occur at night only (nocturnal), during the day only (diurnal), or both night and day.

Encopresis

Encopresis involves repeated passage of feces into inappropriate places; Encopresis may be intentional or unintentional (APA, 2013). For example, a child may experience constipation and soil his pants while sleeping or may choose to defecate in the middle of the kitchen floor. Encopresis may be diagnosed after the chronological and developmental age of 4 years and must happen at least once a month for at least three months. Like Enuresis, Encopresis is not related to a medical condition.

Encopresis is less common than Enuresis, occurring in about 1 per cent of 5-year-olds (APA, 2013). The disorder may be related to concerns with toilet training or stressful transitions such as moving, birth of a sibling, or change of caregiver. Encopresis may occur with constipation (in which it may be less voluntary) or without constipation (in which it may be more intentional).

Treatment

When counselors become aware of youth who are struggling with wetting or soiling, they should first ensure caregivers have consulted with a pediatrician or specialist to ensure there is not a medical explanation for the concern (e.g., urinary tract infection, intestinal blockage). For Enuresis, a urinalysis may help rule out physiological causes. For Encopresis, a physician might focus on treating constipation and ensuring youth are able to empty their bowels. In addition to considering specialized treatments noted below, counselors may help attend to shame and doubt youth may experience related to Enuresis and Encopresis.

Behavioral modification, positive reinforcement, and medication can help children with Enuresis (Tu and Baskin, 2016). Young children may respond well to encouragement and reward strategies (Adamson et al., 2015). Strategies may include encouraging children to use the restroom regularly, stay hydrated, and make sure that they void their bladder before going to sleep for the evening. Parents should be involved in the process by reminding their children to use the restroom and communicating with teachers to ensure children are able to use the restroom as needed. Youth who have difficulty with bedwetting may use an Enuresis alarm that detects moisture and awakens youth, slowly conditioning youth to associate urinary sessions with awakening (Adamson et al., 2015). Finally, physicians may consider medications for those youth who may have a hormone deficiency related to the Enuresis.

Treating chronic constipation by changing dietary habits and/or using stool softeners is an initial step in treatment for Encopresis (Adamson et al., 2015; Freeman, Riley, Duke, and Fu). In some cases, children and families may benefit from toileting education. Behavior management should remain positive, focused on rewarding appropriate behavior and using natural consequences (e.g., involving children in cleaning up). Counselors may also work with children and their families to identify and respond to underlying emotional issues that could be contributing to the Encopresis.

Case Study: Sean

Sean is a 5-year-old kindergartener. Although Sean has been successfully toilet trained for nearly two years, over the past few weeks he has begun having accidents at school involving soiling his pants. One Wednesday, after Sean had been in the class bathroom for an abnormal period of time, the teacher goes to check on him and finds Sean in tears frantically trying to clean a pile of feces out of his pants.

Process Questions

1. What information would be helpful in assessing Sean's needs? How would you go about gathering this information?
2. Assuming you referred Sean for medical evaluation and the physician indicated no known physical cause for the difficulty, how would you proceed to work with Sean?
3. Would your approach change if the physician noted the need to treat Sean for chronic constipation?

Enuresis involves age-inappropriate urination; Encopresis involves age-inappropriate defecation. The first step to treating Enuresis and Encopresis involves consultation with a medical professional. Counselors can provide supportive assistance, helping children to cope with social or psychological consequences of Enuresis or Encopresis and helping parents implement behavioral strategies to address the concerns.

SLEEP–WAKE DISORDERS

Sleep–Wake Disorders are often diagnosed by medical professionals including sleep specialists; however, it is important for counselors who work with youth to be familiar with this category of mental disorder. Some disorders, such as Insomnia Disorder (i.e., difficulty with quality or quantity of sleep), Hypersomnolence Disorder (i.e., excessive sleepiness), and Narcolepsy (i.e., excessive napping or sleep episodes) have to do with the overall pattern or quality of sleep. Other disorders, such as Obstructive Sleep Apnea Hypopnea, Central Sleep Apnea, Sleep-Related, and Hypoventilation are focused on breathing problems related to sleep. Circadian Rhythm Sleep–Wake Disorders are related to problems with timing of sleep that may be inherent to the individual and/or environment (e.g., focused on shift work). Finally, parasomnias involve "abnormal behavioral, experiential, or physiological events occurring in association with sleep, specific sleep stages, or sleep–wake transitions" (APA, 2013, p. 399).

Diagnosis

Parasomnias are among the most common Sleep–Wake disorders impacting youth and include non-rapid eye movement sleep arousal disorders (e.g., sleepwalking, sleep terrors), Nightmare Disorders, Rapid Eye Movement Sleep Behavior Disorder, and Restless Legs Syndrome. We explore diagnosis of two common parasomnias among youth below.

Non-Rapid Eye Movement Sleep Arousal Disorders (NREM)

NREM disorders involve at least one of two primary concerns: Sleepwalking and sleep terrors. Sleepwalking involves just that, walking in one's sleep (some individuals also eat or engage in sexual activity during sleep). Sleep terrors involve "abrupt terror arousals from sleep" (APA, 2013, p. 399) in which individuals have strong physiological responses and do not respond to comfort. In both sleepwalking and sleep terrors, individuals do not recall distressing dreams, and the NREM behavior happens frequently. Both sleepwalking and sleep terrors tend to happen at the beginning of the sleep cycle and may last only minutes. Although the youth's eyes may be open, he or she does not respond to communication from others.

APA (2013) estimates that 10–30 per cent of children sleepwalk at some point in time, and 2–3 per cent sleepwalk often. Similarly, sleep terrors are very common among children, impacting over one-third of 1.5-year-olds and one-fifth of 2.5-year-olds. The presence of NREM behaviors does not necessarily indicate the presence of a disorder. Rather, the behaviors need to be persistent, cause distress or impairment, and happen outside of other concerns such as trauma or phobias.

Nightmare Disorder

Nightmare Disorder involves a problematic pattern of intense nightmares from which an individual awakes and becomes oriented (APA, 2013). Nightmares are a normal part of human experiences and appear to peak in early childhood (ages 3–6). It is quite normal for the frequency and duration of nightmares to increase during times of stress, adjustment, or developmental transition. As with other sleep disorders, Nightmare Disorder is only diagnosed if it causes substantial distress or problems in functioning and is not related to other concerns such as traumas or phobias.

Treatment

Sleep disorders in youth may negatively impact academic functioning, physical health, development, and behavior. These disorders in youth frequently require medical intervention by a physician trained to work with pediatric sleep issues. Counselors working with these disorders should facilitate a referral if the child is not already under the care of a physician. These providers may recommend pharmacological or additional behavioral treatment.

Treatment for sleep disorders should address environmental and familial factors that may be contributing to problems. Treatment for sleep disorders typically involves various interventions associated with CBT (Cortese et al., 2013; Mindell, Kuhn, Lewin, Meltzer, and Sadeh, 2006). For example, counselors may ask parents to keep a record of child sleep patterns in order to identify possible triggers or contextual factors at play. Children may benefit from a structured sleep schedule that is consistent and provides reinforcement for desired behavior, especially when youth resist sleep. Extinction or gradual extinction involves placing a child in bed and not responding to protests, or responding in gradually less frequent intervals. This intervention can assist children with gradually staying in bed longer and thus learning to fall asleep. Scheduled awakenings are sometimes used in decreasing intervals with children who struggle to stay asleep. For some children, therapy that focuses on developing relaxation skills may be beneficial. Finally, for youth struggling with circadian rhythm disorders, intentional use of light may help to assist sleep. Decreasing the use of light at night while increasing exposure to light in the morning may help to regulate sleep in youth (Auger et al., 2015).

Sleep disturbance is developmentally normal for many children; however, recurrent sleepwalking, sleep terrors, or nightmares may cause enough distress to lead parents to seek support. Parents should first visit with a pediatrician or sleep specialist to discuss concerns. Counselors may help parents to identify patterns or triggers for distress and establish healthy sleep routines and rituals.

GENDER DYSPHORIA

Previously known as Gender Identity Disorder, Gender Dysphoria involves distress regarding "incongruence between one's expressed gender and one's assigned gender" (APA, 2013, p. 451). The experience of Gender Dysphoria shifts over time, especially as youth navigate puberty and gain cognitive understanding of their sense of incongruence. There is considerable controversy regarding whether Gender Dysphoria is an actual mental disorder; rather, it may represent a stress response to unhealthy, unrealistic gendered expectations. Prevalence of Gender Dysphoria is quite low (0.002–0.014 per cent) (APA, 2013); however, impacts on those affected may be profound depending on degree of incongruence and acceptance available from caregivers, school personnel, and members of the community (Coolhart and MacKnight, 2015).

Diagnosis

The DSM-5 (APA, 2013) includes two criteria sets for Gender Dysphoria, one specific to children and one focused on adolescents and adults. Gender Dysphoria in children involves a period of at least six months in which a child expresses incongruence in experienced/expressed gender and assigned gender. The child must experience at least six symptoms, including "a strong desire to be of the other gender or an insistence that one is the other gender (or some alternative gender different from one's assigned gender)" (p. 452). Other symptoms may include strong preferences for clothing, roles, or toys or activities typically associated with the other gender. Children may also prefer cross-gender playmates, reject toys or activities typically associated with their gender. Further, children may express concern about their bodies, often rejecting their sexual anatomy and showing a strong desire for characteristics associated with their experienced gender.

Criteria for Gender Dysphoria in adolescents are quite similar, although only two symptoms need to be present to make a diagnosis. These include incongruence in secondary sex characteristics, desire to rid oneself of sex characteristics, desire for sex characteristics of the other gender, desire to be or be treated as the other gender, or belief that one has emotional experiences of the other gender (APA, 2013).

Treatment

Treatment for Gender Dysphoria focuses on reducing distress rather than changing gender-related behavior or thoughts. Due to high rates of comorbidity with other mental health disorders, assessment for Gender Dysphoria should also include assessment for other disorders, including anxiety and depression. Because familial and social support are important parts of treatment for youth, assessment should include an evaluation of environmental, social, and familial supports within the youth's life. Finally, depending on the age and desires of the youth, referral to explore medical interventions may be appropriate.

Approaches to the treatment of Gender Dysphoria in youth differ and are often quite controversial (Drescher and Byne, 2012). For children, Gender Dysphoria often does not persist into adulthood, however professionals currently have no means by which to differentiate between those for whom Gender Dysphoria will persist and those for whom it will not. Therefore, treatment tends to focus on managing distress and incongruence rather than directly addressing gendered behaviors in young children. Counseling may be supportive in nature, helping children to feel comfortable in their own skin and use coping skills when encountering difficult situations. Counselors may also help parents and teachers to ensure safe, supportive environments where youth are free to express themselves and experience minimal coercion or pressure. Depending on the child, social transitioning to the experienced gender may or may not be appropriate.

Caregiver involvement in treatment is a significant predictor of success for youth with Gender Dysphoria, and counselors should take special care to include the family (APA, 2015). In part due to its low frequency, many parents are ill equipped to appropriately support youth displaying symptoms. Counselors can provide caregivers and siblings factual information regarding Gender Dysphoria and encourage family involvement in developing a treatment strategy appropriate for their child.

Additionally, counselors can attend carefully to youths' safety and advocacy needs. This may include a broad range of activities, including educating others regarding pronoun use, securing appropriate restroom and changing space, challenging school policies, and facilitating staff support (Coolhart and MacKnight, 2015).

Case Study: Philip

Philip, a four-year-old child, was born into a home with two older brothers. Philip's parents were excited to have another boy in the home, but as he began to grow they noticed differences between Philip and his brothers. When Philip began walking and talking, these differences became even more noticeable.

Philip would frequently attempt to remove his clothes and would often scream when his parents attempted to dress him. In time, Philip's mother would find him in her room trying on her shoes. When she found him, Philip would often point at her dresses and say "Want that." As Philip got older he became extremely angry with his brothers when they attempted to wrestle with him; he much preferred to play house with his stuffed animals.

Today, Philip destroys most of the toys his parents buy him, states that he doesn't like trucks, and pleads for a Barbie. Philip's preschool teachers report that he often plays with the girls and prefers to play dress up instead of army men with the boys. Teachers have observed him stuffing clothes into his shirt and pretending he is a girl during recess. When Philip's teachers suggest that he play with the boys, he insists "No, I a girl. I play with girls." When well-meaning teachers remind Philip that he has a penis and is a boy, Philip often tantrums and sobs, saying "I no want a penis!" Likewise, Philip often becomes angry when his parents attempt to dress him in the morning, frequently asking for "pretty clothes." The family's monthly trips to the barber shop have become increasingly challenging as Philip desperately avoids attempts to cut his hair.

Philip is supposed to begin kindergarten in a few months, and his parents are concerned about the transition. Friends and family have expressed concern about Philip's gender behavior and frequent anger. Philip's parents are supportive and loving, but aren't sure how to help their child.

Process Questions

1. What are your primary concerns for Philip?
2. How might your personal beliefs regarding gender impact your understanding of Philip and your approach to work with him?
3. Imagine Philip's parents reach out to you to request assistance with the transition to kindergarten. How might you help facilitate the most supportive transition possible? What additional information or supports would you need to do so?

Gender Dysphoria involves "incongruence between one's expressed gender and one's assigned gender" (APA, 2013, p. 451). The experience of Gender Dysphoria shifts with time and development. Sociocultural expectations play a major role in the distress experienced in Gender Dysphoria. Primary treatment strategies for Gender Dysphoria involve reducing distress and enhancing supports rather than changing gender-related behaviors or identity.

SUMMARY

Counselors will encounter youth who have neurodevelopmental disorders, experience early signs of severe mental illness, or engage in difficult behaviors. In most cases, these disorders will be evaluated by physicians and mental health professionals with specialized assessment training. Counselors may work with interdisciplinary teams to provide developmentally sensitive interventions and ensure a unique focus on strengths, wellness, and resiliency.

Additional Resources

American Academy of Child and Adolescent Psychiatry: www.aacap.org
American Counseling Association Practice Brief Series: https://www.counseling.org/knowledge-center/practice-briefs
Autism Speaks: https://www.autismspeaks.org/what-autism
DSM-5 Online Assessment Measures: www.psychiatry.org
KidSense Child Development Overview: http://www.childdevelopment.com.au/home/170
National Eating Disorders Association: http://www.nationaleatingdisorders.org/
National Institute on Deafness and Other Communication Disorders: https://www.nidcd.nih.gov/health/speech-and-language
National Institute on Drug Abuse: www.drugabuse.gov

Substance Abuse and Mental Health Services Administration Evidence-Based Practices KITS: http://store.samhsa.gov/list/series?name=Evidence-Based-Practices-KITs
Substance Abuse and Mental Health Services Administration National Registry of Evidence-Based Programs and Practices http://www.samhsa.gov/nrepp

Suggested Readings

American Psychiatric Association (2013). *Diagnostic and statistical manual of mental disorders*, 5th ed. Alexandria, VA: Author.

American Psychological Association (2015). Guidelines for psychological practice with transgender and gender nonconforming people. *American Psychologist* 70, 832–864. doi: 10.1037/a0039906

Apps, J., Winkler, J., and Jandrisevits, M. D. (2008). Bipolar disorders: symptoms and treatment in children and adolescents. *Pediatric Nursing* 34, 84–88.

Centers for Disease Control and Prevention (2013, May). Mental health surveillance among children—United States, 2005–2011. *Morbidity and Mortality Weekly Report* 62 (2). Retrieved from http://www.cdc.gov/mmwr/pdf/other/su6202.pdf

Coolhart, D. and MacKnight, V. (2015). Working with transgender youths and their families: Counselors and therapists as advocate for trans-affirmative school environments. *Journal of Counselor Leadership and Advocacy* 2, 51–64. doi: 10.1080/2326716X.2014.981767

Couturier, J., Kimber, M., and Szatmari, P. (2013). Efficacy of family-based treatment for adolescents with eating disorders: A systematic review and meta-analysis. *International Journal of Eating Disorders* 46 (1), 3–11.

Jacobson, N. C., Newman, M. G., and Goldfried, M. R. (2016). Clinical feedback about empirically supported treatments for Obsessive–Compulsive Disorder. *Behavior Therapy* 47, 75–90. doi: 10.1016/j.beth.2015.09.003

Lachman, A. (2014). New developments in diagnosis and treatment update: Schizophrenia/first episode psychosis in children and adolescents. *Journal of Child and Adolescent Mental Health* 26 (2), 109–124.

Lindgren, S., and Doobay, A. (2011). *Evidence-based interventions for autism spectrum disorders*. The University of Iowa.

National Institute on Drug Abuse (2014). *Principles of adolescent Substance Use Disorder treatment: A research-based guide* [NIH Publication 14-7953]. Retrieved from https://www.drugabuse.gov/publications/principles-adolescent-substance-use-disorder-treatment-research-based-guide/

Subcommittee on Attention-Deficit/Hyperactivity Disorder, Steering Committee on Quality Improvement and Management (2011). ADHD: Clinical practice guideline for the diagnosis, evaluation, and treatment of Attention-Deficit/Hyperactivity Disorder in children and adolescents. *Pediatrics* 128 (5), 1007–1022. doi: 10.1542/peds.2011-2654

Woo, S. M. and Keatinge, C. (2016). *Diagnosis and treatment of mental disorders across the lifespan*, 2nd ed. Hoboken, NJ: Wiley.

Yager, J., Devlin, M. J., Halmi, K., Herzog, D., Mitchell, J., Powers, P. et al. (2012, August). Guideline watch: Practice guideline for the treatment of patients with eating disorders. Retrieved from http://psychiatryonline.org/pb/assets/raw/sitewide/practice_guidelines/guidelines/eatingdisorders-watch.pdf

Glossary

Applied behavioral analysis: A highly-specialized intervention focused on shaping behavior through application of learning theory

Attention-deficit/hyperactivity disorder: A neurodevelopmental disorder characterized by at least six symptoms of inattention and/or six symptoms of hyperactivity/impulsivity that emerge by late childhood

Autism spectrum disorder: A spectrum of neurodevelopmental disorders in which individuals struggle with both social communication and restricted, repetitive behaviors

Bipolar disorders: Mental disorders involving manic, hypomanic, and/or depressive episodes

Communication disorders: Neurodevelopmental disorders impacting speech (i.e., sounds, articulation), language (i.e., use of spoken or written words), and communication (i.e., verbal and nonverbal behavior)

Eating disorders: A category of mental disorders that involve disruption in quality, quantity, and process of eating

Elimination disorders: Mental disorders featuring developmentally inappropriate urination (i.e., Enuresis) or defecation (i.e., Encopresis)

Gender Dysphoria: Severe and persistent distress regarding "incongruence between one's expressed gender and one's assigned gender" (APA, 2013, p. 451)

Intellectual disabilities: Known as Mental Retardation prior to Public Law 111–256 (Rosa's Law), neurodevelopmental disorders that involve deficits in intellectual and adaptive functioning apparent early in development

Manic episode: A "distinct period of abnormally and persistently elevated, expansive, or irritable mood and abnormally and persistently increased goal-directed activity or energy, lasting at least a week and present most of the day, nearly every day (or any duration if hospitalization is necessary)" (APA, 2013, p. 124)

Neurodevelopmental disorders: A broad range of concerns that manifest early in life and are largely believed to be based in the developing brain

Obsessive–Compulsive Disorder: A mental disorder featuring presence of obsessions and/or compulsions that interfere with daily activities or cause great distress

Schizophrenia: A serious, often persistent, mental disorder involving combinations of delusions, hallucinations, disorganized speech, disorganized behaviors, and negative symptoms

Substance-use disorders: A "cluster of cognitive, behavioral, and physiological symptoms indicating that the individual continues using the substance despite significant substance-related problems" (APA, 2013, p. 483).

Substance withdrawal: Physical and psychological substance-specific symptoms that occur as a result of the body not receiving a substance it is used to receiving

Tics: "Sudden, rapid, recurrent, nonrhythmic motor movements or vocalizations" (APA, 2013, p. 82)

References

Adamson, N. C., Campbell, E. C., and Kress. V. E. (2015). Disruptive, impulse-control, and conduct disorders, and elimination disorders. In V. E. Kress and M. J. Paylo (eds.), *Treating those with mental disorders: A comprehensive approach to case conceptualization and treatment* (pp. 384–420). Upper Saddle River, NJ: Pearson.

American Psychiatric Association (2004). *Practice guideline for the treatment of patients with schizophrenia*, 2nd ed. Arlington, VA: Author. Retrieved from http://psychiatryonline.org/content.aspx?bookid=28&sectionid=1665359

American Psychiatric Association (2013). *Diagnostic and statistical manual of mental disorders*, 5th ed. Alexandria, VA: Author.

American Psychological Association (2015). Guidelines for psychological practice with transgender and gender nonconforming people. *American Psychologist* 70, 832–864. doi: 10.1037/a0039906

Apps, J., Winkler, J., and Jandrisevits, M. D. (2008). Bipolar disorders: symptoms and treatment in children and adolescents. *Pediatric Nursing* 34, 84–88.

Auger, R. R., Burgess, H. J., Emens, J. S., Deriy, L. V., Thomas, S. M., and Sharkey, K. M. (2015). Clinical practice guideline for the treatment of intrinsic circadian rhythm sleep–wake disorders. *Journal of Clinical Sleep Medicine* 11, 1199–1236.

Barkoukis, A., Reiss, N. S., and Dombeck, M. (2008a). *Feeding and eating disorders of infancy or early childhood: Pica*. Retrieved from https://www.mentalhelp.net/articles/feeding-and-eating-disorders-of-infancy-or-early-childhood-pica/

Barkoukis, A., Reiss, N. S., and Dombeck, M. (2008b). *Rumination disorder*. Retrieved from https://www.mentalhelp.net/articles/rumination-disorder/

Barrett, P. M., Healy-Farrell, L. J., and March, J. S. (2004). Cognitive–behavioral family treatment of childhood obsessive–compulsive disorder: A controlled trial. *Journal of the American Academy of Child and Adolescent Psychiatry* 43, 46–62.

Bennett, S. M., Keller, A. E., and Walkup, J. T. (2013). The future of tic disorder treatment. *Annals of the New York Academy of Sciences* 1304 (1), 32–39.

Berman, N. C. and Abramowitz, J. S. (2010). Recent developments in the assessment and treatment of pediatric obsessive–compulsive disorder. *Child and Youth Care Forum* 39, 125–126.

Burrows, R. D., Slavec, J. J., Nangle, D. W., and O'Grady, A. C. (2014). ERP, medication, and brief hospitalization in the treatment of an adolescent with severe BDD. *Clinical Case Studies* 12, 3–21. doi:10.1177/1534650112460911

Centers for Disease Control and Prevention. (2013, May). Mental health surveillance among children—United States, 2005–2011. *Morbidity and Mortality Weekly Report* 62(2). Retrieved from http://www.cdc.gov/mmwr/pdf/other/su6202.pdf

Coolhart, D. and MacKnight, V. (2015). Working with transgender youths and their families: Counselors and therapists as advocate for trans-affirmative school environments. *Journal of Counselor Leadership and Advocacy* 2, 51–64. doi: 10.1080/2326716X.2014.981767

Cortese, S., Brown, T. E., Corkum, P., Gruber, R., O'Brien, L. M., Stein, M., and Owens, J. (2013). Assessment and management of sleep problems in youths with attention-deficit/hyperactivity disorder. *Journal of the American Academy of Child and Adolescent Psychiatry* 52, 784–796.

Couturier, J., Kimber, M., and Szatmari, P. (2013). Efficacy of family-based treatment for adolescents with eating disorders: A systematic review and meta-analysis. *International Journal of Eating Disorders* 46 (1), 3–11.

Drescher, J. and Byne, W. (2012). Gender dysphoric/gender variant (GD/GV) children and adolescents: Summarizing what we know and what we have yet to learn. *Journal of Homosexuality* 59, 501–510. doi: 10.1080/00918369.2012.653317

Evans, S., Owens, J., and Bunford, N. (2014). Evidence-based psychosocial treatments for children and adolescents with Attention-Deficit/Hyperactivity Disorder. *Journal of Clinical Child and Adolescent Psychology* 43 (4), 527–551.

Freeman, J., Garcia A. M., Coyne L., et al. (2008). Early childhood OCD: Preliminary findings from a family-based cognitive–behavioral approach. *Journal of the American Academy of Child and Adolescent Psychiatry* 47, 593–602.

Freeman, K. A., Riley, A., Duke, D. C., and Fu, R. (2014). Systematic review and meta-analysis of behavioral interventions for fecal incontinence with constipation. *Journal of Pediatric Psychology* 39, 887–902. doi: 10.1093/jpepsy/jsu039

Jacobson, N. C., Newman, M. G., and Goldfried, M. R. (2016). Clinical feedback about empirically supported treatments for obsessive–compulsive disorder. *Behavior Therapy* 47, 75–90. doi: 10.1016/j.beth.2015.09.003

Jairam, R., Prabhuswamy, M., and Dullur, P. (2011). Do we really know how to treat a child with bipolar disorder or one with severe mood dysregulation? Is there a magic bullet? *Depression Research and Treatment* 2012.

Jorgenson, A. G., Hsiao, R. C. J., and Yen, C. F. (2016). Internet addiction and other addictions. *Child and Adolescent Psychiatric Clinics of North America* 25 (3), 509–520.

Ko, C. H., Liu, T. L., Wang, P. W., Chen, C. S., Yen, C. F., and Yen, J. Y. (2014). The exacerbation of depression, hostility, and social anxiety in the course of internet addiction among adolescents: A prospective study. *Comprehensive Psychiatry* 55, 1377–1384.

Lachman, A. (2014). New developments in diagnosis and treatment update: Schizophrenia/first episode psychosis in children and adolescents. *Journal of Child and Adolescent Mental Health* 26(2), 109–124.

Lindgren, S. and Doobay, A. (2011). *Evidence-based interventions for autism spectrum disorders*. The University of Iowa.

Mindell, J. A., Kuhn, B., Lewin, D. S., Meltzer, L. J., and Sadeh, A. (2006). Behavioral treatment of bedtime problems and night wakings in infants and young children. *Sleep* 29, 1263–1276.

Moreno, C., Laje, G., Blanco, C., Jiang, H., Schmidt, A. B., and Olfson, M. (2007). National trends in the outpatient diagnosis and treatment of bipolar disorder in youth. *Archives of General Psychiatry* 64, 1032–1039. doi:10.1001/archpsyc.64.9.1032

Murphy, T. K., Lewin, A. B., Storch, E. A., and Stock, S. (2013). Practice parameter for the assessment and treatment of children and adolescents with tic disorders. *Journal of the American Academy of Child and Adolescent Psychiatry* 52 (12), 1341–1359.

National Institute on Drug Abuse (2014). *Principles of adolescent substance use disorder treatment: A research-based guide* [NIH Publication 14-7953]. Retrieved from https://www.drugabuse.gov/publications/principles-adolescent-substance-use-disorder-treatment-research-based-guide/

Pediatric OCD Treatment Study Team [POTS]. (2004). Cognitive-behavior therapy, Sertraline, and their combination with children and adolescents with Obsessive–Compulsive Disorder: The Pediatric OCD Treatment Study (POTS) randomized controlled trial. *Journal of the American Medical Association* 292, 1969–1976. doi: 10.1001/jama.292.16.1969.

Rossler, W. (2011). Management, rehabilitation, stigma. In W. Gaebel (ed.), *Schizophrenia: Current science and clinical practice* (pp. 217–246). Hoboken, NJ: Wiley.

Schizophrenia Medications (2013, March). Retrieved from http://health.nytimes.com/health/guides/disease/schizophrenia/medications.html

Stafford, M., Mayo-Wilson, E., Loucas, C., James, A., Hollis, C., Birchwood, M., and Kendall, T. (2015). Efficacy and safety of pharmacological and psychological interventions for the treatment of psychosis and schizophrenia in children, adolescents and young adults: A systematic review and meta-analysis. *PloS One* 10(2), E0117166.

Subcommittee on Attention-Deficit/Hyperactivity Disorder, Steering Committee on Quality Improvement and Management (2011). ADHD: Clinical practice guideline for the diagnosis, evaluation, and treatment of Attention-Deficit/Hyperactivity Disorder in children and adolescents. *Pediatrics* 128(5), 1007–1022. doi: 10.1542/peds.2011-2654

Tanner-Smith, E. E., Wilson, S. J., and Lipsey, M. W. (2013). The comparative effectiveness of outpatient treatment for adolescent substance abuse: A meta-analysis. *Journal of Substance Abuse Treatment* 44, 145–158.

Theule, J., Ward, M. A., Cheung, K., and Lee, J. B. (2015). Psychosocial treatments for tic disorders: A meta-analysis. *Journal of Psychiatric Research* 74, 8–9.

Tiffin, P. and Welsh, P. (2013). Practitioner review: Schizophrenia spectrum disorders and the at-risk mental state for psychosis in children and adolescents: Evidence-based management approaches. *Journal of Child Psychology and Psychiatry* 54 (11), 1155–1175.

Tu, N. D. and Baskin, L. S. (2016). Nocturnal enuresis in children: Management. Retrieved from http://www.uptodate.com/contents/nocturnal-enuresis-in-children-management.

Valencia, M., Jarez, F., and Ortega, H. (2012). Integrated treatment to achieve functional recovery in first-episode psychosis. *Schizophrenia Research and Treatment* 2012. doi: 10.1155/2012/962371

Winkler, A., Dörsing, B., Rief, W., Shen, Y., and Glombiewski, J. A. (2013). Treatment of internet addiction: A meta-analysis. *Clinical Psychology Review* 33, 317–329.

Woo, S. M. and Keatinge, C. (2016). *Diagnosis and treatment of mental disorders across the lifespan*, 2nd ed. Hoboken, NJ: Wiley.

Yager, J., Devlin, M. J., Halmi, K., Herzog, D., Mitchell, J., Powers, P., et al. (2012, August). Guideline watch: Practice guideline for the treatment of patients with eating disorders. Retrieved from http://psychiatryonline.org/pb/assets/raw/sitewide/practice_guidelines/guidelines/eatingdisorders-watch.pdf

Youngstrom, E., Findling, R., Kogos Youngstrom, J., and Calabrese, J. (2005). Toward an evidence-based assessment of Pediatric Bipolar Disorder. *Journal of Clinical Child and Adolescent Psychology* 34 (3), 433–448.

PART V

Issues of Social Justice and Advocacy and Youth with Significant Needs

CHAPTER 12

Issues of Social Justice and Advocacy
Selma d. Yznaga and Deryl F. Bailey

> There can be no keener revelation of a society's soul than the way in which it treats its children.
>
> Nelson Mandela, 1995

CHAPTER OBJECTIVES

After reading this chapter, students will be able to:

- compare and contrast indicators of well-being for White, Black, and Latino children
- identify sources of personal and institutional discrimination affecting youth development
- recognize federal social services available to disenfranchised children
- interpret the disparities in health, educational attainment, and socio-economic indicators in the context of marginalization and oppression

---

INTRODUCTION

This chapter will discuss issues of social justice and advocacy when working with children and adolescents. Issues that influence disparities such as homelessness, poverty, and limited healthcare will be included.

Children represent one of the most vulnerable populations globally, and for children who have voluntarily or forcibly migrated to the United States, the vulnerability intensifies. This includes children of color who have a generations-long history of American citizenship as well as recent immigrants. Despite the United States' status as a child-protective country, full reliance on the adults around them can be uncertain for ethnic-minority children, especially when persistent poverty, addiction, marginalization, and oppression are chronic challenges (Lacey, 2010).

This chapter focuses on two distinct groups of children in the United States: African Americans and Latino/a immigrants. These two ethnic groups collectively encompass 39 per cent of the nation's child population. By 2020, fewer than half of the nation's children will be comprised of White, non-Hispanic ethnicity (Federal Interagency Forum on Child and Family Statistics, 2016). While African Americans have a long history in this country relative to Latino/a immigrants, there remains significant overlap in the ecological circumstances that shape these youths' emotional, social, and cognitive development. In particular, citizenship, economic status, healthcare, education, and discrimination will be discussed in this chapter relative to the identity formation of African American and Latino/a children. Additionally, advocacy strategies for capitalizing on their frequently unrecognized intellectual and social capital are provided.

CHILDREN IN CONTEXT: EXPANDING BRONFENBRENNER'S ECOLOGICAL MODEL FROM CHAPTER 1

Youth development occurs in the relentless tide of contextual stimuli, and for a vast majority of African American and Latino/a immigrant children, this usually means the context of poverty, truncated resources, and the unremitting stress of institutional and personal discrimination that perpetuate these circumstances (Locke and Bailey, 2013). The association between social factors in early childhood as predictors of academic and economic success in adult life are well documented. For example, Chapman (2003) hypothesized that high school students would be able to identify poverty as a contributing factor in their academic performance; the authors' findings indicate that poverty influences not only academic achievement, but its underlying correlates such as attendance, school meaning, and neighborhood support. According to McGee (2004), the achievement gap between White and African American and Latino/a students is not due to inherent students' abilities, but educational systems that provide poor-quality services in low socioeconomic areas in which children of color are overrepresented. The disparities in selected social indicators provide evidence for the challenges faced by African American and Latino/a children. Table 12.1 identifies social indicators by ethnic group that increase children's risk for cognitive, behavioral, and socio-emotional difficulties.

The effects of these disparities manifest in the educational achievement gaps experienced by African American and Latino/a children. Table 12.2 presents statistics for academic success indicators by ethnic group, corroborating the disparities presented in the Table 12.1 social indicators of wellbeing.

Table 12.1 Socio-economic indicators of wellbeing in U.S. children

	White Non-Hispanic	Black Non-Hispanic	Hispanic
Poverty	12%	37%	32%
Food insecurity	15%	34%	29%
Child maltreatment	9%	16%	10%
Single-parent household	21%	55%	31%

Sources: Adapted from Federal Interagency Forum on Child and Family Statistics (2016) and Vespa, Lewis, and Kreider (2013).

Table 12.2 Educational indicators of wellbeing in U.S. children

	White Non-Hispanic	Black Non-Hispanic	Hispanic
Out-of-school suspension	5%	16%	9%
Students enrolled in at least one advanced placement class	59%	9%	18%
High school completion	87%	73%	76%
Bachelor's degree completion	73%	10%	9%

Sources: Adapted from U.S. Department of Education Office for Civil Rights (2014a; 2014b) and U.S. Department of Education, Office of Elementary and Secondary Education (2016).

The disparity trajectory continues with income levels. In 2014, the median income was $60,265 for non-Hispanic Whites, $35,398 for African Americans, and $42,491 for Latinos/as. Income levels are associated with level of education; 29 per cent of people aged 25 and older living in poverty were not high school graduates, while 10 per cent of individuals with some college and only 5 per cent of those with at least a bachelor's degree met the criteria for living below the poverty level (DeNavas and Proctor, 2015). When income level is aligned with educational attainment for African Americans and Latinos/as, the figures are consistent across all indicators. African American and Latino/a children have access to fewer educational opportunities, which in turn leads to restricted prospects for employment and income. Poverty and the physically demanding jobs reserved for those without educational credentials are highly correlated with toxic stress, child maltreatment, substance abuse, and parental negligence, and the cycle of negative social determinants is perpetuated (Duffee, Kuo, and Gitterman, 2016).

Bronfenbrenner's theory of human development posits that individuals' physical, emotional, and intellectual growth depends largely on the environment in which that individual lives and participates. Using nested concentric circles to illustrate his model, Bronfenbrenner identifies the microsystem, mesosystem, exosystem, and macrosystem as settings that influence the way we develop, with each setting having a broader structure than the one before. In other words, the microsystem represents the environmental setting closest to the individual (placed at the center of the model) and comprises the home, school or workplace, with the concentric circle farthest from the center representing the broadest setting, i.e., economic, social, educational, legal, and political systems (Bronfenbrenner, 1977). According to Bronfenbrenner, the individual is a product of his or her environment, regardless of inherent intellectual capacity. This model elegantly explains why the educational and economic achievement gaps persist. Take, for instance, Jodie Foster's 1991 film *Little Man Tate*. The plot revolves around the tension between two women—Fred Tate's single mother, Dede, and Jan Grier, the founder of a school for exceptional children. Dede knows that her inner-city neighborhood cannot provide the educational enrichment in which her son can thrive and eventually allows him to move in with Jane so that his intellectual capacity can be fulfilled. On a less dramatic scale, American families face the same dilemma: How can we maximize our children's intellectual capital in environments that cannot adequately stimulate them for lack of resources and quality teachers?

Understanding the relationship between environment and capacity is critical to the development of a social justice perspective. In the next section, we explore some of the resources that families living in low socio-economic areas take advantage of in order to provide basic necessities for their children.

Dependence on Family, Community, and State

The first experience of security, whether negative or positive, occurs largely in the context of the family system for children. The Universal Declaration of Human Rights (1948) states that everyone has the right to basic necessities, identified as adequate food, housing and medical care. In other words, the population must be able to obtain water, food, shelter and health services in adequate quantity and quality to ensure survival and the right to "life with dignity." For those whose families cannot provide the basic necessities, reliance on the social services of the community and state is substantial. Schools often-times are expected to provide resources such as clothes, school supplies, basic health and mental health care, and additional academic resources for children. Many of these resources are provided by the schools or districts but also through partnerships with non-profits like Boys and Girls Clubs and organizations such as Kiwanis Club.

One specific non-profit, Communities in Schools, offers wraparound services that include basic needs, behavioral interventions, life skills, family engagement, and mental health services. Communities in Schools served 1.5 million students in 25 states in 2015 (Communities in Schools, 2016). Another program is 21st Century Community Learning Centers, present in 50 states. These centers serve students who attend high-poverty and low-performing schools. The program provides after-school and out-of-school assistance in core academic subjects, such as reading and math. Enrichment activities including financial literacy and other project-based learning activities are required of the families of participating children (U.S. Department of Education, n.d.).

Programs providing nutritional support are also necessary for many American families. The United States Department of Agriculture Supplemental Nutrition Assistance Program (SNAP) operates food distribution centers in all 50 states, supplementing schools, community and faith-based organizations in high-need areas to ensure that community members have access to nutritional assistance (U.S. Department of Agriculture, n.d.). Perhaps the most recognizable supplemental food program is The National School Lunch Program (NSLP), a federal meal program operating in public and nonprofit private schools and residential childcare institutions. Established under the National School Lunch Act, signed by President Harry Truman in 1946, it provided nutritionally balanced, low-cost or free lunches to more than 31 million children each school day in 2012 (U.S. Department of Agriculture, n.d). This school-based program might be more widely known as the "free or reduced lunch" offered to students whose families have lower incomes.

Health insurance is another critical social service provided by the state or federal government for children whose families cannot afford it. The Children's

Health Insurance Program (CHIP) is a federal program providing health coverage to eligible children. The program, concurrently funded by states and the federal government and administered by the states, insured 8.4 million children in 2015 (Medicaid.gov, n.d.). Without this support, the probability of children receiving adequate healthcare would be greatly diminished. Childhood preventable illnesses cause substantial disruption to the family system in terms of work and school absenteeism, loss of income, unnecessary suffering, and possible long-term health effects (Federal Interagency Forum on Child and Family Statistics, 2016). The most prevalent chronic health condition for youth is asthma, which can be effectively treated and managed should the access to health care be provided.

Medicaid is a joint federal and state program that, together with the Children's Health Insurance Program, provides health coverage to Americans, including children and their parents. The Affordable Care Act of 2010 created the opportunity for states to expand Medicaid to cover nearly all low-income Americans. In spite of these federal and state resources, African American (4 per cent) and Latino/a children (10 per cent) remain uninsured, compared to 4 per cent of their White, non-Hispanic counterparts (The Kaiser Family Foundation, 2014; U.S. Department of Health and Human Services, 2014). Lack of health insurance contributes to higher absenteeism rates (23 per cent for African American students and 22 per cent for Hispanic students) than for White students (19 per cent) because children are not practicing preventive health care measures like obtaining flu shots or treating wounds. Children who are frequently absent from school may experience academic difficulties and are less likely to complete school if no intervention takes place.

Health disparities describe the increased presence and severity of certain diseases, poorer health outcomes, and greater difficulty in obtaining health-care services for those races and ethnicities typically underserved in health care: African Americans, Latinos, Native Americans, and Asian Americans. Studies have shown that diagnoses, treatments, and quality of care can vary greatly depending on a number of factors that affect minority communities, including language barriers, transportation and childcare needs, lack of insurance coverage, and differential treatments based on the population group (Sacks, 2009). These challenges can be summarized by comparing the median life expectancy age for White and Black Americans, 78.8 and 75.2 respectively (Arias, 2016).

Children in the U.S. embody similar health disparities as adults, manifesting in particular in childhood obesity, asthma, and depression. The prevalence of obesity was highest among Black, non-Hispanic (23 per cent) children and Hispanic (24 per cent) children. In 2014, Black, non-Hispanic were reported to currently have the highest rates of asthma, compared with White, non-Hispanic (8 per cent) and Hispanic (8 per cent) children. Rates of depression in U.S. children were highest for White, non-Hispanic children (12 per cent) and Hispanic children (12 per cent) when compared to African American children (9 per cent). However, racial/ethnic minority youth with a major depressive disorder are less likely to receive depression care compared with their White counterparts (Federal Interagency Forum on Child and Family Statistics, 2016).

Case Study: Juan Pablo

Juan Pablo is an eight-year-old whose parents entered the country without proper documentation. The family lives in a heavy industrial area of the city, a Mexican enclave where they feel more welcome and can afford the rent. Unfortunately, the manufacturing plants in the area emit substantial exhaust and at a young age, Juan Pablo began having trouble breathing. Although Juan Pablo was born in the United States, his parents have not obtained medical insurance for fear of discovery and deportation. Juan Pablo frequently misses school because of his respiratory illnesses and asthma, which go untreated except for frequent emergency room visits. His absences in school have caused him to fall behind his peers academically in spite of Juan Pablo's curious nature and capacity for catching on quickly. His health problems also cause his parents to miss work because of fatigue and unpredictable emergency room visits and long wait times. Getting ahead does not seem possible for this young immigrant family.

While the U.S. government provides families in need with basic necessities and resources, it is important to keep in mind that these are the very minimum that a child and his family need to survive and do not provide opportunities to thrive, as seen in the case study above.

Next, we consider children and families that fall through the cracks of governmental assistance and lose the ability to maintain the most basic necessity—shelter.

Homelessness

The National Coalition for the Homeless defines homeless youth as individuals under the age of 18 who are not in the care of parents (biological or foster) or in institutional care (National Coalition for the Homeless, 2008). The three leading causes for homelessness among youth are family problems (physical and sexual abuse, strained parental relationships, addiction, and parental neglect), economic problems (parental loss of employment or underemployment), or some form of residential instability. Another term, "couch surfing," also refers to youth who are homeless but piecing residential stays together. While it is difficult to provide an accurate statistic regarding homeless youth, it is estimated that approximately 1.3 million U.S. students were homeless at the start of the 2013–2014 academic year (Endres and Cidade, 2015). It can be reasonably assumed that some homeless youth may not be enrolled in school, which increases the difficulty of obtaining a solid count on the number of youth who meet the criteria for homelessness. In academic year 2013–2014, 75 per cent of homeless students were living with other families, commonly known as "doubling up" (Covenant House, n.d.). Another 21 per cent either lived in shelters, hotels, or motels, and the remaining three per cent were "unsheltered," meaning that they were living outside, in abandoned buildings, in cars, or in other places not meant for human habitation (Covenant House, n.d.).

With regard to race, in 2013, African American families and Latinos were disproportionately represented among homeless families with children. It has been reported that children from African American families represented 48 per cent of families living in shelters even though African American families with children only represented 14 per cent of the U.S. population and less than 30 per cent of families with children in poverty (Covenant House, n.d.). Latino families with children represented 23 per cent of families with children, and of that group 36 per cent lived in poverty. However, they represented 22 per cent of the families living in shelters.

Life on the streets presents many challenges for young people. Among these are a lack of basic needs (i.e., inadequate nutrition and health care, both physical and mental). Basic survival may require that homeless children and adolescents resort to exchanging sex for food, clothing, and shelter. On a global level, homeless youth have become easy targets for human trafficking. While this issue seems to have no racial, ethnic, cultural, or socio-economic boundaries, the data presented above indicates that the majority of these youth are from poor families and families of color. The National Center for Missing and Exploited Children (n.d.) has suggested that one in five homeless youth become victims of sex trafficking, an increase from one in six in 2014. It is also reported that approximately 74 per cent of these youth are in the care of some social service agency when they are involved in sex trafficking.

IMMIGRATION

The "immigrant" label is complex and can take many forms depending on country of origination, generation, documentation status, detention status, and age. In 2014, immigrants comprised 13 per cent of the U.S. population. Some 42 per cent of the nation's foreign-born population are from Mexico, Central America, and South America. Of the 69.9 million children under age 18 in the United States, 25 per cent are first- (foreign-born with foreign-born parents) or second-generation (native-born with at least one foreign-born parent) immigrants (Zong and Batalova, 2015). The vast majority (88 per cent) of children living with at least one foreign-born parent are born in the United States.

The phenomenon of unaccompanied asylum-seeking children (UACS) in recent years has challenged the American paradigm of a protected and roman-ticized childhood. In the past five years, over 200,000 children between the ages of 12 and 16 have surrendered at the U.S. border seeking asylum from violence, terminal poverty, and full adult negligence. The majority of these children have traveled from Central America and through Mexico, alone or with age peers, a distance of approximately 3,500 miles on foot and on the tops of trains, many of them in the custody of child traffickers, or coyotes, working for Central American drug cartels. The surge of refugee children defies our perception of how the United States perceives and treats children, as well as our notions about culture and the constructs we have carefully built around them (Suarez-Orozco, Abo-Zena, and Marks, 2015).

While fewer undocumented children are arriving in the U.S. without an adult parent or guardian, the number of undocumented families apprehended with children has increased dramatically. In 2014, approximately 30,000 children traveling unaccompanied by an adult were apprehended at the

U.S.–Mexico border; in the first six months of fiscal year 2016 over 32,000 apprehensions of children traveling with their families have been reported (Krogstad, 2016). Since 2014, 74 per cent of the children entering the country are from El Salvador, Guatemala, and Honduras (Zong and Batalova, 2015). In contrast, the migration of Mexican children and families with children has decreased sharply, most likely due to the lack of economic opportunity in the U.S., immediate repatriation, and increased border security (Pew Research Center, 2015). Based on the migration trends of the last two years and the efforts of the United States government to curb the tide, the population of Central American children arriving with and without adult companionship is projected to remain steady or increase (Krogstad, 2016). What makes children, some as young as two years old (D. Salgado, personal communication, July 29, 2016), take the risk to travel 3,500 miles on foot to reach the United States? As one Honduran adolescent put it, "We're running for our lives" (Cammisa, 2010).

Central American unaccompanied alien children (UAC) comprise a relatively small proportion of immigrants to the United States; however, they are the majority ethnic group of child migrants in the world, and they are in many ways representative of the global migration trends of children (Zong and Batalova, 2015). The number of Mexican children who arrive unaccompanied by an adult is difficult to ascertain; the proximity allows border enforcement officers to repatriate or return the children to their home country with less than a day in detention (Krogstad, 2016).

Immigrants from Central America have repeatedly asserted that they are leaving their homes in Honduras, El Salvador, and Guatemala fearing violence, extortion, and involuntary recruitment into gangs. Child migrants from this area, called the Northern Triangle for its geographical configuration, include family reunification in their reasons for leaving; however, they also report that if they had no family in the United States, they would still flee due to the threat of violence. The majority report witnessing murder and other violent crimes, losing members of their immediate family to violence, and threats of gang recruitment or its alternative, death. The United Nations High Commission for Refugees (n.d.) confirms that UACs indeed present valid reasons to seek international protection related to violence, weak law enforcement, social hardships, and lack of available institutions to care for or protect these children.

The pre-migratory, in-flight, and post-migratory experiences of Central and South American UACs each present a high risk for mental health concerns; however, each phase can also have a cumulative effect and manifest in complex trauma for children. Pre-migratory push factors motivating emigration include severe poverty, homelessness, parental neglect, and the threat of harm or death owing to ubiquitous gang violence (Collier, 2015). Children fleeing Central and South America must navigate their way through Mexico to get to the U.S. border, and are likely exposed to in-flight risks of exploitation by human traffickers, physical battery, rape, hunger, illness and disease, and prolonged exposure to harsh natural elements.

Once a UAC is apprehended in the United States, he or she is placed in detention, usually a residential facility, until an immigration court hearing can be held or the child is reunited with family. Post-migratory, the child might undergo adjustment disorder, acculturative distress, and frustration with the lack of autonomy. In addition, feelings of guilt for being apprehended, uncertainty about the future, and separation and loss issues can be prevalent. A disproportionate number of immigrant children present with post-traumatic stress disorder, including symptoms of restlessness, sleep disorders, anxiety, depression, and dissociation (Collier, 2015).

The Office of Refugee Resettlement (ORR), U.S. Department of Health and Human Services, is charged with the care and placement of UACs. The majority of children are cared for through a system of ORR-funded care provider facilities, most in close geographic proximity to area of apprehension, e.g., the U.S.–Mexico borders. The facilities "provide children with classroom education, health care, socialization/recreation, vocational training, mental health services, family reunification, access to legal services, and case management" (U.S. Department of Health and Human Services, 2012).

Case Study: Rodolfo

Rodolfo, 17, has lived on the streets of Honduras without adult protection since he was seven years old. His mother was killed to avenge her boyfriend's drug debt, and he has never known who his biological father is. He has survived eating garbage and prostituting himself for money when he cannot find or steal what he needs. When he was 10, Rodolfo began using inhalants as a means of escaping his dire circumstances. After years of watching his age peers disappear due to gang-related violence and migration, Rodolfo was convinced by a street missionary to stop using drugs and escape the streets of Honduras by immigrating to the United States, where at the worst he would at least find shelter and food in a detention center. Rodolfo successfully traveled across Mexico and surrendered himself at the U.S. border, claiming he was 14 years old. With his small stature and no documentation to prove otherwise, Rodolfo was classified as an Unaccompanied Alien Child (UAC) and sent to a detention facility for unaccompanied minors where he awaits an immigration hearing to determine if he qualifies for asylum. His dream is to be adopted by an American family that will provide him with brothers and sisters and a traditional Christmas.

Due to our relative privilege, it is difficult, if not impossible, for Americans to conceive of children who are living on the streets of their home countries without any adult care or supervision and fleeing for their very lives. It is easier for some to believe the anti-immigrant rhetoric about foreigners entering the country for the purpose of exploiting or terrorizing the U.S. Unfortunately, immigrants often have unrealistic expectations about life in the U.S., and are susceptible to depression and substance abuse as they experience the struggle of penetrating the social and cultural borders of the "land of opportunity."

In the next section, we consider the transition from one ethnic and cultural identity to another, including the obstacles constructed and maintained by an increasingly xenophobic American society.

Acculturation and Identity Formation

Identity formation for children and adolescents of color necessarily includes the subjective exploration of culture and ethnicity. Whether individuals of color have grown up in the United States or have migrated to this country, they are constantly challenged to identify themselves in ways that differ from mainstream White American children. Challenges come in the form of discrimination when they deviate from the American cultural script by participating in cultural events like quinceañeras, eating traditional food from the home country, or have parents who speak with an accent. The "perpetual foreigner syndrome" identifies children of color, even when they have lived in the United States their whole lives, as "different," and forces them to consider their differentness continuously (Schwartz, Cano, and Zamboanga, 2015). Because White children are associated with being American, ethnic identity is less salient for them, and they are not likely to be confronted by questions of where they came from or made to feel like outsiders; White adolescents have the option to subjectively consider their ethnicity, but are more likely develop in terms of a more global personal identity (Berry, Phinney, Sam, and Vedder, 2006).

Ethnic identity develops on a continuum from the "unexamined attitudes of childhood" to exploration of one's culture and later to a secure ethnic identity (Phinney, Horenczyk, Liebkind, and Vedder, 2001, p. 496). Pride in belonging to a particular ethnic group is typically promoted by parents who choose which of the home country values and traditions to maintain. People of color tend to live in ethnic enclaves due to perceived discrimination, housing policies, socioeconomic factors, and reunification with or proximity to family members. Living among others who hold the same cultural values and traditions offers little opportunity for direct exposure to the dominant country values, leaving adolescents to acculturate on media representations of the dominant culture in a sort of segmented assimilation and serving to maintain the perpetual foreigner syndrome.

Eriksonian psychosocial theory (1994) classifies the adolescent period from ages 12 to 18 as the most prolific time of identity exploration, when adolescents navigate conflict between parental and peer values and the transition into adulthood. Phinney (2001) classifies ethnic identity as a critical component of personal identity development. While ethnic identity is elemental to personal identity development for adolescents of color, it departs from the Eriksonian aspiration of individuation: Ethnic identity can be conceptualized as the subjective sense of belongingness to a particular ethnic group (Phinney, 2001; Schwartz, et al., 2015). Acculturation, in contrast, is the way that an individual changes as a result of interaction with a new culture (Birman and Addae, 2015).

Upon arrival in a new culture, the individual must choose cultural maintenance or contact and participation with the new culture. This choice, along with the confluence of personal and social factors affecting acculturation, result in four possible identity categories: (1) separation, (2) assimilation, (3) marginalization, and (4) integration. When the individual retains a strong sense of the home country or ethnicity and does not identify with the host country, a separated identity ensues. Conversely, when the individual over-identifies with the host country and retains none of the ethnic values, the individual has achieved assimilation to the new culture. A third category of acculturation is marginalization, in which the individual identifies with neither the host nor the home country but rather lives in constant limbo. The individual rarely chooses this state; rather, he or she is forced out of inclusion by either group.

Three of the four categories above can have unfavorable outcomes. For example, a separated identity prevents the individual from fully experiencing life in the new context. Next, assimilated individuals may not be accepted as members of the new culture, and can be frequently reminded that it is the dominant group that decides who is allowed to belong. Another unfavorable outcome includes those individuals who value neither culture are relegated to the margins of society and experience the powerlessness that accompanies this position. Berry (1997) proposes one positive outcome—integration. Acculturative integration is possible when the individual maintains desirable characteristics of the home country while integrating desirable characteristics of the host country, i.e., combining the best of both worlds.

Phinney (2007) corroborates, indicating that the best outcome is for immigrants to retain elements of their home culture while incorporating valued aspects of the host culture. Individuals with a bicultural or adaptive perspective have fewer emotional, behavioral, and physiological problems than in any other acculturation category. Personal and social factors influence the manner in which immigrants are able to adapt and acculturate favorably.

For immigrant adolescents, acculturation is contingent upon personal variables such as age of migration, gender, education level, and the degree of exposure to the host country's cultural values and sentiment toward cultural plurality. Positive acculturation experiences are associated with younger ages, possibly because they have less cultural accrual and subsequently less cultural shedding upon arrival. Gender can impact acculturation, especially when the home country has negative stereotypical gender roles that devalue women and girls. Political climate impacts immigrants' perception of their reception in the host country; for example, the current debates and presidential campaigns regarding immigration have resulted in a negative climate, not only for immigrants but for all Latinos, typically viewed by the dominant culture through a panethnic lens (Schwartz, et al., 2015).

In addition to personal variables, acculturation is significantly impacted by the geographical distance of the two cultures (Berry, 1997). The less two cultures are alike, the more difficult it will be for immigrants to adapt and the probability of conflict and resistance on the part of both the immigrant and the native increases. The pace of the dominant culture's willingness to accul-turate to immigrants and people of color is sluggish in the best cases, and most research applies only to the acculturation of non-White ethnic groups. In the United States, the White ethnic group is still perceived to have more value than non-White ethnic groups, with adverse effects on acculturation. Successful adaptation to a new culture requires that the receiving country be supportive, open, and inclusive in its approach to cultural diversity (Berry, 1997). As mentioned above, this is not the case in the current American political climate.

A notable example of acculturation can be found in the television person-ality Nicole Polizzi, also known as Snooki, who stars in the MTV reality shows *Jersey Shore* and *Snookie and Jwoww*. Polizzi is a Chilean by birth who was adopted and raised by Italian American parents. The reality show relies heavily on Snooki's cultural identity as Italian American, which is popularly known as "guido" for males and "guida" for females. Snooki personifies the guida cultural stereotype by dressing in a flashy manner, including an abundance of jewelry and voluminous hairstyles. In 2014, the incongruence between Snooki's American Italian cultural identity and her Chilean phenotype was questioned, and an episode of *Snookie and Jwoww* was devoted to sampling her DNA and airing the results. Polizzi is a solid example of the "perpetual foreigner syndrome" introduced above, in which individuals with visible ethnic features are challenged to prove they are American.

People of color undergo an additional layer in the struggle for identity formation and frequently experience a social double bind: American society demands that people of color assimilate to national culture when they devalue individuals or groups seeking to maintain their cultural values, e.g., language, folk healing, or dress. On the other hand, American society can segregate those who do not fit the dominant stereotype, and refuse to allow acculturation based on visible and audible differences. This double bind is felt more when the political and cultural climate is anti-immigrant and perpetuates fear of the "foreigner." In the next section, we will identify vehicles for maintaining and extending the social double bind.

Personal and Institutional Discrimination

Children as young as 10-years-old are able to identify both personal and institutional discrimination, and can provide examples like name calling, unequal distribution of resources, and social exclusion (Brown and Bigler, 2005). Children of color are often members of several negatively perceived groups concurrently, including ethnicity, poverty, and social segregation, multiplying the likelihood of being targets of discrimination.

Case Study: Eric

Eric is a-fifth year African American high school senior. He has been the target of bullying from other students because his parents are not able to afford the latest student gear, pay for after school activities, and because his younger brother has a disability. Most recently, talk has started regarding Eric's sexual orientation. Unfortunately, the school head administrator has been heard making extremely homophobic comments such as Eric is asking for the trouble by the way he dresses.

Process Questions

1. As a mental health or school counselor, how might you assist Eric in resolving or dealing with his systemic recent issues?

As supported by the educational attainment in the tables provided earlier in the chapter, African American and Latino/a children are frequent objects of the institutional discrimination that is inherent in the public school system. Schools reinforce the "myth of meritocracy," which asserts that individuals have equal opportunities to advance in educational and vocational aspirations based on their own merit. Merit is defined as innate factors, hard work, the right attitude, and high moral character (McNamee and Miller, 2013). Ironically, the concept of meritocracy was conceived as the crux of the American Dream, in which immigrants could escape countries ruled by impenetrable monarchies and caste systems to a land where anyone could progress based on their own strengths (Liu, 2011).

In McNamee and Miller's (2013) definition of merit, hard work is frequently cited as the most salient factor in success. Yet, the jobs requiring the hardest work are frequently the lowest paid. Alvarado explains that in the context of meritocracy, hard work refers to one's ability to "create a future for oneself" (2010, p. 12); however, the hard work that the working class is often engaged in rarely results in upward social mobility. The ideology of meritocracy also assumes that motivation to work hard is innate. Pablo Freire (1970) disagrees, pointing to the inevitable and insidious inertia ensuing from the internalization of the oppressor's negative perceptions. For children and adolescents, Freire's assertions are manifested at the micro levels of school and neighborhood. Lowered academic expectations and fewer educational opportunities exist for African American and Latino/a children, who tend to live in poorer neighborhoods. The narrative is further perpetuated by corresponding low academic achievement, high disciplinary referrals, and overrepresentation in special education programs, resulting in an infinite cycle of poverty and injustice (Kozol, 1991). Outside of the school environment, children of color are more likely to be arrested for criminal activity than their White counterparts (Office of Juvenile Justice and Delinquency Prevention, 2014).

Institutional discrimination is also evident in the neighborhoods and communities where children of color spend the majority of their time. In 2010, minority youth accounted for 75 per cent of the juveniles held in custody for violent offenses (Office of Juvenile Justice and Delinquency Prevention, 2013). Lacey questions the likelihood that children of color are more predisposed to commit crimes than White children, pointing instead to a "legacy of years' of racial segregation, discrimination, and mistreatment" (2013, p. 3).

Personal discrimination is characterized by negative actions and practices that are based on phenotypic characteristics or ethnic affiliation (Pachter, Bernstein, Szalacha, and Garcia-Coll, 2010) and have been shown to adversely affect physiological and psychological functioning (Pachter, et al., 2010; Saleem and Lambert, 2016; Umaña-Taylor and Updegraff, 2007). It is well documented that the majority of American non-dominant children have experienced at least one incidence of racial discrimination, citing verbal insults and racial slurs as the most commonly experienced discriminatory behavior (Bogart, et al., 2013; Brown, 2005; Saleem and Lambert, 2016; Umaña-Taylor and Updegraff, 2007). Examples of this discrimination might include being bullied because of one's facial features, hair texture, and/or accent. Institutional discrimination might include announcing students who receive free or reduced lunch publicly and therefore identifying them as economically disadvantaged.

In the clinical setting, this would include the practice of routinely assigning counselors in training with the less amount of clinical experience to clients at the lower end of the sliding fee scale, while routinely assigning counselors in training with the most clinical experience to the more affluent clients.

SPIRITUALITY AND WELLNESS

Wellness is defined as "a way of life oriented toward optimal health and well-being in which body, mind, and spirit are integrated by the individual to live more fully within the human and natural community" (Myers, Sweeney, and Whitmer, 2000, p. 252), and is an underpinning of the unique counselor identity (American Counseling Association, n.d.). Myers, Sweeney, and Whitmer (2000) propose three salient reasons for including wellness in counseling practice: Persistent disparities in illness and health care for the uninsured, validation of nontraditional therapies as cost-effective and life-saving, and the suitability of counselors to provide wellness strategies such as stress management, communication improvement, and modification of lifestyle (Myers, Sweeney, and Whitmer, 2000).

School counselors' access to a captive audience of children may present the best chance of proactively impacting health disparities evident in ethnic-minority children and adults by teaching them wellness and lifestyle habits. Clinical mental health counselors also have opportunities to reduce health disparities by working closely with multiple agencies and providing resources for health and behavioral health care. Murphy and colleagues (2014) present wellness as analogous to a bank account in which stressors act as withdrawals and wellness interventions act as deposits. As in banking, transactions take place continuously and are not fixed or stable but fluctuate. Both clinical mental health and school counselors are in a unique and beneficial position to make systematic deposits in children's wellness accounts by providing research-based interventions and working collaboratively across allied professions.

Evidence for the efficacy of wellness training which includes stress management and problem-solving interventions, is promising (Kragg, Ven Breukelen, Kok, and Hosman, 2009; Ray, 2007). Reddy, et al. (2013) used Cognitive-Based Compassion Training (CBCT) to teach children and adolescents how to calm down and regain composure in stressful situations by using deep breathing techniques or meditation to avoid aggressive interpersonal conflict. Additionally, adolescents between the ages of 10–14 showed less perceived stress and increased adaptive coping after participating in Anti-Stress Training (Hampel, Meier, and Kummel, 2008). Kaplan, Turner, Piotrkowski and Silber (2009) increased Latina adolescents' self-esteem and cultural identity via a mentoring intervention called Club Amigas.

Advocacy Strategies

The American Counseling Code of Ethics includes a mandate to advocate for clients, citing a professional responsibility to "address potential barriers and obstacles that inhibit access and/or the growth and development of clients" (2014, p. 5). Mental health practitioners who are familiar with community resources can augment their clinical work with children and adolescents by providing their clients' parents with referrals to social services. In addition to providing individual and group counseling interventions with students at the immediate micro level, school counselors and clinical mental health counselors are in an ideal positions to advocate for students of color at the meso and macro levels as well. The meso level is described as the larger context of the school and community in which the student/client spends the majority of his or her time (Lewis, Arnold, House, and Toporek, 2003), while the macro level refers to the institutions encompassing the more intimate ecological settings, e.g., government or culture. Students of color are especially in need of advocates since they might have parents who face challenges with heavy work schedules, language barriers, or lack of familiarity with advocacy processes (Ratts, deKruyf, and Chen-Hays, 2007). School and community advocacy includes strategies to

- implement school-wide approaches to promote positive school climate and the mental wellness of all students
- offer comprehensive mental health services within schools, and increase partnerships with additional community resources
- lead efforts to develop community gardens, playgrounds, community centers, and other youth-friendly facilities
- provide mental health awareness training to adults who work with youth

At the macro level, counselors work to change policy in the public arena. Advocacy includes working with state and federal legislators and professional counseling organizations. Clients/students and their families rarely have the professional networks and contacts that professional counselors have, and acting at the macro level ensures that children benefit from the counselor's efforts on a much broader scope. Advocacy interventions at the macro level include:

- building relationships with state and federal legislative representatives; providing information about policy changes that would improve the lives of clients/students in your community
- partnering with interdisciplinary community agencies to develop models of healthy living
- collaborating with university faculty to evaluate and publish efficacy of models for wider impact

It is clear that school and mental health counselors not only have the skills needed to provide the much-needed services for the mental and emotional health for children and adolescents. By partnering with local faith-based organizations and colleges and universities they can obtain state and federal funding to provide after-school and weekend programing for young people and their families. This might include additional opportunities located at churches and other facilities in the community. For example, community-based yoga, zumba, and tai chi classes exist and are free to the public.

The following are case studies that include many of the issues presented in this chapter.

Case Study: Ximena[1]

Ximena is a 14-year-old Guatemalan female unaccompanied alien child who was apprehended by Immigrations and Customs Enforcement (ICE) agents near the Mexican border when she attempted to enter the United States without proper documentation. She was traveling with the mother and sister of her 22-year-old common-law husband, who had successfully entered the country undetected and sent money to a human smuggler (coyote) for their passage. Because Ximena was not a blood relative of her husband's family, nor lawfully married, she was not allowed to accompany them to a family detention center to await processing, but was assigned to a residential shelter for UACs, or Unaccompanied Alien Children. The term "alien" is used throughout this chapter to align with federal language in order to familiarize students with accurate terminology. The term "alien" dates back to 1798 and the Alien and Sedition Act, when it was first used to describe individuals outside of national citizenry. While the Alien and Sedition Act was repealed under Thomas Jefferson's administration, the Alien Enemies Act is still in effect, and the term "alien" is the official technical term selected by the U.S. Office of Refugee Resettlement to describe children who are in the country unlawfully without adult company at the time of their apprehension by U.S. Customs and Border Patrol (U.S. Department of Health and Human Services, 2012).

Ximena was living and working independently in Guatemala by the age of 9. She had a history of sexual abuse by her mother's boyfriends, her cousins, and her uncles. Her mother, grandmother, and aunts blamed and subsequently beat her for each instance of sexual abuse, accusing her of instigating it, starting when she was 4-years-old. Her mother eventually demanded that she either leave the house or get a job and contribute to the family's budget. Ximena found work as a live-in housekeeper, where she says she was treated well. When I [S. Yznaga] asked her what that looked like, she stated that she was not beaten.

When Ximena was 11, the 20-year-old son of her boss asked her to be his common-law wife. Ximena confided in me that she considered this offer very carefully and then accepted, stating that she had nowhere else to go.

As is typical for South and Central UACs, Ximena was exhausted when she arrived at the shelter. She and her traveling companions spent two weeks traveling through Mexico to arrive at the U.S. border, and the stress of constant threat and exploitation was evident in her restless and fretful behavior. For the first month of her detention, Ximena engaged in self-harm, cutting herself to relieve the frustration of being detained and immobile. She also presented with passive suicidal ideation (thoughts of suicide with no specific plan) and social withdrawal, refusing to talk to anyone, including me, for weeks. Ximena was referred to a psychiatrist who works with the ORR residential facility and prescribed an antidepressant, after which the self-harm and suicidal ideation ceased. In addition, Ximena began interacting with her housemates and increasingly participated in counseling.

In counseling sessions, the priority was to restore Ximena's sense of security and trust in her surroundings. This was accomplished through several tours of the compound, where security measures were presented to her as provisions for her safety as opposed to her containment. Facility staff introduced themselves to Ximena and, each time they met, patiently explained their role in her care, e.g., case manager, mental health clinician, house mother, teacher, or child advocate. When possible, staff members were careful to offer choices to offset the lack of autonomy imposed by her detention.

Trust-building activities to develop therapeutic alliance continued for weeks. As her clinical mental health counselor, I took a non-directive stance, empowering Ximena to direct our time together. Our initial sessions centered on creative arts in which we painted, made beaded bracelets, or used clay to form animals. These were quiet times, and I was careful not to pry into her history. Four weeks into our time together, Ximena told me her story without prompting as we colored mandalas. Never taking her tearful eyes off of her mandala, she spoke of the early abandonment of her mother and grandmother, and the moment when she realized that she had no choice but to accept the offer of common-law marriage.

I introduced trauma-informed cognitive behavioral therapy to reduce her persistent symptoms of anxiety. Relaxation, mindfulness, and breathing strategies were utilized in order to help Ximena regain composure when experiencing intrusive thoughts or autonomic symptoms.

Ximena expressed frustration and resentment at being detained and asked repeatedly to join her husband's family. An element of the clinical work was to facilitate her acculturation, including the United States' perception of children and rights afforded to them. This cultural reconstruction included the prohibition of child marriage, and Ximena's outlook improved markedly upon understanding that she was not going to be allowed to join the man she thought was her legal husband and to whom she felt obligated.

An additional therapeutic goal was the deconstruction of her self-narrative of deserving the chronic sexual abuse by the men in her life, and the ensuing physical abuse by the women. This was accomplished through narrative therapy, allowing Ximena to tell increasingly empowering iterations of her history as she regained her sense of security and trust, and was able to consider the reality of a world where she is not at risk of sexual and physical abuse.

Ximena remains in the residential facility, awaiting a transfer to the adoption system after being award asylum by a U.S. immigration court. She continues to develop her English skills and looks forward to attending and completing high school when she is released from the ORR shelter to the adoption and foster care system.

Case Study: Jimmie[2]

Thirty years ago, while working as a high school counselor, I [Deryl Bailey] developed an enrichment program for African American high school boys, called Empowered Youth Programs. The catalysts for the development of this program were the following:

1.   *high academic failure of African American males*
2.   *high rate of discipline problems for this group and*
3.   *the seeming lack of support for these young men*

Since this time I have worked with thousands of young people. The young man that I will be discussing in this case study is Jimmie.

Jimmie was a 12-year-old middle school student who was initially referred to EYP by his school counselor due to his poor academic performance. In addition to this poor performance, Jimmie was an "active fighter," meaning that he was involved in physical, violent fights in school and the community. Jimmy's mother was a single mom who lost her oldest son in a car accident with his grandmother when he was 12 years old. After the first year in EYP, Jimmie's grades had improved, his personal appearance was one that his mother was proud of, and he had developed several close friends. The next few years proved to be good years for Jimmie. Unfortunately, as he entered high school, things changed. His father remarried (without notifying Jimmie), his mother had started dating again, and Jimmie got involved with a rough group of guys. For a while, we suspected that he was experimenting with drugs and sex. Before long, his mom was being summoned to the school almost every day. As a participant in EYP, one of the benefits was that I (as Director of EYP) would participate in these meetings, usually to support the mom. As time passed and Jimmie reached the age of 17 with only a few high school credits, our suspicions of his drug use and unprotected sex were confirmed. To make matters worse, Jimmie had also become an active member of one of the most violent gangs in town. His mother had been fired from her jobs twice because of the amount of time that she either had to leave work or miss work to address Jimmie's problems. This created a serious financial crisis for the family. In the past, Jimmie had got anything and everything he wanted, with the exception of having his father in his life. Now, with his mom's reduced income, the "things" that his mother could provide for him were also reduced. At the same time, his drug use increased, and so did the number of nights that he stayed away from home. We would later learn that Jimmie had been stealing money from his mom's bank account and had stolen her hand gun. There were rumors that he had been sexually abused by an older male in the community (his probation officer, who was also a family friend … it is important to note that this was never confirmed).

After meeting with his mom on a regular basis, we devised a plan of action. First, we agreed that Jimmie needed to be in counseling. As a professor in a university counseling department that operated a community-based counseling center, I was able to get him and his mom an intake appointment within a few days. Shortly thereafter, they entered individual and family counseling. One of the key goals of therapy was to make sure that Jimmie complied with his appointments. As a result of my personal relationship, I was able to convince Jimmie to show up for his appointments.

After several months of counseling, the counseling center staff, his mom, a family friend who was a police officer, and I agreed that our first priority was to keep Jimmie off of the streets. This meant that when he did not come home his mom would contact the police to find him. Most of the time this worked; however, there were times where he slipped by them or fought with them. Our goals were as follows:

1. *not to give up on this young man*
2. *to keep him off of the streets*
3. *to make sure we knew where he was at all times (as best we could)*
4. *for mom to feel supported by the school and the justice system, and, most importantly*
5. *that he continue with therapy*

Jimmie is now 17. In the past year I have been to court with him eight times. The first four times the judge accused the mom of being a "bad mom." Eventually, the judge placed him in detention, but only after he had destroyed two ankle monitors and posted videos of his drug use on Snapchat and Facebook. On several occasions I discussed with his mom a program for young men in Jimmie's situation called Youth Challenges.

Youth Challenges is a National Guard dropout recovery program for teens who are experiencing difficulty in completing traditional high school. The program uses a very disciplined and structured program embedded in a military model. Challenge also provides post-graduation assistance in career or military placement. It is the only program of its kind that provides graduates with a personal mentor for one year to help in the transition into adulthood. I have agreed to serve as Jimmie's mentor. Working with this program, my goal is to help Jimmie embrace responsibility, motivate him to achieve, and increase his use of positive behavior.

I selected this program because Youth Challenge has shown encouraging outcomes: A multi-year study by MDRC found the program's participants achieve impressive results in educational attainment and employability. Key findings of that study include GED or high school diploma attainment increased by 29 per cent, college attendance increased by 86 per cent, and annual earnings increased by 20 per cent.

While Jimmie is not too excited about being in Youth Challenge, he agreed to participate as long as I agreed to be his mentor. As thrilled as I am about our relationship, I truly feel that this should be a role that his father should play. We don't know what the future holds for Jimmie, but what we do know is that he is not on the streets, that—hopefully—he doesn't have access to illegal drugs, and he is away from the gang activity. Based on the aforementioned Youth Challenge program results, I am hopeful for his recovery and his overall future.

SUMMARY

Native-born American citizens are raised with the concept that children are a vulnerable population that is to be protected and raised with intentionality and care. This chapter presents numerous challenges to the social construct of the vulnerable child. Immigrant children who travel for thousands of miles without adult supervision defy the precept that children are not capable of survival. Furthermore, if all children are valuable and vulnerable, how is it possible that African American children continue in the generational cycle of poverty and lack?

As was illustrated in this chapter, not all children are included in the American ideal of necessary care and protection. The glaring data confirming the surplus of neglected children in the United States pours in from educational, economic, and social institutions, demonstrating persistent and significant disparities between White children and ethnic minority children, particularly African American and Latino children. Awareness and acknowledgement of the foundational institutional structures that maintain the disparities is essential if there is to be change and a true effort to protect and care for all children.

Additional Resources

Amnesty International: People on the Move: https://www.amnesty.org/en/what-we-do/people-on-the-move/?gclid=CjwKEAjwlq24BRDMjdK7g8mD6BASJABBl8n3-ezCRVd2i26kgLWwLj5oEi9gg7Bu-73HFXD76bpvlBoCwNHw_wcB

Child and Adolescent Mental Health Project: http://nccc.georgetown.edu/projects/camh.html

Child Stats: http://www.childstats.gov/

Empowered Youth Programs, Inc.: http://empoweredyouthprograms.org/

Migration Policy Institute: http://www.migrationpolicy.org/

Model School Wellness Policies: http://www.schoolwellnesspolicies.org/Wellness Policies.html

The Center for Health and Health Care in Schools: http://www.healthinschools.org/

Suggested Readings

Berry, J. W., Phinney, J. S., Sam, D. L., and Vedder, P. (2006). *Immigrant youth in cultural transition: Acculturation, identity, and adaptation across national contexts*. Mahwah, NJ: Lawrence Erlbaum Associates.

Birman, D. and Addae, D. (2015). Acculturation. In C. Suarez-Orozco, M. M. Abo-Zena and A. K. Marks (eds.), *Transitions: The development of children of immigrants* (pp. 122–141). NY: New York University Press.

Cohn, D. (2015). *Future immigration will change the face of America by 2065*. Retrieved from http://www.pewresearch.org/fact-tank/2015/10/05/future-immigration-will-change-the-face-of-america-by-2065/

Duffee, J. H., Kuo, A. A., and Gitterman, B. A. (2016). *Poverty and child health in the United States*. Pediatrics 137 (4), 59–72.

Kena, G., Musu-Gillette, L., Robinson, J., Wang, X., Rathbun, A., Zhang, J., Wilkinson-Flicker, S., Barmer, A., and Dunlop Velez, E. (2015). The Condition of Education 2015 *(NCES 2015-144)*. U.S. Department of Education, National Center for Education Statistics. Washington, DC. Retrieved on May 16, 2016 from http://nces.ed.gov/pubsearch

Kozol, J. (1991). *Savage inequalities: Children in America's schools*. New York: Crown.

Lacey, C. (2013). *Racial disparities and the juvenile justice system: A legacy of trauma*. Los Angeles, CA, and Durham, NC: National Center for Child Traumatic Stress.

Lewis, J., Arnold, M. S., House, R., and Toporek, R. (2003). *Advocacy competencies*. Retrieved on October 3, 2006, from http://www.counseling.org/Publications

Office of Juvenile Justice and Delinquency Prevention (2014). *Statistical briefing book*. Washington, DC: U.S. Census Bureau.

Saleem, F. and Lambert, S. (2016). Differential effects of racial socialization messages for African American adolescents: Personal versus institutional racial discrimination. *Journal of Child and Family Studies* 25 (5), 1385–1396.

Glossary

Acculturation: A bidirectional process of an individual's psychological adaptation occurring with respect to both the host and the home country

Advocacy: The act or process of supporting a cause or proposal

Assimilation: Over-identification with the host country; loss of home country values

Asylum: The protection granted by a nation to someone who has left their native country as a political refugee

Bicultural: Retention of home country values with simultaneous incorporation of host country values

Cultural plurality: The willingness to value multiple ethnic groups and their values

Cultural script: The assumptions and values underlying a specific cultural group

Ethnic identity: A person's beliefs, attitudes, and feelings about the meaning of his or her ethnicity

Health disparity: The inequalities that occur in the provision of healthcare and access to healthcare across different racial, ethnic and socioeconomic groups

Home country: The country of origination for an immigrant

Host country: The country of destination for an immigrant

Immigrant Detention Center or Facility: A secure residential facility maintained or contracted by the U.S. government to house asylum seekers and/or undocumented immigrants

Marginalization: Identification with neither host nor home country

Panethnic lens: The perception of multiple nationalities as one ethnic group. For example, considering Mexicans, Puerto Ricans, and Cubans as Latinos

Perpetual foreigner syndrome: The perception of an ethnic minority individual to be a foreigner despite years or generations of residence in the U.S.

Personal identity: Ways that individuals explore and make choices regarding career, values, friendships, and dating relationships

Refugee: A person who has been forced to leave their country in order to escape war, persecution, or natural disaster

Separated identity: Maintaining a strong sense of home country values at the expense of incorporating host country values

Social identity: The positive feelings that individuals derive from group memberships

Unaccompanied alien child (UAC): An individual who is less than 18 years old, has no lawful immigration status in the U.S., and has no parent or legal guardian in the U.S.

Notes

1 Written in the first person (counselor) by Dr. Selma Yznaga.
2 Written in first person (counselor) by Dr. Deryl Bailey.

References

Alvarado, L. A. (2010). Dispelling the meritocracy myth: Lessons for higher education and student affairs educators. *The Vermont Connection* 31, 10–20.

American Counseling Association (n.d.) What is counseling? Retrieved on from https://www.counseling.org/about-us/about-aca

Berry, J. W. (1997). Immigration, acculturation, and adaptation. *Applied Psychology: An International Review* 46 (1), 5–68.

Berry, J. W., Phinney, J. S., Sam, D. L., and Vedder, P. (2006). *Immigrant youth in cultural transition: Acculturation, identity, and adaptation across national contexts.* Mahwah, NJ: Lawrence Erlbaum Associates.

Birman, D. and Addae, D. (2015). Acculturation. In C. Suárez-Orozco, M. M. Abo-Zena, and A. K. Marks (eds.), *Transitions: The development of children of immigrants* (pp. 122–141). NY: New York University Press.

Bogart, L. M., Elliott, M. N., Kanouse, D. E., Klein, D. J., Davies, S. L., Cuccaro, P. M., and Schuster, M. A. (2013). Association between perceived discrimination and racial/ethnic disparities in problem behaviors among preadolescent youths. *American Journal of Public Health* 103 (6), 1074–1081.

Brown, C. S. and Bigler, R. S. (2005). Children's perceptions of discrimination: A developmental model. *Child Development* 76 (3), 533–553.

Cammisa, R. (2010). *Which way home.* United States: White Buffalo Entertainment.

Chapman, M. V. (2003). Poverty level and school performance: Using contextual and self-report measures to inform intervention. *Children and Schools* 25(1), 5.

Cohn, D. (2015). Future immigration will change the face of America by 2065. Retrieved from http://www.pewresearch.org/fact-tank/2015/10/05/future-immigration-will-change-the-face-of-america-by-2065/

Collier, L. (2015). Helping immigrant children heal. *Monitor on Psychology* 46 (3), 58–62.

Communities in Schools (2016). 2015 Annual report. Retrieved from https://www.communitiesinschools.org/about/publications/publication/annual-report-2015.

Copeland, E. P., Nelson, R. B., and Traughber, M. C. (2010). Wellness dimensions relate to happiness in children and adolescents. *Advances in School Mental Health Promotion* 3 (4), 25–37.

Covenant House (n.d.). Statistics on homeless youth in America. Retrieved from https://www.covenanthouse.org/homeless-teen-issues/statistics.

DeNavas-Walt, C. and Proctor, B. D. (2015). *U.S. Census Bureau, current population reports, P60-252, income and poverty in the United States: 2014.* U.S. Government Printing Office, Washington, DC.

Duffee, J. H., Kuo, A. A., and Gitterman, B. A. (2016). Poverty and child health in the United States. *Pediatrics* 137 (4), 59–72.

Endres, C. and Cidade, M. (2015). Federal data summary school years 2011–12 to 2013–14. The University of North Carolina at Greensboro: National Center for Homeless Education. Retrieved from http://nche.ed.gov/downloads/data-comp-1112-1314.pdf

Erikson, E. H. (1994). *Identity and the life cycle.* London: W. W. Norton.

Federal Interagency Forum on Child and Family Statistics (2016). *America's children in brief: Indicators of well-being.* Washington, DC: U.S. Government Printing Office.

Freire, P. (1970). *The pedagogy of the oppressed.* New York: Continuum Publishing.

Goldthorpe, J. (2003). The myth of education-based meritocracy. *New Economy* 10(4), 234.

Hampel, P., Meier, M., and Kümmel, U. (2008). School-based stress management training for adolescents: Longitudinal results from an experimental study. *Journal of Youth and Adolescence* 37 (8), 1009–1024.

Kena, G., Musu-Gillette, L., Robinson, J., Wang, X., Rathbun, A., Zhang, J., Wilkinson-Flicker, S., Barmer, A., and Dunlop Velez, E. (2015). *The Condition of Education 2015 (NCES 2015-144).* U.S. Department of Education, National Center for Education Statistics. Washington, DC. Retrieved on May 16, 2016 from http://nces.ed.gov/pubsearch

Kozol, J. (1991). *Savage inequalities: Children in America's schools.* New York: Crown.

Krogstad, J. M. (2016). *U.S. border apprehensions of families and unaccompanied children jump dramatically.* Retrieved June 6, 2016 from http://www.pewresearch.org/fact-tank/2016/05/04/u-s-border-apprehensions-of-families-and-unaccompanied-children-jump-dramatically/

Lacey, C. (2013). *Racial disparities and the juvenile justice system: A legacy of trauma.* Los Angeles, CA, and Durham, NC: National Center for Child Traumatic Stress.

Lewis, J., Arnold, M. S., House, R., and Toporek, R. (2003). Advocacy competencies. Retrieved October 3, 2006, from http://www.counseling.org/Publications

Liu, A. (2011). Unraveling the myth of meritocracy within the context of US higher education. *Higher Education* 62 (4), 383–397.

Locke, D. C. and Bailey, D. F. (2014). *Increasing multicultural understanding*, 3rd ed. Los Angeles: Sage Publishing.

Mandela, N. (1995). Speech by President Nelson Mandela at the launch of the Nelson Mandela Children's Fund. Retrieved from http://db.nelsonmandela.org/speeches/pub_view.asp?ItemID=NMS250&txtstr=Mahlamba&pg=item.

McGee, G. W. (2004). Closing the achievement gap: Lessons from Illinois' golden spike high poverty high-performing schools. *Journal of Education for Students Placed at Risk* 9(2), 97–125.

McNamee, S. J. and Miller, R. K. (2004). *The meritocracy myth*. Lanham, MA: Rowman & Littlefield.

Medicaid.gov. (n.d.) Children's Health Insurance Program (CHIP). Retrieved from https://www.medicaid.gov/chip/chip-program-information.html

Migration Policy Institute (n.d.) *Frequently requested statistics on immigrants and immigration in the United States*. Retrieved on June 10, 2016 from http://www.migrationpolicy.org/article/frequently-requested-statistics-immigrants-and-immigration-united-states

Mitchell, K. (2013). Race, difference, meritocracy, and English: Majoritarian stories in the education of secondary multilingual learners. *Race, Ethnicity and Education* 16(3), 339–364.

Morgan, H. (2012). Poverty-stricken schools: What we can learn from the rest of the world and from successful schools in economically disadvantaged areas in the US. *Education*, 133(2), 291–297.

Nehrkorn, A. M. (2014). CDC: Mortality in the United States. *The International Journal of Aging and Human Development* 79(4), 334–335.

Nguyen, N. (2015). Education scholars: Challenging racial injustice begins with us. *Education Week* 34 (36), 27–32.

Office of Juvenile Justice and Delinquency Prevention (2013). *Census of Juveniles in Residential Placement.* Washington, DC: U.S. Census Bureau.

Office of Juvenile Justice and Delinquency Prevention (2014). *Statistical briefing book.* Washington, DC: U.S. Census Bureau.

Pachter, L. M., Bernstein, B. A., Szalacha, L. A., and García Coll, C. (2010). Perceived racism and discrimination in children and youths: An exploratory study. *Health and Social Work* 35 (1), 61–70.

Pew Research Center (2015). More Mexicans leaving than coming to the US. Retrieved on June 18, 2016 from http://www.pewhispanic.org/2015/11/19/more-mexicans-leaving-than-coming-to-the-u-s/

Phinney, J. S., Horenczyk, G., Liebkind, K., and Vedder, P. (2001). Ethnic identity, immigration, and well-being: An interactional perspective. *Journal of Social Issues* 57 (3), 493–510.

Ray, D. C. (2007). Two counseling interventions to reduce teacher–child relationship stress. *Professional School Counseling* 10 (4), 428–440.

Reddy, S., Negi, L., Dodson-Lavelle, B., Ozawa-de Silva, B., Pace, T., and Cole, S. (2013). Cognitive-based compassion training: A promising prevention strategy for at-risk adolescents. *Journal of Child and Family Studies* 22 (2), 219–230.

Sack, K. (2009). Doctors miss cultural needs, study says. *New York Times*, June 10, 2009. Retrieved on May 26, 2016 from http://www.nytimes.com/2008/06/10/health/10study.html?_r=0

Saleem, F. and Lambert, S. (2016). Differential effects of racial socialization messages for African American adolescents: Personal versus institutional racial discrimination. *Journal of Child and Family Studies* 25 (5), 1385–1396.

Schwartz, S.J., Cano, M. A., and Zamboanga, B. L. (2015). Identity development. In C. Suarez-Orozco, M. M. Abo-Zena, and A. K. Marks (eds.), *Transitions: The development of children of immigrants* (pp. 142–164). NY: New York University Press.

Suárez-Orozco, C., Abo-Zena, M. M., and Marks, A. K. (eds.) (2015). *Transitions: The development of children of immigrants*. NY: New York University Press.

Sylvester, K. (2001). Caring for our youngest: Public attitudes in the United States. *Caring for Infants and Toddlers* 11 (1).

The Henry J. Kaiser Family Foundation (2014). *Distribution of the nonelderly with Medicaid by race/ethnicity*. Retrieved May 24, 2016 from http://kff.org/medicaid/state-indicator/distribution-by-raceethnicity-4/?currentTimeframe=0&sortModel=%7B%22colId%22:%22Location%22,%22sort%22:%22asc%22%7D

Umaña-Taylor, A. J., and Updegraff, K. A. (2007). Latino adolescents' mental health: Exploring the interrelations among discrimination, ethnic identity, cultural orientation, self-esteem, and depressive symptoms. *Journal of Adolescence* 30 (4), 549–567.

United Nations General Assembly (1948). Universal Declaration of Human Rights. Retrieved from http://www.refworld.org/docid/3ae6b3712c.html

United Nations High Commissioner for Refugees (n.d.) Children on the run: Unaccompanied children leaving Central America and Mexico and the need for international protection. Retrieved from http://www.unhcr.org/en-us/about-us/background/56fc266f4/children-on-the-run-full-report.html?query=children%20on%20the%20run

Unterhitzenberger, J., Eberle-Sejari, R., Rassenhofer, M., Sukale, T., Rosner, R., and Goldbeck, L. (2015). Trauma-focused cognitive behavioral therapy with unaccompanied refugee minors: a case series. *BMC Psychiatry*, 151–159.

U.S. Customs and Border Protection (n.d.). Southwest border unaccompanied alien children statistics fy 2016. Retrieved on June 13, 2016 from https://www.cbp.gov/site-page/southwest-border-unaccompanied-alien-children-statistics-fy-2016

U.S. Department of Agriculture (n.d.). National School Lunch Program. Retrieved from http://www.fns.usda.gov/nslp/national-school-lunch-program-nslp

U.S. Department of Agriculture (n.d.). Supplemental Nutrition Assistance Program (SNAP). Retrieved from http://www.fns.usda.gov/snap/supplemental-nutrition-assistance-program-snap

U.S. Department of Education (n.d.) 21st Century Community Learning Centers. Retrieved from http://www2.ed.gov/programs/21stcclc/index.html

U.S. Department of Education, National Center for Education Statistics (2016). Consolidated state performance report, 2013–14. Retrieved on May 16, 2016 from http://nces.ed.gov/programs/coe/indicator_coi.asp.

U.S. Department of Education Office for Civil Rights (2014a). *Civil rights data collection: Data snapshot (school discipline)*. Washington, DC: U.S. Government Printing Office.

U.S. Department of Education Office for Civil Rights (2014b). *Civil rights data collection: Data snapshot (college and career readiness)*.Washington, DC: U.S. Government Printing Office.

U.S. Department of Health and Human Services (2012). Divisions—unaccompanied children's services. Retrieved on August 2, 2016 from http://www.acf.hhs.gov/orr/resource/divisions-unaccompanied-childrens-services

U.S. Department of Health and Human Services Centers for Medicare and Medicaid Services (2014). *2014 CMS Statistics*. Washington, DC: U.S. Government Printing Office.

Vespa, J., Lewis, J. M., and Kreider, R. M. (2013). America's families and living arrangements: 2012. Current population reports, P20-570. U.S. Census Bureau, Washington, DC.

Yu, J. J. and Gamble, W. C. (2010). Direct and moderating effects of social affordances on school involvement and delinquency among young adolescents. *Journal of Research on Adolescence* 20 (4), 811–824.

Zong, J. and Batalova, J. (2015). Central American immigrants in the United States. Migration Information Source. Retrieved on August 11, 2016 from http://www.migrationpolicy.org/article/central-american-immigrants-united-states

CHAPTER 13

Special Populations of Children and Adolescents Who Have Significant Needs

Brandie Oliver and Nick Abel

> We must have a place where children have a whole group of adults they can trust.
>
> Margaret Mead

CHAPTER OBJECTIVES

After reading this chapter, students will:

- be able to understand the impacts of trauma and other stressful life experiences on children and adolescents
- have learned strategies and interventions that are appropriate when working with children and adolescents presenting with specific traumas and adverse life experiences
- have gained knowledge about the long-term impact of risk and protective factors present in the lives of children and adolescents

---

SPECIAL TOPICS IN CHILD AND ADOLESCENT COUNSELING

The periods of childhood and adolescence are times of physical, cognitive, and social growth. Numerous developmental needs are critical during this span of time. Parents/guardians, school communities, friends, and society have significant impact on the development of these youth. The extent of the presence or absence of positive support and healthy influences can have long-term consequences. Emerging capabilities, confidence, and capacities are nurtured throughout life experiences both during childhood and adolescence. However, a young person's development can be disrupted with the presence of conflict, trauma, or other life events that can be detrimental and require interventions and extra supports that can be met by helping professionals. This developmental time is charged with opportunity and hope, but can be equally complicated.

Risk and Protective Factors

During child and adolescent development, healthy behavior can be modeled and nurtured by supportive families, peers, and community involvement.

Understanding common risk and protective factors can assist counselors working with youth in making healthy behavior choices. Risk and protective factors include psychological, biological, family, social, and cultural characteristics, some of which are fixed (e.g., genetic predisposition, personality traits, etc.), while some are variable and can change over time (e.g., income level, self-esteem, etc.).

Risk factors are defined as characteristics at the biological, psychological, family, social, community, or cultural levels that are commonly associated with an increased likelihood of negative life outcomes (Substance Abuse and Mental Health Services Administration [SAMHSA], 2015). Adverse childhood experiences (ACEs) contribute to risk factors that negatively impact youth development. The toxic stress caused by ACEs can impede the typical healthy development of an adolescent, and each additional risk factor introduced into a youth's life increases the probability of developing a mental and/or substance use disorder.

Just as risk factors place an adolescent at higher risk for negative outcomes, *protective factors* help safeguard them by preventing problems or reducing the impact of a particular risk factor (SAMHSA, 2015). Examples of protective factors include parental/family support, positive adult relationships that model healthy behavior, opportunities to participate in meaningful participation such as athletics or arts programming, and positive self-image. Protective factors are commonly connected to the concept of *resilience*, or the ability to "bounce back" or persevere following adverse events (e.g., trauma, tragedy, stressful life experiences, etc.). By focusing on the development of protective factors, resilience can be developed or enhanced in youth in an effort to help manage common stressors and counteract the effects of toxic stress.

Table 13.1 illustrates risk and protective factors common in childhood and adolescence, specifically linked to the three contexts most prevalent during these periods of life: Individual, family, and school community/peers.

When counseling children and adolescents, it is important to not only identify existing risk and protective factors, but also work with clients to increase the number of protective factors in their lives. In some instances, clients may need encouragement to recognize existing strengths because their perspective can be easily clouded by the stress and trauma of their presenting issue(s). By helping youth understand their capacity to change the course of their lives, counselors can instill hope and resilience. Additionally, youth feeling a sense of connectedness with at least one adult is essential in equipping them with the necessary traits to overcome risk factors that may be present.

In this section, risk and protective factors are defined and described. Risk factors are characteristics that may inhibit typical growth and development as well as impede learning and social–emotional functioning. Protective factors are characteristics that act as safeguards and improve the likelihood that youth will develop healthy behaviors and resiliency skills. Throughout this chapter, a variety of topics are discussed, most of which would threaten youth development and be considered risk factors. As you read each section, keep in mind how counselors may assist in fostering the development of protective factors to counteract challenging and traumatic life events that may impact the lives of young people.

Table 13.1 Risk and protective factors

Childhood	Risk Factors	Protective Factors
Individual	low emotional regulation hyperactivity/ADHD aggressive reactions poor cognitive development	mastery of academic basic skills (reading, writing, math) ability to make friends follow rules
Family	permissive parenting harsh or inconsistent discipline child abuse/domestic abuse	consistent discipline and expectations strong extended family connections
School community/ peers	low commitment to school accessibility to illegal substances lack of adequate resources at school	positive and consistent teacher expectations strong school to family partnerships high academic standards
Adolescence		
Individual	antisocial behavior impulsivity early substance use rebellious behavior	high self-esteem emotional regulation conflict resolution skills strong communication skills
Family	substance use poor attachment untreated mental health disorder lack of adult supervision	firm boundaries provides clear expectations strong attachment with family adult supervision
School Community/ Peers	poor academic performance for school few close friends no postsecondary plans	strong relationship with at least one teacher participation in extracurricular activities strong peer social support

Source: SAMHSA, 2015.

List two protective factors for both children and adolescents that will help
build resilience.

Exercise 13.1

TRAUMA

Traumatic events are those that are likely to be highly stressful and potentially threatening to a person's emotional and/or physical wellbeing. Outcomes of *traumatic events* include feelings of helplessness, anxiety, and concerns about safety. While there are many types of childhood trauma, the topics discussed in this section are among the most common and are associated with some of the most detrimental outcomes for children and adolescents.

Unfortunately, trauma is quite common in the lives of young people. According to data from the Adverse Childhood Experiences Study (ACE Study), nearly 60 per cent of Americans are exposed to at least one traumatic event before the age of 18, with over 22 per cent facing three or more such events during that time (Centers for Disease Control and Prevention [CDC], 2015). While significant trauma can stem from a single event (such as a disaster or exposure to violence), the most severe forms of trauma are those that occur repeatedly over time (i.e., physical/sexual abuse or neglect). These pervasive, ongoing traumas are referred to as *complex traumas*.

Regardless of the particulars, ACEs data indicate that each exposure to trauma increases a person's risk for a number of negative outcomes, including health ailments (e.g., asthma, stroke, heart disease), mental health issues (e.g., depression, mental distress), and consequences at school and work (e.g., decreased educational attainment, academic achievement, and income). As such, it is clear that traumatic experiences during childhood are a serious barrier to wellbeing, and that all counselors must be prepared to recognize and respond to signs of trauma in young people. Complicating this issue is the fact that no two children are likely to respond to trauma in the same way. Even siblings who experience the same event might present with vastly different symptoms—or none at all. This is because a child's unique demeanor, support systems, relationships, and coping strategies all influence resilience, which in turn influences trauma response. The most typical reactions to specific traumas are discussed in the sections below, but common symptoms among children and adolescents include anger, the need to control situations/maintain order, and problems with peers, including lashing out verbally, bullying, and/or hitting other children. Victims of trauma may also turn their anger inward and abuse themselves. These feelings can surface in a number of ways, including self-harm.

Therapeutic approaches to trauma vary widely based on children's responses. Many victims return to previous levels of functioning naturally, while others experience ongoing impairment and symptoms consistent with post-traumatic stress disorder (PTSD). Table 13.2 lists common responses to trauma by age and includes recommendations for counselors working with each population. While more specific guidelines for responding to various traumas are discussed throughout this section, the following apply to most.

- ■ The therapeutic alliance is critical. Trust, respect, and rapport must be established before any healing can take place.
- ■ A trauma victim's primary concern is generally safety and security. Spend time exploring feelings of safety at school, in your office, and at home. Help clients develop safety plans to avoid future exposure to their specific trauma, and/or to respond when a traumatic event has taken place.

■ Oftentimes, victims have experienced more than one type of trauma over their lifetimes. It may be helpful to screen for various types of trauma, as well as symptoms of PTSD before selecting a therapeutic approach.

■ Do not push clients to share more than they are comfortable with. Carefully monitor their anxiety and avoid subjects or situations that elevate stress past a moderate level.

■ Assess the presence of factors that contribute to resilience, such as emotional coping strategies and social connectedness. When necessary, teach the client ways to recognize and regulate emotions such as fear, anxiety, and anger through mindfulness, progressive relaxation, diaphragmatic breathing, and other relaxation strategies. Encourage positive social connections and involvement in enjoyable activities.

■ Help clients identify *triggers* (e.g., people, places, and/or things) that are likely to remind them of the trauma and cause distress. When necessary, identify and/or teach the client coping strategies to deal with triggers.

■ Especially with children and preadolescents, consider creative counseling approaches such as play therapy, bibliotherapy, and art therapy. Even among older teens, techniques such as music therapy and journaling can supplement traditional forms of talk therapy.

Table 13.2 Childhood and adolescent trauma: typical responses and suggestions for counselors

Age Group	Typical Responses	Suggestions for Counselors
Childhood (elementary school)	■ worries others will die or be injured ■ concerned about own safety ■ separation anxiety ■ sleep disturbances ■ fear of the dark ■ sadness ■ anger/irritability ■ reenacting trauma in play ■ developmental regression	■ simple, developmentally appropriate explanations ■ allow free play, including reenactment of the trauma ■ creative/expressive therapies— books, art, play, journaling, drumming ■ work with primary caregivers to assess safety, security, and support at home ■ teach basic coping strategies for anxiety, anger, etc.
Adolescents (middle/high school)	■ anger (arguments, fights) ■ mood swings ■ difficulty concentrating ■ withdrawal from friends, activities ■ headaches, stomachaches ■ depression ■ decreased school performance ■ increased risk-taking ■ questions about spiritual beliefs and/ or state of the world	■ establish trust, support, safety ■ active listening ■ monitor their anxiety in session and encourage, but don't push them to share ■ encourage connectedness and social support systems ■ assess triggers and develop coping strategies as necessary ■ cbt ■ mindfulness ■ groups for those who have experienced similar traumas

The National Childhood Traumatic Stress Network (NCTSN; http://www.nctsn.org) maintains a database of promising practices for counselors, as well as organizations that deliver counseling and/or social services using a *trauma-informed* approach that trains staff members to understand, recognize, and respond to signs of trauma. Below is a list of evidence-based approaches for counseling survivors of trauma:

- Trauma-Focused Cognitive Behavioral Therapy (TF-CBT)
- Trauma-Focused Cognitive Behavioral Therapy for Traumatic Grief (TG-CBT)
- Parent-Child Interaction Therapy (PCIT)
- Child and Family Traumatic Stress Intervention (CFTSI)
- Trauma Affect Regulation: Guide for Education and Therapy (TARGET)

Traumatic events are fairly common, and are associated with a host of negative outcomes related to both physical and mental wellbeing. Common signs of trauma among young people of various ages were presented in this section. Keep these in mind as you read some of the upcoming sections related to trauma, but consider how each is unique with regard to impact, symptoms, and counseling approach.

Exercise 13.2

List three common symptoms of trauma in childhood and adolescence and discuss when you have seen these symptoms in people you know or clients you have worked with.

GRIEF AND LOSS

It is natural that a young person's focus is on life and the infinite possibilities ahead. Death can be seen as the antithesis to this outlook. Grief is very personal and is as diverse as the student experiencing it. Despite the uniqueness of grief, there are common grief responses and a wide range of feelings often experienced during the grief process. The reactions to grief are not linear in nature, and emotions can vary both in frequency and duration. Some common grief responses in childhood and adolescence include anger, sadness, confusion, denial, questioning, and—through time—acceptance of the loss. It is natural for there to be a quick switch in emotional responses, where a youth may go from crying to becoming angry. Additionally, it is critical to keep in mind that it is typical for youth to re-grieve throughout each developmental stage in life.

Childhood Grief

Children in the early elementary years (typically until 9 years of age) often have an unclear idea about death. It is common that students in this age group may believe death is temporary and their loved one will return. Due to this belief, it is important to use concrete language when discussing the death experience rather than abstract terms. During the later elementary years (through 11–12 years of age), death begins to become more real, and students can sometimes be curious about death and ask several questions about the details surrounding the loss. Regardless of the age of the child, it is common for *grief bursts* to occur throughout the grief journey. You may notice children playing and returning to normal activities following a death, yet during the play the child has frequent bursts of grief. The behavior of play allows the child to take needed grief breaks and, in a way, indicates the ability to engage in healthy self-soothing behaviors. Additional considerations when working with a younger child include the following:

- It's important not to use euphemisms when explaining the death of a loved one. Phrases like "went to sleep" or "left us" can be confusing and can cause even greater feelings of sadness, confusion, and fear for the young person. Another common response "went to heaven" may also have the opposite effect meant because the young person can begin to fear heaven or ask when their loved one will return home from heaven. Additionally, using this term has a religious connotation. Encourage open expression of feelings. Bibliotherapy is an excellent tool to help students through the grieving process. While some youth may share emotions verbally, invite other outlets for emotional expressions (e.g., art, puppet play, sand tray, storytelling, etc.). Sample titles include *The Invisible String*, *When Dinosaurs Die*, *My Yellow Balloon*, and *Tear Soup: A Recipe for Healing After Loss*.
- Involve parents/guardians and any other loved ones that support the child in their grief work in the therapeutic process. Adults often think that showing their own sadness or other emotions will only hurt the child more. In reality, children need to see their loved ones openly grieve and are open to talking and sharing about the deceased loved one.
- Help the child understand that grief is not an act that they will "get over" but instead is a lifelong journey.

Adolescent Grief

Kubler-Ross (1969) referred to adolescent grievers as the "forgotten ones." Adolescents represent a unique group of grievers that have particular developmental needs that confound the normal grieving process. Many times the adolescent grief experience is inaccurately described similarly to those of younger children or can also be assumed merely a less intense form of adult grief. Adolescents do uniquely express and experience grief, often in ways that are intermittent and ensue over a longer period of time than that of adults. Adolescent grief may manifest in multiple forms that can include anger, confusion, exhaustion, emptiness, loneliness, sleep disturbances, and eating disturbances. What follows are examples of potential adolescent grief responses:

- *anger*—aggression toward others or loud verbal outbursts
- *denial*—withdrawal or fantasizing the deceased relationship
- *denial*—can also be displayed as regression
- *bargaining*—may try to atone for past mistakes in hopes of bringing back deceased
- *depressive symptoms*—adolescents may display somatic symptoms
- *withdrawal*—may remove themselves from normal social activities
- *acting out*—engaging in risky behaviors or atypical behaviors such as aggression toward others

Youth entering into the acceptance stage of grief are able to discuss the death in a realistic and healthy way. They understand that death is inevitable, and they have adjusted their life patterns and routines to accommodate for their loss. While they will undoubtedly still feel strong emotions from time to time, they understand that this is a normal part of the grieving process, and they have developed healthy ways to cope.

Potential complications associated with adolescent grief may include heightened impulsivity leading to self-destructive behaviors (e.g., substance use, reckless driving, sexual promiscuity, etc.) or even suicidal ideation. It is important to foster an open discussion that includes causes for despair, reasons for hope, and the meaning of life.

Generally speaking, when working with grieving adolescents, encourage the open expression of feelings. Teens often work to hold in their emotions for fear of what others may say or think. Providing a safe and secure space that accepts each feeling and reaction as being valid is critical in the grief journey. Teens can especially benefit from group counseling to help normalize the grief experience (Perschy, M., 2004). It can be a relief for adolescents to learn that others of the same age share similar grief stories, responses, and coping strategies. Additionally, counselors should be cognizant of the resurfacing of grief feelings around the holiday times, anniversaries, the birthday of the person who died, or the death anniversary.

Specific counseling strategies include narrative counseling that allows the bereaved to share the grief story in a personalized way and over the course of time. It is encouraged to allow the story to be told over and over as the grieving process can evolve and change. Additionally, the meaning-making process can be another helpful counseling strategy that is made up of the content of the meanings discovered in the loss and are divided into three major categories, according to Neimeyer and Anderson (2002): Sense-making (exploring the "why" the death happened), benefit finding (discovering the "silver lining" in the grief experience), and identity reconstruction (developing a modified identity reflective of the grief process).

Regardless of the age of the grieving youth you are working with, it is important to be aware of your own potential triggers or countertransference. Grief affects everyone and working with a grieving teen can evoke the helper's past loss so seeking supervision or personal counseling may be needed or beneficial.

Activity

Memory boxes

First find a box (can be any kind of box) that the child can decorate. Offer a variety of supplies to allow the child to make the box special and personal. Next, the child is encouraged to explore memory items of their loved one. This may include pictures, letters, artwork, death announcement, prized possessions, or any other items that the child connects with the loved one. These items are placed in the memory box as a way to honor the loved one. The memory box can be visited whenever the child wants to reconnect with the loved one and items can be removed or added at any time.

Develop three creative counseling strategies for working with grieving children. Make sure to include strategies for both children and adolescents, and to create a reference list or supply list so others can easily replicate the strategies.

Exercise 13.3

Grief is a personal and unique experience for children and adolescents. However, this section describes typical reactions as well as symptoms of complicated grief. Strategies and approaches are discussed to provide counselors skills and resources to be prepared to work with grieving youth. Grief can result from death but as the remaining sections describe, youth may have grief reactions when faced with other devastating life experiences.

NATURAL DISASTERS

Disasters such as hurricanes, tornadoes, floods, and earthquakes strike various parts of the U.S. on a regular basis. No community is immune to such events, and counselors everywhere must be prepared to respond to the needs of young people who have faced these traumas. While each disaster is unique, they share common traits with regard to their impact on the wellbeing of children and adolescents. In addition to the typical trauma responses listed earlier in this section, young people who have experienced a natural disaster are more likely to exhibit the following behaviors:

- fears that another disaster will strike
- worries that they will be suddenly separated from their loved ones
- in young children, clingy or regressive behavior

■   in older adolescents, increased risk-taking based on irrational beliefs that they will either die soon or that they are somehow immune to harm

Counselors working in schools or mental health settings impacted by a natural disaster should be prepared to assess the extent to which the trauma has impacted each student/client. While many are likely to return quickly to previous levels of functioning with only normal social support, others will have experienced heavy losses such as the death of a loved one, destruction of their home, or damage to prized possessions. These children will likely require more intentional, prolonged support as they work to overcome both the mental strain associated with experiencing the disaster, as well as the secondary losses they might face, such as moving, changing schools, or making new friends.

General guidelines for working with trauma victims apply to children and adolescents who have faced a natural disaster, including teaching targeted coping strategies based on symptoms (e.g., progressive relaxation or diaphragmatic breathing for anxiety). In addition, it is important that counselors work with the adult caregivers of their clients to encourage the following:

■   Monitor conversations about the disaster and carefully consider how much information to give children based on developmental level and coping skills. When young children are present, encourage adults to focus on the positives ("I'm thankful that …").
■   Take breaks from media coverage of the disaster, as repeated exposure can heighten anxiety and/or re-traumatize victims. Young children watching the news may even believe the disaster is happening again.
■   Maintain and/or establish a regular schedule, as routines can be helpful in establishing feelings of safety and security. Whenever possible, assign duties to children and adolescents so they feel like they are contributing to recovery efforts.
■   Schedule breaks for enjoyable activities, including time outdoors.

In addition to the above, there are a variety of resources available to counselors working with disaster survivors. A partial list appears in the Resources section of this chapter.

Exercise 13.4

Identify the most likely natural disaster in your area and compile a list of resources you could use (or share) with families who survive such an event.

Case Study

"Other people were leaving, but we stayed. We didn't have money for a hotel or car trip. When it looked like it would be a direct hit, we were all scared. The power went out right away, so we didn't have lights or TV. The wind was blowing so hard I thought our house would collapse. Windows were breaking. It was raining so hard. My little sister was screaming. But we couldn't go anywhere. We were trapped. That night, you could see the water near our front door. What if we had to swim? Would our stuff be destroyed? I started wondering if we'd die."

This 16-year-old client may have survived, but she and her family suffered heavy losses as a result of a hurricane. Their home, car, and possessions were destroyed, and they've been living in a makeshift shelter at a hospital for over a week. She has no idea what's next. They have no place to live. Her school was flooded, and most of the students are displaced. She has an aunt in a northern state, so they've talked of heading there, but how? She's barely slept since the storm. Everyone is so stressed, they're constantly bickering. Of course they're happy to be alive, but what will they do? She cries when she thinks about it.

As a mental health counselor working in the hospital, you have been talking with survivors, including this client.

Process Questions

1. What trauma symptoms are present? What others are likely to manifest?
2. After drawing out the story and showing empathy, how might you support this client?
3. Considering the client may relocate, what goals are realistic?

Natural disasters can strike virtually any part of the country at any time. Counselors should be prepared to work with survivors and their families on addressing feelings of safety, anxiety, fear, and helplessness. General tips for approaching this work were provided in this section, and a variety of other resources to support counselors can be found at the end of the chapter.

VIOLENCE

Findings from the most recent National Survey of Children's Exposure to Violence (U.S. Department of Justice, 2015) indicate that in any given year children under the age of 18 experience (41.2 per cent) or witness (22.4 per cent) violence at fairly high rates. The numbers are even more staggering when considering lifetime exposure to violence, as a majority (54 per cent) of young people having experienced some type of assault, while 39 per cent have witnessed violence such as physical assaults/intimidation, bullying or other types of relational aggression, or domestic violence. As with all traumas, each violent experience is unique and will manifest differently in the life of the survivor based on a number of factors. For example, witnesses to violent crimes resulting in death may simultaneously be grieving the loss of a loved one while worrying about their own safety. Like disaster victims, persons who experience violence may be dealing not only with the direct impact of the event (whether physical, mental, or emotional), but also secondary losses associated with it. For example, a person who experiences physical violence or bullying may withdraw from a friend group or extracurricular activity to avoid the perpetrator.

Victims of or witnesses to violence are at risk of the same outcomes as other trauma survivors, including decreased academic performance, mental health issues such as depression and anxiety, and substance abuse. And while no two children will respond to violence in exactly the same way, those who have faced this type of trauma are especially prone to the following:

- Constant worries about safety; always "on edge" or in "fight or flight" mode. May manifest as skittishness (e.g., jumps out of seat at a loud noise), irritability, and/or inability to concentrate.
- Anger, both towards the perpetrator and towards self for allowing it to happen.
- Physical symptoms such as stomachaches and headaches.
- Difficulty sleeping. May have nightmares related to violence.

In addition to the general guidelines for working with trauma victims given above, the following suggestions may be helpful when working with survivors of violence:

- Safety is often the primary concern. Establish safety in your therapeutic environment and help clients identify safe people and places in their lives. Help create safety plans to avoid or cope with dangerous situations.
- Teach relaxation techniques such as diaphragmatic breathing, mindfulness, and progressive muscle relaxation.
- Help clients identify and process their feelings about the event they experienced, being careful not to push them beyond a moderate level of anxiety at reliving the event. With younger clients, this often involves the use of play or other expressive techniques.
- Help normalize the experience through group counseling, bibliotherapy, popular media, or other ways of showing clients they are not the only ones to have experienced such a trauma.

CHILD ABUSE AND NEGLECT

Abuse or neglect of a child can take many forms. In the simplest terms, child abuse is commonly understood as physical or emotional battery, or sexual (see section below) contact that results in harm to a child, while neglect is a deliberate failure to provide care that is typically required by children of that age (e.g., food, shelter, clothing, medical care, education, etc.). According to the Child Maltreatment Report (U.S. Department of Health and Human Services, 2016), state child welfare agencies took action in over 500,000 cases of neglect and 119,000 cases of physical abuse in 2014. In addition, the most recent ACEs data indicate that approximately 35 per cent of those under the age of 18 have experienced emotional abuse in their lifetime (CDC, 2015).

Clearly, there are wide-ranging consequences for children and adolescents who experience abuse and/or neglect, up to and including death (2.13 per 100,000 children in 2014; U.S. Department of Health and Human Services, 2016). In addition to any outward scars that abuse victims might carry as a result of physical harm or neglect of their basic needs, they must also wrestle with the mental and emotional repercussions of being hurt by adults who are meant to care for and nurture them. It is no surprise then that cases of child abuse and/or neglect are some of the most challenging for a counselor. While entire texts have been dedicated to these complex topics, below are some considerations for counselors working with these students, beginning with the impact of such traumas, including common symptoms and warning signs.

- Common signs of physical abuse include marks or injuries that cannot be explained (or are explained in ways that are not believable), and baggy or heavy clothing that is inappropriate for the season (to cover physical marks). Signs of neglect include poor personal hygiene, inadequate/tattered clothing, and frequent discussion of heavy responsibilities at home.
- Attachment disorders are common among this population. Because of the harm they have suffered at the hands of trusted adults, abuse/neglect victims are likely to have issues bonding with teachers and other adults.
- Typical trauma symptoms are likely, including anger and withdrawal. Children who have been physically abused may be anxious or startle easily.
- Children may talk around the abuse or neglect and provide vague generalities about difficulties at home. Probe for information when necessary, and do not be afraid to ask direct questions such as, "Is someone hurting you?" and "Who provides things like food and care at home?"

The following are suggestions for counselors working with children or adolescents who have experienced abuse and/or neglect:

- School counselors and other mental health providers are mandated reporters of abuse and neglect in all states. Become familiar with your state's specific statutes and reporting procedures at https://www.childwelfare.gov.
- Train teachers, primary care physicians, and other frontline service providers on the importance of recognizing and responding to abuse. Inform them of their duty to report (as applicable), and provide information about warning signs of abuse and neglect.
- When allowed by child welfare authorities, work directly with parents or caregivers in a partnership framework. Provide services in the home when possible, and work on multiple levels to first carefully understand possible reasons for the abuse or neglect, and then tailor services as appropriate. When you suspect issues such as severe mental illness or substance abuse, connect the adult with a service provider. When help is needed with necessities such as food, clothing, housing, childcare, transportation, etc., provide information about social services in the neighborhood, helping facilitate contact when possible. In cases of inadequate parenting skills,

work with the parent to both recognize their beliefs about children and expectations for behavior (CBT/REBT), and train them on productive strategies for child-rearing, including appropriate discipline, positive communication, and methods for enhancing engagement/attachment.

■ Recognize that trust is likely to be the client's main concern, following stabilization of physical needs and safety. Use basic counseling skills like empathy and positive regard to slowly establish rapport. Reassure the child that you want to help, and that there are other adults in the world who also want to help, such as teachers, law enforcement officers, child welfare workers, and health care providers.

■ If a physical abuser still lives in the household, help the client create safety plans that include recognition of caregiver emotional state, and specific steps that can be taken to minimize the risk of harm in situations when physical or emotional outbursts are likely.

■ Consider partnerships between schools and community organizations to provide food and other necessities for children and families in need.

■ Assess the child's behavior patterns in various situations and put interventions in place to modify as necessary. While children are never at fault for abuse or neglect, their emotional or behavioral patterns may be contributing to caregiver stress.

SEXUAL ABUSE AND SEXUAL VIOLENCE

Similar to other forms of abuse and neglect discussed above, sexual abuse and violence are highly damaging to children and adolescents, but are all too common in our society. According to ACEs data, 15 per cent of females and 6 per cent of males experience sexual abuse or violence before the age of 18 (CDC, 2015). In total, over 58,000 cases of sexual abuse were acted on by child welfare agencies in 2014, representing 8.3 per cent of all abuse/neglect cases handled that year (U.S. Department of Health & Human Services, 2016). As is the case with all types of child abuse, counselors are mandated reporters of sexual abuse and violence in all 50 states. For more specifics on reporting procedures and questions about what constitutes abuse in each state, consult http://childwelfare.gov.

While children may display physical signs of sexual abuse, it is more likely that a counselor or other attentive adult would notice the following emotional and behavioral signs, some of which are unique to cases of sexual abuse, but many of which are common in other types of trauma:

■ unexplained anger, anxiety, or depression
■ dissociative symptoms
■ nighttime issues such as bed-wetting and nightmares
■ compulsions, such as frequent washing or masturbation
■ unexplained fear of certain people and/or places
■ loss of appetite
■ sexual symptoms, such as reenactment of the abuse, unusual interest in (or avoidance of) sexuality, and unexpected expression of sexual ideas in drawings and/or play

Counseling victims of sexual abuse is delicate, challenging work. As is the case with other types of abuse, these children are often dealing with multiple physical and emotional wounds, and have likely suffered profound losses such as broken relationships with family and friends, shattered trust or faith in people—even those they know well—and a lack of interest in activities that used to be enjoyable. They are also likely dealing with intense feelings of anger, both at the perpetrator and at themselves for "allowing" the abuse to happen and/or not reporting it sooner. Below are general considerations for counselors:

- Report all suspected cases of sexual abuse to your local child welfare agency.
- As with other types of abuse, recognize that trust and safety are likely to be primary concerns. Slowly establish rapport through active listening and positive regard. Do not push the client to share too quickly or to discuss the abuse if it causes more than a moderate level of distress.
- Since survivors will respond to abuse in different ways, tailor your approach to each client according to their needs. Common issues include self-esteem, basic emotional coping skills, anger management, trust and attachment, depression/withdrawal, and PTSD. No single counseling approach is "right" when it comes to sexual abuse. See the Resources section for NCTSN promising practices/interventions in trauma therapy.
- When the abuse is profound or beyond your realm of expertise, do not hesitate to refer to a therapist who is more experienced with this type of work.

List one critical consideration for working with a childhood abuse victim and explain how a counselor might approach the issue.

Exercise 13.5

Research your state's procedures for reporting child abuse or neglect. Who are mandated reporters? What agency handles these cases? How does someone make a report? What information would a "screener" ask for? What are the likely outcomes given clear evidence of physical, emotional, or sexual abuse?

Exercise 13.6

Case Study: Marna

Marna is a 14 year-old female in the eighth grade. Over the past few weeks her family, teachers, and friends have noticed a change in behavior. She has been overly sensitive to touch (e.g., hugs from family and friends), easily agitated, and sleeping in class. Most recently, she has refused to attend an upcoming family event that is usually one of her favorites, and she becomes extremely anxious around middle-aged men. On the recommendation of her mother, Marna reluctantly agrees to meet with her school counselor. After the second meeting, she breaks down and discloses that her uncle forced her to touch him and he also touched her breasts. She is embarrassed, feels ashamed and doesn't want her parents to know. The school counselor reports the incident to the Department of Child Services/Child Protection Services, contacts her family, and provides a referral to a community mental health counselor that specializes in counseling victims of sexual abuse.

Process Questions

1. Upon meeting Marna, it is evident she is guarded and reluctant to share. How would you work to build rapport with Marna? What questions or strategies may be helpful to gather Marna's story?
2. What counseling strategies might the mental health counselor employ?
3. How should the school counselor follow up with the student? How can the school counselor provide support to Marna during the school day?

Counseling Activity

Art therapy provides an outlet for emotional expression and provides opportunity for the child to process the abuse event witnessed and/or experienced.

YOUTH IN FOSTER CARE

Youth in foster care have been removed from their home due to experiencing some form of serious abuse and/or neglect or the loss of a parent. The placement process in foster care is a difficult and stressful life experience for any child. According to the Child Welfare Information Gateway (2016), 415,129 children were in foster care in 2014, with approximately 29 per cent placed in relatives' homes, and nearly half placed in non-relative foster care. Other foster care placements can include group homes, residential facilities, emergency shelters, and pre-adoptive homes.

Commonly, youth in foster care have experienced traumatic events that contribute to the likelihood of emotional, behavioral, and/or developmental problems. Physical health problems may also be present, which add another layer of potential complications. The removal of the young person from home is a risk factor in itself. Being removed from a parent represents the loss of an attachment figure, even though this attachment may be unsafe and harmful to the youth. Or, youth may be experiencing loss of a parent while, at the same time, not able to find housing with relatives and subsequently entering the foster care system.

Most children in foster care experience numerous feelings, including confusion, fear of the unknown, loss, sadness, anxiety, and stress. These feelings and experiences must be addressed early to prevent or minimize poor developmental, academic, and mental health outcomes. In addition to the trauma experienced, children in foster care are further susceptible to further wounds if placed in unstable or unhealthy environments, increasing the risks of an already fragile and vulnerable group. The transition from foster care to early adulthood can be another complicated process. At age 18 youth are out of foster care and often find they have little to no adult support and struggle to find ways to be self-supportive.

Counselors in all settings can support youth in foster care by working to form a therapeutic relationship that demonstrates healthy boundaries, unconditional positive regard, and acceptance. It is important to screen for trauma and assess for mental health related disorders (e.g., post traumatic stress disorder, anxiety, depression), and to address those as needed via typical counseling interventions such as client-centered or cognitive–behavioral therapy. In schools, counselors can help advocate for ongoing mental health counseling despite if the youth in foster care has multiple placements and frequently moves. Additionally, considerations relevant to the school setting need to include number of schools attended by the student, truancy or high absenteeism, ensuring the student record is complete (e.g., special education services are being provided if applicable, all school transcripts are included so credits will be granted) to confirm all appropriate supports are in place for the student. Clinical mental health counselors working with youth in foster care may want to explore the use of trauma focused cognitive behavioral approaches, as well as assess for attachment and connectedness issues possibly present in the youth's behaviors.

Youth in foster care often have exposure to traumatic experiences. They may have developmental delays and complications with secure attachment. An essential task of a counselor is to establish trust and rapport demonstrating to the foster youth acceptance and unconditional positive regard.

SUICIDE AND SUICIDE RISKS

The Centers for Disease Control and Prevention (2013) reports suicide as the third leading cause of death among persons aged 10–14 and the second among persons aged 15–34 years. Although suicide deaths and attempts for children under the age of 10 is infrequent, there are at-risk students in elementary schools across the nation that need support and intervention. Depression is the leading cause of suicide in teenagers; however, suicide is complex. There likely are several underlying or co-occurring disorders. In addition, the impulsivity common in adolescence is a tremendous added risk. Since the prefrontal cortex is not fully developed, a teen is more likely to make a rash emotional response following a stressful life event (e.g., relationship break up, fight with parent/guardian, school problem, etc.). It is important to remember that the vast majority of teens who experience even very stressful life events do not become suicidal.

Suicide can be prevented. Early detection and appropriate mental health counseling are key factors. Advocating for comprehensive suicide prevention programming in schools and communities is a critical element in the prevention effort. In schools, all employees, parents, and students, need to receive training about both the risk factors and warning signs. Furthermore, suicide prevention training within emergency rooms, community clinics, and other community serving organizations should be included to build capacity regarding suicide prevention and intervention. By providing accurate information to assist in early detection, referrals can be made to appropriate mental health professionals that can lead to appropriate diagnosis and mental health treatment as well as help reduce the stigma commonly associated with the topic of suicide. One communication tool that can help reduce stigma is explaining the best terminology to use when there is a death by suicide is to state "died by suicide" instead of "committed suicide". The term committed carries a negative connotation that is often associated with committing a crime. Since suicide already places the bereaved in a heightened state of sensitivity concerning the death, using this updated terminology is best practice.

Both legal and ethical obligations apply when working with suicidal youth. Limits of confidentiality apply. Parents/guardians must be contacted when a young person discloses suicidal ideation and appropriate next steps should be discussed. In school settings, a student's privacy needs to be protected. Teachers and other caring adults may have good intentions by asking about the details of a student situation, but information about the suicidal student cannot be shared without the permission of the student or family.

A common myth about suicidal talk and suicide attempts is that it is merely a cry for attention and students are often dismissed as being dramatic. No matter how many times a student shares suicidal ideation, a threat of suicide should never be dismissed. Each situation needs to be taken seriously because it is important to respond to any threat of suicide and other warning signs in a thoughtful manner. Not all suicidal talk leads to an attempt, but it's a chance counselors cannot take.

What factors do we know that increases the chance a young person may be at risk of suicide? What do we know about youth that die by suicide? What factors help protect youth from suicide? Understanding the risk factors, warning signs, and protective factors that are associated with suicide is critical in our work. The majority of suicidal young people give warning signs of their despair. According to the American Association of Suicidology (2016), a majority of those thinking about suicide let others know their intent because they are ambivalent and want others to know about their emotional pain and stop them from dying. A warning sign does not automatically mean a person will attempt suicide, but it should be taken very seriously and treated as a call out for help.

When counseling a student presenting with suicidal ideation, it is vital to stay calm, stay with the young person at all times, and provide unconditional positive regard. Below are some important considerations when intervening.

■ Use active listening skills and seek to gain an understanding of the presenting problem. Additionally, assess to check if a plan is present and if the young person has access to the lethal means indicated in the plan.

■ Explore if the student has any prior suicide attempts.

■ Use reflecting skills to ensure you have an understanding of the client's information.

■ Focus on the central issue. This is not the time to explore other aspects within the presenting issue. The focus needs to be solely on keeping the young person safe.

■ Listen for ambivalent feelings about this decision. Seek to find at least one person, place, or thing that has kept the student alive to this moment.

■ Work with the youth (and family members) to develop a safety plan that all persons supporting the youth agree to follow.

■ Do not leave the youth alone and immediately involve parents/guardians.

Table 13.3 lists numerous risk factors, warning signs, and protective factors of adolescent suicide. The possibility of suicidal ideation increases when a youth has numerous risk factors yet presents with a low number protective factors.

Table 13.3 Risk and protective factors for suicide

Risk Factors	Warning Signs	Protective Factors
Behavioral cues		
■ prior suicide attempt ■ family history of suicide ■ recent death ■ access to lethal means ■ substance use	■ increase of substance use ■ giving away possessions ■ searching internet for ways to kill oneself ■ sudden withdraw from social group ■ change in eating or sleeping patterns	■ effective communication skills ■ strong family and community connections ■ conflict resolution skills ■ school connectedness ■ access to effective health care (includes medical/physical, mental/psychological, and substance abuse)
Verbal cues		
■ delinquent behavior—trouble with the law ■ school suspension or expulsion ■ undiagnosed, untreated or ineffectively treated mental disorder (depression is most common) ■ school failure—potential for school dropout ■ impulsive and/or aggressive tendencies	■ talking about dying ■ "I can't stand living anymore." ■ "I wish I were dead." ■ ■ "I can't go on." ■ "I wish I could go to sleep and never wake up."	

Other situational/stressful factors include:
■ target of bullying
■ victim of sexual/physical abuse
■ multiple adverse childhood experiences
■ breakup of romantic relationship
■ sexual orientation (e.g., coming out as LGBT in an intolerant environment)

Discuss differences between risk factors and warning signs associated with suicide.

Post-Suicide Intervention

When an adolescent dies by suicide, surviving family members and friends are left with many unanswered questions and a range of emotions. Survivors are susceptible to developing symptoms of depression and posttraumatic stress. Grief associated with suicide is often complex in nature, may last longer, and is more intense. Multiple emotions can range in intensity and duration including anger, sadness, guilt, blame, and embarrassment. Other concerns associated to grieving suicide survivors include:

- shame due to stigma
- guilt and/or blame over inability to prevent death
- difficulty understanding why/obsession with finding answers
- relief
- feelings of rejection/abandonment
- uncertainty what information about the death to share with others due to stigma

Another factor, according to the American Foundation for Suicide Prevention and Suicide Prevention Resource Center (2011), to consider following a suicide is the possibility of contagion, the process by which one suicide may set off others. Adolescents are more susceptible to imitative suicide or cluster suicide, especially in cases where media has glamorized the death (e.g., Stack, 2003). In school communities that have experienced a student suicide, it is important to be on high alert and assess those students that have past suicidal ideation and/or attempts, referring to mental health providers if deemed at-risk. Another higher risk group to check-in with would be the peers in the same social group as the student that died by suicide.

Suicide is a leading cause of death among adolescents. Counselors in all settings must be prepared to recognize and respond to warning signs in young people, and to assist families, schools, and communities in responding when a suicide attempt or completion has taken place. This section covered risk factors, warning signs, and suggestions for intervening.

NON-SUICIDAL SELF-INJURY

Non-suicidal self-injury (NSSI) is highly prevalent and viewed as a significant adolescent social problem. Youth that self-injure intentionally destruct the body or skin. They do not have intent to end their life, but rather are seeking a way to relieve stress or escape problems. Deliberate self-harm among adolescents—including such actions as cutting or scratching oneself, burning, self-hitting, and biting—are among a few of the common self-harming methods. Although youth NSSI is not intended to be fatal, this behavior is a strong risk factor to suicidal ideation (Guan, Fox, and Prinstein, 2012).

Recent investigation into the etiology of NSSI has revealed there is not a clear profile of a youth that engages in this behavior. The complex nature of NSSI resulted in the disorder not being included in the Diagnostic and Statistical Manual of Mental Disorders (DSM-5); it instead appears in the research section so further investigation can be completed. Because NSSI is typically something adolescents work to keep secretive, it is difficult to have solid prevalence data. Current research estimates a variance between 15–30 per cent of adolescents report engaging in NSSI yearly.

When working with a youth that is engaging in NSSI, it is important to be supportive and nonjudgmental. The focus of your interaction should not be on stopping the NSSI but instead helping the adolescent find alternative coping strategies. In addition to this communication, it's also important to conduct a thorough assessment that includes questions about methods of self-injury, places on body where harm has occurred, how the wounds are being cared for, and if the youth has ever required medical attention following the NSSI. In addition to these questions, it is also helpful to ascertain information about the precipitating factors or events that lead to the NSSI actions, including frequency and duration of these behaviors and the perceived benefits the youth gains from engaging in NSSI. Since NSSI is a risk factor associated with suicidal thoughts and behaviors, a suicide assessment may also be warranted.

Social contagion is often commonly associated with adolescent self-injury behavior. Within a social group, the behavior becomes normalized or can even be glamorized. Social media adds another layer to the problem. Understanding social contagion is important so intervention strategies are individualized in nature and do not include group counseling or large scale school convocations to discuss this topic.

Case Study: Travis

Travis is a 12-year-old male in the sixth grade. Two of his friends met with the school counselor to express concern about Travis. They shared that he has been burning himself with matches and they have seen him use an eraser at school to rub his skin until it leaves burn marks. The school counselor meets with Travis and discovers he has been using burning as a way to cope with a stress and worry. She contacts his parents to discuss what she has learned. The school counselor plans to meet with Travis on a weekly basis, but she believes Travis would strongly benefit from seeing a clinical mental health counselor outside of school. She offers the family a list of referrals for practitioners in the local community.

Process Questions

1. As the school counselor, how do you approach Travis? What questions do you use to engage in assessing what his friends have shared with you?
2. What information do you share with his parents?
3. What counseling strategies might the mental health counselor employ?
4. How can the school counselor provide support to Travis during the school day?
5. What information could be shared between the school counselor and the mental health counselor to best support Travis? What would be required to share information?

Examples of evidence-based programs for children exposed to violence include:

■ Al's Pals: Kids Making Healthy Choices
■ Child–Parent Psychotherapy
■ Cognitive Behavioral Intervention for Trauma in Schools (CBITS)
■ Functional Family Therapy (FFT)
■ Motivational Interviewing (MI)

BULLYING

Bullying is a repeated (or highly likely to be repeated), unwanted, aggressive behavior where there is either a real or perceived imbalance of power (Gladden, Vivolo-Kantor, Hamburger, and Lumpkin, 2014) between the target and student exhibiting the *bullying behavior*. As you may have noticed, the term "student exhibiting bullying behavior" was used in the definition rather than the student being labeled as a bully. This shift in terminology is important because labeling a student causes only more harm and can induce continued bullying behaviors as the student demonstrates the self-fulfilling prophecy of the label assigned.

Bullying behavior generally takes one of four forms:

■ physical (e.g., hitting, kicking, breaking someone's possessions, etc.)
■ verbal (e.g., name calling, insults, threats, etc.)
■ social (e.g., spreading rumors, exclusion, embarrassing someone, etc.)
■ cyber (e.g., fake profiles, social network posts, sending unwanted pictures, etc.)

Despite educational and legislative efforts to address bullying, it remains a significant problem. Almost one in four students (22 per cent) report being bullied during the school year (National Center for Educational Statistics, 2015b). Many potential reasons surround why a student may be a target of bullying including an overall perception of "being different" from peers, perceived sexual orientation, body shape, disabilities, and race. The person who is bullied may also be perceived as weaker or in a submissive position or status such as a student who is going through a break up or another student who might be adopted. Possible characteristics of a student exhibiting bullying behavior include aggressive tendencies, low parental involvement or attachment, views violence positively, and challenges authority. It is also plausible that students who display bullying behavior may have been a target of bullying previously (including by a sibling). One way to think about students that engage in bullying behavior is they are hurt and feel that lashing out on others will relieve their pain. The saying "Hurt people, hurt people" can be associated with bullying behavior. When youth have been the recipient of peer maltreatment or other forms of abuse (i.e., verbal, emotional, physical), then these hurt and painful feelings may be turned outward by looking to cause harm to others.

In counseling children and adolescents on either side of this issue, it is critical to gain an understanding of the level of emotional pain associated with the bullying. The Center for Disease Control (2015) report that targets of bullying are at increased risk of poor school adjustment, sleep difficulties, anxiety, and depression, and youth who engage in bullying behavior are at increased risk of academic problems, substance use, and violent behavior later in life. Bullying sometimes is said to result in suicide. However, this is not accurate. The prevalence of bullying is an additional risk factor to consider if assessing for suicidal ideation as necessary, but it cannot be said to be the only reason.

When working with youth that have been targets of bullying, ongoing individualized support is necessary. A counselor can help youth build resiliency through self-esteem skill development, finding healthy coping strategies, and increasing protective factors. Individual counseling that emphasizes empathy training, social–emotional skill development, positive communication, and aggression replacement training can be appropriate for youth exhibiting bullying behavior. Furthermore, counselors in the school setting need to advocate for systemic change that intentionally changes the culture of an entire school community. To do so, a comprehensive school-wide bullying prevention and intervention program needs to be implemented. This program would include training for all school professionals, students, and parents. Additionally, it is important to utilize all existing programs and resources available in the school such as restorative practices, culturally responsive positive behavior interventions and supports, character education, the parent-teacher organization, school-wide positive discipline programs, social–emotional learning curricula, grade-level teams, professional learning communities, and any other meaningful supports to eliminate bullying from the school.

The following are prevention programs that can be implemented in schools to address bullying.

- Olweus
- Bully Busters
- Get Smart, Get Help, Get Safe
- The Kinder and Braver World Project
- Bully Safe USA

Exercise 13.8

What types of bullying have you witnessed? List a specific example of the four types of bullying as discussed above.

Bullying continues to be a problem for today's youth. It is essential to have an understanding of the definition of bullying as well as recognize symptoms of a student that has been both the target of bullying and the student exhibiting bullying behavior. Schools need to implement comprehensive programming to prevent and equip educators with the abilities to intervene if witnessing a bullying event.

SEXUAL ORIENTATION AND GENDER IDENTITY

Lesbian, gay, bisexual, or transgender (LGBT) youth commonly face challenges at home and at school, in foster care, and in the juvenile justice system. It is important to remember this topic is also applicable to young children. Aina and Cameron (2011) share that gender identity expression begins between 3 to 5 years of age, and it is natural for a youth to have the first romantic crush around the age of 10. As early as kindergarten, students may hear derogatory comments about LGBT students (Willoughby, 2012). *Gender-variant* youth, children and adolescents who do not look or traditionally behave in ways that males and females are expected to behave by their families and by society, are at a greater risk of becoming the target of bullying and future school and social problems.

With the onset of puberty and feelings of emotional and sexual attraction toward others, adolescence can be a difficult time. This is perhaps no truer for any group than those who identify as LGBT. For many of these students, adolescence brings not only the typical developmental challenges, but also elevated risk for a number of serious issues related to physical, emotional, and mental health. While a complete rundown of risk factors is beyond the scope of this section, counselors should know that LGBT youth are statistically more likely than their peers to experience physical and verbal harassment and assault, decreased self-esteem, lowered GPA (Gay, Lesbian, and Straight Education Network [GLSEN], 2013), homelessness or "couchsurfing" (Ray, 2007), suicidal thoughts, ideations, and attempts (CDC, 2011), and a host of other issues. While many LGBT youth are able to navigate these challenges with the support of family and friends, some lack the necessary social connections and coping mechanisms and will seek the assistance of a counselor. The following are suggestions for working with the youth LGBT population:

■ Maintain an open, nonjudgmental attitude. Both the ACA (2014, A.4.b.) and ASCA (2010, A.1.c.) ethical standards require counselors to respect the diversity of their clients and avoid imposing values/beliefs upon them. Like other youth who seek out counseling, LGBT youth want to be heard and empathized with, and as such, a great deal of healing can take place simply through the formation of a positive therapeutic alliance.

■ Given the evidence of possible bullying of LGBT youth, it may be appropriate to scan for academic, social, behavioral, and emotional issues early in the counseling process. Counselors should also assess each client's current coping strategies and when needed, teach positive techniques for managing stress, anxiety, decreased self-esteem, and anger.

■ Like all adolescents, LGBT youth benefit from positive, supportive peer relationships. Encourage clients to seek out like-minded peers and become involved in school or community activities. To promote these types of positive relationships, advocate for the formation of LGBT-affirming clubs such as Gay and Straight Alliance in your school or workplace.

■ The process of "coming out" or telling one's family and friends about their sexual orientation or gender identity is a life-changing step for LGBT youth. Allow clients to make this decision in their own time when they are ready—do not push them or "out" them without their knowledge. When a client is ready, offer your support in the form of brainstorming strategies for sharing, role-playing, or offering to be present for the discussion. Family support is a critical protective factor for LGBT youth, so it is important that counselors continually assess this area of a client's life and offer assistance when needed.

■ Help make your school or work environment a safe place. Use inclusive language (e.g., partner instead of boyfriend/girlfriend), display LGBT-affirming materials, and do not tolerate slurs or offensive language. Encourage other staff to do the same. Additionally, support and/or lead efforts to change or institute inclusive policies around non-discrimination and inclusion. One example would be a bathroom and locker room policy that invites students to use facilities that most closely align with their gender identity.

■ Some adolescents may ask about "reparative" or "conversion" therapies, which purport to change a person's sexual orientation. Counselors should recognize that no rigorous scientific data exists to demonstrate that these therapies are ever successful, and in fact, they can have wide-ranging negative consequences for clients. Every major professional association for mental health practitioners (i.e., ACA, ASCA, APA, AAP, NASW) has issued a statement discouraging its members from attempting to change a client's sexual orientation.

■ Professional counselors are also called to advocate for systemic change that supports the rights and wellbeing of all marginalized persons, including LGBT youth (Ratts et al., 2015). Be on the lookout for policies, rules, laws, etc. that intentionally or unintentionally discriminate against this population, and speak up! Whether in your school, workplace, town, or state, your efforts can make a difference.

Discuss several strategies counselors can use when working with LGBT youth at various levels: Individual, school, community, and state.

YOUTH WITH DISABILITIES

In the most recent school year for which statistics are available (2011–2012), almost 6.5 million children and adolescents were being provided services through federally funded special education programs (U.S. Department of Education, 2015a). With this number representing roughly 13 per cent of the total public student population, it is clear that a counselor providing services to children and adolescents is very likely to encounter a young person with a disability. As such, counselors must be familiar with the challenges faced by these students, as well as the laws and terminology that govern special education.

Federal oversight and funding for special education largely began in 1975 with the passage of the Education for All Handicapped Children Act, later renamed the Individuals with Disabilities Education Act (IDEA) upon its reauthorization in 1990. Although the legislation has been improved and renamed many times over the years, its core principles and requirements have remained largely unchanged. First and foremost is the requirement that schools provide a free appropriate public education (FAPE) to all students with disabilities. Prior to IDEA, it was not uncommon for public schools to either deny educational services completely, or to charge families the costs of educating students with disabilities. Schools are now required to not only educate all students, but also to do so in a manner that is consistent with state standards and tailored to a child's specific needs based on disability. Furthermore, IDEA requires that students provide this education in the *least restrictive environment* (LRE). This means schools educating students with disabilities alongside nondisabled students to the greatest extent possible, even when that means providing accommodations and modifications in the form of materials, assistive technology, and/or additional staff. Essentially, LRE is in place to ensure that students are not continually placed in "pull-out" or "self-contained" special education classrooms or buildings when they are capable of learning in a general education setting with proper supports.

IDEA also requires schools to provide an appropriate evaluation for special education to all students who might benefit. Evaluation comes in many forms, including the administration of standardized tests and instruments, developmental interviews with the student and parents, and a review of school records.

This process that must be completed within a specific timeline as specified by IDEA. It is typically carried out by a diverse team of specialists that includes special education teachers, a school psychologist, school nurse, school administrator, and school counselors. Many types of disabilities could potentially qualify a student for special education services, but the most common are specific learning disabilities (e.g., a math or reading disorder), speech or language impairments, "other" health impairments (e.g., ADHD, asthma, epilepsy), and autism spectrum disorders. Once a student has been found eligible for services, IDEA requires the team to develop an individualized education program (IEP) for the eligible student. An IEP is the foundation for a student's education. It outlines the impacts of the student's disability on current levels of academic and social performance and sets concrete goals for future performance. It includes accommodations and modifications, either in the classroom or school environment, that will be necessary for the student to succeed, as well as services that will be provided by school staff to help the student meet his/her goals.

With such a wide variety of disabilities being fairly common among children and adolescents, it is difficult to give broad recommendations for counselors working with this population. That said, the following are general suggestions to keep in mind.

- Treat students with disabilities as individuals. Just as a mental health diagnosis does not define a person, neither does the presence of a disability. A "label" does not mean a child will act in stereotypical ways or experience the same challenges as another person with the same disability. Take time to get to know each individual, including exploring strengths and aspirations. When discussing challenges, try to focus on a client's strengths when designing interventions that target specific areas of academic, emotional, and personal–social wellbeing. The needs of students with disabilities are as wide and varied as that of the general student population, and could include things like academic achievement/graduation, social issues, self-esteem, anger management, post-secondary planning and transition, etc.
- Advocate for the needs of students with disabilities. Educate yourself on IDEA and state rules, regulations, and processes that are in place to protect these students. Speak up when something is not right or someone is being treated unfairly.
- Special education team meetings can be overwhelming. Offer to meet individually with parents and students, ensuring they understand what is happening in meetings, what is contained in the IEP, and what their rights are with regard to IDEA.
- Connect with other important adults in the student's life, including teachers, coaches, and the school-assigned case manager. Offer to help in any way you can, including as a service provider on the IEP when it is appropriate.
- When called up to counsel these students, focus on empowerment strategies. This could take many forms, but is frequently focused on helping a student build self-advocacy skills working to discover own needs and find solutions to presenting challenges. Teaching a client counseling

approaches such as Solution-Focused Brief Therapy, CBT, and/or mindfulness could be appropriate.

■ Differentiate classroom lessons and group sessions to effectively reach all learners and to specifically accommodate the needs of students with disabilities. For example, counselors might need to prepare large print copies of materials for a student with a vision impairment. Check with teachers in advance of classroom lessons to become aware of any needs and adjust lessons accordingly.

Exercise 13.10

Think about your high school experience. What types of interactions did you have with students with disabilities? Did you share classes, play sports, or socialize with these students? Discuss with a peer.

MILITARY FAMILIES

There are approximately two million youth under 18 living with a parent or primary caregiver in the military. These children and adolescents typically face numerous challenges unique to military life, and while most are able to cope with these issues in developmentally appropriate ways, others may require additional support. Below is a brief overview of the two most common challenges faced by military families, followed by suggestions for counselors working with this population.

■ **Frequent relocation.** Military families are often required to relocate every few years, or even more frequently during times of conflict. These moves may take families to new states or even overseas, causing children to experience both emotional strain and losses such as friends, schools, homes, neighborhoods, and routines. In extreme cases, children may exhibit attachment issues or an unwillingness to engage peers or school staff after a move. Others may be depressed or anxious before or immediately after a move. Adults may notice typical trauma symptoms such as anger, "clinging" or developmental regression, and difficulty concentrating.

■ **Deployment of a loved one.** In times of conflict, it is not unusual for a military member to be deployed for weeks, months, or even years at a time. Families typically endure three stages of deployment, each of which brings unique challenges. During the pre-deployment stage, families typically try to draw closer, but it is not unusual for at least one member to pull away in an attempt to prepare for the extended absence. Anxiety and tension may also run high as arrangements are made for things like child care and finances, and as the non-deploying parent begins to imagine the burden of an increased workload at home. During the deployment, the primary concern is typically safety, both for the deployed parent and for the family left behind without their "protector." Children may also exhibit typical signs of separation anxiety during this time, ranging from bedwetting and unexplained fear or crying in younger children to physical complaints (stomachaches, headaches) and decreased school performance in older children and adolescents. Post-deployment, the immediate joy of being reunited can sometimes be overshadowed by the challenges of readjusting to life as a family. These challenges might include difficulties the deployed parent is having with a return to civilian life, including coping with traumas experienced in a combat theater. During this time, young children may have trouble reconnecting with the deployed parent, and may even have difficulty recognizing them or submitting to their authority. Older children and adolescents may resent the deployed parent for having left them, made them worry, and may lament the return to old parenting routines and modes of discipline.

Suggestions for working with military children will now be outlined.

- Counseling strategies for coping and resilience are generally enough to support a child before or after a move or parental deployment. Creative methods such as play, bibliotherapy, art, journaling, and music could be helpful ways to facilitate sharing. For example, a family took one photo per day while a parent was deployed and created an album that both recognized the strength and resilience of the family during this time and also celebrated the parent's return. Writing letters or emails to old friends or a deployed parent can be therapeutic. Group counseling or other organized opportunities for kids to process these challenges with their peers can also be extremely helpful.
- Emphasize confidentiality since military families frequently worry that seeking out counseling or therapy could be a detriment to the service member's career. It is part of the military culture to be strong in the face of challenges, so even seeking out the help of a counselor can be a difficult step. Reassure children and families that you will remain impartial, keep their information confidential, and stand at the ready to be helpful in any way possible.
- Do your best to learn military acronyms, jargon, and ways of life. While military families frequently appreciate the opportunity to interact with those outside the "chain of command," it can be frustrating for them to adjust the language and behavior to do so. The more misinformed a counselor is, the more of an "outsider" they will seem to the family—and the more difficult it will be to establish rapport.
- Since children frequently take emotional cues from adults during difficult times, counselors may do well to connect with a child's caregivers during times of transition to remind them that a positive outlook and attitude could be one way of helping their child cope. When faced with a move, parents might emphasize the positives, such as the perks of career advancement and opportunities to experience a new culture (seeing new places, trying new foods, meeting different types of people, etc.).

Case Study

You are working in a community with a large military population and have been asked by the principal of the local elementary school to set up supports for K-5 students who are having social, academic, or behavioral difficulties.

Process Questions

1. What might be your primary concerns with this population?
2. What types of interventions might you set up to address these concerns?
3. How would your interventions look different with older students, such as those in high school?

The previous three sections discussed three unique groups of young people (LGBT, youth with disabilities, and those in military families). While many children and adolescents belonging to one of these groups are leading perfectly healthy and well-adjusted lives, each group is susceptible to various negative outcomes with regard to academic, social, and mental wellbeing. Counselors should be aware of the typical needs and risk factors of these groups, and should provide interventions and/or advocate on their behalves as needed.

SUMMARY

Risk factors are life circumstances that threaten to harm the physical or mental wellbeing of a person. Protective factors (such as family and social support, high self-esteem, and emotional coping skills) can instill resilience, or the ability to "bounce back" after experiencing difficulties in children under 18. Counselors should assess for risk factors as well as resilience, continuously working to increase the presence of protective factors in each client's life.

Trauma is highly prevalent in childhood and adolescence, and its negative impacts on the physiological and emotional wellbeing of survivors is well documented. Counselors should be aware of these facts and ready to recognize and assess the symptoms and impacts of trauma.

Grief is a personal response and unique to each person. However, counselors need to be able to recognize typical responses to grief for children and adolescents that include grief bursts expressed by anger, sadness, confusion, denial, and questioning. It is common for youth to re-grieve as they reach each developmental milestone.

Natural disasters can strike virtually any community at any time. In addition to the direct impacts of the disaster, young people often experience secondary losses such as their community of residence or school friends. Various nonprofit and government agencies such as the Red Cross and FEMA provide a plethora of resources for helping survivors cope.

Over 40 per cent of persons under the age of 18 experience some form of violence in any given year. Survivors are at risk for a variety of outcomes, including anxiety, anger, and insomnia. A good first step for helping professionals is establishing safety and trust in the counseling office, and helping the client identify strategies for doing so at home and school. Child abuse and neglect takes many forms, from physical or emotional battery to sexual abuse to failure to provide for basic needs. Counselors should be on the lookout for signs of abuse and neglect, such as physical marks, clothing worn to hide certain body parts, and attachment issues. Counselors should be frank in asking about abuse and should never hesitate to report suspected cases of abuse/neglect to the proper authorities.

Before turning 18, 15 per cent of females and 6 per cent of males experience sexual abuse or violence. While outward physical signs are rare, counselors may suspect such abuse when clients present with nighttime issues (bed-wetting or nightmares), unexplained fear of certain adults or places, and certain sexual symptoms. Counseling survivors of sexual abuse is difficult, delicate work. Counselors should report all suspected cases of sexual abuse and refer these clients to trained professionals if they feel the work is beyond their scope of practice.

Young people in foster care are likely to have had exposure to a traumatic event. They may have challenges with trust, attachment, and engaging in healthy relationship practices. By providing unconditional positive regard and acceptance, counselors can begin to build an effective and productive therapeutic relationship allowing the counselor to address any mental health concerns.

Suicide is a leading national problem facing our youth. Suicide is preventable and having knowledge and skills for early identification (including risk factors and warning signs) is vital. Depression is the leading cause of suicide in teens. When counseling a student presenting with suicidal ideation, it is vital to stay calm, stay with the young person at all times, and provide unconditional positive regard.

Youth that are demonstrating non-suicidal self-injurious (NSSI) behaviors may be engaging in behaviors such as cutting or scratching oneself, burning, hitting self, and biting (a few of the common self-harming methods). Counselors need to approach these youth with openness and withholding judgment. The focus should be on building the relationship rather than on stopping the NSSI behavior.

Young people who identify as lesbian, gay, bisexual, or transgender (LGBT) are likely to face many difficulties during their school years, including bullying, decreased self-esteem, and drops in school performance. All counselors are called to be non-judgmental and to work to form a healthy therapeutic alliance with LGBT students. Possible issues to address include self-esteem and identity formation, "coming out" to family and friends (when the client is ready), and advocating for fair practices and systemic change as needed.

Almost 6.5 million school-aged youth receive federally funded special education services. The Individuals with Disabilities Education Act (IDEA) projects the rights of these students and provides guidance and mandates for public schools who educate them. Students who are assessed and found to be eligible for protections under IDEA are entitled to a Free Appropriate Public

Education (FAPE) in the Least Restrictive Environment (LRE), and with a course of education designed to meet their needs via an Individualized Education Program (IEP).

Approximately two million youth live with a parent or primary caregiver who is part of the military. These families face numerous challenges, including frequent relocation and deployment. Counselors can support these youth before, during, and after transitions such as these by forming support groups and using creative strategies such as bibliotherapy, art therapy, letter writing, etc.

Additional Resources

Risk and Protective Factors

Search Institute: http://www.search-institute.org/research/developmental-assets
Provides research and resources regarding the 40 Developmental Assets youth.gov: http://youth.gov/youth-topics/youth-mental-health/risk-and-protective-factors-youth. Website offering information and resources specific to the mental health needs of youth

General Trauma Resources

American Counseling Association (ACA) Traumatology Network: http://www.counseling.org/aca-community/aca-groups/interest-networks#Traumatology
The National Center for Trauma-Informed Care (NCTIC): http://www.samhsa.gov/nctic. NCTIC is a division of the Substance Abuse and Mental Health Services Administration (SAMHSA) and provides training and support to a wide variety of community organizations who serve trauma victims, including community mental health agencies
The National Childhood Traumatic Stress Network (NCTSN): http://www.nctsn.org/about-us/network-membersatabase of trauma-focused service providers. An organization that provides data sheets, reading lists, and a variety of other resources for trauma victims, their families, and those who provide service to them. http://www.nctsn.org/resources/topics/treatments-that-work/promising-practices. Promising practices in trauma treatment

Books for Bibliotherapy

A Terrible Thing Happened, Margaret M. Holmes
Reactions, Allison Salloum
Why Did it Happen?, Janice Cohen

Grief and Loss

Center for Grieving Children: http://grievingchildren.org/grief-resources/
Mental Health America: Helping Children Cope With Loss: http://www.mentalhealthamerica.net/conditions/helping-children-cope-loss. This site provides tips and other resources for grieving children
National Alliance for Grieving Children (NAGC): https://childrengrieve.org

The Dougy Center: The National Center for Grieving Children and Families: http://www.dougy.org. This national center provides tremendous grief resources, information, books and training

Disasters

NCTSN, Natural Disasters: http://www.nctsn.org/trauma-types/natural-disasters
Red Cross, Disaster Response Training (including disaster mental health): http://www.redcross.org/take-a-class/disaster-training
SAMHSA, Disaster Distress Helpline: http://www.samhsa.gov/find-help/disaster-distress-helpline#sthash.f1zKF1ER.dpuf

Violence

NCTSN, Community and School Violence Reading List: http://www.nctsn.org/resources/online-research/reading-lists/community-and-school-violence
NCTSN, Interventions for Children Exposed to Domestic Violence: http://www.nctsn.org/content/interventions-children-exposed-domestic-violence-core-principles

Abuse and Neglect

NCTSN, Physical Abuse Reading List: http://www.nctsn.org/resources/online-research/reading-lists/physical-abuse-and-neglect
NCTSN, Sexual Abuse Reading List: http://www.nctsn.org/resources/online-research/reading-lists/sexual-abuseNCTSN, Sexual Abuse Resources: http://www.nctsn.org/trauma-types/sexual-abuse#q9
Prevent Child Abuse America: http://preventchildabuse.org/resources/

Foster Children

Child Welfare Information Gateway: Website providing information, resources, and tools to best support foster children. https://www.childwelfare.gov
Foster Care to Success: Reading and Resource List: http://www.fc2success.org/knowledge-center/resources-for-students-state-workers/

Suicide

American Association of Suicidology: http://www.suicidology.org
Columbia Suicide Severity Rating Scale (C-SSRS): http://www.cssrs.columbia.edu/index.html. Anyone, anywhere can use the C-SSRS. Hospitals, schools, jails, armed forces and many other public health settings are using the scale for suicide risk identification. The C-SSRS has been administered several million times and has exhibited excellent feasibility—no mental health training is required to administer it
National Suicide Prevention Lifeline 1-800-273-TALK: http://www.suicidepreventionlifeline.org/. The National Suicide Prevention Lifeline's mission is to provide immediate assistance to individuals in suicidal crisis by connecting them to the nearest available suicide prevention and mental health service provider. It is the only national suicide prevention and intervention telephone resource funded by the Federal Government

Non-Suicidal Self-Injury

Self-Injury Outreach and Support: http://sioutreach.org. A non-profit outreach initiative providing information and resources about self-injury to those who self-injure, those who have recovered, and those who want to help

The Cornell Research Program on Self-Injury and Recovery: http://www.selfinjury.bctr.cornell.edu/index.html. A website that provides links and resources to self-injury information

Bullying

Association for Behavioral and Cognitive Therapies (ABCT): http://www.abct.org/Information/?m=mInformation&fa=fs_BULLYING_PRO. ABCT provides fact sheets, podcasts, and other helpful strategies specific for mental health counselors working with bullied youth

Connect Safely: Smart Socializing Starts Here: http://www.connectsafely.org/cyberbullying/

National Bullying Prevention Resources: http://www.pacer.org/bullying/resources/

U.S. Department of Health & Human Services: http://www.stopbullying.gov

Violence Prevention Works! Safer Schools, Safer Communities: http://www.violencepreventionworks.org/public/bullying_prevention_resources.page

Sexual Orientation and Gender Identity

American Psychological Association (APA), Promoting Resiliency for Gender Diverse and Sexual Minority Students in Schools: http://www.apa.org/pi/lgbt/programs/safe-supportive/lgbt/resilience.aspx

Gay, Lesbian, and Straight Education Network (GLSEN): http://www.glsen.org. GLSEN provides research and resources to support students, educators, and community members interested in creating positive, affirming school environments

Youth with Disabilities

Understood.org: https://www.understood.org/en. Fifteen non-profit agencies banded together to create Understood.org to provide support and tools for parents raising a child with a learning or attention difficulty

U.S. Department of Education, Office of Special Education and Rehabilitative Services: http://www2.ed.gov/about/offices/list/osers/osep/index.html

Military Families

Military Kids Connect: http://militarykidsconnect.dcoe.mil/. A place for children of military members to learn from and connect with one another online. Includes groups for all age categories

National Military Family Association: http://www.militaryfamily.org/. Resources for families of military members. Includes tools for a wide range of topics including healthcare, education, scholarships, support during deployment, etc.

NCTSN, Childhood Traumatic Grief Resources for Military Children and Families: http://www.nctsn.org/trauma-types/traumatic-grief/military-children

Sesame Street for Military Families: http://www.sesamestreetformilitaryfamilies.org/. Includes many resources about relocation, deployment, injuries, grief, etc.

Suggested Readings

Brymer, M., Jacobs, A., Layne, C., Pynoos, R., Luzek, J., Steinberg, A., Vernberg, E., and Watson, P. (2006). *Psychological first aid: Field response guide*, 2nd ed. Washington, DC: National Childhood Traumatic Stress Network and National Center for PTSD.
National Center for Trauma-Informed Care (2012). Changing communities, changing lives: NCTIC 2012 report. Washington, DC: Author. Retrieved from http://www.nasmhpd.org/sites/default/files/NCTIC_Marketing_Brochure_FINAL(2).pdf
Office on Child Abuse and Neglect (2006). Child neglect: A guide for prevention, assessment, and intervention. Washington, DC: Author. Retrieved from https://www.childwelfare.gov/pubs/usermanuals/neglect/
Siegel, D. (2011). *Mindsight: The new science of personal transformation*. New York: Bantam.

Glossary

Complex trauma: Severe, pervasive trauma that accumulates over time through repeated exposure to traumatic events such as abuse or violence
Foster care: Placement when a youth has been removed from their home due to experiencing some form of serious abuse and/or neglect
Gender variant: Children and adolescents who do not look or behave the way that girls and boys are expected to behave by their families and by society
Grief bursts: A sudden feeling and expression of grief, typically lasting short periods of time
Least restrictive environment (LRE): A requirement of IDEA that schools educate students with disabilities alongside their nondisabled peers to the greatest extent possible
Non-suicidal self-injury: Act when youth intentionally destructs the body or skin but does not have intent to end his or her life; he or she rather is seeking a way to relieve stress or escape problems
Protective factors: Conditions or attributes that mitigate or eliminate risk and can increase the health and wellbeing of individuals.
Resilience: Adapting well in the face of adversity, trauma, tragedy, threats or significant sources of stress—the ability to "bounce back".
Risk factors: Characteristics at the biological, psychological, family, social, community, or cultural level that are commonly associated with an increased likelihood of negative life outcomes
Trauma: Emotional or physical harm resulting from exposure to highly stressful events.
Triggers: People, places, and things that are likely to cause distress by reminding a trauma victim of previous experiences
Warning signs: Cues that can be observed, heard, or viewed in behavior or social changes that commonly connect to suicidal attempts

References

Aina, O. E. and Cameron, P. A. (2011). Why does gender matter? Counteracting stereotypes with young children. *Dimensions of Early Childhood* 39, 11–19.

American Association of Suicidology (2016). Warning signs and risk factors. Washington, DC: Author. Retrieved from http://www.suicidology.org/resources/warning-signs

American Counseling Association (2014). 2014 ACA code of ethics. Alexandria, VA: Author. Retrieved from https://www.counseling.org/resources/aca-code-of-ethics.pdf.

American Foundation for Suicide Prevention and Suicide Prevention Resource Center (2011). *After a suicide: A toolkit for schools.* Newton, MA: Education Development Center, Inc.

American School Counselor Association (2010). Ethical standards for school counselors. Alexandria, VA: Author. Retrieved from https://www.schoolcounselor.org/asca/media/asca/Resource%20Center/Legal%20and%20Ethical%20Issues/Sample%20Documents/EthicalStandards2010.pdf

CDC (2011). Sexual identity, sex of sexual contacts, and health-risk behaviors among students in grades 9–12: Youth risk behavior surveillance. Atlanta, GA: U.S. Department of Health and Human Services.

Centers for Disease Control and Prevention (2013). Web-based Injury Statistics Query and Reporting System (WISQARS) [Online]. National Center for Injury Prevention and Control, CDC (producer). Retrieved from http://www.cdc.gov/injury/ wisqars/index.html.

Centers for Disease Control and Prevention (2015). Behavioral Risk Factor Surveillance System Survey ACE Module Data, 2010. Atlanta, Georgia: U.S. Department of Health and Human Services, Centers for Disease Control and Prevention. Available from http://www.cdc.gov/violenceprevention/acestudy

Child Welfare Information Gateway (2016). Foster care statistics 2014. Washington, DC: U.S. Department of Health and Human Services, Children's Bureau.

Gay, Lesbian and Straight Education Network (2013). 2013 national climate survey. Washington, DC: GLSEN.org. Retrieved from http://www.glsen.org/sites/default/files/2013%20National%20School%20Climate%20Survey%20Full%20Report_0.pdf

Gladden, R. M., Vivolo-Kantor, A. M., Hamburger, M. E., and Lumpkin, C. D. (2014). *Bullying Surveillance among Youths: Uniform Definitions for Public Health and Recommended Data Elements, Version 1.0.* Atlanta, GA; National Center for Injury Prevention and Control, Centers for Disease Control and Prevention and U.S. Department of Education.

Guan, K., Fox, K. R., and Prinstein, M. J. (2012). Nonsuicidal self-injury as a time-invariant predictor of adolescent suicide ideation and attempts in a diverse community sample. *Journal of Consulting and Clinical Psychology* 80, 842–849.

Kübler-Ross, E. (1969). *On death and dying.* New York: Macmillan.

Neimeyer, R. A. and Anderson, A. (2002). Meaning reconstruction theory. In N. Thompson (ed.), *Loss and grief: A guide for human services practitioners* (pp. 45–64). London: Palgrave.

Perschy, M. (2004). *Helping teens work through grief.* New York, NY: Brunner-Routledge.

Ratts, M. J., Singh, A. A., Nassr-McMillan, S., Butler, S. K., Rafferty McCullough, J. (2015). *Multicultural and social justice counseling competencies.* Alexandria, VA: American Counseling Association.

Ray, N. (2007). *Lesbian, gay, bisexual and transgender youth: An epidemic of homelessness.* New York: National Gay and Lesbian Task Force.

Stack, S. (2003). Media coverage as a risk factor in suicide. *Journal of Epidemiology and Community Health* 57 (4), 238–240. Washington, DC: National Gay and Lesbian Task Force. Retrieved from http://www.thetaskforce.org/downloads/HomelessYouth.pdf

Substance Abuse and Mental Health Services Administration (2015). Prevention and behavioral health: Risk and protective factors. Retrieved from http://www.samhsa.gov/capt/practicing-effective-prevention/preventionbehavioral-health/risk-protective-factors

U.S. Census Bureau (2013). Age and sex composition in the United States: 2012: Table 1. Retrieved from census.gov/population/age/data/2012comp.html

U.S. Department of Education, National Center for Education Statistics (2015a). *Digest of Education Statistics, 2013* (NCES 2015-011), Chapter 2. Retrieved from https://nces.ed.gov/fastfacts/display.asp?id=64.

U.S. Department of Education, National Center for Educational Statistics (2015b). Student Reports of Bullying and Cyberbullying: Results from the 2013 School Crime Supplement to the National Victimization Survey. Retrieved from: http://nces.ed.gov/pubsearch/pubsinfo.asp?pubid=2015056.

U.S. Department of Health and Human Services (2016). Child welfare information gateway. https://www.childwelfare.gov/

U.S. Department of Health and Human Services, Administration for Children and Families, Administration on Children, Youth and Families, Children's Bureau (2016). Child maltreatment 2014. Retrieved from http://www.acf.hhs.gov/programs/cb/research-data-technology/statistics-research/child-maltreatment

U.S. Department of Justice, Office of Juvenile Justice and Delinquency Prevention (2015). Children's exposure to violence, crime, and abuse: An update. Retrieved from http://www.ojjdp.gov/pubs/248547.pdf.

Willoughby, B. (2012). *Speak up at school: How to respond to everyday prejudice, bias and stereotypes.* Montgomery, AL: Teaching Tolerance project of the Southern Poverty Law Center.

PART VI

Creativity, Expressive Arts, and Play Therapy

Evidence-Based Strategies, Approaches and Practices with Youth, and Future Directions and Trends in Counseling Youth

CHAPTER 14

Creativity, Expressive Arts, and Play Therapy

Kimberly M. Jayne and Katherine E. Purswell

It is in playing and only in playing that the individual child or adult is able to be creative and to use the whole personality, and it is only in being creative that the individual discovers the self.

Donald Woods Winnicott, *Playing and Reality*, 1996

Play is the highest expression of human development in childhood, for it alone is the free expression of what is in a child's soul.

Friedrich Froebel, *The Education of Man*, 1898

CHAPTER OBJECTIVES

After completing this chapter, readers will be able to:

- understand the role and purpose of creativity, expressive arts, and play in child and adolescent counseling
- identify benefits, procedures, and considerations for incorporating expressive arts into child and adolescent counseling
- identify benefits, procedures, and considerations for incorporating bibliotherapy into child and adolescent counseling
- identify benefits, procedures, and considerations for incorporating games, music, drama, and puppets into child and adolescent counseling
- understand the history of play therapy and major philosophical and theoretical approaches to play therapy
- identify the goals of play therapy and understand the fundamental nonverbal and verbal counseling skills used in play therapy
- understand the purpose and benefits of additional applications of play therapy in child and adolescent counseling including sandtray, filial, Theraplay, and Kinder therapy
- access additional resources to increase knowledge and skill in child and adolescent counseling and for use in practice with children and adolescents

INTRODUCTION

Children and adolescents grow, develop, and heal through creativity, art and play (Gladding, 2008; Landreth, 2012; Malchiodi, 2005a; Ray, 2011). Each of these counseling approaches allows youth to explore and express their experiences in mediums that honor the way they naturally encounter, interact, and understand the world and themselves. Utilizing these essential and developmentally responsive approaches is critical for effective counseling with children and adolescents in both clinical and school settings. The purpose of this chapter is to introduce readers to the fundamentals of utilizing creativity, art, and play in counseling to promote the wellbeing and development of children and adolescents in a variety of settings.

CREATIVITY

Counseling is, in and of itself, a creative endeavor. No two people are alike, thus no counselor–client dyad is alike. Both counselors and clients spend their time together trying to find unique ways of describing and addressing life's problems. In fact, Gladding (2008) argues that the history of counseling is a creative endeavor to find increasingly effective ways to address life's challenges. Thus the use of approaches beyond talk therapy is merely an extension of a long history of finding unique ways to help people.

Although creative practice in counseling has formally existed for almost half a century (Rosen and Atkins, 2014), limited research exists demonstrating the effectiveness of creative approaches. One reason for the lack of empirical research in art therapy and related fields could be the scarcity of professionals trained in research procedures as well as the difficulty measuring the variable of import (Eaton, Doherty, and Widrick, 2007). Notable exceptions to the limited research in the field of creative interventions include the strong research base for child-centered play therapy (CCPT), filial therapy, and Theraplay. Although much of the research for other modalities, such as art therapy (Eaton et al., 2007), are positive, the majority of the research involves case examples or single-group designs that lack the research rigor required to demonstrate effectiveness. However, the limited research does not indicate these creative approaches are not effective; it merely suggests that we do not yet know the extent to which they help clients beyond other approaches. Creative approaches to counseling certainly have considerable acceptance in the field of counseling— there is an entire American Counseling Association division—The Association for Creativity in Counseling—dedicated to creativity.

In this chapter, the term "creativity in counseling" is used "as a broad term for practices that typically include a variety of therapeutic approaches used in a creative way" (Rosen and Atkins, 2014, p. 298).

Regardless of theoretical orientation, most counselors would agree that the ability to be creative is an indicator of mental health. When people feel anxious, depressed, defeated, or hopeless, creativity is suppressed. The accepting, caring relationship established in counseling can provide people with the safety to be creative, and creativity in the counseling process can help people grow and heal so that they can feel a greater level of self-expression

> **Process Question**
>
> 1. Think about your own perception of creativity. Do you see yourself as a creative person? Has your creativity grown or waned at different points in your life? Can you connect those changes to any life events or seasons of your life?

in their lives outside of counseling. Creativity in counseling can help clients express themselves in new ways and develop new ways of seeing themselves and others (Karkou and Sanderson, 2006).

Creative arts therapy is a broad term that describes the use of a variety of methods beyond talk therapy to help clients creatively address their life concerns. These approaches can be particularly useful when working with young people because creative arts naturally appeal to children and adolescents' developmental needs. Child and adolescent counselors work to provide environments where young people can access and express their own creativity through a variety of means. Although a strong research base does not exist for all creative modalities, scholars have begun to discuss the need for research in these areas and to propose appropriate methodologies. Expressive arts, a field closely related to creativity in counseling, will be discussed next.

Creativity in counseling can help clients express themselves in new ways and develop new ways of seeing themselves and others (Karkou and Sanderson, 2006).

EXPRESSIVE ARTS

In contrast to general use of creativity in counseling, expressive arts therapy refers to the use of a variety of media, such as art supplies, clay, painting, and others, to facilitate a deeper therapeutic process. Compared to those who endorse creative practice, counselors who utilize expressive arts believe that the process itself can be healing when conducted in the context of a safe, caring relationship (Rosen and Atkins, 2014). Expressive arts can help clients to represent their internal experience externally, with enough distance to engage with challenging and painful material in a way they might not be able to do if they simply talked about their internal processes. Indeed, from a developmental perspective, children and even some adolescents may not be able to verbalize their internal processes in a way that leads to emotional healing (Ray, 2011).

The use of expressive arts can vary along a continuum of very directive to very non-directive interventions. That is, the counselor may take sole responsibility for determining what the client will do in the session, the counselor may allow the client to interact with the materials in the way the client chooses without giving suggestions, or the counselor may fall anywhere in between. The non-directive use of expressive arts will be discussed in the section on play therapy below. Thus, the first part of this chapter will focus primarily on the use of expressive arts elsewhere on the continuum.

Expressive arts can be a powerful tool for a counselor. However, expressive arts can also bring up thoughts or feelings for the client that are unexpected and that may sometimes feel unsafe. Therefore, ethical counselors will be certain they have received proper training in foundational counseling skills as well as the expressive modality they would like to employ. Ongoing supervision and consultation is recommended.

Expressive arts are often viewed as fun techniques to engage the client, but they should be used within a counselor's established theoretical framework, philosophy of counseling, and scope of training. The use of expressive arts merely to give the client something interesting to do may not be as effective, and at worst can be harmful. When expressive arts are intentionally integrated into a counselor's theoretically based case conceptualization of a client, the approaches can be powerful tools for facilitation of client growth, healing, and change. Although games and bibliotherapy are not expressive media *per se*, they are explored in this section as well.

Art in Counseling

Counselors who feel self-conscious or embarrassed about their own art abilities may have more difficulty being present and accepting of their clients' differing art abilities. This concept does not mean counselors have to be great artists—just that they need to be OK with not being excellent artists.

To explore your feelings about your own art abilities, try this activity. Think about your first experiences with art and the messages you received about art as a child or adolescent. Perhaps you see art as a way to express yourself or maybe something to be feared. Try expressing yourself using any form of art you choose and notice what feelings come up for you as you work. Then notice what feelings come up for you as you look at your finished produce. Maybe you feel embarrassed or satisfied, inhibited or relaxed. How might your feelings about yourself as an artist positively or negatively impact your work with clients?

An introduction to the use of art in counseling must include a discussion regarding the difference between art therapy and the use of art in counseling. Art therapy is a professional field of study, and an individual may receive a degree in art therapy. Art therapists take courses in art, art theory, and in the therapeutic use of art, whereas a counselor who uses art in counseling need not have extensive training in art techniques. Furthermore, some art therapists may tend to focus more on the product than the process (Moon, 2008). Here, the focus is on art in counseling.

Art can be used as visual communication that helps clients express feelings and experiences that are difficult to explain with words (Malchiodi, 2005a). Many children and adolescents enjoy using art materials and, when given the opportunity, readily employ art to express themselves. In addition, the use of art in counseling has been utilized from a variety of theoretical frameworks (Moon, 2008). In school or office settings where counselors may not have resources or space for a wide variety of play materials, a relatively small number of art materials can provide a wide range of expression for clients. For example, construction paper, office paper, crayons, markers, prepackaged paint sets, scissors, glue, pipe cleaners, and leftover egg cartons or cardboard boxes are all relatively inexpensive and small. These few items allow for a broad variety of expressive projects.

The number and use of art activities in counseling is dependent only on the creativity of the client and counselor, and an overview of even the more common art activities is beyond the scope of this chapter. Some examples include family drawings, mandalas, rosebush activity (Oaklander, 1978), family genograms, career genograms, draw your feelings, personal logo, clay creatures, masks, group murals, body outline drawings (Gladding, 2011), etc. The possibilities are endless and include providing a range of art materials without giving any specific direction and allowing clients to create whatever they wish.

> The number and use of art activities in counseling is dependent only on the creativity of the client and counselor.

The primary consideration for a counselor wanting to use art in counseling is to receive proper training and supervision. An individual does not need a knowledge of art, but does need knowledge of how to process arts effectively in counseling. Understanding how development impacts the use of art in counseling is very important. Although art is appropriate for most ages, very young children will have an extremely short attention span for drawing and coloring. For young children, their interaction with the counselor while they create the art will be more important than the actual art itself. For example, if a child tests limits around use of glue, this process will likely be more therapeutically beneficial than what the child actually made. Young children should not be expected to be able to process their art beyond concrete descriptions of what they created. Pre-adolescents, with their budding abstract reasoning skills, may be able to engage in some cognitive discussion of their art, but for them the primary value of artwork will likely be in the process of creation rather than in an ensuing discussion. Adolescents, however, may be able to engage fully in both the process of creation and a discussion of what they created. Some adolescents may want to make direct connections between what they created and their own lives, but others will want to stay in the metaphor. Regardless of client age or setting, counselors employing art in counseling will want to allow the client to make personal meaning from the art rather than imposing the counselor's meaning on the project (Malchiodi, 2005a).

In summary, the use of art in counseling is developmentally appropriate for children and adolescents. With children and some adolescents, the process of creating art is likely to be more important than the finished product. Many adolescents will be able to engage in an abstract level of processing with regard to their finished products. To use art effectively and ethically in counseling, practitioners should receive training and supervision. Individuals wishing to pursue a career in the related yet distinct field of art therapy must pursue a specified field of study, including courses in art theory. The next medium to be discussed is bibliotherapy.

BIBLIOTHERAPY

Bibliotherapy refers to the use of the written word (literature, poetry, self-help books, autobiographies, etc.) to aid in the therapeutic process and involves a connection between literature, counselor, and client so that therapeutic growth occurs in both the reading and the application of what was read (Gladding, 2011).

The primary purposes of bibliotherapy are to provide information, help clients develop greater insight into self, increase in empathy for self and others, and grow in awareness of possible solutions for a particular problem (Gladding, 2011; Mardiziah Hayati, 2002). Bibliotherapy is only a part of the therapeutic process and is not intended to be used as the sole modality for counseling. Further, the decision to use bibliotherapy should be guided by an overarching theory or philosophy of counseling, and the counselor must receive sufficient training and supervision before using the modality (Pehrsson and Pehrsson, 2006).

Types of Bibliotherapy

Professionals generally refer to three types of bibliotherapy: Developmental, clinical, and client-developed (Vale Lucas and Soares, 2013). Developmental bibliotherapy consists of providing reading material to help relatively well-adjusted children better cope with normal transitional changes or typical childhood/adolescent concerns. Individuals utilizing developmental bibliotherapy, or any form of bibliotherapy, should have training in human development as well as training in choosing books and facilitating discussions. To implement developmental bibliotherapy, a health teacher might have a middle school class read and discuss a book about their changing bodies. Similarly, during a guidance lesson, a school counselor might read a picture book about a child who was able to effectively deal with bullies.

Clinical bibliotherapy involves use of the written word with individuals who have increased emotional and/or behavioral concerns. Counselors working with children or adolescents referred by teachers or parents would likely be using clinical bibliotherapy individually, or in small groups. For example, with a small group of children who are struggling to adjust to parental divorce, a counselor might read a picture book about an animal who has to live in two homes because her parents divorced and then engage the children in an activity to help them express and process their feelings around divorce. Another counselor might provide an adolescent who witnessed domestic violence with a fictional or autobiographical book about someone who experienced a similar trauma. Clearly the clinical level of bibliotherapy requires a substantial foundation in mental health knowledge. In the example of children from divorced families, the counselor would need to be prepared to address empathically and effectively strong feelings that might come up. In the second example, the counselor would need the clinical skill to assess whether the client was ready for a potentially triggering book as well as the ability to respond therapeutically to the client's reactions to the book.

Client-developed bibliotherapy refers to the client making changes to the storyline or writing a different ending to the book. This type of bibliotherapy can help the client find creative solutions to difficult problems and expand critical thinking around the problem the client or the main character in the book is facing. This use of bibliotherapy may be indicated if the ending of a story is not a good fit for the client or if the counselor wants to help the client think in multiple ways about the problem in the story. For an adolescent client who is struggling with anxiety, a counselor might provide a story about another adolescent who dealt with anxiety in a successful way, and then ask the client to rewrite the end of the story. This activity could both help the counselor to assess the client's problem-solving skills and provide the client the opportunity to think in new ways about the topic.

Process of Bibliotherapy

The first step in implementing bibliotherapy is to receive sufficient training that will prepare the counselor for the phases of bibliotherapy described below (Mardiziah Hayati, 2002). First, the counselor must assess the issue that seems most relevant to the client. Once the counselor has identified this concern of focus, the counselor creates a list of potential literature sources and then carefully reviews for developmental appropriateness, relevance to the client's life, and relevance to the issue of focus. A counselor should never provide reading material the counselor has not thoroughly read ahead of time.

After the counselor has selected material appropriate for the client(s), the counselor develops a plan for helping the clients make the most of the material. For example, the counselor might think of questions to ask during the reading to keep the client(s) engaged and connected to the material. The counselor will also want to plan a follow-up activity. For older adolescents, this could include a discussion of the text. For younger children as well as all ages of adolescents, the counselor could prepare another type of expressive arts activity to help the clients make the most of the experience (Vale Lucas and Soares, 2013).

Bibliotherapy Considerations

Counselors implementing bibliotherapy may confront some challenges. First, bibliotherapy may not be appropriate for all clients, and care should be taken to utilize bibliotherapy within a larger therapeutic context. Further, counselors using bibliotherapy may have to work to ensure that the use of a book does not damage the therapeutic relationship. Some clients may perceive the counselor's use of a book as sending a message that the client should deal with their problem on their own or that the counselor and client should not talk directly about the problem. Other clients may dislike reading or have a reading disability or visual impairment, and being asked to read a book outside of session may seem like onerous homework rather than a therapeutic experience. Counselors using bibliotherapy should also be aware of their own needs for the client(s) to change. Is the counselor trying to get the client to see a point of view the counselor believes is right? If so, the use of bibliotherapy could send a message that the client needs to change in order to be accepted by the counselor, a situation that is unconducive to therapeutic growth.

Research indicates that many clients respond positively to bibliotherapy (McCulliss and Chamberlain, 2013), and most of the considerations mentioned above can be addressed through adequate training and counselor self-awareness. For example, even children who dislike reading themselves or have difficulty reading due to a physical or learning disability often enjoy being read to by another person. Thus, a counselor working with children could read aloud books with many pictures, few words, and an engaging message. As with any other therapeutic intervention, bibliotherapy must be used with intentionality and adequate training. When these conditions are met, bibliotherapy can be a valuable resource for working with children and adolescents and even their parents.

Process Question

1. Think about a book that was particularly meaningful to you at some point in your life. How do you think that book had therapeutic value for you?

Three types of bibliotherapy exist, and all require a knowledge of child development and training. Developmental bibliotherapy is the use of books to assist individuals to continue to cope in healthy ways with typical developmental challenges, such as puberty or moving to a new school. Clinical bibliotherapy refers to a mental health professional's use of books and processing activities to help clients successfully deal with challenging life events with which they might be struggling. Client-directed bibliotherapy involves the client adding to the story, such as writing a new ending or adding another plot line. Counselors using bibliotherapy need to consider ethical issues as well as the client's reading capabilities and attitude toward reading before implementing bibliotherapy. Although research shows bibliotherapy to be useful, it should not be used as the only therapeutic intervention within a counseling relationship. Board games are another activity some counselors use with children. Their use will be discussed below.

Table 14.1 Children's literature organized by topic

Family and Life Transitions	*The Family Book*, Todd Parr *Rosie's Family: An Adoption Story*, Lori Rosove and Heather Burrill *Living with Mom*, Melanie Walsh *Living with Dad*, Melanie Walsh *Two Homes*, Claire Masurel *Kindergarten Here I Come*, D. J. Steinberg *You're Finally Here*, Melanie Watt *Alexander, Who's Not (Do you hear me? I mean it!) Going to Move*, Judit Viorst
Peer Relationships and Bullying	*Enemy Pie*, Derek Munson and Tara Calahan King *Stick and Stone*, Beth Ferry and Tom Lichtenheld *The Invisible Boy*, Patrice Barton *How to Lose All Your Friends*, Nancy Carlson *Lacey Walker Nonstop Talker*, Christianne C. Jones and Richard Watson *The Recess Queen*, Alexis O'Neill and Laura Huliska-Beith *The Name Jar*, Yangsook Choi *A Bad Case of Tattle Tongue*, Julia Cook and Anita DuFalla *Those Shoes*, Maribeth Boelts and Noah Z. Jones

Empathy and Emotional Awareness	**Elementary** *Bear Feels Scared*, Karma Wilson *The Way I Feel*, Janan Cain *In My Heart: A Book of Feelings*, Jo Witek *Alexander and the Terrible, Horrible, No Good, Very Bad Day*, Judith Viorst *My Mouth is a Volcano*, Julia Cook *Too Shy for Show and Tell*, Beth Bracken *Hurty Feelings*, Helen Lester **Middle to high school** *Wonder*, R. J. Placio *Mockingbird*, Kathryn Erskine *Out of My Mind*, Sharon M. Draper *Counting by 7s*, Holly Goldberg
Grief and Loss	*Lifetimes: The Beautiful Way to Explain Death to Children*, Bryan Mellonie and Robert Ingpen *I Miss You: A First Look at Death*, Pat Thomas and Leslie Harker *The Invisible String*, Patrice Karst and Geoff Stevenson *Sad Isn't Bad*, Michaelene Mundy and R. W. Alley *I'll Always Love You*, Hans Wilhelm *When Dinosaurs Die*, Laurie Krasny Brown and Marc Brown *A Terrible Thing Happened*, Margaret M. Holmes and Sasha J. Mudlaff
Self-Esteem	*You*, Sam McBratney *Giraffes Can't Dance*, Giles Andreae *The Most Magnificent Thing*, Ashley Spires *The Girl Who Never Made Mistakes*, Mark Pett and Gary Rubinstein *Beautiful Oops*, Barney Saltzberg *Spaghetti in a Hot Dog Bun*, Maria Dismondy and Kathy Hiatt *The Dot*, Peter H. Reynolds

USE OF GAMES

The use of games in counseling with children and adolescents is generally intended to serve one of three purposes: To occupy client's energy and encourage verbal communication, to teach specific skills, or to provide an opportunity to assist clients in gaining insight into their ways of relating to themselves and others. Regardless of the reason a counselor chooses to use games, the decision should be made with intentionality and attention to the needs of the specific client (Bellison, 2002). Here, the focus is on the last two purposes.

> Regardless of the reason a counselor chooses to use games, the decision should be made with intentionality and attention to the needs of the specific client (Bellison, 2002).

Developmental Considerations

From a developmental perspective, children begin to understand games with rules around age 6 with the onset of Piaget's Concrete Operational stage. Even though elementary-aged children are able to understand games with rules, and may enjoy them, the developmental needs for movement and dramatic play tend to supersede their ability to sit still and play games for extended periods of time. Of the three purposes mentioned above, none seem to have a strong rationale for elementary-aged children. Verbal language is not children's primary means of communication, so occupying their energy/hands to increase verbal communication would not be likely to be as productive as providing the children with imaginative play materials. Children in the concrete operational stage do not have the ability for abstract thinking. Thus, while they may be able to learn a skill, they are less likely to be able to transfer it to another situation (Ray, 2011). With regard to facilitating insight into relational patterns, imaginative play material would also better serve this purpose.

From a cognitive perspective, pre-teens and adolescents have increasing abilities for verbal communication and abstract thought. Depending on the purpose of counseling, games could be appropriate for these age groups, but should be chosen and introduced with intentionality and care. Pre-teens in particular may be in transition between developmental stages and some pre-teens may benefit from interventions targeting younger children while others may be moving more rapidly toward abstract thought.

Competitive Games

As with any games, competitive games should be used with intention and not just to provide mutual fun (Berlin, 2001). Many therapists choose to provide a range of board games in their counseling rooms for pre-teens and adolescents. Therapists likely do not want to choose games that require lengthy set up or lengthy rule explanation due to limited time in counseling sessions. They also will not want to choose games for which they have a personal disliking, as their feelings toward a game may get in the way of acceptance toward a child who chooses that game. Some counselors choose not to provide games at all, reasoning that, in a permissive environment, if a client wants to invent a game with rules, he or she will do so. Electronic games are discouraged in relationship-based counseling for a variety of reasons including the limited interpersonal interactions available in many electronic games as well as the fact that it is almost impossible to break the rules (Bellison, 2002).

Clients' manipulation of or disregard for the rules often provides the primary source for therapeutic work around competitive game play. Bellison (2002) suggests that clients should be allowed to cheat as this provides room for the counselor and client to have open conversations about the client's need to cheat and the underlying desires or feelings that prompt the cheating. Many other adults exist in the client's life to teach him or her the importance of following rules. This is not to say that the counselor should ignore the cheating.

Case Study: Michael

As an example, if the counselor observes 13-year-old Michael secretly discarding two cards per turn in order to run out of cards and win, the counselor might reflect how important it is for Michael to win. Depending on the counselor's relationship with Michael, the counselor might reflect that it is so important for Michael to win that he would rather win by not following the rules than win at all. The counselor might even reflect that Michael feels bad about himself if he doesn't win, even though much of the game is based on luck. These kinds of reflections can be more helpful to Michael and further therapeutic work than telling him he is not allowed to break the rules.

When implementing games in therapeutic settings, the counselor must be aware of his or her own process. Some counselors may find it challenging to balance natural competitiveness, a desire to let the client win, and congruence. The counselor should not play to win, but should also not play to lose (Bellison, 2002). Adolescents in particular may be offended if they realize that the counselor is allowing them to win. Counselors may find it helpful to focus on the process rather than on the game play, thus distracting themselves from fully engaging in the content of the game. Use of games is contraindicated for counselors who are unable to successfully focus primarily on the therapeutic process and who are unable to engage genuinely in game play without competitiveness.

Process Question

1. How would you feel if a child or adolescent cheated during a game? What feelings would immediately come up for you, and how could you deal with them so that you could remain therapeutic?

Games Developed for Therapeutic Use

Some games, such as the Talking, Feeling, Doing Game (Gardner, 1973), have been developed specifically for therapeutic use. These games tend to encourage sharing of feelings or thoughts or teach specific skills and often require that the counselor participate in self-disclosure. When used appropriately, games requiring counselor self-disclosure may help strengthen the therapeutic relationship between counselors and adolescents, who often like to know something about their counselors. Bellison (2002) suggests that responses by the counselor should be just as intentional as any other responses in counseling. For example, the counselor may not want to share details of their life, but may want to share certain feelings and general experiences with which the client can connect. For example, if a counselor draws a card about the worst part of his day, the counselor might say, "I had an argument with someone in my family this morning, and afterward I was so mad at myself for getting upset over something that wasn't really a big deal. I think I was feeling jealous of the person, so I lashed out." This kind of response does not share personal details, but it does share something of the person of the counselor. It also models elaboration in responses and a building of rapport rather than giving the quick, easy answer.

Although children often enjoy games with rules, from a developmental perspective games tend to be less helpful for children than other more expressive and kinesthetic interventions. Adolescents, however, may benefit from

Table 14.2 Games for use in counseling with children and adolescents

Game	Brief Overview and Potential Relationship Concerns
Uno by Mattel	Try to discard all one's cards. Call "Uno" when the other person has only one card. May require counselor to decide whether to use a "skip" card on the client.
Trouble by Hasbro	Move spaces to try to get all one's pieces home before opponent. May require counselor to choose whether to send a client's piece back to start.
Chutes and Ladders by Hasbro	Move one's game piece from start to finish. Landing on a "chute" requires one to go backward. Landing on a "ladder" allows one to move forward. Primarily based on luck.
Checkers	Remove opponent's checkers by jumping them. Fairly simple rules.
The Thinking Feeling Doing Game by The Guidance Group	Earn tokens by answering questions or following directions for cards designed that range from fun to moderately stressful issues. Client may choose not to answer and forfeit a token.
The Ungame by Talicor	Non-competitive. Respond to cards on various topics. Promotes communication and connection.
Jenga by Hasbro	Simple rules and can be utilized in various manners to facilitate interaction. May be competitive.
Ringtoss	Engages children physically. Client may create own rules and degree of challenge. Potential to be competitive.
Lifestories by Talicor	Facilitates expression and storytelling. May require counselor to share some personal information.

playing games when the therapist is able to respond in a therapeutic manner. Games introduced into the counseling room should be carefully chosen for therapeutic value and used according to the counselor's guiding theory. Traditional board games or card games can have therapeutic value when the counselor responds to situations, such as cheating, in an accepting, caring way. Additionally, games have been developed for therapeutic use and can be a helpful starting place in building the relationship and beginning to discuss meaningful topics. As with any new modality, counselors should receive adequate supervision when beginning to introduce games into the counseling room. This may be particularly important in monitoring one's own competitiveness.

USE OF MUSIC

Music therapy is the integration of musical concepts and psychotherapy. Music can help to improve physical, cognitive, psychological, and social functioning (Degges-White, 2011). To become a licensed music therapist, an individual must have a background in music and go through a specific training program, but a counselor does not need a background in music to incorporate certain aspects of music into sessions. Counselors who do not wish to become music therapists but do wish to incorporate music into sessions with children and adolescents should also seek out appropriate training and supervision.

Individuals receiving music therapy may compose and play their own music, or they may engage in activities related to music (Degges-White, 2011). Typically, a counselor without specific training in music therapy will use music in more informal ways. For example, the counselor may provide instruments for the client to use to express the self, or may encourage the client to respond to the music by singing, dancing, or an expressive arts activity (Karkou and Sanderson, 2006). Music may be particularly useful to incorporate into sessions with adolescents whether as a way of connecting with the adolescent or providing a culturally relevant means of expression. One way of using music in this way would be to ask an adolescent to create a musical autobiography by putting together a playlist of songs (with lyrics when applicable) that describe who the adolescent is (Gladding, 2011).

Many other uses for music in counseling exist. A school counselor could use songs to help children remember key concepts in a guidance lesson (Gladding, 2011). For example, a school counselor may use Echosmith's *Cool Kids* to promote perspective-taking, develop empathy, and discuss concepts of bullying and social relationships at schools. Listening to music can also help set the stage for other expressive activities or provide opportunities for physical and emotional regulation. A counselor might want to have a group of energetic 12-year-olds do a minute or two of guided breathing while listening to calming music before creating mandalas. Another counselor might play various types of music and ask adolescents to tune into the emotions in the music to build emotional awareness. This activity could be adapted for younger children by asking them to express a particular emotion by dancing (for small groups) or moving their fingers (for large groups) to the music. Although rare in general counseling practice, some clients may enjoy bringing in a musical instrument and composing music to express themselves. Others, especially children, may enjoy making their own impromptu music using play xylophones, drums, maracas, cymbals, or other instruments that typically come in a youth music kit.

Some adolescents may feel more comfortable when they have their favorite music playing in the background during talk therapy or expressive arts sessions, although doing so may bring up the issue of explicit lyrics and discriminatory messages in the songs. Such lyrics may be particularly relevant in school settings where a higher expectation for setting limits around language exists. Yet, if the counselor views the lyrics as a form of self-expression, much could be lost by limiting the use of what the counselor might consider negative lyrics. Counselors in both private and school settings may choose not to limit the use of explicit lyrics, but rather to engage the client in a discussion of those lyrics including what the client connects with in the song and how the lyrics impact the client. This approach tends to be appropriate for individual counseling, but more formal ground rules around the inclusion of explicit material may need to be implemented in group settings to maintain the emotional safety of everyone in the group.

Typically, a counselor without specific training in music therapy will use music in informal ways.

In summary, music has a wide variety of uses in counseling and can be a useful tool for many clients, especially adolescents. Music can be used as a medium for exploration or as a calming force. Counselors choosing to invite clients to bring music into sessions must be prepared to deal with explicit lyrics and discriminatory messages. When counselors have a coherent philosophy for how to address such issues, more "negative" lyrics can be a mechanism for therapeutic growth. Regardless of how music is used by counselors, it should be used with intentionality and attention to unique client needs. Similar to the use of music in counseling, drama can help clients express themselves in many ways. Thus, drama will be discussed next.

USE OF DRAMA

Drama therapy is the intentional use of drama in psychotherapy and includes techniques and props like those a drama teacher might use (McFarlane, 2005). As with art and music therapy, drama therapy is a mental health specialty in its own right, and one can receive a degree in Drama Therapy. However, any counselors who receive adequate training and supervision may utilize drama in their counseling practice.

The use of drama in counseling can help a child revisit challenging stages of development (McFarlane, 2005). Drama may also help a client find creative ways to deal with challenges they are experiencing in their lives. It can also help children and adolescents feel less alone through identification with an individual in the drama (Gladding, 2011). Drama can help clients become more comfortable expressing emotions and allow them to explore challenging personal situations while providing some psychological distance from the situation. McFarlane (2005) describes drama therapy as the "use of fiction to express a truth" (p. 3).

> Drama can help clients become more comfortable expressing emotions and allow them to explore challenging personal situations while providing some psychological distance from the situation.

One way drama can be used in counseling is to have the client role-playing real situations. For example, a child who is struggling with a bully might role-play how to respond to the bully with the counselor and client taking turns playing the role of the bully. If a client seems overwhelmed by a situation to the extent that playing out the real situation seems too threatening, the counselor and the client might role-play an imaginary situation that is somewhat similar to the real one. For example, if a child is feeling scared because of parental fighting, the counselor and client might role-play a situation in which a baby rabbit is scared because the big rabbits are fighting. Drama activities can be used with groups as well. For a group focusing on emotional awareness, a counselor might pass out a different emotion to each participant and have the participants take turns acting out short scenarios in which they can only demonstrate the emotion they have been assigned. The others in the group try to guess which emotion each participant is portraying. Counselors working with groups may also want to ask pairs or triads to create a brief play acting out a particular problem and how to deal with it. Then, members of the group could watch each of the small groups perform and discuss the various ways of dealing with the problem. For counselors working with families, family sculpting is a drama activity in which the family describes a situation and one member gets to "sculpt" all the other family members in that situation by arranging them in frozen poses as desired and then adding oneself to the scene. This activity can help family members understand one another's perspectives.

Counselors need to consider whether a client is ready to engage in a particular activity. For example, if an adolescent has low trust in the counselor and low self-esteem, then role-playing an interaction between the adolescent and his mother may result in the adolescent resenting the counselor for trying to interfere in something the counselor does not fully understand. The counselor must also be prepared to respond to client reactions and emotions that might come up during these activities. For example, if a child who is experiencing bullying begins to play out a story about a rabbit who is being bullied, the child may feel more comfortable expressing feelings of anger or fear than if she were speaking directly to the counselor. Thus, the counselor needs to be able to respond both to the feelings and to the content of the play. As can be seen, a strong therapeutic relationship is necessary for successful use of drama in counseling (McFarlane, 2005). Counselors also need to be aware of the differences between using drama in individual versus group settings. In individual settings, the clients may be able to get more deeply into the drama and express higher levels of vulnerability. In group settings, the counselor needs to be careful not to require that clients express too much without having the emotional support to accompany the expression. In addition, drama and group settings can get out of control quickly and lead to some individuals not feeling supported. Thus, it is recommended that counselors introducing drama to groups begin with less threatening types of drama, such as the emotional awareness activity described above, and assess the appropriateness of incorporating drama with deeper levels of expression, such as playing out a story about bullying, before using such activities.

In summary, drama can allow for unique expression and the ability to work through real life problems in a low-stakes or fictional environment. Drama can also help clients become more aware of feelings and can be used to engage both individuals and groups. By carefully assessing the needs of the client, counselors can introduce drama activities that are useful and enjoyable. Counselors wanting to become drama therapists can pursue special training, but any counselors can incorporate drama into sessions with appropriate training and supervision.

Therapeutic writing, which will be discussed next, is similar to the use of drama in that it provides creative expression and storytelling. Therapeutic writing may be appropriate for clients who enjoy expressing themselves, but do not prefer the more kinesthetic mode of drama.

THERAPEUTIC WRITING

Sometimes called scriptotherapy, therapeutic writing may include creative writing and/or poetry writing (Degges-White, 2011). It can allow a client to reflect on and express the self, and it can also help with the resolution of a specific problem (Gladding, 2011). In general, therapeutic writing involves the counselor providing a prompt and the client responding to that prompt. Some clients, such as those with a physical disability, may not be able to write fluently with pen and paper, but these clients could dictate or type the words and thus still participate fully in the activity. Therapeutic writing is most appropriate for adolescents with a command of written language (White and Murray, 2002) because younger children and those who struggle with writing may be so focused on the mechanics of writing that the expressive piece becomes less salient. Of particular concern for school counselors is to communicate that the client's written work is not being evaluated or graded in any way. If therapeutic writing is to be done with elementary or middle school children, the writing aspect should be minimized. For example, children of this age could be asked to respond to sentence stems, and the therapist could write their answers. This strategy might be appropriate for assessment, but more developmentally appropriate strategies for providing a means of expression for children and pre-adolescents exist and are discussed in this chapter.

> Therapeutic writing is probably most appropriate for adolescents with a command of written language.

Therapeutic writing for adolescents can take many forms. Clients might be asked to write a haiku poem about their day or they might be encouraged to journal. An adolescent could re-write an ending to a story to explore different ways of responding to a particular issue (Gladding, 2011). Yalom (2002) reported that he and one client would write letters to one another after each session. The letters described each person's perception of and reactions to that session, and they would discuss the letters with one another. Additionally, the counselor might ask a client to write a letter to the future, current, or past self (White and Murray, 2002).

Case Study: Steph

Steph, a 14-year-old female, is attending individual counseling because she recently revealed that she was physically abused by her previous stepmother. Steph is working through self-blame, and the counselor thinks that writing a letter to her 10-year-old self might help Steph have more compassion and less blame toward herself. In her letter, Steph wrote, "Don't let her tell you you're a bad person. She is just angry at the world and she is taking it out on you. Keep being strong, and don't let her get you down. This will be over soon." Through therapeutic writing, Steph was able to take a different perspective on the abuse. This new outlook allowed her to continue on in her healing process. Similarly, the counselor could have asked Steph to write a letter to her current self from a more experienced future self or the counselor could have asked her to write a letter to her future self about how to deal with self-blame when it comes up.

For many clients, writing can be a powerful tool. However, some clients, particularly those struggling in school, may see themselves as poor writers and may find more work than catharsis in any kind of writing. Counselors need to be sensitive to the extent to which writing can be an effective medium for a particular client. Counselors new to therapeutic writing also need to seek out supervision on the purposeful use of writing so that the client gets the most out of the experience.

Process Question

1. Try keeping a journal for a few days and see if you find it helpful. Perhaps process the experience with a classmate.

In summary, therapeutic writing is most appropriate for adolescents who feel comfortable with the mechanics of writing, whether the "writing" be through typing, dictation, or handwriting. However, some forms of therapeutic writing may be useful for older children and adolescents with learning disabilities or lack of confidence in writing skills. When using therapeutic writing with such clients, the counselor should not expect lengthy or well-developed writing, and plan accordingly. However, for most of these clients who struggle with writing, other expressive activities may be more beneficial. Working with puppets is one such activity.

PUPPETS

A review of literature on the use of puppets in child and adolescent counseling reveals a steady stream of publications in the 1970s through the early 1990s, with fewer manuscripts published in recent years. Nonetheless, puppets are frequently a part of a counselor's toy supply, and may be used in a variety of ways. Specifically, they can be useful in facilitating the symbolic play of children (Kjellstrand Hatwig, 2014). As with most expressive techniques, puppets can be used in both directive and non-directive ways. This section will focus on directive techniques for the use of puppets. The sections below concerning child-centered play therapy and play therapy skills describe how a counselor would engage in non-directive play, including puppet play.

As with most expressive techniques, puppets can be used in both directive and non-directive ways.

Due to the association of puppets as toys for children, puppets may not be well received by adolescents, although some adolescents with lower social/ emotional maturity may enjoy their use. Puppets may be animals and people. Animals allow children to play out their feelings at a deeper level of metaphor than do people, so it is desirable to have a variety of animals in a puppet collection. Animal puppets also tend to be less expensive than human puppets. If people puppets are included in the collection, they should represent as broad a range of ethnicity, gender, and ability as budget/space allows.

Although counselors are likely to gain much important information about the child and the child's view of the world through a child's spontaneous use of puppets, some counselors also use puppets when they want to gather specific information from the child. For example, Kottman and Meany-Walen (2016) suggest puppets as one possible way of gathering information about the family atmosphere in Adlerian play therapy. The counselor might ask a child to use puppets to tell a story about her family or ask to choose a puppet to represent each member of his family.

Puppets may also be used to help a child find new ways to respond to a problem. For example, a counselor might use puppets to tell a story about how a sheep learned that throwing a temper tantrum was not the way to get what he wanted. This technique should not be used until the counselor and child have a strong relationship and the counselor has a basic understanding of how the child views the world and why the child responds to disappointment with a temper tantrum, for example. Counselors wanting to use puppets in directive ways, such as the two examples presented here, should seek out training and supervision. Kottman and Meany-Walen's (2016) *Partners in Play* provides a helpful example of how to integrate directive techniques into a coherent theoretical framework.

In summary, puppets are most appropriate for children and pre-adolescents who still enjoy engaging in imaginative play. Puppets can be used as a way for the child to express the self, as a way to gather information about the child, and as a way to explore problems in the child's life. More directive use of puppetry should be avoided until the counselor and client have established a strong therapeutic relationship. Puppets, art, drama, music, bibliotherapy, therapeutic writing, and games can be useful tools for counselors working with children and adolescents. In addition, counselors need to have a thorough understanding of child and adolescent development as well as a coherent theoretical framework so that they can intentionally choose interventions that are best for individual clients.

Process Question

1. How do you see expressive arts fitting within your theoretical orientation or overall philosophy of counseling?

PLAY THERAPY

Play therapy and play-based approaches are other ways counselors incorporate creativity into child and adolescent counseling. The development of play therapy and its preeminent use in child counseling originated through the early practice of psychoanalysis with children. Specifically, through the research, writings, and teaching of Melanie Klein (1932) and Anna Freud (1946), play therapy was expanded as a structured approach to working with young children. Following the development of the psychoanalytic approach to play therapy, release therapy was developed by David Levy (1938) as a means to promote cathartic release through play. The primary goal of release play therapy was to allow children to process traumatic experiences through play and reach the resolution through catharsis. Proceeding the psychoanalytic and catharthic approaches to play therapy, the person-centered approach to play therapy was developed by Carl Rogers' student and colleague Virginia Axline (1947). Axline applied the key principles of person-centered theory in her work with young children, providing an accepting and empathic environment where children could express themselves verbally and nonverbally through the use of play. Originally developed as non-directive play therapy, Guerney (2001) and Landreth (2002) extended the person-centered approach to play therapy to what is known today as Child-Centered Play Therapy (CCPT).

Process Question

1. Reflect on your favorite toys and play activities as a child at different points in your development. What role did play have in your life? What purpose did play serve?

Play therapy is an evidenced-based (Ray and McCullough, 2015) modality for counseling children between the ages of 3–12 that utilizes play as the primary means of interaction and communication between a child and a counselor in school and clinical settings. In play therapy, children utilize play to symbolize, express, and integrate their experiences as, "toys are used like words by children, and play is their language" (Landreth, 2012, p. 12). In order to meet children within their natural range of communication, social interaction, and developmental capacities, play is the context that allows the counselor to understand and enter the world of the child. Within play therapy, children are provided toys and materials that facilitate creativity, expression, and represent a variety of experiences and feelings within the following categories: Family/nurturing, scary, aggressive, expressive, and pretend/fantasy. Ray (2011) recommends that every toy and material in the playroom is evaluated by the following criteria:

1. What therapeutic purpose will this serve for children who use this room?
2. How will this help children express themselves?
3. How will this help me build a relationship with children? (p. 80)

Toys and materials are selected intentionally to facilitate the relationship between child and therapist and to provide a variety of symbols for a child to express, process, and integrate his or her experiences. Comprehensive lists of toys and play room materials are presented by Landreth (2012) and Ray (2011), including how to create mobile play therapy sets and address needs specific to setting up a play room within a school environment. Play space and materials are organized in a manner that allows a child easy accessibility to materials, freedom and creativity to use the materials in a variety of ways, and to promote predictability, consistency, and safety in the environment.

> Toys and materials are selected intentionally to facilitate the relationship between child and therapist, and to provide a variety of symbols for a child to express, process, and integrate their experiences.

Theoretical Approaches to Play Therapy

Play therapy continues to be approached and practiced from a variety of theoretical orientations including Child-Centered Play Therapy (CCPT), Adlerian Play Therapy (AdPT), Cognitive Behavioral Play Therapy (CBPT), Gestalt Play Therapy, and Jungian Play Therapy (JPT).

Child-Centered Play Therapy

Recognized as the most widely used (Lambert et al., 2005) and well-researched approach to play therapy in the United States, Child-Centered Play Therapy (CCPT) was first conceived as non-directive play therapy by Virginia Axline (1947). Axline wanted to develop a person-centered approach to working with children based on Carl Rogers' (1951) theory of development and conditions for personality change. Within CCPT, the counselor works to create an environment characterized by empathy, unconditional positive regard, and genuineness to facilitate the child's ability to explore and express experiences freely, integrate experiences into their understanding of self, their relationships, and their world, and access their internal resources for growth and change.

First and foremost, the play therapist seeks to provide an environment where the child feels safe, understood, accepted, and valued.

Within CCPT, the therapeutic relationship is considered the context for change, as the child experiences an environment absent of threat then the child is able to access and actualize their own capacities for growth and healing. According to Landreth (2012) the goals of CCPT are to promote the child's self-concept, personal responsibility, self-acceptance, self-direction, decision-making, self-control, coping skills, self-confidence and trust, and internal locus of evaluation. CCPT is the theoretical approach with the strongest empirical evidence supporting its use and effectiveness with children in a variety of contexts and with a range of developmental, emotional, and mental health challenges (Bratton and Lin, 2015; Ray et al., 2015; Ray and McCullough, 2015).

Adlerian Play Therapy

Adlerian Play Therapy (AdPT) is a play therapy approach based on Individual Psychology, as developed by Alfred Adler. According to Adlerian theory, individuals are born with an innate capacity to move towards growth, purpose, and social connection (Kottman, 2011). Each individual's unique perspective and abilities inform his or her view of self and the world, approach to life, and whether the person approaches his or her environment with confidence or a sense of inferiority.

Through the phases of AdPT, the therapist establishes a strong relationship and connection with the child, observes and interacts with the child through the play therapy process to better understand the child's lifestyle, uses techniques to promote the child's self-awareness and understanding, and finally teaches the child new attitudes and skills to engage relationships and their environments differently (Kottman and Meany-Walen, 2015). The goals of AdPT are to foster the "Crucial Cs" for children to feel connected, feel capable, feel they count, and develop courage (Lew and Bettner, 2000). AdPT has a growing research base supporting its use with children experiencing behavioral and emotional difficulties (Kottman and Meany-Walen, 2015).

Cognitive Behavioral Play Therapy

Growing in popularity due to the use and research of cognitive behavioral approaches with adults, Cognitive Behavioral Play Therapy (CBPT) has less research evidence to support its use with children and has limited applications with younger children due to the emphasis on cognition (Ray, 2015). CBPT practice typically incorporates cognitive behavioral techniques utilizing aspects of play, play materials, or a play setting to promote comfort and safety for the child, to support the child's verbal expression, and to teach and model cognitive-behavioral concepts and strategies to the child.

Knell (2009) identifies CBPT as a brief play therapy approach that is directive and structured and aims to modify a child's maladaptive beliefs and behavior through specific treatment goals, selected play activities, education, and praise and interpretations provided by the therapist within the context of a safe and trusting therapeutic relationship. The goal of CBPT is to help the child identify and modify irrational beliefs and to support the child's ability to exercise responsibility for behavior change.

Gestalt Play Therapy

Gestalt Play Therapy is based on the philosophy that the organism acts as a whole, naturally moving towards self-regulation and growth (Blom, 2004). As the child experiences needs and seeks to satisfy those needs, the child either comes into conflict with his or her environment, or is able to resolve one's needs and reach homeostasis. Interaction with the environment or contact is the core context for the development of the child's self-concept (Carroll, 2009). A primary focus of Gestalt play therapy is to help children develop awareness of their needs and processes for getting needs met. The goals are to help the child develop and restore self-regulation, develop awareness of both internal and external experiences, and to utilize the environment to satisfy needs.

Utilizing both nondirective and directive approaches, the Gestalt play therapist encourages play and creativity as the primary means to allow the child to express and experience aspects of self in relationship to their environment, to develop awareness of their own needs and efforts to resolve and satisfy their needs, to develop a stronger sense of self, and to develop the capacity for contact with the counselor and the environment (Carroll, 2009). Play is the mode of communication and context for self-exploration and understanding, and interaction with the environment.

Jungian Play Therapy

Emphasizing the use of symbolic meaning and the self-healing archetype (Green, 2014), Jungian Play Therapy (JPT) is an approach to play therapy that attends to the symbols that children express through their play and access to support positive growth and development. According to Green (2009), "a self-healing archetype is an innate symbol that promotes healing by recognizing and achieving a balanced communication between the ego and the Self" (p. 83). The symbols that children express through play and creative activities reflect the aspects of the child's unconscious that are in need of the most attention.

Throughout the counseling process, the Jungian play therapist attends to the symbols the child utilizes and to the child's movement towards symbols that reflect the self-healing archetype. Through the reconciliation of polarities, differences between a child's internal and external experiences, and integration of the shadow self, a child may experience and express a more balanced and whole sense of self and engage in relationships and environments with greater ease (Green, 2014). The goal of JPT is for a child to move towards individuation, becoming a whole, integrated psychological individuation through the use and transformation of symbols.

Process Question

1. What theoretical approach to play therapy resonates most with your belief system about how children develop, struggle, and change? What approach is most consistent with how you work with individuals across the life span?

There are many theoretical approaches to play therapy. All play therapy approaches utilize play as the means for building a therapeutic relationship, communicating, and interacting with children. Although more theoretical approaches to play therapy exist and are used in practice, CCPT, AdPT, Cognitive Behavioral play therapy, Gestalt play therapy, and JPT are among the most widely discussed in literature with varying empirical evidence for their use with children. Further exploration of theory, training, and supervision is necessary to understand the best approach for an individual counselor and within specific settings. Beyond understanding theoretical approaches to play therapy understanding the goals and fundamental skills utilized in play therapy is essential for effective practice.

Goals of Play Therapy

While the goals of play therapy may differ according to the applications and theoretical approaches utilized, most play therapy approaches incorporate the following opportunities and objectives for supporting children's growth and development.

1. A first and primary goal of play therapy is to allow the child to express a range of feelings, thoughts, and experiences utilizing the child's natural language and means of communication and honoring the child's developmental process and capacities. By allowing the child to express one's self through play, the counselor is able to fully engage and enter the child's world. Play therapy provides the opportunity for the child to express his or her thoughts and feelings symbolically in the same manner that adults may use words and verbal expression to symbolize their experiences.
2. Play therapy provides the opportunity for a child to explore and work through the issues and experiences that are of importance to the child.

Play allows the child to lead and collaborate more fully and equally in the therapeutic process.

3. Through the use of play, the child is able to communicate more fully and freely with the counselor, engage within the therapeutic relationship, and develop social skills. Play is a natural context for social relationships and connection in childhood that promotes a strong therapeutic alliance between the child and counselor.

4. Children utilize play to develop a sense of mastery, control, and order over their world and environments. Through fantasy, children can create and experience in play what may not be possible in reality allowing them to develop new perspectives, learn new skills, gain self-understanding, increase self-esteem, and regulate their emotions and behavior.

Play is a natural context for social relationships and connection in childhood that promotes a strong therapeutic alliance between the child and counselor.

Play Therapy Skills and Techniques

While each theoretical approach to play therapy may incorporate unique skills and techniques, several fundamental attitudes and skills are utilized across most approaches to play therapy. First and foremost, the play therapist seeks to provide an environment where the child feels safe, understood, accepted, and valued. To convey these attitudes, the play therapist utilizes a variety of nonverbal and verbal skills.

Child-Centered Play Therapy is the theoretical approach with the strongest empirical evidence supporting its use and effectiveness with children (Bratton and Lin, 2015; Ray et al., 2015; Ray and McCullough, 2015).

Body Position

Counselors provide safety and warmth by positioning themselves in a consistent chair or location in the playroom. He or she maintains an open and inviting stance towards the child, allows the child to invite the counselor into his or her space and play, and conveys engagement and interest in the child's play by leaning forward toward the child and keeping his or her eyes and body focused on the child.

Tone of Voice

Counselors utilize tone of voice to match the child's affect conveying emotional understanding and awareness of the child's experience in the moment. Counselors also aim to utilize the tone of their voice to express congruently their own thoughts or feelings, speaking in a manner that is natural and reflective of the child's and one's own experience.

Matching

Counselors naturally and consciously work to match the child's affect, facial expressions, body position, and movement. An essential component of demonstrating empathy, understanding, regard, and care to the child is subtle and intentional eye and micro expressions and physical movements that are congruent and reflective of the child's own expressions and movements. These matching behaviors communicate to the child that the counselor is truly "with him or her" in their play.

Verbal Skills

Utilizing concise and simple verbal responses allows the counselor to convey understanding, empathy, and acceptance to the child while also facilitating the child's therapeutic process and self-awareness. In addition to keeping verbal responses concise and utilizing developmentally appropriate vocabulary, counselors should also attend to the rate of responses, communicating verbally in a manner that matches the affect, activity level, and pace of the child in their play. Fundamental verbal skills include reflecting non-verbal behavior, reflecting content, reflecting feelings, returning responsibility, esteem-building, and limit-setting.

Reflections of Nonverbal Behavior

The counselor conveys understanding and regard for the child by responding to the child's nonverbal and play behaviors. As play is the child's primary mode of communication, the counselor responds to the play by verbally responding and reflecting the child's action by stating what is observed through the child's play. For example, if Javier pours sand into the bucket, the counselor may respond, "You dumped it in there."

Reflections of Content

When children choose to verbalize their thoughts, feelings, and experiences, the counselor may respond to the child by paraphrasing or restating the content of the child's statement. For example, if the child says, "I had pizza for lunch today," the counselor may respond by reflecting "You ate pizza." Reflections of content are utilized to convey empathy and understanding for the child, validate the child's experience, and promote the child's self-awareness.

Reflections of Feeling

As the child expresses emotion nonverbally and verbally, the counselor responds by verbally stating the child's feelings and emotional state. Children primarily express emotion through tone, facial expression, and energy level. Through attunement and careful observation, the counselor identifies the child's emotional experience and states it to convey acceptance, empathy, and help the child express and understand their experience. For example, if Jayda crosses her arms and stomps away from the paint easel, the counselor may respond "You're angry the paint dripped on your picture."

Returning Responsibility

Returning responsibility to the child allows the child to experience self as capable and trustworthy and to develop decision-making skills. Within the context of play therapy, the counselor promotes the child's self-direction by allowing the child to explore and experiment with choices and developmental tasks towards mastery. If Isabel asks the counselor to define a toy or how it is used, or to help with a task that is within her capacity to accomplish, the counselor returns responsibility by saying "In here, you can decide," or "That's something you [or we] can do [together]." Play therapists avoid doing tasks or making decisions that are within the child's capacity.

Esteem-building

Esteem-building responses are utilized to encourage the child and promote his or her self-esteem and positive self-concept. Rather than evaluating the child or using praise, the play therapist responds to the child's efforts and actions with encouragement and recognition for the person of the child rather than the outcome. For example, if the child knocks down all the bowling pins, the counselor may say, "You did it." Or if the child struggles to unlock handcuffs and finally masters the task, the counselor may say, "You worked really hard to get those open."

Therapeutic Limit Setting

Limits are communicated within play therapy to promote the child and the counselor's physical, emotional, and psychological safety, to protect the playroom and materials, to provide structure within the play therapy process, and to protect the therapeutic relationship. Limits are only established as needed and presented to the child in a manner that conveys trust, empathy, and predictability. Although several limit-setting models exist, the primary goal of limit-setting is to provide the child with an opportunity and support to develop self-control and skills to regulate their own emotions and behavior. When setting limits, the counselor verbally acknowledges and empathizes with the child's desire, feelings, or motivation for the behavior (Landreth, 2012; Ray, 2011)—"I know you're really angry with me." Next, the counselor communicates the limit calmly, clearly, and concisely, "But *I* am not for kicking." He or she then provides one or two choices or alternatives for the child to express his or her feelings—"You may kick the stuffed animals or the puppets." The counselor establishes and communicates the limit multiple times as needed to allow the child the opportunity to regulate behavior.

Process Question

1. Observe how you typically communicate with children. What nonverbal and verbal play therapy skills seem the most accessible or natural for you to use and convey? What skills seem the most challenging? Practice using some nonverbal and verbal play therapy skills.

Depending on theoretical orientation, play therapists may use these fundamental skills more frequently or with varying timing to facilitate a child's growth in individual or group play therapy. Additional skills and techniques, specific to each theoretical orientation, may also be used. These fundamental play therapy skills are also utilized in sandtray, filial and theraplay approaches, and in the context of counseling are used both in individual, group play therapy, family counseling, assessment, and classroom guidance programming.

Mastery of the fundamental nonverbal and verbal play therapy skills requires dedication, practice, supervision, and self-reflection. Although synonymous to some skills used in counseling for adolescents and adults, play therapy skills allow the counselor to enter the world of the child through play and facilitate their growth and wellbeing without reliance on the child's ability to verbalize his or her own experience.

Additional Applications of Play Therapy

Play therapy may be utilized with children in both individual and small-group formats. Additional approaches and applications of play therapy include sandtray therapy, filial therapy, and Theraplay. Sandtray therapy is a play therapy approach that is appropriate for children and adolescents to communicate nonverbally and interact through play, and may be a more practical play therapy approach in settings where space or access to materials are limited. Play therapy approaches are utilized to enhance the child–parent relationship and engage parents/caregivers and significant adults in the therapeutic process with the child through filial therapy and Theraplay.

Sandtray

Sandtray is a counseling approach that incorporates aspects of play therapy through the use of sand and miniatures, allowing children and adolescents to express their thoughts, feelings, and experiences through objects and symbols within a safe and contained space. Sandtray (sometimes referred to as sand play) is facilitated by counselors of various theoretical orientations and in a variety of settings to allow children and adolescents a nonverbal, developmentally responsive medium of expression. Homeyer and Sweeney (2011) define sandtray therapy as an "expressive and projective" (p. 4) counseling approach that allows children to express self in a safe and contained environment.

Similar to play therapy, the counselor provides specific categories of miniatures that facilitate expression and creativity and allow for a range of experiences and feelings to be expressed. Recommend categories of sandtray miniatures include people, animals, buildings, transportation, vegetation, fences/walls, natural items, fantasy, household items, and landscaping items (Homeyer and Sweeney, 2011). Fine to small-grain sand is provided within a small to medium container with 2–4 inches depth for the child to place and interact with the miniatures throughout the therapy process.

When facilitating sandtray therapy, the counselor provides an open-ended or specific prompt for the child to select miniatures and place them in the sand. The counselor carefully observes and attends to the child including affect, nonverbal and verbal responses, decision-making processes, timing, and sequencing as they select and place their miniatures in the sand. Following the selection and placement of miniatures in the sand, the counselor verbally responds and explores the child's creation by attending and responding to the child's description and verbalization about their sandtray, the child's creative process, the child's affectual and nonverbal expression, the child's placement and selection of symbols, and the child's reaction to individual miniatures and the sandtray as a whole.

Care is given to avoid over-interpreting the child's sandtray, to stay in and with the child's metaphor throughout the sand tray process, and to regard and prize the child's creation as reflective of the child's sense of self and the world. General guidelines for facilitating dialogue and exploration of the child's created sandtray is to allow the child to describe his or her creation in his or her own words, to gently offer concrete observations related to the selection and placement of the miniatures, to consider the meaning of the miniatures individually and in relationship to one another, and to expand the symbols and metaphors used by the child in the sandtray to the larger context of the child's direct experience, life, and environment.

> Care is given to avoid over-interpreting the child's sandtray and to regard and prize the child's creation as reflective of the child's sense of self and the world.

Process Question

1. How does sand tray therapy compare and contrast with other play therapy, expressive art, and creative counseling approaches?

Filial Therapy

Guerney (1964) developed one of the first filial therapy models for utilizing play therapy with parents and caregivers. Building on Guerney's work, Landreth and Bratton (2006) created a 10-session group counseling filial therapy model called Child–Parent Relationship Therapy (CPRT). In filial therapy and CPRT, parents or caregivers are taught fundamental play therapy attitudes and skills to practice and use in regularly scheduled play sessions with their child. Through the filial therapy process, parents receive play therapy instruction and

Filial therapies strengthen existing significant relationships within the child's life and influence change within the systems and environments that most directly impact the child's development.

supervision from a trained play therapist in a group or individual format. The parent or caregiver learns specific skills to promote a strong relationship with the child, to better understand the child's worldview and experience, and to facilitate the child's expression and integration of his or her thoughts, feelings, and experiences through play. Parents, caregivers, or teachers learn how to follow the child's lead, use empathic listening skills, facilitate the child's creativity and decision-making, and to promote the child's self-confidence and self-esteem.

Several researchers and practitioners have adapted the filial or CPRT models of play therapy for use with teachers and trained adult volunteers to utilize with elementary students within school settings (Coggins, 2016; Morrison and Bratton, 2010). By using established relationships between parent and child or teacher and student to promote growth and change, filial models strengthen existing significant relationships within the child's life, and influence change within the systems and environments that most directly impact the child's development.

Theraplay

Theraplay is a relationship-focused approach to play therapy that incorporates parents within the therapy process to promote healthy attachment, self-esteem, and positive interactions and relationships for the child (Bundy-Myrow and Booth, 2009). Based on principles of attachment theory and healthy parent–child interactions, Theraplay incorporates aspects of attunement and regulation to promote connection and positive interactions between therapist and child and/or parent and child.

Through the Theraplay process the counselor provides or teaches the parent to provide structure and safety for the child, to incorporate nurture and positive touch, to create positive, fun, and interactive opportunities for play, to engage and challenge the child, and to promote secure attachment within the parent–child relationship (Booth and Jernberg, 2010). The goals of Theraplay include helping the parents provide a secure base for the child, attune to the child's needs and co-regulate affect, and interact with the child in ways that support positive self-concept and a positive view of his or her relationships and environments. Theraplay has a growing body of research supporting its use and researchers have demonstrated some promising evidence for its effectiveness. Theraplay differs from filial therapy in that the counselor may be the primary person delivering the intervention to the child if a parent or caregiver is unavailable or not in a position to engage therapeutically with the child. Filial therapy focuses on the parent–/caregiver–child relationship as the primary relationship. Additionally, Theraplay may be parent- or therapist-directed, whereas in filial therapy the child leads the play and interaction and the parent learns to respond and facilitate the child's process.

Process Question

1. What are some potential benefits of engaging parents/caregivers in play therapy with children?

Kinder Therapy

Kinder Therapy is an Adlerian approach to filial therapy that utilizes teachers as therapeutic agents in the child's life through one-on-one play interactions between teachers and students and in the general classroom (White, Flynt, and Jones, 1999). Counselors train and consult with teachers to support their use of filial and play therapy skills with the child in individual play sessions and in the way they respond to the child in the general classroom. In this way, the counselor supports the pivotal role of the teacher in the student's life, promotes the student–teacher relationship, and impacts change in the classroom environment for all students.

The use of play extends beyond play therapy to include sandtray therapy, filial therapy, Theraplay, and Kinder therapy. Sandtray therapy allows play to be readily accessed by children and adolescents of all ages. Through the use of filial, Theraplay, and Kinder therapy, caregivers, parents, and teachers become essential partners in the therapeutic process and the counselor trains, consults, and supervises key adults in the child's life to be thereapeutic agents. In this way, the counselor is able to multiply the benefits of counseling and play therapy and directly promote systemic change in the child's life.

Case Study: Ronaldo[1]

This case study is about an adolescent and counselor using sand tray in private practice.

Ronaldo is a 14-year-old male Latino client. His parents brought him to counseling because his grades had been slipping and he had been staying out past his curfew and refusing to tell them where he was.

His parents had immigrated to the United States from El Salvador to escape growing gang violence in their city. They met during the difficult journey, and Ronaldo was born two years after they arrived in the United States. Both parents left the country before they had a chance to finish high school, and neither pursued further education once they arrived in the U.S. due to the pressing need to earn money. Ronaldo's parents have worked outside the home for his whole life, and they report that they work hard to build a better life for their son and that they believe education to be the key to a successful future. The family speaks Spanish in the home, but both parents speak conversational English. Ronaldo is bilingual and almost exclusively speaks English outside the home.

Ronaldo told the counselor he prefers to be called Ron. He reports that he receives average grades in school. His parents report that his teachers indicate he could get better grades if he applied himself more. Ron says he enjoys running track, but knows that his father wishes he would play soccer, even though Ron has explained that he does not particularly enjoy soccer. Ron also complains that his parents do not give him as much freedom as other kids his age. He describes his 10pm weeknight curfew as restrictive and expresses frustration over his parents' rule that he return from school and complete his homework before spending time with friends. "They even make me put my phone away while I do homework," he says. "No one else's parents make them do that." He admitted that he does sometimes connect with his friends over social media when he does homework on the computer as long as his parents are not in the room.

After enough sessions to establish rapport with Ron, the counselor noticed that he seemed to have difficulty discussing his feelings about his family and kept returning to this theme every session. Ron seemed to stumble over his words and get caught up in multiple trains of thought. The counselor thinks that sandtray therapy might provide a way for Ron to express himself without having to get caught up in trying to find the right words to describe what is clearly a complex concern for him.

After the counselor explains the process of creating a sandtray and why she thinks it would be helpful for Ron, he says that he is willing to try out the activity. The counselor asks Ron to use the sand and/or miniatures to create his world in the tray. Ron first placed a house in the top left corner of the tray. He then added some flowers, an owl, and a purple heart made of glass near the house. He fenced in that corner of the tray and placed a school building and school bus in the center of the tray. He surrounded the school with various human figures of different ethnicities and with various types of clothing. He placed a radio on the outskirts of the school area and a modern-looking building in the opposite corner from the house. He worked fairly quickly and decisively, but took his time choosing the people placed around the school.

When Ron had completed the tray, the counselor took a few seconds to connect with the feeling of the tray. Looking at his tray, she had a sense of isolation—each scene in the tray was separated from the other scenes, with little cohesiveness between them. She asked Ron if he would be willing to tell her about what he had created. Ron said that the house represented his home, with the dad representing his dad "because he has a lot of experience" and the heart representing his mom because "she likes us all to get along." He said the school building was his school and the people surrounding it were his friends. Ron noted that he had a lot of friends, and they were really important to him. He said he liked to listen to rap music with his friends (hence the radio), but that his parents did not like it when he listened to that kind of music at home. They were always playing music from their home country, and he thought it was "lame." He said the building in the bottom-right corner represented his dream to be an architect. He reported his dad wanted him to be a businessper-son, but he did not have any interest in business. As Ron described his tray, the counselor listened attentively, sometimes paraphrasing his responses or reflecting his feelings as he talked.

When Ron and the counselor had finished processing Ron's description of the tray, the counselor decided to point out one detail she had noticed by saying, "I noticed you didn't put yourself in the tray." This statement was an invitation, but not a request, for Ron to respond.

"You're right. I didn't," he responded. "I wonder what that means about me." The counselor continued to use reflective responding to help Ron process this realization. Ron decided to put a male figure with a backpack in the tray. He placed the figure within the gateway of the fence with his back to the house, flowers, owl, and heart. The counselor noted that it looked like the figure was between two worlds. One world seemed to have a sense of nurture and care while the other was fun and exciting. There didn't seem to be much connection between the two. Ron agreed this was true, and a conversation about his mixed feelings of love and resentment toward his parents ensued. This was a conversation he had seemed to feel guilty having before, but the visual representation of his love for his parents seemed to make talking about his resentment toward them easier. Although Ron did not use sandtray in every following session, he would sometimes return to the tray to work through a particularly difficult issue.

Case Study

This next study looks at an elementary school counselor using play therapy in meeting career standards.

The first graders at Sherwood Elementary school were exploring traditional and nontraditional career options, vocational pathways, and personal interests, skills, and abilities. The school counselor used the weekly guidance lesson to provide an opportunity for the students to explore a variety of careers through "career centers." The school counselor set up centers with dramatic play items including costumes, toys, and objects related to a variety of careers including medical careers, educational careers, service careers, science and technology careers, manufacturing and industrial careers, business careers, and artistic careers. For example, for medical professions, the counselor included scrubs, white lab coats, surgical masks, a stethoscope, medical gloves, an empty medicine syringe, band-aids, an ace bandage, a microscope, EKG readouts, x-rays, tongue depressors, a blood pressure cuff, toothbrushes, floss, a dental mirror, a stuffed animal cat and dog, and a leash. In groups of three to four students, the children rotated from one center to the next.

At each center, children were instructed to take turns trying on various parts of the uniform, to play with the various items related to each career, and to identify how the objects may be used by people in their jobs. After exploring the center freely for several minutes, the students were given laminated cards that showed a variety of pictures representing diverse people in each job field. At the medical professions center, the cards included a doctor, a nurse, a dentist, a lab technician/phlebotomist, medical researcher, x-ray technician, paramedic, and a veterinarian. On the back of each card were specific characteristics that each professional needed to be successful at their job. For examples, on the back of the nurse card, the words read "caring, brave, attentive, kind, and responsible." Below the characteristics, pictures were included to show the steps one would need to take in order to have each specific career. On the nurse card, the pictures included a report card to represent good grades in school, a picture of a college to represent 2–4 years of secondary education, a picture of a beaker to represent a background in science, a "2 + 2" math equation to represent a background in math, and a picture of ears and a mouth to represent good communication skills.

The school counselor rotated frequently to each group of students as they explored the career centers, providing guidance, direction, and utilizing nonverbal and verbal play therapy skills to facilitate the students' exploration of various careers. The school counselor also encouraged the kids to use their communication and relationship skills with one another that were taught and practiced in previous classroom guidance lessons, including sharing, listening, noticing other's feelings, using one's words to express thoughts and feelings, and being kind with our hands.

Children picked their top three careers from all the centers they were most interested in and kept a checklist of their favorite careers as they moved from each center. At the service career center, the school counselor noticed Sophia, Noah, and Marcos playing with all the uniforms and objects. Marcos put on the fire fighter's jacket and then practiced locking and unlocking the handcuffs from the police officer uniform. Marcos then picked up the ambulance and chased it around with the fire truck and police car. Finally, Marcos picked up the teddy bear, the tissue box, and a cut-out paper heart. Marcos asked the school counselor "What job are these for?"

"Hmm. You're wondering what jobs all those belong to. Well, I wonder what they could each be used for?"

Marcos thought about it. Then Sophia chimed in, "Well, they seem like things that might make someone feel better if they're sad."

The school counselor said, "Oh, there's an idea. Things that can bring comfort to someone. Can you match those items to any of the job cards you see on the table?"

All the kids started to sort through the job cards at the service career center. They agreed that all the jobs needed a big heart to help other people. As they sifted through the cards for each service career, they found a counselor card. "That's it!" said Marcos excitedly. "Counselors need Kleenex for when people cry."

"You did it, Marcos! You figured it out. Now can you find the steps you need to take to become a counselor on the back of the card?" asked the school counselor.

Marcos and the rest of the students in his group, looked at the back of the card and read it together. The school counselor continued around the room checking in with the other groups of students.

At the end of the guidance lesson, the school counselor collected the students' "Top 3 Careers for Me" lists to utilize in a future guidance lesson and then read "I Can Be Anything" by Jerry Spinelli as students sat on the floor in a circle. After finishing the story, the school counselor encouraged the students to tell three grown-ups—moms, dads, grandparents, teachers, and other significant adults in their lives—about the careers and jobs they liked the most and why they liked them.

SUMMARY

Creativity, expressive arts, and play therapy are essential approaches for effective and developmentally responsive intervention and prevention with children and adolescents in both school and clinical settings. Each of these modalities requires extensive training, practice, and supervision in order to be ethically and effectively utilized in practice with children and adolescents.

The key points in this chapter were:

- Regardless of the creative media used, the counselor must have a clear therapeutic goal for its use.
- Expressive modalities should not be used to get the child or adolescent to talk, but rather to provide an opportunity for deeper client expression and better counselor understanding. Talking is not always necessary.
- Counselors using expressive modalities must receive adequate training and supervision in order to practice that modality in an ethical manner.
- Play therapy is an effective counseling intervention for children that utilizes play as the primary means of communication and interaction between the child and the therapist. Play therapy allows the counselor to speak the language and enter the world of the child.
- Play therapy approaches may also be used with adolescents through sandtray therapy and with families through filial therapy, Child–Parent Relationship Therapy, and Theraplay.

Additional Resources

Association for Child and Adolescent Counseling: acachild.org
Association for Creativity in Counseling: www.creativecounselor.org
Association for Play Therapy: www.a4pt.org
International Expressive Arts Therapy: www.ieata.org
National Coalition of Creative Arts Therapies Associations Inc.: www.nccata.org
The Center for Play Therapy: www.centerforplaytherapy.com

Suggested Readings

Gladding, S. T. (2011). *The creative arts in counseling*, 4th ed. Alexandria, VA: American Counseling Association.

Kottman, T. and Meany-Walen, K. (2016). *Partners in play: An Adlerian approach to play therapy*, 3rd ed. Alexandria, VA: American Counseling Association.

Landreth, G. L. (2012). *Play therapy: The art of the relationship*. New York, NY: Routledge.

Landreth, G. L. and Bratton, S. C. (2006). *Child–parent relationship therapy (CPRT): A 10-session filial therapy model*. New York, NY: Routledge.

Malchiodi, C. A. (2005). *Expressive therapies*. New York, NY: Guilford Press.

Moon, B. L. (2008). *Introduction to art therapy: Faith in the product*. Springfield, IL: Charles C Thomas.

Morrison, M. and Bratton, S. (2010). Preliminary investigation of an early mental health intervention for Head Start programs: Effects of Child–Teacher Relationship Training on children's behavior problems. *Psychology in the Schools* 47 (10), 1003–1017.

Oaklander, V. (1978). *Windows to our children*. Gouldsboro, ME: Gestalt Journal Press.

Ray, D. C. (2011). *Advanced play therapy: Essential conditions, knowledge, and skills for child practice*. New York, NY: Routledge.

Ray, D. C. (2016). *A therapist's guide to child development: The extraordinarily normal years*. New York, NY: Routledge.

Glossary

Adlerian play therapy (AdPT): An approach to play therapy based on the theoretical approach of Alfred Adler. AdPT counselors emphasize a strong relationship and sharing of power in the relationship

Art therapy: A professional field of study that includes courses in art theory, art history, and the therapeutic use of art. Many counselors choose to use art activities in counseling without pursuing a degree as an art therapist

Bibliotherapy: Use of the written word (literature, poetry, self-help books, autobiographies, etc.) to aid in the therapeutic process

Child-centered play therapy (CCPT): An evidence-based approach to play therapy that emphasizes an open, accepting, understanding relationship between the counselor and client as the primary healing factor. CCPT is based on Carl Roger's person-centered theory

Cognitive behavioral play therapy: An approach to play therapy in which counselors incorporate cognitive behavioral techniques into counseling with children. Research supporting the use of the approach with young children is limited

Creativity in counseling: A term used to describe a range of therapeutic interventions that emphasize the use of means other than talk therapy in the therapeutic process

Drama therapy: A professional field of study in which therapists use drama techniques and props as a primary part of the therapeutic process. Many counselors choose to integrate drama concepts into their counseling without a degree in drama therapy

Esteem building (play therapy): Rather than evaluating the child or using praise, the play therapist responds to the child's efforts and actions with encouragement and recognition for the person of the child rather than the outcome

Expressive arts: The intentional use of a variety of media, such as art supplies, clay, painting, and others to facilitate a deeper therapeutic process in the context of a safe, caring relationship. Expressive arts counselors believe the process of expressive arts themselves can be healing

Filial therapy: An approach in which a qualified play therapist teaches parents skills to engage in therapeutic play with their children with the intention of strengthening the parent–child relationship

Gestalt play therapy: An approach to play therapy based on Gestalt theory and the idea that the organism acts as a whole, naturally moving toward self-regulation and growth

Jungian play therapy: An approach to play therapy based on Jungian theory. Counselors utilizing Jungian play therapy emphasize the use of symbolic meaning and the self-healing archetype

Kinder therapy: Kinder therapy is an Adlerian approach to filial therapy that utilizes teachers as therapeutic agents in the child's life through one-on-one play interactions between teachers and students and in the general classroom.

Matching (play therapy): The counselor naturally and consciously works to match the child's affect, facial expressions, body position, and movement

Music therapy: a professional field of study in which the therapist integrates musical concepts and psychotherapy. Many counselors choose to integrate music into counseling settings without a degree in music therapy

Play therapy: A modality for counseling children between the ages of 3 and 12 that utilizes play as a primary means of interaction and communication between a child and a counselor in school or clinical settings

Reflection of content (play therapy): When children choose to verbalize their thoughts, feelings, and experiences, the counselor responds to the child by paraphrasing or restating the content of the child's statement

Reflection of feeling (play therapy): As the child expresses emotion nonverbally and verbally, the counselor responds by verbally stating the child's feelings and emotional state

Reflection of nonverbal behavior (play therapy): The counselor responds to the play by verbally responding and reflecting the child's action by stating what is observed through the child's play

Returning responsibility (play therapy): The counselor promotes the child's self-direction by allowing the child to explore and experiment with choices and developmental tasks towards mastery

Sandtray therapy: A counseling approach that incorporates aspects of play therapy through the use of sand and miniatures, allowing children and adolescents to express their thoughts, feelings, and experiences through objects and symbols within a safe and contained space

Scriptotherapy see Therapeutic Writing

Therapeutic limit setting (play therapy): The counselor sets limits on the child's behavior as needed and presented to the child in a manner that conveys trust, empathy, and predictability

Therapeutic writing: The use of writing in the therapeutic process to facilitate self-awareness, creative problem solving, and general therapeutic growth

Theraplay: A relationship-focused approach to play therapy that incorporates parents within the therapy process to promote healthy attachment, self-esteem, and positive interactions and relationships for the child

Note

1   To protect confidentiality, Ronaldo is a purely fictional character loosely based on several clients whose identifying details have been changed.

References

Bellison, J. (2002). *Children's use of board games in psychotherapy*. Northvale, NJ: Jason Aronson.

Berlin, I. (2001). The use of competitive games in play therapy. In C. E. Schaefer and S. E. Reid (eds.), *Game play: Therapeutic use of childhood games* (pp. 109–129). New York, NY: John Wiley & Sons.

Blom, R. (2004). *The handbook of Gestalt play therapy: Practical guidelines for child therapists*. London: Jessica Kingsley.

Carroll, F. (2009). Gestalt play therapy. In K. O'Connor and L. Braverman (eds.), *Play therapy theory and practice: Comparing theories and techniques*, 2nd ed. (pp. 283–314). Hoboken, NJ: Wiley.

Coggins, K. (2016). *The efficacy of child–teacher relationship training as an early childhood mental health intervention in head start centers* (Order No. 10113687). Available from ProQuest Dissertations & Theses Global. (1801725449). Retrieved from http://stats.lib.pdx.edu/proxy.php?url=http://search.proquest.com.proxy.lib. pdx.edu/docview/1801725449?accountid=13265

Degges-White, S. (2011). Introduction to the use of expressive arts in counseling. In S. Degges-White and N. L. Davis (eds.), *Integrating the expressive arts into counseling practice: Theory-based interventions* (pp. 1–6). New York, NY: Springer.

Eaton, L. G., Doherty, K. L., and Widrick, R. M. (2007). A review of research and methods used to establish art therapy as an effective treatment method for traumatized children. *The Arts in Psychotherapy* 34 (3), 256–262. doi:10.1016/j. aip.2007.03.001

Freud, A. (1946). *The psycho-analytical treatment of children*. New York: International Universities Press.

Froebel, Friedrich (1898). *The education of man*. New York: D. Appleton & Company.

Gardner, R. A. (1973). *The talking, feeling, doing game*. Cresskill, NJ: Creative Therapeutics.

Gladding, S. T. (2008). The impact of creativity in counseling. *Journal of Creativity in Mental Health* 3 (2), 97–104. doi:10.1080/15401380802226679

Gladding, S. T. (2011). *The creative arts in counseling*, 4th ed. Alexandria, VA: American Counseling Association.

Green, E. J. (2014). *The handbook of Jungian play therapy with children and adolescents*. Baltimore, MD: John Hopkins University Press.

Guerney, B. (1964). Filial therapy: Description and rationale. *Journal of Consulting Psychology* 28 (4), 303–310.

Guerney, L (2001). Child-centered play therapy. *International Journal of Play Therapy* 10 (2), 13–31.

Guerney, L. and Ryan, V. (2013). *Group filial therapy: The complete guide to teaching parents to play therapeutically with their children*. Philadelphia, PA: Jessica Kingsley Publishers.

Karkou, V. and Saderson, P. (2006). *Arts therapies: A research based map of the field*. Philadelphia, PA: Elsevier.

Kjellstrand Hatwig, E. (2014). Puppets in the playroom: Utilizing child-centered facilitative skills as a metaphor for healing. *International Journal of Play Therapy* 23 (4), 204–216. doi: 10.1037/a0038054

Klein, M. (1932). *The psychoanalysis of children*. London: Hogarth Press.

Knell, S. (2009). Cognitive-behavioral play therapy. In K. O'Connor and L. Braverman (Eds.), *Play therapy theory and practice: Comparing theories and techniques*, 2nd ed. (pp. 203–236). Hoboken, NJ: Wiley.

Kottman, T. (2011). *Play therapy basics and beyond*. Alexandria, VA: American Counseling Association.

Kottman, T. and Meany-Walen, K. (2016). *Partners in play: An Adlerian approach to play therapy*, 3rd ed. Alexandria, VA: American Counseling Association.

Lambert, S., LeBlanc, M., Mullen, J., Ray, D., Baggerly, J., White, J., and Kaplan, D. (2005). Learning more about those who play in session: The national play therapy in counseling practices project. *Journal of Counseling and Development* 85, 42–46.

Landreth, G. L. (2012). *Play therapy: The art of the relationship*. New York, NY: Routledge.

Landreth, G. L. and Bratton, S. C. (2006). *Child–parent relationship therapy (CPRT): A 10-session filial therapy model*. New York, NY: Routledge.

Lin, D. and Bratton, S. (2015). A meta-analytic review of child-centered play therapy approaches. *Journal of Counseling and Development* 93, 45–58.

Malchiodi, C. A. (2005a). Art therapy. In C. A. Malchiodi (ed.), *Expressive therapies* (pp. 16–43). New York, NY: Guilford Press.

Malchiodi, C. A. (2005b). Expressive therapies. In C. A. Malchiodi (ed.), *Expressive therapies* (pp. 1–15). New York, NY: Guilford Press.

Mardziah Hayati, A. (2002). Bibliotherapy. ERIC Digest. Bloomington, IN: ERIC. ED470712

McFarlane, P. (2005). *Dramatherapy: Developing emotional stability*. London, UK: David Fulton.

Oaklander, V. (1978). *Windows to our children*. Gouldsboro, ME: Gestalt Journal Press.

Ray, D. C. (2011). *Advanced play therapy: Essential conditions, knowledge, and skills for child practice*. New York, NY: Routledge.

Ray, D., Armstrong, S., Balkin, R., and Jayne, K. (2015). Child-centered play therapy in the schools: Review and meta-analysis. *Psychology in the Schools* 52, 107–123.

Ray, D. C. and McCullough, R. (2015). Evidenced-based practice statement: Play therapy. Association for Play Therapy. Retrieved from: http://c.ymcdn.com/sites/www.a4pt.org/resource/resmgr/About_APT/APT_Evidence_Based_Statement.pdf

Rogers, C. R. (1951). *Client-centered therapy: Its current practice, implications, and theory*. Boston: Houghton Mifflin.

Rosen, C. M. and Atkins, S. S. (2014). Am I doing expressive arts therapy or creativity in counseling? *Journal of Creativity in Mental Health* 9, 292–303. doi:10.1080/15401383.2014.906874

White, J., Flynt, M., and Jones, N. (1999). Kinder Therapy: An Adlerian approach for training teachers to be therapeutic agents through play. *Individual Psychology* 55 (3), 365.

White, V. E. and Murray, M. A. (2002). Passing notes: The use of therapeutic letter writing in counseling adolescents. *Journal of Mental Health Counseling* 24 (2), 166–176.

Winnicott, D. W. (1996). *Playing and reality*. New York, NY: Routledge.

Yalom, I. (2002). *The gift of therapy*. New York, NY: Harper Collins.

CHAPTER 15

Strategies, Approaches, and Evidence-Based Practices

Jolie Ziomek-Daigle and Tameka Oliphant

How are students different as a result of what school counselors do?
American School Counselors Association

CHAPTER OBJECTIVES

As a result of reading this chapter, readers will:

- understand the utility of employing evidence-based strategies
- be able to identify evidence-based practices for use in school and clinical settings
- understand the role of consultation in the work of counselors
- be able to describe new and emerging counseling interventions

---

INTRODUCTION

Strategies, approaches, and evidence-based practices will be introduced in this chapter. We will begin with specific examples of evidence-based practices for more common issues that present with children and adolescents in both school and clinical mental health settings. Then, consultation will be discussed, as well as models of prevention.

PREVENTION AND INTERVENTION IN COUNSELING

The counseling profession is now recognizing prevention science and borrowing from the mission of the public health discipline in reducing problematic behaviors and disorders and promoting health and wellness. Prevention-focused interventions fit well with the professional identity of counselors and the services counselors offer. Prevention-based efforts move past the focus on the individual and are developmental in nature, population or group-based, and interdisciplinary (Mason and Nakulla, 2008). Focusing less on the individual not only removes stigma, blame, and defensiveness but considers ecological influences such as communities, schools, health, and culture in treatment approaches. The spectrum of mental health interventions will be discussed next in order to assist counselors-in-training conceptualize the range of interventions, preventative and treatment-based, that can be offered to clients.

The Spectrum of Mental Health Interventions

The spectrum of mental health interventions is a useful resource for clinicians to refer to as they conceptualize "the sequencing of mental health interventions in relation to the severity and classification of the presenting problem" (Mason and Nakkula, 2008, p.3). The classification systems consist of three levels—prevention, treatment, and maintenance. The prevention level includes universal, selective, and indicated intervention. Positive Behavioral Interventions and Supports (PBIS) is an example of a universal (i.e. school-wide) intervention. A selective intervention may include a substance prevention program for youth who live in a community lacking after-school and enrichment programs (Mason and Nakkula, 2008). A social skills small group for youth with emotional/behavioral disabilities is an example of indicated intervention as these youth have an already documented and identifiable risk factor.

The treatment levels of the spectrum for mental health interventions include the diagnosis and subsequent treatment of the mental health-related disorder. For example, a youth might be diagnosed with post-traumatic stress disorder as a result of an automobile accident, and the clinician may treat this client by using trauma-focused cognitive behavioral therapy (https://tfcbt.musc.edu). Finally, the maintenance levels of the spectrum for mental health interventions include compliance with long-term treatment and after-care. Examples of compliance and aftercare may include on-going individual counseling, attendance in small group counseling (i.e. support groups), medication management, and healthy wellness practices.

EVIDENCE-BASED PRACTICES AND APPROACHES

The use of evidence-based practices (EBPs) or evidence-based approaches (EBAs) are more and more used by counselors and in school and clinical mental health sites and endorsed by government agencies and healthcare companies. However, there seems to be a lack of exposure in the use of EBPs/EBAs in counseling training programs. Many students report being introduced to EBPs/EBAs for the very first time during their internship experience or the first year of a full-time position. During internship or the first year of employment is far too late for new counselors to become familiar with and begin using EBPs/EBAs.

Different factors may drive counselors' use of EBPs/EBAs at school and clinical mental health sites. Counselors working at clinical mental health sites may use EBPs/EBAs such as CBT and Parent–Child Interaction Therapy (PCIT) (http://www.pcit.org). In clinical mental health settings, insurance companies may require the use of certain programs for reimbursement or grant guidelines may stipulate the use of specific interventions. Whereas, in school settings, counselors collect data to inform decision making on the use of EBPs/EBAs in the delivery of services. Some examples of EBPs/EBAs used in school settings include universal instruction (i.e. classroom guidance programming) and applying a social skills curriculum, Positive Behavioral Intervention and Supports (PBIS) (http://www.pbis.org), and initiating a wrap-around plan (https://www.pbis.org/school/tier3supports/wraparound) for students with elevated needs.

Cultural Considerations in Providing Evidence-Based Practices

Often times, the question is raised whether all evidence-based practices can be used with youth in general, and specifically with culturally diverse youth. Research studies are inconclusive, with some citing that adapting interventions for specific populations can increase effectiveness and others concluding that changing an intervention could alter the original treatment effectiveness (Ngo, Langley, Kataoka, Nadeem, Escudero, and Stein, 2008).

For illustrative purposes, one specific study and evidence-based program will be further discussed to assist readers in understanding the importance of cultural responsiveness in designing interventions. Cognitive-Behavioral Intervention for Trauma in Schools (CBITS) was originally developed for youth of color and immigrant youth who were exposed to trauma. The intervention is delivered through small group in the school setting. Research findings suggest that CBITS participants who completed the program reported a reduction in post-traumatic stress and depressive symptoms (Ngo, et. at., 2008). The CBITS program, in its delivery, is ideally culturally responsive and encourages counse-lors to embed culturally relevant material to increase participant engagement and program meaningfulness.

Ngo et al. (2008) provide the following cultural enhancements to the CBITS implementation and treatment components. One CBITS treatment component includes social program solving. The researchers suggest includ-ing aspects of spiritual coping such as prayer, meditation, and meeting with a religious leader. These specific strategies of spiritual coping are important components in ethnic culture and context and can aid the problem-solving process. The trauma narrative is another CBITS treatment component and participants can be encouraged to create a rap, song, poem, or graphic novel about a traumatic event and its ending.

Specific Evidence-Based Practices and Approaches

Counselors provide services to youth in various settings and focus on issues of academic achievement, mental health, motivation, problem-solving, and so on. The following sections present a number of EBPs/EBAs that can be used across counselor settings.

The Second Step Violence Curriculum Program is an intervention for K–8-grade students designed to reduce student aggressive behavior and behavioral referrals and improve school climate. Researchers found that schools that use the Second Step Violence Curriculum Program saw reduced aggres-sive behavior in playground and cafeteria settings and increase in neutral or prosocial behavior in the same school areas (Dimmitt, Carey, and Hatch, 2008), reduced behavioral referrals, bullying incidents, and improved academic achievement (i.e. grades) and effort via report cards (Zyromski and Mariani, 2016).

The Student Success Skills Program (SSSP) (Webb and Brigman, 2007) yielded strong outcomes on overall student achievement and, more specifically, with lower-achieving students by teaching cognitive, social, and self-management skills in small groups and classroom settings. The goals of the SSSP for fourth–twelfth grade include increased math and reading abilities, behavioral outcomes, self-management skills, and internal perceptions and emotions (Zyromski and Mariani, 2016). Part of the larger SSSP, Ready to Learn, serves pre-K through first grade, and the goals of the program are to enhance both academic and behavior through reading, listening, paying attention, and focusing. Program outcomes revealed significant gains in academic achievement and social skills through teacher, parent, and student self-reports, surveys, standardized test scores, and discipline referrals (Zyromski and Mariani, 2016).

The Too Good for Drugs (TGFD) and Too Good for Violence (TGFV) programs, for students in grades K–8, have goals that include a reduction in at-risk factors and an increase in built-in protective factors, pro-social behavior, and problem solving related to decision-making and conflict. Evidence of program effectiveness revealed that participants had more positive interactions with peers, higher social competence and conflict resolution skills, more knowledge on the harmful effects of drugs and violence, and a change in behaviors and attitudes (Zyromski and Mariani, 2016).

The Why Try (WT) Program aims to boost resiliency through gaining social, emotional, and leadership skills for students across K–12 grade levels through the collection of teacher and student self-reports, student surveys, achievement data (i.e. school completion rates, grades, GPA), and student behavior reports. This classroom and small-group approach has yielded the following results: Higher school completion rates, increased GPA and social/emotional competence, and reduced suspensions, expulsions, and bullying incidents.

The PeaceBuilders Program (Dimmitt, Carey, and Hatch, 2008), a program that aims to reduce aggressive behavior by increasing social competence in the elementary grades, revealed improved prosocial behavior, school climate, peace-making behaviors, and reduced teacher-reported aggressive and violent behavior.

To address bullying in the school setting, the Bully Busters Program implemented in grades K–5 changed teacher and student perceptions related to bullying, reduced peer aggression, and enhanced school and classroom climates (Newman-Carlson and Horne, 2004).

Another evidence-based bullying prevention program, the Olweus Bullying Prevention Program, includes teacher and student reports and a host of other data collection sources, reports positive intervention outcomes such as a reduction in student reports of bullying, antisocial behaviors and an improved classroom climate, peer relationships, attitudes toward school, and standardized test scores in language arts, math, science, and history (Zyromski and Mariani, 2016).

The Incredible Years (IY) program includes a curriculum for parents, teachers, and students (Webster-Stratton and Herman, 2010). The program seeks to promote both academic and social–emotional competence while reducing discipline problems. The program has both classroom and small group applications. An offshoot of the IY program, the Dina Dinosaur program, can be implemented by teachers in the classroom and incorporated into whole-classroom instruction. Intervention outcomes included increased school readiness, emotional regulation, social competence, and improved parent interaction and family relationships (Zyromski and Mariani, 2016).

The Promoting Alternative Thinking Strategies (PATHS) Program is for students in kindergarten through fifth grade. Skills addressed in the PATHS program include emotional literacy, positive peer relationships, problem solving, and self-control (Macklem, 2011). Teachers implement the program in classrooms during, for example, homeroom advisory periods or teacher-as-advisor periods.

For students of 3–18 years of age, The Positive Action (Flay and Allred, 2003) program teaches social–emotional literacy skills and character development. Program components include a curriculum, school-wide climate intervention, parenting classes, and kits for school stakeholders. Additionally, the program promotes learning through positive behaviors, but also through thoughts, feelings, and actions. Evidence-based outcomes of the Positive Action Program include increased academic achievement and a reduction in violent behavior (Zyronski and Mariani, 2016).

The check in/check out (CICO) program, although different in its approach—being implemented by school staff rather than a clinician—is facilitated and organized by a counselor. The CICO intervention improves student behavior through frequent feedback and monitoring by school personnel who interact regularly with students (Hawken and Horner, 2003). Through ongoing progress and data monitoring, counselors can facilitate the CICO intervention for students who do not respond to universal supports, such as PBIS, by pairing students with a mentor who has been provided CICO-related materials and training. The CICO intervention is effective across grade levels in reducing discipline referrals, minimizing attention seeking behaviors, and increasing more desirable behaviors.

For youth with behavioral disorders such as oppositional defiant disorder, conduct disorder, and attention deficit disorders, researchers found that functional family therapy, multi-systemic therapy, or parent management were effective treatments (Eber and Whiston, 2006).

Research indicates that family-based interventions are effective in supporting students' academic progress and that family involvement promotes student achievement (Dimmitt, Carey, and Hatch, 2008). It has also been reported that increases occurred in academic achievement, attendance, graduation rates, and post-secondary enrollment when families were involved in the counseling process (Henderson and Berla, 1995). Further, family counseling and parent consultation is effective in increasing student motivation and classroom behavior. Student achievement can be further impacted by small group interventions that teach specific learning strategies such as taking notes and organization skills (Ziomek-Daigle, 2015).

In terms of linking career education and academic achievement, younger students benefit more from participating in career exploration and activities and by having these activities integrated into math and language arts classes (Dimmitt, Carey, and Hatch, 2008).

Case Study: Joe

This case study focuses on student success skills.

Joe is a fifth-grade African American male student. He is in school with his appropriate age cohort but has always struggled with reading comprehension. He does not have any psychological diagnoses, but does have mild asthma issues. His reading comprehension skills have also impacted his ability to master the material in his science and social studies classes. Joe often chooses to disengage and doodle in his notebook rather than ask for assistance from his teacher or a peer when he does not understand. He makes average grades in these subjects. However, he excels in mathematics. According to Joe, he also enjoys playing with his friends in gym class and drawing in his art elective. When asked about his strengths, the teacher notes that Joe is well liked by his peers, has a good sense of humor, and has a supportive home environment.

Joe attends a regular K–5 public elementary school. The school is located in a suburban area and is diverse in its racial and ethnic demographics. He has attended the school since second grade. There are 18 students in his class. He rotates between two teachers to take his core subjects during the school day, remaining with the same group of students for the majority of the day. His teachers are very organized and structured and work to provide a caring and welcoming environment.

As a result of his third-grade test scores, Joe has been placed in an early intervention program at his school. He receives extra support in reading and reading comprehension skills with the hope of improving his scores enough to get him past the "bubble" to passing scores for his grade-level state exams. When the school year began, Joe was doing well in most of his classes. He still demonstrated struggles with reading comprehension, but was making consistent progress according to his assessments. However, as the second quarter began, Joe's grades began to drop, even in his math class. Joe's teacher initially incorporated a reward system in the hope of reinforcing positive behaviors such as completing classwork and homework assignments. Now the teacher has reached out to the school counselor to seek further guidance on how to work with Joe. The counselor is currently utilizing the Student Success Skills program as a whole-school approach, but thinks that Joe will benefit from an opportunity to practice the classroom instruction in a small-group setting.

After meeting with Joe's teacher and then speaking with Joe one-on-one to assess his appropriateness for the upcoming small-group cycle, the school counselor determines that Joe will likely benefit from the Student Success Skills (SSS) small group and receives parent permission. The areas she hopes to highlight in particular are goal setting, recognizing improvements, and cognitive/memory skills.

The initial small-group session begins with an introduction of the SSS logo to provide a visual foundation for the group. The logo also provides a visual of the group goals, which include: (1) creating a supportive group environment; (2) learning skills to improve academic and relational success; and (3) sharing successes that result from consistent effort in applying the learned skills (Webb and Brigman, 2007). Following this introduction, students will each introduce themselves using a name game. This activity provides an opportunity to begin building the group rapport. Third, the school counselor leads the group in a discussion of the group expectations and norms, highlighting the importance of active listening, respect for and towards others, and confidentiality. Finally, the students interview and introduce another group member. Again, this provides an opportunity to build rapport among group members. During the remainder of the time in the first session, the counselor explains the purpose of the group, introduces the key concepts of Kaizen and Keep Kool Tunes, and introduces the Seven Keys to Course Mastery. Using the Seven Keys, students are able to track their improvement on the program's success skills throughout the eight weeks of group.

Each week, the small group will open with check-ins to gauge how students have been feeling during the past week. Keep Kool Tunes will also be utilized to help set the tone of the meeting each week. During the opening, students will also be asked to report on the progress they have made on their goals during the past week. If a student has not made any improvements, the group can brainstorm ideas that the student can try during the upcoming week. Finally, the counselor can use the Looking Good Feeling Good chart to have students track their own progress on the SSS Life Skills. One goal during this time can be to help students recognize any behavioral patterns from week to week, and develop strategies to address any consistent issues. The remainder of the session can be used to reinforce skills that were covered during the classroom guidance lessons. For this small group, these lessons would center on goal setting, recognizing improvements, and sharpening cognitive and memory skills. Role playing various scenarios can be helpful during this stage.

The final SSS small group should serve as a closure session. The group will open with a Keep Kool Tune and a check-in for students' feelings about the events of the past week. Rather than discussing the weekly success, this final session can be used to assess what students have learned from the group, what they have liked about the group, and what goals they would like to set going forward. A closure activity highlighting the things learned from each member in the group can be a helpful way to wrap up the small-group experience.

Monthly follow-up sessions for the small group, as well as check-ins with Joe's teacher, can be used to monitor the impact and effectiveness of the small group. Additional support services could be provided in an individual format if Joe's grades continue to decline.

Anxiety and Mood

The Oregon Resiliency Project (ORP) emphasizes prevention and the promotion of positive mental health. Different curriculums of the (ORP) include: Strong Start, Strong Kids, and Strong Teens and lessons are taught weekly in the classroom. Program components include cognitive restructuring, empathy training, and relaxation techniques (Merrell, 2010), and the program can be implemented in the classroom or in small groups based on the needs of the school and the students.

The Coping Cat Program is a cognitive behavioral manualized and comprehensive treatment program for youth who experience anxiety disorders (e.g., generalized anxiety disorder, separation anxiety disorder, social phobia). Parents are involved in the treatment and are trained to become "coaches." The CCP relies heavily on the cognitive behavioral approach and uses modeling, exposure, role-play, relaxation, and *in vivo* exposure as techniques to reduce anxious behaviors (Kendall, 2000). Outcomes of implementing the CCP include a decrease in anxiety, fear, negative thoughts, and depressive symptoms and improved coping skills. The CCP also includes the following curriculums that cross age ranges: (a) Coping Bear and (b) Coping Koala.

Implementing a wrap-around plan is an example of a structured intervention for 1–5 per cent of youth with complex emotional/behavioral disorders, mental health problems, and high needs (Eber and Nelson, 1997). Wraparound is conceptualized as a team-based service planning and coordination process and is a treatment plan that blends home, school, and community interventions. The approach is rooted in cultural competency, is strengths-based, values family voice and choice, and addresses the complex needs of this youth population rather than focusing attention on one individualized problem such as chronic absenteeism or problematic behavior (Suter and Bruns, 2009). This "holistic prevention tool" offers a systems framework to address multiple areas in a child's life and actively involves family and community entities (West-Olatunji, Frazier, and Kelley, 2011). Wraparound has been widely used in implementing systems of care models by designing individualized and flexible services and interventions for youth and families (Eber and Nelson, 1997). The wraparound approach can be effective for youth with complex emotional and behavioral problems and schools are ideal settings for interagency collaboration and individualized care (Epstein, 2011). Positive outcomes of the wraparound approach include improvement in living situations, healthcare access, academic progress, mental health, resiliency, and juvenile justice-related outcomes (Suter and Burns, 2009). Using wraparound is especially relevant with transitional aged youth (i.e. ages 17–25), as this is the age when youth "age out" of foster care, juvenile justice programming, move from youth to adult social services, and often end special education services. Furthermore, transitional age youth appear to have the highest rates of both psychiatric and substance use problems, with rates of mental illness as high as 28 per cent (SAMSHA, 2013). The high prevalence and severity rates of psychiatric and substance use disorders in this age group underscore the need for early intervention for this vulnerable population.

The Anger Coping Program (ACP) is a small group approach based on cognitive behavioral therapy for children in elementary and middle school in need of anger management treatment. Studies show that ACP reduces aggressive and disruptive behaviors compared to students in control groups (Larson and Lochman, 2005).

Researchers found that anxiety, fear, specific phobias and depression are effectively treated by using these specific cognitive behavioral therapy techniques—systematic desensitization, modeling, and reinforcement schedules (Eder and Whiston, 2006).

Trauma

Trauma-focused cognitive behavioral therapy (TF-CBT) is an example of targeted intervention for youth who have experienced trauma. In one study, children and young adolescents of 8–14 years of age who were sexually abused experienced greater reductions in PTSD, depressive symptoms, and behavior disruptions after completion TF-CBT small group compared to peers provided child-centered play therapy (Macklem, 2011).

Applications of Cognitive–Behavioral Therapy

Cognitive behavioral therapy (CBT) is a widely used and empirically valid counseling approach for a variety of presenting concerns such as anxiety, depression, eating disorders, behavioral disorders, and academic motivation. CBT can be adapted to various settings such as clinical mental health and school settings and is an effective treatment for children and adolescents with a focus on prevention and early intervention. While there is existing research using CBT to manage challenges related to mental health-related disorders, emerging research highlights the significance of the CBT approach on academics. One such program used in the school setting, Student Success Skills (Webb and Brigman, 2007), focuses on meta-cognitive and self-management education, self-monitoring, self-efficacy, automatic thoughts, muscle relaxation, and role playing.

One specific approach to treating trauma, trauma-focused CBT, employs the efficacy of CBT and is characterized as an individualized treatment that conceptualizes clients or students within the context of their familial, social, and cultural ecological settings. Essential components of trauma-focused CBT include parental involvement and the therapeutic alliance. Trauma-focused CBT can be used across settings and subpopulations that have reported successful research outcomes including immigrant children, children traumatized from natural disasters like Hurricane Katrina, children who had been refugees, and those who have been sexually abused or assaulted.

To help counselor trainees become familiar with the various evidence-based practices, one additional CBT approach, used mostly with juvenile offenders and rooted in prevention of future criminal activity, will be briefly presented. Thinking for a Change (TFAC) is a manualized program, rooted in CBT, and includes 22 sessions that focus on didactic instruction, homework assignments, role plays, and reviews from previous lessons. The main objective of the program is to identify and mitigate deficient interpersonal or social problem solving skills that lead to problematic behaviors. TFAC is a program used in over 45 states with juvenile offenders and uses strategies and skills that promote reasoning, social awareness, and problem solving. Results of outcome studies indicate that participant repeat offenses were reduced and, on a micro level, the program improved problem solving skills and interpersonal skills.

Functional Behavioral Analysis

Functional Behavioral Analysis (FBA) serves as an assessment strategy that examines the antecedent events, as well as maintaining events, associated with problem behaviors in students (Sugai et al., 1999). FBAs are often utilized when a student has not been responsive to Tier 1, and in some cases Tier 2, interventions in the behavioral Response to Intervention (RtI) process (Pearce, 2009). FBAs can serve as a "systematic and informed means by which targeted interventions can be developed and monitored" (Sugai et al., 1999, p. 13). Once the functional behavioral assessment has been conducted, details from the analysis can then be used to brainstorm possible strategies to address the identified behaviors (Parker, Skinner, and Booher, 2010; Pearce, 2009). For instance, if the FBA suggests that behavior problems are due to a deficit in social skills, social skills training can be used as an intervention strategy in the school or clinical setting (Pearce, 2009).

According to Sugai et al. (1999), the FBA process includes six steps: (1) collecting information to determine the conditions under which the behaviors are and are not observed, (2) developing testable hypotheses, (3) collecting direct observation information, (4) designing behavior support plans, (5) developing implementation scripts, and finally (6) evaluating the plan and redesigning as necessary. In one recent study, Parker et al. (2010), an FBA was utilized to identify problem behaviors and develop objectives for the consultation process that would happen between the research team and the teacher seeking consultation. The consultant on the research team was able to use the information collected during the interview with the teacher to determine a cluster of target behaviors for the student, as well as procedures for the teacher to use within the classroom. Throughout the consultation process, the consultant completed three one-hour antecedent–behavior–consequent observations, collected data using multiple standardized assessments, and finally completed direct observation sessions. Using the data collected through the FBA, the teacher and consultant were able to develop a hypothesis for the student's behavior, namely "negative" teacher attention. From there, the teacher and consultant were able to develop and monitor an intervention addressing the specified behaviors gathered from the FBA.

As with the consultant in this research study, counselors may serve in the consultant role during the assessment or intervention stage of FBA. Counselors may be asked to go into classrooms to complete observations of students to assess antecedent events, problem behaviors, and consequences. During the treatment phase, counselors may be needed to perform direct services, such as individual counseling, or indirect services, such as teacher and administrator consultation (Stage et al., 2008). However, because many school personnel are not trained in functional behavioral analysis, having a counselor or consultant who is knowledgeable regarding the process can increase the fidelity of implementation (Lee and Jamison, 2002; Pearce, 2009).

This section discussed prevention-based activities and those more focused on interventions and treatment. Evidence-based practices and approaches and the importance of cultural relevance in these practices were highlighted. Finally, several evidence-based practices and approaches were presented that both school and clinical mental health counselors can use across settings to effectively manage a variety of presenting issues and concerns. Next, additional programs and strategies that are rooted in prevention, intervention, and advocacy on behalf of youth and families will be further explored.

MENTAL HEALTH FIRST AID

One in four youth have a mental health-related disorder that interferes with daily living (Merikangas, et al., 2010). A 2009 report by the National Research Council and the Institute of Medicine estimated that 13–20 per cent of children living in the United States experience a mental health challenge in a given year. Additionally, suicide is the second leading cause of death for youth aged 10–24 years (Kann, et al., 2014). Furthermore, youth of color and youth from low-income backgrounds are less likely to receive mental health services compared to their white counterparts (Zambrano, Castro-Villarreal, and Sullivan, 2012). Youth who have significant mental health needs pose serious problems to themselves, disrupt classroom environments, challenge school safety and routines, and impact communities (Fuchs and Fuchs, 2006).

Additionally, youth who experience disaster-related trauma are affected in profound ways given their dependence on others for help and recovery and their developmental levels. Programs exist to train all walks of life including individuals who teach or provide counseling services to youth to interested individuals who want to play an active role in their communities. Disaster Mental Health, Psychological First Aid, and Mental Health First Aid are all curriculum-based programs that train individuals to work with others in crisis or post-crisis situations. Mental Health First Aid will be discussed next, in more detail.

Mental Health First Aid (MHFA) is an international evidence-based prevention educational program that increases the public's knowledge of mental health and substance use issues and connects people with mental health-related disorders with treatment resources and healthcare providers. Originally created in Australia, MHFA is global in its use, translated into two languages, and housed within the National Council on Behavioral Health in the U.S. Individuals who complete the eight-hour MHFA course learn risk factors, signs, and symptoms of mental health and addiction challenges.

MHFA program evaluation results indicate that the training increases understanding of mental health issues and treatment, reduces stigma, connects people with concerns to resources, and, overall, improves individuals' mental health. The program provides a clear understanding to participants that their role is not to diagnose, but to be more aware of signs and symptoms of budding mental health or substance use concerns and to connect that individual with help and resources. Participants in the eight-hour training learn a five-step action plan to assess situations as crisis or non-crisis, use techniques to gain more information, and secure appropriate care for an individual experiencing a mental health-related disorder or substance use issues. The trainings are designed for individuals who come in contact with others in work or social settings such as school personnel, law enforcement, faith-based communities, hospital staff, community leaders, and business owners. As of 2016, more than 550,000 people have been trained in MHFA by a group of 9,000 trained instructors. The author of this edited textbook, Dr. Daigle, is a certified instructor for Youth Mental Health First Aid (YMHFA). She has provided several trainings to both undergraduate and graduate students, school resource officers, police officers, and members of faith-based organizations.

Check out the Mental Health First Aid site (https://www.mentalhealthfirstaid. org/cs/). Peruse the site including the different trainings offered (Adult and Youth), program outcomes, and endorsements. Think about the counselor role as leader and catalyst of systemic change. Discuss your views on counselors becoming MHFA trainers. What groups of people should counselors provide trainings for? Why?

Activity

This section discussed Mental Health First Aid, an evidence-based prevention program that provides knowledge to the general public about mental health and substance use issues. This program has been shown to increase understanding of mental health issues, reduce stigma, and promote overall improvement in individuals' mental health. The next section will consider the role of consultation in counselors' work. As counselors work systemically to improve the lives of their clients, other allied professionals must be involved and work collaboratively.

COUNSELOR AS CONSULTANT

Consultation can be described simply as an interpersonal helping relationship focused on problem-solving (Carlson, Dinkmeyer, and Johnson, 2008; Dougherty, 2014). Consultation is a relationship involving three players—the consultant, the consultee, and the client. Consultation is considered an indirect treatment model because service delivery is administered by the consultee as opposed to the clinician him or herself (Auster, Feeney-Kettler, and Kratochwill, 2006). For example, a school counselor may serve as a consultant to a teacher who is having difficulty managing the classroom culture. A clinical mental health counselor may work as a consultant with a local principal who has noticed an increase in depressive symptoms among students in the school. Resistance to the consultation process may come from both teachers and parents. However, by emphasizing the value of these individuals' contributions to the process and ensuring a collaborative environment, consultants are more likely to be successful in facilitating the consultation process (Carlson et al., 2008).

Mental health consultation was originally identified and differentiated from other forms of mental health services by Gerald Caplan in 1962. In 1962, Caplan (1995) recognized consultation as a process between two individuals in which "the consultant, who is a specialist, and the consultee, who invokes his help in regard to a current work problem with which the latter is having some difficulty, and which he has decided is within the former's area of specialized competence" (p. 7). The consultant provides recommendations that the consultee is allowed to accept or reject as the consultee maintains responsibility for the client's welfare in the consultation relationship (Caplan, 1995). Current writers, however, agree that the consultant has an ethical obligation to make informed recommendations because he or she oversees the professional welfare of the consultee and the client system (Dougherty, 2014). At that time, Caplan proposed four main types of consultation—*client-centered case consultation*, *program-centered administrative consultation*, *consultee-centered case consultation*, and *consultee-centered administrative consultation* (Caplan, 1995). These will be discussed in further detail later in this section.

While consultation is seen as an integral element in the role of those who work in community-based settings, this view is less prominent in educational settings. In clinical mental health settings, consultation is often utilized as a method to facilitate managed care, provide the best resources to their clients, as well as to advocate for and assist with certain populations and or causes (Dougherty, 2014). In school settings, however, consultation is often seen as a supplemental, as opposed to a principal, role (Dougherty, 2014). However, the American School Counselor Association's School Counselor Competencies (2005) uses the term consultation six times as a role that school counselors both perform as well as receive. Undoubtedly, ASCA's stance indicates that consultation is an integral part of the school counselor's role as well.

In fact, consultation can be used as a way to reframe the mental health professional's role, particularly in a school setting, from one of reactive, problem solver to a systems level, prevention-focused worker (Clemens, 2007). Consultation service provides an opportunity to give consultees a skill set that can be used in the future with other clients (Auster et al., 2006). The consultee becomes more knowledgeable, self-reliant, and more effective in working with the client in the future (Carlson et al., 2008). Given that there are often many students and clients in need of services, and only a limited amount of service providers, counselors, and mental health professionals increase their range of services through the use of consultation.

Stages of Consultation

Although all authors do not agree on the names of the stages of consultation, a general progression through initial, middle, and closure stages constitute most models. Consultation models tend to follow a linear progression; however, there is some provision for flexibility and movement back through previous stages. Perera-Diltz, Moe, and Mason (2011) highlight that the initial stage involves rapport building to establish a collaborative environment, the middle stages require problem-solving skills as goals, strategies, and interventions are identified, and, finally, the closure stage requires assessing, evaluating, and terminating. For example, Dougherty (2014) uses a four-stage model that encompasses entry, diagnosis, implementation, and disengagement stages.

Although the model employed is generic in creation, Dougherty notes that the implementation of the consultation process must incorporate the unique needs and perspectives of the consultee and the client.

Kratochwill and Bergan (1978) provide a similar stage model using a behavioral framework. The four stages are (1) problem identification, (2) problem analysis, (3) plan implementation, and (4) problem evaluation. In the problem identification stage it is most important for the goals to be well defined and operational, with specific outcomes determined. The problem analysis stage is based on a problem analysis interview that identifies variables and intervention(s) that will influence the achievement of the determined goals. During the problem analysis stage, the consultant is able to bring in their expertise, experience, and empirical data, as well as any theoretical frameworks that might provide additional insight into the issues. In a collaborative consultation orientation, this might be a point where the consultant relies on the expertise of the consultee to provide unique insights specific to the client and the organization in which the consultation relationship is occurring.

Throughout the plan implementation phase, the consultant's main goal is to ensure valid and reliable implementation of the intervention (Kratochwill & Bergan, 1978). The consultant must work to maintain continuous contact with the consultee. Data should be collected to use as formative assessments to track the progress of the intervention. The final phase, problem evaluation, provides an opportunity to assess if the selected intervention was successful in alleviating the initial issue.

Similarly, Scott, Royal, and Kissinger (2015) propose a five-stage model of consultation that flows in a circular nature and includes the preliminary stage, exploration and goal-setting stage, intervention and implementation stage, outcomes stage, and termination stage. Scott et al. visualize consultation as a process of back-and-forth movement with permeable boundaries between the stages. This model acknowledges that there may be roadblocks in the consultation process that consultant and consultee must overcome to navigate the consultation process successfully. As stated previously, allowing the consultee to see his or her contributions at play in the process can help the consultant avoid such roadblocks.

In the preliminary stage, the consultee recognizes that there is a need and seeks to find someone with the needed expertise who can serve as a consultant. The purpose of the exploration and goal-setting stage is to get to know the consultee. This may mean utilizing basic counseling skills to establish rapport with the organization or setting up new boundaries if the consultant is already a member of the organization (Perera-Diltz et al., 2011). Goal setting may work from a collaborative or expertise approach. In a collaborative approach, the consultant works as a co-expert or partner in the process, whereas in an expertise approach the consultant is the sole expert in regards to the issue (Perera-Diltz et al., 2011). Goal revision should be expected and should not be considered a failure in the consultation process (Scott et al., 2015). Keeping a file of resources and developing relationships with individuals on a local, national, and international level are integral to one's success in this stage. Although this step may take the most time, ensuring that all parties involved are on the same page from the start will decrease complications in later phases of the process.

Following these two stages, the process moves into the intervention and implementation stage. In this stage, consultants will be expected to have a breadth of knowledge on the various types of interventions that can be used in any given setting. The setting, needs, and structure of the organization will determine the type of interventions that are employed to reach the consultation goals. Things to consider during this stage of the process are cost and feasibility of the intervention, as well as the approach that will need to be taken to implement the intervention. From a counseling standpoint, the implementation stage is the opportune time to begin empowering the consultee by facilitating growth and awareness by supporting rather than doing (Scott et al., 2015). It is also vital to acknowledge that everyone within the organization may not be favorable to the changes that are being made, and that this feedback, in the form of resistance, is normal (Carlson et al., 2008).

The outcomes stage is the opportunity for the consultant to document that the consultation process has been successful. Although evaluations and feedback may have been conducted throughout the process, the outcomes stage provides a formal opportunity to gather data and document effectiveness. Finally, in the termination stage, consultants will need to conduct final evaluations and close the consultative relationship. As with counseling, addressing closure at the onset of the consultation process can ease the termination process. Final evaluations should not only center on the success of the interventions, but the consultant should also ensure they collect information regarding the process and impact of consultation. In this way, the consultee as well as the consultant benefit from the termination process. The information collected during the final evaluation can assist the consultant in providing stronger consultation services to the next consultee.

While various researchers have created different versions of these stages, the main point is that consultation, like counseling, is a process that requires attention to rapport building, creative thinking, and final assessment. Now we will consider some of the models of consultation, many of which are based in counseling theory themselves.

Models of Consultation

Just as with counseling, consultants should employ evidence-based approaches and strategies to ensure that the services they provide are both legal and ethical. Various models of consultation have been established and tested, resulting in a number of different options for approaches to be utilized in the field. No matter which model of consultation one might decide to utilize, it is imperative, both from an ethical as well as practical standpoint, to know the theoretical tenets undergirding that particular consultation model (Scott et al., 2008). This section will briefly detail four different models of consultation. Additional resources will be provided at the end of the chapter to use as further study.

Caplan's Mental Health Consultation

One of the first models of consultation was developed by Gerald Caplan in 1962 and came to be known as *mental health consultation*. Caplan believed that consultation is "primarily preventative and that consulting relationships are fundamentally collaborative and egalitarian" (Scott et al., 2008, p. 163). The model developed by Caplan details four different orientations—*client-centered case consultation*, *program-centered administrative consultation*, *consultee-centered case consultation*, and *consultee-centered administrative consultation*. Each orientation is distinct in its focus and overall goal.

Client-centered case consultation assumes that the consultant is the expert. The consultant is given the responsibility of assessing the client, selecting the appropriate diagnosis, and offering treatment suggestions. Although the consultant determines the intervention, the consultee is still responsible for implementing the intervention. While client-centered consultation focuses on one individual, program-centered administrative consultation considers the larger organization or program. In this case, the consultant still takes the role of expert; however, they must also use skills in data collection and action-planning to establish a well-orchestrated plan for resolving the program's or organization's issue and ensuring more effective functioning (Scott et al., 2008). Taking yet another focus, consultee-centered case consultation considers the consultee first, client second, with the goal of professional development for the consultee. In these cases, consultants could assist the consultee in developing their lack of knowledge, confidence, or objectivity about a particular situation. Finally, in consultee-centered administrative consultation, the focus is on the professional competencies of those involved in an organization with the goal of creating enduring organizational change.

Developmental

Based in Piagetian thought, Developmental Counseling Theory (DCT) is predicated on the idea that there are four primary cognitive developmental modalities—sensorimotor, concrete, formal—operational, and dialectic—systemic (Clemens, 2007). While an individual may have access to each of these cognitive developmental modalities, the person is more likely to prefer one modality over another, depending on the situation. DCT has been utilized in school settings as a means of intervention as well as education. By utilizing this consultation model, mental health professionals can maximize their time, while also providing support that can effect positive change for the long run. Presenting the strengths and limitations of each cognitive developmental modality, the consultant and consultee are able to develop an appropriate intervention while also developing the consultee's perspectives for future client interactions.

An individual operating from a sensorimotor perspective will focus on the feelings and emotions conjured during an experience. Someone with a concrete operational focus will be very attuned to the facts of the story and likely to present information in a linear cause—effect fashion. A person who operates from a formal–operational standpoint is likely to consider patterns of behavior but miss the dynamics of the interaction in a particular instance. Finally, the person who prefers a dialectic modality examines larger systemic issues that may be influencing the child or adolescent's behaviors, but may not consider individual or classroom-level influences.

Within the consultation context, the goal is to broaden the perspectives from which a consultee understands the behavior(s) in question. A three-step framework is used to meet this goal. The first step is assessing the consultee's current modality in describing the behavior. The preferred modality can usually be determined in fewer than 100 words. The second step is determining which modality would best help the consultee to expand his or her view of the situation and lead to substantive change. Finally, the consultant constructs a plan grounded in the analysis of the modalities (Clemens, 2007). As stated previously, the final decision of how to proceed is left with the consultee.

Behavioral Consultation and Conjoint Behavioral Consultation

Behavioral consultation is a problem-solving model in which the consultant assists the consultee in defining problems and evaluating attainment of goals. Consultation services may be directed at all levels of the organization, including client, staff members, administration, social system, or community (Kratochwill and Bergan, 1978). Behavioral consultation has been empirically researched and is the model most often employed in school settings. The specificity found within the model makes it easier to create protocols, trainings, and evaluations, all elements valued in a school setting (Holcomb-McCoy and Bryan, 2010; Rosenfield and Humphrey, 2012).

Behavioral consultation is considered an indirect form of service delivery and operates with four distinct characteristics: "(a) use of a standard problem-solving process, (b) adherence to behavioral assessment techniques, (c) adherence to behavioral intervention strategies, and (d) evaluation of outcomes based on behavioral analysis and related methodologies" (Holcomb-McCoy and Bryan, 2010, p. 259). Following from these ideas is a four-stage process: (1) problem identification, (2) problem analysis, (3) plan implementation, and (4) problem evaluation. The primary focus of the work is to change behavior perceived as inappropriate (Kratochwill and Bergan, 1978).

An extension of behavioral consultation is Conjoint Behavioral Consultation (CBC). CBC combines the resources of home and school, involving the consultant, family, and teachers in influencing outcomes for the child. This model is collaborative in nature, requiring parents and teachers to serve as joint consultees in a cooperative, constructive manner (Auster et al., 2006; Holcomb-McCoy and Bryant, 2010). CBC problem solving meetings are thought to "improve the communication and interactions between the child, family, and school personnel" while promoting "joint and shared responsibility for problem solution" (Sheridan, Eagle, Cowan, and Mickelson, 2001).

CBC is usually initiated at a teacher's request and the mental health consultant works to connect the teacher and parent(s). As identified earlier in the chapter, CBC utilizes a stage process similar to other models of consultation. There are four structured meetings encompassing four stages in the CBC process. The first stage is *conjoint problem identification* where all involved parties come together to identify and prioritize concerns for the child as well as identify goals. The second stage is *conjoint problem analysis* in which baseline data is reviewed, a functional behavioral analysis is given, if necessary, and an intervention plan is created. In the third stage, *conjoint treatment implementation*, data is collected and used to monitor the progress of the intervention implementation. Any modifications are made based on a collaborative evaluation process. Finally, the last stage, *conjoint treatment evaluation*, calls on consultant and consultees to evaluate the intervention effectiveness, as well as address concerns around sustaining the effects of the intervention.

The four main goals of CBC include "(a) sharing the responsibility for the problem solution, (b) improving communication and interactions among the child, family, and school personnel, (c) obtaining comprehensive and functional information related to the identified problem, and (d) improving the skills of all parties" (Auster et al., 2006, p. 247). CBC creates connections between teachers and parents while building a skill set for both entities that promote empowerment to provide effective interventions in the future without the assistance of the consultant.

CBC has been used with a diverse set of problem behaviors, including anxiety and behavioral disorders, as well as social skills deficits, inattention, and academic concerns (Auster et al., 2006; Holcomb-McCoy and Bryant, 2010). Research has shown that there is some variability in respect to the effectiveness of CBC based on severity of symptoms and developmental level of the client; however, most research investigating the impact of CBC on behavioral changes has been promising (Sheridan et al., 2001). Further research with culturally diverse populations will continue to increase its viability (Holcomb-McCoy and Bryant, 2010).

Adlerian Consultation

Based in the theory of Alfred Adler, Adlerian consultation is based on the belief that everyone wants to belong to a group (Holcomb-McCoy et al., 2010). According to Carlson et al. (2008), Adlerian consultation is based in three guiding principles: (1) behavior is goal-directed and purposeful, (2) effective change occurs when the individual believes he or she is capable of change and can identify this ability as a strength while identifying other strengths, and (3) the consultant understands the school setting in a holistic manner—no student, no teacher, no parent operates in a vacuum independent of the others in the system (p. 484).

Through the use of Adlerian consultation, consultants can help teachers, parents, and other individuals in a child or adolescent's life recognize the goals of their misbehavior and implement interventions that focus on this underlying belief. These four goals include to gain attention, to gain power, to gain revenge, or to display inadequacy (i.e. avoid failure) (Carlson et al., 2008; Holcomb-McCoy and Bryan, 2010).

Solution-Focused Consultee Consultation

Solution-Focused Consultee Consultation (SFCC) is based on postmodern philosophy found in the tenets of solution-focused brief therapy. The work of Steve de Shazer and Insoo Kim Berg, this theoretical orientation posits that perspective is important, thus a consultant utilizing this model would place a strong emphasis on the consultee's worldview and understanding of the concerns brought to the consultation relationship (Scott et al., 2008). Unlike other consultation models, SFCC requires a greater level of cultural competence because much of the work is grounded in the consultee's perspective. Another unique aspect of this approach is the strengths-based focus that is incorporated throughout the process.

In the initial phases of this model, the consultant's main goal is to gain an understanding of the consultee's strengths and assets and any solutions they have used in the past to solve problems. Searching for these solutions may involve seeking exceptions to the current situation and/or the use of the miracle question to encourage the consultee to conceptualize the issue differently. During the goal-setting stage, the consultee is the individual responsible for setting goals; however, the consultant should collaborate with the consultee on determining how these goals will be met. Scaling questions, commonly utilized in solution-focused therapy, may be one technique a consultant can employ to gain baseline data that can lead to brainstorming possible interventions. In the end, however, it will be the consultee's use of his or her own strengths that will lead to sustainable change (Scott et al., 2008). Finally, considering possible obstacles to success is vital to setting the stage for problem resolution in SFCC. The earlier these discussions occur, the more likely it is that the process will be successful.

Sessions throughout the remainder of the consultation process will highlight progress made by the consultee. If attempted solutions have not been successful, consultation dialogue should center on determining other viable solutions. Termination occurs once the consultee attains his or her goal or the consultee believes he or she is capable of problem solving on his or her own.

Case Study: Middle School Counselor

The following scenario is based on consultation in the school setting.

You are a middle school counselor who is approached by the seventh-grade lead teacher because she is concerned about an increase in aggressive behaviors of female students that she has recently noticed. The teacher is concerned that the aggressive behaviors may lead to bullying or fighting. In order to better understand the teacher's concerns, you meet with the teacher during her planning time to discuss the instances in more detail. As you talk more with the teacher, you notice that the incidents seem to happen, most often, after lunch and between the same three students. Initially, you develop a plan with the teacher to meet with each of the students individually to get an understanding of their points of view. The teacher will continue to monitor the students' behavior, making note of any instances that occur over the next week.

Using a behavioral consultation approach, you recognize that knowing the behaviors immediately before and after the aggressive behaviors will be helpful in identifying a plan for behavioral change. During your meetings with each student, you seek information about the antecedent behaviors and consequences. You ask the teacher to note specifically what happens before and after the aggressive behaviors that are concerning her. Once these points have been identified, you work with the teacher using a problem-solving process to determine strategies that could be used to promote positive behavioral changes. For example, the teacher may choose to create more structure during the transition from lunch back to the classroom. Alternatively, positive reinforcements, such as tokens or privileges, could be implemented to encourage students to enter the classroom quietly, keeping their hands to themselves. You would work with the teacher to track any changes in behavior as a result of the implemented strategies, and make any adjustments as necessary.

Process Question

1. Take a few minutes in class and review the above case scenario. Think, pair, share. Read on your own, talk over key points/further recommendations/questions you may have, and share with the larger group.

Case Study: Consultation in a Clinical Mental Health Agency

You are a counselor working in an out-patient substance abuse treatment program for youth and adolescents. A co-worker, Mark, has come to seek your input because he feels that he is struggling to connect with one of his newest clients. The client, Randy, is a 16-year-old White male who was recently mandated for treatment after being caught on school grounds with marijuana and under the influence of alcohol. Mark has been meeting with Randy for the last three weeks, but still feels that he has not made any progress in getting Randy to open up. Mark's usual approach with adolescent clients is to employ motivational interviewing, but he believes there may be some other approaches he could consider that might work better for Randy. You are known around the agency for having success with moving clients into the working stage of counseling, and Mark hopes that you will be able to provide some new perspectives for him.

As Mark's consultant, you determine that using Caplan's consultee-centered case consultation process would be most beneficial. Listening to Mark's situation, you recognize that it would not only be important for Mark to be able to address Randy's needs, but to also be able to develop his own professional skills in this area (Dougherty, 2014). You agree to meet with Mark next week to talk more in depth about his client. In order to gain a better understanding of the counseling process, you ask Mark to bring one or two specific examples of instances that happen during the week where he believes he gets "stuck" with Randy. In the meantime, you agree to review Randy's case file to gain a more holistic picture of his situation.

Based on your conversation with Mark, as well as your past experiences working with him, you determine that Mark's issue may be a lack of skills. During the follow up meeting, you work with Mark to explore the problem using the examples he provides, discuss what techniques he has tried thus far to help the client, and create a list of possible interventions he could select from to try to move the counseling process forward. Mark acknowledges that he has never used some of the techniques you have suggested, so you offer to provide some resources and/or training should he pick one of those techniques. You and Mark agree to meet in two weeks to determine if his selected intervention is working or if another approach would be better.

Process Question

1. Take a few minutes in class and review the above case scenario. Think, pair, share. Read on your own, talk over key points/further recommendations/questions you may have, and share with the larger group.

In this section, you have been introduced to the consultation role of counselors. Consultation occurs in both school and clinical mental health settings and is one way in which counselors can provide indirect services to clients. Particularly in school settings, consultation allows counselors to reach a greater number of individuals. Consultation happens in three general stages—initial, middle, and closure stages. There are various models of consultation, including Mental Health, Developmental, Behavioral, Adlerian, and Solution-Focused, among others.

The next section describes new and emerging interventions that are at the initial stages of becoming evidence-based practices and approaches such as neurofeedback and mindfulness.

NEUROFEEDBACK

The brain is not a fixed entity, but rather changes in response to external, environmental events, and actions. Brain research in the field of neuroscience has shown that effective counseling can produce new neurons in the brain. Neurons fire when we have any type of experience or stimulus. Different brain wave patterns are associated with different arousal states in the brain (Butnik, 2005). Neurofeedback can be used alone, but is more likely to yield greater results when combined with traditional counseling and stress management interventions (Matuszek and Rycraft, 2003). As mental health professionals work with clients, the changes that develop in the brain occur through the development of new neural networks, thus producing client changes (Ivey, Ivey, and Zalaquett, 2010). Neuroscience provides direct information about and direct influences on these brain processes (Fultz, 2009).

According to Butnik (2005), the goal of neurofeedback work is to train the individual to normalize abnormal brain wave frequencies by learning to regulate their mental states. Through this process, children and adolescents can gain a more concrete understanding of the mind–body connection, making sense of the relationship between what they think and how they feel physically, through the data provided from neurofeedback sessions (Matuszek and Rycraft, 2003). In essence, the individual becomes more mindful of their level of attentiveness. The data provided from neurofeedback readings consists of electronic signals that are amplified to create frequency bands or wavelengths that can be presented to clients in a graphic or auditory format (Fultz, 2009; Hammond, 2011; Matuszek and Rycraft, 2003). These readings are created from electro-encephalogram, or EEG, readings. EEG readings are most commonly created from a measurement of the electrical activity of the brain measured by a number of electrodes on the scalp. Technology such as PET scans and fMRIs allow these changes to be observed as they are occurring (Ivey et al., 2010).

Neurofeedback sessions typically occur twice weekly and last about one hour (Butnik, 2005). Neurofeedback training can last anywhere from 15 to 20 sessions for a diagnosis such as anxiety or insomnia to 30 to 50 sessions for a condition such as ADD/ADHD or learning disabilities (Hammond, 2011). The total number of sessions depends on a number of factors, including diagnosis, severity, and other co-morbid diagnoses (Butnik, 2005). Neurofeedback training, however, requires a trained clinician in order to avoid harmful side effects of this work. Within the process, there are various assessments that should be done prior to initiating biofeedback training, as biofeedback work should be uniquely attuned to each client. The neurofeedback process itself should also include an assessment, the results of which are then used to develop goals with the client. By completing in-depth assessments, clinicians can statistically compare the collected brainwave data to a large normative database that provides an objective comparison of how the brain should be functioning at the client's age. Such information can be used to determine if the child or adolescent is significantly different from normal, and, if so, how and where he or she is different (Hammond, 2011).

Neurofeedback was initially used in the 1970s to train children with ADHD after researchers noted improvements in academics and behavior for school children with seizure disorders who were being treated with neuro-feedback (Butnik, 2005). Since that time, neurofeedback training has been demonstrated to be effective with a variety of diagnoses, including ADD/ADHD, anxiety, and learning disabilities (Hammond, 2011). Research has shown that there are distinct patterns in EEG readings that differentiate various diagnoses. However, much of the produced research literature around neuro-feedback with children and adolescents examines training for ADHD diagnoses. For example, Hammond (2011) demonstrated that there are a minimum of three different subtypes of ADD/ADHD, which cannot be identified by simply observing a person's behavior. Each of these subtypes requires a different treatment protocol. By using neurofeedback data, a counselor can more accurately differentiate between the subtypes, and provide a more specific treatment plan.

A randomized control trial conducted by Steiner, Frenette, Rene, Brennan, and Perrin (2014) examined the use of in-school neurofeedback training for ADHD. Their research compared outcomes for students who received neuro-feedback training with those who received cognitive training or were in a control group. Results indicated that neurofeedback participants made improvements more quickly and displayed greater improvements in their ADHD symptoms, which were sustained at the six-month follow up, in comparison to the cognitive training group, as well as the control group, participants. As of the writing of this chapter, this study was the first to use neurofeedback training in a school setting as opposed to a laboratory or clinical setting.

While these technologies hold promise for determining the impact of counseling on brain development, neurofeedback was not originally backed as a plausible treatment because it carried a hefty price tag (Hammond, 2011). However, the practice has gained popularity over time, and is currently utilized in various settings by a number of professionals (Butnik, 2005). The beauty of neurofeedback is that it provides immediate information to children and adolescents about the ways in which their brain activity is being influenced by the counseling process (Butnik, 2005). Additionally, neurofeedback training provides an alternative to medication to alter brain patterns (Hammond, 2011), and can be used as a strengths-based intervention as opposed to a medial model of treatment (Matuszek and Rycraft, 2003). Most past research on neurofeedback training has been done with single-subject designs and small groups of clinical subjects. Additional research utilizing large-scale, double-blind, or controlled studies, as well as studies examining the long-term effects of neurofeedback training, will continue to increase the validity of this option and provide support for its effectiveness (Butnik, 2005).

MINDFULNESS

As a practice, mindfulness has been defined in many ways. While the practice originally began in the Eastern traditions of Buddhism, it was popularized in a Western context by Jon Kabat-Zinn from the University of Massachusetts (Weare, 2013). The general consensus is that mindfulness is the awareness and nonjudgmental acceptance of an experience, in the moment, with a clear, calm mind (Singh et al., 2007; Thompson and Gauntlett-Gilbert, 2008). Mindfulness "rebalances emotionality and thoughtfulness as a nonjudgmental focus" and allows one to detach unpleasant thoughts and feelings from the self-identity, thereby reducing their power and impact (Swart and Apsche, 2014, p. 9). It is believed that the nonjudgmental awareness that is a key element of mindfulness raises awareness of one's own impulses and thought patterns, thereby decreasing emotional reactivity (Thompson and Gauntlett-Gilbert, 2008). A core assumption of mindfulness is that people move through life in an "autopilot" way, unaware of their automatic behavioral responses (Thompson and Gauntlett-Gilbert, 2008). Therefore, engaging in a practice such as mindfulness provides a space in which children and adolescents can become more aware of their emotional habits and learn to choose their response rather than react automatically, resulting in more flexible, adaptive behavior.

Mindfulness interventions have been used with adults for a long time, but more recent research is now exploring their use with children and adolescents. Some research has used mindfulness as an element of a larger treatment approach; however, research conducted in the last 10 years has explored the direct impact of mindfulness training on aggressive behaviors with students diagnosed with conduct disorder (Singh et al., 2007), Asperger syndrome (Singh et al., 2011b), and autism (Singh et al., 2011a), as well as with adolescents in in-patient treatment experiencing chronic pain (Thompson and Gauntlett-Gilbert, 2008) and incarcerated sexual offenders (Jennings, Apsche, Blossom, and Bayles, 2013). These research studies have taught the technique to both the student, as well as adults in the student's life, and shown promising outcomes, even three to four years post-treatment.

However, the use of mindful practice must be developmentally appropriate when used with children and adolescents. As with adults, mindfulness practice tends to focus on teaching children and adolescents skills such as paying attention, focusing on breathing, and focusing on being in the moment, among other things (Weare, 2013). However, mindful practice with children and adolescents tend to last for shorter periods of time and focus more on fun as opposed to long periods of silent meditation. Additionally, the focus for younger children is on the concrete experience of mindfulness, while older children and adolescents can also discuss the meta-cognitive aspect of their mindfulness experience (Weare, 2013).

Mindfulness programs have been used in both school and clinical settings. In clinical settings, Weare (2013) highlights multiple research studies demonstrating decreased levels of rumination and intrusive thoughts, anxiety, depression, substance abuse, and behavioral issues, while there were increases in trust amongst friends, self-esteem, and sustained attention as a result of mindfulness training. Most of these studies used or incorporated Mindfulness Based Stress Reduction (MBSR). Within school settings, mindfulness programs that have been found to be effective with children include Susan Kaiser Greenland's "Inner Kids" and Schonert-Reichl and Hymel's "MindUP." Programs geared towards adolescents include the "Learning to BREATHE" curriculum. If working with very young children, ages 5–8, one might consider exploring the Attention Academy Program intervention. A current study of the United Kingdom-based program ".b" also shows promising preliminary results of a significant impact on wellbeing, depression, and anxiety in high school-aged adolescents (Weare, 2013). As these practices begin to influence the social–emotional aspects of student's lives, decreasing anxiety and increasing attention, positive results for academic outcomes also increase.

While mindfulness training and use does not alter one's feelings, the practice is able to help children and adolescents recognize when an emotion is happening and allow them to choose a different reaction from their immediate, initial reaction. One limitation, however, to using mindfulness practice with children and adolescents in a school setting is the amount of time required for the practice to become automatic. Singh et al. (2011b) note that consistent practice and use are necessary to see a significant change. In essence, mindfulness practice must become a way of life, not just a reactive response to a triggering event (Singh et al., 2011b). On a positive note, mindfulness is a relatively cheap practice to introduce, and is likely to have an impact fairly quickly with long-term benefits for students' social–emotional as well as academic success. Previous research has shown that as little as five days of twenty-minute mindfulness meditations can lead to significant changes in functioning (Weare, 2013). It is vital, however, that mindfulness instruction be taught by trained professionals, and that those who teach have a sustained mindfulness practice themselves (Bell, 2016; Weare, 2013).

In conclusion, mindfulness research with children and adolescents, though limited, has demonstrated positive changes in psychological and physiological wellbeing, and that the practice is generally enjoyed by the young people who participate (Weare, 2013). Advances in neuroscience have demonstrated the benefits of mindful meditation as well, showing that practice over time actually changes the way the brain sustains attention and reacts to sounds in the environment (Davidson and Lutz, 2008; Weare, 2013). Additionally, a preliminary review of research on mindfulness conducted by Burke in 2009 indicated support for the use of mindfulness with children and adolescents, but also highlighted a lack of empirical evidence for the efficacy of these approaches. Burke, like more current studies (Singh et al., 2011a; Singh et al., 2011b; Weare, 2013), note that more well-designed, large-scale studies should be conducted using various methodologies in a way that they can be easily replicated and compared to continue to increase our understanding of mindfulness practice with children and adolescents.

This section presented two current and timely approaches used in counseling, neurofeedback and mindfulness, and both are being further validated as evidence-based.

SUMMARY

This chapter provided an introduction to a variety of evidence-based strategies and techniques that counselors in both school and clinical settings can use to support youth and adolescents. The goal of these strategies is to create prevention interventions that move past the individual, focusing on more ecological perspectives. Evidence-based strategies considered in this chapter included Cognitive Behavioral strategies, Functional Behavioral Analysis, Mental Health First Aid, and Student Success Skills, among others. Consultation was also presented, as well as other innovative interventions such as mindfulness and neurofeedback. As a counselor-in-training, staying abreast of well-researched, evidence-based practices and approaches will assist you in providing the most effective services to youth and adolescents in your care.

Additional Resources

Evidence-Based Programs

Centers for Disease Control and Prevention—Adolescent and School Health: http://www.cdc.gov/healthyyouth/stories/index.htm?s_cid=hy-homepage-005
Collaborative for Academic, Social, and Emotional Learning—Effective Social–Emotional Learning Programs Guide: http://www.casel.org/guide/
Inner Kids: http://www.susankaisergreenland.com/inner-kids.html, a curriculum for using mindfulness within school settings
Mind Up: http://thehawnfoundation.org/mindup/, using cognitive neuroscience, positive psychology, and mindful awareness training to teach social and emotional learning

National Registry of Evidence-based Program and Practices via SAMHSA: http://www.
samhsa.gov/nrepp
Responsive Classroom: www.responsiveclassroom.org
Student Success Skills: http://studentsuccessskills.com, a whole-school and small-
group curriculum to improve cognitive, social, and self-management skills
The What Works Clearinghouse: http://ies.ed.gov/ncee/wwc/

Best Practice Documents and Websites

Best Practices: Behavioral Health Guidelines for Children and Adolescents from Birth
to 17 Years of Age: https://www.tn.gov/assets/entities/behavioral-health/
clinical-ls/attachments/Best_Practice_Guidelines_Children-Adolescents.pdf,
compiled by Tennessee Department of Mental Health and Substance Abuse
Services
Center for School Counseling Outcome Research and Evaluation (CSCORE): http://
www.umass.edu/schoolcounseling/index.php
SAMHSA: http://www.samhsa.gov/nrepp, National Registry of Evidence-based
Programs and Practices (NREPP)

Suggested Readings

Black, D. S. and Fernando, R. (2014). Mindfulness training and classroom behavior
among lower-income and ethnic minority elementary school children. *Journal of
Child and Family Studies* 23 (7), 1242–1246.
Crone, D. A., Hawken, L. S., and Horner, R. H. (2015). *Building positive behavior
support systems in schools: Functional behavioral assessment*, 2nd ed. New York,
NY: The Guildford Press.
Guillermo, B. and Domenech Rodriguez, M. M. (eds.) (2012). *Cultural adaptations: Tools
for evidence-based practice with diverse populations*. Washington, DC: American
Psychological Association.
Jaycox, L. H., Kataoka, S. H., Stein, B. D., Langley, A. K., and Wong, M. (2012). Cognitive
behavioral intervention for trauma in schools. *Journal of Applied School Psychology*
28 (3), 239–255.
Ngo, V., Langley, A., Kataoka, S. H., Nadeem, E., Escudero, P., and Stein, B. D. (2008).
Providing evidence based practice to ethnically diverse youth: Examples from the
cognitive behavioral intervention for trauma in schools (CBITS) program. *Journal of
the American Academy of Child and Adolescent Psychiatry* 47 (8), 858–862. doi:
10.1097/CHI.0b013e3181799f19
Pfeiffer, S. I. and Reddy, L. A. (eds.) (2012). *Innovative mental health interventions for
children: Programs that work*. New York, NY: Routledge.
Saxe, G. N., Ellis, B. H., and Brown, A. D. (2016). *Trauma systems therapy for children
and teens*, 2nd ed. New York, NY: The Guilford Press.
Steele, W. and Malchiodi, C. A. (2012). *Trauma-informed practices with children and
adolescents*. New York, NY: Routledge.
Wisner, B. L. (2014). An exploratory study of mindfulness meditation for alternative
school students: Perceived benefits for improving school climate and student
functioning. *Mindfulness* 5 (6), 626–638.

Glossary

Conjoint behavioral consultation: A collaborative form of behavioral consultation that combines the resources of home and school

Consultation: Interpersonal helping relationship focused on problem-solving

Evidence-based practices: Research-based techniques and approaches for working with clients

Functional behavioral analysis: Assessment strategy that examines the antecedent events, as well as maintaining events, associated with problem behaviors in students who have not been responsive to tier-one interventions in the behavioral Response to Intervention process

Intervention: Action or programs undertaken to improve a situation

Mental Health First Aid: International evidence-based prevention educational program that increases the public's knowledge of mental health and substance use issues, and connects people with mental health-related disorders with treatment resources and healthcare providers

Mindfulness: Awareness and nonjudgmental acceptance of an experience, in the moment

Neurofeedback: A form of biofeedback in which brain wave frequencies are made visible through monitors allowing clients to develop self-regulation skills

Prevention: Proactively stopping something from happening or arising with the goal of reducing problematic behaviors and disorders and promoting health and wellness

Spectrum of mental health interventions: A continuum of interventions, from preventative to treatment-based, that can be offered to clients

Wraparound: Team-based service planning and coordination process that uses a treatment plan that blends home, school, and community interventions

References

American School Counselor Association (2005). ASCA School Counselor Competencies. Retrieved from https://www.schoolcounselor.org/asca/media/asca/home/SCCompetencies.pdf.

Auster, E. R., Feeney-Kettler, K. A., and Kratochwill, T. R. (2006). Conjoint behavioral consultation: Application to the school-based treatment of anxiety disorders. *Education and Treatment of Children* 29 (2), 243–256.

Bell, P. (2016). Mindfulness in schools is giving children the vital tools to protect their mental wellbeing. *Huffington Post*, February 18. Retrieved from http://www.huffingtonpost.co.uk/2016/02/17/mindfulness-schools-good-mental-health-children-_n_9184916.html

Butnik, S. M. (2005). Neurofeedback in adolescents and adults with attention deficit hyperactivity disorder. *Journal of Clinical Psychology* 61 (5), 621–625. doi: 10.1002/jclp.20124

Caplan, G. (1995). Types of mental health consultation. *Journal of Educational and Psychological Consultation* 6 (1), 7–21.

Carlson, J., Dinkmeyer Jr, D., and Johnson, E. J. (2008). Adlerian teacher consultation: Change teachers, change students. *The Journal of Individual Psychology* 64 (4), 480–493.

Clemens, E. (2007). Developmental counseling and therapy as a model for school counselor consultation with teachers. *Professional School Counseling* 10 (4), 352–359.

Davidson, R. J. and Lutz, A. (2008). Buddha's brain: Neuroplasticity and meditation. *IEEE Signal Process Mag* 25 (1), 176–174. Retrieved from http://www.ncbi.nlm. nih.gov/pmc/articles/PMC2944261/

Dougherty, A. M. (2014). *Psychological consultation and collaboration in school and community settings*, 6th ed. Belmont, CA: Brooks/Cole.

Eber, L. and Nelson, C. M. (1997). School-based wraparound planning: Integrating services for students with emotional and behavioral needs. *American Journal of Orthopsychiatry* 67, 385–395.

Epstein, J. L. (2011). *School, family, and community partnerships: Preparing educators and improving schools*, 2nd ed. Boulder, CO: Westview Press.

Flay, B. R. and Allred, C. G. (2003). Long-term effects of the Positive Action program: A comprehensive, positive youth development program. *American Journal of Health Behavior* 27 (1), 6–21.

Fuchs, D. and Fuchs, L. (2006). Introduction to Response to Intervention: What, why, and how valid is it? *Reading Research Quarterly* 4, 93–99.

Fultz, D. E. (2009). The current status of behaviorism and neurofeedback. *International Journal of Behavioral Consultation and Therapy* 5 (2), 160–163.

Hammond, D. C. (2011). What is neurofeedback: An update. *Journal of Neurotherapy* 15, 305–336. doi: 10.1080/10874208.2011.623090

Hawken, L. S. and Horner, R. H. (2003). Evaluation of a targeted intervention within a schoolwide system of behavior support. *Journal of Behavioral Education* 12 (3), 225–240.

Henderson, A. T. and Berla, N. (eds.) (1994). A new generation of evidence: The family is critical to student achievement (A report from the National Committee for Citizens in Education). Washington, DC: Center for Law and Education.

Holcomb-McCoy, C. and Bryan, J. (2010). Advocacy and empowerment in parent consultation: Implications for theory and practice. *Journal of Counseling and Development* 88, 259–268.

Ivey, A. E., Ivey, M. B., and Zalaquett, C. P. (2010). *Intentional interviewing and counseling: Facilitating client development in a multicultural society*, 7th ed. Belmont, CA: Brooks/Cole.

Jennings, J. L., Apsche, J. A., Blossom, P., and Bayles, C. (2013). Using mindfulness in the treatment of adolescent sexual abusers: Contributing common factor or a primary modality? *International Journal of Behavioral Consultation and Therapy* 8 (3–4), 17–22.

Kann, L. Kinchen, S., Shanklin, S. L., Flint, K. H., Hawkins, J., Harris, W. A., and Zaza, S. (2014). Youth risk behavior surveillance—United States, 2013. *Morbidity and Mortality Weekly Report* 63 (4), 1–168.

Kendall, P. C. (2000). *Cognitive-behavioral therapy for anxious children. Therapist manual*, 3rd ed. Ardmore, PA: Workbook Publishing.

Kratochwill, T. R. and Bergan, J. R. (1978). Evaluating programs in applied settings through behavioral consultation. *Journal of School Psychology* 16 (4), 375–386.

Larson, J. and Lochman, J. E. (2002). *Helping school children cope with anger: A cognitive–behavioral intervention*. New York: Guilford.

Lee, S. W. and Jamison, T. R. (2002). *Working toward improvements in the student assistance team (SAT) process: A preliminary investigation incorporating functional behavior assessment (FBA) into a structured team process*. Washington, DC: US Department of Education.

Macklem, G. L. (2011). *Evidence-based school mental health services: Affect education, emotion regulation training, and cognitive behavioral therapy*. Springer-Verlag: New York.

Mason, M. and Nakkula, M. (2008). A risk and prevention counselor training program model: Theory and practice. *Journal of Primary Prevention* 29 (5), 361–374.

Matuszek, T. and Rycraft, J. R. (2003). Using biofeedback to enhance interventions in schools. *Journal of Technology in Human Services* 21 (1/2), 31–56.

Merikangas, K. R., He, J., Burstein, M., Swanson, S. A., Avenevoli, S., Cui, L., Benjet, C., Georgiades, K., and Swendsen, J. (2010). Lifetime prevalence of mental disorders in US adolescents: Results from a national comorbidity study—adolescent supplement. *Journal of the American Academy of Child and Adolescent Psychiatry* 49 (10), 980–989.

Merrell, K. W. (2010). Linking prevention science and social and emotional learning: The Oregon Resiliency Project. *Psychology in the Schools* 47 (1), 55–70.

Newman-Carlson, D. and Horne, A. M. (2004). Bully Busters: A psychoeducational intervention for reducing bullying behavior in middle school students. *Journal of Counseling and Development* 82 (3), 259–267.

Ngo, V., Langley, A., Kataoka, S. H., Nadeem, E., Escudero, P., Stein, B. D. (2008). Providing evidence-based practice to ethnically diverse youths: examples from the cognitive behavioral intervention for trauma in schools (CBITS) program. *Journal of the American Academy of Child and Adolescent Psychiatry* 858–862.

Parker, M., Skinner, C., and Booher, J. (2010). Using functional behavioral assessment data to infer learning histories and guide interventions: A consultation case study. *International Journal of Behavioral Consultation and Therapy* 6 (1), 24–34.

Pearce, L. R. (2009). Helping children with emotional difficulties: A response to intervention investigation. *The Rural Educator* 30 (2), 34–46.

Perera-Diltz, D. M., Moe, J. L., and Mason, K. L. (2011). An exploratory study in school counselor consultation engagement. *Journal of School Counseling* 9 (13), 1–24.

Rosenfield, S. A. and Humphrey, C. F. (2012). Consulting psychology in education: Challenge and change. *Consulting Psychology Journal: Practice and Research* 64 (1), 1–7. doi: 10.1037/a0027825

Scott, D. A., Royal, C. W., and Kissinger, D. B. (2015). *Counselor as consultant.* Washington, DC: SAGE.

Sheridan, S. M., Eagle, J. W., Cowan, R. J., and Mickelson, W. (2001). The effects of conjoint behavioral consultation results of a 4-year investigation. *Journal of School Psychology* 39 (5), 361–385.

Singh, N. N., Lancioni, G. E., Joy, S. D. S., Winton, A. S. W., Sabaawi, M., Wahler, R. G., and Singh, J. (2007). Adolescents with conduct disorder can be mindful of their aggressive behavior. *Journal of Emotional and Behavioral Disorders* 15 (1), 56–63.

Singh, N. N., Lancioni, G. E., Manikam, R., Winton, A. S. W., Singh, A. N. A., Singh, J., and Singh, A. D. A. (2011a). A mindfulness-based strategy for self-management of aggressive behavior in adolescents with autism. *Research in Autism Spectrum Disorders* 5, 1153–1158. doi: 10.1016/j.rasd.2010.12.012

Singh, N. N., Lancioni, G. E., Singh, A. D. A., Winton, A. S. W., Singh, A. N. A., and Singh, J. (2011b). Adolescents with Asperger syndrome can use a mindfulness-based strategy to control their aggressive behavior. *Research in Autism Spectrum Disorders* 5, 1103–1109. doi: 10.1016/j.rasd.2010.12.006

Stage, S. A., Jackson, H. G., Jensen, M. J., Moscovitz, K. K., Bush, J. W., Violette, H. D., and Pious, C. (2008). A validity study of functionally based behavioral consultation with students with emotional/behavioral disabilities. *School Psychology Quarterly* 23 (3), 327–353. doi: 10.1037/1045-3830.23.3.327

Steiner, N. J., Frenette, E. C., Rene, K. M., Brennan, R. T., and Perrin, E. C. (2014). In-school neurofeedback training for ADHD: Sustained improvements from a randomized control trial. *Pediatrics*, 133 (3), 483–492.

Sugai, G., Horner, R. H., Dunlap, G., Hieneman, M., Lewis, T. J., Nelson, C. M., and Wilcox, B. (1999). *Applying positive behavioral support and functional behavioral assessment in schools: Technical assistance guide 1.* Washington, DC: Center on Positive Behavioral Interventions and Support (OSEP).

Suter, J. C. and Bruns, E. J. (2009). Effectiveness of the wraparound process for children with emotional and behavioral disorders: A meta-analysis. *Clinical Child and Family Psychology Review* 12, 336–351.

Swart, J. and Apsche, J. (2014). Mindfulness, mode deactivation, and family therapy: A winning combination for treating adolescents with complex trauma and behavioral problems. *International Journal of Behavioral Consultation and Therapy* 9 (2), 9–14.

Thompson, M. and Gauntlett-Gilbert, J. (2008). Mindfulness with children and adolescents: Effective clinical application. *Clinical Child Psychology and Psychiatry* 13 (3), 395–407. doi: 10.1177/1359104508090603

Weare, K. (2013). Developing mindfulness with children and young people: a review of the evidence and policy context. *Journal of Children's Services* 8 (2), 141–153.

Webb, L. and Brigman, G. A. (2007). Student success skills: A structured group intervention for school counselors. *The Journal for Specialists in Group Work* 32 (2), 190–201. doi: 10.1080/01933920701227257

West-Olatunji, C., Frazer, K. N., and Kelley, E. (2011). Wraparound counseling: An ecosystemic approach to working with economically disadvantaged students in urban school settings. *The Journal of Humanistic Counseling* 50 (2), 222–237.

Zyromski, B. and Mariani, M. A. (2016). *Facilitating evidence-based, data-driven school counseling: A manual for practice.* Thousand Oaks, CA: Corwin.

CHAPTER 16

Future Directions and Trends in Counseling Children and Adolescents
Jolie Ziomek-Daigle and Russ Curtis

Mental health is a person's ability to function and to be productive in life; to adapt to changes in his/her environment; to cope with adversity; and to develop positive relationships with others. Without good mental health, one cannot have good health and well being. Therefore, the primary care and mental health partnership is crucial for overall balanced health.

Surgeon General David Satcher

CHAPTER OBJECTIVES

As a result of reading this chapter, students will be able to:

- understand the current state of the counseling profession and the complex issues of licensure, portability, and standards; counseling identity will also be presented
- gain awareness of how online counseling can be used across settings and also examples of how technology can be utilized in the counseling process
- understand how integrated care can be applied across counseling settings
- understand the importance of self-care, resiliency, and mindfulness strategies for counselor psychological health and wellness

---

INTRODUCTION

This chapter will discuss future trends in counseling children and adolescents in school and clinical mental health settings. The chapter begins with information pertaining to the growth and influences of the counseling profession such as standards, licensure, and counselor identity. Next, the chapter discusses online counseling and the use of technology in counseling. Integrated care is then discussed and applications of how integrated care is established in schools and clinical mental health sites are presented. Self-care, mindfulness, and resiliency are topics discussed at the end of the chapter as well as specific strategies for counselors-in-training to maintain a positive perspective along with health and wellness.

PUBLIC AWARENESS AND ADVOCATING FOR THE COUNSELING PROFESSION

For over 30 years, leaders in the counseling profession have discussed issues of counselor identity, counselor licensure and portability, and the future direction of the field (Mascari and Webber, 2013). In the last decade, both counseling organizations (i.e. ACA) and accrediting bodies (CACREP) were asked to consider the future trajectory of the counseling profession, clearly define and resolve the licensure issues listed above, and provide a unified voice for counseling professionals and training programs. Outcomes of those discussions and subsequent decisions are discussed next.

Counseling leaders first looked at the definition of counseling and the role of counselors. Counselor identity, involving a core set of beliefs and values about the characteristics of the counseling profession, is grounded in the therapeutic relationship, typical development, empowerment and advocacy, and health and wellness (Mascari and Webber, 2013). Counseling programs cultivate counselor identity through maintaining program standards and faculty engagement in the counseling profession. The Council for Accreditation of Counseling and Related Educational Programs (CACREP) has set the national standard of programs since 1982 and promotes the counseling profession and counselor identity by providing standards for master's- and doctoral-level preparation programs and a rigorous peer initial accreditation and reaccreditation review process.

Currently, 50 states license professional counselors. Issues of counseling licensure reciprocity and portability have beleaguered the profession for years. The licensure reciprocity and portability issues and deviations among states include having different titles for the counseling credential such as licensed professional counselor (LPC) and licensed mental health counselor (LMHC), varying program hours requirement (48 or 60 hours), requiring a standard number of supervision hours and years of experience, and deciding on a common examination such as the NCE (National Counselor Examination), NCMHCE (National Clinical Mental Health Counselor Examination), or state-administered examination.

> Think about your program and classes. Does your program have a counseling identity? If so, describe it. What are some key characteristics of your program? What types of professional engagement activities is your faculty involved with? Local, state, and national counseling involve ment? Or private practice? Can you state their research interests? How does their involvement and research interests relate to the counseling identity and these characteristics: interpersonal relationships, therapeutic interventions, typical development, empowerment and advocacy, and health and wellness?
>
> Activity

Entering into a CACREP-accredited program and graduating from one is the first step in forming a counseling identity. As of 2016, approximately 20 states require a degree from a CACREP-accredited program for licensure and another dozen require graduation from a program equivalent (i.e. courses with similar content areas internship requirements). Studies indicate that graduates of CACREP-accredited programs have increased internship and job placement opportunities, sustained involvement in private practice, higher acceptance into counseling doctoral programs, and score higher on the NCE than students from non-CACREP-accredited programs (Mascari and Webber, 2013).

TRICARE

One of the benefits of strengthening the counseling profession's identity was the 2015 recognition of the counseling profession by the Department of Defense (DOD) as a legitimate provider who could bill TRICARE, the healthcare program for military personnel, military retirees, and their dependents (Terrazas, Todd, Harp, and Nickel, 2016). Over a decade ago, TRICARE was in need of counseling professionals to provide services to the military and their families and the recent change in TRICARE policy allows these individuals expanded access to mental healthcare. This provision to the TRICARE policy was also another further indication of the legitimization of the counseling profession by the federal government. In order for LPCs to become independent practitioners under TRICARE, counselors must:

1. hold a master's degree in counseling;
2. obtain current licensure to practice in their state; and
3. have practiced as a professional counselor in good standing for five years.

The National Defense Authorization Act of 2016 allowed Licensed Professional Counselors who graduated from CACREP accredited programs the ability to independently provide services to military personal and their dependents (Terrazas, et al., 2016). TRICARE refers to the health insurance system provided by the Department of Defense (DOD) to military personnel and their dependents. Mental health counselors who graduated from non-CACREP programs will also be allowed to bill TRICARE independently, meaning they will not need physicians or other behavioral health providers (e.g., psychologists, social workers) to oversee and sign off on their work in order to bill TRICARE (Terrazas et al., 2016).

The previous section discussed current issues and future directions in the counseling profession. Enhancements to the counseling profession include licensure reciprocity and portability. Counselor identity and common characteristics of the counseling role were also presented. Finally, the changes in the TRICARE system, a health insurance program provided by the Department of Defense (DOD) to military personnel and families, that expands access to counseling services was briefly explained.

In the next section, the authors will explore online counseling and the use of technology in delivering counseling services.

ONLINE COUNSELING AND TELEHEALTH

Youth of today integrate technology into every aspect of their lives from academic learning in the classroom to interacting with peers and family through social media. Some studies suggest that youth increasingly utilize the internet for academic and mental health resources and support groups. Technology competence varies greatly among counselors and it is important to keep in mind that certain work settings either limit or allow access and use of the internet. Additionally, counselors in school and clinical mental health settings can utilize online tests and digital tools that can increase accessibility and services to clients.

Did you know?

Many instruments, tools, and apps are available through internet-connected devices. Several advantages are inherent to using applications including lower testing cost, less materials, integrated process of administration, scoring, and interpretation, and time/efficiency. Some drawbacks may include cost of technology such as computers, possible networking challenges, and client technological competence.

Telehealth has also been referred to as telemedicine and telepsychology and is defined as counselors delivering medical and counseling services through technology media such as video conferencing, the internet, and telephone (Slone, Reese, and McClennan, 2012). Telehealth has shown to be an effective service medium as an alternative or adjunct to in-person mental health services. Interestingly, given that youth tend to be more open to technology and comfortable using technology in educational settings, this age group might be more apt for receiving services through this modality.

Videoconferencing, using a real-time connection, allows individuals or groups to interact with each other on a screen or monitor. Research indicates that videoconferencing is very promising in providing direct counseling services and, in some cases, show better outcomes than face-to-face interactions (Reese, Slone, Soares, and Sprang, 2015). Telehealth services delivered through the internet format includes synchronous chat services, asynchronous communication as in email or discussion boards, and video/audio such as gaming and psycho-educational materials. For example, in one study, the use of email or real-time chat was helpful in adolescents benefitting from smoking cessation programs (Slone, Reese, and McClennan, 2012). Additionally, participants in the smoking cessation program reported satisfaction interacting with other participant's online and viewing vignettes produced by other teenagers. In another study, youth with eating disorders benefitted from telehealth internet services by receiving psycho-education and networking opportunities (Burke, Bynum, Hall-Barrow, Ott, and Albright, 2008). In one final study, telephone-based interventions were effective for youth experiencing anxiety and mood disorders (Slone, Reese, and McClennan, 2012). Mostly positive results have been reported in the literature regarding youth's response to telehealth services. More focus in the area of telehealth needs to include providing telehealth services to youth in rural areas and to diverse populations.

In regards to working with parents, research reporting on outcomes related to parent education and training delivered through telehealth modalities has been positive. These trainings or educational sessions focus on parenting skills, shaping youth behavior, and social support and specific examples include Parent–Child Interaction Therapy (PCIT), the Incredible Years Parent Training, and the Triple P Positive Parenting Program (Reese, Sloane, Soares, and Sprang, 2015). The telehealth modalities more commonly used were telephone consultation, self-directed internet websites, and videoconferencing. Overall, counselors in both school and clinical mental health settings may need to increase access to services and should consider training in telehealth as an effective and viable alternative to face-to-face counseling.

Aligning integrated care, behavioral health, and telehealth: Counselors working across settings

Schools are ideal settings for the application of integrated care and behavioral health services. With the advances in telehealth, more schools can expand to include this model of health care delivery especially in remote, rural, poor, and health-disparate areas of our country. Telehealth offers the same level of face-to-face standard care and affords opportunities to individuals to receive clinical health care and professional health-related education through telecommunications. Barriers exist for those living in remote areas or of lower income including travel distance, lack of transportation, work constraints, lack of finances, limited healthcare insurance, and lack of access to a variety of medical care providers. Adding telehealth services in schools where integrated care is established bridges some of these well-known barriers and makes quality health care attainable and affordable for families. Burke, Bynum, Hall-Barrow, Ott, and Albright (2008) recommend a seven-step process when communities are considering adding telehealth to existing integrated care sites and clinics:

1. access local and regional healthcare needs;
2. secure community support and partnerships and establish community goals;
3. evaluate existing resources;
4. examine logistics and steps to be made;
5. train existing staff;
6. engage and inform parents through multiple media; and
7. open clinics based on student needs and stakeholder support.

The previous section discussed online counseling and telehealth. Several positive study outcomes related to youth and telehealth services were presented. The next section describes integrated care and provides examples of integrated care in school and clinical mental health sites.

INTEGRATED CARE

Counselors need to recognize the potentially powerful role they play in helping people heal, not just from mental and behavioral issues, but physical illnesses as well. Emerging evidence indicates how clients' thoughts, perceptions, and early childhood experiences directly affect physiological processes and health (Crum, Corbin, Brownell, Salovey, 2011; Crum, Salovey, and Achor, 2013; Felitti et al., 1998; Paquette et al., 2003), and counselors are uniquely trained to help people evaluate and change self-defeating thoughts and beliefs. As such, the artificial divide between medical and mental health care is quickly disintegrating, which is providing the impetus for the integrated care (IC) trend in health care.

Integrated care refers to the close collaboration, often located within the same practice, of medical and behavioral health professionals. Research indicates that integrated care improves client and physician satisfaction with care (Chomienne et al., 2011; Kates, Crustolo, Farrar, and Nikolaou, 2001; Kenkel, Deleon, Mantel, and Steep, 2005), improves client outcomes (Bogner, Morales, de Vries, and Cappola, 2012; Katon et al., 2010; Wang et al., 2007), increases clients' perceived quality of life (Chomienne et al., 2011), decreases the length of hospital stays (Nickel, Thiedemann, and Knesebeck, 2010) and reduces healthcare utilization and cost (Chomienne et al., 2011; Hwang, Chang, LaClair, and Paz, 2013; Katon et al., 2002). These studies are not limited to the treatment of adults. In one study, for instance, depressed adolescents who received care in an integrated setting reported significantly less depressive symptoms, increased quality of life, and were more satisfied with the care they received at the six-month follow up compared to a treatment as usual group (Asarnow et al., 2005). Another study found that 5–12-years-olds who were experiencing behavioral health problems demonstrated significant improvement among those treated in an integrated care practice versus treatment as usual (Kolko, Campo, Kilbourne, and Kelleher, 2012). Integrated care, then, is obviously advantageous to not only clients but for the entire counseling profession. Thus what follows are some of the essential components necessary for counselors to begin preparing for this new and improved healthcare delivery system.

Economic and Health Care Literacy

Before describing the process by which counselors can work within integrated care practices, counselors should be aware of several health care initiatives that are paving the way for increased integration of medical and behavioral health care within traditional primary care settings. To begin, the primary purpose of the Affordable Care Act (ACA), often referred to as Obamacare, was to expand the number of people who are insured so they can receive routine healthcare without having to rely on expensive providers such as, hospitalization or emergency departments (Miller and Auxier, 2012). The philosophy guiding the ACA is that increasing access to primary care will enable more people to receive routine care before minor illnesses become more complicated. For example, if people experience persistent chest colds, they can go to their primary care doctor and receive a minimally invasive treatment, perhaps an antibiotic, for instance, which then could reduce the chance that the persistent cough turns into pneumonia, a much more serious illness, which often requires hospitalization. Thus, when people have insurance they are more likely to go to their primary care physicians (PCPs) for regular examinations, which are far less expensive than receiving routine care within the emergency department (ED) of a hospital.

There is, however, controversy surrounding the ACA primarily because some question whether insuring more people will actually slow the rising cost of healthcare. Automobile liability insurance is an analogy that can help clarify the philosophy guiding the ACA. Although not a federal program, all states in the United States require people who own cars to carry liability insurance. The reason liability insurance is required is because the states want all drivers to be able to pay for any damage they may cause when driving. So, if a car owner caused an accident, the owner's insurance company will pay for the damages. If liability insurance was not required, only those who could afford insurance would be able to pay for damages, and many innocent victims would be left without help to repair their cars or pay hospital bills. This then would result in higher premiums paid by those who could afford insurance because the cost of unpaid hospital bills, lawsuits, and property damage eventually gets passed on to the consumers through higher insurance premiums and healthcare costs. Thus, the goal of the ACA, as with automobile liability insurance, is to require healthcare coverage for more people so that the few who can afford insurance do not have to pay higher rates to cover the uninsured.

The ACA includes other provisions that specifically impact counselors. First, the ACA stipulates that people cannot be denied coverage because of pre-existing conditions such as mental and substance abuse issues, meaning more people can receive the counseling they need. Second, insured people would receive initial services at their Primary Care Medical Home (PCMH), where they go for routine visits, so that potential illnesses can be treated before they evolve into more serious illnesses. The PCMHs can bill at higher rates if they demonstrate they are providing quality care. One such service PCMHs can offer is to screen for substance abuse and depression and then provide treatment or referrals, when needed. This particular provision is one reason why integrated care is such a hot topic right now, because it recognizes that the artificial barriers erected to segregate mental and physical care no longer work. It should be noted, however, that the ACA has in some cases significantly increased premiums for small business owners and people who are self-employed. Thus, although the philosophy of expanding coverage to more people as a way ultimately to halt the drastic increase of healthcare costs down the road, the current policy has several flaws, which will need to be addressed.

Mental Health Parity

Another term all counselors should know is mental health parity. The Mental Health Parity and Addiction Act was introduced into congress by the late Paul Wellstone and Pete Domenici and was signed into law in 2008. This bill stipulates that mental health and substance abuse treatment should be provided on equal basis to other conditions (i.e., diabetes, cancer). Prior to this law, people could receive virtually as much care as needed for illnesses such as cancer, but the number of counseling sessions and substance abuse inpatient treatments was severely limited (Miller and Auxier, 2012). The ACA stipulates that mental health and substance abuse treatment parity should continue and expands the definition of care to insure that mental health and substance abuse costs and care management (i.e., authorizations for treatment) must be equitable between behavioral health and other medical conditions (see www.yourhealthcare simplified.org/news/obamacare-and-mental-health).

Integrating Primary Care within Behavioral Health Settings

This type of IC arrangement is often referred to as reverse integration because medical professionals (physicians, certified physician's assistants, family nurse practitioners) work within specialty mental health care settings. It is not uncommon for medical professionals to work within the mental health agency several days per week, where they meet with clients to perform routine physical examinations to diagnose and/or monitor for common comorbid conditions such as diabetes, heart, lung, and gastrological conditions, and chronic pain. Counselors work in tandem with PCPs to help insure the coordination of care and to reinforce medical advice provided by the PCPs. Also, since counselors often have much more contact with clients than PCPs, they coordinate care to insure vital client information is accurately communicated, with client consent of course, creating a more seamless integration of care.

Telemedicine as it Relates to Integrated Care

The national shortage of psychiatrists and the general lack of PCPs in rural areas have inspired the use of synchronous online visits between clients and PCPs. This way, clients who need medical or specialty psychiatric care can go to their local health clinic and meet online with a PCP, who is often located in a larger city where it is cost prohibitive to drive long distances to meet with a few clients face to face in remote areas. Counselors are often a part of this online visit to insure that both client and PCP are adequately informed about client concerns and so the faxed prescription and medical advice can be properly managed in the local clinic. The practice of telemedicine is particularly helpful when PCPs working in IC settings lack the training needed to treat clients who present with more complicated psychiatric issues such as schizophrenia and schizoaffective disorder.

Integrating Behavioral Health within Primary Care Settings

In this more traditional form of integrated care, the BHP works within a primary care practice conducting brief screening for depression, anxiety, and substance abuse, and then provides counseling for clients and consultation with PCPs. In this way, clients, many of whom would never go to a mental health or substance abuse treatment agency, can be screened for mental and substance abuse issues and treated before these issues become severe. As indicated in the aforementioned research review, both clients and medical staff prefer this type of one-stop health care. PCPs know that mental and substance abuse issues complicate medical treatment, if not properly addressed and managed, but may not screen for these issues without the presence of BHP on staff because if an issue is diagnosed they are legally liable to provide care. Clients prefer this one-stop form of health care because they often do not want to attend several appointments at various disparate locations, or the stigma of receiving behavioral care prevents them from keeping other appointments.

Counseling Skills Needed to be Effective IC Providers

Counseling programs, in our opinion, provide ideal training for those who are wishing to work within integrated care settings because of their emphasis on providing direct client care. Most counseling programs require students to take classes in cross-cultural counseling, helping skills, theories and techniques, addiction counseling, and assessment, all of which provide the basic building blocks for successful counseling in IC practices. And counselors who desire to work within IC can be successful if they are willing to develop, enhance, and utilize the following skills: empathy, open-mindedness, conscientiousness, confidence in the value of counseling, and interpersonal effectiveness.

In addition to these specific classes and personal characteristics, there are areas unique to working within IC settings that counselors should heed in order to increase confidence and effectiveness. First, counselors should become skilled in conducting brief assessments using common IC screening instruments such as the Patient Health Questionnaire-9 for depression (PHQ-9: Kroenke, Spitzer, and Williams, 2001) and Generalized Anxiety Disorder-7 (GAD-7; Spitzer, Kroenke, Williams, and Lowe, 2006). A new more comprehensive brief assessment is currently being piloted and holds great promise for IC practitioners as it can be completed, scored, with the results presented in an easy to read graph that compares scores to patient norms. The 36-item Minnesota Behavioral Health Screen assesses for anxiety, depression, suicidal ideation, mania, paranoia, and substance abuse (MBHS; D. McCord, personal communication, October 10, 2015). Counselors should also become familiar with substance-screening instruments such as the CAGE (Ewing, 1984) and the Alcohol Use Disorders Test (AUDIT; Bohn, Babor, Kranzler, 1995), and an evidence-based method for conducting brief substance abuse intervention using the Screen, Brief Intervention, and Referral to Treatment model (SBIRT; Babor, Higgins-Biddle, Higgins, Gassman, and Gould, 2004).

It is important for counselors to learn about psychopharmacotherapy, including the side effects of medicine so you help determine if after administration clients are experiencing further symptoms and/or side effects. Much like school counselors who have to work effectively with students, parents, teachers and administrators, IC counselors must demonstrate interpersonal effectiveness when collaborating with physicians, nurses, physician's assistants, other behavioral health specialists, front-office staff, and documentation compliance officers. Just as counselors must keep clients' readiness for change in mind when providing treatment, they should also consider a practice's stage of change related to how staff members view the necessity of BHPs in their practices. It is not uncommon in IC practices for there to be the IC supporters, sometimes referred to as "physician champions," who strongly support BHPs, but there may be medical staff who do not believe in the efficacy of counseling. Skilled counselors know that the best way to work with reluctant clients or staff is to spend ample time getting to know them to strengthen personal connections. In time, counselors can ask the staff about times when they had received mental and emotional support as a segway into the importance of providing such care in all healthcare practices.

While it is important for BHPs to receive extensive graduate education, this does not mean that providing IC services is complicated. In fact, Goetz (2015) offers simple steps she takes every day in her mental health center to insure optimal care for her clients. Goetz suggests the following recommendations for counselors:

- be curious about your clients and health and be open to having them teach counselors about their condition
- acknowledge how difficult it is to follow health care and nutrition recommendations
- ask clients what good health means to them in terms of every day functioning (i.e., walking up steps, playing with their children)
- call clients after physician appointments to check in and see if they need assistance with physician recommendations
- use staff meetings to provide brief education about common comorbid conditions (e.g., diabetes, heart disease, chronic pain)
- when providing health information, keep it simple and allow time to process clients' understanding and concerns

Curtis and Goetz (2016) are currently creating brief health information cards and public domain training videos utilizing positive priming and motivational statements that counselors can give clients to remind them of the purpose for improving their health. Smoking cessation information, for instance, would be shared by counselors using the positive aspects of reducing or quitting smoking. A few brief motivational statements about smoking cessation, such as reducing the number of cigarettes smoked saves money, or quitting smoking makes it easier to play with children and grandchildren without getting tired, are printed on attractive health information cards, which are approximately the size of index cards so as to not overwhelm clients with handouts that get thrown away immediately upon leaving their appointments. Each card includes a question related to the client's readiness and confidence in making one or two healthy decisions as a way to subtly, yet effectively, increase clients' contemplation toward choosing healthier behavior.

Case Study: Charlene

The following is an inpatient adolescent case study.

Charlene is a 16-year-old cisgendered female who identifies as "liberal–southern–White with Scots–Irish and Cherokee Indian heritage" and has an older brother, Patrick (19), a college student, and a younger sister, Gaylyn (13), who is in advanced placement classes and is considering leaving home to attend a prestigious math and science high school. Charlene lives with her biological parents, who have been married for 21 years. Her mother is a high school math teacher and her father is a plumber who owns his own company. Charlene was diagnosed with type 1 diabetes when she was 9 years old and is insulin dependent. Although Charlene's parents report that each of their children has unique personalities and interests, Charlene was the most intro-verted, melancholy, and impulsive. Beginning in the ninth grade, Charlene started exhibiting problematic behavior by not doing homework, acting out in class, and becoming violent with her parents when they attempted to uphold boundaries. Later, Charlene was charged with marijuana possession at school. After a family counseling session where the possibility of therapeutic boarding school was suggested, Charlene became enraged and started trashing the counselor's office and shouting that she was going to kill herself, resulting in her parents taking her to the hospital emergency department, where she was assessed and committed to a private psychiatric treatment facility.

At the hospital, Charlene was diagnosed with mixed anxiety and depression, which she was apparently self-medicating with marijuana. After Charlene was stabilized and discharged, the hospital staff recommended she receive care in an integrated care practice, where her diabetes could be treated in close co-ordina-tion with her emotional needs. Fortunately, the counselor at the integrated care practice was skilled in using neurofeedback assessment to determine in consul-tation with her medical provider what, if any, might be the best medication for Charlene while they worked on cognitive, emotional, and behavioral strategies to help her heal and thrive. The counselor developed strong working relationships with the medical team, which allowed for seamless coordination of Charlene's medical and mental health treatment. The counselor was also aware of the strain Charlene's parents felt because of their love and concern for their daughter and, as such, she provided counseling to them as well with the hope that she may one day include them in sessions with Charlene.

Process Questions

1. Skilled counselors recognize that adolescent behavior is influenced by many variables, including, but not limited to, genetics, the family system, media, peers, and spiritual influ-ences. As a counselor, how do you make sense of troubled adolescents who come from loving and supportive families? How do you make sense of well-adjusted, kind, and thriving adolescents who were raised in abusive families? How will considering the aforemen-tioned disparities help you counsel clients and their parents in an integrated care setting?
2. How might learning about the side effects of commonly prescribed medications help you work with clients in integrated care practices?
3. What counseling skills and knowledge will you use to quickly develop productive professional working relationships with medical providers?
4. What counseling skills may hinder your working relationship with medical providers?

COUNSELOR WELLNESS AND SELF-CARE

More research is being published in the area of counselor wellness and self-care, especially integrating wellness in counseling graduate programs through curriculum changes and experiential learning (Fulton and Cashwell, 2015; Merriman, 2015). Myers, Sweeney, and Witmer (2000) describe wellness as the integration of mind, body, and spirit into healthy balance. In order for professionals to be effective in counseling and prevent burnout or compassion fatigue, wellness and self-care should be learned and practiced early on. It is imperative that counselors-in-training learn wellness strategies and begin these practices while enrolled in graduate programs to find a balance in managing their professional and personal lives. This section will discuss counselor wellness and present the signs and symptoms of compassion fatigue to assist counselors-in-training in managing work-related stress. Examples of mindfulness and resiliency strategies related to self-care will also be explored.

Compassion Fatigue

Compassion fatigue has been well established as a cause of burnout and impairment for counselors. Additionally, new counseling professionals are especially susceptible to compassion fatigue, and may not be aware of common self-care strategies (Fulton and Cashwell, 2015) to combat this work-related stress. Some of the triggers of compassion fatigue for counselors-in-training may stem from performance anxiety, the transition from student to professional, and exposure to real-life client events. Experiencing compassion fatigue may lead many professionals to exit the profession early in their careers, encounter ethical violations, engage in severe professional and personal impairment, and potentially harm clients (Merriman, 2015).

Compassion fatigue may include characteristics of secondary traumatic stress disorder, which is described as the counselor exhibiting certain emotions and feelings from learning the client trauma and the subsequent stress of providing counseling services (Merriman, 2015). Compassion fatigue can also result in a state of exhaustion from working with and over empathizing with clients who have elevated needs. Keep in mind that *vicarious traumatization*, a more serious form of compassion fatigue, is noticed as a significant change in counselor behavior and affect as a result of overexposure to client material. Practicing counselors and counselors-in-training are susceptible to compassion fatigue when supervision, self-care, and professional development opportunities are not provided. When not afforded these opportunities, counselors can accumulate risk factors that contribute to compassion fatigue. Certain protective factors to reduce compassion fatigue exist and daily rituals, including journaling, supervision, self-awareness, and practicing self-care through wellness, mindfulness, and resiliency strategies, may help shield counselors from this work-related stress.

Activity

Examples of self-care/wellness practices for counselors

Mindfulness, meditation, yoga, massage therapy, acupuncture, exercise, leisure, healthy eating, creativity and art, social support, spirituality.

What self-care activities do you engage in? Are you interested in learning more about any of the self-care activities listed above? If so, which ones?

Mindfulness

Increasing self-awareness is an important step in maintaining wellness and practicing self-care. Being aware of our own reactions to stressors—whether the stressors manifest emotionally, cognitively, or physically—and accepting those experiences with peace and positivity can help reduce stress, contribute to a better quality of life, and increase a sense of vitality.

As discussed in Chapter 15, mindfulness-based interventions have shown to be an effective method to help children and adolescents reframe stress and improve focus. Some goals of mindfulness-based interventions include:

1. providing organized movement with an emphasis on body awareness, rhythm, and coordination;
2. maintaining relaxation and focus; and
3. encouraging self-expression through art.

Sitting, movement, body scan meditation, and relaxation exercises are examples of strategies to increase mindfulness. Research suggests that mindfulness-based interventions may reduce test anxiety, lessen problematic classroom behavior, improve attention, increase social skills, and heighten academic performance. More specifically, in one study, elementary aged children who practiced mindfulness-based interventions had improved attention, reduced teacher-reported problem behavior, and increased emotional regulation (Campbell and Christopher, 2012). In another study, for adolescents at the high-school level, self- and parent-reported measures of sustained attention, behaviors, personal goals, subjective happiness, and mindful awareness were reported as a result of engaging in mindfulness-based interventions.

More recent research and literature has emerged detailing courses and experiential activities for students in counselor training programs in the areas of wellness and mindfulness. Mindfulness programs have been applied in training programs over the last few decades. Studies reveal that students who participated in mindfulness activities while in graduate training had reduced anxiety and depression, increased empathy and positive affect, lessened stress, and enhanced self-kindness (Campbell and Christopher, 2012; Davis and Hayes, 2011). Mindfulness training also assists trainees to learn self-care practices that could prevent counselor burnout, compassion fatigue, and vicarious traumatization (Campbell and Hayes, 2011).

Counselors-in-training are encouraged to seek out admission to CACREP programs that emphasize wellness practices not only in work with clients but throughout the counseling curriculum. The practice of mindfulness not only enhances one's mental and physical state but increases attention and empathy, which are also elements critical to the therapeutic alliance (Campbell and Christopher, 2012). Additionally, one study suggested that mindfulness training sustained with counselors up to six years post-graduation (Campbell and Christopher, 2012). The long-term practice of mindfulness could also assist in the early stages of compassion fatigue and counselor burnout.

Resilience

As counselors-in-training contemplate self-care and consider mindfulness strategies to increase wellness and positivity, resilience should also be discussed. Resilience has been defined as one's ability to manage changes and ambiguity and move forward. Some individuals refer to resiliency as one's "bounce-back factor" from challenging and traumatic events. Researchers have compiled traits of resiliency and the more common characteristics include the following: having a healthy lifestyle (i.e. nutrition, exercise, sleep, stress reduction), goal setting and positive orientation, problem solving, emotionality and creative expression, self-efficacy, social competence (i.e. maintaining friendships and relationships), and a positive, optimistic outlook of the future or optimism (Griffith, 2010).

As previously discussed, counselors-in-training should seek out CACREP-accredited programs that promote health and wellness both in curriculum and in experiential activities. Those in counseling training programs should seek opportunities to enhance their resiliency skills, not just for their own health and wellness, but to foster stronger relationships with clients, supervisors, peers, and program faculty.

SUMMARY

The future for counselors is bright and the need for skilled and healthy counselors to provide an array of services in non-traditional settings is increasing. As this chapter suggests, the practice of counseling is gaining in acceptance and expanding to exciting new areas that will potentially reach many people who would never consider receiving services within a mental health center. As such, the need for counselor understanding of the complex issues that they will face, counseling trends, and the imperative for counselor self-care while meeting new challenges will continue to evolve. It is hoped, then, that this chapter serves as a catalyst for counselors to continue to consider the promising future of counseling and the skills needed to thrive in this profession.

Additional Resources

American Counseling Association: https://www.counseling.org
Center for Connected Health Policy, Telehealth: http://www.cchpca.org/what-is-telehealth
Center for Integrated Health Solutions, What is Integrated Care? http://www.integration.samhsa.gov/about-us/what-is-integrated-care
Council for Accreditation of Counseling and Related Educational Programs: http://www.cacrep.org
Council for Accreditation of Counseling and Related Educational Programs, Directory of Programs: http://www.cacrep.org/directory/
Council for Accreditation of Counseling and Related Educational Programs, Information on State Licensing Boards: http://www.cacrep.org/for-students/getting-licensed-after-you-graduate/
Mindfulness, Getting Started: http://www.mindful.org/meditation/mindfulness-getting-started/
National Board for Certified Counselors: http://www.nbcc.org
Tricare: http://www.tricare.mil
U.S. Department of Health and Human Services, About the Law: https://www.hhs.gov/healthcare/about-the-law/read-the-law/

Suggested Readings

Counseling Today, online, Ray, B. (2014, April). One stop shopping Q & A. http://ct.counseling.org/2014/04/advocating-for-one-stop-shopping-health-care-qa-with-acas-interest-network-for-integrated-care/
Curtis R. and Christian, E. (eds.) (2012). *Integrated Care: Applying Theory to Practice*. New York: Routledge.
Curtis, R. and Christian, E. (American Counseling Association) (2012, August). *Integrated care: Applying theory to practice* [audio podcast]. Retrieved from http://www.counseling.org/Counselors/TP/PodcastsHome/CT2.aspx
Rollins, J. (2010, January). Reconnecting the head with the body. *Counseling Today*, 44–49.
Shallcrosse, L. (2013, October). Counseling today. *Total Health Care*, 31–37.

Glossary

Affordable Care Act: The Patient Protection and Affordable Care Act, more commonly called the Affordable Care Act, often nicknamed "Obamacare," is a federal statute and was signed into law by President Barack Obama in 2010. The goal of the Affordable Care Act was to provide more accessible and affordable healthcare to consumers

Integrated care: The systematic organization of general and behavioral health-care including primary care, mental health, and substance abuse. This approach is effective for treatment of individuals with multiple, complex, and compounded health needs, decreases barriers or lack of access to health care, provides a seamless process of therapeutic services, and helps individuals navigate complex health care systems and specialties

Mental health parity: The Mental Health Parity Act (MHPA) requires annual or lifetime dollar limits on mental health benefits to be no lower than any such dollar limits for medical and surgical benefits offered by a group health plan or health insurance issuer offering coverage in connection with a group health plan

Mindfulness: To focus one's awareness on the present moment, to be fully present and aware of one's present state and surroundings, and accepting and paying attention to one's thoughts or feelings without judging them

Resilience: One's ability to adapt to change, conflict, discourse, and stress. Often referred to as one's "bounce-back" factor. Resiliency traits, characteristics, and behaviors can be taught and learned

TRICARE: A healthcare program for the US Department of Defense (i.e. active and retired military members and their families) that includes mental health benefits

References

Asarnow, J. R., Jaycox, L. H., Duan, N., LaBorde, A. P., Rea, M. M., Murray, P., and Wells, K. B. (2005). Effectiveness of a quality improvement intervention for adolescent depression in primary care clinics. *JAMA* 293 (3), 311–319. doi10.1001/jama.293.3.311

Babor, T. F., Higgins-Biddle, J., Higgins, P., Gassman, R., and Gould, B. (2004). Training medical providers to conduct alcohol screening and brief interventions. *Substance Abuse* 25 (1), 17–26.

Bogner, H. R., Morales, K. H., dr Vries, H. F., and Cappola, A. R. (2012). Integrated management of Type 2 diabetes mellitus an depression treatment to improve medication adherence: A randomized controlled trial. *Annals of Family Medicine* 10 (1), 15–22. doi 10.1370/afm.1344

Bohn, M. J., Babor, T. F. and Kranzler, H. R. (1995). The Alcohol Use Disorders Identification Test (AUDIT): Validation of a screening instrument for use in medical settings. *Journal of Studies on Alcohol* 56 (4), 423–432. doi: 10.15288/jsa.

Burke, B., Bynum, A., Hall-Barrow, J., Ott, R., and Albright, M. (2008). Rural school-based telehealth: How to make it happen. *Clinical Pediatrics* 47 (9), 926–929.

Campbell, J. C. and Christopher, J, C, (2012). Teaching mindfulness to create effective counselors. *Journal of Mental Health Counseling* 34 (3), 213–226.

Chomienne, M.-H., Grenier, J., Gaboury, I., Hogg, W., Ritchie, P., and Farmanova-Haynes, E. (2011). Family doctors and psychologists working together: doctors' and patients' perspectives. *Journal of Evaluation in Clinical Practice* 17, 282–287. doi:10.1111/j.1365-2753.2010.01437.x

Crum, A. J., Corbin, W. R., Brownell, K. D., and Salovey, P. (2011). Mind over milkshakes: Mindsets, not just nutrients, determine ghrelin response. *Health Psychology* 30 (4), 424–429.

Crum, A. J., Salovey, P., and Achor, S. (2013). Rethinking stress: The role of mindsets in determining the stress response. *Journal of Personality and Social Psychology* 104 (4), 716–733.

Davis, D. M. and Hayes, J. A. (2011). What are the benefits of mindfulness? A practice review of psychotherapy-related research. *Psychotherapy* 48 (2), 198–208.

Ewing, J. A. (1984). Detecting alcoholism: The CAGE questionnaire. *Journal of the American Medical Association* 252 (14), 1905–1907.

Felitti, V. J., Anda, R. F., Nordenberg, D., Williamson D. F., Spitz, A. M., Edwards, V., Koss, M. P., and Marks, J. S. (1998). Relationship of childhood abuse and household dysfunction to many of the leading causes of death in adults: The Adverse Childhood Experiences (ACE) Study. *American Journal of Preventative Medicine* 14 (4), 245–258. doi:10.1016/S0749-3797(98)00017-8

Fulton, C. and Cashwell, C. S. (2015). Mindfulness-based awareness and compassion: Predictors of counselor empathy and anxiety. *Counselor Education and Supervision* 54, 122–133.

Goetz, K. (May, 2015). Recommendations for working effectively in an integrated care agency. *ACA Interest Network, Integrated Care*. Retrieved from http://www.wcu.edu/WebFiles/CEAP-HS-COUN-RussCurtis-ACA-ICNewsletter201505.pdf

Griffith, K. (2010). Small group counseling to enhance resiliency skills (unpublished doctoral dissertation). University of Georgia, Athens, Georgia

Hwang, W., Chang, J., LaClair, M., and Paz, H. (2013). Effects of integrated delivery system on cost and quality. *The American Journal of Managed Care* 19 (5), 175–184.

Kates, N., Crustolo, A., Farrar, S., and Nikolaou, L. (2001). Integrating mental health services into primary care: Lessons learnt. *Families, Systems and Health* 19 (1), 5–12.

Katon, W., Russo, J., Von Korff, M., Lin, E., Simon, G., Bush, T., Ludman, E., and Walker, E. (2002). Long-term effects of a collaborative care intervention in persistently depressed primary care patients. *Journal of General Internal Medicine* 17 (10), 741–748.

Katon, W. J., Lin, E. H., Von Korff, M., Ciechanowski, P., Ludman, E. J., Young, B., Peterson, D., Rutter, C. M., McGregor, M., and McCulloch, D. (2010). Collaborative care for patients with depression and chronic illnesses. *New England Journal of Medicine* 363 (27), 2611–2620. doi: 10.1056/NEJMoa1003955

Kenkel, M. B., Deleon, P. H., Mantell, E. O., and Steep, A. E. (2005). Divided no more: Psychology's role in integrated health care. *Canadian Psychology/Psychologie canadienne* 46 (4), 189–202.

Kolko, D. J., Campo, J. V., Kilbourne, A. M., and Kelleher, K. (2012). Doctor–office collaborative care for pediatric behavioral problems: A preliminary clinical trial. *Archives of Pediatrics and Adolescent Medicine* 166 (3), 224–231. doi:10.1001/archpediatrics.2011.201

Kroenke, K., Spitzer, R. L., and Williams, J. B. W. (2001). The PHQ-9: Validity of a brief depression severity measure. *Journal of General Internal Medicine* 16, 606–613.

Mascari, J. B. and Webber, J. (2013). CACREP accreditation: A solution to license portability and counselor identity problems. *Journal of Counseling and Development* 91 (1), 15–25.

Merriman, J. (2015). Enhancing counselor supervision through compassion fatigue education. *Journal of Counseling and Development* 93(3), 370–378.

Miller, B. F. and Auxier, A. (2012). Integrated care policy. In R. Curtis amd E. Christian (eds.), *Integrated care: Applying theory to practice* (pp. 281–295). New York: Routledge.

Myers, J., Sweeney, T. J., and Witmer, M. (2000). The wheel of wellness counseling for wellness: A holistic model for treatment planning. *Journal of Counseling and Development* 78 (3), 251–266.

Nickel, S., Thiedemann, B., and Knesebeck, O. (2010). The effects of integrated inpatient health care on patient satisfaction and health-related quality of life: Results of a survey among heart disease patients in Germany. *Health Policy* 98 (2–3), 156–163.

Paquette, V., Levesque, J., Mensour, B., Leroux, J., Beaudoin, G., Bourgoin, P., and Beauregard, M. (2003). Change the mind and you change the brain: Effects of cognitive-behavioral therapy on the neural correlates of spider phobia. *Neuroimage* 18(2): 401–409.

Reese, R. J., Slone, N. C., Soares, N., and Spring, R. (2015). Using telepsychology to provide a group parenting program: A preliminary evaluation of effectiveness. *Psychological Services* 12 (3), 274–282.

Slone, N. C., Reese, R. J., and McClennan, M. J. (2012). Telepsychology outcome research with children and adolescents: A review of the literature. *Psychological Services* 9 (3), 272–292.

Spitzer R. L., Kroenke K., Williams J. B. W., and Lowe B. (2006). A brief measure for assessing Generalized Anxiety Disorder: The GAD-7. *Archives of Internal Medicine* 166, 1092–1097.

Terrazas, A., Todd, G., Harp, D., and Nickel, K. (January, 2016). New law expands number of LPCs who can practice independently under TRICARE. *Counseling Today* 58 (7), 8.

Wang, P. S., Simon, G. E., Avorn, J., Azocar, F., Ludman, E. J., McCulloch, J., Petukhova, M. Z., and Kessler, R. C. (2007). Telephone screening, outreach, and care management for depressed workers and impact on clinical and work productivity outcomes. *JAMA* 298 (12), 1401–1411.

Index